TODAY'S
BEST
NONFICTION

TODAY'S
BEST
NONFICTION

THE READER'S DIGEST ASSOCIATION, INC.
PLEASANTVILLE, N.Y., MONTREAL

The condensations in this volume have been created by The Reader's Digest Association, Inc.,
by special arrangement with the publishers, authors, or other holders of copyrights. Letters,
documents, court testimony, etc. may have been edited for space.

The original editions of the books in this volume are published and copyrighted as follows:

Circle of Fire: Murder and Betrayal in the "Swiss Nanny" Case
Published by William Morrow and Company, Inc.
distributed by Gage Distribution Company at $34.95
© 1994 by Joyce Egginton

The Camera Never Blinks Twice: The Further Adventures of a Television Journalist
Published by William Morrow and Company, Inc.
distributed by Gage Distribution Company at $34.95
© 1994 by DIR Enterprises, Inc.

Nuremberg: Infamy on Trial
Published by Viking Penguin, a division of Penguin Books USA Inc.
distributed by Penguin Books Canada Limited at $32.99
© 1994 by Joseph E. Persico

Autobiography of a Face
Published by Houghton Mifflin Company
distributed by Thomas Allen & Son Limited at $29.95
© 1994 by Lucy Grealy

Contents

JOYCE EGGINTON

CIRCLE

Murder and Betrayal in the "Swiss Nanny" Case

. . . At first glance his house looked intact. Bill saw no flames, only smoke, so it had to be all right to go inside. He ran up the driveway, only to be blocked near the front entrance by a fireman.

"You don't want to go in there," the man said.

There was such a grave tone in his voice that Bill, suddenly fearful, tried to brush past him into the house.

"You don't want to go in there," the fireman repeated, not budging.

Bill stopped, trying to grasp what he wasn't being told. Suddenly he realized why Olivia was alone and why she was still crying. The baby must still be in the house.

—*Circle of Fire*

PART I: THE FIRE
Chapter One

MOST days Bill Fischer went home to lunch. As the senior partner in the family business, he could pick his time, and this was usually late, after the employees had eaten. At about 1:30 on this damp and gray afternoon, December 2, 1991, he walked around to the back of the auto repair shop, climbed into his Chevrolet Blazer, and made the familiar five-mile drive from North White Plains, New York, to Thornwood: left on Route 22, up the hill, then left again onto West Lake Drive and over the long stone bridge across the reservoir. It was a curiosity of local geography—to become of crucial importance later in the afternoon—that West Lake Drive, the long winding road where he lived, would soon seem to disappear and merge into Columbus Avenue. But then two sharp right turns would get him back onto the far end of West Lake Drive.

Bill Fischer had lived in this part of Westchester County for most of his forty-seven years, seeing it develop from a scattering of rural hamlets into an exurb of New York City. He had grown up in North White Plains, in the old colonial-style house next to Fischer's Garage where his father, Willie, and sister, Barbara, still lived, and which at times of rejoicing or grief was still the family gathering place for up to four generations of Fischers. Bill's current home on West Lake Drive was very different. It was built by his former father-in-law, Jan Menting, who as a contemporary artist and designer, had a strong sense of light and space; its large skylights and windows were intended to let nature into the living room. The house was surrounded by a generous landscaping of bushes and trees to give it a sense of peace and isolation.

Over the years Bill had added improvements to the house, and in his spare time he was usually doing some kind of carpentry or electrical work. He kept his building materials with organized precision. In the murder trial in which he would be a leading witness—a trial as yet beyond his imagining—the prosecuting counsel would describe Bill Fischer as a careful craftsman who knew at any given time what tools and supplies he owned, and exactly where to find them.

Recently he had driven home for his lunch breaks with more joyous anticipation than he had felt in a long time. For almost three years after his first wife moved out, he had often come into an empty house; although his two grown children, Troy and Leah, had still lived there, they were usually at college or working. But more than a year ago Bill, a man of deliberate actions and few words, surprised his family by introducing into the household Denise—a slender, pretty woman who had the same quiet ways that he had, but was not afraid to express her opinions with a disarming directness. Bill had met her as a customer at his garage; she was eight years younger than he and had long been divorced from an early and childless marriage. She worked as an accountant in the nearby town of Stamford, Connecticut.

All that most people in the family knew, after the wedding, was that he and Denise went off to Nantucket one weekend and got married. Soon after Troy moved out of his old room, Bill turned it into a nursery. When Leah, his younger child, was twenty-two, William Fischer became a father again. And on this December afternoon he was hurrying home not just for lunch, but to spend a little time with his new baby daughter.

If asked, he would have said that he wanted to make sure that Olivia Riner, the Swiss au pair who had been with the family for a month, was managing all right, now that Denise had gone back to work. But Olivia had already shown herself to be so dutiful and solicitous of the baby that he and Denise felt confidence in this young woman who seemed to be the perfect baby-sitter.

No, he wasn't worried about Olivia. It was Kristie he wanted to see.

KRISTIE Rebecca Fischer was born in White Plains Hospital on September 11, 1991. An early snapshot of her shows an engaging infant with a delicate fair complexion, the vivid blue eyes of both parents,

Denise's cute little upturned nose, and perfectly formed features. Denise had a difficult pregnancy. Years earlier she had suffered several miscarriages, and bringing this first baby to term in her fortieth year required a lot of caution. The birth had to be by cesarean section. She wanted Bill to be with her through labor and delivery, and having missed the experience when his older children were born, he was anxious to be supportive.

Bill stayed at his wife's side through surgery, and he was the first to be given their new daughter to hold. Denise asked Bill to choose a name for her, and he suggested Kristie. Denise added Rebecca.

ON THIS December afternoon, almost twelve weeks later, Bill let himself into his house and went straight to the nursery. The front door led directly into the family room, at the opposite end of which was a short, narrow corridor with doors on the left opening onto a laundry room, bathroom, and nursery, in that order; on the right were a heater room, Olivia's room, and Leah's room. The living room, kitchen, and master bedroom were upstairs.

At the nursery door Bill came upon Olivia sitting on the floor, folding freshly laundered baby clothes. Kristie was lying on the rug beside her, looking pink and clean and happy, playing with the mobiles on an infant jungle gym. Olivia did not seem startled by Bill's appearance. She would surely have heard the front door open and close, and his footsteps on the vinyl tiles of the corridor. There was such resonance to that flooring, laid directly on concrete, that anyone walking around could be heard through most of the house.

"Hi," Bill greeted Olivia as he walked into the room. He bent down and spoke to Kristie, feeling a flood of tenderness toward her when she recognized his voice. She gave him a big, happy smile—a smile he would never forget or afterward be able to recall without tears coming to his eyes. He could not have imagined, before she was born, how special this renewed experience of fatherhood would make him feel. In his twenties he had been too concerned with working hard, too immature to appreciate the wonder of his babies. Now he had so much more to give a child: financial security and time for loving.

He smiled back at her and went upstairs to the kitchen to fix lunch. While he was eating, he heard Kristie fussing a little. Olivia was clearly taking care of her, because the whimpering soon subsided.

Olivia looked younger than her age of twenty, with her hair worn straight down her back, her scrubbed complexion, and her teenage style of dressing in jeans, sneakers, and a sweatshirt. But she seemed to be responsible and self-sufficient. Before they contracted to sponsor her one-year stay in the United States, Denise had been concerned that this girl might become bored and homesick, and she telephoned Olivia's home in the small town of Wettingen, near Zurich, to warn her of the possibility. "It's real countryside where we live. You won't see many people around. It's very quiet. What will you do when you are alone in the house with the baby?"

"I shall talk to her," Olivia replied in her softly accented English.

Denise had been impressed with that response, and since then Olivia had given the Fischers no reason to doubt her competence or sincerity. "We felt we had found the perfect nanny," Denise said.

AT ABOUT 2:45 p.m. Bill prepared to return to work. Stopping by the nursery, he saw Kristie peacefully asleep, strapped into the reclining infant seat where she often napped in the daytime. It rested on the floor in such a position that Olivia, relaxing in her bedroom across the hallway, could easily watch the baby. Right now she was sitting at the desk by her window, reading.

Bill hesitated by the nursery's open door, tempted to go inside for a last look at his daughter. But fearful of waking her, he turned toward Olivia's room. "I'm leaving now," he said. "See you later."

She acknowledged the comment and went back to her book.

Later, blaming himself, Bill Fischer said again and again that if he had noticed anything in the least bit wrong, he would not have left the house that afternoon.

Chapter Two

IT WAS hard to tell whether Olivia was happy. She gave the impression of a dutiful, serious child who lived in a world of her own. She had none of the poise or instant friendliness of Bill's elder daughter, Leah, who at that time was the other member of the household. At twenty-two Leah had a sophistication that Olivia did not remotely possess and probably never would.

Denise had been reassured to find that Olivia "wasn't the kind of baby-sitter who would have her coat on, waiting to get out of the house the minute we got home." Leah proffered a couple of invitations, to go shopping and to see a movie, but both times the response was a monosyllabic no. Leah did not ask again.

So far as Bill and Denise could tell, Olivia was content to spend her evenings in the house, having polite conversation with the family, then retiring to her room. She kept it neat and clean, unlike Leah, whose mess really bothered Denise. They asked Olivia about her life in Switzerland and learned that she was an only child who seemed to be devoted to her father and somewhat critical of her mother. She loved animals and played affectionately with the Fischers' four cats.

In her free time Olivia enjoyed reading thrillers, and was currently immersed in a German-language copy of Thomas Harris' recent best seller, *The Silence of the Lambs*. She also kept a diary—a thick volume with a mock-leather cover and a lock.

Her isolating activities seemed to be at odds with her stated desire to learn about America, which she had visited twice before, as a tourist. Knowing that the agency that sent her was putting her in touch with other au pair girls, the Fischers told themselves that she would soon make friends and become more adventurous.

Olivia was physically small, with dark blond hair and features that were interesting rather than pretty. When she smiled, her eyes would sparkle and she could look vivacious. More often she had a downcast expression, with a way—when spoken to—of looking up behind lowered eyelids, like a scolded child. The straight bangs, which fell almost to her thick dark eyebrows, intensified the impression.

She was naturally shy, the more so because she still felt awkward about expressing herself in English. But although her syntax was sometimes strange, she had a good command of the language. There was a forthrightness about her that at best could be refreshing, at worst judgmental. Lacking insight into how middle-aged parents might feel about the only child they were likely to have, her first impression was that their concern for Kristie was excessive. Sometimes when Denise ran to pick her up at the first whimper, Olivia would look quizzical and faintly disapproving. But after a few weeks of helping to look after this baby, she, too, seemed to be drawn into a loving, protective relationship toward her.

What else was there in her life? No boyfriend back home, and a prudish attitude toward men, which was unlikely to invite romance. Leah had a steady boyfriend, John Gallagher, who saw her almost daily and who obviously loved her. Leah also had her own car and a closet full of clothes. Was Olivia envious? Did she feel like Cinderella when the adults drove off to work, leaving her stranded in this house?

Denise still worried about this. For the first few weeks of Olivia's stay, she had been there with her. But last week, finishing her maternity leave, she had eased herself back into her job by working for three days, then taking the Thanksgiving holidays. Today, Monday, December 2, was the beginning of Olivia's first full week alone with Kristie. If she was intimidated by all those days of loneliness looming ahead of her, Olivia gave no hint of it.

AFTER Bill returned to work that afternoon, there was one known caller at the house: a deliveryman bringing a supply of propane gas that had been ordered. After filling the outside tank, the driver stopped by the front entrance to leave his delivery slip. Nothing about the house struck him as unusual. He made a note of his delivery time, 4:20 p.m., and drove off.

Shortly after five o'clock the telephone rang at Fischer's Garage.

"Meester Fischer, Meester Fischer." The voice was female, excited, and foreign. It was Olivia, hysterical. "Fire, fire!" she cried.

Unable to tell whether she was reporting a small accident or a major explosion, Bill did not waste time calming her down enough to find out. It went through his mind that having got herself to a telephone, she must be safe and would have baby Kristie with her.

"I'll be right there," he assured her. "Have you called the fire department?" He thought of the list of emergency numbers that Denise had pinned up by the kitchen phone.

An operator cut in and told him that, yes, help was on its way.

Bill hurried out to his van and drove home as fast as he dared, worrying all the way about how a fire could have started on a damp day like this. It must have ignited within the house. Only a few days earlier he had been working on the first-floor wiring; maybe he had omitted some safety precaution. He was appalled at the thought.

The first fire truck was already there when he reached the house. So was John Gallagher's elderly Ford pickup truck. John, who was an auto mechanic, worked for a nearby Jaguar dealer, and on the nights when Leah was not going to classes, it was his habit to drive directly from work to the Fischers' house to spend the evening with her. As Bill got out of his van, John came running toward him from the house. His eyes were streaming, and he looked ready to collapse.

"Mr. Fischer, you'd better get over there," he gasped.

Olivia was standing outside the front door, by the patio, sobbing. In the background Bill saw his next-door neighbor, George Fries, and a lot of activity in the Frieses' house. He hoped that Kristie had been taken there. Kitty Fries, George's wife, must be looking after her. At first glance his own house looked intact. Bill saw no flames, only smoke, so it had to be all right to go inside. He ran up the driveway, only to be blocked near the front entrance by a fireman.

"You don't want to go in there," the man said.

There was such a grave tone in his voice that Bill, suddenly fearful, tried to brush past him into the house.

"You don't want to go in there," the fireman repeated, not budging.

Bill stopped, trying to grasp what he wasn't being told. Suddenly he realized why John Gallagher looked so shocked and defeated, why Olivia was alone, and why she was still crying. The baby must still be in the house, and no one was trying to rescue her, because she was dead. He could think of only one possible cause of the fire—an electrical fault—and only one person who could have caused it.

"Oh, my God," he said to himself, "I have killed my own baby."

"WHAT happened?" Bill was standing next to Olivia on the patio, trying to take in the horror of the scene.

Her response was different from the story she later gave the police. She told Bill that in the late afternoon, while Kristie was still sleeping, she started to feed the cats. Before putting out their food in the laundry room, Olivia said, she closed the nursery door to keep the cats away from the baby. A few minutes later she smelled smoke, went to investigate, and saw a fire on her bed. Then, she said, she realized there was another fire in the nursery, but she couldn't open the door.

"After that," Bill related, "I do not remember what she said." The emotional overload was more than he could handle. He became aware that Leah had arrived and was standing at his side listening to Olivia's story, and that a policeman was trying to shepherd them to the Frieses' house. Bill refused to leave, and Leah insisted on staying with him. Denise would soon be arriving from work, and he wanted to be there to comfort her.

John Gallagher—soot stained and shaking—walked across to the place where Olivia was still standing. He was not feeling kindly toward her. "Did you tell Bill Fischer?" he asked.

"Yes, yes, yes," she sobbed.

He turned his back on her and walked away. It was beyond his comprehension that she had failed to save the baby.

JOHN had been one of the first to see Kristie after she was born. He and Leah arrived at White Plains Hospital only five minutes before Kristie was helped into the world. After a while Bill came out to them in the waiting room, all smiles, carrying his newborn daughter. He handed her to Leah, who adored babies. Many of the tensions about having to deal with a stepmother had diminished during Denise's pregnancy. It was typical of Leah's warmhearted enthusiasm that she had organized a surprise baby shower for Denise.

"Before this baby was born, it was all Leah would talk about," John Gallagher recalled.

Having been around the Fischers' household for four years as Leah's steady boyfriend, John was almost part of the family. Like Leah, he watched Kristie's development over the ensuing weeks with childlike delight. After Kristie's death, memories of her kept painfully flooding back to him. "I would sit and play with her feet and her fingers. She had Denise's tiny little hands. She was a very good baby."

ON THE night of the fire John left the repair shop of White Plains Jaguar at about 5:00 p.m. His mother, Carol Gallagher, was due to go into the hospital for throat surgery the following morning, and he and Leah wanted to spend some time with her that night. So they arranged to meet at Leah's home and, later, to make the thirty-minute drive north to the Gallaghers' house in the village of Mahopac.

Leah, who had a secretarial job in White Plains, usually arrived home a few minutes before John, close to 5:15 p.m., but today she was delayed at her office. John parked in his usual spot, at the end of the long driveway. As he had made the sharp left turn from West Lake Drive onto the Fischers' driveway, a bag of auto parts on the passenger seat had fallen to the floor. He now bent down to pick it up and, from this unlikely vantage point, saw out of the corner of his left eye what appeared to be a burst of orange flames coming from the far side of the house, the side of the nursery. He peered over the dashboard and realized that the flames were real. He ran toward the house, thinking, I hope that girl got the baby out.

Olivia opened the front door as he reached it, crying, "Fire, fire!" Through the door, which was almost solid glass, he had seen her scurrying around the family room with a fire extinguisher in her hand. Now she held it limply at her side as she stood motionless.

"Where's Kristie?" he yelled. He was shouting to be heard over the alarm noise of a smoke detector.

"She's in the room." Her voice was panicky, and her body was quivering. In answer to his questions she told him that she had telephoned the fire department and Bill.

Grabbing the fire extinguisher, John dashed down the hallway to the nursery. The door was shut. He twisted the knob, but it would not yield. It was locked. There was a gap under the door, and inside the nursery a strip of vinyl tile before the area rug began. John could see the reflection of flames on the floor's surface.

Frantic, he shouted to Olivia, "Why did you lock the door?" There was no answer. She was now outside on the patio, nervously watching him from a safe distance.

The door was new, of the hollow-core variety. Bill had hung it about ten days previously, not entirely to his satisfaction. The new hinges were a little short, so that the locking mechanism barely reached the strike plate on the doorjamb. It was still possible to lock the door, but the lock was not secure. Bill had painted the door with polyurethane, cleaning his brushes with paint thinner from the storage closet off the family room. He kept most of his supplies there, including other flammable liquids, all of the cans tightly capped and neatly lined up on the shelves. Olivia had watched while he worked on the door.

The lock was keyless, secured on the inside by turning a little button in the center of the knob. If anyone were to turn the button with the door open and then close the door, no one on the outside could get in. And that was the situation John Gallagher found when he tried to enter the nursery.

He was a rangily built twenty-six-year-old, six feet two inches tall and a hundred and fifty-five pounds. Bracing himself against the opposite wall of the narrow hallway, he gave the door a sharp kick close to the latch, and the ill-fitting lock yielded instantly.

He was so traumatized by what he saw in the nursery that he could barely speak of it that night. Kristie was lying in her infant seat on the rug, so totally engulfed in flame, so horribly destroyed by it, that at first he was not sure whether what he was seeing was human. He wanted to believe that the charred and disfigured shape was the remains of a doll, and he looked across to the crib in the vain hope of seeing Kristie there. If she had been in that crib, he might have saved her. The sole source of the flames that he had seen from his truck was this inexplicable blaze on the rug: an almost perfect circle of fire, with Kristie in the middle like a sacrificial offering.

He sprayed the fire extinguisher around the baby, as close as he dared, without letting the powder touch her. As the flames died down, he knelt beside her, hoping against all logic that she was still alive. The heat had been so intense that the gray plastic shell of her infant seat was melting and twisted, gluing it to the rug.

"I knew I was too late," he said, describing the scene months later. "She was already dead. It was horrible. I cannot get the sight out of my mind. I felt like I had been put in somebody's nightmare. I almost got sick to my stomach. I had to get out. And all I could think about was how the Fischers would feel when they got home."

IN THE house next door the fire department pager was sounding urgently. George Fries, one of Thornwood's volunteer firemen, was at home with Kitty when the alert was broadcast: a house fire at Five West Lake Drive. He grabbed a flashlight and ran outdoors, skirting the bushes that separated the two properties.

He came face to face with John Gallagher as John stumbled out of the house, coughing and choking, tears running down his cheeks.

"What happened?" George asked.

"There is a fire in the nursery and it does not look good for the baby," John replied. He could not bring himself to say "dead."

"Is she still in there? Which room is it?"

"Third door on the left-hand side."

When George Fries entered the nursery, the flames had been quenched, but there was a great deal of heavy smoke. Even with his flashlight it was not possible to see across the room. He felt around the crib and realized it was empty. Turning to leave the room, he almost stumbled into the blackened shape on the floor that had been at the heart of the inferno.

He was so shaken by this experience, thinking of his own small grandchildren, that when he saw John Gallagher outside the house, he, too, could not say the word.

"Did you see the baby?" John wanted to know.

"Yes, and it does not look good."

Within the next few minutes the Thornwood fire chief arrived in his car, followed by the first fire truck, followed by Bill Fischer, followed by Leah.

After Olivia had told Bill her halting, incomplete story, she was led across to the Frieses' house, accompanied by an ambulance worker. She was no longer hysterical; in fact, Kitty Fries was struck by her self-control as she sat demurely at the dining table, making occasional little whimpering sounds.

John, meantime, went back to his truck, and there in the cold and dark he, Bill, and Leah sat, waiting for Denise.

Chapter Three

AT THE time, there was no 911 emergency telephone system in the area. The procedure that Denise had explained to Olivia was to make a direct call to the Mount Pleasant police at 769-1998 or to dial the operator. The second option would inevitably take longer. To obviate this, Denise duplicated the list of emergency numbers by the kitchen phone and put the second copy on Olivia's desk.

At about 5:10 p.m., while the nursery fire was raging, Olivia tried to call the police from the phone in her room. But she could not make her desk light work. Just when she needed it most, the bulb had blown. She took the list to the family-room telephone, but was so panicky that she dropped it, gave up, and dialed 0.

She gave the operator the address in Thornwood, one of several villages in the Mount Pleasant police district, and was transferred to police headquarters in neighboring Pleasantville. This conversation was recorded:

Pleasantville police officer: "Police department."

Olivia: "Hi. Fire."

"Where is this, ma'am?"

"In Thornwood."

"What's the address?"

"West Lake Drive."

"What number on West Lake Drive?"

"Five."

"Okay, I'll send the fire department. What's your name?" He assumed her to be the homeowner.

"Riner." She pronounced it the Swiss-German way, Reener, which the officer misheard.

"Leland?" he queried.

"Reener," she repeated. By now she was crying, and her words were getting swallowed by sobs.

"What's your phone number?"

Hearing her distress, an operator broke in: "769-5939."

The officer repeated, "5939. Five West Lake Drive. Okay, I'll send the fire department."

Olivia: "Yes."

"Okay. Bye."

"Bye," Olivia replied. In this whole conversation she had said nothing about a baby being in danger, just as she then failed to report this to Bill after the operator put her through to Fischer's Garage.

While the Pleasantville police officer was getting information from Olivia, his colleague was telephoning Mount Pleasant police headquarters. This officer passed on the message—with the correct address but with the garbled name of Leland.

"This is yours, isn't it?" he asked.

"I think so," replied the Mount Pleasant desk sergeant. "I'll check." The sergeant was being cautious. The address he was given did not sound right. From his knowledge of West Lake Drive, he doubted that there was a Number Five in Thornwood.

He looked up the name of Leland on West Lake Drive, but there was no such listing. With valuable minutes slipping away, he decided to call back and check the address. Olivia picked up the phone.

"Yes?" she said nervously.

"All right," the sergeant began. "What's your address?"

"Five West Lake Drive," she stated again, unaware that she was dealing with a different police department.

"What street is that near?"

"Nannyhagen Road."

"You're near Nannyhagen?" He sounded dubious.

"Nannyhagen, yes."

"How far off Nannyhagen?" he pursued.

She was beginning to sound frantic. "It's the next street, and then you come"—the next phrase was inaudible—"to Nannyhagen and West Lake Drive is on the right."

"Yeah. How far in on West Lake?" the sergeant inquired, wondering whether this was a prank call.

"Five."

Did she mean five houses? "The first house?"

Her voice rose in panic. "The first, the corner, and then the second," she said.

"Is it right near Nannyhagen?" he persisted.

"Yes," then a few more words that were muffled by her sobs.

Now he, too, was beginning to sound frustrated. "Ah, boy," he said. "Do you have any smoke in the house?"

"Yes," she cried, almost shrieking.

His next question turned her tears into hysteria. "I don't have a Five West Lake Drive. Can you tell me exactly where the house is?"

"The baby's in the room!" she screamed, by now frantic. It was her first mention of anyone being trapped in the fire.

"All right," he said. Only then did he punch out the code that set off the pagers of volunteer firemen throughout Thornwood.

After she hung up the phone, Olivia acted with a rare presence of mind. She went upstairs and put on all the lights to direct the fire trucks to the house. Unlit, the place was hard to find after dark, being set back from the road and surrounded by shrubbery. But with the lights streaming through the skylights and the upstairs plate-glass windows, it stood out like a beacon in the night.

Most people in Olivia's situation, with a baby trapped in a smoke-filled room, would not be so aware of the fire department's needs as to go upstairs in a burning building and put on lights. Most people would have a different, overwhelming priority: to rescue the baby. There were two ways into that nursery—through a door that could be kicked open, or by going outside and breaking a window that was less than two feet from the ground. Olivia attempted neither.

Given her state of panic, putting on the lights was an extraordinary inspiration. Or perhaps this emergency procedure came to her automatically. Not until months later, when it could do her no harm, did it become known that Olivia was a fireman's daughter.

THE house where Kristie died had been given the unlikely number of five by the man who built it, Bill Fischer's former father-in-law, Jan Menting. In that time of haphazard postwar development Menting was left to pick his own house number, any odd figure from one to twenty-five. He chose five because he liked the way it sounded with the street name, thus creating the only address on that side of West Lake Drive that did not have a double-digit number.

If there had been a computerized address system in the Mount Pleasant Police Department, the desk sergeant could have resolved his doubts in a second. This was one of many pieces of technology the town board refused to get on grounds that it would cost too much. Even if a computerized system had existed that day, Kristie's death was inevitable. She was lost as soon as the flames started licking around her, which must have been happening when Olivia picked up the telephone. But prompter police action would have minimized the damage to the house and allowed for more evidence of arson to be preserved.

More important, John Gallagher would not have been the first on the scene. George Fries and probably most of the Thornwood Fire Department would have arrived ahead of him; thereafter no one else would have been admitted to the house. John would have been spared a sight he would never forget, and a great deal more besides.

Chapter Four

MOUNT Pleasant is not a town in the literal sense, but an administrative area covering twenty-eight square miles. At its hub are the three adjoining villages of Thornwood, Valhalla, and Hawthorne. The traffic between them is quiet but constant, and the community so stable that almost everyone knows everyone else.

Although much would be made of it later, it was not unusual that the first police officer on the fire scene and the lieutenant in charge that night both knew John Gallagher. Scott Carpenter, a rookie patrolman, had worked for the same construction company as John's brother Michael. The lieutenant, Louis Alagno, was the popular swimming coach in a Mount Pleasant summer program. As a teenager, John was on his team. They knew and liked one another, but it was a casual acquaintance.

The three of them came together at the fire scene, among the mess of hoses and floodlights and trucks accumulating across the front lawn. Carpenter had been out cruising in his patrol car when the radio call went out. He arrived at the Fischers' house shortly after Gregory Wind, the Thornwood fire chief.

"I pulled up in the roadway to leave room for the fire trucks to come in," Carpenter recalled. "In the front yard I saw Greg Wind looking so upset that he was almost like a zombie. He told me, 'There's a dead baby in the house.' I ran to the house and in at the front door. There was so much smoke I couldn't see a thing. I couldn't even see a door, so I had to turn around and leave. At this point I ran into John Gallagher. He was nervous, pale, and sick-looking.

" 'There's a dead baby in the house,' he said. I asked him to stick around until I could take his statement. Later I saw him staying close to the Fischers, and him and Leah hugging a lot."

Carpenter called police headquarters. "There's a D.O.A. baby and we need detectives," he reported. In the Fischers' front yard, he was relieved to see another police officer, Robert Miliambro. He, too, had been touring the neighborhood in a radio patrol car. Then Carpenter noticed Olivia standing on the patio, crying loudly. He asked her what happened, and she replied at some length in a language he did not understand. The only word that came through to him was cats. He was probably hearing *Katze*, the German word for a cat. What was all this about cats? he wondered.

He went back into the house with Miliambro. They separated, groping through clouds of smoke, searching for the baby. Miliambro found the nursery and called Carpenter to join him. The carpet around Kristie was still smoldering. So were the remnants of her undershirt and cloth diaper. The burn pattern on the carpet formed a circle around the melting infant seat, as though a flammable liquid had been carefully poured to enclose the baby in flames. This fire was no accident. Reluctantly they moved a little closer.

"I didn't see how that baby could be alive, but I leaned over to check for vital signs," Carpenter related. "You want to save a baby's life, and when it turns out you can't . . ." He left the sentence unfinished.

Outside, Miliambro spoke to Fire Chief Wind. "There's a crime scene in there," Miliambro said. "The fire in that room has been extinguished, so keep the guys out of it if you possibly can."

An ambulance worker had been giving Olivia oxygen. She no longer seemed to need it and had stopped crying entirely. Now she was quiet and self-controlled.

Carpenter was amazed at the speed of the transformation. Again he asked her what had happened, not expecting to be understood. "But she spoke English. It really took me aback. And I thought it was weird that she wasn't crying any longer. She said that she had just fed the cats, and that one had run away. Then she said she found a small fire on her bed. She noticed that the baby's door was closed, but did not appear concerned about it. She never once asked about the baby."

Carpenter led her to the Frieses' house and asked her to wait there. So far as he could tell, she was the only witness to whatever happened in the nursery, and he did not want her talking to anyone else until a detective arrived to interview her.

SEVERAL of the Mount Pleasant police officers were also volunteer firemen. The most experienced was Sergeant Brian Dwyer, with twenty-five years in the fire service, twenty-two of those years as a full-time officer in the Mount Pleasant Police Department. On call as a fireman, he was on the first fire truck to reach the Fischers' home.

As soon as Dwyer jumped out of the truck, Miliambro took him into the house and to the nursery. They noted a second, smaller burn pattern on the carpet near the nursery door. About six inches from the baby's foot was a one-liter plastic seltzer bottle, empty and partially melted, and a charred box of Diamond kitchen matches. They left these items undisturbed, to be photographed as evidence.

In Olivia's room they saw the remains of another strange fire. There was a burn area about two feet square in the middle of her bed. Someone had put out this blaze with a fire extinguisher, leaving a residue of chemical foam around the scorch marks. Nothing else in the room was damaged. Although this fire, too, appeared to have been deliberately set, there was no evidence of an intruder. As in the nursery, the window in Olivia's room was closed and latched.

Later Dwyer noticed a sizable hole in the nursery window, which must have been caused by a heat break, not only because of the closed latch but also because the shattered glass was outside the house. If anyone had broken in, the shards would have been inside the room.

ONE of the first priorities of firefighters involves checking every room to make sure that no one is trapped and that there are no extension fires behind furniture or in closets. Leah's closed door aroused the suspicions of the first firemen who came into the house, but their attention was drawn away from it to the body in the nursery. The size and helplessness of the victim magnified their sense of shock. The knowledge of what lay inside the nursery dominated the consciousness of every fireman present that evening, coupled with a feeling of helplessness that they had all arrived too late to save this baby.

Initially no one noticed that the latch on Leah's door was similar to the nursery's and that it, too, had been locked from the inside. In fact, Leah never latched her door in the daytime, let alone locked it, because she was more concerned about the cats being trapped in her room than with forestalling comments about her untidiness.

While fireman Jim Lawrence was standing in the hallway, Thornwood's second assistant fire chief, Joseph Rod, tried Leah's door. It was locked. Joe's reaction was the same as John Gallagher's had been about forty minutes earlier. Without hesitating, he kicked the door in.

Both men were startled by a rush of intense flame that leaped out of the doorway and chased them down the hall. They ran for their lives. This third fire had been burning in Leah's room until it had exhausted all the oxygen and subsided to a mass of smoldering residue, ready to burst into an inferno as soon as fresh air was let in.

The door to Leah's room, unlike the one to the nursery, fit tightly on all sides. If either her door or her window had been slightly open, the fire would have fanned down the corridor or outside the house in search of more oxygen.

There were several moments of confusion before all hoses were directed to this new fire. Then the powerful force of water drove the flames back into Leah's walk-in closet, which was separated from

the nursery closet by a thin wooden partition. Fueled by her clothing, the fire raced through this partition and emerged out of the
baby's closet, starting a second blaze in the nursery. As soon as the
firemen trained their hoses on this, the crime scene became thoroughly contaminated. The force of water dislodged the empty soda
bottle and the matches, created piles of debris, and washed away any
footprints or fingerprints an arsonist might have left behind.

The evidence of the heat break in the nursery window also became
confused as Brian Dwyer, fighting the fire from outside the house,
smashed out the rest of the broken pane with the end of his folding
ladder to make enough space for another hose to be brought in. Now
there were shards of glass on the nursery carpet as well as on the
ground outside, leaving Dwyer with a visual memory that would later
cause him, and the prosecution, a great deal of trouble.

Only Kristie's pathetic remains were carefully avoided.

THAT night the Mount Pleasant Police Department was short of staff.
Lieutenant Louis Alagno had struggled through an eight-hour shift
feeling terrible and had gone straight home to bed. He did not know
it then, but he had pneumonia. Detective Bruce Johnson had finished
his day's work at 4:30 p.m. When Scott Carpenter called the police to
report what he had seen in the nursery, the desk sergeant telephoned
Alagno and Johnson and asked them to come back on duty.

In fairness to himself, Alagno should have declined. He had a fever
of 102, and the dampness of this December day was turning into a
steady rain. But it was part of his job to take charge of a crime scene.
So he got out of bed, hurriedly dressed, and walked to Five West Lake
Drive, which was around the corner from where he lived.

The desk sergeant's call reached Detective Bruce Johnson at his
home in Valhalla before he had a chance to eat. He flung on a jacket,
strapped his pistol on his hip, and drove to the fire scene. He knew
exactly where to find it. He had grown up seven houses away.

Lou Alagno was there about ten minutes before him and had already determined that there were two witnesses to be interviewed:
John Gallagher and Olivia Riner. Alagno remembered Gallagher
from the swimming team and from Gallagher's having amassed some
speeding tickets, and he told Scott Carpenter not to let him leave
without getting a written statement. This was standard procedure.

Alagno had learned that the nursery fire was already raging when Gallagher came upon it, whereas Olivia was there when it started. He decided that interviewing her would be a detective's job. "At this stage she was not a suspect, but the best witness we had," he said.

When Bruce Johnson arrived at about 5:40 p.m., Brian Dwyer took him around outside to the broken nursery window and invited him to peer through the hole. The fire in Leah's room had not yet erupted, so the hole was exactly as Dwyer had found it: about a foot across and jagged at the edges. Johnson warily stuck his head through the hole and beamed his flashlight into the room. The beam fell upon the ravaged infant carrier and on the charred body of its occupant.

As a detective, he was trained to observe and remember as much detail as possible. As a father, he would afterward wish that he wasn't. His strongest memory of the scene, the one he could not afterward shake no matter how hard he tried, was the position of the baby's arms: outstretched, with the tiny fingers clenched in defenseless anguish. He hoped she had not suffered, that the smoke overcame her before the fire. He checked for footprints on the windowsill and on the muddy earth below. There were none. But near his feet were fragments of glass from the heat break, and he noted that the window was latched. It was beyond his comprehension how anyone could have broken in without a trace and committed so outrageous a crime.

"I'm GOING to let Brian do the crime scene and select the evidence, and you can do the interviews," Alagno told Johnson.

Johnson walked to the Frieses' house, where he found Olivia sitting at the dining table, still a little tearful but essentially calm. He sat next to her and pulled out his notebook. "I'm a police detective and I'd like to ask you some questions," he told her.

She answered quietly, telling him her name, her home address in Wettingen, and the fact that she had arrived in the United States on November 1, four days before her twentieth birthday. He found her English quaint but comprehensible, and she seemed to have no difficulty understanding him.

This was her story.

From the time Bill Fischer finished his lunch break, she was alone in the house with the baby and the four cats. At about 5:00 p.m. she fed the animals in the laundry room; then Oliver, the black cat, went to her room, where he liked to sleep on the bed. After a few minutes he came running out into the hallway, "very angry." She went to see what had disturbed him and found a circle of bright orange fire burning fiercely in the middle of her bed. Upstairs, in the kitchen, there was a fire extinguisher, one of three in the house. She ran to get it, pulled the pin with some difficulty, and put out the fire. She noticed that her bedroom window was open about ten inches, although she had left it closed.

Then she went to check on the baby and found the nursery door locked. She was positive that she had left it open. This significant detail differed from her earlier account to Bill, in which she said she herself had closed the nursery door to keep out the cats. She told Johnson that she saw smoke coming from under the door and telephoned for help. She had no idea how the fires started or how the door became locked, and she neither heard nor saw anything suspicious before Oliver's warning of the blaze on her bed.

It was an odd tale. Johnson was struck that she seemed to have made no attempt to rescue the baby. Surely, he argued to himself, it would be instinctive for a person in charge of an infant to try to save that child from certain death. This girl had not even tried.

Olivia did not ask Bruce Johnson whether Kristie had been rescued. Nor did she mention hearing her cry or choke, although, as he would later discover, a working monitor in the baby's room was directly connected to a receiver in hers.

At about 7:00 p.m. Brian Dwyer came looking for him. "Joe Butler has arrived," he told Johnson. "I think you should talk to him."

Joseph A. Butler, Jr., the arson investigator from the Westchester County District Attorney's Office, was a welcome sight at any fire scene. He had an encyclopedic knowledge about the causes and behavior of fire. In his seventies, he had the energy and enthusiasm of a man half his age. His stocky figure commanded the respect of every police officer and firefighter in Westchester.

At the fire scene, Bruce Johnson learned from Joe Butler that all three fires were separately and intentionally set by the ignition of a liquid accelerant. Butler could tell from the pour patterns that the arsonist was an amateur and had worked from inside the house, moving deliberately from room to room.

By the time Butler arrived, the fire in Leah's room had been extinguished, leaving a mass of charred and smoldering rubble. He pointed to the elliptical pour pattern on the carpet around the bed, similar to the one that encircled the infant seat on the nursery floor. More flammable liquid had been used in Leah's room than anywhere else.

The localized blaze in Olivia's room was very different. In the center of the large burn on her bed, there was a smaller area that the fire had not penetrated so deeply, as though some item lying on top of the bedspread had protected it.

Detective Johnson went into the nursery and saw the partially melted plastic soda bottle and the charred box of matches. He took video photographs of the body, working in a routine, mechanical way to avoid dwelling on those tiny outstretched arms.

In the laundry room he saw that Olivia had indeed fed the cats. Their feeding bowls were empty, but in the sink was an empty cat food can that someone had recently washed out. Johnson's attention was drawn to a plastic recycling bin in which there were about eighteen empty one-liter soda bottles, similar to the bottle on the nursery floor.

Checking around the house, he noticed that while the nursery and Leah's windows were latched, Olivia's was open. A couple of firemen told him that they had opened it.

Johnson stopped to speak with Scott Carpenter, who repeated what John Gallagher had just told Carpenter about the locked nursery door and the fire around the baby. Sitting beside his friend's brother in a patrol car, smoking one of his cigarettes, Carpenter had elicited the story in painful detail. Gallagher had choked up badly, and Carpenter had felt concerned about him; he looked so dazed and sick.

RETURNING to the house next door, Bruce Johnson found Olivia still seated at the dining table. He repeated his questions about the events leading up to the fire, and she retold her story in the same chronology but with a difference. This time she said she was not in the laundry room when Oliver ran out of her bedroom in fright, but was in the family room, playing with O.J., the marmalade cat.

They were barely fifteen minutes into this second conversation when his attention was diverted by the sight of Lieutenant Louis Alagno entering the Frieses' house by the back door, ushering in a very distressed couple. The man was sobbing and the woman crying hysterically. He did not need to be told who they were.

"I knew I had to get Olivia out of there quickly, because I wanted to avoid a confrontation at all costs," Johnson recounted. "We had a rapport going, and I didn't want anything to break it."

He led her to the front door, explaining that he would like to continue the interview in his office. She did not demur. His manner toward her had been quiet and affable, and he was making an effort to inspire confidence. He assessed her as a compliant but reluctant witness who knew more than she was telling.

It was almost 8:00 p.m. when Johnson sat Olivia down beside his desk in the detectives' office and began a more probing interrogation. He was increasingly suspicious about the inconsistencies in her story. By about 8:30 p.m. he had ceased to think of her as an innocent bystander and, while still addressing her politely as Miss Riner, was framing the kind of questions that he would put to a suspect.

Chapter Five

JOE Butler had reached the fire scene at almost 7:00 p.m. His immediate task was to establish whether this was arson and, if so, whether a life had been lost as a direct result of the criminal action. Unlike the firemen and the police, he was able to walk around the nursery without flinching. Not that the sight failed to disturb him, but in his experience of thousands of fires, he had seen so much worse. He paced around the room with professional curiosity, documenting the details in his mind. Tomorrow he would write his report from memory, the way he always did.

What he saw was clearer proof of arson than he had expected.

"On the rug was a distinctively placed flammable liquid which I would attribute to a pour and not a throw," he observed. "There had been another fire coming from the closet, but there was not much burned in the room except near the baby."

That meant someone had entered the room and virtually walked around the baby, dribbling flammable liquid in a circle that enclosed her as she lay in the infant carrier on the rug. It was a carefully executed, purposeful act. No one leaning through the window or standing by the door, flinging fluid from a bottle, could have achieved this result. Whoever set the nursery fire intended to kill Kristie or to destroy all evidence of something that had already happened to her.

It took Butler less than an hour to establish that, in the phraseology of his formal report, "there was no plausible, natural, mechanical, electrical or accidental causation for this fire which was deliberately set with the use of a flammable fluid as an accelerant." Furthermore, he felt certain that Kristie's death was murder. He judged that about three pints of volatile liquid had been used, most of it in Leah's room, a small amount on Olivia's bed, and the contents of the soda bottle in the nursery. He smelled the empty bottle and decided that it had contained a petroleum-based distillate.

The police had already put in a request for the medical examiner to come to the scene. Joe Butler was appalled to learn that instead of making a personal trip, the medical examiner had sent an investigator, William Fazzalaro, with a van to transport the body to his laboratory.

"Do not move this body," Joe Butler told him. "Before you touch it, I must notify my office and find out what they want to do about it."

Butler recounted, "He thought I would get clearance immediately. But the phone in the house was not working, so I went across the street to a neighbor. I called John Keating [chief criminal investigator in the D.A.'s office], but he was not at home. So I called the assistant district attorney on duty. He was not at home either. I tried three others. It was terrible. An A.D.A. called back fairly soon, and he said, 'Well, I don't know what to tell you. I'll have to call one of my superiors for advice.'

"I was then advised to call A.D.A. James McCarty. I could not get him immediately, had to put a beeper call out for him. The police thought I had disappeared, and I had told them not to move anything. The firemen were champing at the bit because this was delaying cleanup. McCarty called back and said, 'Don't let anyone move the body. I want to look at it first.' So that was more delay. I got back to the scene after at least an hour of relatively wasted time. It was about ten p.m. before McCarty arrived."

Lieutenant Alagno, the police officer in charge, also wanted the medical examiner to come personally, concerned that important evidence might be lost if the body was moved before a pathologist saw it. Alagno asked Fazzalaro to telephone his office. "Tell them I want the medical examiner to come out here," he urged.

Minutes later Fazzalaro returned from making the call, with a report that the medical examiner would not be coming.

Finally, after a chilling three-hour wait, Fazzalaro went through the grisly mechanics of his task. Working in near darkness, sometimes ankle-deep in water, he made his diagrams, took his photographs, and, as best he could, checked the body for trauma. It is arguable whether a forensic pathologist would have picked up additional information, but Louis Alagno would always blame himself for not being more insistent that the medical examiner come.

As Bill Fazzalaro gently lifted Kristie's body from the infant seat, a portion of her cloth diaper fell off. It had escaped the fire because she had been lying on it. Sergeant Brian Dwyer, one of the small group of police officers in the nursery, picked it up and instantly recognized a familiar odor. He passed it to Officer Robert Miliambro.

"What does that smell like to you?" he asked.

"Paint thinner," Miliambro promptly replied.

Dwyer nodded. Paint thinner was exactly what he had in mind.

Joe Butler had an interesting observation to add. Whatever was on the diaper was not the same flammable liquid that had been in the soda bottle on the nursery floor. They had distinctly different smells. In his experience arsonists did not encumber themselves with more than one kind of accelerant, not if they were bringing it into a building from outside.

After Bill Fazzalaro had made a discreet departure, carrying the tiny body in a small wooden box, Dwyer and Miliambro went through the house taking videos and photographs, and searching for evidence. It was an eerie scene. There was no electricity in the house, and the firemen's floodlights cast bright beams and long shadows as they moved from room to room. Outside, it was still raining heavily, and bitter cold.

In the wreckage of the family room the two men soon found the closet where Bill Fischer kept some of his construction supplies. They were impressed by its orderliness, with clearly labeled cans of oil and paint placed in logical arrangement. It came as a shock to see a two-liter white plastic container lying on its side on the closet floor. It had contained paint thinner and was almost empty.

On a shelf above, there were two containers for other flammable liquids. One held charcoal-lighter fluid; the other, a metal can of Coleman appliance fluid for camping stoves. Both were virtually empty. The last person to use the Coleman fluid had set the cap loosely on top of the can, as though too hurried to be bothered. The two officers carefully placed the containers in their evidence cans for laboratory testing. The burned box of matches and the partially melted soda bottle were put in separate cans.

They looked indecisively at the infant seat, which Fazzalaro had left behind. "What about the baby carrier?" they asked Joe Butler, who, as a representative of the D.A.'s office, was nominally in charge.

"No need for that," Butler replied, meaning that since Fazzalaro had not taken it with the baby, he saw no reason to send it to the laboratory for separate analysis. He knew the plastic would not yield any trace of a volatile substance, though he shared Lou Alagno's silent outrage: Why hadn't this man brought an adult-size body bag so he could have taken the infant seat with the baby still in it? Maybe there were clues in that seat, in the way it was burned, in the way the baby was positioned, that could be important to a forensic pathologist.

Nevertheless, Butler assumed that the police would take the carrier for their own collection of evidence. "It would be normal police work to take it," he said. "When I saw them gathering up lab samples in the nursery, I presumed they would also take what they needed for themselves. I never dreamed they would leave that infant carrier."

Butler had no sense of the awe in which Westchester policemen held him. He was so knowledgeable that no officer ever questioned his judgments. What they heard him say that night became incontrovertible. Afterward they would regret leaving the seat glued to the charred remnants of the nursery rug, to be seen and wept over by Bill and Denise Fischer. But it remained there until later in the week, when it was realized that there would probably be a murder trial and that it would be important for a jury to see this horribly heat-deformed object that had so recently cradled a living child.

Chapter Six

OVER his forty years in the Mount Pleasant Police Department, twenty-five of them at its head, Police Chief Paul Oliva had built up a reputation for straight dealing and a demanding standard of professionalism. He was widely respected among his peers, stubborn, and suspicious of any authority but his own. Soon to retire, he had run the department

The Fischers' house at Five West
Lake Drive, Thornwood, New York.

John Gallagher and Leah Fischer

Denise and William Fischer leaving
court on the day before the verdict.

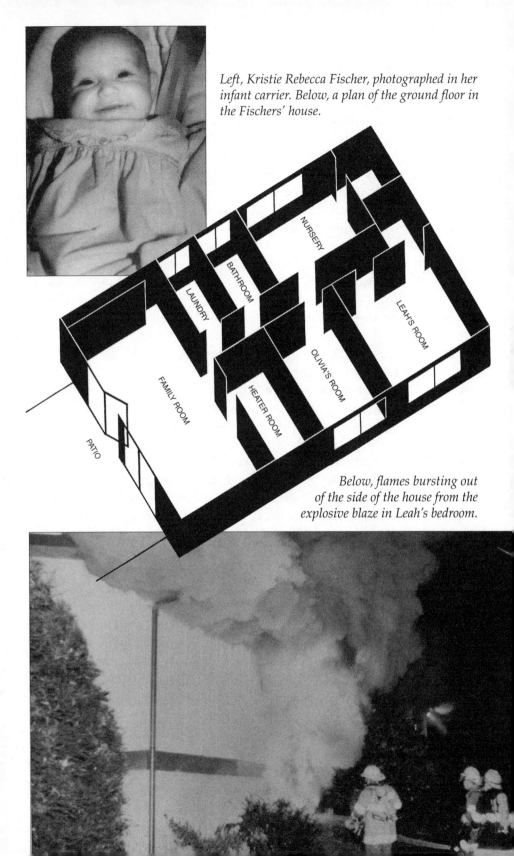

Left, Kristie Rebecca Fischer, photographed in her infant carrier. Below, a plan of the ground floor in the Fischers' house.

NURSERY

BATHROOM

LAUNDRY

LEAH'S ROOM

FAMILY ROOM

HEATER ROOM

OLIVIA'S ROOM

PATIO

Below, flames bursting out of the side of the house from the explosive blaze in Leah's bedroom.

like his private fiefdom. As an administrator, he sometimes had his critics, but in one area he could not be faulted.

"He is an excellent, excellent cop," said Bruce Johnson, who was trained by him. "He is from the old school, a cop's cop, self-taught, with a good sense of judgment and a nose for criminal investigation." When it came to solving a complex case, it was the inborn sagacity and the sixth sense of Paul Oliva that were most likely to be on-target—to the extent that smaller police departments in the county called on him for advice.

On the evening of December 2, 1991, Lieutenant Louis Alagno called Paul Oliva at home. The police chief was spending a quiet evening with his wife at home in the neighboring village of Valhalla. Minutes after Alagno's call he was back in his office.

BRUCE Johnson was already in the detectives' room, questioning Olivia. It was sparsely furnished, with four metal desks, vinyl tiling on the floor, and a general impression of drab monotony. The police department furnishings were a low priority on the town budget.

Johnson was seated at his desk in a swivel chair, with Olivia in a straight-backed chair to the side of him. He swung around to face her and, in the brightness of the recently installed neon strips, was startled to notice that her eyelashes were singed. He had not been able to see this in the subdued lighting of the Frieses' dining area, and it instantly recalled a memory for him—that of preparing a barbecue in his own backyard and not being sufficiently cautious. As he put it: "How many times have I lit my gas grill and it poofed up in my face and singed my eyelashes?" He remembered the immediate reaction of needing to rub his eyes. And he saw that Olivia's eyes were still quite red.

The combustion that causes singed eyelashes is an entirely different phenomenon from that of being burned by flames, which, he conceded, might have happened to Olivia when she extinguished the fire on her bed. That would most likely singe her long hair, perhaps also her eyebrows and bangs, but not her eyelashes alone. Singed eyelashes meant only one thing to him—that she had bent over an incendiary liquid and the vapors had risen and pooled, as they automatically will, in her eye sockets. She would not have been aware of this until a source of flame, like a lighted match, ignited those vapors. To Johnson singed eyelashes were the mark of someone who had lighted explosive material, not of a person using an extinguisher to douse the fire.

Bruce Johnson was not yet ready to draw Olivia's attention to her eyelashes, especially since she seemed unaware of their ragged appearance. If he brought out his camera now, she would realize that he suspected her. If he delayed too long, she might rub her eyes and remove the evidence. His impression that she had guilty knowledge of the crime was getting stronger by the minute, and he knew that his best chance of getting her to tell him about it was to maintain a friendly, inquiring manner. He decided to risk postponing a question about the eyelashes until later in this interrogation.

Again he asked her to describe the events leading up to the fire. She recalled preparing an eight-ounce bottle of formula shortly before Bill's arrival for lunch at about 1:45 p.m. She sat on the nursery floor feeding Kristie, while Bill ate upstairs in the kitchen. After the baby had taken about five and a half ounces of formula, Olivia burped her, then put her in the infant seat on the rug, with a rolled-up cloth diaper to prop one side of her head. Soon Kristie fell asleep.

After Bill left, Olivia said she sat in her bedroom reading and writing until about three o'clock, when the baby wakened. She offered her the remainder of the eight-ounce bottle, and Kristie drank most of it. She changed the baby's diaper, but not the rest of her outfit, which she described as a light green one-piece suit with ruffles and white stripes at the wrist, worn over a white undershirt.

She then warmed up a smaller, four-ounce bottle of formula and sat in the family room with Kristie in her arms, feeding her the contents of this second bottle. While doing so, she heard "the propane man" make his 4:20 p.m. delivery. Kristie soon fell asleep, and at about 4:30 p.m. Olivia put her back in her carrier near the nursery window. She was now positive that she left the nursery door open.

Bruce Johnson's naturally benign expression betrayed none of his incredulity. Remembering the infancy of his daughters, he was thinking, How on earth could a three-month-old baby ingest twelve ounces of formula in two and a half hours? He wondered whether Kristie regurgitated the excess and choked to death, whether the nursery fire was a cover-up for an act of carelessness or stupidity that Olivia was afraid to admit. He pressed on with his questions.

Olivia did not react like any young person he had ever met, even allowing for the fear she must have felt in this alien place, traumatized

by whatever she had seen of the fire. He was used to young people
who act affronted and defiant when interrogated about a crime in
which they deny involvement. This girl sat passively still except for the
constant twirling of her hands in her lap, twisting a sodden tissue. In
a quiet voice that rose a little with each denial, she protested that she
had no idea how the fires started or how the nursery door became
locked. The mystery became more mysterious when she volunteered,
"If anyone else was in the house I would either hear or see them from
any place I would be downstairs." Those were her exact words, as
Johnson carefully remembered them.

He made few notes during this extended conversation. Note-taking
was not a practice Paul Oliva encouraged. In Oliva's reasoning, "A
seasoned police officer is trained to observe, to keep information in
his head. He will do his report later, and most cops do it from memory. Otherwise, the other side can subpoena his notes."

Throughout this interview a woman civilian dispatcher sat in the
room—a police requirement when a female is interrogated. On several occasions Johnson stopped his questioning to inquire whether
Olivia would like anything to eat or drink, or to have the dispatcher,
Betsy Hoagland, take her to the ladies' room. But every time, Olivia
refused. Again Johnson privately marveled at her inner fortitude.

Johnson had her go over and over the story. All her versions tallied
until she finished telling about going into the laundry room to feed
the cats. Then the narrative would shift back and forth, as it had done
earlier, with no satisfactory account of that crucial half hour before the
fire. There was the version in which she was in the laundry room when
the black cat, Oliver, came rushing out to warn her of the blaze on her
bed. And there was the version in which this happened while she was
in the family room with the television on, playing with O.J.

Her stories became consistent again when she told about finding
and extinguishing the fire on her bed, hearing the smoke alarms go
off, and discovering that she could not open the nursery door.

Watching her intently, he observed that whenever he asked about
the baby in relation to the fire, she shrank into an attitude of avoidance and withdrawal. Her voice sank to a whisper, and her head bent
so far forward as to hide her face behind the lank curtain of hair.

"All the time I was interviewing her, there was no emotion, no eye
contact, and her body language was that she was lying," Johnson

recalled. "She just sat there with this stoic stare, as though she was not really there. She was talking in a monotone all the way through. I don't believe that she thought I suspected her, not at that time. I had read John Gallagher's statement and had ruled him out, simply because of the layout of the house. It was so small. There was no way that anyone could have come in without her knowing. And she herself was admitting that she would have heard or seen if anyone else had been downstairs. She was adamant about that."

AFTER about an hour Police Chief Oliva arrived. Johnson stopped by the chief's office down the corridor and summarized what Olivia had told him and what he had observed. When he described her singed eyelashes, the chief became excited.

"Bruce, that could be the most crucial piece of evidence in this entire case!" he exclaimed.

Back in the detectives' room, Johnson asked Olivia where she was standing when she put out the fire in her room. Was she at the side of her bed or at the foot of it? At the foot, she replied. Johnson was thinking, The bed has a footboard at waist level to a person of Olivia's height. She could not have bent over it low enough to get her eyelashes singed. No way.

"If she had told me that she was at the side of her bed when she put out the fire, I might have believed that was how she got her eyelashes singed," he related. "But I asked where she was standing again and again, and she was dead sure."

By this time a small group had gathered in the police chief's office. Louis Alagno and Joe Butler had come in from the fire scene, along with two assistant district attorneys. Bruce Johnson stopped by again and filled them in on Olivia's story.

They all assumed that Kristie was dead before the blaze began. The thought that a living baby was deliberately set on fire was unacceptably abhorrent to everyone in the room.

"We discussed it back and forth, trying to figure what the hell happened," Paul Oliva related. "This was a twenty-year-old girl, not much more than a child herself. We went over what we had: the matches left at the scene; her admission that she was alone in the house; her statement that she gave the baby twelve ounces of formula, which sounded more like she was trying to explain away time; her conflicting accounts of where she was when the fire started. But most of all, the singed eyelashes."

Paul Oliva picked up on a clue that everyone else had missed. "This girl calls the police and is screaming fire. She has already put out the fire on her bed. How does she know that a fire is raging behind a locked door in the other room?"

"She saw smoke coming from under it," someone suggested.

"The fire was near the window," Oliva countered. "And smoke does not come out at the bottom of a door unless the room is saturated. And when a fire is really raging, the smoke is minimal." The police chief had not yet heard John Gallagher's account of seeing flames, not smoke, reflected on the tiled floor beneath the nursery door, even after Olivia had telephoned for help.

All this added up to a persuasive collection of circumstantial evidence, in addition to the direct evidence of Olivia's singed eyelashes. There was a strong feeling in the room that she was the arsonist.

The police chief was faced with a decision that might have waited until the next day if Olivia Riner had not been a foreign citizen. If she were an American, he might have let her go, keeping a careful watch on her while his department tried to find more evidence. He dared not take that risk with Olivia and could not hold her overnight without charges. This left him no option but to have her arrested. Who knew who might spirit her off on the next plane to Switzerland?

Bruce Johnson was in his office down the corridor, still trying to extract a confession, when shortly after 10:00 p.m. his private-line telephone rang. It was Brian Dwyer calling from the fire scene to tell him about the odor of paint thinner on the fragment of Kristie's diaper. Johnson muttered a quick thank-you and rang off, not wanting Olivia to hear of this dramatic discovery. He went back to the chief's office for another brief conference, returned to the detectives' room, advised Olivia of her legal rights, and at 10:30 p.m. told her that she was under arrest for arson.

LIKE most detectives, Bruce Johnson had the words to the Miranda warning committed to memory.

"You have the right to remain silent and refuse to answer questions. Anything you do say may be used against you in a court of law. You have the right to consult a lawyer before speaking to the police and to have a lawyer present during any questioning now or in the future. If you cannot afford to hire an attorney, one will be provided for you without cost.

"You can decide to stop answering questions at any time. Do you understand each of these rights that I have explained to you?"

"Some I don't," she told him.

"What don't you understand?"

"Some words. What's remain?"

"Be quiet, you can just be quiet."

"What's court of law?"

"That is the, ah, the American judicial system."

"The lawyer?"

"The lawyer is someone who can represent you for legal purposes. Do you understand these now?"

"What's afford to hire?"

"If you don't have money, the court will appoint an attorney for you."

"Oh. Decide?"

"It's a yes or no. It's up to you whether you, you can decide to answer questions or not answer the questions."

"That all?"

"Yes." Continuing with the formal warning, he added, "Having explained these rights to you, do you wish to still talk to me? I'm going to ask you the same questions I have been asking since I've seen you."

"I can't say anything different."

"So you wish to still discuss it with me?"

"I can talk, but I can't say anything different."

"Okay, okay." He switched on the tape recorder behind his desk. During the next fifty-seven minutes, all of them now on the record, he had her go over the afternoon's events once more.

She seemed almost eager to tell him the domestic details of her day, as in her description of Bill's arriving home for lunch. "He come into Kristie's room and talk with her. Then he go upstairs and she begin drooling badly. Sometimes she make noises, and then I put her on the shoulder and then she got quiet."

And again when she prepared the first bottle: "She eats about five, five and one half ounces. Then she make two big burps. Then she sleep and I put her in the seat. And then I give her the pacifier. And then I go in my room. And the door is open. She sleeps where I can see her. Bill looks in room and see that she is sleeping and then he waitens, quiet, like he wants to see her and says 'See you later.' "

She had a precise memory about Kristie's waking up and being fed the second bottle that afternoon. "I go upstairs and put her in the swing because I want to make another bottle. And she was happy in the swing, and I go downstairs to the living [family] room. And then she a little hungry so I give her a bottle. But she don't really want to drink. Then I play with her, talk with her, and then she sleep in my arms."

It sounded so innocent and dutiful. Olivia went on to tell how she put Kristie back in the infant seat on the nursery rug before feeding the cats in the laundry room. In this final version she had let two of the four cats out of the house and was in the family room, playing with O.J. and watching TV, when "I see Oliver run out from my room and I go to look why and I see fire in my bed."

She described running upstairs to the kitchen for a fire extinguisher, conveying the panic she felt when she was not immediately able to make it work.

After putting out the fire, she said, "I try to make the light on in my room because it is dark. The light didn't go, and then I see the door from Kristie's room is locked, closed. And I try. It's locked. I try. It's locked." With every successive word "locked" her voice rose a little higher. "Then I run and then I see the smoke. The smoke. And I run for my room and look for telephone number. A little note for telephone numbers. And then around, around the living room for a phone to call operator and tell him fire. And then I tell another man and tell him fire and give him address. And he asked me many times.

"And then the telephone rings. The man say he has no address for Five West Lake Drive. I tell him near from Nannyhagen Road. The first house. Then I put it down. And then, so maybe they can find it, it's dark, and I run upstairs and make light. All the lights I make."

As soon as she got back downstairs, she opened the front door to let Oliver out. Then John Gallagher arrived, and O.J. scampered out of the house as John ran in.

"What did he say to you?" Johnson asked.

"Oh, I don't know what he say. I was very nervous."

"Prior to John coming up the driveway, there was nobody in the house with you?" he asked her.

"I see nobody. I don't see someone."
He repeated the question several times, always getting a negative response.
"Then you don't know how the fire started on your bed?"
"No."
"And you don't know how a fire started in Kristie's room?"
"No, I don't."
"And her door got closed?"
"No."
"And the smoke coming out from under Kristie's door?"
"Yes, I see only smoke."

THE taping finished at 11:37 p.m. Toward the end of it Betsy Hoagland went off duty, and another civilian dispatcher, Marie Solimando, took her place in the detectives' room.

After turning off his tape recorder, Bruce Johnson ventured the question that had been on his mind for more than three hours: How did Olivia get her eyelashes singed? She looked startled, thought for a moment, then said it must have happened when she put out the fire in her room. Marie walked across to take a look and noticed that the singed ends of Olivia's lashes were an ashy white. Johnson brought out his Polaroid, took a shot of Olivia's face, wasn't satisfied with the result, and took more photographs with his 35-mm camera.

Olivia's ordeal was far from over. Next he told her to undress and left her alone with Marie. Officer Scott Carpenter, who had accompanied Johnson and Olivia from the fire scene, had already been sent back to the Fischers' house to bring her a change of clothes. Olivia removed her black pants, hooded purple shirt, and purple sneakers. Then she took off her underwear. Marie folded the clothing and put it in a brown paper bag. Subsequent laboratory analysis would find no traces of flammable liquid on anything Olivia was wearing; however, the tests for accelerants were not considered conclusive, because there was a delay of several days before they were carried out.

While she changed, Johnson had another conversation with his chief. They were joined by Sergeant Brian Dwyer, just back with news of his discovery of the disturbed and emptied containers of paint thinner and other accelerants in Bill Fischer's storage closet. Everything was pointing to this arson being an inside job and to Olivia Riner as the culprit. Bruce Johnson still hoped to get a confession that night. "Let me take a shot at her," Paul Oliva offered.

They went back to the detectives' room and tackled the prisoner together—Bruce Johnson playing the tough guy and Paul Oliva acting avuncular. It was their strategy that, needled by Johnson's change of attitude, Olivia might confide in the chief. Soon Brian Dwyer joined in the questioning—three strong men verbally battering a shy young girl who had only a limited knowledge of their language and their laws. She continued to give direct answers until the questioning got close to the fire in the nursery; then again she looked into her lap, letting her hair fall forward and screen her face.

"I questioned her for six hours," Johnson recounted. "For four of them I was very gentle with her, and for two I acted like a bastard. But nothing worked."

Shortly after midnight Bruce Johnson asked her, harshly and directly, "Did you kill the baby?"

Her denial was vigorous, conveying no grief or shock. He pressed on, enumerating the ways Kristie could have died, assuming her dead before the fire started. "Did you drop the baby?" "Did you strike the baby?" "Did you suffocate the baby?" "Did the baby choke?"

The answer was always a vehement no. He asked whether she was sexually attracted to anyone in the Fischer family or to John Gallagher, whether she was jealous of Leah or anyone else. All these suggestions were firmly denied. He accused her directly of setting fire to the house, and she protested, "I didn't light no fire." Again and again she said this, her fractured English emphasizing her negative response. Was she covering for someone else, even—in a question he would come to regret—John Gallagher? No, no, no, she told him. She didn't light no fire, and she didn't know who did. In a house where she believed herself to be alone with a baby and four cats, bedrooms were set ablaze and doors locked as if by some supernatural force.

After a while the others gave up. Johnson was running out of steam, but Olivia looked alert enough to go on all night. At 3:00 a.m. he conceded defeat, unable to establish any kind of rapport with her. It helped him to know that Paul Oliva had done no better.

"None of us could get close to her," Johnson remarked months later. "But I had no doubt that she was guilty. Her, or someone else inside her." His last words to her, at about 3:30 a.m., were "Olivia, you need help." Then he drove home to Valhalla, utterly exhausted.

Olivia spent the rest of the night in the female holding cell at the end of the hallway from the detectives' office. It was a very small room, with blank walls on three sides and iron bars on the fourth, a toilet and washbasin behind a screen, and a bare wooden bench that was scarcely wide enough to serve as a cot. No blankets or pillow were provided. The New York State Department of Corrections does not require these comforts for overnight prisoners.

Olivia did not show outrage, anxiety, or fear at being locked in this place—none of the usual emotions that police experience from those who claim to be innocent. She stretched out on the bench, her head turned away from Marie Solimando, who sat on the other side of the bars, keeping an uneasy watch.

PART II: THE FAMILY
Chapter Seven

EVEN before she learned of the fire, Barbara Donnelly had been dreading this week. This was Monday, and Wednesday would be the first anniversary of Kim Marie's death. The pain of it had become so much part of her that she and her husband, Jim, had almost forgotten what it was like to live without it. Kimmy was the last of their three children, born long after Debra and Jimmy, on the brink of their middle age. Kimmy was so precious to them because her coming had been a surprise. On this gray Monday in December, a year after her death, it seemed the worst of fate's cruelties that a similar tragedy should shatter the lives of Barbara's brother Bill and his wife, Denise.

In the Donnellys' living room, where Bill and Denise and Leah and John took refuge on that night of the fire, a photograph of Kimmy sat on top of the large television set—a portrait of a pale and delicate child wearing a blue-and-white pinafore dress and a little pink turban that she had fashioned for herself.

She was ill, on and off from the time she was three, with childhood leukemia. For the next four years she was in and out of hospitals, and toward the end, mostly in. Barbara had been grateful for the comfort of the church during Kimmy's last illness. But it was beyond her understanding that God would let Kimmy die when so many people were praying for her. While Barbara's faith had wavered, Jim became a regular churchgoer again; day after day he would go alone to an early Mass, hoping to find healing and peace.

Like all the Fischers, Barbara did not show her feelings. Of the three in her generation, she was the middle child, Bill the eldest, and her other brother, Bob, the baby. They all had a muscular leanness, fresh complexions, and light blue eyes of a rare intensity.

In her early childhood and through all the periods of remission, Kimmy and her maternal grandfather, Willie, were frequent companions. Now in his seventies, Willie had been a widower since middle age. Illness had caused Kimmy to drop out of school in first grade, so she had not formed childhood friendships. Willie lovingly filled the gap, and she followed her grandfather around the garage workshop, where he loved to putter, fixing things.

Debra, the oldest child of Barbara and Jim, courageously volunteered for a bone-marrow transplant in the hope that it would help her sister. Debra's type matched Kimmy's, and Kimmy went into remission for eleven months after the transplant. Then, when recovery seemed most likely, the symptoms returned. But there were some comforting memories. When Debby married Edward "Rick" Huntington, her father got six-year-old Kimmy out of the hospital for a few hours to be her sister's flower girl. Kimmy was so excited, and they were all so proud when she managed to walk down the aisle alone. The Donnellys did not know it then, but she was coming out of remission for the last time. The cancer had spread to her knees. Soon after the wedding she lost the use of her legs, and never walked again.

Barbara and Jim's first grandchild was born to Debby and Rick at 9:20 on the evening of September 30, 1990. It was an irony and a blessing that a new life should come into the family as Kimmy was preparing to leave it. The baby boy was named Edward James, which was soon abbreviated to E.J. On December 4 Kimmy died.

EARLY the following summer word went around the family that there would soon be another child. The way Bill told it was, "Denise is pregnant, and we are going to get married." He had always been a man of few words.

When Kristie was three days old, Barbara and Jim visited Denise in

White Plains Hospital. It was a Saturday evening, and various friends were gathered around, eager to hold the new baby. Somebody asked who would be the godparents. Denise, who had long since turned away from her Roman Catholic upbringing, replied that there would be time enough for Kristie to decide about that when she was older.

Jim stood apart from them, with the baby in his arms. Out of his own bitter experience he knew that there is not always time enough, that children can die. There was a cup of water on Denise's bed table. On impulse Jim turned away from the others, dipped his finger into the cup, made the sign of the cross on the baby's forehead, and quietly said the words of the only sacrament that a layperson can administer.

"I don't know why I did it," Jim recalled. "But I knew I couldn't let that baby out of my arms until I had baptized her."

AFTER serving dinner to her father on the evening of December 2, Barbara went to her part-time clerical job for a couple of hours. When she came back at about 8:00 p.m., she was surprised to see Jim standing at the front door, anxiously waiting for her.

"What's the matter?" she asked.

"Your brother's house caught on fire," he told her.

"What?" she asked, incredulous.

"Your brother's house caught on fire," Jim repeated. "And the baby is dead."

By the time Barbara and Jim reached West Lake Drive, the blaze had been extinguished, but the fire trucks were still there. Directed next door, they found Bill, Denise, Leah, and John Gallagher in the Frieses' family room. Kitty Fries was serving coffee and snacks.

"What happened?" Barbara asked her brother.

"I don't know if it was an electrical fire, or what," he told her.

She was full of questions. "Where's Olivia?"

"She's at police headquarters."

"Why?"

"Barbara, I don't know. I don't know what happened." He looked dazed, bewildered, and sadder than she had ever seen.

Denise was numb and silent. She wept a little but most of the time sat staring into space. Nobody knew what to say or how to be of comfort. There was a lot of conjecture about how the fire could have started. Someone suggested that Olivia might be a secret smoker. Or that she had an accident with matches. Arson had not yet entered their speculations. When all the likely possibilities had been exhausted, the conversation returned to the nagging questions: Why didn't Olivia try to get the baby out of the house? What was she doing when the fire broke out? "She was always so good with the baby," Bill kept saying.

The group was soon joined by Barbara and Bill's younger brother, Bob, and his wife, Betsy, from whom he was separated. Bill's son, Troy, was the last family member to come. He had a job as an industrial designer in nearby Mount Vernon, and he was still at his office when his maternal grandmother telephoned at about 6:30 p.m.

"There's been a fire at the house, and the baby is dead," she told him. She sounded very distressed.

"I took the train there," Troy said. "I found everyone sitting around and nobody talking. Denise kept going into the kitchen to make phone calls. We realized that it was her way of coping. My father was in the group, and when I came in, I embraced him. He was sobbing. That was a shock to me—I had only seen him cry once before."

For Troy his father's tears evoked the painful memory of his decision to leave the house after Denise moved in. His father had told him about Denise's being pregnant and their plan to get married. Neither Troy nor Leah was invited to the wedding. Shortly after that, Bill set about turning Troy's room into a nursery. Shelves where Troy had kept boyhood treasures were ripped out, and the mementos of his twenty-four years put in boxes and stored in the basement. Troy felt helplessly dispossessed. He left angrily a few weeks before Kristie was born. On returning to pick up his last few possessions, he had a frank talk with his father, and to his surprise Bill became tearful.

"I didn't realize that his feelings ran that deep," Troy said.

That was the beginning of a better relationship between father and son. Troy had visited White Plains Hospital a few hours after Kristie was born, and felt a stronger sense of family than he had known since before his parents' divorce. Tonight he felt in Kristie's loss the loss of part of his own identity. Suddenly he wasn't her brother anymore.

DURING the evening Lieutenant Louis Alagno stopped by to tell the family, "There's a possibility that it was arson."

"Is that what you think?" Leah asked, surprised.

Alagno avoided a direct answer. "It's a possibility," he repeated.

After he left, they began to speculate. If there was an arsonist, John Gallagher felt it had to be Olivia because he had seen no one else around the house. Bill Fischer was reluctant to believe that, but he blamed Olivia for failing to try to rescue Kristie.

While they were talking, Kristie's body was quietly removed from the Fischers' house. After the firemen had gone home and a police guard was left on their property, there seemed no more reason for them to wait next door. At about 11:00 p.m. they drove to the old family house in North White Plains. "We have three spare bedrooms, and you can stay as long as you need," Barbara told her brother.

Nobody felt like going to bed. Denise was struggling with the denial stage of grief, unable to accept that she no longer had a baby. It was more than she could grasp, that she had said good-bye to a healthy daughter before going to work and had returned to a total void. She kept saying that she wouldn't believe Kristie was dead until she saw the body. The others exchanged glances, horrified at the thought.

John Gallagher was in no state to drive home to Mahopac, and no one suggested it. The Fischers were deeply touched that he had risked his life to try to save Kristie, and felt very protective toward him.

They talked until past 3:00 a.m., trying to absorb the shock and to share the grief. Suddenly Jim remembered the one close relative who did not yet know about the fire. In a sad, tired voice he asked, "Who's going to tell Willie this time?"

"I'll tell him," Bill said. "She was my daughter. But let him sleep tonight. I'll tell him in the morning."

Chapter Eight

MOST of the relatives heard of Olivia's arrest for arson on Tuesday's early morning radio news and gathered at the Donnellys' home to offer sympathy and help. Barbara and Jim's daughter, Debby, was among the first to arrive.

Soon after 9:00 a.m. Debby, Leah, and John Gallagher set off for the Fischers' home in search of the cats. For reasons of their own the police were also interested in finding the cats. Police Chief Paul Oliva was developing a theory that Olivia may have hated cats and started the fire by pouring flammable liquid on the animal sleeping on her bed. He needed to have the Fischers' four cats rounded up and examined for burns and accelerants.

Unaware of this, Leah was walking around in the woods at the back of the property, holding out a can of tuna fish and calling the cats. There was a shed next to the Fischers' carport, raised from the ground on cinder blocks, and after a while O.J. came crawling out from beneath it, soaked and frightened. Peering under the shed, Leah, Debby, and John spotted two other cats huddled out of reach. After a long time, they were able to coax them out. But there was no sign of Oliver, the black cat who, according to Olivia, was lying on her bed immediately before the fire in her room started. All three animals were checked by a police officer before Leah was allowed to take them away.

In the meantime Detective Bruce Johnson had been interviewing Bill and Denise. He was shocked by their changed appearances when they arrived at the police station.

"I could not recognize Denise Fischer from the lady I had seen the night before," he said. "She looked as though she had been crying until she could not cry anymore. Her eyes were black. I have never seen anyone look so bad. Bill looked terrible, too."

Johnson had to put aside his sympathy and get on with the investigation. One of the first clues had been the charred box of Diamond kitchen matches found near Kristie's body. It was important to know if they belonged in the house or were brought in from outside. Almost casually he asked Bill whether he kept stick matches around.

"Yes," Bill told him. "There were two boxes of Diamond matches and two boxes of long fireplace matches in the bookcase cabinet in the upstairs living room."

Johnson recounted, "I took them up to the house, opened the door to the cabinet, and there was just one box of Diamond stick matches, with the same bar code as the box we found in the nursery." Both boxes of fireplace matches were still there.

In the downstairs work closet, there was further evidence of the fire being an inside job. As a meticulous workman, Bill had a good memory for the quantities of liquid in the various containers and knew instantly that a considerable amount of flammable fluid was missing. He told Johnson that the plastic container of paint thinner, found almost empty and lying on its side, had been full and standing upright. He said that the emptied can of Coleman appliance fluid had been about a quarter full and that the cap, now loose, had been firmly screwed in place. The one-gallon jug of charcoal-lighter fuel, now virtually empty, had contained about three quarts.

Told of these findings, Chief Oliva observed, "It is possible that someone came into the house and set one of those fires. But not all three. And someone else would have brought his own matches."

The police had already been at work in the house, cutting out the locks from Leah's door and Kristie's. They were hoping to find fingerprints, knowing that the last person who had activated the lock had to be the arsonist. Subsequent laboratory tests would show nothing.

Bruce Johnson, meantime, had gone through Olivia's room. Other than her burned bed, everything was intact. In addition to her casual wardrobe, he found several clues to her personality. There was the locked diary, written in her neat printlike hand. Along with *The Silence of the Lambs* were several Western-style paperbacks, also in German.

On a shelf in her closet he found a pile of baby clothes, neatly folded. Olivia had told the Fischers that since she had left Switzerland, her cousin had had a baby. Denise had said that she would be glad to contribute some of Kristie's clothes as soon as they were outgrown. Denise was not yet ready to do this, and when Johnson showed her the items, she instantly recognized them as sweaters, overalls, and suits of Kristie's that had never been worn.

In the top drawer of Olivia's dresser Johnson found a cache of junk food—candy bars, potato chips, and a large quantity of marshmallows. Confronted by this evidence of an apparent eating disorder, he wondered whether it was triggered by homesickness or by an older unhappiness that Olivia had tried to escape by coming to America.

He also confiscated her camera. When the film was developed, there was one surprise among the snapshots. The first few were family pictures, including some of herself, taken in Switzerland. Then came the American ones—of the house on West Lake Drive, the baby, her new bedroom. What baffled Johnson was a close-up shot of the fire hydrant outside the Fischers' house. What was Olivia's interest in it?

He reported these findings to his superior, Louis Alagno. From the snapshots in Olivia's camera and from his view of her last night, Alagno estimated that she had gained close to twenty pounds in about a month. He wondered what inner turmoil might have caused her to shut herself in her room, stuffing food.

THAT TUESDAY AFTERNOON, THERE was a telephone call for Bill at Barbara's home from the medical examiner's office. He listened in shock to the autopsy report. Kristie had died of massive burns and smoke inhalation. She was not, as the police first assumed, the victim of a prior accident. She was a victim of the fire itself, doused by a liquid accelerant apparently while she was still alive. There was a lethal level of carbon monoxide in her lungs, which she could not have inhaled if she was already dead when the fire started. And since Olivia Riner already stood accused of arson, Bill drew the inescapable conclusion. He collapsed sobbing in Barbara's arms.

"She murdered my baby!"

EARLIER the same day, Tuesday, December 3, an unusual phone call was received at the Mount Pleasant police headquarters. The caller was Kurt Riner—or possibly an English-speaking friend representing himself as Riner—chief of civil defense for the town of Wettingen. He had heard from E. F. Au Pair, the agency that had arranged Olivia's employment, that his daughter was in police custody. In accented but fluent English he spoke to Bruce Johnson.

"He wanted to know what had happened, and I told him that his daughter had been charged with arson," Johnson said. "I asked him if she had any history of lighting fires, any problems whatsoever. He was very defensive and said no to all my questions."

Olivia was brought from her cell to take the call in Louis Alagno's office. Standing on guard by the doorway, Bruce Johnson was surprised to see her burst into floods of tears as she spoke to her father—and at this point the speaker evidently was Kurt Riner—in a language Johnson wished he understood. All that came through to him were her sobbing protests: *"Nein . . . nein . . . nein."* It was an uninhibited display of emotion, the first he had seen from her.

A few hours later, at 4:00 p.m., Olivia was taken to Mount Pleasant's small courtroom to be arraigned for first-degree arson and second-degree murder. The murder charge had been added upon receipt of the medical examiner's report. This baby did not die by accident. Whoever killed Kristie Fischer wanted her dead.

Olivia did not seem apprehensive as she was led into court. Her emotions were under control again. "I would have expected her to be tearful and frightened, surrounded by these strange people accusing her, not speaking her language," remarked Teresa Signorelli, clerk of the court. "But there was no expression, no emotion on this girl's face. Her whole personality was blank."

After the brief arraignment she was taken, unprotesting, to the county jail in nearby Valhalla, to be held without bail.

WITH hindsight Louis Alagno regretted not assigning a second detective to the investigation. "Bruce was overwhelmed," he said. But the small police department's resources were already strained, and the early evidence in this case seemed strong enough for a conviction. What was lacking with Olivia Riner was motive.

Paul Oliva was not seriously worried about this. "So far as I am concerned, we had sufficient evidence to charge her," he said. "The rest is up to the prosecution."

Although he saw the case as highly unusual, he did not envision the widespread publicity that it would generate on account of its strong emotional content and its relevance to working mothers. At that time, there were ten million women with children under the age of six in the U.S. workforce, all dependent upon a patchwork of childcare arrangements. The murder of Kristie Fischer absorbed and appalled them, as a manifestation of their worst nightmares.

DENISE Fischer had researched infant-care options with even more thoroughness than most working mothers. "I read every magazine article I could find on the subject, every book in the library," she said.

Toward the end of her pregnancy she followed up on a magazine advertisement for E. F. Au Pair, one of eight agencies in the country designated by the Immigration and Naturalization Service to place young European women in American homes. She received a prompt and informative response, outlining a program that was officially described as a cultural exchange. In reality it was a government-approved source of mothers' helpers: European girls who were willing to take care of children in exchange for the experience of living with an American family. These young women were limited to one-year cultural-exchange visas that could not be used for any other job. An au pair unhappy with her situation was not free to find other employment; she simply had to go back home.

It was an illusion to describe them as nannies, although many mothers did. What, in fact, E. F. Au Pair and competing agencies promised was a carefully evaluated English-speaking young woman between the ages of eighteen and twenty-five who was essentially a competent baby-sitter who would live as a member of the family.

In line with its standard procedure E. F. Au Pair asked Denise for information about her family, home, interests, and childcare needs. The agency claimed to have a "unique matching process" for its au pairs and host families.

"They would give us as many résumés as we wanted, but only one at a time," Denise recalled. "Olivia's were excellent, so we did not ask for more. She had worked for a pediatrician and wanted a career working with children."

They were assured that Olivia's references had been carefully checked and that before leaving Switzerland, she would be instructed in infant supervision, first aid, and emergency procedures. In the United States an agency counselor would introduce her to other au pair girls in her neighborhood and be available to resolve any problems that she or the host family might have.

Kristie was seven weeks old when Olivia arrived at New York's Kennedy Airport. Bill and Denise instantly recognized her from her photograph and felt reassured that she looked so friendly and sensible, so eager to hug the baby, whom they had brought to meet her.

For the next few weeks Denise was with Olivia every day, showing her how she wanted Kristie cared for. In all this time, she saw nothing to make her doubt the wisdom of her choice.

At the beginning of her fourth week Olivia attended one of the monthly E. F. Au Pair meetings for European girls in her area. The meeting was held at the home of an agency counselor, and Olivia was driven there by a German-speaking girl named Helga, who worked for a family in the nearby town of Greenburgh. Helga was charming and vivacious, and the Fischers hoped that this would be the beginning of a friendship.

Many months later they would see a copy of the report that E. F. Au Pair's local counselor asked Olivia to write at that meeting. Its sentiments were exactly what they might have wished for in a person entrusted with their baby. Asked what issues or concerns had arisen for her since she arrived in Thornwood, she had written, "I have no problems with my family." In answer to the question "What is it like to be an au pair?" she wrote this enthusiastic response: "For me it is an experience to see the babies first year. All the mistakes, the fun, how the baby learn, to understand what a baby think, see and talk. Every day I can see something new or different. It's simply the best thing on the world to look on a little child!"

E. F. AU Pair was the offshoot of a large international organization, Educational Foundation for Foreign Study, based in Stockholm, which ran student-exchange programs and language schools across Europe and the United States. The future of all this could be at stake if one of its au pair girls were convicted of murdering an infant in her charge. And so from the beginning a decision seems to have been made to provide Olivia Riner with the best defense that money could buy.

E. F. Au Pair went to the prestigious Manhattan law firm of Morrison Cohen Singer & Weinstein and hired Laura Brevetti, a skilled and aggressive defense attorney whose previous experience included nine years as the attorney in charge of the federal government's Organized Crime Strike Force for the state of New York. In this unusual job for a younger woman, she had developed toughness and insight. Now in private practice, she could apply her inside knowledge of prosecution strategy to build an unassailable defense. And she had a reputation for total commitment to her job.

She appeared at the Mount Pleasant police station on the afternoon of Tuesday, December 3, in time to see Olivia formally charged. A tall, impeccably groomed forty-year-old with blonded hair, she made a sharp contrast to the waiflike creature in jeans, her face pale and strained, who was led into court in handcuffs.

Laura Brevetti returned to Mount Pleasant three days later for a preliminary hearing. She had already worked out an agreement with the district attorney's office for the hearing to be waived in favor of the case going straight to a grand jury. If the grand jury failed to find a case against Olivia, she would be released immediately. If it handed up an indictment, she might be freed on bail.

By this time Kurt and Marlise Riner had arrived to see their only child. They were a quiet, unpretentious couple, jet-lagged and washed up by a tide of circumstance that seemed to overwhelm them. Kurt Riner had something of the look of Bill Fischer, except that the lines of his face were harsher and his features pinched. Bruce

Johnson tried to talk to him, but now Riner indicated that he did not speak the language. Johnson was puzzled. The man who had called from Switzerland had said that he would like to meet with Johnson soon after he arrived.

Marlise looked younger than her husband. She had been nineteen when she gave birth to Olivia; twenty years later she still had the gawky posture of a teenager.

The Riners sat near the front of Mount Pleasant's small courtroom, ill at ease but trying to project encouragement. Like their daughter, they kept their emotions hidden. But as Olivia was led back to jail, Marlise smiled at her and gave a thumbs-up sign.

Chapter Nine

HAVING salvaged what they could from the fire, the Fischers reassembled at the family house. Only Willie was absent, stricken by a grief too intense to be shared. He had not been seen since Bill broke the news to him that morning. Tomorrow would be the anniversary of Kimmy's death, and the loss of another grandchild was more than he could face. While he mourned in the solitude of his bedroom, the others sat in Barbara and Jim's living room, going over the events of the past twenty-four hours and weaving a tale around Olivia.

As the Fischers went over the story of her last few days in the household, there was one piece of unexplained time that gave rise to a variety of speculations.

Denise had gone back to work the previous Monday, exactly a week before the fire. She was at home that Thursday for Thanksgiving, and Friday was another holiday. In an effort to make the celebration pleasant for Olivia, Denise had responded to a local newspaper advertisement by inviting a German-speaking student to the Thanksgiving meal. Coincidentally, the advertisement was placed by an affiliate of the au pair agency, the E. F. Language School, which operated out of Marymount College in Tarrytown, eleven miles from Thornwood. In response to Denise's Thanksgiving invitation, it selected an East German student named Iris. Bill drove to the college to pick her up.

Iris turned out to be a cheerful, friendly girl with limited English. Olivia chatted freely with her in German and seemed so comfortable in her company that by the end of the day, they made plans to spend the next day together. In the hope that it would be the beginning of some social life for Olivia, Denise offered the use of her car.

At about 11:00 a.m. on the day after Thanksgiving, Olivia set off in Denise's car to pick up Iris. Two hours later, there was an anxious telephone call from Marymount College: Iris had been waiting all this time, but there was no sign of Olivia. She should have reached the college before 11:30. Bill had taken her to Marymount with him the previous day to show her the route. Deeply concerned, Denise telephoned the Tarrytown police, and Bill drove to the college himself, vainly searching for her.

Olivia arrived home at 3:30 p.m., unconcerned.

"Where were you?" Denise asked her.

She looked surprised. She told them that she had gone straight to the college, but could not find her new acquaintance. So she drove into White Plains, parked the car, and strolled around. On Mamaroneck Avenue, the town's main shopping street, she said she bumped into Helga, the girl who had taken her to the au pair gathering, and they chatted for a while. Then she came home.

Denise thought this an odd story, but did not question it. Four days later, after the fire, some of the Fischers began to raise doubts that had not occurred to Denise. They wondered if Olivia had actually gone to Marymount and what she did in White Plains other than encounter Helga. Several hours were unaccounted for.

ONE priority was to plan the funeral service. Neither Denise nor Bill had been to church in years. They wanted a Christian burial, but did not know anyone they could ask to officiate.

Betsy, the wife of Bill's brother, Bob, volunteered, "If you don't mind what denomination, let me make that my job." She had in mind an Episcopal rector who had baptized her son, Christopher. She remembered this priest as a caring and sensitive man. And she knew that the Fischers did not simply need an ordained minister to read the funeral rite. They needed one who would speak to their pain.

ON THE morning of Wednesday, December 4, Barbara and Jim slipped out of the house and made the short drive to Gate of Heaven Cemetery in Hawthorne to put flowers on Kimmy's grave. They went through the day acutely aware that it was the first anniversary of her death, yet feeling constrained from talking about it. The family had so much else to mourn. Denise was in a terrible state, crying most of the time. There were long periods that day when the family simply sat around, mutually supportive but barely communicating.

"After Bill and Denise learned that it was murder, it was very quiet here," Barbara remarked. "We were all numb. We could deal with Kristie's death up to that point, thinking it was an accident. But to find out this little baby was murdered . . . What goes through a person's mind to do a thing like that? We just kept asking why. Why?"

Barbara needed to be alone with her memories of Kimmy, but there was no privacy to be had. "All that week our house was wall-to-wall people," Jim said. "Bill's friends, Denise's friends, the Fischer relatives, lots of neighbors. Bill said they didn't want a wake, but every night there was a wake in our living room."

And there were the cats. Barbara felt uncomfortable if cats were anywhere near her, and now there were four in the house. Denise's longtime pet, Oliver, had finally been found—terrified, sodden, and famished—under the shed where the others had hidden. A police officer looked him over, but found no trace of accelerants. That dispelled the theory about a cat's being doused with paint thinner on Olivia's bed. It also added credence to her story about Oliver's being frightened by a mysterious source of fire. If only that cat could talk.

BARBARA and Jim had the master bedroom on the main floor. The upstairs bedrooms and bathroom became home for Bill, Denise, and Leah through most of December. John slept in the guest room. In deference to Barbara the cats were shut in Leah's room. Unaccustomed to this strange, confined space, they cried night after night.

"It was hard on all of us," Leah said. "We were crowded into that house, we had none of our own belongings, and we felt helpless."

Betsy commented, "Leah was still trying to realize that it was not a bad dream. And whenever anyone turned on the news, there was their story. It was impossible to get away from it."

Fascinated against their will, they kept tuning in to find out whether the reporters knew more than they did. It was an odd experience for them—sitting in front of a television set, seeing the wreckage of their home and of their lives exposed to curious strangers.

Their story had also made prominent headlines in the morning newspapers: BABY'S DEATH IN FIRE CHARGED TO AU PAIR. FIRE KILLS TOT; BABY-SITTER CHARGED WITH ARSON. BABY'S NANNY SET FATAL FIRE, POLICE CHARGE. And that was only the beginning.

Bill's relatives were beginning to feel under siege. Earlier in the day reporters had approached some of them outside the burned-out house; now other reporters were calling at Fischer's Garage. They wanted to know the whereabouts of Bill and Denise, but nobody was talking. None of the media people made the connection between the garage in North White Plains and the house next door, there being no listing under the name of Fischer at the house. All this made it possible for Bill, Denise, Leah, and John to slip in and out of the Donnellys' rear entrance unseen.

THE Reverend Steven Jay Yagerman was driving his three small daughters to school, with his car radio tuned to the local news. He heard the beginning of an item about a baby-sitter accused of setting fire to a house with an infant in it, and instantly switched stations. This was nothing he wanted his children to hear.

After dropping them off, he went to work out at a health club before starting his day as rector of All Saints Church in the Westchester village of Briarcliff Manor. In the hallway of the club he encountered a parishioner, Pamela Knoll. Tearfully she began to tell him about the very incident that he had heard on the radio. Her sister, Betsy Fischer, she explained, was the dead baby's aunt, whom he would remember from the baptism of Betsy's son, Christopher.

"The Fischer family does not have a priest. Can you help them?" Pam asked. She knew he would not refuse.

"I'll do as much or as little as they want," he assured her.

Later in the day Betsy telephoned. She told him this was the first anniversary of the death of another child in the family. "You will be walking into a house full of people who need a lot of help," she warned him.

When he called at the Donnellys' home a few hours later, he was shown to an upstairs bedroom, Kimmy's old room, for a private conversation with Bill, Denise, Leah, and John.

"I didn't know what to say, so I told them that this experience was new for me and that I would be struggling with it along with them.

They all told their stories. They spoke about their feelings so honestly. The room was thick with emotion, and I was conscious of being in the presence of something very unusual, very special."

After listening to them for more than an hour, he offered a prayer. They seemed to welcome it. It was evident that they wanted him to conduct the funeral service, and he promised to return the following evening to discuss details. Denise made it very clear that she did not want it said that Kristie's death was God's will or that her baby had gone to a happier place. She was offended by such platitudes.

He assured them that it was all right for them to be angry, and sensed that this was something they needed to hear.

The funeral was arranged for Friday morning, at the same time as Olivia's second court appearance so that Kristie's burial would escape the attention of the media.

On Thursday evening the Reverend Yagerman returned to the Donnellys' home and enlisted Denise's help in planning the funeral. He observed that giving her some control over the arrangements absorbed and calmed her. With an open Bible between them they searched the Scriptures for passages that were meaningful to her.

Eventually she settled on a particularly stark translation of Psalm 55, expressing the bitterness of a man betrayed by a friend he trusted. It ended with a cry for retribution: *But you, O God, will bring these murderers and liars to their graves before half their life is over.*

The following morning Steven Yagerman delivered his funeral sermon before about two hundred people, overflowing two large adjoining rooms at the Ballard-Durand Funeral Home in White Plains. "Oh, if only words could heal," he began, wishing it were so. He developed the thoughts that had come to him the night before about the willful destruction of innocent life, and he tried to make sense of this by pointing out that from such tragedy can come strength and grace and healing.

"When we come through this deep disillusionment we reach a new wisdom that places an obligation upon us," he said. "An obligation to share how it was that we made it through this. I guarantee you that others in future will need to know how you did it. And part of your healing will be in helping those others to face the unfaceable."

Some of the Fischers mentally filed his remarks as a future source of comfort. Right now it was as much as they could manage to get through today. After the brief service a small procession of them drove to the Mount Pleasant Cemetery, where Kristie was to be buried.

It was a cold day, flaking with snow, and the wind that blew across the high ridge of the cemetery was bitter. It was Kimmy's funeral all over again. Only the place was different.

The funeral urn had been placed in a small white casket for burial. Everyone was tearful as Steve Yagerman said the words of committal. Denise sobbed inconsolably. Leah clung to John for physical support. Troy held Bill in an emotional embrace.

Chapter Ten

DETECTIVE Bruce Johnson was trying to find out what Olivia did and whom she saw in the days before the fire. At his request Iris came to the Mount Pleasant police station to be interviewed, accompanied by the E. F. Language School's director of student activities, a young Englishman named Richard Polley, who spoke fluent German.

With Polley's help as translator, Iris told Johnson of her certainty that Olivia had not shown up for their planned meeting the previous Friday. The language school had an obvious place for people to meet at its entrance. Iris had waited there for some time, but saw no sign of Olivia. Polley, whose office was nearby on the main floor, confirmed her story.

Finding him receptive, Johnson asked him a favor. Would he translate the recent entries in Olivia's diary? The detective handed him the book, open to a page of her precise handwriting. Johnson already knew that its contents were innocuous, because Mount Pleasant's only German-speaking police officer, Claudia Bolwell, had read off a translation to him. He showed Polley the diary to make certain that there was no nuance of phraseology that his colleague might have missed. Apparently there was not. The last month of entries, covering Olivia's time with the Fischers, told the expected story of a young woman who had looked forward to a year in the United States but was having a hard time settling in.

"That period started with her being extremely homesick over several days," Johnson summed up. "She wrote that she wished to go home, but couldn't, because her father would not accept her failure to fulfill her obligation to stay for a year. She would cry at night, but did not want anyone to see. All her emotions were kept inside.

"She was wishing that Denise would go back to work, so that she could be alone with the baby to raise it the way she wanted. She seemed to have strong opinions about infant care.

"She seemed to be more content as time went on. She wrote that she loved the baby and that the baby was beginning to recognize her. And toward the end, she was feeling that this year would not be as bad as she had feared."

Continuing his check into Olivia's activities, Johnson located Helga. She was astonished at Olivia's story about the two of them meeting on the street in White Plains and denied it vehemently. She said she had not been anywhere near White Plains on that previous Friday, but had remained in Greenburgh for the entire day, which was confirmed to Johnson by the mother of the family she lived with.

He wondered why Olivia had lied so elaborately. She might have lost her way to Marymount and been embarrassed to admit it, or she might not have wanted to spend her day off with a girl she barely knew. That he could understand. What puzzled him was her invention of a chance meeting with Helga. It was an unlikely encounter in a busy town of fifty thousand people. Why pretend that it happened?

IN THE days immediately following the fire, Bruce Johnson made several return visits to the house on West Lake Drive. The more he paced around the downstairs area, the less likely it seemed to him that an intruder could have moved from room to room unobserved. The hallway leading to the three bedrooms, bathroom, and laundry room was only nineteen feet long, and narrow. Footsteps echoed on those vinyl tiles. The sliding windows slid noisily.

He retraced Olivia's account of the fire. He also inspected the burn patterns on beds and carpets, and estimated that "an incredible amount of accelerant" was used—probably close to two gallons.

Johnson was struck by the horseshoe-shaped burn pattern around Leah's queen-size platform bed. "One of the things the textbooks tell you is that burning somebody's bed is a sign of jealousy. And I think this girl was mad as hell at Leah. According to her diary, she thought of her as a typically spoiled young American.

"After Leah's room I think she went to the baby's room, using a lot more fluid, then to her own room. Then I think she put the cans back in the closet, ignited the fires in the order they were set, and locked the doors behind her. The only door that wasn't locked was the one to her own room, and that was the only fire she put out."

Hindsight led him to wish that he had taken more samples of carpet and bedding from Leah's room. Forensic tests would confirm it was indeed paint thinner that soaked Kristie's diaper, and that to a ninety-nine percent certainty it was the same paint thinner as the residue in the can in Bill Fischer's storage closet. "But you can't say that in court. Legally, ninety-nine percent isn't good enough. It has to be a hundred. If we had tied another accelerant, like the charcoal-lighter fuel or the Coleman appliance fluid, to the fire in Leah's room or to the one on Olivia's bed, it would have been important evidence. But we could not make that connection. There was enough soot and water in that house to destroy most of the evidence."

Johnson regretted that Kristie's infant carrier was not removed on the night of the fire, if only to spare Bill and Denise the pain of seeing it. He felt compassion for the Fischers and a strong empathy with Bill. He and Bill were of the same generation, born into the same community, shaped by the same work ethic and family loyalties. His desire to see justice done in this case came not only, as it always did, from pride in his job but also from his personal desire to help this couple to recover and get on with their lives.

He was back at the ruined house with the Fischers on the Thursday after the fire, the day before Kristie's funeral, making videotapes of the scene as the family searched the debris for personal treasures. As he moved around the house, his microphone picked up snatches of their conversation. After he had finished in the house, Johnson took a shot of Leah and John outdoors, sorting among the rubble of charred furnishings that the firemen had jettisoned out windows.

These details seemed inconsequential at the time. A more memorable incident was the arrival of a Federal Express messenger with a letter from a syndicated talk program, *The Maury Povich Show*, offering Bill and Denise the opportunity to tell their story on national television. Sickened by the intrusion, Bill flung the letter aside. And that, he assumed, was the end of his contact with the TV media.

He would soon be proved horribly wrong.

Chapter Eleven

IT WAS a little more than half a mile from the Fischers' home to the nearest shops, but not a journey to be done on foot. Most of it was on Nannyhagen Road—a two-lane highway without a sidewalk—which twisted down a steep hill. And yet for a girl in Olivia's position, lonely and in need of human contact, this was the obvious walk to take. At the bottom of Nannyhagen Road was the Rose Hill Shopping Center, a functional strip of shops behind a large parking lot.

After Olivia's arrest, when her photograph had appeared in the newspapers, the proprietor of Rose Hill's cigarette-and-candy store identified her as someone she had twice seen at the shopping center and remembered clearly because of her unusual behavior.

The first occasion was late one morning, when the young woman, who she felt sure was Olivia, came into the shop alone. She hung back by the entrance for several minutes, then nervously picked up a pack of cigarettes from a display stand, where the price was marked on a handwritten sign. Without a word she put the exact money on the counter and left. Later the storekeeper asked her assistant, "Is it my imagination, or is there something wrong with that girl?"

"She looked really out of it," the assistant replied.

Initially Bruce Johnson might have discounted the incident. Olivia said she did not smoke, and there were no cigarettes among her belongings. However, the storekeeper had an additional recollection that confirmed Johnson's impression that her silent customer was indeed Olivia Riner. She told him that she saw this same girl a second time, on Saturday, November 30, two days before the fire. That morning, as the storekeeper was driving into the parking lot, she passed Olivia walking along the road toward the shopping center, carrying a baby. It was a troubling sight. No woman in her experience would walk on a trafficked street with an infant in her arms. And the baby was in only a light blanket, with no head covering.

"It was bitter cold, and the wind was unbelievable," the storekeeper recalled. This girl was as poorly clad as the baby, wearing only a jacket with her jeans. And thus Olivia must have carried Kristie down the treacherous hill of Nannyhagen Road.

After about half an hour the cigarette-store owner was looking out through her shopwindow when she saw Olivia leave the shopping center, carrying the baby across the parking lot in the direction of Nannyhagen Road. "Such a cold day!" she remarked to her husband. "Why doesn't that baby have something on its head?"

Olivia's entry in her diary for this Saturday made no mention of her walk to the shopping center. "Today was what I would call a horribly normal working day. I was watching the little girl," she wrote.

"Every day I am taking care of her I feel closer and closer to her. I really do love her. If one considers how we are created and how fast we develop in the first years of our life. Life is the most beautiful thing this world has ever brought forward. It is something every human receives and which he should protect as well as possible."

BRUCE Johnson was trying to make sense of these contradictions when another ingredient was added to the mystery. It was a telephone call to the Mount Pleasant Police Department from *New York Times* reporter Lisa Foderaro. She stated that in reaction to her account of Olivia's arrest, a New Jersey reader had telephoned to point out a striking similarity between the circumstances of the Thornwood fire and a short story, "The Heroine," written by the American author Patricia Highsmith more than twenty years earlier.

According to the New Jersey informant, a Highsmith collection of short stories—titled *Eleven*—including "The Heroine," was being sold in Switzerland. He had purchased a copy when recently traveling there. This Paris edition had English text faced by a German translation, intended for people trying to perfect a second language.

Johnson obtained a copy of "The Heroine" and read it with mounting astonishment. It was an eerie tale whose plot came uncannily close to the case he was working on. Forever after he would be nagged by the thought that Olivia could have read the story and, consciously or otherwise, acted it out.

"The Heroine" opens with a twenty-one-year-old woman named Lucille Smith being hired as nanny to a family in Westchester. The two small children in her charge quickly become fond of her, and the children's mother thinks she has found a treasure. The reader, however, is let in on a secret. Lucille's mother has recently died in a mental institution. And Lucille may have inherited some of her instability.

Desperately needing to feel loved and appreciated, she works unusually hard to give the impression of being the perfect nanny. But nothing she does is sufficient to satisfy her need for approval. While playing a game with the children, she imagines herself in the role of their rescuer and begins to wish for some real catastrophe so that she can prove her great courage and devotion.

Alone in her room one evening, she dwells on the fantasy. Although she has told the mother that she is not a smoker, she smokes three cigarettes from a secret hoard. Idly she sets a small fire in her ashtray, and this gives her an idea—that there might be a fire in the house to endanger the children.

By now the house is in darkness. She goes down to the garage, rolls out the heavy gas tank, and splashes its contents around the walls.

"Then," the author relates, "she struck her match and walked back, touching off the wet places. Without a backward glance she went to stand at the door of the servants' house and watch." She waits there, intending to let the flames leap up to the nursery window before rushing in on her rescue mission.

"The fire crept up the house like the fingers of a hand, warm and flickering. Then suddenly the gasoline tank exploded with a sound like a cannon and lighted the scene for an instant.

"As though this had been the signal for which she waited, Lucille went confidently forward."

Thus the story ends.

CHIEF Oliva was fascinated with this tale, but it was not admissible as evidence and not all of the details fit. But those that did appeared to go well beyond coincidence. He was particularly struck by the multiple fires lit with a flammable solvent, in both instances directed at an occupied nursery. Some similarities were glaring: girls of much the same age, newly employed in Westchester households where they were trusted, appearing to love the children in their care, yet uncomfortable within themselves and essentially lonely.

There was even the tantalizing detail about the cigarette smoking. At first Bruce Johnson had some doubt about this. And yet was it too far-fetched to suppose that before leaving Switzerland, Olivia bought this collection of stories and was drawn to the one about a girl close to her age taking the same kind of job in the same American county?

And that subsequently she copied Lucille in having an occasional cigarette, lighting one or two as an adventure, and then a larger fire to prove herself a heroine? But had Olivia read "The Heroine"?

Johnson searched through her possessions, but could find no trace of the book. He telephoned the police department in Wettingen, her hometown. Initially he spoke to a police officer surnamed Suter, who was very cooperative. Johnson asked him whether the Patricia Highsmith book was currently available in Wettingen. Suter told him that very close to Olivia's home there was a kiosk that sold popular fiction, and he offered to call the woman who managed it, while Johnson held on. He came back with the response that there had been two copies of the Patricia Highsmith book in her inventory, one of which was sold in October. The second copy was still in stock.

"Does she know who bought it?" Johnson asked. He felt the excitement of being on the edge of a discovery.

The bookseller did not have an immediate answer to his question. But she would try to recall.

Johnson asked Suter for the second copy of the Highsmith book to be sent to him. "Mail it to me, overnight express, and I will reimburse you," he promised. But the package never came.

When he telephoned another time, he said, "I asked the Wettingen police if they would find out some background on Olivia Riner. They said they would get back to me, but didn't. As soon as these people understood what was at stake, they clammed up."

Johnson called Interpol, which suggested he should contact the U.S. Federal Bureau of Investigation station in Bern.

"I really hoped that FBI office would help," he said. "The man there said he would check into how many Highsmith books sold in Switzerland, but he never did. I asked if he could interview the lady at the kiosk, but I never got an answer to that either."

A few days later Johnson checked into his office and was told that a woman had called him from Switzerland, leaving her home number. He couldn't believe his luck. It had to be the bookseller, with information she didn't want to send through the Swiss authorities.

When he tried to return the call, he got a wrong number. Then he realized: "Whoever took the message at our front desk got one of the digits wrong. I didn't know the woman's name or the name of the kiosk. And she never called again."

There was almost nothing to be learned about Olivia in the United States. Johnson telephoned the headquarters of E. F. Au Pair in Boston and spoke with the agency's director, Louise Jakobsson. She had already told *The New York Times* that Olivia Riner had "an impeccable record and lovely recommendations saying that children loved her, and she was so nice and mature." She had nothing to add, except to refer Johnson to her agency's legal department. He was not given access to Olivia's references.

Now Johnson badly wanted to go to Switzerland. It was a bold proposal to put to a small-town police department whose budget was already trimmed to the bone.

"I thought it was extremely important," he said. "When you are investigating a homicide, you always research your background first. Here we didn't have much, but in this girl's hometown we could have talked to neighbors, people who knew her in school, people she worked with. It would have meant bedding down there for quite a few days, but what would that have cost? A couple of thousand dollars? That's nothing in an investigation like this."

It was Paul Oliva's view that if anyone went to Switzerland, it should be from the Westchester County District Attorney's Office. But he wasn't pressing for it. "Based on the evidence we already had, I felt we were in pretty good shape for trial," he said.

DISTRICT Attorney Carl Vergari had assigned his senior trial lawyer, George Bolen, to this case, and Bolen had begun to spend several hours a day working with the Mount Pleasant police. Out of the thirty assistant district attorneys, he was widely regarded as the best prosecutor, with a reputation for being diligent, dedicated, and legally correct. His most famous case was his successful prosecution of Jean Harris, headmistress of an elite girls' boarding school, for the murder of her lover, Dr. Herman Tarnower, at his Westchester home.

Vergari, operating his department under severe new budgetary restrictions, was as reluctant as Paul Oliva to send an investigator to Switzerland. "It won't achieve anything," he argued. "The Swiss authorities are being far too protective."

The country's newspapers were taking the same kind of editorial stance. The German-language tabloid *Blick* quoted a neighbor of the Riners' as saying, "The family is without blemish and works hard.

Olivia was always friendly and caring. It is simply impossible that this girl did such an atrocity." And the pediatrician for whom Olivia had worked told Swiss reporters that it was outrageous to suggest that she could have harmed a baby.

Bruce Johnson continued to believe that elsewhere in Wettingen might be people who knew a darker side of her. He was angry and frustrated about being denied the chance to search for them.

Chapter Twelve

LINDA Sawyer, freelance television reporter and producer, was one of the first mass-media journalists to take up the story. Young, vivacious, and hardworking, she was the embodiment of what the readers of popular fiction and the watchers of TV dramas expect women reporters to be. She was tall, blond, and attractive, with a trusting look in her clear blue eyes that seemed to compel people to reveal themselves to her. She was skilled at quickly getting the story, presenting it, and going on to the next.

At the beginning of December, 1991, she was working for a nationally syndicated program, *Now It Can Be Told,* presented by the popular talk show host Geraldo Rivera. This series, a mixture of straight reporting, speculation, and voyeurism, was aimed at revealing new information about a variety of emotionally appealing news stories.

The newspaper account of Kristie Fischer's terrible death and Olivia's alleged involvement grabbed Sawyer's attention—not only as the kind of story that might provide material for the program but because it spoke to her personally. She was a single mother with sixteen-month-old twin daughters, whom she adored and saw too rarely. As the family's only breadwinner, she had to earn enough money to support the twins, the help, and herself.

The help in this case was Annie McKee, an impeccably trained young woman from a prestigious nanny school. With steadfast faith in her beloved Annie, worrying if her daughters were properly cared for had never crossed Linda's mind. But there in the newspaper was a photograph of a young woman close to Annie's age, charged with murdering a baby while the infant's mother was at work.

"That story horrified me because of my personal situation," she said. "The thought suddenly crossed my mind, How well does any mother truly know her nanny? Reading about what happened to Kristie Fischer made me realize how vulnerable working mothers can be. We bring strangers into our homes to care for our children, and no matter how thoroughly we do the research, we never really know."

Linda dwelt on this obsessively, imagining how outraged she would feel if Annie were accused of harming a child and how dedicated she would be to proving her nanny's innocence. It became imperative for her to discover exactly what happened to Kristie Fischer, even though she wanted a different explanation for this baby's death than the one suggested in her newspaper. She wanted Olivia to be innocent.

"I knew that I would walk into my editor's office and say, 'I have to do this story,' " she recounted.

She was given the assignment and began making phone calls.

She found, as all the other reporters did, that no one in the district attorney's office was talking and that Police Chief Oliva would add nothing to his original statement—that the police had positive evidence of Olivia's guilt, but would not disclose what it was.

Laura Brevetti was not talking either. Telephone calls to her Manhattan office were taken by a secretary. But Linda Sawyer was more persistent than most. "I called her office at seven o'clock one evening," she said. "As I hoped, she picked up her own phone, and I knew that this was my chance.

"It was obvious why she had not been responding to the media. There was a police chief saying that he had a clear-cut case against Olivia Riner, and she was still figuring out how to defend it. She knew she had to wait, perhaps for just the right journalist to walk into her office. And I was the one. Nobody had the reasons I had. She told me to come to her office the following day."

Their meeting took up the afternoon and continued beyond dinner. "We went to a late café with a group of Laura's friends and sat talking until the small hours of the morning."

Linda went home believing this to be the most important assignment she had ever undertaken. Every investigative reporter hopes to uncover hidden truths and, by exposing them, to make a difference. Linda assumed she knew the truth before the uncovering began.

Over the ensuing weeks Linda was given a rare insight into how a skilled defense lawyer prepares for a major trial. At first all the legal maneuvers were concentrated on getting Olivia out of jail, a task that seemed overwhelming in light of the $500,000 bail set by Westchester County Court judge Donald Silverman. This high figure was thought necessary to deter Olivia from attempting to leave the country.

If the bail money could not be raised, Olivia would have to remain in prison until her trial, several months hence. Her plight was sympathetically reported in the Swiss-German newspapers, and soon promises of loans for bail money started pouring in from concerned Swiss citizens. Before long the legal presumption of her innocence became, for most of her fellow countrymen, a fact.

The Riners were portrayed as a decent, law-abiding couple. His salary as a small-town public official, coupled with hers as a clerk in a garage, gave them a modest standard of living. They were the epitome of the middle-class German Swiss, with a daughter whose school and work record seemed to be impeccable. In the German sector of Switzerland, there was a collective sense of outrage about the unlikely charge against her.

In this gathering sympathy for Olivia, her status subtly changed. Newspapers on both sides of the Atlantic elevated her from au pair to nanny. And nanny stuck. The word was more familiar and unintentionally helped her image. There is a mystique about a Swiss nanny. The phrase conjures a vision of a starched and smiling children's nurse. The reality in this case was a girl of barely twenty whose uniform was jeans and a sweatshirt.

To Linda Sawyer, however, Olivia was as much a nanny as her own. And she was totally committed to her defense.

ON CHRISTMAS Eve, Laura Brevetti announced an agreement she had worked out through the legal system and diplomatic channels. Bail was reduced to the $350,000 covered by the private loans that had been pledged by Swiss donors, and conditions were set to ensure that while Olivia was technically free, she would remain under surveillance.

Her mother would have to remain in the United States as her guardian and companion. Both their passports would be impounded until the trial was over. Olivia was restricted to living within the Westchester–New York City area and obliged to wear an electronic device that would sound an alarm at the monitoring company if she should attempt to go outside her prescribed boundaries.

For the next six months she and her mother lived anonymously above the New York City headquarters of the Swiss Benevolent Society. This charitable organization occupied an old brownstone on a quiet street to the west of Central Park. They were provided with a shabbily furnished twin-bedded room and a makeshift sitting room on the same floor. A forbidding security system on the front door protected them from any possibility of intruders. Kurt Riner had returned to his job in Switzerland but kept in touch by telephone.

Reporters assumed that Olivia was still in Westchester and, after checking the local motels, gave up trying to locate her. Only TV journalist Linda Sawyer was let in on the secret. Through Laura Brevetti she was given frequent access to Olivia. During the next few weeks she came to know her well and to feel very protective toward her. She took her out to restaurants and over various meals learned about Olivia's lonely childhood, her rigid perfectionism, her earnest desire to please, and her propensity to criticize others as well as herself.

Linda thought it outrageous that Olivia could be suspected of arson and murder. She seemed to be so trusting about the outcome of her trial. "I believed in her so much I would have hired her to look after my children," Linda recalled months later. "I wanted to rescue her. I felt she was wrongly accused and that if I worked hard enough on the story, I could put it right."

Linda began doing her own investigation in the Thornwood area, gathering material for a television program that she believed would clear Olivia's name and uncover a very different explanation of how and why Kristie Fischer was murdered.

BILL's reconstituted family—Denise, Leah, John, and himself—had moved out of the Donnellys' home a few days before Christmas. Through a real-estate-agent friend they had been offered temporary refuge in a three-bedroom condominium next to the Rose Hill Shopping Center, conveniently close to the house on West Lake Drive for Bill to oversee its cleanup and rebuilding. But emotionally it was a long way from home.

The condominium was pleasant enough, but Leah felt ill at ease there. Still deeply traumatized, she would have been uncomfortable anywhere. Her father and Denise were preoccupied with their own tragedy, and though John was a comfort, he, too, was still in shock. He and Leah found security of a sort in the familiar but crowded space of the Gallagher home in Mahopac and increasingly drove the fifty-mile round-trip to stay there overnight.

Leah's overnight visits there had become more frequent even before the fire. With the arrival of Olivia, Bill and Denise had made it clear that they did not want John to continue sleeping on their family-room sofa. It was the area Olivia would use as a sitting room.

Leah commented, "I understood the reason for that request. So did John. We spent more time at his house after that."

EARLY one morning in January, after an overnight visit in Mahopac, Leah and all the Gallaghers were preparing to go to their various jobs. It was barely 6:45 a.m., still dark outside, and as usual, cars had to be shifted around so that those who needed to leave first could get out of the driveway. When John went to move his car, he heard other automobiles at the entrance to the driveway. He looked up and saw several strangers piling out of their cars and advancing toward him.

John ran to the back door to get inside before the intruders caught up with him. Leah, who had watched the scene from behind the wheel of her parked Toyota, got out of her car and also hurried toward the house. One man, holding a microphone, ran after John, breathlessly shouting, "I have a question for you concerning the Fischers' baby. I mean, you're a hero. You were there. You went into the room, right? What did you see?"

John had been instructed by the D.A.'s office not to discuss the case with the media. But he was unprepared for an onslaught like this. "I have no comment," he replied, anxiously tapping on the back door, hoping someone would open it.

The reporter persisted. "You say you went in. Did you see the baby in the room? How come nobody's heard from you, John, when you're a hero?"

At that moment Carol Gallagher opened the door for her son and Leah.

"John, you're the hero," the reporter called after him. "You're the hero, man."

Carol Gallagher recalled, "There were two cameramen, a black fellow, and a white woman, and they all left their cars blocking our driveway. We asked the reporters to go away, but they continued to sit out there. One of them ran up onto the deck to try and get photographs of John and Leah through the window."

The woman in the group outside was Linda Sawyer, and she had a very different perception of the confusion around her—one that in part was colored by hearing someone in the Gallagher family ask rhetorically, "How did they find out where we live?"

Carol related, "Eventually we called the police, and two patrol cars showed up within five minutes."

They thought that was the end of it.

ASSISTANT District Attorney George Bolen had feared something like this. He had explained to the Fischers and to John Gallagher why he did not want them talking to reporters. From his prosecution of Jean Harris he knew what could happen to people who were caught up in a sensational murder trial—how an off-the-cuff comment could come back to haunt them as a headline.

Also, in these early weeks of 1992 murderous nannies were in the news. In January a sensational new movie, *The Hand That Rocks the Cradle,* premiered, and was drawing packed audiences across America. The film told the bizarre tale of a nanny who wreaks havoc in a household as her way of settling a personal vendetta. After endearing herself to the mother and children, she suddenly attempts to destroy their house and to kill them. Inevitably, the movie recalled last month's headlines about Olivia's arrest, bringing that story—and all the anxious questions it raised—back into public consciousness. Americans who had not previously heard of the events in Thornwood heard about them now.

Making a direct link between the known facts of Kristie's death and the movie, *People* magazine commented, "Until the trial the Fischers must live with the wrenching possibility that, if Riner is indeed guilty, they delivered their daughter into the hands of a killer."

This was nothing young parents wanted to contemplate. The movie, after all, was fiction. It would be a comfort and a relief to learn that the charges against Olivia Riner came into the same category.

In this climate of public opinion, on February 14, 1992, Valentine's Day, Geraldo Rivera devoted half of his *Now It Can Be Told* program to the Kristie Fischer case.

RIVERA WAS BETTER KNOWN AS THE star of *Geraldo,* a daytime television interview program widely regarded as the most sensational of the network talk shows. Rivera's new program, *Now It Can Be Told,* promised the same approach to current news stories. His presentation of the "Swiss nanny" case was produced by Linda Sawyer and was largely the result of her research.

Prosecutor George Bolen had obtained a copy of the transcript from a courthouse reporter a day or two before the show was aired. He had alerted the Fischers to watch the program and warned them that they would find it offensive. But what came on the screen that Valentine's night was far more damaging than Bolen had feared.

The program opened with the stark announcement by Rivera, "Today we find a key suspect in a horrifying crime that mirrors the terror of one of the country's hottest movies."

The camera closed in on his lean face, crossed by an expression of concern.

"It's one of our worst nightmares, leaving our child in the care of a nanny or a baby-sitter who ends up neglecting, abusing or even, God forbid, murdering the kid," he confided to his viewing public. "That certainly was our impression in the case of a horrifying incident which took place in an affluent New York suburb this past December. But our Alexander Johnson has uncovered new evidence that the authorities apparently chose to ignore."

Appearing on screen, Alexander Johnson was immediately recognized by the Gallaghers as the reporter who had chased John up to the back door of his home, calling, "You're the hero, man." But tonight he was telling viewers a different story.

He claimed to have obtained exclusive information that the Mount Pleasant police deliberately ignored a possibility that John Gallagher could have been the arsonist. "Sources tell us that Chief Oliva has a long-standing friendship with the Gallagher family," Alexander Johnson observed meaningfully.

This unverified—and untrue—statement was juxtaposed with clips from *The Hand That Rocks the Cradle* and with the police recording of Olivia's emergency call, her voice rising to hysteria as the desk sergeant argued back that Five West Lake Drive did not exist. This impression of police ineptitude was followed by a comment from Laura Brevetti describing the arrest of her client as "a rush to judgment for no apparent reason other than she was the convenient suspect."

Rivera interpolated. "The nanny Olivia Riner really thought that she was alone with three-month-old Kristie Fischer when that fatal fire broke out. But we've uncovered a shocking possibility. Someone else may have been there."

The scene shifted to the exterior of the Gallagher family home at the time of the early morning invasion by the television team. John Gallagher was photographed averting his face as Alexander Johnson asked him, "You went into the room, right?"

From his studio Rivera posed the rhetorical question, "Who is this mystery man and why won't he talk?"

After a station break Johnson returned to identify this mystery man in the preceding pictures. "His name is John Gallagher, and he frequently visited the Fischer house to see his girlfriend. *Now It Can Be Told* has exclusively obtained the police report that contained Olivia Riner's statement to law enforcement on the night of the fire. She told officers that when she ran outside to get help, John Gallagher was standing right in front of the Fischer house. She reported that Gallagher ran inside and tried to rescue the infant. Though he was unsuccessful, he acted very much like a hero that night. But oddly his name has never come up in any newspaper account of the case."

This was the first time that John had been publicly identified as the young man who was first on the scene at the Fischers' home. Now millions of viewers were hearing that, as the boyfriend of Kristie's half sister, he may have had a motive to cause the fire.

Before the cameras shifted back to the early morning scene outside the Gallaghers' house, a copy of John Gallagher's application for a pistol permit was flashed on the screen. Juxtaposed with photographs of the fire raging at the Fischers' house, the implication was obvious: This young man could be a killer.

The cameraman had caught a final shot of John and Leah retreating to the house. As presented, their behavior began to look like guilty avoidance. Alexander Johnson observed, "Gallagher turned out to be a very reluctant hero. The woman with him is Leah Fischer, baby Kristie's stepsister. The same two were captured on this police video, shot the morning after the tragic fire. Their voices indicate a mood anything but tragic."

The next segment of the program was devastating.

Parts of Bruce Johnson's police film were shown, with voices his sound track had picked up. There was a shot of Leah and John, and one of Leah's burned-out bedroom, with people talking off-camera. Their conversation was so muffled that what was said and whose voice it was thought to be was spelled out in a caption: JOHN GALLAGHER: "YOU AND I WILL STAY AT MY HOUSE FOR A WHILE, AND WE'LL HAVE BARBECUES."

Then a woman's laughter. In fact, John had never made the remark and the woman's laughter was not Leah's. But the way this was presented, it seemed as though John and Leah were making jokes—gloating, or worse—over the burned-out house and the dead baby.

John was in Hawthorne watching the program with a group of friends. One of them, a policeman who had not been involved in the case, was as shocked as the rest of them. "I can't believe this," he said.

"I can't believe it either," John responded, shaking his head.

Leah saw the show with her father and Denise, in the living room of their rented condominium. "I felt sick to my stomach," she said.

"Now we're not indicting this guy Gallagher," Rivera summed up. "The fact that he runs away from the camera or the fact that he's sifting through the wreckage and laughing the next morning—we don't mean to attribute guilt to him. However, has he been questioned to this date?" he asked Johnson.

"As far as we know, no," Johnson replied.

Again they were wrong. On the night of the fire John Gallagher was indeed questioned by the police.

"Stay on this one," Rivera urged his reporter. And he concluded, "We alert all the other journalists in the New York City area to take another look at this case. I smell a rat."

This comment so enraged Jim Donnelly, watching the program in his living room, that he might have flung something hard at his twenty-six-inch screen if Kimmy's portrait had not been in its customary place on top. Instead, he limited himself to arguing back at the image of Geraldo Rivera. "So do I," he yelled. "And it's you."

MOST of the material in that program was privileged information. Bruce Johnson's videos of the fire scene had been turned in to the district attorney's office, and under the evidential rules of discovery the district attorney had sent copies to Laura Brevetti.

It would have been a serious breach of legal ethics for either side to publicize evidence prior to criminal proceedings, especially in ways that could influence the outcome of a trial. Yet someone had made available to Rivera two of Bruce Johnson's videos, his taped interview with Olivia, the recording of Olivia's frantic telephone call to the Mount Pleasant police, and John Gallagher's application for a pistol permit, which he had filed months earlier, when he wanted to go hunting. When these items were presented together, linked by photographs of John evading reporters, the effect was damning.

Overnight there was a perceptible shift in public opinion. It was the boyfriend who did it. And by implication it was Leah who helped him. From that supposition a scenario was invented—the daughter of this house and her boyfriend were so resentful of the new wife and so jealous of the new baby that they conspired to ruin the life of the mother by eliminating the child. The program confirmed what most parents wanted to think—that Olivia was innocent—and the expression of this opinion on national television gave it authenticity.

Chapter Thirteen

THE morning after *Now It Can Be Told* was aired, prosecutor George Bolen received a telephone call from Linda Sawyer, asking if he would participate in a follow-up report. He responded by asking where she got the videotape.

"You have to be kidding," she said. "I can't reveal my sources."

"You should know that you misidentified the voices," he told her. "That was not John Gallagher or Leah Fischer."

"Then whose voices were they?" she asked.

She recalled, "If he had given me the information, I could have made a retraction. But he said he would not give the question the dignity of a response. And hung up."

Linda's assumption about John and Leah's involvement seemed to confirm gossip that she had been picking up around Thornwood about some of John's male contemporaries being involved in petty crime. One of them was widely suspected of some of the arson that had plagued the neighborhood for months. There had been a rash of nuisance fires, and the police believed all of them to be the handiwork of this same young man, a known troublemaker. They were equally sure that he was not responsible for the fire at the Fischers' house. Bruce Johnson commented, "Forget that fellow as a suspect. Been in trouble since he was a little boy. He's a sick kid, not a murderer. And he's not smart enough to carry through anything as premeditated as this."

Linda Sawyer, however, had learned that John and this suspected arsonist had been in high school together and shared an enthusiasm for car racing, which could have made them friends; there was also barroom talk about outstanding favors that this young man was said to have owed to John.

Direct involvement by John Gallagher seemed much more plausible to Linda Sawyer than criminal action by Olivia. Digging deeper, Linda found that John had left high school before the end of his senior year, without graduating. And he had a reputation for a hasty temper that had involved him in teenage fistfights. As Linda saw it, everything pointed to his having guilty knowledge of the fire at the Fischers' house. Why else would he be sitting in his truck, waiting, while Kristie was burning to death? It seemed outrageous to charge Olivia with murder and to cast him in the hero's role.

Immediately after Linda revealed John Gallagher's identity, television and newspaper journalists from New York to Switzerland took up her story, assuming it to be true. And that assumption created a lasting public image of Olivia Riner's innocence.

"After the show Laura [Brevetti] called me," Linda said. "She told me that I had done even more than I had promised and that she would be forever grateful to me. She knew I would break the case."

A few days later George Bolen met with Bill and Denise, Leah and John, and Jim Donnelly at the Mount Pleasant police headquarters. Bruce Johnson was also there.

Jim explained that it was he who had made the taped remark about a barbecue when they were outside the house the day after the fire, trying to coax a smile from Denise. He told Bolen that he wanted to call all the newspapers and television stations and publicly take responsibility for his disastrous attempt at a joke, explaining the woman's nervous laughter as Denise's hysterical reaction to it. He was eager to do whatever it might take to lift the suspicion from John Gallagher.

Bolen saw only a risk of spreading the damage. It would be even worse to admit that it was the *mother* of the dead baby who was laughing. How would *that* be understood by the public? Better to hope that the damning TV show would be forgotten before the trial began. Which is why Bolen argued that, hard as it might be for them to keep silent, the Fischers should continue to avoid speaking to the press.

There was no peace for the Gallaghers or the Fischers after the Geraldo Rivera show. Reporters and photographers hung around Fischer's Garage and around the Gallaghers' home in Mahopac. John Gallagher was pursued by every journalist on the story. Day after day they were waiting outside the Jaguar service department before he clocked in at 8:30 a.m. and again when he was due to leave.

"One day Channel Four news came looking for me on my job," John said, "and asked people who knew me, 'Do you think John Gallagher could have done it?' Another day a woman from Channel Five told the foreman she had an interview set up with me. I walked up to the front with him to see who it was, and he asked me if I knew her. When I said no and started to go back in, they photographed me walking away and showed the picture on TV."

At his garage, Bill was besieged by requests for interviews, comments, opinions, and photographs of Kristie. "Is that Bill Fischer?" one anonymous call began. "Don't hang up. I want to tell you about John Gallagher. Did you know that years ago he burned his brothers and sister?" There were other sick messages of this kind.

At the White Plains auto dealership where Leah worked as assistant to the president, most of her colleagues were ominously silent. She wished they would ask her about John so she could tell them what really happened. She was getting such mixed reactions from friends. A few were supportive, but most of them excused their awkwardness with a hasty remark like "I know you don't want to discuss it."

"But they didn't know," Leah said. "They had no idea. And there were other friends, close girlfriends, who I expected to hear from, and didn't. And that hurt."

All this drew her closer to John and to everyone else in the larger Fischer family. They had begun to feel like shipwreck survivors, alone against a hostile world. A single hope remained, and it helped to keep them going. In a few months' time Olivia would be tried for murder; then, they believed, the truth would be told and justice done.

PART III: THE TRIAL
Chapter Fourteen

OLIVIA had been indicted on four counts of second-degree murder and one count of first-degree arson, and Laura Brevetti had entered a plea of not guilty on all five. The murder charges presented alternatives for a jury to determine whether, if found guilty, Olivia killed Kristie intentionally, or as the result of a careless or malicious action that knowingly put the infant's life at risk. George Bolen had his doubts most jurors would accept that a young, unsophisticated girl could have killed deliberately. He judged that they would probably agree to this being a case of arson but would want to believe that Kristie's death was somehow accidental.

There was no doubt in Bolen's mind that Olivia deliberately set the fires. What he lacked was motive. The most persuasive theory was that Olivia started a fire intending to rescue Kristie but, finding the baby dead from smoke inhalation, lit the other fires to cover up. Bolen was impressed by the correlation between Patricia Highsmith's story "The Heroine" and the known facts of this case. That short story might provide jurors with an acceptable scenario. But he could not introduce the Highsmith book into evidence unless he could prove it had been in Olivia's possession.

It angered and offended him that in advance of Olivia's trial Laura Brevetti had expressed her opinions on a national television program. There was also the matter of John Gallagher's application for a pistol permit—which had been denied because of an accumulation of speeding tickets—flashed onto the screen during the Rivera program. This was classified information, available only to law-enforcement officials. Someone must have punched into the state's computerized police statistics and run a criminal-history check on John Gallagher.

Bolen refrained from public comment about this violation of John Gallagher's civil rights. He did not want to draw any more attention to this young man. What irked him was how easy it was for the theory about Gallagher's involvement to be believed and how hard it would be to select a jury who had not heard it.

PREPARING HER DEFENSE, LAURA Brevetti made formal motions to have as much damaging evidence excluded from the trial as possible. Because this was a circumstantial case, Judge Silverman had promised that he would consider all her objections, and he scheduled a pretrial hearing for mid-May 1992.

Brevetti's main contention was that Olivia was unlawfully arrested and had not understood the Miranda warning, with the result that she responded to Bruce Johnson's lengthy interrogation without knowing that she had the right to remain silent.

Brevetti alleged that the Mount Pleasant police did not seal off the crime scene until the defense's investigators were given an opportunity to examine it. Referring to Bruce Johnson's video, she charged that Leah and John were permitted to "rummage through the fire scene without supervision" on the day after the tragedy. The wording of this charge perpetuated one of the errors of the Geraldo Rivera program. The shots of Leah and John searching through the wreckage were not taken the day after the fire, as Brevetti charged, but three days later, when—as the video showed—there was snow on the ground, which had only just fallen.

Brevetti maintained that there was no physical evidence linking Olivia to the crime—no fingerprints, no trace of flammable liquid on her clothing—and "the autopsy report establishes that the infant died from the smoke, and burns. There is no evidence that she had been injured, poisoned, abused, or otherwise harmed."

She criticized the fact that the police eliminated John Gallagher as a suspect and "seized no evidence from him although he was present during the fire." This was clear warning that she intended to cast suspicion on him at the forthcoming trial.

What the police regarded as the one piece of direct evidence, Olivia's singed eyelashes, was ridiculed in Brevetti's statement: "It defies credulity that eyelashes would be singed while her full eyebrows, long hair, hands and clothing would be totally undamaged."

This argument might well convince a jury. It took a knowledge of the dynamics of combustion to appreciate the significance of Olivia's eyelashes alone being singed. After reading Brevetti's statement, Paul Oliva gave his detective a piece of advice: "Bruce, those eyelashes are a very important factor in this case. It was why we made the arrest. This whole case hangs on those eyelashes."

THEY WERE NOT AN ISSUE AT THE pretrial hearing, which concentrated on the admissibility of other evidence. As is common procedure, at the end of the hearing the judge gave his ruling, determining how much of the known evidence would be allowed at the trial.

Laura Brevetti petitioned to have all the charges against her client dismissed. She gained almost nothing. George Bolen agreed that Olivia's diary and personal photographs would not be presented as evidence, but Brevetti lost all her other arguments, including her contention that her client did not understand the Miranda warning.

Olivia sat demurely through the hearings, dressed in a plain white blouse, navy blue tailored jacket, and a matching pleated skirt. The strange, boxlike shape of the electronic monitor strapped to her left ankle was an incongruous reminder that she was not the convent schoolgirl she appeared to be. Her mother, Marlise, sat near the front of the courtroom's public section, watching tensely.

The only witnesses to be called at this stage were police officers who had been at the fire scene. The first was Scott Carpenter, the young patrolman who reached there before any of his colleagues. This was the first time he had given evidence in court. Hesitantly he described seeing "a severely charred object which appeared to be a doll" on the nursery floor. "Then I saw it was a baby." Even now, he had difficulty talking about it and was easily shaken by the sharp cross-examination by Laura Brevetti.

"Did you close the door to the baby's room?" she asked.

"I don't know. I just wanted to get out of the house. I was choked up, and my eyes were burning as I came out."

He was shifting in his seat on the witness stand, and the muscles of his jaw were tensing. In contrast, Laura Brevetti seemed entirely at ease, elegantly attired in a softly draped beige dress and jacket. She had a way of thoughtfully pacing the floor before moving to the next line of questioning, adding to a witness's apprehension.

After such a pause she returned to the traumatic moments in the nursery. "Did you observe the window when you were in that room?"

"No."

"And there is only one wall where the window is, correct?"

"Yes."

"And you did not examine it?"

"No."

Olivia Riner leaving Mount Pleasant Justice Court following her arraignment for arson and murder. Police Lieutenant Louis Alagno is in the background.

Detective Bruce Johnson

Assistant District Attorney George Bolen

Judge Donald N. Silverman

Olivia's parents, Marlise and Kurt Riner, at Mount Pleasant police headquarters shortly after their arrival from Switzerland.

Laura Brevetti being interviewed on the day of the jury deliberations, with her private investigator, Christopher Rush.

Olivia at Westchester County Courthouse on the first day of the trial.

She was building up the case that an intruder could have entered the nursery through the low window and that the first police officer on the scene failed to look for clues.

Pressing on, she led Carpenter into his interview with John Gallagher in the police car while the house was still smoldering. Carpenter indicated that he never doubted the story his friend's brother told him. From the prosecution's viewpoint it was becoming evident that the police should have covered themselves—and Gallagher—by having his clothes and hands tested before letting him go.

She concluded by having him tell how he went back into the house later that evening and walked around. Brevetti asked him why he did this, and he admitted that he had no reason other than curiosity.

"You stepped on things?" she inquired, implying that on this unnecessary return visit he may have destroyed evidence.

He paused, trying to remember. "I stepped where I stepped," he replied belligerently.

That was when George Bolen must have decided not to call Scott Carpenter as a witness at the forthcoming trial.

DETECTIVE Bruce Johnson was much more experienced at giving evidence. His bland expression through an entire day on the witness stand gave no hint of his emotions, and he did not permit himself to be ruffled by questions implying that he deliberately intimidated Olivia. His answers gave a fair image of himself—a senior officer observing police regulations governing the treatment of a suspect, always keeping his feelings in check, never allowing Olivia insight into what he was thinking. Only late in the evening, after he had formally charged her with arson, did the tone of his interrogation change.

Brevetti prodded him about those two hours. "Did you tell her she might as well admit to killing the baby because there would be an autopsy?"

"Yes."

"Did you tell her there would be fingerprints at the scene that would show she had committed the crime?"

Johnson paused. "It is possible," he conceded.

"And all these things you asked for one purpose?"

"Yes."

"You wanted her to confess?"

"Correct."
"And she did not confess?"
"Correct."

THE most dramatic part of this pretrial hearing was when Johnson's taped interview was replayed for the judge's benefit. Although Laura Brevetti argued, "My client did not always understand his [Johnson's] questions," the judge was impressed by Olivia's reactions when she didn't. He ruled against all the defense motions, explaining that in his opinion Olivia fully understood the Miranda warning.

Judge Silverman commented, "I am struck by the fact she appears to understand everything that is said, and that when she comes on a word which is not understandable she asks for an explanation."

He determined that she was not coerced or intentionally intimidated by Detective Johnson during their long interview. "It is my feeling that she was willing to cooperate. At no time did she indicate that she did not want to remain or to answer questions."

Laura Brevetti made a brave attempt to turn the judge's ruling to advantage. After the hearing she gave one of the first of many press conferences in the large lobby of the courthouse. Briskly she told reporters, "While a defense attorney is disappointed when a motion is denied, I get a great deal of satisfaction from the judge's comments—his saying that through many hours of questioning this girl was fully cooperative. This behavior is totally consistent with innocence."

A WEEK later there was a surprise item on New York City's *Fox News*. It concerned the high incidence of fires in the Thornwood area and named the Mount Pleasant Police Department's suspect as Eric Trimpe, who lived with his parents on Nannyhagen Road. The television reporter, Rosanna Scotto, made a direct link between these cases of arson and the fire at the Fischers' house. She described Trimpe as "a friend of John Gallagher" and emphasized that the outbreak of Thornwood fires began before Olivia came to the neighborhood. This report would form a renewed basis for local gossip: Maybe John Gallagher hired Trimpe to set fire to the Fischers' house. Maybe they did it together.

The timing of this TV report was a gift to the defense. Jury selection had just concluded, and the judge had yet to instruct the twelve prospective jurors and four alternates not to read or listen to anything touching this case. They were free to watch that news program or to hear about it from others. They would, of course, undertake to go into this trial with open minds. But suspicions had now been planted that might subliminally influence their thinking.

Chapter Fifteen

IN THE clothes she wore for court, Olivia looked very different from the girl Laura Brevetti had met on December 3, and that was intentional. Linda Sawyer had taken her shopping. Combing through Bloomingdale's, Linda had picked out three basic outfits that created the image Laura Brevetti wanted to project—that of a correct and obedient schoolgirl. Linda chose matching skirts and jackets in quiet colors of a flattering cut and classical design: one each in navy, cream, and a light silvery gray, with pumps to match. "I spent eight hundred dollars on Laura's credit card buying those clothes," she said.

It was also an important part of defense strategy that Olivia should wear her hair long and loose, with bangs almost to her eyebrows. So long as a jury could see all that hair surrounding Olivia's face, Laura Brevetti could minimize Bruce Johnson's testimony about her singed eyelashes, even when a scientific explanation was offered. Only on weekends, when the court was not sitting, did she braid her hair down her back, the way she had often worn it at the Fischers' home.

Olivia was not privy to the painstaking preparation for her defense and had little sense of its complexity. But Linda was included in conferences behind closed doors; in turn, she brought in information, like the gossip she was picking up about John Gallagher and about certain young men engaged in illegal activities who were said to be his friends.

Linda was a little shaken when she attended a mock trial, staged in Brevetti's law office, about a month before the pretrial hearing.

"Laura played the prosecutor, and her assistant played the defense attorney," she recalled. "I was sitting there and listening to her summation. She went into details of how small this house was, how difficult it would have been for someone to break in and set those fires without Olivia knowing. Who but she could have committed the crime? I thought to myself, Holy cow, when you hear it in those terms, the girl has to be guilty. But none of us wanted to believe it."

Linda's allegiance did not fail even after her reading of pretrial evidence raised some troubling questions. With her experience as a young mother, she picked up a serious discrepancy that everyone else missed, including the police. During his interrogation of Olivia, Bruce Johnson had asked her about the clothes Kristie was wearing when she was set down to sleep in the nursery for the last time, about half an hour before the fire. Olivia had described the light green one-piece suit, worn over a diaper and a white undershirt. What struck Linda was that not a shred of this or any other outer garment was found on the baby's burned body, although those pieces of her undershirt and diaper that had been pressed between Kristie and the infant seat remained intact. If Kristie had been wearing an outer garment, a portion of that would surely have been preserved too.

On a damp December afternoon, chill enough for Olivia to be wearing a long-sleeved sweatshirt around the house, did she really put a baby down to sleep dressed only in her underclothes? Was the outfit an invention to explain her neglect? Or worse, had she decided that this child was about to die, so what she wore didn't matter?

Linda's journalistic curiosity demanded an explanation. "But I was so psychologically connected to Olivia that I let it go."

Linda was not alone in her empathy with Olivia. The trial attracted an unusual group of supporters who, for a variety of personal reasons, made her cause their own. Day after day they filled most of the seats in the public section of the courtroom, smiling approval at her. Influenced by pretrial television coverage and by their own emotions, many people perceived her as a victim. They came to court to see justice done and genuinely believed that meant her acquittal.

In the meantime the real victims, the baby's parents, were ignored. Following George Bolen's advice, they had declined to deal with the media; as a result, people had no sense of who they were or what Kristie's death had done to them. Thus the Fischers never connected with the general public, never became real to them, never told their story, and all the sympathy that should have been theirs went to Olivia.

A FEW weeks before the trial Bill and his family had to move out of the Thornwood condominium and find another temporary home. The owner, a colleague of Bill's, offered them the use of a large old house in the neighboring village of Valhalla—a gray and shadowy colonial-style building that stood back from the road behind an overgrown garden. It was the antithesis of the house on West Lake Drive, still being rebuilt, which in happier times seemed to have been filled with sunshine and laughter.

The trial was scheduled to begin on June 2, 1992, exactly six months after Kristie's death. The Fischers approached the ordeal hopefully, expecting a resolution that would bring them healing. From the beginning George Bolen had determined that Bill, Denise, Leah, and John would be his only family witnesses. He liked them all, but he worried about the impression they would make in court. He judged that Bill would be the most effective of the four. He was the only one who could testify about the quantities of paint thinner and other accelerants that were missing from his utility cupboard; also, he was the last member of the family to see Kristie alive. He was strictly truthful, and it showed on his face.

Denise was more complex: intelligent, analytical, and utterly devastated by her baby's death. Predictably, she would weep on the witness stand. Bolen could not bring himself to put her through a public exposure of her grief merely for the dramatic effect of it—which, given the tactics the defense was using, may have been overly protective on his part.

But he was also looking beyond the emotional impact. He knew that his case would depend upon what she said. Denise could give no direct evidence about the events leading up to the fire. And he was worried about the questions that Brevetti would put to her and the answers she would feel constrained to give. Before the fire were you happy with Olivia? Was she loving and attentive with the baby? Did you feel confident about leaving her alone with Kristie? And Denise, who until the night of the fire believed she had found the perfect baby-sitter, would have to answer yes to every one. Bolen decided to defer a decision about calling her as a witness until the trial was under way.

Leah, he judged, was a warm and giving person. She would be controlled and straightforward. But her staunch defense of John was a serious hazard. If Brevetti could persuade the jury to suspect him of murder, Leah's loyalty to her boyfriend could make her look like his co-conspirator, and that could be bad for both of them.

THE JURY-SELECTION PROCESS produced a predominantly middle-aged team of seven men and five women. It was just the kind of jury that Brevetti wanted, intelligent and aging. Older jurors might have less sympathy for a mother who went back to work so soon after the birth of her child. They might also be more critical of the Fischers' lifestyle.

That was another problem for the prosecution. While Bill had the outward appearance of a traditional parent, his was a very unorthodox household. It was hard to predict what a jury might make of a father who condoned his daughter's having her boyfriend as a regular overnight guest, then invited a woman to move in and delayed marrying her until two months before their baby was born.

Another challenge for Bolen was that "Olivia Riner did not fit the profile of a criminal. She was a young female, and there was a ready male suspect. Somehow I had to get the jury beyond that to look at all the bits and pieces of evidence which pointed to her." He acknowledged that while "the prosecution is not required to show motive, people still want to know why." And he could not answer that.

"Did she mean to kill this child?" he wondered. "Or did something else occur which Olivia intentionally or accidentally caused to happen? Maybe the baby was overcome by smoke in another room. Maybe Olivia set a fire to cover." If only the medical examiner had gone to the scene that night. . . . He might have noticed something about the body and the way it was placed to provide a better insight into the cause of death.

At one point he mused, "They say a trial is a search for the truth. But is it really? The jury has only limited information. Some evidence is suppressed because it is hearsay or might be prejudicial. A prosecutor can rarely tell the whole story."

BEFORE and during the trial Bill, Denise, Leah, and John had a compassionate mentor and counselor in Marianne Walsh, who ran the homicide crisis program for Victims Assistance Services in White Plains. A strikingly attractive blonde in early middle age, she formed a deep bond with the Fischers, guiding them through the trial preparation, listening to their pain and their fears. She told them they were fortunate to be represented by George Bolen, but disagreed with his insistence that they should avoid talking to the press.

"I told them that the case was going to be tried in the media whether they talked or not," she related. "I said that they should look for one person in the media whom they could trust and give them a story. I could see that Brevetti was using the press, and I knew that would escalate when the trial began. I asked Denise and Bill if they could release a picture of the baby. But they said no, and I understood why. But at some point Kristie should have been given some reality."

Afterward she agonized over whether she should have argued more forcefully. She had been around courthouses enough to know that justice can be perverted. Lacking her sophisticated knowledge, the Fischers held on to their trust in the judicial system. "They thought that once they got to trial, all the ugly rumors would be dispelled and people would see the truth," Marianne commented.

In that expectation Bill Fischer left his home on the morning of June 2, 1992, to be the prosecution's first witness.

THIS is the point at which most journalists came into the story. In the six months since the fire very little had been added to their understanding of what had happened. The police had said all they intended to say during the week of Olivia's arrest. George Bolen had refused to discuss the case. The Fischers were consistently unavailable. Laura Brevetti was the only principal who was talking, and to only a few reporters. Perhaps some carefully hidden truth would come out in testimony. If so, the nanny trial could be an unusually good story.

Thus, on Tuesday morning, June 2, 1992, the press seats in the courtroom were filled with American and Swiss reporters, television commentators, and—cameras being banned—artists. It was a relatively small room on the fourteenth floor of a modern white building.

Judge Silverman had given his customary advice to jurors during the previous week: "The defendant is presumed to be innocent. She need not prove anything. The burden of proof is on the prosecution to prove beyond a reasonable doubt that the defendant is guilty."

The morning session on this first day of the trial was taken up with George Bolen's opening statement. He bluntly told the jury that the prosecution was relying entirely on circumstantial evidence. "No one witness will be able to tell you what occurred on a dreary, rainy, dismal day in December of 1991. But it will come together like pieces of a puzzle, and then you will know beyond a reasonable doubt that this defendant, Olivia Riner, murdered Kristie Fischer."

It was fine courtroom rhetoric. Bolen went on to describe the layout of the Fischers' house. After the fire, he said, "there was no sign of forced entry, no locks picked, no broken windows, zilch. The baby's room windows were kept closed and locked. . . . You walk through that front door to a combination playroom, family room, living room. To the left was a series of closets that were for storage. There Mr. Fischer kept his fishing tackle, tools, containers of turpentine, paint thinner, lighter fuel. Everything had its place. If the paint thinner was used it would be securely capped and put back."

Bolen explained how the Fischers came to employ Olivia and how Bill showed her the workings of his house, including the contents of his utility closet, as well as the shelf by the upstairs fireplace where he kept his household matches. She was also told of the precautions in place for an emergency: three fire extinguishers, three smoke detectors, six telephones with a list of emergency numbers, a baby monitor in Kristie's room, with one receiver in the master bedroom and another in the au pair's room. Bolen went on to describe the new hollow-core door to the nursery, which inexplicably became locked from the inside. "One punch would have put a hole in it."

All this was new to the press and the public, who were hearing for the first time about the half-spent box of matches found on the nursery floor, identical to a box missing from upstairs, along with the remains of a soda bottle, identical to some of the empty bottles in the recycling bin, except that this one had contained an accelerant.

Bolen alleged that Olivia took flammable liquids from the utility closet, transferred some of them to a discarded soda bottle, and set fires in three separate rooms downstairs, locking the doors to the nursery and Leah's room behind her.

He stated, "Olivia had the presence of mind to get the fire extinguisher and put out the fire in her room; yes, she had the presence of mind to get emergency personnel to that scene. But what about Kristie? She says the door was locked, and that she had left it open." Earlier, however, she told Bill Fischer that she had shut it herself.

What really happened, Bolen insisted, was that "between four and five o'clock the defendant set about intentionally, knowingly, and willfully in acts that ended in murder and arson." He glanced across the courtroom at Olivia, dressed in her new navy suit with a white blouse, and commented, "As you look at Olivia Riner, the way she is attired, her apparently angelic face, you will be thinking it cannot be her. It must have been Bill. It must have been Denise—postpartum depression. It must have been Leah—she was jealous. Or else some unknown murderer, some unknown arsonist. Appearances are deceptive."

He had made a convincing presentation. During the lunch recess a reporter remarked to a colleague, "If I had to vote on this case right now, I'd vote guilty on the basis of what George Bolen said."

It WAS a hard act to follow. Laura Brevetti seemed nervous, at times addressing the jurors so softly that they had to strain to hear her.

"You will come to learn," she told them, "that from the first hour the police department set out not to solve the crime, but to build a case against Olivia Riner. Mr. Bolen has told you of a matchbox and a soda bottle, that doors were locked, that windows were closed. Listen to the conclusion that is drawn from this: She did it. Without any doubt. End of story. But there will be no expert, no witness, who will tell you beyond all doubt that these items came from the house. This girl was not the only one who had access."

She pointed to Olivia's cooperative behavior on the night of the fire—how she telephoned for help, turned on the lights to guide the fire trucks, and was compliant during seven hours of interrogation. Were these the actions of a guilty person? Brevetti suggested that the police themselves had doubts, citing Bruce Johnson's unfortunate questions: Was she covering up for someone? John Gallagher? "This," Brevetti said cynically, "to the person who they are sure did it!"

She was making some strong points, but her speech lacked impact. She kept it brief and sat down abruptly. Then the prosecution called its first witness, William Fischer, and the story so many people had been eager to hear began to unfold.

Chapter Sixteen

BILL walked stiffly up to the witness stand, treading warily when he approached the defense table, where Olivia was sitting. This was a very private person, yet unable to hide his pain. The expression in his light blue eyes was of one so deeply wounded that there was no joy left in him. It was impossible to look at him without feeling compassion.

Over the next three days he told his story. In response to George Bolen's sympathetic questioning, he came across as a responsible, caring husband and father, a model homeowner who could give immediate answers to a barrage of questions about all his door and window latches, his heating system, and the contents of his utility cupboard, including the number of cans of paint thinner, charcoal-lighter fluid, turpentine, and other flammable liquids, and their approximate levels. Thus he was able to confirm, with believable certainty, which accelerants had been taken from the utility closet and the approximate quantities.

On the day of the fire he remembered saying "Hi" to Olivia when he walked into the house and "See you later" when he left. He spent the intervening forty-five minutes in the kitchen, upstairs, while she remained on the ground floor, near the baby. His version of their brief encounter gave a sense of her isolation, alone in a rural area where she had no friends and where the only family member who came home during the day was not very communicative.

He was asked whether he had used his front-door key when he arrived home for lunch. No, he said, that door was never locked in the daytime. Laura Brevetti made sure that the implications of that unsecured door were fully understood.

"This house is not the fortress that is being portrayed," she remarked to a group of journalists outside the courtroom. "Not just Bill Fischer but anyone could have walked in without her knowing."

Brevetti latched onto her own phrase and used it repeatedly through the rest of the trial. "That house was not a fortress. Anyone could have walked in." No one had directly claimed that it was, but her denial created the unspoken assertion, at the same time making it seem too extravagant to be true. It was a clever strategy that led the jury far away from one of the prosecution's best arguments: the contention that no one could move around in the house without being seen or heard.

In his testimony Bill stated that Grada moved out of the house in the fall of 1987. Leah had continued to live there with him, but eventually Troy had moved to Manhattan. Denise moved in during the summer of 1990; they married in July of 1991, and Kristie was born that September. Bill said that Leah was happy about the new baby. But he conceded that she and Denise "did not always see eye to eye" and that when Olivia joined the household and John was told to discontinue sleeping over, Leah began to spend more nights in Mahopac. Although they had been dating seriously for some time, the relationship between these two young people had its stormy passages.

Bill was questioned about another cause of family friction.

"Did you smoke?" Bolen asked him.

"I have never smoked," he replied.

"Did your wife smoke?"

"No, sir, she did not."

"Prior to December the second did Leah smoke cigarettes?"

After an uncomfortable pause Bill muttered, "She didn't admit to it but she did smoke."

"Did you see her smoke?"

"No."

Outside the courtroom, Laura Brevetti's private detective and chief investigator, Christopher Rush, hinted to journalists that there were other, more serious tensions in the Fischer family. None of the press had heard the half of it, he said.

TOWARD the end of Bill's second day on the witness stand, George Bolen asked him to identify a photograph.

"Do you recognize what this is?" he asked.

His voice breaking, Bill replied, "Yes, my daughter Kristie's car seat." He was referring to the infant carrier in which she died.

There was a smiling Kristie cradled in the carrier, reminding him of the last time he saw her, but he couldn't bring himself even to mention that she was in the picture. Bolen wanted to get the photograph entered into evidence, knowing it would have an emotional impact upon the jury. Laura Brevetti objected for the same reason, and the judge upheld her objection. He asked what purpose the photograph would serve, and Bolen gave the convoluted answer "To show what portions of the baby would be affected by whatever it was that burned her."

"There is no real controversy as to how this baby died," Judge Silverman observed. And so the jury had no sense of how Kristie looked and was left to think of her only in the abstract. With that, the emphasis of this trial shifted, and it became more a case about arson than one about murder.

BILL'S APPEARANCE IN COURT WAS the beginning of daily television coverage of the nanny trial. It brought out a new breed of journalists— slender young women of flawless appearance who positioned themselves with their camera crews on the ground floor of the courthouse. There would be a scuffle of activity as Laura Brevetti came importantly down the escalator with a retinue of aides at her heels; microphones would be held up to her, cameras trained on her.

Her version of the case was virtually the only one to be aired on the nightly news programs, since George Bolen, observing protocol, was consistently unavailable to the media. One program reported that Leah was jealous of the new baby—which was exactly the opposite of what Bill had just said in court. But no one on the prosecution side spoke up to correct the impression.

LAURA Brevetti and her staff worked late into the night, analyzing Bill's testimony, comparing what he stated at the trial with what he had said before a grand jury almost six months earlier. When Brevetti's turn came to cross-examine Bill, she revealed several minor discrepancies, sufficient to cast doubt on Bolen's carefully presented image of a homeowner who knew every screw in the place.

She reminded him that at the grand jury hearing he had not been certain about how many boxes of matches there were by the fireplace. Now he was positive there were four. He had told the grand jury that there were three bottles of paint thinner in the closet. Now it was "two, three, or four."

Bill tried to explain. "I don't believe they were all paint thinners. There were different chemicals in the house."

Silverman asked, "Do you consider turpentine a paint thinner?"

"Yes," Bill replied. Then he remembered, "There's a large bottle of paint thinner, a small bottle of turpentine, and a small bottle—I don't know what it was."

By now, most of the jurors were looking confused.

THROUGH several hours on the witness stand, almost directly facing Olivia, Bill avoided any eye contact with her. But from time to time she looked across at him with a kind of detached curiosity. His pain was palpable, yet it did not seem to touch her. It was as if she had never known him or his baby. She sat upright, hour after hour, feet side by side on the floor, hands in her lap, like an obedient child. There was only one outward sign of her nervousness. The hands, which from a distance seemed to be quietly folded, were in fact never still, the fingers constantly twining around one another.

While her hairstyle, her clothes, and her demeanor made her look young and innocent, her lack of emotional response was troubling. Linda Sawyer urged her to act as though she were grief-stricken by Kristie's death. "I looked into Olivia's eyes, and I implored her to show emotion in court. I told her that she must no longer act like a Swiss, because she was facing an American jury who would not understand. She listened to me as though she was a student listening to an authority figure. There was no emotional reaction."

The following afternoon the tape recordings of Olivia's two frantic telephone conversations with the desk sergeant at the Mount Pleasant police station were played to the jurors. They heard her disembodied voice become hysterical, trying to convince the desk sergeant that Five West Lake Drive did indeed exist. Suddenly the Olivia at the defense table seemed overcome by this replay of her own anguished cry for help. She became tearful and was ushered out of the room.

This incident made the next day's headlines: NANNY SOBS HEARING TAPED CALL. "It was just too much," Laura Brevetti explained to reporters. "It was very, very emotional evidence for her to hear."

THE next exhibit was even more theatrical: a twenty-minute film of the fire itself. It was an amateur videotape whose sequences were jerkily connected because the photographer, Henry Flavin, had switched his video equipment on and off as he moved around the burning house. An instructor of volunteer firefighters for Westchester County, Flavin had made the film solely for his own records, with the idea of replaying it during one of his training sessions.

A large television set was wheeled into court, and the room darkened. What the judge and jurors saw was a confusion of flame, noise, heavy smoke, searchlights stabbing the darkness; firemen dragging their equipment around, hacking at the building with axes, shouting instructions. All told, there seemed little to be learned from this videotape. So it was assumed as the television set was switched off.

Later Henry Flavin's film would become the most crucial piece of evidence at this trial.

THERE WAS A STIR IN COURT WHEN the next name was called—John Philip Gallagher III, the witness everyone had been eager to hear. He looked groomed and correct, dressed in a silvery gray suit, white shirt, and conservative tie. Everyone in court stared at him as he took his place at the witness stand. They saw a tall, lean young man with a pale complexion and thick red-gold hair, slightly receding at the forehead and worn low on the nape of his neck.

Bolen's questioning began gently, then led into some of the controversial areas of John's life. Brevetti was certain to probe them in her cross-examination, so it was politic for the prosecution to put them out in the open. There was the fact that twelve years earlier, when John was fourteen, his swimming coach had been Lieutenant Louis Alagno of the Mount Pleasant police. It was an irrelevant detail, but the defense could make it seem significant.

Bolen moved to his witness's failure to graduate from Westlake High School. At first John told the court he did graduate, then amended his response. He was asked why he did not complete his senior year.

"I was asked to leave," he replied.

"You were asked to leave?" Bolen was giving him a chance to rephrase his answer. John had not been expelled. He had dropped out.

John simply said, yes, he was asked to leave.

Bolen tried again. "You were expelled? What did you do?"

"Cutting classes."

Bolen moved on. He had John tell that in 1989 his family had moved from Mount Pleasant to Mahopac; how he and Leah Fischer met in 1987, broke up for seven months in 1988, and had dated steadily ever since. John admitted that it had been "an up and down relationship," including an argument during the month before the fire.

John stated that he smoked cigarettes and sometimes lit them with matches. He was not allowed to smoke at Leah's home. That seemed to diminish the possibility of his walking into the Fischers' house with a box of matches. He was asked if Leah smoked. No, he said. Had she ever smoked? Yes.

He testified that on Sunday, December 1, he and Leah spent the night at Mahopac. He drove her home the following morning, arriving there between 6:45 and 7:00 a.m. He did not accompany her into the house, but went directly to work.

This left a gap in his account of the day. Given the facts that John Gallagher clocked in for work at 8:04 a.m. and that it took fifteen minutes to drive from the Fischers' house, there remained about an hour of unexplained time.

Ignoring it, Bolen quickly moved the narrative to 5:00 p.m., when John left work and drove back to West Lake Drive. He had him tell about pulling into the driveway, seeing a burst of fire from the hole in the nursery window, running up to the house, taking the fire extinguisher from Olivia, kicking open the locked nursery door.

"The baby was on the floor," he recounted. "On fire."

There was a long pause before he was able to continue. Yet his emotions were so tautly controlled that his telling of the tale seemed almost dispassionate. He described kneeling down beside the remains of Kristie and spraying foam from the extinguisher around her. "But I knew it was too late. I then backed out."

"What motivated you to leave the room?" Bolen asked.

"The smoke," John replied. "And the smell of the burned baby."

Bolen had no more questions. This was a propitious moment to let his witness go, allowing the horror of that scene to sink in. Judge Silverman announced that he was adjourning court for the day. No explanation was offered, but later some of Laura Brevetti's aides let it be known that she had requested the break because she felt ill from a virus.

It was Wednesday before the court resumed.

On the evening before John Gallagher went back on the witness stand, there was a replay of Linda Sawyer's segment on Geraldo Rivera's *Now It Can Be Told* suggesting that John should be a suspect in the murder of Kristie. Yet again viewers were treated to Rivera's innuendos about "this guy Gallagher" and to his suggestion that the police and the press should take a harder look at him.

Later Sawyer explained. "The show was canceled in midseason, and the contracts ran until September. So they had to do reruns to fill in airtime. The Geraldo people, thinking this was a topical subject because the trial was on, decided to dump in my twelve-minute package. It was their decision. I was no longer working for them."

That was not the end of it. As if by collusion, the morning after the segment was shown, *Newsday,* a New York daily newspaper widely circulated in White Plains, carried a prominent article headed A NANNY VS. A LIAR: WHO TO BELIEVE? It named John as the liar, and the misinformation he had initially given about his high school record as evidence of his mendacity. Copies of this newspaper were on sale in the streets of White Plains and at the newsstand in the courthouse building.

Against this background of renewed suspicion John returned to the witness stand—agitated, angry, and exerting all his energy to keep his negative feelings in check.

Every seat in the courtroom's public section was filled. Two rows were always set aside for people attached to the defense team, which meant there was always a place for Marlise Riner and for friends and colleagues of Laura Brevetti, including Linda Sawyer. But the Fischers and the Gallaghers were often obliged to stand in line with the general public. At times even Bill had to argue his way into court, although, having testified, he was free to attend the rest of the trial.

LAURA Brevetti began her cross-examination with an acerbity that jurors had not previously seen in her. She wanted to discredit John Gallagher, and she knew exactly how to do it.

If he was expelled from school, why did he at first say he graduated? she wanted to know.

"It was a mistake on my part," John replied. He was expelled from school after cutting classes "four or five times."

"Nothing else?" she asked. After a pause to allow jurors to share her incredulity, she went on to probe another dubious area of his life.

There was the matter of the insurance on his pickup truck, with Leah named as the primary driver. Under relentless questioning, John admitted that he had used Leah's name for insurance purposes because of his own poor driving record. He "didn't recall" signing his own application for insurance and being refused, until Brevetti produced papers showing that he had amassed five traffic violations in as many years. He told her he "didn't remember" to include these violations on his insurance application, as required by law.

Under Bolen's interrogation John had been clear and prompt with his answers. Now, with no prior warning of what he would be asked, he was flustered and confused.

At the opposite end of the courtroom Carol Gallagher agonized as

John flubbed Brevetti's searching questions. Across the aisle were Olivia's self-appointed supporters, exchanging knowing looks as he sank deeper into his own confusion. His most frequent responses were "I don't know," "I can't recall," "I don't remember." He didn't even recall Denise's objecting to his overnight visits, until he was reminded that this was the cause of the big argument in which he and Leah were involved. As to his own feelings about Denise, "It was not a great relationship, but I got along with her."

Brevetti picked up on it instantly. "You did not have much in common?" she pursued.

"No, we did not." Outwardly impassive, George Bolen must have been wincing.

John was asked about his activities on the day before the fire. He said he had planned to take Leah to brunch, but they sat talking until it became too late for a restaurant meal.

Brevetti led him into the events of the morning of December 2. She asked him to account for that hour between dropping off Leah and checking into work at 8:04 a.m. Although he had testified on the previous Friday that he did not enter the Fischers' house that morning, she prodded him into remembering that "it was possible" he did go in and have a cup of coffee while Leah showered and dressed. He had sometimes done so in the past. He also admitted to being in the habit of going into Leah's room. This time he "believed" he didn't and that he left the house before she finished showering.

Again Brevetti was several steps ahead of him. She was laying the foundation for a theory that, alone in Leah's bedroom, he could have slipped the catch on her window, so that later in the day he or someone else could have entered the house undetected.

"Is it not a fact that on Friday you said that you went directly to work?" Brevetti demanded.

John was turning red and shifting in his seat. "I don't recall," he said.

After the trial he explained. "When I said I didn't remember, it was because I didn't remember. After the fire I couldn't place when things happened. Brevetti was talking to me, and there was this murderer sitting five feet away from me, and I was wanting to say to her, 'What the hell did you do that night?' But I didn't want to screw up. I wanted to hold back my temper."

Sensing his antagonism, Brevetti pressed on relentlessly. "Did you make any plans with Miss Fischer that morning?"

"No, I don't recall making any plans with her." He seemed to have forgotten their arrangement to have dinner with his mother before she went into the hospital.

"Did you call her at lunchtime?"

"It's possible that I did, and possible that I didn't."

Now he was really doing badly. And so it went on, until Brevetti led him into the episode of the fire. He was able to recount every detail at the heart of the trauma with considerable clarity. The rest eluded him. And it was the rest she was grilling him about, in such a way as to avoid any suggestion of his own heroics that night.

Finally she apprised the court about the Mount Pleasant police officers he knew: Scott Carpenter, and Louis Alagno, who taught him to swim. She mentioned the recently retired police chief, Paul Oliva, who knew John's grandfather. (Of course he did, since the elder Gallagher was custodian of the only high school in town.) And—her moment of triumph—the new acting chief, Anthony Provenzano. "You call him Uncle Tony?" she asked with a meaningful look.

He conceded that he did. All these relationships were small-town stuff. Provenzano had known John's parents since the three of them were in Westlake High School together, almost thirty years before. But the friendship between the two families drifted after the Gallaghers moved to Mahopac. Provenzano did not inherit the Olivia Riner case until after it was scheduled for trial, but the impression of a police cover-up had been registered.

Bolen's redirect examination was brief and dramatic.

"You were asked about your relationship with Leah. After Olivia entered the household it was made clear to you by Bill and Denise that it would be better if you did not sleep over?"

"Correct," John replied.

"Did you dwell on that for a long time—"

"No."

"—to such a point that you set three separate fires, doused an infant in some flammable liquid, and set fire to her. Did you do that, sir?" He was shouting now.

"*No,*" John replied, almost shouting back.

It was a staged effect. Bolen was trying to redeem all that had gone before, but some of it was beyond redemption. One of the few family members to recognize this was Barbara Donnelly. "I think we lost the case when John was on the stand," she observed later. "He got flustered and couldn't remember a lot of stuff. And I think George Bolen gave up after that."

She was wrong about Bolen. He was too stubborn a prosecutor to give up. But he did appear to change direction. From now on he seemed to be defending John Gallagher rather than prosecuting Olivia Riner.

Chapter Seventeen

THE next witnesses were volunteer firemen, describing the scene before the police investigation began. Thornwood's second assistant fire chief, Joseph Rod, confirmed that the window in Olivia's room was closed when he arrived there. This contradicted her statement to the police that she had found it open when she put out the fire on her bed.

Rod told of kicking Leah's door open and causing the flash fire that sent both him and James Lawrence running back down the hallway. Lawrence was asked by George Bolen, "What does it mean when a fire flashes?"

"It means," he replied, "that there was not sufficient oxygen for the fire to continue burning. It reignites when you let oxygen in by opening the door, and that would blow the windows out." It was an important point in light of later developments at the trial.

POLICE officer Robert Miliambro recounted his part in the story—of finding the nursery door latch in the locked position, of smelling paint thinner on a fragment of Kristie's diaper, and of noticing that several containers of accelerants had been almost emptied, including a two-liter plastic container of paint thinner. Again Laura Brevetti led the witness into peripheral details.

After Miliambro described the evidence he collected on the night of the fire, including the partially melted soda bottle, the charred box of matches, the diaper fragment, and the residues of accelerants, Brevetti asked what else he had looked for. Hair samples? Bloodstains? Did he remove the knob from the nursery door? No, he said to all three.

"Did you secure the crime scene before you left?"

"No, it was not my responsibility." He was a good witness, but she was making him look inept.

He had been told to answer the questions and only the questions. This was his first experience of testifying in court, and he was following the rules. He wanted to say that the reason he didn't secure the crime scene was because other police officers had been delegated to the task and that it was no use looking for hair samples or bloodstains in a waterlogged house in the dark.

After Miliambro's testimony the baby carrier was brought into court and placed in front of Judge Silverman's bench. At the judge's request the jurors got up and silently walked around it. What they saw was a twisted mess of metal and plastic, still attached to the portion of burned carpet into which it had melted. Nothing displayed in court gave a more graphic sense of what had happened to this baby. When the exhibit was removed, it left a trail of ashes on the beige-carpeted floor of the courtroom. Olivia turned her head from the sight.

The next police witness was Sergeant Brian Dwyer. Tall, graying, with a military bearing, he gave an impression of competence. He was forty-seven and had spent virtually all of his adult life in the Mount Pleasant Police Department while also serving as a volunteer fireman. He confirmed Miliambro's testimony and described his first glimpse of the dead baby through the nursery window. He saw no signs of an attempted entry, but noticed that the glass had fractured, creating a hole. Later, Dwyer said, he used a folding ladder to break out the rest of that window in order to vent the room.

Bolen asked him about the hole in the window. When he first saw it, were the fragments of glass inside the nursery or outside on the ground? It was a crucial question. If the window had been ruptured by the heat of the fire, shards of glass would have been blown outdoors. If the break was caused by an intruder, they would be inside the room.

Dwyer said they were inside. Baffled, Bolen repeated the question and got the same reply. As he left court, Dwyer realized that he had momentarily lost his concentration and was thinking of the glass fragments he saw after he smashed the remains of the window from the outside. It was a mortifying mistake for a veteran police officer. He went straight to Bolen's office in the courthouse building.

"George, I messed up," he said. He was due back on the witness stand the following morning and could predict that Laura Brevetti would capitalize on his mistake.

In fact, she was doing so already. While he was talking to George Bolen, she was giving her usual informal press briefing downstairs. "The prosecution stated the broken window occurred other than someone breaking in. But this evidence, elicited by the prosecution itself, is contrary to their position. The defense theory is that this was not a thermal break but a mechanical break." Now, she added triumphantly, Brian Dwyer had confirmed this.

In court the following morning Dwyer did his best to backtrack. He stated that he had made an error about the nursery window. The broken glass was on the ground outside the house.

"Who or what refreshed your memory?" Brevetti asked.

He replied, "When I walked out at recess it dawned on me what I had said, and I knew I was wrong."

She stared at him, incredulous. "Did it dawn on you because you realized the significance of what you said, that it was not a heat break because the glass was on the inside?"

"It dawned on me that I made a mistake."

As he had feared, the media took up the story. A four-column headline in *Newsday* read NANNY COP RECANTS. Laura Brevetti was quoted as saying that Dwyer's amended testimony was "too convenient." What was widely believed was that his first statement about the window was correct. There had indeed been evidence of an intruder, but now the police wanted to cover it up.

Looking back on the trial, Brian Dwyer remarked, "I was on the stand about four hours one day and eight hours the next, and the only thing the newspapers brought up was my change in testimony. But what was important was my evidence about the way those containers in the closet had been disturbed, and the paint thinner on the baby's diaper, and that the accelerant was poured around her in such a way that it must have been done from inside the house.

"Brevetti criticized the police for not collecting more evidence. But you can't collect evidence while you're fighting a fire. It's organized chaos. Windows were torn out. Furniture was ruined. In all that mess we're supposed to dust for fingerprints?"

His point about the inevitable loss of evidence in an arson case was never made clear during the trial, and Laura Brevetti was able to strengthen her argument that the police had done a sloppy job. She capitalized on their failure to remove the infant carrier, the lapse of time before materials were sent to the laboratory for testing, the desk sergeant's delay in calling the Thornwood Fire Department because he doubted the address that Olivia gave him. These became Brevetti's themes for the trial: her allegations of police incompetence and her contention that the house was not a fortress. It was just what the media needed to give new interest to the tale. She couldn't lose.

THE defense had lost all its pretrial motions, but this early advantage soon slipped away from Bolen. Laura Brevetti had the superior resources, both in finances and organization. Consultants were hired, and quantities of sophisticated tests ordered. Henry Flavin's amateur videotape of the fire was taken to a studio and run in slow motion on a large screen, many times over, in the hope of picking up some clue.

As adversaries, Brevetti and Bolen could not have been further apart. She was aggressive, and he withdrawn. She used the media constantly, judiciously, and boldly. He kept his own counsel. Her method of interrogation was dogged and incisive. His could be so convoluted that it was easy for his listeners to get lost.

His direct examinations dodged around in time and place, sometimes complicated by a tortuous phraseology that the trial reporters dubbed Bolenspeak. Occasionally the judge stopped him to act as interpreter, as he did after Bolen's question to Bill Fischer about the nursery door: "During the time when you purchased it, and while you were working on it, and during the process of your hanging it, were you able to determine the depth of the inside and the outside of the door that was hollow between the two?"

"How thick was the door?" Judge Silverman translated.

While Brevetti's team had researched the backgrounds of all the witnesses, particularly John Gallagher, Bolen was prosecuting a total stranger. He went to trial knowing nothing about Olivia Riner. But District Attorney Vergari's office had the material at hand for Bolen to be better informed than he was about the young woman on trial.

Olivia's diary, which the police passed on to Bolen, covered the entire year. But the D.A.'s office translated only her entries for the last month, starting with her arrival in the United States—a period that reflected her eagerness to learn more about the country, her home-sickness, her impatience with the Fischers' indulgence of Kristie, and her growing affection for the baby. On the basis of these entries the prosecution decided not to introduce the diary as evidence.

But there was earlier material in that diary that might have helped Bolen's case. Like this comment about a doctor for whom Olivia worked in Switzerland: "He is sometimes unbearable, and every day I hope that he will have a fatal accident and we will get time off. If I believed in God I would even pray for that. But nothing has happened so far. Unfortunately."

Bolen also seemed unaware of the contents of the brief telephone conversation between Olivia and her father on the morning after her arrest. Kurt Riner's call to the Mount Pleasant police station was routinely taped. But no written translation appears to have been made of it. Months after the trial it was revealed that Riner asked his daughter, "How did you see the fire?"

Sobbing, she replied, "I don't know how the fire traveled, but somehow there was a liquid there."

"Somebody threw a liquid there?"

"Yes," she told him.

It is possible, but unlikely, that she had heard about the use of a liquid accelerant during the few hours since her arrest. Bruce Johnson was positive that he did not tell her during the interrogation. Nevertheless, no attempt was made to enter that tape as evidence.

The prosecution also lost the opportunity to show the jury the most telling piece of evidence. Bolen tried hard to get Judge Silverman's approval for jurors to visit the Fischers' house. He told the judge that it was crucial to the prosecution's case for them "to get a true, overall picture of the house. Without seeing it, it is hard for the jury to grasp how open this house is."

He did not seem to have anticipated Brevetti's argument that the recently rebuilt house was no longer the crime scene. Different construction materials had been used. Bill had decided to enlarge Leah's bedroom. The shape of her closet had been changed. The new window frames were not quite the same size. The new floor covering gave footsteps a different sound. These renovations had made enough of a difference for Judge Silverman to rule in Brevetti's favor.

"Rather than having the benefit of seeing what could have been seen on that day," he conceded, "we would be giving them the opportunity to speculate on how it might have been."

Seated in the back of the courtroom, Bill Fischer was utterly dismayed. Why hadn't anyone warned him of this? If he had had any idea that he could hamper the prosecution's case by making those small structural changes, he would never have suggested them. Now he felt angry with himself for what he had done and with George Bolen for letting him do it.

This was yet another defeat for Bolen. As if that weren't enough, there was an important piece of evidence that he did not learn about until shortly before the trial: an accelerant-soaked diaper found under Olivia's bed. Unfortunately for him, the police had failed to notice it, and it remained there until the defense team's investigators discovered it several days later. They had it analyzed and learned that it had been soaked in paint thinner. As part of the process of legal discovery, Laura Brevetti had the diaper delivered to the district attorney's office, which ordered its own laboratory tests. These revealed not only paint thinner but the same kind of charcoal-lighter fluid that was kept in Bill's closet.

It was further evidence of an inside job. But only too late did the police realize the importance of proving that the same accelerants were used to set the fires as were missing from Bill's closet. Paint thinner alone could have been brought in by an intruder. The discovery of charcoal-lighter fluid in the diaper under Olivia's bed could have been a gift to the prosecution, except that Bolen would have to call the defense's witnesses to testify how and where that diaper was found. They could be counted on to use the opportunity to make the police and prosecution look inept, reiterating Laura Brevetti's theme.

JOSEPH Butler was one of the memorable witnesses of the trial. His experience as an arson expert went back more than half a century— the most recent as criminal-arson investigator for the district attorney of Westchester County.

Butler's knowledge of fire was encyclopedic. He described the scene at the Fischers' house room by room and confirmed that there were three, possibly four, fires set in the three downstairs bedrooms. He described "a very pungent odor" of flammable fluid on the baby's carrier, the nursery rug, her clothing, and on the infant herself.

Butler asserted that flammable liquid had been poured on the carpet around the carrier by someone standing close to the baby. If the liquid had been thrown from across the room or through the window, the burn on the carpet would have been fan shaped. And he confirmed the amended testimony of Brian Dwyer that the nursery window was initially blown out, not broken in. And he said that he had not suggested taking samples from Leah's room for analysis "because of the volume of debris." Viewing the scene as an arson, but not a homicide, expert, "We already had unusually good evidence."

In cross-examination Brevetti brought out the fact that Butler took no notes at the fire scene. He left Thornwood at midnight and wrote his report the following morning. Later he explained, "From years of experience I can easily do it from memory. That night it was raining, there was water coming down inside the building, and if I had tried to take notes, they would probably have been illegible." Outside the courtroom, Brevetti hinted that a man of his age should not be trusting his memory. She commented to reporters, "A total investigation was made by this individual with nothing to refresh his recollection— no notes, no photographs. If that evidence had been carefully documented it would have led away from my client to another individual instead."

During his second day of testimony Butler stated that although he saw fire-extinguisher residue in Olivia's room, he found none in the nursery. He explained that this was not necessarily significant. "It leaves a dry powder, and air and water could blow it away."

This became the subject of Brevetti's next impromptu press conference. "We heard that John Gallagher sprayed residue all over the nursery," she told the reporters, "but now we hear there was no fire-extinguisher residue in that room. Mr. Butler was the authority on the scene. But we found out today that his opinions have no forensic basis, and as the result of those opinions my client is sitting there today in that courtroom."

Butler had testified in more courts than any of the other witnesses, but this trial was unique in his experience. "It appeared to be the easiest case I had ever had," he reminisced. "There was absolutely no doubt that it was arson. There was a suspect, and the evidence of her guilt seemed incontrovertible. Yet in court we were losing ground every day. It was a foolproof case which exploded."

THIS WAS NOT THE WORST OF IT. Another national television program, *Hard Copy,* replayed the videotape of the fire scene with the same interpretation as Geraldo Rivera's—that John and Leah had been laughing about making a barbecue as they sorted through the ruins of her home. It was the third time this damaging film had been shown.

"It's much too early to know what the jury will do in this case," commented Doug Ruttner, the show's reporter. "But those who have followed the trial seem to be convinced that the wrong person has been charged with murder."

The trial was nearing the end of its third week. Arriving in court the following morning, George Bolen looked preoccupied and angry. He would usually acknowledge journalists covering his case with a curt nod or a thin smile. Today he ignored them.

"What's that about?" one of them asked on the elevator ride to the fourteenth floor. In the courtroom a few minutes later, before the jury was called in, Bolen answered the question with a tirade against the media. Focusing on Geraldo Rivera's interpretation of the police videotape, he charged that it was full of "outright lies and distortions." His voice rose to a shout as he described the repetition of part of this program during the trial as "an incredible act on the part of a section of the media, without any attempt to verify the accuracy."

He added, "I would like to state that the voices and the laughter in question are not those of John Gallagher and Leah Fischer."

In the four months since that Geraldo Rivera show was first aired, this was his first public denial. His initial reaction, to let it pass, had been a misjudgment. Now he was furious. At one point he accused the reporters of "misrepresentations, distortions and falsehoods." Glaring at Laura Brevetti, he added, "I'm biting my tongue and not stating what I surmise."

IT HAD become a game of legal strategy in which reputations of people unsuspected by the police and the prosecution were being attacked in the cause of disproving the charges against Olivia Riner. The next victim was Eric Trimpe, because of his history of arrests for petty crimes. But despite the police's suspicions about his connection with fires in old barns and trash cans around Thornwood, Trimpe had never been charged with arson.

With the jury absent Brevetti argued before Judge Silverman that testimony about these other local fires should be brought into the trial. Like the Fischers' fire, most of them were started after dark by the ignition of a flammable fluid. Brevetti described Trimpe as "a pathological fire setter." She suggested a close association between Trimpe and Gallagher, based on the facts that they attended the same high school and shared an interest in car racing. She theorized that Gallagher could have "used" Trimpe to set fire to the Fischers' house. Then she made the direct accusation: "It is our submission that Eric Trimpe was involved in the fire at Five West Lake Drive, and that there is a connection between Trimpe and Gallagher."

It was a bold claim that sent the district attorney's staff chasing down another tangent, researching the background of Eric Trimpe. It was a tiresome task, but Brevetti's allegations had to be answered, creating another unwanted diversion for George Bolen. It was becoming harder and harder for him to follow his own agenda in the prosecution of Olivia Riner.

Judge Silverman ruled against Laura Brevetti's request for the admission of evidence about the other fires. He saw no pattern of arson that might link the Fischers' fire to Trimpe or to the other fires, so he was proceeding with the trial.

At the same time, the Swiss people were being fed a popular version of Olivia's trial by their own newspapers, which, governed by stricter libel laws and motivated by national pride, did not make a serious effort to research the background of Olivia and her family. They assumed her to be innocent and her parents to be law-abiding people.

Swiss journalists must have been aware of a fact that the American reporters did not learn until after the trial—that Kurt Riner was one of the senior firemen in his canton, a man fascinated by the art and science of his profession. He had firefighting equipment on display in his home, hung around the walls of a spare bedroom. Growing up in that household, Olivia would surely have acquired knowledge of arson methods and fire prevention. Perhaps it was for him that she took the snapshot of the stubby fire hydrant outside the Fischers' house. Perhaps it was because of what she had learned from him that Olivia switched on upstairs lights to guide the fire trucks to the Fischers' house. Most people would not think of that. A fireman's daughter might.

Using some of his vacation time, Kurt Riner was on a flying visit to White Plains. As he sat in court, Riner's inner tension showed only in the rhythmic flexing of his jaw muscles. The bleak expression on his face reflected that of Bill Fischer, seated a few rows farther back. Seen in such proximity, their likeness was striking—blond, muscular, Germanic, controlled, and stubborn.

The thought nagged: When Bill came in for lunch, did Olivia expect him to behave like her father, brightening her day with familiar conversation? And did her loneliness and her longing for home become less tolerable when he didn't?

Chapter Eighteen

DENISE Fischer drove to the courthouse with her husband every day of the trial. Arriving there at 8:30 a.m., they took an elevator to the district attorney's suite on the third floor, sat there together for a while, then parted. Bill went to Judge Silverman's courtroom to hear the day's evidence; Denise remained in the room reserved for prosecution witnesses, and waited. Prospective witnesses are not allowed in court until they have testified, and George Bolen indicated that he was saving Denise's testimony until last. She assumed he was thinking in terms of dramatic impact. The jury would retire to consider their verdict, wrenched by a mother's tears.

There was little for Denise to do all day. She badly wanted to take part in this trial and felt unjustly excluded. Marianne Walsh of Westchester's Victims Assistance Services was there for her, trying to ease Denise's anxiety.

"My heart went out to her," Marianne said. She wondered how this woman and her husband could get up in the morning and force themselves through another day, grieving and not knowing how this case would end and being surrounded by people who thought that John Gallagher and Leah Fischer had conspired to cause their baby's death. It was so unjust. It pained her that the image of Kristie, this lovely lost child who should have been central to the trial, had been replaced by the image of Olivia Riner.

Her sadness was turned to anger by the court officers' treatment of the Fischer family. Every day some of Bill's relatives came to court and were ordered to stand in line with people who had no reason to be there, other than curiosity. Waiting, unrecognized, sometimes for an hour or two, they could not avoid hearing what some of the spectators thought about people they knew very differently.

"It was horrendous," Jim Donnelly remembered. "We had to stand there and listen to the general public saying that John Gallagher committed this crime because he was not allowed to have sex any-more with Leah, which was absolutely ludicrous."

Marianne Walsh concurred. "People were saying horrible things. I have never seen victims' families treated so badly. Generally, seats are reserved for them behind the prosecutor. It is highly unusual for court officers to make them wait."

Nevertheless, the family turned out in force, including the Menting side, when it was Leah's turn to testify. She had been waiting with Denise for the ominous telephone message from the fourteenth-floor courtroom: "You're on in a few minutes." She was so pale and tense that Marianne advised her, "Put on a bit of blush before you go up."

Leah had dressed carefully for her day in court. With a navy blue suit, she wore a white V-necked blouse, some discreet jewelry, and high-heeled navy leather pumps. Her lightly waved brown hair was drawn back and tied with a white bow. She looked older than twenty-two and of a different generation from Olivia, who, only two years younger, was more child than woman.

Bolen had advised John Gallagher to stay away from court after he finished giving evidence. "He wanted the jury to get him out of their minds," Leah said. "But John wanted to be there for me and for all of us, so he came anyway."

Bolen began his interrogation by dealing with the details of Leah's biography. He elicited that she had grown up in the house at Five West Lake Drive and that after her mother moved out in 1987, it was her decision to continue living there with her father. She seemed accepting about Denise's entry into the household three years later and mentioned the baby shower that she gave for her new stepmother before Kristie was born. It had been her own idea, she said.

Questioning Leah about her daily routine, Bolen asked whether she usually closed her bedroom door before leaving the house. No, she said, she always left it slightly open in case one of the cats was trapped inside. Early on the morning of December 2, Leah related, she came home from her overnight visit with John's family to have a shower and change her clothes. She reached her office at about 8:30 a.m. On her return to the house at 5:25 or 5:30 p.m., she saw fire trucks in the front yard. John was standing in the driveway, waiting for her. Her father and Olivia were in the patio area.

Bolen asked whether she heard her father say anything to Olivia.

"My father asked her what happened," Leah related. "She said she fed the cats, and she closed the door to the baby's room so the cats would not go into the room because the baby was on the floor. She sounded hysterical."

Leah's memory of this incident was better than her father's. She recalled hearing Olivia not only say that she closed the nursery door but explain why she did so. It was an important piece of testimony that passed almost unnoticed.

LAURA Brevetti's cross-examination started almost gently, like a woman-to-woman conversation, except that Brevetti was in charge. She led Leah through the circumstances of her life since her parents separated. Much of it had been said before, but Brevetti wanted to be certain that the jury understood how the lifestyle of this family had changed since Denise moved in and how there might be grounds for a daughter's jealousy and a boyfriend's revenge.

Brevetti asked where John used to sleep.

"He slept on the couch," Leah replied.

"Never anywhere else?"

"No."

"Are you going to marry him?"

Leah was offended by the question. "Maybe," she snapped.

On the defensive, Leah was beginning to sound tart and snippy. From their places at the back of the courtroom her parents and grandparents agonized for her.

Referring to the cancellation of John's overnight sleeping arrangement after Kristie was born, Brevetti asked, "Do you recall coming home one night before Thanksgiving and being very angry?"

"It's possible. I don't recall." Her answers were beginning to sound like her boyfriend's.

"Both you and John Gallagher smoked?" Brevetti inquired.

"At one time, yes."

"John used matches and a lighter?"

"Yes, he did."

"Your father did not permit smoking in the house?"

"Correct."

"But you smoked in the bedroom, didn't you?"

"No."

"You left the window open to smoke, didn't you?"

"No."

In response to Brevetti's questions Leah stated that she wasn't sure whether John came into the house on the morning of December 2 while she took a shower.

"Before you left that morning, did you check the lock on the window?" Brevetti asked.

"No."

What about her bedroom door? Did Leah really leave it open for the cats, or did she close it to avoid Denise's criticism about her untidiness? "You kept it closed to hide the mess," Brevetti accused.

She questioned Leah about a brunch plan that did not materialize on the day before the fire, a plan to which John had testified earlier.

"On Sunday, December first, John came over to your house to take you to brunch, right?"

"Yes."

"Isn't it a fact that you did not go out that day?"

"Yes, we did."

Where? Without hesitation Leah replied that they ate at the Travelers Rest in Millwood, an upscale restaurant in the Westchester countryside. How could John have forgotten that meal? Now a spectator in the courtroom, he felt mortified. "When Brevetti asked me about it," he said later, "I couldn't remember for the life of me. After the fire, stuff like that didn't seem very important."

When it was George Bolen's turn, he used for his redirect examination the same tactics he had adopted for John Gallagher, and hurled two final dramatic questions at Leah.

"Did you murder your half sister?"

"No, I did not."

"Did you set fire to your own house?"

"No!"

It had been a worse ordeal than she had feared. Leaving the witness stand, she walked down the center aisle of the courtroom, past the rows of jurors, reporters, and spectators. All of them were watching her. It felt like the longest walk in the world.

OUTSIDE the courthouse at the end of the day, Laura Brevetti shared her impressions with a small group of reporters. She was more forthright than usual.

"You have to feel sorry for this girl. She's stuck with this bum. Some of the discrepancies in their stories are so glaring. It all adds up to a couple who have tried to agree on a story and haven't got it right. How can neither of them remember, on the day this thing happens, whether or not John came into the house that morning?

"Then about lunch that Sunday. Gallagher said they left it too late to have any. Then she comes along and not only says they went out together but she gives me Travelers Rest. *She gives me Travelers Rest!* I could have kissed the girl."

THE autopsy report on Kristie Fischer was presented by Dr. Kunjlata Ashar, as assistant medical examiner for Westchester County. Her gentle manner softened the grisly details of her examination, which revealed that between eighty and eighty-five percent of Kristie's body was severely burned. The only uncharred portion of her skin was on her neck and back, protected by the infant carrier, where a portion of her undershirt remained.

Bolen asked whether Kristie had been injured before the fire. Dr. Ashar said she could not tell about bruises or abrasions because so much of the skin was destroyed, but there were no fractures. The infant died from burns and from asphyxia due to the inhalation of smoke containing carbon monoxide. She was still breathing when the fire started.

Some jurors were looking pained at this description of an agonizing death. Judge Silverman asked, "Is it possible for a baby that size to lose consciousness in two or three breaths?"

"Yes."

Her response strengthened Bill's hope that this was how Kristie died. A few quick breaths, then oblivion. He tried to put the rest of that autopsy report out of his mind, thankful that Denise was not in court to hear it.

Although neither of them yet knew it, George Bolen was close to a decision not to call her. His last witness, and in evidential terms his most important, would be Bruce Johnson.

JOHNSON's testimony was spread over four days, longer than anyone else's. As at the pretrial hearing, he was calm and unemotional. His largeness seemed to fill the witness stand, but not aggressively. He left a memory of a moon-shaped face, impossible to read, with mild blue eyes focused straight ahead, avoiding Olivia's interested gaze.

He was remembering his former chief's injunction to make sure that his evidence about her singed eyelashes came out right: "This whole case hangs on those eyelashes." Johnson had urged George Bolen to subpoena an ophthalmologist to explain how combustible vapors will pool in the eye sockets. Otherwise he was prepared to do the explaining, provided he was asked the right questions. Trial witnesses may not volunteer information on their own.

The direct examination began with a detailed description of the Thornwood area, the layout of the Fischers' house, and what he saw when he was summoned there in the late afternoon of December 2. Asked about the windows, Johnson stated that when he went back to the house between 7:00 and 7:30 p.m., the center catches of the broken nursery window and Leah's window were in the locked position.

From here on, Bolen's questions moved from one unrelated topic to another, defying chronology. Were there tree houses in the immediate vicinity of the Fischer house? On the day of the fire were any suspicious cars seen in the neighborhood? And on to the crucial question, phrased in Bolenspeak: "I want to take you back to a point in time between eleven-thirty and twelve midnight, a point in time when you were in the detective division with Marie Solimando—around that time did you have occasion to utilize a certain type of camera?"

Johnson replied that he took one or two Polaroid pictures of the prisoner's eyelashes, which were singed.

"Did that picture represent fairly accurately what you saw that evening?"

"No," Johnson admitted. "The picture came out dark, and the eyelashes did not show."

He wanted to say more about those eyelashes; instead, Bolen was asking who else was in the detectives' office. The next question was about the Miranda warning, followed by "Now I want to go back to the scene of the fire."

Olivia's eyelashes were not mentioned again until the end of the following day. Finally Johnson had the opportunity to say, "I asked her if she knew how she singed her eyelashes. She said she did not know. Then she said she probably did it when she put out the fire on her bed. I asked her if she put the fire out from the foot end or the side. She said the foot end."

He had given the lead to Bolen and was expecting some follow-up questions that would bring out the significance of where Olivia was standing, how, with the footboard in the way, she could not have leaned over that small blaze far enough to get her eyelashes singed. But Bolen moved on to another topic, and the police's one piece of direct evidence linking Olivia to the crime—the clue that had determined her arrest—fell between the cracks in the prosecution's case.

WHILE Bruce Johnson was on the witness stand, his tape-recorded interview with Olivia was replayed, and again a courtroom was hushed by the sound of her high, small voice relating how she cared for Kristie on the last afternoon of this baby's life.

From the witness stand, Johnson glanced across at Olivia. She was still sitting upright, both feet on the floor, elbows lightly resting on the arms of her metal-framed chair, hands in her lap—in the same position she had held from the beginning of the trial.

After the recording was finished, Laura Brevetti, beginning her cross-examination, asked Olivia to stand up. "Would you say that she looks the same as on December the second?"

"Essentially the same," Johnson replied. Except, he recalled, that then her hair was pushed back behind her ears. "It is longer now."

Olivia was looking at him gravely.

"Eyebrows essentially the same?" Brevetti inquired.

"Yes."

"Did you notice anything unusual about her clothing?"

"No."

"Did you smell any flammable liquid on her?"

"No."

After the jury had had a good look at Olivia, Brevetti asked her to sit down and began to pick away at Johnson's recollection of his interview with her. He had already said she told him, "If anyone else was in the house I would either hear or see them from anyplace I would be downstairs," contrary to the defense's contention that there had been an intruder. Now Brevetti tried to discredit his memory of that statement. She asked if it was an exact quotation.

Johnson replied that it was. She looked at him dubiously. "Inspector Johnson, did you write that quote down?"

"No."

"So you are relying on your memory?"

"Yes." But he was not to be budged.

A few minutes later, during the midafternoon recess, five big television sets were rolled into the courtroom, and Laura Brevetti announced that she was going to replay Henry Flavin's eleven-minute video of the fire scene. She reminded the court that it was shot before Bruce Johnson returned to take a second look at the damage. Enhanced by the superior equipment, this film showed a fire that looked more fearsome and overwhelming than it had when Bolen showed it, with an orange inferno spilling out of Leah's bedroom. Standing in the middle of the courtroom with a remote-control switch in her hand, Brevetti stopped the video abruptly, freezing the scene with a shot of Leah's window lit by raging flames from within. She had rehearsed for this moment, and her timing was perfect.

Addressing Bruce Johnson, she said, "Now concentrate on the frame of the window in Miss Fischer's room. Looking at the center bars of that window, would you tell me what position they are in relation to each other?"

He gulped. What he was seeing on the screen was not what he remembered seeing that night, after this video was made. At that time he was certain that this pair of sliding windows was firmly shut. Now he was looking at a picture of a gap between the two glass panels.

"I don't know," he said hesitantly. "They look like they are back to back, but separated."

It was an illusive image. They had looked shut when the videotape was run straight through, earlier in the trial. But the longer one stared at this frozen shot of them, the more obvious was the center gap of about three or four inches between the two panes.

"As you look at them now, Inspector Johnson, do those windows appear to be separated?" Brevetti persisted.

"Yes," he agreed.

Brevetti ran the video back and forth, repeating the view of Leah's slightly open window. She was relishing the witness's discomfort.

"Who closed the window, Inspector Johnson?"

"I don't know."

"It was open before you saw it?" She framed this as a question, but she was making a statement.

"I can only tell you what I saw," he replied.

"So if you made the observation at seven o'clock that the window was closed and locked, you had no way of knowing if it was closed and locked before the fire—is that correct?"

She had everyone's rapt attention. All those hours when Brevetti's assistant Chris Rush had scrutinized this film, scene by scene, had paid off. Rush had noticed this one quick shot of the gap down the center of Leah's window, which was not discernible on a normal run-through of the videotape. Cleverly Brevetti delayed bringing it to the jury's attention until her cross-examinations had revealed that Leah did not check her window latch that morning and that John may have gone into her room while she was taking her shower. It did not take much imagination for jurors and reporters to fill in the rest.

Johnson was abashed. "When I saw Leah's open window on that video, I felt like someone had punched me in the stomach," he admitted later. "I am one hundred percent sure that the latch was in the locked position between seven and seven thirty. The only way I can explain it is that the hasp became burned and melted down to make the windows spread apart when the fire was raging. But after Leah's fire was put out, before I got there the second time, the window frame must have gone back into place."

This was not an explanation that jurors and reporters were likely to accept. They would conclude that the window was open all along. It was the window that an intruder with knowledge of the house would choose—low to the ground, at the back of the building, opening into the one room where Olivia was not likely to be. Leah's room would make an ideal hiding place until it was possible to slip into the nursery next door, unobserved. All that was needed was the inside assistance of someone who would leave the window latch undone.

The script Brevetti had written for herself was impeccably timed. She led Johnson directly back to the subject of John Gallagher.

"After my client was placed under arrest, did you ask her if she was covering up for someone else who had committed the murder? Did you mention the name of John Gallagher?"

"I believe I did, yes," Johnson muttered.

"And the answer was no, right?"

"Yes."

"Was anybody else, that evening, taken to police headquarters for questioning?"

"Not to my knowledge." She had amply made her point.

From the beginning of Johnson's testimony it had been his habit, every time the judge announced a recess, to nod in the direction of Bill Fischer as he walked down the center aisle and out of the courtroom. It was his indication that the case for the prosecution was going well. At the end of this afternoon he avoided Bill's questioning gaze and strode straight to the swing doors and into the lobby.

THE following morning George Bolen tried to demonstrate Bruce Johnson's interpretation of the Flavin film. But instead of the defense's five state-of-the-art televisions, he had only the elderly set provided by the court. On its smaller screen the shot of Leah's bedroom window was again blurred.

"Can you go back?" Judge Silverman inquired. Bolen fiddled impatiently with the knobs, trying to coax the set into stopping at the right place, visibly annoyed at the indignity of his situation.

"In the middle of the window you see two bars coming down. They are separate?" the judge asked Johnson.

"No," Bruce Johnson replied. "That is the reflection, your honor."

It was almost anybody's guess, with no way of ending this ongoing trail of doubt spread by a cleverly organized defense. Afterward it was said of George Bolen that he had always played by the rules and that when the rules were suddenly changed, he was lost. At the end of Bruce Johnson's evidence he rested his case.

The court was unprepared for Laura Brevetti's announcement that there would be no defense witnesses. "The defense rests," she said, almost echoing her opponent's words.

Her bold decision was made "as soon as I heard Detective Johnson. He was Bolen's strongest witness, but on cross-examination he became a witness for the defense."

Chapter Nineteen

THERE is a perceptible shift of gears at this point in a major trial. The witnesses relax, their duties done, and all their discarded tension is taken on by the attorneys as they prepare for the last stage of this marathon. Their summations must somehow catch and distill the essence of their cases, in speeches powerful and succinct enough to leave an impression.

As the trial of Olivia Riner drew toward its close, there was a spontaneous convergence of her supporters—strangers with a common faith in her innocence and a desperate desire to see it proved. They began to introduce themselves to one another. They exchanged stories and, as the verdict approached, talked about staying in touch, and did.

On the other side of the courtroom the Fischers rearranged themselves as Denise was finally permitted to join them. Neither she nor her in-laws could understand Bolen's decision not to call her. They vehemently disagreed with him but continued to trust that he would pull all the loose ends together and bring his case to a successful close.

In a move both actual and symbolic Linda Sawyer shifted sides. Detaching herself from the defense team, she began to sit across the aisle with the journalists and the Fischer relatives. There had been a falling-out with Laura Brevetti, and the exclusive television interview that Linda believed she was promised was no longer likely to materialize. She felt hurt and betrayed.

Seated with members of Laura Brevetti's team, Kurt Riner was again in court, on his third visit from Switzerland. This had been a strange time for Marlise, with little to do but think and fret. Inwardly, she worried about her daughter, yet she seemed unable to get close to her. During breaks in the trial, there were no reassuring hugs and only an occasional exchange of glances. When Kurt was in town, her daughter seemed to have even less need of her.

Olivia herself had changed since her arrest. She had lost her pudginess and was very conscious of her slim new figure. This young woman who had tried to assuage her loneliness with marshmallows and chocolate bars was now restricting herself to half a small sandwich at lunchtime, worrying about her weight.

By Thursday, July 2, one month after the trial began, all evidence had been heard and all the attorneys' motions had been dealt with. The trial was adjourned for the Independence Day holiday, and jurors were again told not to read or discuss anything about the case.

The pro-Olivia journalists, however, continued to keep the nanny story in the news. The following Monday the entire front page of *Newsday* was filled with a close-up photograph of Olivia, looking pretty and thoughtful, alongside a headline-size quote from her diary, which had been kept secret up to this point, as it had not been entered as evidence: I Feel Closer and Closer to Her . . . I Really Do Love Her. An inside section was headed Accused Nanny's Diary Unlocked—But Not for Jury. Theoretically, that was true. But any juror who passed a newsstand on the way to court could not have failed to see Olivia's photograph and her quote about how much she loved the baby.

The attorneys' summations took most of that day. Brevetti spent the entire morning arguing the case for Olivia's innocence and for the probable guilt of John Gallagher. She claimed that she had known "from the beginning" that the prosecution's evidence would exonerate her client and "point the finger at others, known and unknown."

Brevetti noted that Bill Fischer had seen no problem with Olivia. Would he have left his baby with her if he had? "Of course not. Olivia was a good kid, an unlikely killer." Moreover, she had no motive.

This led to an attack on John. "This is a man who, when he cannot get insurance, lies on his application. No problem. He has Miss Fischer to cover up so he can drive a truck with commercial plates. Why does he drive without a license? Because he knows all the cops.

"This is a man who forgets being expelled from high school, who then remembers he cut classes. Who is expelled from high school in this day and age for cutting classes four or five times? What is being covered up? Why is an alibi needed for Mr. Gallagher?"

In response to her own question Brevetti stated, as if it were fact, that on the morning of the crime John "admitted he was in Leah's bedroom, that he waited there while she was in the shower." (In fact, he had testified that he doubted if he went into her room that morning.) "Well, what was he doing while she was in the shower?" Brevetti implied that he was opening the window.

She took her tale a stage further, imagining an episode to explain the melted soda bottle on the nursery floor. Brevetti implicated John Gallagher, whom she described as "a walking reasonable doubt." Paint thinner, she stated, was a clear liquid. The soda bottle was "used to transfer it out of the house, and then to transfer it back in without anyone knowing it was paint thinner rather than seltzer."

She reiterated that Five West Lake Drive was not "an impregnable fortress" and concluded by frankly facing Olivia's failure to try to save the baby. "Ladies and gentlemen, she is not a heroine. She is just innocent of murder, that's all. She is not Superwoman who busted through walls and doors. There is abundant evidence that Olivia Riner loved the child, treated the child well, and was cooperative. And there is something rotten when the police do not look far, and base their initial actions on what seems to be wild speculation."

GEORGE Bolen had a neat introduction to his closing speech, a quotation from Sir Arthur Conan Doyle's detective story *The Sign of Four*. Sherlock Holmes, lecturing his disciple, Dr. John Watson, remarks, "How often have I said to you that when you have eliminated the impossible, whatever remains, *however improbable*, must be the truth?"

This had been Bolen's strategy throughout the trial—to eliminate the impossible—and the task was overwhelming him. It was also unnecessary. Whether the Fischers' house was a fortress or Leah's window was open—neither of those things was as significant to his case as the improbability of Olivia's tale. If her story was to be believed, a stranger entered this small house unheard and unseen, picked up matches from a cabinet on one floor and paint thinner from the closet on another, opened and closed doors and windows, went up and down the stairs and hallway, set three separate fires with accelerants whose odor must have penetrated the building, and, finally, lit a blaze around an active, healthy baby within earshot of a monitor that amplified every sound—all this while Olivia was no more than sixteen feet away.

Instead of stressing the incredibility of this story, Bolen argued defensively. Brevetti's theory about the soda bottle was material for ridicule, but Bolen addressed it seriously, thereby conceding it was plausible. "Is Brevetti suggesting that Gallagher would pour paint thinner into a clear plastic bottle, get into the house after work, set a fire, exit by Olivia Riner's window, get back in the truck, and then get out and go to the front door? This is what she surmised."

Again falling into Brevetti's trap, he was so involved in explaining why John was not a walking reasonable doubt that he was forgetting to prosecute Olivia. He could not even suggest a motive for her.

"No one," he acknowledged, "could possibly have a logical reason to do what was done in this case. But I submit to you, ladies and gentlemen, that the police did not overlook any other suspect. It had to be Miss Riner."

Most members of the Fischer family were satisfied with George Bolen's speech. They had come to this trial with their own kind of innocence. They believed that the American judicial system was even-handed and that right would prevail.

Chapter Twenty

ON TUESDAY morning, July 7, the jurors began their deliberations. Judge Silverman explained the charges, which had been reduced to three second-degree murder charges and one first-degree arson. The first two counts were alternatives, describing either reckless or intentional conduct resulting in loss of life. The third was a felony murder count, based on the assumption that in the course of a deliberate act of arson a person was killed. The fourth—the most serious of all arson charges—on which Bolen was pinning his hopes, presumed that the defendant set a fire knowing that it posed a serious threat to the life of another person. At 10:47 a.m. the jurors withdrew to the jury room.

At the beginning of the lunch recess Denise decided to break her silence. For seven months she had respected George Bolen's advice and kept quiet. Now she could contain herself no longer. She had picked her time carefully—too late for her to be accused of trying to influence the jury and while reporters were hanging around with not much else to do. She chose a few whom she trusted and, accompanied by Bill, Leah, and John, took them to the third-floor waiting room. There she told the reporters what she knew about the other side of Olivia—about the missing baby clothes and the lie she told about whom she saw and what she did on the day after Thanksgiving. "She is not as sweet as you might think," Denise expostulated, on the edge of tears. "She stole baby clothes, a whole shopping bag full. They were found in her closet after the fire."

A reporter asked whether she thought Olivia was guilty.

Bill responded for the two of them. "Absolutely. No one else could have gotten into the house without her knowing it."

"She ran out from the fire," Denise added. "The baby was twelve feet away from her, and she did not get the baby. . . . Nobody can understand how we feel about losing Kristie."

All of them insisted that there was no discord in this household. "We are a happy family," Leah said.

"We have normal disagreements but no major problems," Denise added, making clear that her statement included John.

Also close to tears, Leah spoke up for him. "You sit and watch a man dragged through the mud. Brevetti made him look like an idiot."

John had been standing there looking distressed. "She made up a very big fictitious story about me," he said.

"What would you like to say to her?" a reporter asked him.

"I would like to punch her in the mouth," he replied.

IGNORING Bolen's advice, John went back into the courtroom with Leah after the lunch break. It took courage; the day before he had been booed out of the building by Olivia's supporters. "How can you sleep at night? We all know you did this!" one woman had shouted.

The long wait for a verdict was punctuated by the jurors filing back to rehear passages of testimony read in a fast monotone by the court reporter, then filing back to the jury room for more discussion.

Kurt and Marlise Riner sat in the front of the public section, craning forward, trying to comprehend the language and the legal system and what was happening to their daughter. Olivia was seated with her back to them, rigidly upright in her chair, immobile and expressionless except for her twisting fingers.

Shortly before 7:00 p.m. the courtroom was prepared for a replay of the Flavin videotape. The jurors had indicated that they wanted it stopped at the segment showing the separation of Leah's windows.

As if at a prearranged signal, the five handsome new rental TVs reappeared, courtesy of Laura Brevetti. She was taking no chances with the court's makeshift equipment. Again she stood up with the remote-control switch in her hand, in command. The judge got up and stood in front of one of the large screens for a better view. "Looks open to me," he observed. Brevetti was smiling.

SHANNETT YANCY, THE JURY'S forewoman, said afterward, "I felt from the beginning that she was not guilty, and after that film of the fire was shown, my mind was kind of made up." At 7:40 p.m. the jury sent a note to the judge: "We are near a decision and think we can conclude deliberations tonight."

Silverman urged them to take their time. "If you feel the need to go overnight, we shall go overnight. This is too important a matter to rush a decision." He emphasized his point by calling a dinner break.

The Fischers left the building with Marianne Walsh, the homicide crisis counselor. Drained, they all needed a change of scene and some fresh air. By now they had been joined by Barbara and Jim. After having something to eat, they went back to the district attorney's suite. George Bolen was hurrying down the hallway, looking preoccupied.

He nodded a greeting to Jim Donnelly, who had become separated from the others. "Jim, I'm glad you're here," Bolen said as they came face to face in his office hallway. "In case I don't get a chance to tell the others myself, the judge has asked them to remain seated after the verdict, no matter what it is. He wants to speak to the family."

Jim guessed what this was about, and so did Marianne when he told her: If the verdict was guilty, the judge was likely to overturn it and would want to explain his reasons.

"Right up to this point we had all been hopeful, but now I began to prepare Bill and Denise for the worst," Marianne recalled. "I told them it did not look good."

AT 10:10 P.M. the jurors filed back into the courtroom for a readback of part of Gallagher's testimony. At 11:00 p.m. they withdrew for a final conference. Theirs was a thoughtful, well-educated group. Shannett Yancy, the only black juror, was a grandmother and a secretary, and she defended Olivia strenuously.

Along with several other jurors Ms. Yancy discounted all of John's and Leah's evidence. "Nobody said 'I don't remember' so many times as they did, and that disqualified their testimony so far as I was concerned. I couldn't believe anything else they said." She could not imagine a motive and saw this as an unsolved crime, with the murderer still at large.

"There were so many gaps in the story," said Alfred Carapella, a juror who had recently retired from being dean of students at a large public high school. "We wanted to know: If her eyelashes were singed, why wasn't her hair also? Could Gallagher really see flames from the nursery if he was bending down and there were trees in the way? Why didn't we have testimony from Lieutenant Alagno, who was in charge of the crime scene? Why were the police in such a hurry to arrest Olivia? If she had used paint thinner from the house, wouldn't there have been some residue on her? Why didn't the prosecution send someone to Switzerland so that we could have known more about her mental state?

"What disturbed everyone on the jury was that every question we raised came to a dead end. I don't know how anyone will ever get to the bottom of this case, unless at some future date Olivia decides to come out with a statement."

The jury focused on the arson charge, on the theory that if Olivia was not guilty of arson, the three murder charges were irrelevant.

"The baby never became part of the issue," one juror admitted. "This baby was dead, and we were not talking about it. We concentrated on whether or not Olivia set the fires."

At 11:10 p.m. a note was sent to the judge stating that the jury had reached a verdict.

WHEN the jury filed back into the courtroom at 11:25 p.m., Bill and Denise held hands, and in a chain reaction other hands were grasped all the way down the row as the Fischer family and their few supporters braced themselves for whatever they would have to hear.

Slowly the three murder charges were read.

"Not guilty." "Not guilty." "Not guilty," Shannett Yancy replied.

Then the arson charge, the most likely one, the charge that hung in the balance.

"Not guilty."

In the public section a gray-haired woman in an orange dress stood up, let out a jubilant cry, and clapped her hands. Everyone around her joined the cheering. Judge Silverman smiled. Laura Brevetti hugged Olivia, and Olivia was suddenly transformed into a radiant young woman with sparkling eyes and a joyous smile.

The group in the back row continued to hold hands, not looking at one another. Denise's body sagged visibly, all energy drained from it. Bill stared straight ahead, expressionless, in shock. It was torture to sit there and listen to the cheering while trying to comprehend that the murder of his child might never be resolved.

Judge Silverman dismissed the jury and gave Olivia permission to remove the electronic monitor from her ankle. She bent down to unstrap it, smiling again at the relief of being freed. The atmosphere was entirely one of celebration. Bitterly Denise remarked, "People seem to have forgotten that a baby was murdered."

She would have walked out but for the judge's request for the family to wait. He had gone into his chambers to disrobe, and they assumed he would be back. Marianne Walsh and the Reverend Steven Yagerman waited with them while the court emptied.

"You have to leave," a court officer told them.

They explained why they were waiting. "I'm sorry," the officer replied. "I've had no instructions about that. I've been told to escort you out."

Denise got up. "I've had enough," she said. "Let's get out of here."

Back in the district attorney's office, the Fischers encountered George Bolen. He looked exhausted and sad. "I'm very sorry," he said. "If you're going to blame anybody, blame me." On his way out of the room he added, "Now I have to put on my smiling face for the reporters." And he was gone.

Barbara was crying. Jim put his arm around her, consoling.

Leah kept repeating, "It's not fair, just not fair. We do everything we are supposed to do, and look at what happens."

Marianne tried to comfort them. "I know this isn't going to make sense to you right now, but what goes around comes around. I was thinking of something I have seen in other cases—in some way, shape, or form, there is a kind of justice. For you it did not happen in this court, but in time it will."

The group in the district attorney's office prepared to leave. In the large lobby, they had to walk past a triumphant press conference being given by Laura Brevetti, seated at a table beneath a battery of television lights, with Olivia at her side.

Brevetti was having her last word about the Mount Pleasant police. "They should not close the book on this case. There is an arsonist running around in that community, and they should start pounding the pavements like good policemen to try and solve this crime."

Only two reporters saw the Fischers hurry by, and followed them

The defense team's triumphant press conference on the night of the
verdict. Front, from left: Laura Brevetti, Olivia, and Patricia Meier,
a friend of the Riner family. Back row, center: Olivia's father, Kurt
Riner; the others in the picture are members of the Brevetti entourage.

down the escalator to the garage. How did they feel about the verdict?

"I felt as if they were all cheering at my baby's funeral," Denise
replied.

It was past midnight when, in the shadows of the vast garage, the
weary little group of relatives and friends parted, and walked to their
separate cars. On most of the windshields there were parking tickets.

Chapter Twenty-One

OLIVIA went home a heroine. Eight days after the verdict she was
greeted at Zurich International Airport by relatives, friends, reporters, rounds of applause, and bouquets of flowers. In a few weeks she
had become the kind of celebrity who is recognized by her first name
alone. OLIVIA FREI! the headline of one Zurich paper declared.

In her hometown of Wettingen, her father's colleagues drove her
through the streets on a fire truck, like a carnival queen. Relayed to
the United States in a television newscast, this scene was the first
intimation to the Fischers, the Mount Pleasant police, and the West-

chester district attorney's office that Olivia was a fireman's daughter, and they were shocked.

Laura Brevetti had traveled to Zurich with the Riners, ensuring that her client said as little as possible to the press. "My advice to her is not to speak to anyone," she said. "I am protecting her monetary interests." There was an American film contract pending. Three months later Olivia, acting through Laura Brevetti, initiated a $20 million lawsuit against the town of Mount Pleasant for "unlawful and malicious" criminal prosecution.

Implicit in this action was an assumption of Olivia's innocence, although her trial left it in doubt. Judge Silverman explained that although he might have overturned a guilty verdict for legal reasons, he was still puzzled by the case.

"It is very rare for me to end a trial without having a strong feeling that the person is either guilty or not," he stated. "This time I don't know. I spent a lot of time looking at Olivia Riner for her reaction to certain testimony—testimony about her, about the baby—and she was expressionless. Every so often she would catch me looking at her and put her eyes down. There was no smile. Nothing.

"Laura Brevetti manipulated the press skillfully," Silverman commented. "She did a good job of steering public opinion toward her client. There was a spin put on this case, a distortion of there being great turmoil in the family, enough to make John Gallagher commit a horrendous murder in the household of people who had opened their home to him. But there was no evidence to support it.

"Here there was intent to kill a baby—not someone tossing something through a window, but a definite pour pattern around her, and no rational explanation for this act. No one benefits from it. No one could be seeking revenge against a baby. But if it was only the baby, why set other fires in that house? Why run the risk of being caught setting them? All these things point toward Olivia Riner having done this. But Brevetti was able to play the case in such a way that by the time the prosecution rested, the defense was won."

The judge was severely critical of the media coverage. "The TV people were off the wall. They made no effort to be accurate or objective, but saw the defense theory as a good story and ran with it as though it were fact. They destroyed the character of John Gallagher, then moved out of the community without a care in the world."

THE FAMILY HAD BEEN NUMB AND unprotesting through most of the trial, but the verdict released an outburst of uncharacteristic rage. They had not only lost Kristie, they had lost faith.

"I don't trust the courts," Bill said. "I don't trust the media. I don't trust anyone. It was not Olivia who was on trial. It was us."

And from Denise: "You trust someone with your baby, and they betray you. The media, the D.A., the justice system—they all betray you. It's as though the world isn't working anymore."

"This is how a rape victim must feel," Bill added. "You have been violated, and yet you are made to feel that you should have known better than to let it happen, that somehow it is all your fault."

Jim Donnelly empathized with them. "So many times at that trial I wanted to scream out, 'Forget Olivia. Think about my brother-in-law. You have no idea what he and his wife are going through. And you don't care.' If I were John, I would have blown my brains out. I couldn't handle it. He was part of our family, and there's no way anyone can convince me that he set that fire. But that man was crucified. He was brutally taken apart."

During the succeeding weeks the Fischers and the Gallaghers heaped their frustrations on the person who had invited blame, George Bolen. They argued that if only he had done this or said that, Olivia would have been convicted. Bolen, meanwhile, was undergoing his own agony of self-doubt.

"I have tried a lot of circumstantial cases," he recalled. "Usually it's possible to come up with a reasonable scenario of what you think occurred. This time I racked my brains, and couldn't. I was hoping the jury would see that only Olivia Riner could have done it, despite the fact that they could not come up with a reason."

Bruce Johnson was devastated by the verdict. As the lone detective on the investigation, he felt he had failed the Fischers. "We had a lot of evidence, but so much of it didn't get presented. I was throwing things around George Bolen's office. I was saying, 'Dammit, this is very important.' The Fischers have been done a great injustice."

There were other consequences of the trial. Four months later Judge Donald Silverman was elected to the state supreme court. What undoubtedly tipped the vote in his favor was his public exposure as the nanny-trial judge and the praise he was given in Westchester newspapers for his skillful handling of the case.

Laura Brevetti's career was given an enormous boost. She became a frequently quoted figure in the legal profession and resigned from her law firm to set up her own New York City practice.

None of the posttrial inquests produced a clue leading to any other possible arsonist, and an increasing number of Westchester residents came to believe that Olivia Riner may have got away with murder. This view was strengthened by the withdrawal of her lawsuit against the town of Mount Pleasant. In an exclusive CBS television network interview—courtesy of Laura Brevetti—Olivia gave her reasons: "I must [would have to] go back to New York. I must go to court. It would take a long time, and I do not want to do it." She was photographed in Switzerland, back at her old job as a physician's assistant.

"I am not angry," she told CBS. "I am sad. They may have made a mistake, but I am not mad about it."

"What would you say to Bill and Denise Fischer?" the interviewer asked.

She hesitated. "I did not do it. I do not know how it happened."

NOT all the media remained sympathetic to Olivia. In the weeks after her acquittal, journalists who had thought her innocent at the outset began to question her story. Linda Sawyer began to dwell on details that, earlier, she had pushed to the back of her mind. The baby monitor that Olivia didn't hear. The light green outfit in which Kristie wasn't dressed, which Denise said she didn't own. These things brought her to the distressing question "Have I been defending a guilty person for all these months?"

She wanted to be assured of the truth. The Riners had invited her to visit them anytime, so on impulse she flew to Switzerland and showed up on their doorstep. They were surprised to see her and as hospitable as they had promised. In their apartment she saw a great deal of Kurt's firefighting equipment on display, much of it hanging from the walls of the spare bedroom in which she slept.

"Olivia was happy to see me," Linda recalled. "She had come to think of me as the sister she never had." The two of them talked for hours. In response to Linda's questions Olivia revealed a sophisticated knowledge of fire and the use of accelerants.

While in Wettingen, Linda tried to check on the two Swiss references Olivia had supplied to E. F. Au Pair. At one address the name given in the reference was not known. The other address did not exist. She also visited the bookstall whose proprietor had talked on the telephone to Bruce Johnson, and learned that Olivia was a frequent customer. But she could not discover whether a book containing "The Heroine" was sold to her.

Back in the United States, she shared her information with Bill and Denise Fischer. By now she had come to believe Olivia guilty and wanted to make amends. She told the Fischers that she was in a unique position to help them get justice done "because if I hadn't believed in Olivia's innocence so desperately, I wouldn't know what I know now." They were contemplating a lawsuit against E. F. Au Pair, and she could be very persuasive.

In an extraordinary reversal of allegiances, they appeared with her on two editions of a national television program—the same *Maury Povich Show* that they had turned down during the week after the fire. In the first program Linda made an abject public apology to John Gallagher. For the second she returned to Switzerland and had herself videotaped as she waylaid Olivia outside her apartment house.

Linda approached her bluntly, becoming more and more emotional as she spoke. "I have questions to ask, questions that are haunting me," she said. "Did you buy this book, Olivia?" She was holding a volume containing "The Heroine." "How did you know how the fire was started? When you talked to your father on the phone, how did you know a liquid was poured? Eight months of my life I protected you. I believed in you. Olivia, I deserve the truth. Tell me the truth. What happened to Kristie? What happened, Olivia?"

She was trying her utmost to get the confession the police had failed to achieve. But this time Olivia had nothing to say. She had her head bent down and walked indoors without a sign of recognition.

FOLLOWING up on Linda's lead, Bill and Denise hired an investigator to research Olivia's references. His report stated that "even the most casual screening" should have revealed that they were fictitious. Both signatures appeared to have been written by the same person, in a handwriting resembling Olivia's. One reference was signed with the surname Meier, the other Reinert. No first names were given. As Linda Sawyer had found, Meier's address was that of a commercial building where no Meier was listed. Reinert's address did not exist.

On the second anniversary of Kristie's death, December 2, 1993, in a news conference arranged by Linda Sawyer, Bill and Denise Fischer announced that they had filed a $100 million lawsuit against E. F. Au Pair. The suit alleged that despite the agency's claim of a rigorous screening process, it sent them an au pair who was unqualified and psychologically unstable, and who caused the death of their baby.

There was no expectation of a speedy settlement.

THERE were certain immutable occasions when members of the Fischer family got together. One was the Christmas Eve tradition of gathering at one home or another, with Jim Donnelly, jovial, portly, and exuding good cheer, playing Santa Claus.

Bill's sister-in-law, Betsy, remembered the Christmas Eve following the trial: "At seven p.m. the front door opened, and Santa came in doing his 'Ho! Ho! Ho!' routine. Then his voice cracked. Tears ran down his face, and he made a quick departure. He came back wearing his usual clothes."

The next day the family gathered at Bill and Denise's new home. They had moved again, permanently this time, to a condominium with an adjoining apartment for Leah and John. The usual keepsakes were noticeably missing. All those treasures had perished with Kristie. The house was being rented until it could be sold.

"Denise had done a beautiful job with the tree," Betsy recalled. "She did not shy away from the children. She was teary, but she made an effort."

When Denise was in the kitchen preparing the meal, Jim took the opportunity to speak to her privately. "There's something I have to tell you," he said. "I don't want you to think I was intruding, but that time when Barbara and I visited you in the hospital, I baptized Kristie. I don't know why I did it, but I had this sense of urgency."

She grasped his hand, and there were tears in her eyes. Nothing was said. Others came into the kitchen, and the moment passed. He was worried about how she'd react. But it was all right. She understood.

SETTLED in their new home, Bill and Denise began to rebuild their lives. Her feelings were poignantly described in a letter written eighteen months after Kristie's death. "My mind has replayed those events over and over again like a broken record. My hands have written down words that appear to come from another world, from a wretched, tormented creature. I will never, ever lose sight of what happened. I have only learned to live with a higher level of pain."

Bill avoided discussing the murder. The pain etched on his face when he testified in court had, over ensuing months, softened a little, only to become absorbed into the rest of his body, where it seemed to have lodged as a lasting part of him.

Leah lost the job she had held for three years. Her employer told her she had taken too much time off to attend the trial; she wondered whether the suspicion surrounding her was an unspoken factor. The shock of dismissal forced her to rethink her career, and she went back to college to train as a social worker.

The stories about her and John did not disappear. "When I think about what happened to me," John said, "I wonder if I shouldn't have stayed outside that night. But if it would have saved Kristie, I would have gone through that experience many times over."

At family gatherings the Fischers began to make a conscious effort to talk about other things. Even so, every celebration seemed to be a reminder of pain.

"There are constant reminders," Jim acknowledged. "Every time something happens to a nanny, the newspapers mention this case. It will never stop. It will haunt us. It will follow us to our graves."

Part IV: THE CRIME
Chapter Twenty-Two

There is a motive, but we don't know what it is. Perhaps she was angry at me. Or she was angry at Bill. Perhaps she was insane, or manic depressed. Perhaps she was an abused child who had some crazy idea about wanting to save this baby from abuse. We may never know. But there *is* a motive.

—DENISE FISCHER

IT WAS the missing link in the chain of evidence, and without it none of the rest made sense. In the absence of a motive George Bolen was lost and Laura Brevetti could weave a tale that won an acquittal. Her intruder theory did not bear close analysis, but it was easier for people to accept than the guilt of her client. Even in a society as violent as that of the United States, it was beyond imagining that a shy young girl who said she loved babies could do anything so calculated and terrible as to set an infant on fire.

Whatever happened in the Fischer household that winter afternoon was beyond comprehension. In his twenty-five years as Westchester County's district attorney, Carl Vergari had not encountered a crime remotely like it.

"This case is truly extraordinary," he said. "It is one of a kind, thank God. And why it happened, I do not think we shall ever know."

It was hard to leave it at that. Months after Olivia's acquittal the research for this book led to the discovery of an extraordinary collection of old case histories shockingly similar to the crimes with which she was charged.

These case histories form the basis of a medical thesis by Dr. Karl Jaspers, published in Germany in 1907. In it Jaspers discussed the eighteenth- and nineteenth-century phenomenon of young Central European girls, sent away from home to be live-in nursemaids, who set fires and murdered infants in their charge. Jaspers was struck by the contrast between the naïvely innocent demeanor of the girls and the diabolical kinds of murders they planned: the same contradiction that puzzled the prosecution in the case of Olivia Riner. Jaspers summarized the girls' motives in his title *Heimweh und Verbrechen* (Homesickness and Crime).

When it was first published, the report was seen in professional circles as an unusual and important piece of research. It was written as the dissertation for Jaspers' medical doctorate at the University of Heidelberg. He went on to become professor of psychology at Heidelberg and turned to a career in philosophy.

The girls in Jaspers' study were essentially indentured labor. The parents who hired them out may have seen this as a way of offering their daughters a better life. But the girls knew that if they ran away to go home, they would be punished by their parents and sent back to the same situation that made them so miserable.

The contemporary au pair system seems much more free, yet there are strong parallels. In both instances young women of limited worldly experience go to work as nannies in strange environments, cut off from the emotional support of their families. Often they are left for hours with the infants in their charge with no one to talk to.

The program in the United States requires a one-year agreement. In theory a girl longing to go home need only contact her agency and say she wants to quit. In practice that involves awkwardness with the host family and a sense of failure. It is not the kind of decision that a young woman of Olivia Riner's rigid and dutiful personality would easily make.

Olivia confided to her diary that she often cried herself to sleep but felt bound to stay for the promised year because her father would be disappointed in her. And his approval was all-important to her. Like the girls in Jaspers' study, she hid her homesickness and did not think she had any options.

These were her feelings on her third day as Kristie's nanny: "I am missing my home, my room, simply everything. Or nothing? What good is it, I am here and should make the best of it, or . . . ?" Leaving the question unformed, she continued angrily, "Sometimes I am sick of everything! The amiability, the badly pampered baby! All the baby has to do is to scream once and the whole family rushes to feed her, to change her diapers, to play with her or rock her to sleep, as she does not go to sleep otherwise. Damn!"

KARL Jaspers was fascinated by the pathology of those young nurse-maids who, feeling hopelessly trapped, found their own terrible solutions. Their homesickness was so overwhelming that they permanently eliminated their own jobs, either by setting fire to their employers' homes or by killing the infants in their charge within the first few weeks of their employment. Prior to these criminal outbursts all the girls were perceived to be compliant, caring, and trustworthy. Most of them worked conscientiously and behaved affectionately toward the infants.

These crimes were planned, often days ahead. Many of the girls denied any knowledge of the crime and told carelessly concocted stories that were transparently untrue. Those who eventually confessed explained, with a child's imperfect logic, that it was necessary for them to do what they did in order to get back home.

Researchers from previous centuries looked for the usual kind of motives—vindictiveness, hate, envy—but found none. One researcher writing in 1830 concluded that these girls wanted nothing more than to go home and could think of no other way than to destroy their employers' domestic situations and thus put an end to their jobs. The girls' prison sentences were often abbreviated as a result of the medical experts' frequent findings: diminished accountability because of emotionally crippling homesickness.

In an attempt to identify the girls most likely to be susceptible, Jaspers found one constant characteristic: In physical appearance and behavior they were all very childlike for their years. Most of them were quite intelligent, but their reasoning processes had not kept pace with their intellectual development.

Jaspers understood that homesickness of itself does not cause criminal behavior, but that it can be the trigger that makes some relatively benign preexisting disorder, such as depression or anxiety, become violently explosive. He wrote, "What we find is not feeblemindedness but a horizon kept narrow by upbringing and environment." In his analysis Jaspers made the analogy between a child and a young plant, both dependent for survival upon the only environment they have ever known. When either of them is transplanted, all support systems are lost. A child feels threatened, terrified, and cast adrift in unfamiliar surroundings. The homicidal nursemaids of Jaspers' study were not killing out of evil intent, but in a kind of life-and-death struggle for their own sanity.

SOME observations about Olivia Riner may be relevant. She had looked forward to spending a year away from home, with no sense that the humdrum life of Thornwood had a lot less to offer her than the small Swiss town where she grew up.

For the first weeks of her contract she had the constant company of Denise, who took her shopping and showed her the neighborhood. After that, Olivia was to be alone all day with the baby, without a car. There was nowhere for her to go alone and no one to confide in but her diary. The fact that within a month she made five telephone calls, which she had to pay for herself, to relatives in Switzerland suggests how much she missed them.

In happier moments she seemed to have great affection for Kristie, but she felt ambivalent about her. The love showered upon Kristie underlined Olivia's own loneliness. "I turned twenty today!" she wrote on her fourth day at the Fischers' home. "Actually a reason to celebrate, but who's celebrating? Not me. Kristie is a spoiled, pampered tyrant. Most of the times she cries for unknown reasons. I would just let her cry, but the mother won't. But so what? When she's at work I can just let her cry for a while. Nobody will hear it except me."

This festering anger, on her own birthday, surely came from her unfulfilled need to spend the anniversary with people who would make a fuss over her. "Why don't I have children? Why don't I have love?" she wanted to know.

Alone in the family, Jan Menting, Bill's father-in-law from his first marriage, held on to the thought that came to him the morning after the fire, when he walked into the ruins of Kristie's nursery and saw the deeply etched circular scorch mark on the carpet, outlining the charred remains of an infant carrier. He did not know about Jaspers' research, but he did know what a powerful emotion homesickness can be.

"That fire around the baby was an act of insanity," he said. "And homesickness can be such a profound psychological condition that your sanity might break. Then you could do something you would never contemplate in a normal state."

Others had raised this possibility, and it had quickly been dismissed. It was inconceivable that an unhappy employee would kill rather than quit.

"You mean that the motive they attribute to the nanny is that she was homesick?" Geraldo Rivera had sounded incredulous in the television program that turned the tide of public opinion in this case. "That's the best they could do?"

It was indeed. And whoever they were, they could have been right.

Dan Rather

with Mickey Herskowitz

THE CAMERA

NEVER

BLINKS TWICE

The Further Adventures of a Television Journalist

. . . Everything in me said to keep going. Hell, we were on a roll. We were hot. We were out front, exclusive on what might be one of the best stories of our time. This is what a reporter dreams of, works for. This is why you paid the price all those years, standing in the rain, microphone in hand, covering city hall hearings. This is why you left a young wife home with your babies when you knew what a wrench it was. It was all to get to a place such as this, at a moment such as this. Frontline, cutting edge, on a world-class story.

—*The Camera Never Blinks Twice*

OUTTAKE

IT IS morning in a large Florida city. I have flown in late during the night, after midnight, have not slept well, and am now up early to go downstairs in the hotel to make a speech before several thousand people.

I am not in a good mood and am silently asking myself unjustifiably self-pitying questions, such as "Why am I doing this?" I dress hurriedly, gulp down black coffee that tastes like day-old drained transmission fluid, and go to the elevator.

It is crowded. I nod glumly as I get on. Not a word is spoken as we go down ten floors to the lobby, but I feel all eyes on me. In the egocentric way of anchors generally, I am thinking, Okay, I'm on television, but didn't any of these people's mothers teach them that it's rude to stare? Besides, I have the uncomfortable feeling these people aren't just staring; they're looking me over, top to bottom. And why do I have the feeling some of them are smirking?

The elevator reaches the lobby. As it empties, a woman of about forty, crisply and immaculately groomed, gently takes hold of my sleeve. "Mr. Rather," she says quietly, "I don't mean to intrude." Then why are you? I think. She continues. "But I have admired you for years." Well, of course, your anchorman is thinking, now I understand. "And this will only take a moment." It had better, madam, I say to myself. I'm already late to this big important speech I must deliver.

She looks first to one side, then to the other, making sure no one else is listening.

"I don't want this to be awkward or embarrassing in any way." Pause. "But your fly is unzipped, and a piece of your shirttail is sticking out through it."

She smiles and strides away.

Thank you, ma'am, wherever you are.

ONE
If You Can Keep Your Head . . .

ERIK Sorenson was ticking off the day's stories to me, giving me a sense of the way the *CBS Evening News* would probably shape up that day. The last item on his list was, to his mind, potentially the most important: "The cardinal in Chicago has been accused of sexually abusing a boy. The boy is grown now, in his twenties, and he's pressing charges. There was a big press conference this morning. Chicago is reeling."

Erik Sorenson, executive producer of the *Evening News,* is a laid-back, amiable guy, given to blue jeans and loud ties. Most mornings I'm on the phone early, checking in with Erik and the senior producers in the "Fishbowl" (a glassed-in office within the *Evening News* studio) to find out what news has broken and to discuss what will appear on the broadcast. At any minute something could happen—a plane crash, a terrorist attack—that could require us to overhaul our plans. Sometimes we debate, we argue, we bicker, we cajole, we plead, and sometimes we persuade.

This was going to be one of the times we'd debate. All day long.

"There is some sentiment among our senior producers that we may want to lead with the cardinal sex-abuse story," Erik said.

I disagreed. I said, "Erik, that's not a story; that's an accusation."

He came back with a broader view. "Child sex abuse is an important story, and every part of the church's attitude toward sex has been coming in for close scrutiny." He explained that there may be the beginning of a philosophical change of course for the church, seen also in the heated debates over birth control, abortion, women priests, and the celibate clergy. The increasing number of accusations of sex abuse by priests had already colored the debate on celibacy.

This was all well and good, I thought, but the accusations against the cardinal seemed like a slim peg on which to hang the story. In practical terms, what Erik described sounded like a long, thoughtful piece, something that couldn't be ready by airtime this day. Erik and I agreed that we would continue to monitor the story.

When I got into the office a short time later, the debate had expanded from a dialogue between Erik and me to include all the senior producers in the Fishbowl. These are bright, intelligent people, and I love talking issues with them. They're all hardy veterans of fierce campaigns, but none of them are old enough to have worked in the trenches back in the days when almost any mention of sexuality in a national news program was unthinkable. In those days before the sexual revolution, you might have discussed sexual matters with your very closest friends, but people still couldn't discuss sex with their own doctors.

In many ways we're a lot better off today. We *need* to be able to discuss sexual matters with qualified caregivers and with our partners. But I am not one of those reporters who believe that every sex story is another brick in the foundation of wisdom. I know that sex sells. And the competitive side of me is always pushing, as if whispering in my ear, "Don't let 'em scoop you." But I believe that if we do not treat sex stories exactly as responsibly as we would treat a story on any other subject, then we're not helping anybody, least of all ourselves. Our credibility will go, and we won't be able to get it back.

These are more or less the arguments I made in discussions over the course of a long afternoon. Due to a family emergency, Erik Sorenson had to leave command of the broadcast to Kathy Moore, who now had to wrestle with the thorny professional dilemma of how much coverage to allot to a potentially explosive story.

I was pushing for minimal coverage—at most a "tell" (so called because it's not a videotaped report; the anchor simply tells it). I continued to try to explain that an accusation is not a story.

We hear all kinds of accusations—some credible and some not. One viewer has written a couple of times with the theory that President George Bush *died* at the state dinner in Japan where he became so ill; she believed that the real, dead President Bush was replaced by an impostor. This, she explained, is why Bill Clinton *had* to win the 1992 election. The impostor couldn't keep up the deception any longer despite all the help he was getting from Peter Jennings, Tom Brokaw, and myself.

We hadn't broadcast *those* accusations. But back on planet Earth, the sex-abuse accusations against the cardinal, although pronounced by a seemingly earnest, credible young man, could not be independently substantiated.

New York: Dan Rather in the CBS newsroom

In the late afternoon Kathy called me. "The cardinal is holding a press conference to deny the accusations," she said. "That makes the story—if we choose to look at it that way."

"Kathy," I said gently, "that's not a story; that's a denial."

Now Kathy was leaning against big play for the story, and she'd instructed a solid correspondent, Frank Currier, to get working on a piece as sober and unsensational as possible. But she was clearly concerned by the prospect of dropping or burying a story that might be big. I was torn, too.

The debate kept up all day, but a newsroom is not a philosophers' retreat. As the day winds down, the preparations for the broadcast gear up.

There are a couple of scenes in the movie *Broadcast News* in which the actress Joan Cusack has to dash pell-mell across a network's Washington bureau in the final seconds before airtime—scooting past bystanders, slamming through doors, sliding under file-cabinet drawers—to get the videotape to the studio and meet her deadline. For those of us who work in the real broadcast news, such scenes are not comedy. They are reality. All of us, including your narrator, have had to run that race many times.

By the time those races had begun on this evening, the correspondent's report on the accusations was ready. Our writers had drawn up six different lead-ins to the piece, plus a couple of scripts in which we wouldn't use the piece at all. Tape was ready to roll. Kathy and I were still talking it out. Nobody felt good about running hard with the story. Nobody felt good about running light with the story. Nobody thought we could afford to drop it altogether.

Finally, with the clock ticking to airtime, the stage manager ready to count down to the broadcast, I said with as much anchor authority as I could muster, "Kathy, this is not our lead."

And she agreed. We used Currier's piece, but within the body of the newscast, alerting our audience to a story of interest and possible importance, yet by no means the most significant event of the day.

We thought we were striking a blow for responsible coverage in the war of sensationalism that is always raging at the borders of good journalism. We were also, it turned out, doing the prudent thing. Months later the young man withdrew his accusations, said he wasn't sure his memories were accurate, how much was imagination and how much was reality.

This is just one example of the ways in which I've been called upon to act as managing editor of the *CBS Evening News*. That's a part of my job that is not well understood outside our newsroom, and not the kind of thing you can tell adventure stories about, but being a managing editor has turned out to be one of the great adventures of my life.

I have been at CBS News since 1962, have worked with those who became legends in the industry, have tried to preserve their memories even as I have tried to move forward. Besides the *CBS Evening News,* I spend a good deal of my time working on *CBS Reports* documentaries, live special-event coverage, and the weekly documentary series *48 Hours.* I have also worked in radio ever since I came to CBS News. I do spot pieces when I'm covering a breaking story, and I have a daily radio essay called *Dan Rather Reporting.*

What I have sought, over a lifetime in news, is to earn a reputation as a "pull no punches, play no favorites" reporter of integrity. My intent has been to uphold the highest standards of journalism, even when there is reason to believe this will cost me something.

I certainly have made mistakes—may have made more than my share of them. But I have tried hard to be as accurate, fair, and unafraid as is humanly possible. And along the way I have also tried to lead an interesting professional life, including some adventures.

I grew up on adventure stories. I thrived on them. Cowboy movies at the picture show. At home I read Rudyard Kipling. Kipling may be out of fashion now, but I wouldn't trade anything for the color and excitement of his stories—and, most of all, the idea that your integrity, your sense of honor, of justice, of duty to others and to country counted for something. Kipling fired my imagination when I was a little boy in a way that no one else did.

Well, almost no one. The exception, of course, was Edward R. Murrow. To this little boy listening to the radio during World War II, Murrow, risking his life for the *truth*, was a hero right out of the adventure books. His work heightened my sense, even then, that being a reporter was a kind of vocation—demanding sacrifice, needing courage, requiring honor. Only with those qualities could a reporter endure one adventure and go on to the next.

If I'm reckoning up the adventures of my life, I've got to put first on my list the adventure of getting to know, over four decades (so far), Jean Grace Goebel Rather. A gifted artist, a wise mother, a loving partner, whose intelligence has gotten me out of countless scrapes and whose natural beauty and style turn heads and win hearts to this day. I'm blessed just to know her. Actually to be married to her, to share my life with her, is some kind of miracle.

Because most of the adventures in this book took place away from the anchor desk, I think it's important to reemphasize that I think every day is an adventure.

My coanchor, Connie Chung, and I broadcast the *Evening News* in two feeds, one at 6:30 p.m. and one at 7:00. In the second feed, we update with any new information and correct any production errors. Often we update again for broadcasts to the West Coast and Pacific.

Throughout the day I'll have been in conversation with correspondents and producers in the field and in New York, still trying to find out what's going on, but also offering advice when it's solicited. A reporter may be working on a story that has something to do with a story I once covered or may want my ideas on how to treat a sensitive issue. But sometimes the reporter may want nothing more complicated than the name of a good restaurant.

I may prescreen a report or read the script well in advance to make sure it's fair, reflects what I'm hearing from my own sources. All of the staying in touch with the news and with news sources, all of the cross-checking, copy editing, keeping myself available to our news team for consultation on matters large and small—this is what it means to be managing editor, and it is important to me.

I believe it is also important to viewers to know that the person on-screen presenting the news is directly involved in gathering the news and putting the newscast together. A managing editor should help direct coverage, help to set standards, and keep morale up. I would not want to be anchor without also being managing editor.

On most nights around 7:45, once the broadcast is put to bed, and if we're not on standby for any breaking story, I can head for home, a hot meal, and the company of my wife.

But those are typical days—or as near to a typical day as I ever get. The standout adventures, of course, don't much resemble typical days—that's why they stand out. What follows is an account of a few of my standouts, a few adventures I've had lately.

OUTTAKE

HAVE dodged bullets on three continents; I've been maced, mugged, and arrested by the KGB; and I've flown on planes so flimsy that the length of the flight depended on the size of the bugs that hit the windshield.

And I've been frightened every time. Fear is useful to a journalist. It sharpens the senses, gives you an edge. Nervousness just makes you smile harder. One of the only times I get nervous anymore is just before I appear with David Letterman.

Appearing on the *Late Show* is a joy, but also a terror. Anyone who has ever watched Letterman knows he is spontaneous. You have a rough idea of what is planned, but at any moment David can throw out his producers' hard work and jump the tracks. I consulted a friend who had been on the show, and he advised me, "If you're prepared to be yourself, and to laugh at yourself, you'll do fine. If you bring any pretense along, you are asking for it. David is a master at puncturing pretense."

Letterman is thorough, with a humor that is effortless, and he is a gracious host. His entire show hums with excellence.

It didn't take long for David's team to worm out of me the fact that I enjoy, and know the lyrics to, a few old railroad songs. Once, as a gag, I pulled out the cover of a compact disc showing me in a conductor's uniform and standing next to an engine, with the title lettered in red: *Dan Rather Sings His Favorite Train Songs.* This was the handicraft of Letterman's brilliant art department.

For good measure I belted out a chorus of "The Runaway Train" a cappella, and the bit came off better than I had any reason to expect. I joked that the CDs were on sale at the Oklahoma Railroad Museum, and Dave added that you could find them in the CBS gift shop. To my amazement my office received around 250 orders for this product that didn't exist. Ah, show business.

I'm more than relieved to say that appearing on the *Late Show with David Letterman* is only an occasional adventure for me.

TWO
Afghanistan's Plains

WHEN I first walked through the Hindu Kush into Afghanistan in 1980, just after the Soviet invasion, I had no idea what I was getting into.

I came out knowing that Afghanistan had become one of the most dangerous places in the world and believing that it could develop into one of the most important battles of the cold war. It did that and more. The Soviet defeat in Afghanistan was and is an underestimated factor in the sweep of people and events that led to the fall of the Soviet empire.

This is the story of how I came to Afghanistan and what happened when I got there.

Just after Christmas, 1979, the Soviets invaded Afghanistan. It was front-page news but began to fade as a story almost from the first day. For one thing, Afghanistan was a long way off. For another, the United States was absorbed by the hostage crisis in Iran. For another, America's intelligence community and military and diplomatic corps all had been caught by surprise. And besides, they were all in a kind of hiatus—partly because of the holidays.

As for the press, well, almost no major Western news outfit moved into Afghanistan to cover the story.

I was still a reporter for *60 Minutes* at the time. As soon as I heard about the invasion, I said, "This is a big story." It was mostly just hunch, a gut instinct. No reporter can explain these things. You just begin to get a vibration in your reportorial bones.

The Soviets invaded on December 27. On December 29, 1979, I went into the office of *60 Minutes* executive producer Don Hewitt to tell him I wanted to go to Afghanistan. It was late. Don and I were the only two people left in the shop. Christmas lights were blinking outside the windows of his corner office. He was smoking a cigar.

I told him I had a feeling about Afghanistan and that I wanted to go. He looked surprised, took the cigar from his mouth, and looked me over for a long time. Don was there when I first walked into CBS News, in 1961. We had been through a lot together. Now he stared at me, shifted his medium-framed body and his cigar, and said, "Forget it."

He looked at me hard again. He knew from years of working with me that he couldn't just brush off the idea, not this one. The next instant his expression changed and he smiled. "Come on," he said. "It's New Year's. Go home. Enjoy the holidays. Kick back. And then if you still feel the same way, well, maybe we'll see."

After the first of the year, when we came back, I told Don that my feeling about the story had grown, not faded. He still was far from enthusiastic. But he responded along the lines of, "If you're hell-bent to go, then we'll see what we can do." His attitude was, "Let's at least scout it out. Who do you want to work with you?"

On the average *60 Minutes* story the team consists of a correspondent, field producer, researcher, cameraman and soundman, and videotape editor. I told Don I wanted Andy Lack to produce it and that we could talk about the rest of the team later.

Lack and I began making telephone calls, contacting people. We asked a lot of questions and quickly confirmed a problem. It was the dead of winter. All the mountain passes in Afghanistan were blocked with snow. It was frustrating but obvious that January wasn't a smart time to go. Too much risk. So I turned to other things but kept monitoring the situation.

Finally we decided that Lack should go to the Afghan rebels' main staging area in Pakistan—across the border from Afghanistan—get to know people and take a look around. By that time we had some knowledge of who was who and what was what. Everybody we talked to said that there was no getting in. And if by any chance you did get in, you probably would not get out alive. This, to say the least, gave us pause, and all the more reason for Lack to go to Pakistan to check it out.

He went, and soon reported back by telephone and Telex that it was an extremely complex situation, that the rebels were split into a number of different camps and were at one another's throats—loosely, very loosely, united only in their absolute determination to expel the Soviet invaders. They didn't know what they were doing. But he said he was impressed nonetheless. They would never give up. And he added, "You are right about one thing—the Soviets may have bitten off much more than they realize. These Afghans are fanatic in their zeal to do whatever it takes, however long it takes. There are signs of a potentially effective guerrilla army in the making."

As to whether we could get into Afghanistan, Lack said it was odds-against, but he wanted to keep working on it.

Don Hewitt, in the meantime, began saying, "Andy Lack has been over there quite a while. Time and money are wasting. Is this thing going to be or not be?"

Don was hoping it wouldn't be. And in fairness to him, I don't believe that it was only because the fighting was a long way off and, so far, not a story our audience was indicating much interest about. Increasingly, his biggest worry was that the operation looked very dangerous.

Costs and cost control were worries, too—bigger worries in the *60 Minutes* of 1979–80 than they would be later. Through the late 1980s and on into the '90s, *60 Minutes* became such a reliable cash cow that Hewitt and *60 Minutes* pretty much did what they pleased and spent what they pleased. But in the 1979–80 period, costs were monitored closely. The program had a rough budget that included approximately $45,000 per field-produced piece.

An expedition into Afghanistan could not be mounted for anything close to $45,000. It might easily cost twice that or more.

We fairly often were overbudget on pieces, sometimes far over. Nobody raised much if any fuss. There was simply a very loose understanding that if you did an overbudget piece, it would be good if you could bring one in under budget—for example, a big-name interview in New York or Washington. These interviews cost comparatively little and were great to offset a big-ticket piece.

Then Andy Lack telephoned from Peshawar, Pakistan, in late February, 1980. The Soviet invasion was two months old, and there was still virtually no independent reporting coming out of Afghanistan. Lack said, "If we are to do a story, you, Dan, need to come here, and you must come now." He went on to say that he believed it was still odds-against that we could get into Afghanistan and that he couldn't guarantee we would get a story. His point was that it was now or never for trying.

Don Hewitt, with reservations, agreed. Neither he nor I was convinced that those above us at CBS News would agree, so we made a secret plan. We would not tell them I was going. Better, we thought, not to place them in the position of having to approve or disapprove— not before I went, anyway. Few people even in *60 Minutes* knew I was going. Mike Wallace knew. I think Bob Chandler had an inkling, but he was wise enough not to let on.

My wife Jean, my daughter Robin, and my son Danjack had a last family council before I took off. We talked about the danger. Both children had been old enough during my assignments in Vietnam to have clear memories of the fears of their father's reporting from a war zone. But Afghanistan would be different, not least because there would be no U.S. military, no representatives of the U.S. government, not even any other press around to help in case of emergency.

Jean and Robin both said frankly that they had "bad feelings about this one." Danjack said he was worried, but his opinion was, "Since you survived Vietnam, I prefer to believe that you can somehow survive this, too." Jean and Robin wept as I kissed them good-bye.

This may all sound a bit overdramatic now, years later. And perhaps it was. But that's the way it felt. The craft of journalism has its dangers, and flying into hellholes is one of them.

THE flight to the Afghan freedom fighters' base camp in Pakistan was long and lonely—New York to Karachi, then on to Islamabad, and finally, a small plane hop to Peshawar. The minute I stepped off the plane into the dingy grime of Peshawar, I could sense war, desperation, and death. One could feel it, see it, hear it, smell it. It permeated the air and your consciousness.

The Peshawar bazaar was filled with men hawking their wares, often made locally and just as often stolen or traded from afar; men were also trading news and rumor, truth and lies, without any sure way of knowing which was which.

Peshawar was filled with refugees from Afghanistan, mostly living in tents on the sandy plain outside of town. The city was the rear guard for those fighting the Soviets but the front line of the war of information and misinformation. It's the traditional way of fighting in a still ancient world that is part Persian trader and part mountain herdsman, where warriors are both trusting and faithful and at the same time cunning and deceitful. Half of what is said is true, and you'd better believe it. Half is false. Follow the falsehood, and it will be your undoing. The survivors are those who can tell the difference—or if they can't, they can at least be more devious. The twin coins of this realm are treachery and trust. On this dusty plain and in these rugged mountains truth is told with a glimmer of mischief, and lies are told with direct-eyed honesty.

Andy Lack and I immediately began working around the clock. Intrigue and betrayal among the various Afghan resistance forces abounded. The tribal leaders were suspicious of one another and everyone else. We went around and saw the leaders of every major faction—at least seven. This one eyed us and listened as he smoked opium. That one did so with his knife drawn. None gave us much encouragement. We were tired, frustrated, frazzled.

After almost two days and nights it became clear that there were only two groups that might agree to take us inside Afghanistan. We eventually decided on the one we distrusted least. And with that group we pleaded. We begged, just short of groveling. The leader of the faction finally agreed and turned us over to the man who had "volunteered" to try to get us in. His name was Mirwaz. He was twenty years old, a small, wiry man-child with intense dark eyes and broken English. He was a volunteer in the same way U.S. marines volunteer for hard-duty assignments: He was told that he had volunteered.

It was impossible not to like Mirwaz, right from the start. For one thing, he was so energetic and enthusiastic. For another, he never stopped smiling. The more difficult things got—and things were soon to get very difficult indeed—the more he smiled. He was tough, smart—mountain-smart—quick-witted, and a born leader. With God's grace and Mirwaz's leadership we walked into Afghanistan and we walked out.

It began with a fast trip to Peshawar's open-air market. Under Mirwaz's direction we bought secondhand Afghan clothes: loose-fitting, baggy cotton trousers with drawstring waists; long-sleeved pull-over shirts that resembled pajama tops; and the worst-looking hats in all the world. These were wool cap-hats, knit but with a little bit of a brim, the kind Afghans have been wearing at least since the last century. To all of this was added a large combination blanket and wrap. The whole outfit was brownish gray and olive drab in color.

Shoes? Mirwaz said it didn't matter, so long as whatever we chose would be comfortable for us to walk in for long, very long, distances, and provided they weren't new and were dirty. He wore sandals. I had a pair of Clarks Desert boots, fifteen years old, my lucky boots that I had worn all through the Vietnam War. Jean had bought them for me just before I went to Saigon in 1965. Now dirty, beat, and torn, but comfortable, they were my own footwear of choice.

Funny, but the moment I knew I'd be wearing the old Desert boots into Afghanistan, a certain sort of peace and confidence surged. And I knew, just knew, we'd get in and out all right.

Andy decided on a stylish pair of crepe-soled, brown, lace-up brogans. He and Mirwaz scuffed them up and muddied them up appropriately for this trip, and we all had a good laugh.

We worried, though, about the choice made by our interpreter-historian, Eden Naby, who was leaning toward being a member of our CBS team that would be going inside Afghanistan. She chose what looked like a pair of light ballet slippers. Mirwaz smiled, but it was a tight little smile, when she showed them to him. They didn't strike him as built for long hauls. But Eden made an argument about maximum comfort, and he eventually, reluctantly, said okay.

Eden was thirtyish, a short, solid, dark-haired, dark-eyed American of Middle Eastern heritage. We had found her at Harvard in the early stages of our research. She and her husband—who was an older man—were professors at Harvard's School of Near Eastern Studies. Both were experts on Afghan history, culture, and archaeology. She was fluent in Farsi and Pushto, the languages of the region. They had agreed to accompany us to Peshawar to help with translations and setting up the trip, and to tutor us in local history and culture, but they originally made it clear that neither wanted to risk going to the war.

As the time for going in drew near, however, two things became clear. One, Eden was increasingly tempted by the prospect of adventure and of being able to learn firsthand what was going on in the area of her most intense academic interest. And two, we desperately needed her translating skills.

She and her husband debated and argued. In the end, Eden waveringly decided to go with us. Her husband declined to go because of his age and fragile health. I breathed a silent prayer of thanks.

So going in, we would be six: Andy Lack, producer; cameraman Mike Edwards and soundman Peter O'Connor, both out of *60 Minutes'* London office; myself as correspondent; Eden Naby as translator and general resource; Mirwaz as our faithful (we hoped) Afghan guide.

We had another camera crew with us in Peshawar. We could use them as decoys who would keep themselves obvious around the local hotels and draw potential competitors and any other nosy folk, such as intelligence operatives, away from our tracks. But their main role was to be a kind of communications and logistics base camp for us. And if we were not back in Peshawar in twelve days, they were to check as best they could on our safety. They were not to tell even CBS in New York anything, if they could keep from it, for twelve days. Our plan was to steal away after bedtime on a moonless Tuesday night.

On that evening we made a point of being seen in the hotel restaurant for dinner. Later, in our quarters upstairs, we toasted the mission with shots of Wild Turkey from my flask. And then we left the hotel singly, using three separate exits, and rendezvoused with Mirwaz at a prearranged spot.

By the last hour before dawn, we had made it to the Pakistan border with the territories—Pakistani protectorates that are buffers between Pakistan and Afghanistan. Each territory has a regional headman in charge.

To cross a territory, travelers—especially foreigners—are supposed to have permission from the area headman. That permission depends mostly on whether you pass muster from at least one and usually several of his village "precinct captains." This, we were told, could take hours, or it could take days or even weeks. And then again, it might never happen.

Once we had crossed into one of the territories, we halted. Mirwaz herded us into a large mud-and-straw hut. We were to eat and sleep while Mirwaz checked to see if we were being followed, and tried to contact the local authority to win permission for us to proceed.

The food did not look appetizing, to put it mildly. The camera crew and I ate a little from the inside of bread rolls. (Rather's Rules for Survival in strange, distant places—taken from the tutoring of old CBS News correspondents—are: Don't drink the water, don't eat the meat, and don't even look at the women. Eat the bread, but never the outside of it. Many different hands often touch the bread. Eating the crust can cause you more trouble than you can possibly imagine. Trust me. I learned this the hard way.)

Then we slept—some of us, a little—all in one room, with the resident family and their animals. As we were to do throughout the trip, we took turns on watch in one-hour shifts.

Several hours after dawn Mirwaz returned. There were no signs we had been followed; the straightest, shortest route ahead into Afghanistan was reportedly clear; and we had an appointment with the local main man.

On the way to see him, trouble developed. Some of the locals suspected we might be Russians. They stopped us, crowded us, pushed and shoved us. Knives and guns were brandished—theirs, not ours. Mirwaz was the only one among us who had a gun. He and our passports and something about buying a round of tea finally eased the situation, and we moved on. We looked at one another. Nobody had said this was going to be easy.

When we got to the man in charge of this particular zone, there was more trouble. He was watching a cricket match on Pakistani television and refused to meet with us until it was over. I had been stationed in London years before, and I knew cricket.

"This could take days," I told Andy. We all groaned. A fine rain began to fall, what the English call mizzle. We stood outside in the mizzle for more than an hour, hearing the cricket match from inside.

When the match finally ended, we were allowed inside. The local authority was a small, thin man dressed in a dark suit, white shirt, and a tie. Turned out he was British educated, and trained as a British-style bureaucrat—officious and efficient. He made reasonably quick work of giving us notes, complete with an official stamp, that were supposed to give us safe passage to his boss, the territorial chief, at his headquarters miles ahead.

The papers worked. By late afternoon we were in front of the territorial chief. A tall, portly man dressed in local garb, including colorful headgear, he received us warmly and immediately. Speaking through an interpreter, he wanted to know all about us, and he studied each of us with eyes that had the intensity of an owl's.

After the niceties, he spoke directly and to the point. The rough translation was, "You lie, you die." And with that, he proceeded to interrogate us for an hour.

Near the end, he took me alone into another room and, in effect, made me swear on my mother's grave that we were who we said we were and wanted to do what we said: specifically, report accurately and fairly back to the American people the reality of the war. Then he gave his approval and, with a smile and a wave, sent us on our way.

We walked a long way that late afternoon, into the twilight and on into the night. We walked along sorry roads clogged with refugees. The tide of humanity was staggering, and it was against this tide that we walked. Women, children, the elderly, and the crippled. The cries of the children seemed never to stop.

We would try to sleep a couple of hours, on the ground, on the roadside, then walk on.

Later we left the roads and started up into the mountains, and headed into a pass. The refugee lines thinned out. The mountains loomed, dark and foreboding. Soon we were alone, walking with the silence and discipline our guide commanded.

Night turned to day, then to night again, and on we walked. We rested ten minutes out of every hour, and every six hours we stopped and slept for four—minus the one hour each of us stood watch.

Eventually we passed through the territories. I asked Mirwaz if we were now inside Afghanistan, and he nodded yes. No customhouse, no signs, no one announced it. Some jet fighter-bombers flew low overhead, followed by helicopters. We took cover and froze until the choppers passed. The aircraft were from Jalalabad, Afghanistan's fifth-largest city and a Soviet stronghold fifty miles from the border. We reached the mountains that surround Jalalabad, and a place just three miles from where the Afghan resistance forces had been launching attacks on the Soviets. There we hooked up with a small guerrilla band, fourteen men led by a white-bearded man named Yassini.

Yassini was of medium height, with bulging forearms and calf muscles. His physique was that of a halfback. His age was mid- to late forties. He lived on the run, moving from mountain hideouts through tiny villages of straw-and-mud huts to the opium fields that often provided cover from the Soviet aircraft that patrolled continually.

Yassini had what combat correspondents the world over call strong command presence. Frankly, I was relieved. This man was no amateur. He knew what he was doing, and he had tight control over his unit. What he did not have was very much in the way of weapons or ammunition. And he had no communications equipment, no medical supplies. The word ragtag came to mind. But then I thought of Vietnam. Hearts and minds and feet can be the most important weapons, as can the advantage of fighting on home ground.

We filled our canteens from a spring and dropped in our water-purification tablets as the guerrilla band watched in amusement. Soon we were on the move again, now part of a larger group.

Yassini made us walk spread out, with one man far out front, scanning constantly for mines and for signs of possible ambush. Another man stayed far to the rear, scanning constantly backward.

In this fashion Yassini marched us first to a small fort on the outskirts of Jalalabad that he had recaptured from the Soviet-led Afghan army. The regime installed by Moscow in the capital, Kabul, was less than three months into trying to hold and mold a central army of Afghans to fight alongside the Soviet army that had invaded and was trying to occupy the country.

The Soviets were failing—badly. The world at large, including the Carter and, later, Reagan administrations, didn't know this yet. And wouldn't for a long while. The key errors in both administrations were to overestimate the Soviets and underestimate the Afghan resistance.

The Afghan resistance had retaken the fort using classic guerrilla strategy: When the enemy is strong, retreat; when the enemy gets strung out, harass; and when the enemy is weak, attack.

Afghan rebels had abandoned the fort when Soviet-led, air-supported armor and infantry had attacked it. As defections from so-called Afghan loyal army regulars thinned out the fort's defenses, guerrillas began hit-and-run night raids. Yassini told us he and his men had carried out eleven such raids over a one-month period. Then resistance forces overran the garrison early one morning. They said they killed thirty-five and wounded several dozen others, while suffering one dead and one wounded themselves.

Local villagers confirmed this and other things the resistance fighters had said. The Soviets were using not only napalm but gas.

We pressed hard on this latter claim. During our time in Afghanistan we heard many other reports of gas being used on combatants and civilians, including women and children. When we got back to the States and reported this, our stories were greeted with skepticism. There was even outright ridicule. It was only years later that it became evident that the Soviets had used a variety of gases in Afghanistan.

But at the time we were filming around the garrison, gas was not our major worry. Mines were. A child stepped on a buried mine while we were still in the village; he was blown to smithereens. The short, quick explosion in the distance and the news that followed were sobering to us in the extreme.

When darkness came, again we walked on, well into the night. When we finally bedded down on the dirt floor of the main mud hut of a compound belonging to a huge extended family, there was trouble.

The trouble was women. And our historian-translator, Eden Naby. She had been sleeping in the same crowded huts and bombed-out covered places where we did. When we had slept in the open air, she had slept close by, right in the same area. The reasons—obvious, I think—were her safety and ours.

But Afghanistan was oblivious to the modern women's movement. This was a male-dominated Muslim society, and for one thing, women were considered to be chattel. Thus a Western woman had two marks against her: She was both an infidel and chattel.

Eden Naby was not afraid. But we were afraid for her. And, truth to tell, we were even more afraid for ourselves. In case of attack, in the confusion and chaos of sudden flight for our lives, especially in the dark, our chances for survival would plummet without Eden Naby's language skills and her immense knowledge of the place.

There had been rumbles and mumbles before, but a combination of Eden Naby's tact, diplomacy, and knowledge, plus the intercessions of Mirwaz and the formidable Yassini, had put down previous grous-

Afghanistan: Rather meets with Afghan resistance leader Yassini and his band of battle-hardened guerrillas.

ing and potential trouble over the "American woman with the men." Not this time.

In this place, as in so many others in this devoutly Islamic rural world, the women had separate quarters. In this world not only do women remain covered, from head to toe, but even then they are seldom, if ever, seen by anyone, *any*one, other than their husbands and very close family. And no one, *no* one, save husbands and children, is supposed to see them even slightly uncovered.

The women in the compound numbered about twenty (there were many girls, too). They were uncomfortable about our being among them at all. But they had been ordered to accept that these were highly unusual times. So they accepted our presence.

But when it came to Eden Naby's sleeping in the same room with the men, including their men, they revolted. Noway, nohow, was the American woman going to sleep anywhere but in the women's quarters. Period. We were mighty nervous about parting company with Eden Naby, but she insisted we go along with it.

This was the deal: She would sleep with the women. But we would rig between the men's quarters and the women's a makeshift "telephone" system—a collection of tin cans hanging closely together at each end of a rope. Quick jerks on the rope, either end, would set off a clanging noise. This would bring help running from the other end.

After a fitful period of what passed for sleep, we awakened just at daybreak to the unmistakable smell of fresh bread. A woman was baking bread in a low earthen oven outdoors. She was covered completely, even wearing a kind of cloth mask. She was taking the wonderful-smelling bread out with a long wooden spatula.

I saw Andy Lock peeking outside through a crack in the hut's door. "I'm going to ask her for some of that bread," he said, and started to move out the door. I sprang and tackled him.

"Good God, Andy, if you even look at that woman, much less go near her, we will all be buzzard bait," I managed to whisper. He knew instantly that I was right.

We were all tired, edgy, hungry, and constantly trying to suppress the psychological background drone of fear. Andy and I untangled ourselves and got up, careful to keep our backs to the woman baking outside.

Afghan men, who had been tending their animals, came back and brought us some bread. We ate it—from the *inside*—eagerly.

There had been no cause to use our makeshift alarm that night. But we were full of questions for Eden Naby about her time in the women's quarters. She declined to reveal much, except that one of the younger women had some interesting tattoos.

I had mentioned to Yassini that the Russians seemed to have an extraordinary number of aircraft. His answer translated roughly as, "You don't know the half of it."

His plan for this day was that we would find out firsthand. We moved to a tiny village within sight of the end of some runways at Jalalabad's airport. It took my breath away when I realized how close to the Soviets we had gotten.

But we were to get closer still. Following the lead of Yassini and four of his best men, we quietly dropped down into some four-foot-high grass and began crawling toward the nearest runway. Mike Edwards had a hard time crawling with his camera strapped to his chest. Amazingly, we crawled to within about three hundred yards of the runway. It was loaded with helicopters, fighter-bombers, and larger planes. They were parked practically on top of one another. We were awed, and so scared that we were almost literally afraid to breathe.

There were no guards in sight, no airport-security observation posts, and no Soviet perimeter defenses around this end of the runway—none that we could see, anyway.

In whispers we tried to decide whether to risk filming anything. As you would expect of a great TV news photographer, Mike refused to leave before at least trying to get a picture. It was decided that he and Yassini would inch even farther forward, partly to get a better shot, partly to separate them from the group in case they drew fire. They moved up. Mike carefully raised his camera into position to shoot. The rest of us held our breaths. Some couldn't bear to watch, looked at the ground instead.

Nothing untoward happened. Mike slipped the camera down, and we slipped away on our bellies through the grass.

Besides silent prayers of thanks for deliverance, I was thinking anew, The Soviets and their cause are in deeper trouble here than even they may know. Here we had just been within a few hundred yards of the runways at what couldn't have been less than their second most important air base for the war. No patrols, or none that were evident. No perimeter defense or warning systems. What in the hell could they be thinking?

By late afternoon we reached another "safe camp"—as in safe house, but without the house. It was a tiny staging area, base camp for guerrilla hit-and-run operations. Yassini said we would rest a bit and then he would show us something "very interesting." We had already seen enough interesting sights for one day, in my opinion, but he insisted. Afterward, he promised with a twinkle in his eye, we would have "a full, good hot meal."

This promise brightened everyone. We had eaten little since we came into the country—nearly all of it on the run, none of it hot, nearly all of it bad. "A full, good hot meal"? Lead on!

We began a long, slow climb up the mountainside. Part of the lower slope of the mountain was a combination of gravel and hard, crusty soil. Rough going, hard walking.

Suddenly there was the unmistakable whomp-whomp of helicopter blades. Far off, but they struck terror in all of our crew. Not in our escorts. They calmly but instantly froze. So did we. We were in the open, wide open. There was no cover. The choppers came closer.

No way they don't see us, I thought to myself. Closer and closer they came. Then they were directly above us. Decisive moment. Nobody looked up. Nobody moved.

The sound of the blades and motors crescendoed. Then the sound seemed to be moving away. But wait—they were circling. A big, wide circle. We froze hard as stone again. Again they passed.

Did they see us? We couldn't be sure. The Afghans decided to abort our trek up the mountainside. Instead, we turned back and, following a different route, returned to the safe camp just past sunset.

"Sleep now," we were told. "When you wake up, we will have a good meal." Big smile. We dropped our gear, collapsed, and slept like children. I had the watch for the last hour of the three-hour sleep time. Events of the day—what a day!—were playing like reels of videotape in my head. Over and over. All I could think about was how lucky we were to have survived. And I thought of Jean, Robin, and Danjack, and the green, green grass of home.

Soon all of our crew were awake, and we were walked to a small cave about a half mile away. A piece of tarp was stretched tightly over the entrance. Inside, by very low candlelight, food had been spread. Two or three dozen Afghans sat around the food in a circle three-deep. Places had been saved for us front and center, first row. There was rice and bread and two covered dishes. Andy Lack was salivating audibly and looking poised to pounce. I'd long ago dubbed him Champagne Andy, for he loved the good life, especially good food and drink. Then they took the tops off the covered dishes. What was revealed smelled suspicious, a kind of greenish brown gravy-looking mess. There *was* meat barely visible in it. It was not recognizable as anything we had seen anywhere before.

Andy gulped and began moving, easing his way back from the front row. "What do you suppose it is?" he whispered.

"Dunno," came the reply.

Some small animal; maybe a rabbit or a squirrel—maybe. We were served the mystery meat. Whatever it was, it did not smell tasty.

The word rat was never spoken, but it was surely thought. By this time Andy was way back in the third row, gulping repeatedly and turning olive green as he inched toward the entrance to the cave.

Those of us who had been served looked at one another, smiled at our hosts, who by now were watching intently, and finally proceeded to eat. But not before I pulled from my pocket a small bottle of

Louisiana Tabasco sauce that I always carry. I applied it liberally and passed it to my colleagues. They eagerly accepted. By then Andy was already out of there. We later brought him some bread. To this day I know not what it was we ate.

AROUND midnight we were on the move again. We walked awhile, slept awhile, then walked again. Eden Naby's shoes had begun to come apart. We bound them up with twine and gaffer's tape, and she walked on. All of us had trouble keeping up with the long-striding, seemingly indefatigable Afghans. How she managed to keep up, with her short legs, was mystifying. The lady had guts.

With ears cocked and eyes alternating between sky and ground, we walked to a partially concealed, dilapidated lean-to near a small abandoned house. This was on somewhat elevated ground, giving us a good view of the flatland from which we had come.

Seemingly out of nowhere a dozen new Afghans materialized, each well equipped with small arms. There was a council, a group meeting in which it was explained to us through translation that the Afghans had decided to go on a dangerous reconnaissance patrol. Fourteen Afghans, including one with a backpack rocket-launcher rig, would be going. Yassini would lead, and a stocky younger man with the new additions would be second-in-command. The plan was what amounted to a forced march into the nearby mountains. The goal was a ridge that looked down on a Soviet emplacement.

We were told straight out that it would be a difficult march, partly because they wanted to arrive at a precise time. And we were told that it would be extremely dangerous. Some might make it back or none might. "What about *all* making it back?" the leaders were asked. A shrug of the shoulders, followed by the answer, "Could happen."

They wanted to leave immediately. They left us to decide whether we would join them. The second-in-command said quietly, in what he intended to be an aside, that they would prefer the woman not go. Then Eden Naby spoke up. She did not have a good feeling about this operation and would not recommend anybody's going. She believed our chances of coming back alive would be less than fifty-fifty.

Andy and I took her warning seriously. She knew the area stone-cold. But if it made sense for any of us to go—and I wasn't certain that it did—then what made the most sense was for cameraman Mike

Edwards and me to do it. This meant risking the fewest people for the maximum potential gain.

Although I hadn't yet said anything, Mirwaz had already gone over among the other Afghans to ready himself for the march. I went over and offered him a chance to stay behind. He smiled his wide smile and said what amounted to, "Forget it. You go, I go."

So we went: Mike, myself, Mirwaz, and fourteen other Afghans.

The march was as advertised. Steady, fast-paced. At first through rice paddies and opium-poppy fields, then through trees and over rocks, but most of it was a climb nearly straight up. The ridge we wanted was at ten thousand feet. We stopped seldom, rested little. The Afghans expected us to keep up. It was keep up or be left behind. Somehow we managed.

Our unit arrived at the top just as the sun set behind the far mountain. The objective was to scout a possible location of tanks on the perimeter of Jalalabad. We crawled on our stomachs the final few yards to the edge of the ridge. There was the sound of helicopters in the medium distance. Below, on both sides of a small bridge, we could clearly see two tanks, some tents, and big guns.

As Mike and I took in the scene with awe, we were startled by a sudden flare. First one, then another. The Afghans with us opened up with automatic weapons from the top of the ridge toward the encampment below. Another flare, then another. The whole area—the ridge where we were and the tanks with their support below—was bathed in an eerie light. The Afghans fired off one of their antitank rockets. Then another. Silence. Followed by a tremendous explosion near us. Artillery shell. Then another blast near us. Mortar. Dirt flew over and onto us. The Afghans shot another antitank round. There was another earsplitting sound almost on top of us. Another artillery round had struck very close. They were beginning to get our range.

The Afghans began scurrying slightly down and off to the side of the mountain. They didn't want to go down the same way we had come up, partly because of their concern that a Soviet blocking force might be coming around back from down below. As they retreated to the side, the Afghans took turns raking the forward base of the ridge. This was to discourage the enemy from trying to scale it from the front.

After scrambling mostly sideways for a bit, we began heading straight down the mountain. An explosion rang below us and off to the side, in the direction from which we had come. If we had scurried straight down from our original position, that latest shot might have hit us. The Soviets were trying to walk arcing mortar fire down what they figured might be our escape path. Once again the Afghan resistance fighters had demonstrated their guerrilla combat savvy, correctly predicting the Soviets' thinking.

The Afghans were moving surefootedly and swiftly down the mountainside. Mike and I were half stumbling, half tumbling. We were having a hell of a time keeping up. Mirwaz breathlessly explained that we were now in a desperate race against time and a probable Soviet reaction force hoping to catch us coming off the mountain.

Mike and I stumbled and tumbled more quickly. We resembled human pinballs, bouncing off first one big rock and then another, headed down. At the base of the mountain we could hear the roar and rumble of vehicles coming fast along the dirt road we were crossing. We sped across, then sprinted into the darkness beyond and wound up diving into a deep ditch at the edge of a rice paddy.

The lead vehicles of the reaction force came racing along the road, spraying the base of the mountain with heavy machine-gun fire.

The Soviets and their Afghan allies, we learned, were reluctant to leave their ground encampments. When they did, they generally refused to get out of their tanks, personnel carriers, and jeeps. The Soviet troops from purely airborne divisions were said to be an exception, and Afghan rebels were most wary of them.

As soon as the lead vehicles passed, we were out of the ditch and fleeing farther into the darkness. We waded a short ways through rice-paddy muck. Then we were up on the slick, narrow dikes that crisscross such paddies. The Afghans, who had climbed up and down the mountain like goats, were now speeding along these thin, slippery, rounded surfaces like cats. Mike and I couldn't. We were slipping and sliding, falling and crawling between dashes. We finally began to get the hang of it and were beginning to catch up a little when, wham, I slipped at top speed and hit my groin hard against the dike. I doubled over in pain and thought I might faint. Mirwaz half picked me up, half made me get up. "Must keep running," he said with heavy breath. "Must keep running."

I forced myself to block out the pain and kept silently repeating to myself, Get up, don't quit, keep running, don't give up.

Fear motivates as few other things can. This lesson I had learned other times, other places along life's way. This scary night, and especially the run through the rice paddy, was a potent refresher course.

Run until you drop—then walk. That was the Afghans' way. We finally got to a fairly good dirt road, and soon came upon a house. There was an old school bus in the side yard. Yassini and two of his men bounded up to the front door of the house, pounded on it a couple of times, then kicked it in. Some hollering followed. Our second-in-command came out of the door holding the man of the house by the nape of the neck and the seat of the pants, pushing him ahead. With Yassini right behind, they went to the school bus. The man tried to resist, but they popped him a couple of punches to the head, and he got in. They were in no mood to argue or to tarry. This was not a pretty picture, this little reminder that war is not fair. The weakest—those least able to defend themselves—usually suffer most. And so it was here.

We were all motioned aboard the bus as the terrified driver's women, children, and what appeared to be grandparents looked on in even more terror from the porch. The driver was told to move the bus rapidly but not pell-mell out of the yard and down the road and to keep his lights off. After those commands there was silence. Except for the low clanking and grinding sounds of the worn-out bus and the sound of a small caged bird. Little birds in little cages are a favorite of Afghans. I was told later they are especially popular with bus and truck drivers. This one was to the side of the steering wheel. He chirped and sang as if to say, "What's happening?"

Our sentiments exactly. Neither Mike nor I had any idea what was going on or where we were going. We felt awful about what had just happened, but I can't lie and say we were anything but happy to be off our feet and riding.

Yassini obviously wanted to put as much distance as possible, as quickly as possible, between us and the Soviets. He wanted the bus to go fast, but not too fast—no telltale clouds of dust.

The bus driver was told to stop just short of the T-junction where the small dirt road joined a larger one. We were told to get off quickly and take cover in a ditch. As we were disembarking, our second-in-command put the cold steel of the muzzle of his AK-47 flush against the bus driver's chin. The driver was told that if he or any member of his family ever said a word about what they had seen and heard, they would all die. The driver gulped and said the equivalent of, "Yes, sir." There was a long silence. Then there was the sound of the gun being uncocked. And we heard the caged bird sing.

There was a large culvert under the main road. We squirmed through it to the other side and began sloshing across the rice field beyond.

Our destination turned out to be a small, ancient mosque at the farthest corner of the paddy. We crouched just across from it while Yassini whistled some signals. There were signal whistles back. We stood up and went to an animal shed at the rear of the mosque. A man came out of the shadows and took us through a door into a fair-sized room. In the dark he and our leaders had a whispered conference.

Mike and I were near collapse from a combination of exhaustion, tension, and fear—a kind of combined delayed reaction to events of the past couple of days and especially this night. Even the Afghans were showing signs of being tired. They began bedding down on the straw-covered dirt floor. So did we. The straw was old, damp, and musty with the odor of animals. But we wouldn't have any trouble sleeping. Or so we thought. No sooner had we settled into fetal positions and dozed off than there were commotions and harsh words among the Afghans. You didn't have to know the language to know they were cursing. Mike clicked on his tiny camera flashlight. The Afghans were all standing, dusting themselves off vigorously. And then we felt them, Mike and I: creepy-crawly things on our clothing. As we beat them off and away, Mirwaz tried to tell us what they were. But he couldn't find the English word. Suddenly Mike exclaimed, "Scorpions! Gawddam scorpions!" We nearly trampled two Afghans getting out the door.

The group reassembled out under the shed. Yassini and his second shushed everybody as we all continued running our hands over ourselves to make sure all scorpions were off, and stomping on the few that had been carried out with us.

Finally everybody just began smiling and chuckling, Afghans and Westerners alike. We all began to lie down again in the dark, this time outside under the shed. Apparently the scorpions slept only indoors in the straw. I dropped into a deep and dreamless sleep.

The sleep was short. Just past sunup we were urged to prepare to move out. Mirwaz explained that we were headed for yet another group of distant mountains. Our unit would be splitting into three, each headed in a different direction, to make it more difficult to trail us. Mirwaz, Yassini, two other Afghans, Mike, and I were grouped together.

The trek took a day. The last of it was a steep climb through a narrow pass, with armed Afghan lookouts posted on the heights. We arrived at what turned out to be a major command post—the main camp of a large, spread-out guerrilla force of which Yassini was a part.

The heart of the command post was a large cave that ran deep into the side of the mountain. We were given some tea, bread, and rice, and warm water in which to soak our feet. The post commander then produced a pipe, an elaborate hookah. He looked at me, smiled, and offered a friendly puff on his opium water pipe.

I quickly stammered something like, "Thank you profusely, kind sir, but I only smoke cigars these days, and then only occasionally."

The pipe disappeared, and we began looking over the Afghans' store of weapons. The collection was pitiful. They had a few true relics, candidates for museums: a Gatling gun, some old Enfield rifles, and one Chinese mortar. For this, there was no ammunition. (Which explained why they hadn't mortared the Jalalabad airfield, which we had crawled so close to.)

Mostly what they had were Kalashnikovs, Russian-made rapid-fire hand weapons that are the small gun of choice for guerrilla armies the world over because of their dependability and simplicity. Kalashnikov ammunition tends to be widely available in the Third World, and in Afghanistan, Kalashnikovs themselves were in great supply, since they were the Soviet army's standard issue.

But to the Afghans the best weapon was a belief in a cause. The resistance fighters were consumed with expelling the Soviets. For them this was both a deeply patriotic fight to the death for home and hearth—and a holy war, a jihad. Their faith in Islam was complete, and so was their confidence in themselves and the rightness of their struggle.

They were pleading for American weapons. At this time, in 1980, they were getting none. And it would be a long time before they got any to speak of. This was because first President Carter, then President Reagan were convinced by the CIA, plus the State and Defense departments, that the Afghans were destined to lose and that relations with the Soviet Union were of prime consideration and must not be risked by our getting involved in their war. This view—that our diplomatic business with Moscow was paramount and that nothing else much mattered—was what some called the geopolitical context.

Yassini, that wily mountain cat of a combat leader, had a wholly different idea of geopolitical context. He hadn't been to Duke or Harvard, but he knew his history and thought a lot about strategy.

Outside that big cave, in the late winter and early spring of 1980, he told me that if America helped defeat the Soviets and communism on the battlefields of Afghanistan, then America would win the cold war. If the United States did not aid the Afghans, he theorized, then the cold war would continue and the Soviets might eventually win it. "There is no one in the world who can really fight and resist as ferociously and well as we Afghans," he said.

I told him that even if that was true, no American mother wanted to send her son or daughter to Afghanistan. Yassini shot back, "We don't need anybody's soldiers here to help us. What we need, all we need, are American weapons. We can do all the fighting ourselves." His eyes fairly burned with passion now.

"If we don't win, if you allow the Russians to hammer us down, then there is no place in the world that the Russians will not have the courage to go," Yassini said. He believed a Soviet victory in Afghanistan would mean a second wind for the Soviet Union and communism. They would take control of vast new territories and new resources, and they would take on new confidence.

"Look at the map," Yassini urged. "See how Afghanistan opens possibilities for warm-water ports. See how part of eastern Afghanistan juts into western China, and know that the Russians want to put big, new military bases in there. And see how Afghanistan would help the Russians develop a pincer, a half circle around China."

Another Afghan chimed in along these lines: "America after Vietnam and after the Iranian hostage debacle is seen by much of the world now, and perhaps even sees itself, as having gone soft and being in retreat. And throughout Islam, because of the Iranian hostage trouble, America-haters are exploiting all kinds of doubts, including the most infectious propaganda that says America hates Islam and

Islamic people. You help us win, you become allies with us here in our triumph—and we will triumph—then you can go a long way toward reversing the Vietnam syndrome and the worst vestiges of the hostage experience."

Sure, some of this at least was Afghans spinning their own propaganda for their own purposes. And yes, hindsight shows them to have been more right than wrong in what they thought. At the time, however, without the benefit of hindsight, I wasn't totally convinced.

But I *was* convinced that I didn't want to spend any more time around the big cave. It and the compound outside it, where most of the Afghan weapons were kept, were too inviting a bombing target. Also, before we had gone to the mountain firefight, Yassini and company had worked out some prearranged rendezvous times and places with the Afghans who had set out as escorts for Eden Naby and Andy Lack. We needed to move and hook up again with them.

Before leaving, we went to a high vantage point from which we could see the confluence of the Kabul and Kunar rivers, and the Kunar valley beyond. While we stood there, a squadron of Russian bombers pounded a village in the far distance. We caught glimpses of the bombers and heard the low rumble of the bombs.

As we walked back to the big cave and prepared to leave, our Afghan hosts were asked about a leader we had heard might be the most effective, most ferocious of all the current Afghan large-command leaders. We'd heard his name in Peshawar, around camp-fires and back in the ranks. The name was Younas Khalis.

Khalis was becoming a legend among the Afghans. And when we had researched our trip, some defense experts mentioned him as an Afghan leader they had heard was actually fighting Russians inside his country rather than just talking and bickering outside it. I was, of course, intrigued. So I gambled and brought it up.

Our hosts confirmed that Khalis was fighting to the north of where we were and that he was having many victories. Our hosts agreed to send a runner to contact Khalis' outfit while we rejoined the rest of our reporting team.

Yassini stayed at the big cave. One of his lieutenants, a couple of gunmen, and Mirwaz took us on a journey down to the river's edge near where the Kabul and the Kunar met, and we rendezvoused with Eden Naby and Andy Lack. Our spot was back in the trees, and the sound of water rushing reminded me of a spot in Texas close to where Jeannie was born—a place where I taught Danjack to cast live bait for catfish, where Robin and I sometimes walked and talked.

I admit I was a little homesick. We were eight days into Afghanistan by now; the days and nights were dragging. I gave myself a pep talk: "You're doing what you came to do—and this *is* one helluva story."

That night a runner returned from Younas Khalis. (The runners went in relays, carrying messages as the pony express had carried mail.) Khalis would see us.

We made our plans: We were to cross the Kabul River this night at the roughest, least-suspect, and least-watched place. We and our equipment would be ferried across with flotation aids—very unusual flotation aids. We would cling to the inflated bellies of dead cows and water buffalo. These would not only help to get us and our equipment across, they would hide us. The Afghan gunners would go first; they would scout the far bank and establish a kind of beachhead.

At the first mention of the flotation aids Andy Lack looked at me as if to say, "Oh, great, I don't believe what I'm hearing." Eden Naby immediately frowned. I wasn't exactly breaking out in smiles myself.

"If, *if* we make it to the other side," I asked, "realistically, how long in and how long out?"

"Another week or ten days, minimum," came the answer.

"Danger factor?"

"More dangerous than anything you have done so far."

We were near Jalalabad, which now had one of the country's largest concentrations of Soviet troops. That was what lay between us and Younas Khalis.

We didn't want to make a snap judgment.

Too dangerous, Eden Naby opined, way too dangerous. She did not take this assignment to get killed. She had told her husband she would be back in Peshawar within thirteen days. It was now our ninth day. She was going back.

Everything in me said to keep going. Hell, we were on a roll. We were hot. We were out front, exclusive on what might be one of the best stories of our time. This is what a reporter dreams of, works for. This is why you paid the price all those years, standing in the rain, microphone in hand, covering city hall hearings. This is why you left a young wife home with your babies when you knew what a wrench it was. It was all to get to a place such as this, at a moment such as this. Frontline, cutting edge, on a world-class story.

But there were other people involved. I did not want it on my conscience that I had gotten anyone else killed. Andy and Mike and Peter had been brave and wonderful. I had a responsibility to them, and to those who loved them, waiting back home. I myself had no desire to die on Afghanistan's plains. Yet if we went on, things could get dicier. And the chances of our coming back chancier.

And we were out of food and low on water-purification tablets. We also had only a limited amount of film and audiotape left. Two of us had dysentery.

Experience had taught that most times when journalists were killed or maimed, it was by pushing just a tad too far. It's the journalistic version of the old cardplayer's adage "You got to know when to hold 'em, know when to fold 'em, know when to run 'em, and when to walk away."

This was a tough call for our CBS team. And so we put it to a vote. The vote was 4 to 1 against going to Younas Khalis.

After the decision we began moving about, but we did so in silence. For a long time second thoughts about whether we were doing the right thing were at the front of all of our minds.

Mirwaz finally broke the silence. He had no doubt that we had made the right decision, he said, and the other Afghans thought so, too. He would have gone, but he wouldn't have been happy about it.

Whether or not he was saying what he really thought, he made me feel better. We wrote and shot the last of our "in-Afghanistan" stand-ups, a variety of on-camera opens, closes, and bridges to provide for any need we might have when we got back and were piecing together our stories in the edit room.

As we began the crossing out of Afghanistan, back into the territories, we again found ourselves caught up in the great unending tide of refugees. Only, this time we were going with the flow rather than against it.

Ten thousand refugees a day were streaming out of Afghanistan now, in March of 1980, just three months after the Soviets had invaded. There would be a million before that summer was over. Before the war ended, possibly as many as ten million. It was part of the Soviets' strategy to create as large a refugee population as possible, as quickly as possible, as a way of winning the war. Displaced persons, split families—and all of the other havoc, chaos, and misery—sap morale and effectiveness from an enemy's fighting forces and create pressures for surrender. Many years later Serbs, trained by and allied with the Russians, would use the same strategy in their war of aggression in Bosnia.

Six miles inside the territories, we came upon two refugee camps adjacent to one another. The first was filled with widows and orphans whose husbands and fathers had been massacred in the Afghan village of Kerala. Although proof is not absolute, there is evidence that what happened in Kerala happened a number of times over the length of this still underreported war.

Eleven hundred Afghan men reportedly were slaughtered in Kerala just before the Soviets' full, official military invasion. We were told they were massacred for not complying with Russian "reforms." The story was repeated to us over and over.

We moved on to the neighboring camp, where three thousand new refugees had just been settled. They, too, filled our ears with stories of atrocities: villages put to the torch; the men rounded up and shot, often before the eyes of their women and children. "Bombs on our villages, tanks and mines on the land" was how more than one put it.

What we had seen while we were inside Afghanistan were small snatches of a new Russian offensive in the Kunar valley. The refugee and other interviews now were giving us a more complete picture, helping us to piece together the facts of the offensive.

We moved out and began traveling south again—walking in the territories—with images of the Kerala massacre dancing nightmarishly through our heads.

WHEN we got to a trading village at a crossroads, Mirwaz did some business with one of the locals and we were soon ushered through a beaded curtain into an indoor oasis. In there, sitting cross-legged on cushions, we were served tea and biscuits by barefoot women with smiles behind their half-veiled faces, thin bracelets on their ankles, and tiny rings on their toes. The bracelets and rings had little bells. The bells made soft sounds as the women went to and fro.

Mirwaz disappeared; then he returned to tell us that there was a bus that ran to the Pakistan border, and it would be running today.

It was a sight—a 1950s-era converted school or tourist bus. Bald tires, no hood, slightly steaming radiator. The inside was already jammed past capacity with women, children, old people, and a couple of goats. We climbed the back ladder and muscled our way onto the makeshift upper deck.

Still more people got aboard the bus. The driver refused to leave until the goats were put on the upper deck with us. Just what we needed.

Eventually the bus lumbered on its way. The afternoon was clear and hot. The bus stank like a septic tank, and was enveloping us in gasoline and oil fumes while still belching steam from the faulty radiator. The women chattered, the babies squalled, the goats bleated. We were headed for the finish line: the border. But we weren't there yet. Mentally, we were rapidly reaching the last straw.

The bus chugged up an ever narrowing, winding mountain road. It was like being on some old, rickety amusement-park ride. We could not help but gasp when the top of the bus seemed literally to hang over the high mountain ledges. All we could see was blue sky above and rocks thousands of feet below, with an occasional glimpse of the inches between the bus tires and the edge. This was a thrill a minute and as terrifying as anything we had been through.

As we began the downhill part of the ride, it got worse. Worse because the bus picked up speed, careening even more as the driver negotiated the twists and turns. It was better not to think about the brakes.

The bus made it down to a place near Darra, inside Pakistan. It was a town of perhaps two or three thousand, a town as old and as famous in this part of Pakistan as Dodge City was in the American West. There was no law in Darra. The gun and the fastest draw ruled. Guns were bought, sold, traded, and fired around the clock. Imported guns and guns manufactured right there. Afghans had turned Darra into a boomtown, selling their homegrown opium for the best available weapons, then going back into Afghanistan to fight.

We hired a car and driver in Darra, plus a marksman to ride shotgun, and we headed for Peshawar. I told the driver we would double the price for him and the gunman if we got to Peshawar safely in half the usual time. We did.

As we burst back into our hotel, we were stared at by the Western journalists and their camp followers who were gathered around the bar. When we got to our rooms upstairs, we were greeted with hoots and hugs by the CBS News crew who had stayed behind.

"Man, are we glad to see *you!*" they exclaimed. "We were about to give up on you. You're on the agreed timeline, but just barely. We've been plenty worried—heard rumors that you had been killed. New York has been all over us. Eden Naby's husband has been worried sick. He's gone to the U.S. consulate to ask for help." With that, Eden Naby rushed out to find him.

"See if you can get through to New York by telephone," I said to one of the crew. "I want to let Jean know we're back and okay, and I want to talk to Hewitt. Also, let's check when the next plane's out."

"Already know. One leaves for Islamabad in twenty minutes. If we hurry, you can make it."

"Let's go," I said. We hauled for the airstrip.

When we got there, it was a zoo. Many more people wanted on the plane than it could carry. We paid off every airport worker we could collar. I bounded aboard with Andy and a yellow grapefruit bag filled with cans of film and marked CBS NEWS—URGENT in big letters. We breathed deeply and relaxed for the first time in two weeks.

Everything worked. Word spread quickly through New York and then to every CBS News bureau worldwide that we had gotten in and gotten out, had the goods, and were headed for the barn—the huge old milk barn that was now the CBS News Broadcast Center on West Fifty-seventh Street in New York. Andy and I rode the crest back to New York. It was a precious moment and we knew it. How sweet it was.

The trip took something over twenty-four hours, but because we had been flying against the clock, we arrived in New York the same day we had left Peshawar. From the base of the Hindu Kush to the core of the Big Apple—all in the same day. Even the blasé were impressed. We could barely believe it ourselves.

Jeannie was waiting for me at New York's Kennedy Airport when we arrived. She greeted me with a smile as wide as Texas and a great hug and a long, long kiss. She kidded me about my beard.

We were hard against deadlines now. Jeannie dropped us off at the CBS News complex on Fifty-seventh Street. As we entered the *60 Minutes* area, Don Hewitt and Mike Wallace were waiting with warm congratulations. So was CBS News president Bill Leonard.

Within hours after our first stories aired, there were reports that Soviet radio was broadcasting into Afghanistan and the subcontinent offers of rewards for the death or capture of CBS News correspondent Dan Rather. This seemed to be part of an all-out effort by Moscow to deny that the Russians were using gas in Afghanistan. These reports also said the Soviets were accusing me and our crew of all sorts of ghastly deeds inside the country.

At first I didn't believe the stuff about a reward. But it proved to be true. Soviet radio broadcasts were offering thousands of dollars for my death or capture.

I wasn't angry. I was honored. It was the best compliment they could have given me. And having a price on my head was a small price to pay for the truths we told about Afghanistan.

OUTTAKE

W E SELDOM know the precise instant when everything goes wrong. A blunder can be weeks, months, even years in the making. What we can pinpoint is the moment we became aware of it—in my case 6:12 p.m. on Friday, September 11, 1987.

Six minutes of my life disappeared forever that night in Miami, and several years later there is no agreement on what actually happened to them.

For those six minutes—an infinity in television—CBS was off the air while Pope John Paul II was in Miami on his second trip to the United States, and Steffi Graf and Lori McNeil met in the women's semifinals of the U.S. Open tennis tournament. And there a dilemma was born: CBS had two remote broadcasts under way at the same time—one for sports and one for news. There was no direct contact between the broadcasts, no direct phone line, and, at our end, no picture of the tennis match as it unfolded. No one was in command of both broadcasts; they were being produced by two separate divisions under two separate leaderships.

CBS has been and continues to be staffed at every level by some of the smartest, toughest, most dedicated people I've ever known. The trouble was that on September 11, 1987, and the days that followed, none of us had one of our best days.

What may not be clear to the viewer is the chaos that so often takes place behind the scenes, under the best of conditions. It is a combination of a frantic Lucy Ricardo trying to keep up with the chocolates as they roll off the assembly line and a hard night in the control tower at Kennedy Airport. You remind yourself that midair collisions are rare, but based on the number of near misses, you wonder why there aren't more.

To report on this rare papal visit to these shores, CBS News had leased the eleventh floor of the building on Biscayne Boulevard where our CBS bureau was located in Miami. Throughout the day we believed, and had been given every reason to believe, CBS News would be on the air at 6:30 p.m. eastern time with the first of two broadcasts we were scheduled to do. Our second feed would be at 7:00 p.m. At about 6:12 we received the first word from the main facility in New York that the tennis match was tied and might run over, followed by a wrap-up.

I thought the idea was outrageous, given the importance of the timing of this papal visit: "the cold war pope," the first Polish pope, landing in Miami with its large Catholic community and its very large Cuban exile community, with the abortion issue growing more and more divisive across the United States.

And there was one more factor to make us even edgier.

The ratings. Since I had succeeded Walter Cronkite, the *Evening News* had had its share of victories, including over two hundred consecutive weeks ranked at number one. Finally we were overtaken.

But by midsummer and all through August we were coming back. I believe this was mostly because we were producing a stronger newscast, but there were other factors, including the Nielsen Company's new method of measuring the audience. So in September, for the first time in many months, we were expected to win the week. All we needed was to have a reasonably good Friday.

I understand that this emphasis on the ratings may seem about as important as rubber ducks in the bath. But the News Division had been under heavy pressure about not being first. And more pressure means less money. Less money means fewer bureaus, fewer resources for reporting, and fewer people working for the News Division. We'd just weathered a devastating series of personnel cutbacks, like one of those horror movies where the monster strikes widely, indiscriminately, and fatally; you didn't know who'd be next. We wanted no more cuts, and we thought good ratings would provide us with armor.

Now we were in Miami on the verge of breaking through and winning the week with an important story, and the network was going to let tennis take precedence over the pope's coming to America?

Even before he'd told me, Tom Bettag, our executive producer, had already called Howard Stringer, the president of CBS News, in New York. This was the first he'd heard of it. Tom told him that if what we were hearing was true, we were in big trouble. At the least, we needed more time to rearrange the newscast and decide which stories could be cut.

In our makeshift studio in Miami it was unclear where the match was, unclear whether they were going to throw the feed to us or how much time we'd have—five minutes, ten, fifteen—to do the broadcast. To make matters worse, the nearest telephone with a private outside line was in an office down the hall, away from the anchor site. It is safe to say that confusion reigned.

But about these points, there could have been no confusion; that is, Sports had said they intended to run tennis to the end of the match and then do a wrap-up. What I intended was clearly stated, over and over: "If tennis isn't off at six thirty, don't come to us. Give us a chance to regroup and get ourselves together; have Sports hold it until we can know what we're doing."

Tom repeated this to New York with fewer than three minutes to go. I was in place when 6:30 came and went. Tennis still on. I took off my microphone and walked slowly out of the room. I was described in some printed accounts as doing "a slow burn." Maybe so. What I remember was an overwhelming feeling of disappointment. I thought the incident set an incredibly bad precedent. The message we sent our audience was that CBS thought sports was more important than news.

I headed back down the corridor, where I could have a private phone conversation with Howard Stringer. Tom had followed me into the hall, saying, "We need to talk about this." I asked him to return to the control room and monitor the situation. He had just stepped back inside when the director of the *Evening News* said with numbness in his voice, "The network is in black."

"You mean," said Tom, "they're taking a commercial break."

"No. The network is in black. Sports went off the air."

Tom almost tore the door off its hinges getting to the corridor and running me down. He told me what little he knew: There was a blank screen on TV sets tuned to CBS across America.

There were several options that might have been used. The network—meaning New York—could have put up a commercial to borrow time; we had no commercials in Miami. We could have rolled a four-minute tape we'd prepared to introduce the pope's visit. New York could have flashed a "Please Stand By" message. New York could have thrown the signal back to Sports, but Sports wouldn't take it. At 6:33 p.m. they were gone.

All I could think was, We can't let the network go black. In television that is unpardonable. I hurried back to the studio, thinking, This can't be happening. But the whole network was off the air, and no one knew why.

I understood this much: As soon as we turned on the camera, the responsibility for what happened was going to be ours. The place was in a shambles. Six minutes elapsed from the time Sports put us into black until Tom and I could return to the anchor chair, get me hooked up, organize the opening, and get back on the air. I thought it was a wonder that we got through the broadcast.

Even to those who believe they know a good deal about television, much of this must seem like hairsplitting: three minutes over, six minutes off. But this is the world we exist in; our stories are timed to the tenth of a second. We use stopwatches, not sundials.

While I was still on the air, an executive in New York called and told Tom Bettag that CBS had a disaster on its hands and we would need a cover story. Tom and I opposed a cover story on both moral and practical grounds. We would tell the truth: Sports and News were in separate orbits. They had no clear channel of communication. A bad thing happened. Mistakes were made, some by me and some by others. I was prepared to shoulder the blame for mine.

I was encouraged to leave the talking to CBS management. That suited me fine, except that in such a crunch the corporate needs dominate.

Those who spoke to the press laid the guilt squarely on me. The prevailing attitude became "Dan is out front, he gets paid a lot of money, his job is secure, and instead of having five or ten guys taking arrows, let Dan get hit with one big spear. He'll survive."

Maybe I deserved it, but I certainly didn't believe I deserved all that I was getting. My silence, keeping my word about not talking, hadn't helped. I was in trouble now, deep trouble, and hurting.

Relief came when the chief executive officer of CBS, Inc., Larry Tisch, who had the final say, dealt with this clumsy situation calmly. He took the position that it was counterproductive to wallow in the exercise of who said what to whom and why. He refused to believe that it was all my fault. Let's face it: I could have been fired. Much much later, when I suggested that to Tisch, he indicated he didn't think that would have been fair, nor good business.

But I still fault myself for failing to make the point that a matter of principle was involved. There was a growing argument that Sports should take primacy over News. I don't think that should be the case.

In 1992 CBS was the only network to preempt one of the presidential debates. We were committed to the baseball play-offs.

The trend is worrisome. And looking back on that September night in 1987, I fault myself not because I didn't make the case effectively. I didn't make it at all.

THREE
China: Revolt of the Students

THE trip of ten thousand miles begins with a single step, according to an old Chinese proverb. For CBS News the trip to our coverage of the historic drive for democracy in Tiananmen Square in 1989 began with a step—not toward China, but toward Japan.

I have become convinced that the security of the United States, now and well into the twenty-first century, could depend more on whether we are allies with Japan than whether we are allied to any other single nation on earth. But how to tell the story—or, more precisely, the many stories—of modern Japan?

Emperor Hirohito's funeral in the winter of 1989 gave us the hook we needed to take the *CBS Evening News* overseas, not for a day but for a period of time before and after the Japanese paid their final respects. We would involve *60 Minutes, CBS This Morning,* and the *Weekend News;* every show would have at least a segment.

And so we began *The Dawn of a New Era*. For eight telecasts over a period of ten days we transmitted the *Evening News* from Japan. We achieved our goal of wall-to-wall coverage and provided analysis of the rise of Japanese militarism today, a profile of the Japanese middle class, and a look at the rigorous Japanese educational system. We also showed how the Japanese handled the teaching of their defeat in World War II: a sort of Hans Christian Andersen approach. And we carried live coverage of the Emperor's funeral.

At almost the last moment President Bush decided to schedule a state visit to Japan and attend the funeral. His top advisers tried to discourage him from going to Tokyo, thinking it would send the wrong signal to the Chinese, who were brutalized by Japan in World War II. Chinese resentment and suspicion of Japan have never diminished much. But instead, as a gesture to Beijing, President Bush expanded the itinerary to include a stop in China after the funeral. CBS News then decided to make a stop in China, too.

And that was a stroke of unbelievable luck. We had been in Beijing only a short while when I began to feel that something had changed since my last visit. Something was happening. A whiff of discontent was in the air.

"Something is boiling up from below," I said to Tom Bettag. "You can hear it, see it, feel it everywhere."

We talked about the almost breathtaking progress China had made since the death of Mao Tse-tung in 1976. But economic advances had as yet been unmatched by *political* changes. China still lived under the old-line, hard-line Marxist-Leninist-Maoist government. By this time the world had seen glasnost and perestroika in the Soviet Union. But the Chinese leadership didn't seem to have heard the rumblings that would soon lead to the fall of the Berlin Wall and the collapse of the Soviet empire.

I sensed that the Chinese people, unlike their leaders, wanted more change—faster. I could almost feel the tremors beneath my feet.

At Purple Bamboo Park, where people flocked on Sundays to a special corner, not unlike Hyde Park in London, Chinese students and intellectuals were talking about freedom, about democracy, about Leninism, Stalinism, and all the isms, openly and matter-of-factly. They were talking about communism being obsolete politically, discredited intellectually, and unmanageable economically.

They were excited about Gorbachev and had a sketchy idea of what he was doing. There was a consensus in this marketplace of ideas that China needed to move more rapidly toward social and political change.

CBS News crews recorded many of these conversations, and within hours CBS would report that there was something that looked like a democracy movement stirring in China.

When we left China, Tom and I were convinced that we had put a marker down. We were excited, in the way reporters are when they think they are onto a big story and onto it early. We gurgled out sentences that overran each other's speech. We knew we had to come back to China, and soon. Gorbachev and Deng Xiaoping were planning the first Sino-Soviet summit since Stalin and Mao—maybe *then* we could make our move.

And so we waited. Bettag laid out a budget, penciled in the details. In May 1989 we were ready to go. We began to see scattered notes in the newspapers; students in China were staging miniprotests. It was written off as the traditional spring unrest. Tom and I smiled like deacons with four aces, convinced it was much more.

This went on for a few days; then David Burke, who was now president of CBS News, called me into his office. "You have as good a nose for a story as anyone in broadcasting," he said. "Now tell me what you really think about China, because I can't see it."

I leaned over his desk and said, "David, I've never felt stronger about any story at any time. We have to go. I don't know what's there, but I know it's big and it's coming. And I'm so afraid it will happen before we get there, I can't express it to you."

He said, "Then we're going to go." Just like that. I could not have been more astonished if Princess Diana had ridden through the room on a giraffe.

So we set out for China.

We flew eastward, not across the Pacific and into Japan. We scheduled stops in Paris and New Delhi, catching a few winks in both cities. Any experienced TV correspondent knows to catch all the rest you can on the way to a story. When the plane door opens, you need a surge of energy and stamina.

After we landed in Beijing, we dropped off our bags at the Hotel Mandarin and went right to the heart of Tiananmen Square. We wanted to see and listen and find out what had changed in the past two months. The students from the universities had left their class-rooms and started a demonstration; at that point it was nothing more than that—a student demonstration. Our imaginations did not stretch far enough to see what it would become.

There is nothing in the world quite like Tiananmen Square. The Great Hall of the People is on one side, a huge mausoleum of a building. In the days of Mao, the people were not allowed to enter, and to a large degree this is still true. At the top of the square is Tiananmen Gate, which leads from the square directly into the an-cient Forbidden City. Above the gate is a huge portrait of Mao, three stories high, that dominates the entire square.

On the other side of the square is the Museum of the People, and right in the middle of the square is the Monument of the Heroes, a kind of miniature Washington Monument, with inscriptions along the base of it honoring heroes back to antiquity. At the base of the monument the student demonstrators had established their head-quarters. It was a long and laborious process to get there; they had already set up checkpoints—a series of four circles, with fifty yards separating each one from the next. Part of what they were guarding against was being infiltrated by plainclothes police and local intelli-gence agents. Each circle was color-coded, and the last was red.

When we arrived that night in May, 1989, the scene was not particu-larly tense. But as we talked to the leaders of the demonstration, one thing soon became clear: Something big was brewing. And we wanted information.

Several of the students spoke English; the less well-off of the leader-ship did not. At the checkpoints we were asked a few times, "Russki?" And we replied, "No. No Russki." We had to keep repeating our-selves, explaining what we were doing there. Some suspected that we were either CIA or double agents of the Chinese government. Some couldn't make out whether we were British or American, TV or news-paper. A few said, "Oh, CBS, American TV."

When we got through to the top echelon of the student leadership, they spoke quickly and with animation, words tumbling on top of one another. They gestured vigorously, explaining what they hoped to accomplish.

They were saying that they had a passion for self-determination.

China had embarked on major, fundamental changes. More than any other single thought was their conviction that the system and the society were going to change, and soon rather than later.

One of the Chinese students started quoting Thomas Paine. When we talk about students in China, we talk about the treasure of the nation. To even enter a university in China, you have to demonstrate absolute brilliance or have strong political connections. We were talking to nineteen-, twenty-, and twenty-one-year-olds. What they knew about our Constitution, our civil rights, Jefferson and Lincoln and Tom Paine, fewer than 10 percent of American students know.

Do you get the picture? I hope I am never so blasé that I can stand in the middle of a square and not be impressed when I hear a twenty-one-year-old foreign student quoting Tom Paine to me. I am not too proud to admit that I can't quote Tom Paine.

They knew what they believed in, knew what they were willing to die for. How many such people do you meet in a lifetime? They believed it was a time to stand. After about three hours in the square, I began to feel that the government would respond with violence.

One didn't need long to figure out what the boiling point would be in the square. Either the government would cave in and compromise in a way it never had before or there would be violence here. Part of what went through my mind in those hours was thoughts about the power of the individual, of one person with a conviction. In modern life it is easy to forget how much power is there.

The students gave full credit to Deng Xiaoping and those around him for making economic changes over the past ten years. All the while they underscored their belief that even faster *governmental* changes were needed. Marxism, Maoism were dead. But this is what many people missed: The students did not see the U.S.A. as necessarily good. They did not want a United States of China. They were riveted by the ideas of liberty and freedom and a representative government. Yet they wanted a communist system that was uniquely Chinese—Marxism blended with liberty, freedom, democracy. These students were patriots who loved their country.

We talked until dawn and videotaped only a fraction of what we observed. At first they didn't always grasp that we were journalists. Later, when they realized they were being watched by the rest of the world, signs appeared in English. They had studied the techniques of shaping public opinion and believed in it.

Corruption was high on their list of complaints. Corruption was deep and abiding in China. They described the party elite as getting privileges that the people as a whole didn't have. Only members of the elite could get a job, buy a good train ticket, or get a library pass without paying off someone. The students wanted to eliminate corruption.

The student demonstrators were hopeful that with Gorbachev's presence their demands would get attention. There was no open concern yet about violence and no sign that any violence had been threatened. Given what was going on out there, the government had shown some restraint.

The Gorbachev visit was not the reason we had come to Beijing, but it had served as a convenient cover. We were working against the clock, aware that we would be hard-pressed to stay many more days, if any, once the Russian premier left. We went back to the Hotel Mandarin and began to establish a base camp.

My personal feeling was that the meeting of the two troubled communist giants had already paled. China was different. Ideology, governments, even epics and ages come and go, but China somehow stays a mystery. When I had first gone there in 1972, an old China hand had told me to think of the country as a huge glacier that seems motionless for centuries, so slight is the movement. Suddenly there is an avalanche, and the glacier grinds and crashes and stirs with a terrible violence. Then the glacier is quiet once more. So moved China.

Coming off the square, I thought, This is the avalanche. What had triggered the protest was the death in April of that year of Hu Yaobang, the closest the politburo had to a pro-reform member. His death sent many students into mourning, and the mourning had turned into demonstrations, and these were evolving into a movement.

We tried to unravel the central conflict: The goal of the Chinese leadership was to prevent the students' fervor from spreading to the workers and then to the peasants. These were the basic layers of Chinese society, and as long as the government kept them separated, the party was secure. If two of the three started going in the wrong direction, the uprising would be difficult to stop.

As Tom and I talked over green herbal tea, Gorbachev was driving through the streets of Beijing. He was in for a shock. First, there was food in China. At some corners fruits and vegetables were stacked higher than your head. You didn't see that in the Soviet Union. And his eyes were going to be spinning when he saw the throngs of students in Tiananmen Square. No communist leader had ever seen that many students urging the workers to unite behind their cause.

And this is where the Chinese leaders blew it. The masses in the square had little or nothing to do with Gorbachev, but the leaders elected to take no chances. Gorby was given a tour of the suburbs of Beijing, which, like suburbs anywhere else, were not all that interesting. Here was the photo opportunity of their dreams—"Gorby Does China"—and they give him the "B" tour. The visit had its comic aspect: Welcome, glad you're here, but can't wait to get you out of here, because this town may blow at any moment.

Gorby, for all his red-star-rising celebrity, had been reduced to a member of the supporting cast, and a minor one at that. While it certainly wasn't intended to do so, his high-speed, Chaplinesque swing through town provided a springboard for more students to join the protest and gave new energy to their movement.

One thing we suspected, which turned out to be true, was that the government was refusing to crack down while Gorbachev was its guest. I had heard that before Gorbachev arrived, there had been some unusual troop movements. This was our first inkling that the army might be called in. The government had issued several warnings, and in some areas the police had actually busted some heads. A boycott of classes continued. Student and party officials broke off their dialogue. Some of the student leaders were vowing to stage a hunger strike. This was a new thrust by the students. Anyone who has studied Mahatma Gandhi understands that a hunger strike is a fearsome weapon and carries a unique connotation.

The hunger strike and the climax of the Gorbachev visit overlapped and dominated the news in the middle of May. Here were the leaders of the two communist monoliths meeting at the pinnacle for the first time in thirty years. Then came the incredible scene of the seventeenth of May, the massive march that brought into the streets entire workforces, including some government ministries and maverick army units.

And out of the blue, amid questions about his age and health, Deng, the eighty-four-year-old hard-liner, the squatty little survivor, came down from his tower and made clear that he was still running the country. Gorbachev left town almost literally scratching his head.

The number of students in the square was swelling each day. They came by foot, bicycle, bus, and truckload. Once Gorbachev left, you had to know the government was going to crack down. Age is revered in China, but the students were hammering away that the leadership was old and out of touch. The students were prepared to die for their beliefs, they said, but they didn't think it would come to that if only they could be heard. In that, they were sadly, fatally wrong.

And behind the scenes a terrific power struggle had taken place, reinforcing the power of Deng Xiaoping. Zhao Ziyang—the one potential peacemaker who was saying, "You ought to talk to the students"—was purged and removed from his position as head of the party.

Then came the decision to send in the army, and the tanks were standing by outside the city. There were reports of splits inside the army: "They may do it, may not." To eliminate the uncertainty, Deng called in a unit from way out in the provinces, one that barely spoke Mandarin. Which led to the absolutely unforgettable spectacle of the

China: Demonstrations heat up as striking students face the police and even the military in Tiananmen Square.

people of Beijing blocking truckloads of troops with their bodies. And the image most indelibly burned into the memories of people around the world was that of the solitary, slender, short-sleeved young man who stopped a column of tanks from rolling into Tiananmen Square by walking slowly in front of the lead vehicle and standing there. The tank commanders popped out of their turrets like gophers out of their holes and stared at him with a blend of confusion and bemusement.

By this time the home office was on record as being thrilled with the coverage. That's always nice to hear. But Jean Rather was saying by overseas phone, "Yes, but you are coming home, aren't you?" And New York wanted to know how we were going to protect our people.

But this was China. The streets were swarming with people, including vigilante security units. The danger could have been real or imagined, but emotions were running wild. None of the CBS crew wanted to leave their posts, because something might happen and they were afraid of missing it.

It began to get really rough at the beginning of the third week. Airports and seaports were closing, and at Tiananmen Square the noose was tightening. There were arrests and rumors of executions. One more step, you sensed, and this would be a full-blown revolution.

We knew the army would come soon to shut down our ability to telecast from Tiananmen Square, and then would come the pulling of the plugs of foreign satellite installations, such as ours at the hotel. But for now we kept working.

When the soldiers did show up at the hotel, our personnel sounded edgy, and Tom Bettag and I hurried back there. We found that CBS had interrupted a live broadcast to announce that Chinese authorities had pulled the plug from the square. And indeed, they were intent now on shutting down our satellite, too.

The troops had blocked off the streets, were closing in, while crowds chided them with cries of "Shame, shame." The soldiers had shown great restraint on several occasions, but there were also short, ugly clubbing scenes. We didn't know what to expect.

Tom and I ran up to our control room, and there correspondent Susan Spencer and the producer in charge, Lane Venardos, were broadcasting live. Apparently, the army hadn't shut down our satellite—*yet*. When I ducked in, Susan and Lane were explaining to government officials that our main person, Mr. Dan Rather, was not here, and that they had no authority to let them pull the plug on any of our transmissions.

They were broadcasting, viewed by the American audience as they spoke. Back in New York, Howard Stringer, now president of the CBS Broadcast Group, had put our broadcast from Beijing on the air live, interrupting a surefire prime-time-ratings winner: the last-ever episode of *Dallas*. This was one of those occasions when you say you're glad you work at CBS.

I walked into the room, live on the screen, and asked what was going on. Of course, it was pretty clear what was going on. But stalling for time to get our new videotape transmitted to the States, I asked the government representatives to explain to me the nature of the problem. Over their shoulders I could see a small monitor. Videotapes were playing. I recognized our footage of Chinese citizens stopping army trucks and asking, "How can you do this?"

I went through a very polite and deliberate review of the paper the Chinese government had given us, authorizing our broadcasts. Finally Bettag gave me a thumbs-up: The videotapes had been successfully transmitted to New York. Just in time, because the Chinese wouldn't be stalled any longer. The picture went to scramble.

David Burke, back in New York, insisted that we leave; there were two flights still operating, and CBS had arranged for tickets to get us on board and out of the country. But we had a little time before the planes left, and we piled into a car and got back to Tiananmen Square. We had no broadcast facility, but we could perhaps shoot tapes and ship them to Tokyo or Hong Kong, and we could also get the story out by radio and cellular phone.

The mood at Tiananmen Square was tense. Passing the checkpoints looked to be tougher. The guards seemed more than usually suspicious of strangers, especially Westerners. But then we said the magic word, *"Mei guo ren* [American]*."* We were reporters. We wanted to get the story back to the United States.

Suspicion melted instantly into sad smiles. The students knew what was going on, saw and heard the Red Army pulling into position around the city. They fully expected the government crackdown any minute. They weren't going to back down. The only thing they feared was that no one would ever know of the stand they'd taken, the sacrifice they'd made. But here we were, and we would tell the story.

And so they told us the story one last time. They pointed to the makeshift statue of the goddess of democracy that had been erected in the square. You knew she had a kindred spirit with the American Statue of Liberty, but she was all Chinese. She symbolized what the students were trying to achieve.

We shot almost every tape we had, returned to the hotel, and flew out to Japan with our stories.

This was May 20. The army would move in with force around June 4. Lacking support from, among others, the U.S. government, China's student-led movement for freedom and democracy was beaten down and back. It wasn't killed; it didn't die. Overpowered and wounded, it was forced to fall back, go underground, and await another time.

Later President Bush secretly sent a high emissary, Brent Scowcroft, to toast with champagne China's victorious old-line, hard-line communist leaders. When the secret, including pictures, came out, no one in the United States said much. I believe it was because we were, as a nation, embarrassed by what had been done in our name—and what had not.

No one knows for certain how many died during the crackdown, but Amnesty International had the figure most believed—a toll of one thousand. The story won't end there, of course. China will always have more students burning with more ideas, with or without the cameras rolling. And if the spirit of Tiananmen Square can stay alive, someday in China freedom will ring.

OUTTAKE

THERE'S a saying around CBS News so often preached and so often practiced that it seems to have become our unofficial corporate policy: No good deed goes unpunished.

But in the spring of 1993 some fellow Texans did their darnedest to prove otherwise. Thanks to them, I have a new perspective—not to mention a host of new friends and happy memories—all stemming from one of the most unfortunate stories I've ever covered: the armed confrontation between law-enforcement officers and members of

David Koresh's Branch Davidian cult at their compound outside Waco, Texas.

"Outside" is a key word, and one not enough reporters paid attention to in the first days of the standoff. To most of these reporters, who had never been to Waco, ten miles outside of Waco was the same thing as ten steps from the McLennan County Courthouse. When they finally did get around to background research on the area, they continued to blur boundaries. And they thought Waco was *wacko.*

The proof was in the sweeping generalizations and selective fact checking of their reporting. One week into the standoff the Washington *Post* ran a long front-page article that set out to relate every weird thing that ever happened in Waco. It turned out to be a surprisingly short list for such an old town. My favorite example was the attempt to make something weird out of the fact that Bonnie and Clyde, Texas' most famous bank robbers, once had lunch at Leslie's Chicken Shack, a popular local restaurant.

Well, for Pete's sake, I thought as I read the article, every Texas schoolkid knows that Bonnie and Clyde had lunch *all over* Texas. And as far as calling Waco "wacko," even Sam Houston himself used that joke, and it wasn't very fresh then.

But my amusement evaporated as I read on. The article went on to say that because Waco is in the middle of the Bible Belt and in the middle of the gun culture, it was only natural and inevitable for local citizens to "get a message from God," as Koresh claimed to have done, and then haul off and start shooting at people.

The whole thing struck me as pretty unfair—all of these reporters piling on Waco during a crisis. I knew Waco fairly well, and I wasn't seeing the town in most of the press coverage I'd come across.

I sat down and hammered out a radio piece, broadcast it, and kept going. I had in mind pitching an essay to the Waco *Tribune-Herald,* right where the out-of-town journalists would see it first thing in the morning. Here is some of what I wrote:

> Waco is a town of good schools and sturdy homes. Mostly, folks there just try to do right—about like folks in any town in America. Even Waco's wackos are about like wackos anywhere else.
>
> Which is something to remember. Bad things can and do hap-

pen in good places. How can anyone say bad things are more likely to happen in some places than in others? Anybody who does try to say things like that ought to be more careful—especially if they're reporters from New York or Washington. As if those "normal" towns never set eyes on a gun or a cult or a nut case!

Rowland Nethaway, at the Waco *Tribune-Herald,* liked the essay and ran it on the op-ed page on March 10. Almost immediately I started getting wonderful letters and phone calls from the good people of Waco telling me how much they appreciated my speaking up for the city and how much *they* loved Waco, whether they were born there or had only recently arrived. I knew that their kind of civic pride is hard to earn and hard to beat.

The standoff between David Koresh and the law lasted almost two months more. Keeping the vigil became pretty dull. But nobody covering the story could have been happy with the outcome: On April 19 the compound turned into a fireball, dozens of lives were lost, and you could hardly see straight for all the finger-pointing, as most officials tried to pass the blame for the tragedy.

I stayed on the air late that night, and the next day covered the aftermath of the shoot-out and fire. Understandably, Waco was fed up with reporters. For weeks it had been extremely difficult to get phone lines out, every hotel was booked, and the beams from reporters' strange communications devices—from satellites to cellular phones— were causing all kinds of havoc with one another. Waco was still a hospitable place, but that welcoming civic smile was getting just a *little* tight around the corners. As one Wacoan said to me, "If there's any good to come out of the tragedy at the compound, it's this: The reporters will go home."

But Waco was unfailingly friendly to this reporter, who appreciated every kind word. The Greater Waco Chamber of Commerce held its annual fund-raising dinner on June 3 and invited me as a keynote speaker. I prepared some remarks about neighborliness and showing consideration and compassion for the people whose lives touch ours. I'm sure my audience hears better sermons every Sunday.

I was made an honorary citizen of Waco. I was given the key to the city, a crystal eagle, and a proclamation declaring this "Dan Rather Day" in Waco. It was better than Christmas.

The best moment came when Mayor Robert Sheehy, Sr., spoke of reading the Washington *Post* article about the weird history of Waco. His voice grew thick as he described the anger and sorrow he felt when he read this description of his city and others like it. He wondered what, if anything, Waco had done to deserve such treatment.

I remembered the pain that Dallas suffered after 1963, when too many people assumed that Lee Harvey Oswald was representative of the entire city and that all of Dallas had wanted President John Kennedy dead. That reputation was undeserved, and Dallas struggled with it for many years. Since then I've tried especially hard to remember that bad things can and do happen in good towns.

If that's a good deed, so be it. At least in this case I wasn't punished. In Waco they seem to be making an effort to reward good deeds. Here's hoping the philosophy catches on.

FOUR
The Party's Over: Gorbachev and the Fall of the Wall

IN CHINA the unthinkable was now a cherished dream. But in the Soviet bloc, the unthinkable would soon be a reality.

By the autumn of 1989 everywhere I went around the country, I heard people discussing exactly the same subject and saying exactly the same thing: "I can't believe it's happening *so fast!*" "It," of course, was the collapse of Soviet communism. Starting in the spring, what two generations of cold warriors had warned us about—the domino theory—actually happened in reverse. The dominoes fell over in Poland, Hungary, East Germany, Czechoslovakia, Bulgaria, Romania. The Baltic States wanted more than glasnost—they wanted their independence.

The man at center stage in this drama was Mikhail Gorbachev. But I am not absolutely convinced that Gorbachev really meant to change the world or even to change Mother Russia. His policies of glasnost (openness) and perestroika (restructuring) may have been meant only as a fresh coat of paint for the mammoth Soviet system, to placate the grumblers. Surely he didn't mean to set in motion the forces that would implode the communist empire over which he ruled.

The irony then was the fact that Gorbachev was more popular in the West than he was in the Soviet Union, where perestroika had brought disorder and shortages. When we had gone to the Soviet Union in 1988, the economy was free-falling. Gorbachev's favorable ratings had fallen to 12 percent. The rating of his rival and eventual replacement, Moscow party chief Boris Yeltsin, was 70 percent. You could go a long way just listening to the jokes, like this one that was making the rounds in Russia at the time: "What's the difference between the Soviet Union and the United States?" Answer: "In the United States, Gorbachev could be elected President."

In Moscow hope had been squeezed out of the people for too long. Once, there had been some spirit, some faith that hardships like lousy cars and long lines must be endured but that there was an end to the tunnel. Now melancholia had set in. The man on the farm and in the shop no longer believed communism was going to triumph. Things were not going to get better now or at any other time.

You wondered, How can any country that produces rockets that soar into outer space not produce the basics of daily living? After Gorbachev began urging the people to face the hard truths, an unofficial poll was taken to learn what Russians wanted. High on the list was brassieres.

Many journalists never understood that in spite of his brilliance, Gorbachev was and is a dedicated Marxist, handpicked by the KGB (among others) and repackaged as the New Soviet Man. But in trying to salvage the old Soviet system, Gorbachev gambled, exposing to the people all the old failures, as they'd never seen them before. People were confronted with the cruelties that had been practiced on a scale unhealthy to dwell upon. With the openness of glasnost, the Soviets had a much clearer idea of the failure of their own economy. Now they had a whiff of what was really going on, compared with the past promises of happy times to come.

An electrified mass of feelings and events was turned loose that neither Gorbachev nor anyone else could control. He was afraid to initiate the next phase of reforms (as Yeltsin would later try to do, with mixed and bloody results). Gorbachev's position was the opposite of China's: He took the political risk, but not the economic one.

Gorbachev was then widely seen the world over as the picture of glamour and success. But from another view, you could paint him as a tragic figure who led his country to the lip of the cup and then stopped. He could not break with his ideology and training, could not declare himself in favor of private ownership and individual incentives as fuel for the economy.

But for the moment, he was seen as a key interview, the top of the list for almost any reporter in the world, including this one. But how to get to him? He kept turning us down. Ah, but there were fine spring days when he liked to stroll, and there were spots where, if you positioned yourself just right . . .

Actually, we had no idea we'd see him. We happened to be inside the Kremlin, shooting a few stand-ups in one of the most famous but least photographed locations in the world.

The shoot was going well when suddenly my assistant cried out, "There he is!"

Nobody needed to say who "he" was—and we were like a shot out of a cannon, tearing across the quad as if we were a single body, calling out to Gorbachev.

Gorbachev knew he couldn't duck us. If he tried to get out of the interview, he'd look bad on American television. We had him.

A little lesson: Fancy journalism degrees are well and good, but in the end it comes down to luck, reflexes, and shoe leather.

For the people at the top of your wish list of interview subjects, you've always got at least half a dozen questions on the tip of your tongue and ready to ask. Maybe the information minister will finally give you the green light for an interview with the President-for-life. Or who knows? Maybe you'll run into the pope at the Quik Mart. The point is that you've always got a few questions ahead of time because you've been dreaming of just this opportunity.

The only question was who would translate. But Gorbachev happened to have with him a trusted unofficial translator, who seemed tickled to see somebody put the Big Boss on the spot.

We talked about the arms race and superpower relations, and Gorbachev was pleasant and reasonably forthcoming. After several minutes he excused himself; he'd be late for a meeting if he didn't go now. It gave me a kick to get, even briefly, the exclusive interview I'd been refused.

As it turned out, this was only the first of a few times that I managed to land Gorbachev as a "man on the street" interview—and one of

the times Gorbachev realized there could be unanticipated consequences to the openness of glasnost.

Already Gorbachev was allying himself with the hard-liners, the
military, and the KGB. Already he was falling back from glasnost and
perestroika, dumping Yeltsin, and trying to prop up the crumbling
Soviet system. But the rumblings were spreading throughout the Soviet Union and all through Eastern Europe.

IN EARLY February of 1989, I flew to Munich—as curious as this may
sound—to attend a seminar on defense spending. I also wanted to
take a look at the Berlin Wall. A knowledgeable U.S. Senator had said
to me, "Gorbachev loves surprises, loves the bold move."

"Yes, he does," I said, thinking of our interview, "so long as he's
the one moving boldly."

"If you study him," the Senator went on, "what he usually does is
size up what is going to happen anyway, goes ahead and does the
inevitable a little early, and then takes credit for a gutsy move. You
know, he could announce that he is going to take down the Wall."

I expressed doubts, reservations, astonishment, but the Senator
had continued. "I'm not predicting he will, but if he could do it, it
would be another star in his crown."

I didn't have any more solid lead on the Wall, but I did return from
Munich and Berlin with one surprising discovery: the strength of the
undercurrent in favor of the reunification of the two Germanies. I was
now prepared to go out on a limb and say that reunification would
come before the end of the century.

We were starting a new television season, and in news, the season
begins on Labor Day and ends on Memorial Day. The ratings game is
basically played out in the long, dark winter months, when the sets in
use stay on later and the audiences are the largest. This is where you
make and break careers in the squirrelly business called television.

Just in time for the new 1989 season, strange things began happening around the Wall and inside Berlin itself. Pictures started rolling of
people from East Germany actually crawling over the Wall. In the
past, people making such attempts had been shot, and the question
became where were the East German guards. A trickle can turn
quickly into a stream.

The Wall was not down, but it was beginning to totter.

After the newscast one night, Tom Bettag and I caught the next plane for Berlin.

We were a little ahead of ourselves, however. To my surprise we had outrun our own logistics, and there was no CBS camera crew on the ground yet. They were hell-for-leather on their way, but I had no camera to talk into. Such minor details couldn't delay us from going to the Wall.

The trickle of defectors had indeed turned into a stream. No part of the Wall had been torn down physically, but it was clearly just a matter of time.

Willy Brandt, the former Chancellor of West Germany and one-time mayor of West Berlin, was there, and one could not help but try to imagine what that day must have been like for him. I said to Tom, "Let's get him. I'll try to keep him talking, and keep the interview going, while you round up our camera crew."

We got our interview: I managed to stall Brandt, and Bettag charged up in the nick of time, with the camera rolling.

The interview boosted our morale, but in terms of camera locations, we found we were starting well behind on a huge story. Every known television network in the world, and a few no one had ever heard of, were lined up like ducks in front of the Brandenburg Gate, which was in the eastern sector of Berlin. Each had a camera platform or was in the process of constructing one. And we didn't even have a space we could claim as our own. All the good positions were gone.

We were staring at another monumental story, and this time we were not in front. We hadn't been hurt and were not very far behind, but our concentration was on how to get something—and, best of all, something the others didn't have.

From somewhere came the echo of a fundamental of television news big-event coverage: "Get high and shoot low."

"Tom," I said, "we need a high shot." We both spun around and realized the area in front of the Brandenburg Gate was like a park. There were no tall buildings. There was barbed wire at the foot of the Wall, and pavement twenty feet beyond.

"Good idea," said Bettag. "How are we going to do that?"

We would have to improvise. I said to Tom, "Drop whatever you're doing and find me a cherry picker."

I was talking about the kind of truck that has a boom with a space

Berlin: In front of the Brandenburg Gate, East and West Germans celebrate the fall of the Berlin Wall.

at the end where workers can stand and be raised up to change streetlights and do repairs on power lines. And the next thing I know, here is a perfectly handsome cherry picker chugging into place directly behind all the other networks' platforms, with Bettag sitting in the cab, like Mike Mulligan with his steam shovel. For the first time since we reached Berlin, I could smile.

A little bucket—we could get fancy and call it a gondola—was attached to the boom. It gave us a tricky way to hoist our crew. We knew it would be crowded with three of us in there: the cameraman, the soundman, and myself. But when the picker raised us, we got a fabulous shot of the Brandenburg Gate, the milling crowd below, and the other anchor positions. As soon as we were up in the air, photographers from other networks started lining up, asking where we found it and offering us $500 and more to take them up.

It was one of those rare times when work is more fun than fun. The bucket was about five feet long by two and a half feet wide, and steady enough. The crowd around us stood and watched. Some laughed. The anchorman, meaning me, had to lean as far back as possible. The cameraman positioned himself at the other end, setting his butt on the edge and leaning back in order to focus the lens. The soundman just leaned out of the way and prayed the cable didn't break.

We did our live broadcast at midnight Berlin time. It is a small point, but one worth adding, that the music that led into the broadcast was Beethoven—the "Ode to Joy" from the Ninth Symphony. The music soared like a skyburst of fireworks and rockets, but it was nothing compared to what the Germans were feeling that night.

OUTTAKE

ONCE, riding the Cuban countryside in his jeep, Fidel Castro told me he could never understand why African Americans in the United States had not turned to communism in large numbers.

He acknowledged that once, over a period of years in the 1960s and '70s, he had spent a lot of money (most of it supplied by the Soviets) trying to prime the Marxist-Leninist pump among blacks in the United States. But a surge to communism among North American blacks never happened, and Castro said he never understood it, never would. It was one of the many things about the United States and its people he found inexplicable.

Fidel rarely gets in high gear before 10:30 or so at night. And he is a world-class talker. I am not referring to speeches, although Castro is famous for long ones, over many hours, sometimes days. In this he has rivals throughout the Soviet and Chinese communist old guard. But Fidel has no rivals when it comes to sitting down and shooting the breeze with a couple of cigars and a bottle of Chivas Regal. (For image reasons and the fact that Cuba exports rum, he doesn't flaunt this, but he prefers Scotch. And for health reasons he has officially stopped smoking cigars in recent years.) In these bull sessions he'll talk nonstop for hours about everything from boxing to the Marxist dialectic to why the United States is doomed to fail. ("Any country that spends billions of dollars just to advertise mouthwash and deodorant cannot survive," he once told me, although he presides over an economy that cannot produce enough toilet paper.) Among interview subjects, he's a one-man marathon and prefers to talk all night long, and if he's talking to you, you'd better listen—all night long.

I've had several encounters with the "night person" Castro, including two lengthy interviews for *60 Minutes*. And I had the circles under my eyes to prove it.

And you know what? In spite of everything, the man is a great interview. Always a challenge. Pithy when he chooses to be. Generally interesting. Outrageous sometimes, often infuriating. But even when he is wrong, an interview with him can make for lively, informative television. In the vernacular of my trade, he could make it as an anchor in a major market, probably even on a network.

For one of our most recent interviews, in 1985, Fidel wasn't taking any chances on losing the full and undivided attention of our CBS News crew. He's a great student of the United States—tried to move here as a professional baseball player in his youth—and watches a great deal of television. Although I don't pretend he's a great student of Dan Rather, it's true you don't have to know much about me to know I love a scoop. And Fidel had one all ready for me.

At the time, financier Robert Vesco was on the lam after an embezzling scheme went sour in the early 1980s. Vesco also was widely

Cuba: A world-class talker in an interview, Fidel Castro (right) has been aggressive, outrageous, infuriating—but never dull.

suspected of having connections to the drug trade. Officials all over the world were looking for him. "Oh, yes," Fidel said blithely. "He's here—in Cuba."

My eyes probably widened. There it was: my scoop, the lead for my story, a good day's work in a single sentence. Our cameras and microphones weren't set up yet; I was already planning a sequence of questions to draw out more information about the Vesco story over the course of the interview. But Fidel wasn't through with me yet.

"Of course, I'll never say so on-camera," he said, "and I'll deny it if you quote me."

I suppose that if Fidel Castro governed as effectively as he jerks people's chains, Cuba would be a very different place.

FIVE
Iraq: Sleeping with the Enemy

A VACATION is to a newscaster what a trailer park is to a tornado. It's bound to attract havoc. The theory may have no scientific basis, but there is nothing in my experience to disprove that a relationship exists.

In thirty years with CBS, I had never taken a month's vacation. But in the summer of 1990 Jean and I were taking the plunge. With Tom Bettag and his wife, Claire, we had been invited by friends to spend most of August in France and part of that time fishing in the lower region of the French Alps.

Everything started off according to plan.

Our hosts were Jean-Claude and Martine Christiane, and we celebrated our reunion over dinner, with wine and music, on the banks of Lake Annecy. We were all but giddy at the prospect of a holiday. Free, free at last! Gonna have some time off after a really incredible year and a half, which had started with the journey to Japan and carried us through Tiananmen Square, the fall of the Berlin Wall, the convulsions of Eastern Europe, the invasion of Panama, and multiple trips to the Soviet Union.

At 7:30 the next morning the Land Rover was loaded with fishing gear and we had our suitcases in the driveway. As Jean-Claude backed into the road, we listened to the 8:00 a.m. broadcast of the *Voice of America,* which is standard procedure when we are overseas. And the first report was the news that Saddam Hussein had sent his Iraqi troops across the border and invaded Kuwait.

Tom looked at me, and I looked at Tom, and Jean-Claude looked at the both of us. I said, "Stop. Stop right now. You have to take us to Geneva." The nearest large airport was in Geneva, ninety minutes away. Our wives said nothing. Jean and Claire had tolerated a lifetime of this, and they knew. They knew. We unloaded their luggage, and Claire and Jean got out of the Land Rover.

Our friend, bless him, grasped the situation immediately, and from that moment on, we considered ourselves in a race to get inside

Kuwait before the gates slammed shut. We knew we didn't have long. Still, if we couldn't get into Kuwait, we could get close—into Saudi Arabia or Jordan.

Jean-Claude reminded us that there was a small local airport where, if we couldn't charter a plane to Geneva, we could at least work the phones. For the rest of that day and into the night, we tried to get clearance to fly from Annecy or Geneva to Kuwait. Nobody wanted to fly anywhere near a war zone. At one point, we had the clearance and we had a charter waiting in Geneva. But before we could board a chopper to Geneva, the charter's clearance had been pulled.

By then what we knew was this: Iraqi troops had crossed the border and effectively occupied Kuwait in twelve hours. The action was both audacious and astonishing. In the predawn dark of Thursday, August 2, 1990, a force estimated at over one hundred thousand soldiers poured south into Kuwait. In four hours the first of the troops rolled unchallenged along the thirty-seven miles of superhighway that led to the capital, Kuwait City.

Our reports were that Iraq's heavy armor had surrounded the Emir's palace and the nearby U.S. Embassy. The Emir, Sheik Jaber al-Ahmed al-Sabah, and his family had already fled by helicopter to Saudi Arabia.

Meanwhile, I was on and off the phone with CBS News in New York. Back and forth we debated the options. Tom and I argued in favor of getting to the scene. But this debate is a continuing one: Should your anchorman be on top of a big story or is his place in the studio?

I was then and am now dedicated to the idea of being there—seeing, hearing, sniffing the story. When you slip back into your anchor shoes, you at least have a knowledge of the story, and the credibility, you could not get any other way. Besides, from a visceral standpoint, what reporter would want to be anyplace else? Every instinct you have tells you to follow the fire trucks.

In New York the attitude was that the invasion was a one- or two-day wonder. Our major competitors were not inclined to move.

Then Bettag made the persuading argument. "We have a chance," he said, "to be on the front edge of a great story. We have a huge advantage—a one-leg jump. If anybody can get to Kuwait, we can."

My contribution was an educated guess. I said, "The United States will send in troops. George Bush will go to war over this."

Candor requires an admission: I was simply remembering a tip from Senator William "Bill" Cohen, the Republican from Maine, when we met in a New York City coffee shop in the spring of that year. He said to me that day, "You ought to be doing something on Saddam Hussein."

Whatever was left of my reporter's nose, I understood that Bill Cohen was putting me onto a story. At the time, the White House was tilted completely toward Saddam Hussein. We were shipping him billions of dollars' worth of aid and weapons, not all of it legally. Through private channels the government was encouraging various businesspeople to conduct all kinds of advantageous deals with Iraq. And here was Senator Cohen saying, "The guy is a madman. He may be the single most dangerous person in the world."

Let me make it clear that he wasn't leaking any goodies from the Senate Intelligence Committee files to me. Cohen was telling me that if I wanted a challenge, I ought to take a hard look at Saddam Hussein and the company he kept. He said, "This guy is taking us to the cleaners. He's getting all of this military hardware—tanks from the Soviet Union, artillery from Argentina, Mirage jet fighters from the French, and computers and weapons systems from us. But he is stirring up Muslim fundamentalism while presenting himself as a secular Arab leader with whom we can do business. He is playing all ends against the middle, and his dream is to lead a triumphant Arab army into Jerusalem." Mentally I marked Saddam Hussein as a future candidate for the role of global mischief-maker.

Now, near the end of that day in France, our prospects were shrinking. We had to rule out a charter flight to Kuwait. Planes were forbidden to fly over Saudi Arabia, and no insurer would cover them. Besides, we didn't have visas. By nightfall we had two choices: fly home to New York or catch a plane to London and take our chances.

Though there was no hope of getting into Kuwait by air, I thought that if we could get near enough—to Saudi Arabia, Syria, Turkey, Jordan, or even Iran—we might walk in. The reaction from CBS News in New York was, "That's out of the question."

Tom said, "Let's go to London. That way we don't completely give up our advantage. We can keep swinging and we can do tonight's broadcast from there."

The charter, the one we had hoped to take to Kuwait, landed in

London, where that night I anchored the *CBS Evening News*. As soon as the broadcast ended, we climbed back aboard the plane and took off for parts unknown. Our best bet appeared to be Amman, Jordan. Jordan has a border with Syria, Saudi Arabia, and Iraq. Amman long has been a listening post for diplomats and journalists and spies.

I hadn't given up on sneaking into Kuwait. At the least I thought we could set down in Amman and make our way across the top of Saudi Arabia, through the desert.

So we flew to Amman, and from there we did the next night's *CBS Evening News*. We were now operating on no sleep at all, driven by what tomorrow would bring.

"It could all be over in a few days," predicted Tom. Increasingly, it looked as if Saddam had crushed Kuwait without any opposition, the classic lightning strike.

"Maybe so," I said, "but the next question is, will he invade Saudi Arabia? If he's smart, he will. It's a bold move, but if he keeps going now, he can get the major Saudi oil fields—probably without much of a fight. The other question is whether the United States moves and how quickly."

I was absolutely convinced that we would intervene. Earlier Presidents went to war to make the world safe for democracy. Restoring the Emir of Kuwait to his plush throne and repressive rule didn't quite compute. Nor did the idea of holding down the price of oil. But a crisis can make everything seem larger and more important. I believed the moral objections would be overcome.

George Bush could push some hot buttons. There was the need to keep the Middle East from becoming less stable. The trump card would be a call to reduce the threat of Iraq's becoming a nuclear power. And the White House had good reason to know what was in Iraq's military and chemical inventory.

After the newscast Tom insisted that we venture into what was called the Arab Street. "Let's talk to real people," he said, "about how they feel and what they think will happen."

We wanted to talk with as many people as we could, plumb every source we could find. The street was filled with ordinary men and women, a melting pot of Egyptians, Syrians, Moroccans, Algerians. While many of them hated Saddam Hussein and what he had done in Kuwait, they were also torn by Arab pride. In their hearts, at least, here was an Arab warrior who had put it on the line, who had stunned the West and the Israelis, and for the moment appeared to have won. He was an Arab who had done something, and at ground level the early sentiment was with "the thief of Baghdad." It was not what we had expected.

The street piece aired on the second night of what we were calling *The Road to War* broadcasts, and no sooner did we sign off than the complaints began rolling into the CBS offices in New York from the highest levels of the U.S. government. We were accused of taking sides, of being pro-Saddam, pro-Iraq. I considered the charges outrageous. Our interviews did not constitute an endorsement.

We had organized a makeshift Amman bureau—two hotel rooms and a handful of people—but our goal was still to get into the war zone. A window opened in Dubai, one of the Arab emirates, and our plan was to broadcast from there if we could and use Amman as a base camp. Tom had checked into chartering a boat, but it was soon obvious that we had no chance of making our way up the Persian Gulf and slipping into Kuwait from the sea.

When you are chasing a story, trying to keep track of the time is like waking from a fever and not being sure if you've slept for minutes or hours. The picture on the viewer's screen—the orderliness on the set—conceals the craziness around you. It isn't the stress that grinds you down; it is the need to constantly adjust your emotions. We all have our methods of dealing with the fear of failure.

When we flew into Dubai, under circumstances that might best be described as unpredictable, Tom had scribbled a list of early goals into his notebook, then mine. One was to get to the battlefront. Two was to get to Baghdad. Three was to interview Saddam Hussein. Four was to interview as many other principals as we could reach, including President Hosni Mubarak of Egypt and Jordan's King Hussein.

We were still trying to move up the coast, at least as far as Bahrain. A time or two we thought we had arranged for someone to drive us there, but the roads kept closing. Finally we flew back to Amman after learning that we had been granted an interview with King Hussein.

On a Sunday I went to the palace and met with His Royal Highness, about whom I had no special knowledge, although we had met. The atmosphere around that interview was as interesting as any I have ever experienced. Hussein has a reputation of being very guarded—not surprising for a monarch whose grandfather was murdered, whose father was schizophrenic, and who has survived forty years of intrigue and danger.

I found him heavyhearted, pensive, and willing to talk with a candor for which I was not prepared. Before the interview, I shared with him my own early and limited impressions because I wanted to get his reactions. "I have been here only a few days, Your Majesty," I said, "and I did not pretend to come here as an expert on the Middle East. I am here to educate myself."

He smiled.

"Having conceded that," I went on, "and with the little I know about the region, my instinct is that war is inevitable."

To my surprise he said, "I fear you are right."

There was no evasion, no doubt in his words, and so I pressed on. "Your Majesty, there is a widespread belief in Washington, even at the highest levels, that Saddam Hussein is bluffing."

He looked at me with eyes that were chilling. Then he said, "Mr. Rather, I will tell you that Saddam Hussein does not bluff, he is not now bluffing, and it is for that reason I believe there will be a war."

We did the interview, and I was amazed by the nakedness of his feelings. He was morose and fatalistic, and I believe he revealed himself as he had rarely done before or since.

After we finished, he invited me into his private study, and it was clear he wanted to talk more. He told me about his most recent meeting with Saddam Hussein. He cautioned me about Hosni Mubarak of Egypt, who had lied—his word, not mine—to the White House and, at the least, was dealing in sophistry.

Mubarak had been quoted as saying that Iraq would not invade Kuwait. After the fact, he said that Saddam had assured him he would not. Now King Hussein was telling me that Mubarak had been told no such thing. We may never know the truth, but the King of Jordan left no doubt about what he believed. He was convinced that Hosni Mubarak wanted the United States to go to war with Saddam Hussein.

Still, the King said he was trying to arrange another meeting, in Cairo, with the Iraqi dictator in the hope of finding an "Arab solution." Time was short, the hope was slender, but he felt it was possible, depending on whether President Bush really wanted a peaceful solution.

Of course, not all of this was on-camera, but King Hussein's despair and weariness were. The life of his country, and his rule, were hanging in the balance. In his own mind he could not go against Saddam—he had no other option—and this was his lament.

The interview ran on that night's edition of *60 Minutes*.

ABC News suddenly showed up in Jordan in force. After we had heard the King analyze the prospects for war, it was harder to say that this story was going to blow over. For our part, I think the interview sent a clear signal to our Arab contacts that we are here; we are going to stay here; we want to be fair; we want to be right; we will keep our word; we want to be treated seriously.

Most of the news organizations of the world were on hand for the Arab summit in Cairo and stayed on to file reports. But only CBS was there with the anchorperson for its evening news.

The summit broke up with the Iraqi diplomats and at least one other delegation throwing pieces of bread at one another. There is a timeless resentment of the stereotype of Arabs constantly quarreling among themselves, of being unable to get organized or stay together. Sadly, that stereotype was not banished this day.

Before we left Cairo, the rumor surfaced that Ted Koppel, who had flown in from Rome on a 707 with a news team of twenty-three, had met with Tariq Aziz, the Iraqi ambassador to Washington, and firmed up a deal to get ABC into Baghdad. I flew back to Amman and went directly to the Iraqi embassy, where we had applied for our visas. By now the embassy was dealing with a tidal wave of refugees and journalists and even diplomats from around the world wanting to know what was going on. We had to fight our way through milling crowds just to get to the front gate. Tom and I finally maneuvered our way to the desk of the deputy to the ambassador.

He confirmed that Koppel and his staff were heading for Baghdad to do their *Nightline* telecasts. I came at him hard. We were on the scene first, I roared. CBS had been promised by the embassy in Washington that if and when Iraq began to let in Western reporters, we would be at the front of the line. He gave me as many sympathetic shrugs as his shoulders could manage, and then we got down to practical matters.

We made a lot of calls from his office, virtually spent the night there, and left with visas to allow us into Baghdad.

At the airport in Amman the scene was right out of the Old Testament. Refugees choked the road around the airport. People were fighting over bread. Women and small children huddled and slept with their dogs and camels. It was a sight to behold and to break you. Life was spiraling into chaos.

There was only one way to fly into Baghdad, and that was on an Iraqi aircraft. I have to admit, the prospect didn't thrill me. Certain questions danced in my brain: Who maintains this plane? How do I know that one of the other passengers isn't a terrorist, that someone is not going to blow the plane out of the sky? The worries were not easily dismissed.

In the week after the invasion an interesting paradox was being acted out at home. President Bush had decided not to break off his vacation in Maine, where he was photographed casting for bluefish. This signal was meant to assure the American people—and Saddam— that the crisis would not consume him. At the same time, the largest air- and sealift since D-day was taking shape. By August 8 the first of a half-million American military personnel were landing in Saudi Arabia, along with a billion pounds of equipment and 150,000 bottles of sunscreen.

Meanwhile, frustration was fairly general among the media. Journalists were not being allowed into Saudi Arabia except as part of a Pentagon pool out of Washington.

CBS did not win the race to Baghdad. Koppel was able to use his connection with Tariq Aziz to get the invitation first. He was hoping for an interview with Saddam, of course, but instead had to settle for one with the ambassador. We were ten hours behind ABC, and in this kind of competition ten hours is a lifetime. I was disappointed. We thought we had worked hard enough to catch a break. But you can work hard and work smart and the cards still won't fall your way. In the long run ours did.

There was no battlefront now and no resistance to report. All of Kuwait had been secured. But there was one story, one prize, still worth going after: Saddam Hussein himself.

WE FLEW into Baghdad at twilight on the fourteenth of August— Tom Bettag, cameramen Kurt Hoeffler and Jürgen Normand, technical wizard John Smith, and I. On the drive into town we passed Iraq's

Tomb of the Unknown Soldier, where armed soldiers walked their post. We were not likely to stumble across any military secrets riding into town, but armored convoys rolled along the roadways. Above us, we saw antiaircraft batteries hoisted by helicopters with slings, to be lowered onto the rooftops of key buildings. Still, I would find that the Iraqis were almost matter-of-fact about the threat of an American air attack, which they expected at any moment. The city had been seasoned by the murderous eight-year conflict with Iran.

A "handler" from the Foreign Ministry was waiting for us when we checked into the Hotel Palestine. His name was Ali Abdul-Rashad, a pudgy bureaucrat who politely told us we were not allowed to leave the hotel, not allowed to take photographs or film of any kind.

Whereupon we engaged in a series of seemingly foolish negotiations. It is impossible to convey how petty and torturous they were, and yet how necessary. We were in Baghdad for the purpose of broadcasting the evening news, not just to churn out a daily piece.

I will say this for Ali, our baby-sitter–observer. He made it clear that he would do nothing to jeopardize the security of Iraq or Saddam Hussein or, for that matter, himself. But within limits he would give us whatever help he could. So our first negotiation was to loosen the prohibition against pictures. Television tends to lose something without pictures, and Tom convinced him to let the cameraman film me on the balcony outside our room, framed against the sky. There would be nothing that was clearly identifiable in the background. Of course, we would need to take our videotape to the television station and have them put it on the bird (satellite) for us.

It took hours to get him to agree to this, but he did, and we were assured of a Baghdad dateline. More hours were spent getting into the station, which was surrounded by armed guards. Keep in mind that in many developing countries the three most important locations are the presidential palace, the airport, and the television station.

I was less concerned with the armed guards than with a woman we called the Tiger Lady. She was a member of the ruling Baath Party and in charge of the station. Each day you were subject to censorship. There was a censor sitting there with his hand literally on the plug. If you said anything that they disapproved of, out it came. It was a potential nightmare.

After we had moved our first day's tape, we dropped by the U.S.

embassy, where I met Joe Wilson III, whom I consider one of the unsung heroes of the Gulf war. He had been left in charge after April Glaspie, the American ambassador, returned to Washington shortly before the invasion.

We could not have coped in Baghdad without Joe Wilson. He made it clear from the beginning: "Glad to see you, glad you're here, understand why you are here, and I will help you all I can. But that won't be much. I've got my hands full.

"And now let me put on my official hat as a representative of the United States government and tell you that as a U.S. citizen, you are in peril here."

That very day, an Iraqi government official called at the hotel and said, "Let's take a ride." I thought, Well, that's unusual. We climbed into his car and started riding. Another Iraqi was at the wheel.

The government man said, "I am not supposed to tell you this, but I think you should know our leader is considering taking and holding some foreigners, including and perhaps especially Americans. They will be regarded as guests."

I should have figured out that code very quickly, but in the context of the time I merely said, "What do you mean, 'guests'?" There were thousands of Americans living and working in Kuwait—most with oil companies—and hundreds in Iraq.

With no dissembling, he said they would be taken as hostages and dispersed to selected locations as targets. "Human shields, if you will."

My reaction was just utter shock. I returned to the hotel and told Tom, who said, "My God, I can't believe it." I said, "Well, I believe it. I think we just had a story laid on us." But Bettag reminded me that we needed more than one source.

So I telephoned a man I'll call Hamoud, the one person I knew in the Iraqi government. There were the usual delays, and we were getting closer and closer to broadcast time. I was sitting on information I knew to be explosive, and I felt reasonably sure no one else had it. We had been given a desk at the U.S. embassy, and I had been overheard talking by one of the staff—not Joe Wilson—who called me aside and said, "I'm going to say it once and only once. I think this is true." He made it clear that they were trying to get as many Americans as they could into the compound, into the embassy residences, "under the umbrella of the U.S. government."

I was more desperate than ever to reach Hamoud. I had no luck on the phone, and I believed that he was ducking my calls because he did not want to confirm or deny the story.

In short, we were in never-never land. The clock was running. We were in a beleaguered country that might soon be at war with our own. It was a country that had been the cradle of civilization and had sunk into centuries of ignorance, poverty, and upheavals. They were talking about taking American hostages, and I knew the color of my passport.

The *CBS Evening News* was to go on the air at 2:00 in the morning Baghdad time. By 10:30 p.m. we hadn't reached Hamoud or anyone else to confirm the story. And frankly, at the other end of the phone, in New York, our colleagues were telling us, "Don't worry about filing the story. Just get out of there."

Then, within the hour, Hamoud finally took my call. I used a couple of reportorial techniques that are not uncommon. One was to say, "I have this story. I don't know whether to go with it or not, but the one thing I don't want to do is be inaccurate."

Hamoud said, "Well, what is the story?"

I had a feeling that he knew quite clearly what the story was, but I said, "I would prefer to talk about it with you in person. It is a very sensitive subject and involves the lives and perhaps the deaths of many innocent people."

He said meeting with me would not be possible. I said, "Let me ask you this, Mr. Hamoud. I am going to read you the first three paragraphs of my story, and if there is anything wrong with it, please correct me. And your silence will also tell me a good deal."

He said, "I cannot encourage you to do that."

I said, "Well, let me do it anyway." And before he could interrupt, I proceeded to read him the first three paragraphs, which basically said that the government of Saddam Hussein was considering the possibility of taking foreigners, including Americans, as what they called guests, but what other countries would surely recognize as hostages—with the clear inference that the foreigners would be used as human shields and potential targets in the event of bombing raids on Iraqi soil.

There was a long silence. I said, "Mr. Hamoud, I need to do my broadcast, unless you have anything further to say." There was a second long silence. I said, "Thank you very much, and I may need to get back to you before we go on the air."

He said, "I am not sure I will be available."

That stopped me from putting the phone down. "I told you," I said, "that the one thing I wanted to do was be accurate. I beg of you, don't let me broadcast it if what I have is inaccurate."

There was another silence. I waited . . . and waited . . . and waited. I wanted to be as sure as I could that I knew what that silence meant. Then I rang off, and I told Tom, "It's confirmed. I have the second source."

He said, "Did Hamoud confirm it?"

I said, "Not in so many words, but I consider that he did."

Bettag shook his head. "I would be a lot more comfortable if he actually told you yes, the story is true."

The clock was ticking down, and I was getting itchy. The story was huge, and I wanted to unload it because there is nothing worse than being a day late with a story you had first. But Tom kept working on me, and I finally called Hamoud back.

I said, "This story is of such importance that I think I need to talk to the foreign minister or at least the deputy foreign minister."

And Hamoud said, "That will not be possible."

"Then I need you to tell me that this story is true."

He said, "I told you so three times in our previous conversation." Then he added, only half joking, "Mr. Rather, I thought you were a big-time reporter. Do I have to come and color in your book?"

And I laughed and said, "I owe you one. Thanks a lot."

Up to this point the global temper was more or less unchanged. Saddam Hussein had said that he had made his point. He had taken from the Arab rich to give to the Arab poor, casting himself as a desert descendant of Robin Hood. He had been prepared to withdraw his troops and leave in place a broad-based government. Now, with President Bush rattling his sword and demanding the return of the Kuwaiti royal family to the throne, the equation had changed. Kuwait and Iraq, as far as Saddam was concerned, were one nation, indivisible, with oil and dinars for all.

President Bush was continuing the military buildup, and heating up the rhetoric, having compared the Iraqi dictator to Adolf Hitler. Meanwhile, Secretary of State James Baker rallied our allies in Europe and the Middle East, forging what would become a most improbable coalition. Sanctions were already in place; a deadline for the Iraqi withdrawal was in the making.

My daily reports on CBS Radio allowed me a freedom not always available within the structure of a network newscast: I could interpret what I was told. I could conjecture.

From Baghdad, August 16:

> "None of the portents are encouraging. The most important have been: one, the ordering of the British and Americans in Kuwait City to an undisclosed hotel, which many diplomats here fear may mean some kind of internment, possibly in Iraq; two, President Saddam Hussein's tough, vitriolic speech calling Bush a liar; three, the Americans now held in Baghdad see no light, no hope of gaining their freedom of movement."

On August 20:

> "Armed squads of soldiers have been seen knocking on doors on Baghdad's side streets. It is believed that what they are doing is looking for Americans and other Westerners.
>
> "In Kuwait all embassies will be closed as of noon Friday, in a move widely interpreted by diplomats to mean that the four to five thousand American and British citizens there will be transported to Iraq as part of Saddam Hussein's hostages-as-human-shields strategy. CBS News was told by Iraqi sources tonight that they could be dispersed to as many as one hundred military and industrial sites."

Saddam had made a colossal error: He had with one ominous stroke turned world opinion into a solid bloc against him. At first President Bush had avoided using the word hostages, a label that had so wounded and haunted Jimmy Carter. But as the shock and anger mounted, words became a weapon. Within a week Saddam released the women and children but acted on his threat to disperse the men to potential military targets as human shields.

It wasn't long before we discovered that our ranks of Western reporters were thinning. An Iraqi source told us that he knew of only three or four who remained. ABC had left behind a skeleton crew; CNN, one or two staffers. We had the best story in the world almost to ourselves, but the danger was increasing. I made it a point to see as much as I could of Joe Wilson, and I stayed in touch with Hamoud, knowing that I might require his help at any time. I finally managed to see him, alone, and made a hard pitch for the interview with Saddam Hussein.

I said, "You tell me that Saddam is misunderstood; his policies and intentions are misunderstood. And you tell me this is dangerous for the world. I can give him one hour of prime time. He should speak to the people himself. That is his best chance. We are the people to do it: CBS. I am here. I am going to be here. I'll stay in Baghdad for as long as I can. I'm not leaving until you tell me I have to leave."

Hamoud took it all in, and he said, "I will try," which encouraged me greatly. There were several moments when we thought we were really close, and then suddenly the chance went away. Hamoud called and said, "It could happen at any time, but I do not think it will happen on this trip." A day or two later he called and said, "It is time for you to go."

I said, "I'd rather not."

He replied, "It is not for you to say. You must leave."

We left, but not disheartened. Tom and I both had a hunch that we would be back. On our return to Amman we asked for an interview with Hosni Mubarak, whose role in the crisis held some fascination for me.

We flew to Alexandria, the ancient city by the sea where once the oldest library in the world was located and where Mubarak had a home. I had been there on other occasions and always felt it was one of the world's enchanted cities.

We had a leisurely conversation off-camera. Mubarak has a strong and sturdy look, with thick black hair and the hands of a laborer. He asked me how things were in Baghdad and in Saudi Arabia, and in the timeless ritual between journalist and source—particularly a high-level source—you have to give something to get something. It is an interesting exercise and one I rather like.

We both knew the game. I told him of King Hussein's accusation that he had lied to the White House about Iraq's plan to invade Kuwait. He did not seem offended, but insisted that he had not lied about what Saddam Hussein had told him. Then he said, "How long is Bush going to wait?"

"Wait for what?" I asked.

"To go to war," he said.

"Mr. President, I'm not sure he will."

"Oh, yes," he said. "He will. And he ought to go soon." During our actual interview Mubarak was far more cautious, but after we had finished filming and removed our microphones, he returned to the subject. "The longer he waits," he said, "the more difficult it could be. Saddam Hussein does not have a strong army. It is a myth. Who around President Bush has built up so strongly his army?"

Dick Cheney, the Secretary of Defense, had kept referring to the Iraqi army as the fourth most powerful in the world, which made you wonder if the rating was provided by the same people who did college-football polls.

"Yes, Iraq has a lot of equipment," said Mubarak. "But the equipment is not as good as has been advertised. Secondly, the best equipment in the world is only as good as the people who operate it. I am telling you, if it is an air war, it will last three to four weeks. If it is a ground war, ten days to two weeks, at the outside."

This was in late August, four and a half months before the bombs would fall. I said respectfully that his estimate was not what I had been hearing from the U.S. military. But I was impressed with his confidence, his forcefulness. He was saying flat out that Saddam Hussein and his forces were vastly overrated.

I knew that Mubarak had come to power out of the Egyptian air force. He knew about modern equipment, and he knew how good American weapons were. We had conducted military maneuvers in the Egyptian desert. He knew what our fighters and bombers could do.

In his judgment of King Hussein he was as devastating as the Jordanian King had been toward him. "He is of no consequence," said Mubarak. "He believes if you feed a lion meat, he will become your friend. But what you get is a lion you cannot stop feeding."

We left Alexandria feeling fairly pleased. We had gotten an exclusive interview with the President of Egypt, the first he had given on the crisis in the Persian Gulf, and we thought it would play well.

We had been working seven days a week, virtually around the clock. In a twenty-four-hour period, we had gone from Baghdad to Amman to Alexandria and then on to Dhahran, Saudi Arabia. Now at the airport, we were met by a representative of the company that leased us the plane. As soon as the ramp was lowered, he ran right up and popped his head inside and said, "Mr. Rather, you must call your office in Amman. They want you to call immediately."

Bettag and I got off the plane and walked into the airport, apprehensive about the call and the urgency of it. We were operating on maybe an hour and a half of sleep over the past forty-eight hours. It took a while to get a call through to Amman, but I finally reached a senior producer for the *Evening News*, who said, "We've had a strange call. Your man in Baghdad says that he might be able to show you some sights if you come back to Baghdad as quickly as you can." I hung up and turned to Tom. "The Saddam interview."

We sprinted to the plane and told the pilot to get us back to Amman. Once there, we had to claw our way through the airport scene and then to the Iraqi embassy to have our passports stamped with our new visas for Baghdad. Then we had to wade through the crowd outside the embassy, and one more time through the flood of refugees at the airport, and hustle aboard an Iraqi government plane.

Our anticipation was high, but we still had no certain knowledge of what lay ahead. Bettag and I were met at the Baghdad airport by our original handler, Ali Abdul-Rashad, and a driver, which we took as a favorable sign. To our delight they drove us to the newly redecorated Sheraton Hotel.

After two days in Baghdad I was still having trouble getting through to Hamoud, and I was asking myself what the hell was going on here. I had been told to get there quickly, and now nobody was telling us anything.

Reporters were pouring into the city every day, and the mood there had changed dramatically since our first visit. It was almost self-congratulatory. The people had expected to be bombed in early August, and when the bombs didn't come, they thought the Americans had backed down.

My own mood was made no easier by the fact that I had caught a cold, complicated by a strep throat. I was running a fever of between 101 and 104 degrees. I was taking Tylenol and calling around, trying to find erythromycin at any price. I felt really punk.

We were still reporting, getting stories out—in particular, following up on the hostages and those Americans who had taken refuge in the compound of the U.S. embassy. We went to the office of the information minister and did all the obligatory things: you checked in downstairs, then went up one flight and had tea with the deputy minister. And if all the tea leaves fell into place, you would be invited all the way upstairs to meet the minister himself.

It took a while to figure it out, but there were some turf battles going on among the Information Ministry, the Foreign Ministry, the Intelligence Branch, the military—all the Iraqi top brass. We came to believe that in the end, Saddam Hussein made his own decisions, but the single most important character was the information minister. So we began to pay more attention to him.

On our fifth day back in Baghdad, our handler stopped by the hotel around noon and told us, "The information minister wants to see you." That hadn't happened before, and so we went straight to his office. We went through the usual formalities and drank the authentic Persian tea that is as close to kerosene as any liquid I know.

But the end result was somewhat disappointing. He said through a translator, "I can't promise you anything, but I would like you to stay in your hotel for the remainder of the day."

I said, "Fine. We will be happy to do that, Mr. Minister. Thank you very much." And we were out the door.

Back at the hotel, I took my temperature and it was still pushing 104. I was having difficulty talking, and every two or three hours I broke into a cold sweat. I kept popping Tylenol, tried to gargle, napped all I could, and said a little prayer that it not get worse, because this could be the day.

The daylight had begun to fade and so had our hopes. By 9:30 p.m. we had still heard nothing. Tom said, "I think we ought to call somebody." So we called the deputy minister at home, and he said, "Oh, didn't somebody tell you? I don't know that it is going to happen at all, but it certainly isn't going to happen today."

Our hearts dropped a little, but to be honest, I felt relieved. I went to my room and had one of those shivering sweats, and when it subsided, I dropped off to sleep. Shortly after 11:00 p.m. there was a knock at the door and I staggered out of bed, opened it, and saw two uniformed guards standing in the hall. I was in my undershorts and a T-shirt, groggy and unwell and still half asleep.

One of them said in broken English, "Mr. Rather, you are wanted at the Foreign Ministry." I knew that Hamoud was a late-night person, and this had happened before—a knock at the door close to midnight. But this time I said, "I'm not really up to it. If you don't mind, I would prefer to do it in the morning."

He said, "No, no. You must come now. Foreign Ministry. You are expected."

Looking back, one might think I would have brightened right up at that. But I didn't. I really believed we were going to the Foreign Ministry, and I was irritated. I had not shaved since early morning, had not bathed after going through two or three of these cold sweats, felt grubby and intended to stay that way. I didn't bother to put on a fresh shirt, and I almost didn't put on a tie. Unshaven, disheveled, looking and feeling crummy, I slipped into my coat. I figured I was going to see Hamoud and he would understand. The guards kept telling me to hurry. I said I had to get my producer, and the one who spoke English shouted, "No. Nobody else."

We walked outside, and I got into the back of a car, while the two Iraqis sat in front. Both were wearing sidearms, I noticed. The one in the passenger seat also had an AK-47 submachine gun at his feet.

It was now between 11:00 and midnight, and as we drove along, I realized we were not heading in the direction of the Foreign Ministry. I was still fuzzy-headed, but then we started running into roadblocks and checkpoints. Soldiers would stick their heads into the car and look me over. Naturally, I didn't understand a word of what anyone was saying. I finally leaned over and asked the one who had done the talking, "We are headed for the Foreign Ministry, are we not?"

He said nothing. Before I could really zero in on the other possibilities, we circled around and stopped in front of a large building. When they opened the back door, I realized where we were. "Wait a minute, this looks like the Baghdad Palace."

Yet it still did not dawn on me that I was going to meet Saddam Hussein. I already had it firmly in my mind that the interview had been postponed to another day.

As we climbed the steps, I thought, Maybe it's his staff—the last hurdle—and they need to check me out. I was mentally cursing myself for not having shaved or showered or found a fresh shirt. I was trying to soak up every detail—even counting the number of steps that led to the palace, noticing what the door looked like, and then the hallway with the long, plush red carpet.

And then something came back to me that I had said to Hamoud when I made my initial request. I had told him that I fully understood the need for security, that I would go anywhere, anytime, under any conditions to do the interview. I had even said, "If you think it's necessary, blindfold me, put me in the trunk of a car, whatever." I had said any conditions, and I had no squawk coming.

I am no authority on palaces, but this one, I thought, met the old-fashioned image. It had been built in the 1940s for the Iraqi royalty, who had been put on the throne by the British and deposed in the revolution of the late 1950s. It is a world-class palace, large and ostentatious, with high ceilings and marble columns and floors. I *knew* Saddam Hussein was there. I could feel it. The security was extremely heavy. There was an armed guard every fifteen feet. My escorts led me into a combination office and study. One said, "Please, sit down." Almost immediately Saddam Hussein's personal interpreter appeared, although I did not know his identity at the time.

He was obviously well educated; his English was perfect; he had a nice smile, and manners that were almost excessively polite. He said, "Welcome to the palace. You are going to interview the President, and he will be with you in a few moments."

I said, "Well, I'm really pleased to hear that. I'd like to call my producer and camera crew and get them moving right away."

He smiled and said pleasantly, "It will be done with our cameras. We will provide everything you need."

I was stunned. I said, "I respectfully submit, I must have my producer and my crew."

We argued awhile, and he said simply that there was no appeal. In the end, he said, "Mr. Rather, you said you would go anyplace, anytime, and the President is waiting. He is ready for you. You may do the interview now, or you may go."

So I took a deep breath and said, "In that case, we will do it your way. But I must have assurances from the President himself. I say this respectfully. First of all, if you are doing this with your cameras, I must be given every millimeter of videotape from however many cameras you are using. And I want his assurance that I will be allowed to feed every millimeter of it to the United States."

He said, "That is our intention."

I said, "Again, with respect, I would like to hear that from the President."

He said, "Then you may ask him yourself."

With that, we took what I thought was an exceptionally long walk over the red carpets, deep into the palace, to a study that appeared to be small but which was actually quite a bit larger than the study just off the Oval Office at the White House. At one end was Saddam Hussein. Near him, smiling, was the information minister. The first thing that struck me was the number of people in the room whom I had seen under other circumstances. Several of them were Western educated, with fine intellects, but in that room they all literally clicked their heels and tended to bow to Saddam when they addressed him. It was more than a little unsettling. The only one who did not seem scared of him was the information minister.

Saddam had a firm handshake, made eye contact, and through his translator he said, "Welcome."

The everlasting first impression that attached to my mind's eye was not of the desert warrior, but of a man who did not look a great deal different from a successful, well-tailored merchant.

I had noticed quickly that everyone in the room, including Saddam, appeared to have just shaved, showered, or bathed, and had on freshly pressed clothing. Most of them were in civilian dress, and Saddam, whom I had seen on television in nothing but self-designed military uniforms, was wearing a dark blue suit, with a light blue shirt and a striped tie.

I was both looking and feeling as if I had been rode hard and put to bed wet. The information minister made a point of saying to me that I looked tired, and smiled. But my mind was turning now, clicking ahead, trying to put together the serious questions I needed to ask. I was close to being distracted by the idea that they might be trying to trap me. I kept looking around the room, wondering what could go wrong.

As we talked, I said through the interpreter, "Mr. President, I want to get one thing cleared up from the beginning. This is highly unusual to do the interview this way."

His eyebrows seemed to arch, and he said, "What do you mean?"

I said, "Well, to do the interview by myself, with no camera crew."

He said, "But we have camera crews. It has all been arranged."

I said, "I understand that, and I want to do this interview. I consider it important, and I think it can contribute quite a bit to understanding on all sides. But I can't do it unless I have your word that I get every inch of tape from all the cameras."

He answered, "You have my word."

I didn't think about it then, but I had the word of a man who had just gobbled up a neighboring small Arab country, who had gassed undefended villages and executed some of his closest friends. He had been called a madman and compared to Hitler, and even as we talked, he was holding hostage the citizens of a dozen other countries. I looked at my watch and thought again about what I would ask the man who, at that moment, was the villain of the world.

We talked mostly about why Saddam had invaded Kuwait, what he intended to do now (less than a month after the invasion), how he thought things might play out, and what he wanted U.S. leaders and the American people to know.

That night in Baghdad, on-camera and off, Saddam emphasized that he would not withdraw from Kuwait, that he would go to war with the United States if necessary, that he was "not bluffing." And he wanted President Bush and the American people to know that. He warned of much bloodshed and many U.S. casualties. Throughout the interview he never took his eyes off me. He answered every question slowly and deliberately.

The only time I thought I saw Saddam's eyes flicker, even for a minute, was when I asked him how he answered criticisms that he and his regime were similar to Hitler's leadership of Nazi Germany. Sad-

The Persian Gulf: This interview with Saddam Hussein (right) was filmed by Iraqi technicians, then photographed from a television transmission, which accounts for its poor quality.

dam didn't like the question. (He wasn't supposed to.) And his main man gave me a look as if to say, "I can't believe you asked him that." In Iraq nobody asks Saddam tough questions. Certainly not in public, and for sure not on television.

Saddam answered with a stare and a voice thrown deeper, saying that anybody who suggested that he was anything like Hitler, or that what he had done was similar to Nazi Germany's conquest of weaker neighbors in the 1930s, just didn't understand. Didn't understand him, Iraq, or the region.

One of his themes throughout the interview was that Americans, and President Bush in particular, were "ignorant" about his history and the history of Iraq and of all the Middle East. He repeatedly criticized what he said was an "insulting and dangerous" lack of knowledge about Iraqi character and culture.

As he went through this, I silently reminded myself that this was coming from a man who had seldom traveled out of Iraq, whose only in-person brush with the West were two short trips to Paris.

"America is big and strong," he said repeatedly, "but you cannot take the blood," meaning Americans would not support a war with heavy casualties. "America," he said, "has no staying power."

I came away more convinced than ever that there would be a war, that Saddam's ignorance—his lack of understanding of the United States—made war inevitable. I could see that America's role in the Vietnam War was one very big factor in Saddam's belief that Americans couldn't "take the blood" and had "no staying power." Several times off-camera I suggested that Vietnam had, in fact, demonstrated just the opposite—had demonstrated the United States' ability to stick with a war for a decade despite terrible casualties. This was dismissed by Saddam.

But more important than Vietnam in his miscalculations, I believe, was Lebanon. In 1983 President Reagan had responded to the terrorist attack on the marine barracks (in which 241 American servicemen were killed) by immediately withdrawing all American troops from the peacekeeping mission. Whether Saddam had anything to do with the bombing or not, he took away an important lesson from the attack: that the United States would run from a tough fight. It was the wrong lesson, but he took it. Vietnam plus Lebanon had led Saddam Hussein to the mother of all miscalculations.

OUTTAKE

A SURPRISINGLY underreported story of the Persian Gulf War involved an F-15 fighter wing whose very presence may have kept Saddam Hussein from moving on Saudi Arabia.

This was the chronology: The Iraqi forces whipped across the border into Kuwait on the second of August. My crew and I arrived in the region shortly afterward, even as the *Independence* carrier battle group was speeding toward the Gulf.

We were tipped off by David Martin, our Pentagon correspondent, that a wing of F-15s was being moved. A lot has been said about reporters fuzzing the line on national security. David isn't one of them. He told us all he could on our overseas calls, but much less than he knew.

"I'm going to work on some people here," he said. "You work that end. Get to this F-15 wing. Nobody has done them. The commanding officer is Colonel John McBroom. And you need to know: He thinks Dan Rather is a left-wing, antimilitary pinko."

What else was new. Even though, during the Korean War, I volunteered for the marines, I am somehow labeled an antimilitary agitator. I believe the label was first applied when I reported what I saw in Vietnam, and the label adhered even more firmly when I asked President Nixon questions about Watergate. What the latter had to do with the nation's defense isn't clear, but in the early '70s there were still disciples of Joe McCarthy who thought if you could spell Stolichnaya, you were a communist dupe, at the least.

Martin got in touch with Pete Williams at the Pentagon and through him to Dick Cheney, the Secretary of Defense. They convinced Colonel McBroom to let me interview him. They did it, I believe, by saying, "Look, we want to see those F-15s on television—all over television. We want them to look big and dangerous to the Iraqis, to the Saudis, to the Soviets, and, yes, to the American public. Rather is there. He will build a whole broadcast around it—'This is the *CBS Evening News,* tonight with the First Tactical Fighter Wing in Dhahran, Saudi Arabia. . . .' "

I took an instant liking to McBroom. He was silver-haired, jut-jawed, with unblinking blue eyes. He was everything you would expect a warrior to be—smart, tough, prepared to put his own life on the line. He had checked around and heard that, no, I was not the "wrong kind of reporter" in Vietnam, and his attitude changed. When we finished the interview, he waved off an invitation to review the tape. He said, "I'll tell you something. I didn't want to do this. Didn't think I would. But you're welcome back here at any time."

The F-15 is the basic fighter-bomber of the U.S. Air Force and the standard the world over. There were only twenty-four planes on the ground, but moving those F-15s was a critical decision. In those early days of August we had a good deal of air power at sea around the Middle East, but not much of it actually in the Persian Gulf. And carrier-based planes were limited in range. The F-15s had left Langley, Virginia, on the seventh of August and had flown straight through to Dhahran. They refueled in the air. The moment they touched down, the price to Saddam Hussein of taking the next step soared.

When I first saw them on the ground, they were out in the open, with little protective cover. Airfields are vulnerable until you move in the troops with such weapons as the Patriot missiles. Land-based aircraft are never left exposed and in the open, a lesson we learned at Pearl Harbor. But these were. There were not even decent antiaircraft batteries available, and McBroom knew it. After one visit I knew it.

Yet their arrival was a tremendous lift to the Saudi spirit and a downer for the Iraqis. If Saddam had kept rolling through Kuwait, had immediately sent his tanks down the Persian Gulf highway and moved on the Saudi oil fields, he probably could have succeeded. But Iraq had hesitated just long enough for the F-15s to slip in. Historians may long debate whether Saddam ever intended to roll into Saudi Arabia. I was one person who believed he did. He still had time to make a Pattonesque run, but by the time he checked his hole card, the window had closed. The 82nd Airborne was soon on the scene in force.

You can make the case that this was the first war decided almost entirely by air power. And the point of the spear was one bold and uncelebrated wing of F-15s.

It is one of the eternal truths: Wars are often won not by the armies you have, but by the armies your enemy thinks you have.

SIX
Somalia: The Politics of Hunger

I CAN see her face now, can sketch every detail in my mind: the eyes deep and hollow as ashtrays, the cheeks so sunken you appear to be looking directly into a skull. It is the face of a small girl. It is the face of Somalia, of every parched and barren land where life was once, and may be again, worth less than a bowl of rice infested with flies.

Any reporter who hangs around long enough will cover them all: famine, flood, war, and death—not quite the four horsemen of the Apocalypse, but close enough. For sheer horror and helplessness, famine rarely ranks less than a tie for first.

For years I had been struck, as had others around me, by the harrowing stories of starving masses in Africa—in the Sudan, in Ethiopia, in Somalia. Somalia was arguably the worst, but even the thought of comparing misery on such a scale is pointless.

From time to time CBS made an effort to bring this story to the attention of our viewers. But no matter what we did, none of us were ever satisfied with the result.

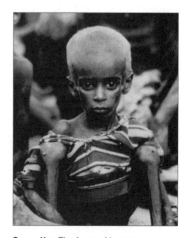

Somalia: The faces of hunger

We moaned about the dilemma of so many stories to cover, so little time and so few resources. This is the endless, ageless problem of journalism. You cannot focus on every story.

In 1992, an election year, most of our resources, psychic and otherwise, were committed to the presidential campaign. Still, a few of us, obsessed with the idea of the African famine, promised ourselves that before the year ended, we would make an all-out effort to bring home the story.

In August, Dr. Bob Arnot went to Somalia for *CBS Morning News*, and Ed Bradley went for *60 Minutes*. The numbers of those dying had been large for a very long time, but there was always someone around to say, "Listen, it's Africa. Starving children have been around since biblical times. There are no ratings for it. No audience."

Arnot, a medical doctor, and Bradley came back with stories that pierced the heart. I was determined now to make the trip. Somalia saddened and outraged me.

I knew that Somalia should have been able to feed itself. The shortage of food, the masses of starving people—these were conditions created by gangsters. This was war between clans, and people were being denied food as a form of terrorism.

Life in rural Somalia was little different today than it was in the fifth century before Christ. Nomads had crossed and recrossed the land. A hundred generations had survived drought and famine, but nothing had prepared the Somalis for modern civil war.

Colonialism had come to Somalia in the late nineteenth century, when Britain took the northern third and Italy the south. Independence was declared in 1960, and the clans quickly seized power. Into the 1980s the United States and the Soviet Union armed the different factions to the teeth, battling for control of the region and its access to the Indian Ocean and the Persian Gulf. When the superpowers pulled out, the warlords kept their arsenals. Food to them was what whiskey was to Al Capone. The clans that controlled the two big ports, Mogadishu and Kismayu, took a 15 percent rake-off on whatever passed through them.

In November 1992 Bill Clinton won the election, and I began doing my homework, not just on Somalia but on the other parts of Africa threatened by famine. It appeared that the earliest I could get to Somalia would be late February or March, after the inauguration.

Then in mid-November, I began to pick up the muffled drums of the Pentagon. What I heard was that the United States might just "do something" in either Bosnia or Somalia.

In the waning weeks of his presidency, Bush and his team were criticized for indecision, confusion, and a general lack of leadership on Bosnia and Somalia. Both were going from bad to worse, but Bosnia posed a risk of longer term. I called a flag-rank officer I had known in Vietnam, who knew the area well. "Frankly," he said, "I don't know if they are going to do either one, but if they do, it will be Somalia. Why? Because it's a 'three-fer': The U.S. military are looking for a role in the postcommunist world to justify their budget; Somalia is doable, particularly if they get in quickly and out quickly; and our presence there would put the lie to the smear that America doesn't care about black Africans and about Muslims."

Logic told me that if the troops were going to Somalia, they would start moving before Christmas. It would be pretty hard for Americans to argue with a humanitarian mission to save starving children during Christmas. We had meetings at CBS twice a day for about ten days, and finally I said, "If we're going, let's go early and in strength, and if I'm wrong, you can put pins under my fingernails."

We geared up to go and attacked our first problem: getting there. Somalia had no airline service. You flew to Nairobi, Kenya, chartered a plane, and hired the best bush pilot around. There was no U.S. embassy in Somalia, no police force, no food you could depend on, no water, no sewage system worth the name. In short, there was no government. And everybody had a gun.

CBS made discreet inquiries to the State Department about what assistance we might expect if we sent a crew to Somalia. A CBS executive gave me their answer: "They say don't go. They say you're crazy if you do. You need to understand, there are people who will kill you for the sport of it. There are, of course, many decent Somalis, but they are helpless. Don't expect any help from the U.S. government."

Our plan was to get in, survive, and wait for the American ground forces to arrive. We started making arrangements before President Bush announced that the United States would join the United Nations peacekeeping force in Somalia. Operation Restore Hope would call upon 28,000 U.S. troops to provide an armed escort for the safe delivery of food to the towns and countryside.

was a small risk, but still a risk. The army didn't send us a telegram saying they would go. There was no guarantee. We had made a commitment to fly halfway around the world on a hunch and some information from our Pentagon correspondent, David Martin, who last made a mistake sometime around Caesar's Gallic campaign.

The country was absolutely disease-ridden. So we had to be totally self-contained. We provided our own food, water, medical supplies, and protection. You handpick a crew for an assignment of this kind, people who can do several jobs and do them under pressure.

In Nairobi, we hired our pilot, a daredevil who had to fly us into an airport that wasn't open. The Mogadishu airport lies hard by the sea. It was the largest airport in the country, but hadn't operated in years. Private planes attempting to land nearly always drew sporadic gunfire.

Bush pilots didn't come cheap. The trick was not to barter with them on the money, but to find one who was good and trustworthy and fearless. Since the airport wasn't operating, our pilot had to carry his own drums of aviation fuel in the cabin of the airplane so he could refuel and fly out.

We had to have additional gasoline of our own for the vehicles we would be renting. When we boarded, we were literally sitting among the cans of fuel. There were twelve of us in the original contingent, with ten to follow. Four had gone ahead to Mogadishu, including Allen Pizzey, one of our most experienced and toughest correspondents. The advance party would set up some kind of camp and at least try to figure out a way to get us from the airport to the interior of the city.

There was no place to stay in Mogadishu, so far as we knew, and we were prepared to sleep outdoors on the ground. We had sleeping bags and a few personal articles, but mostly I carried lots of U.S. currency—in denominations up to $1000 bills—and some gold coins. My experience has been that while the dollar is still almighty in many remote places, when you absolutely, positively have to pay for what you can't do without, gold is better. From the most brutal warlord to the smallest street urchin, everyone knows gold.

We took off for Mogadishu on December 4, 1992, on a billowing, cloudy day. The pilot immediately told us the air was rough and we might not get in. "What I'll try to do," he said over the wind and the hum of the propellers, "is fly halfway, and at that point if the weather doesn't look any better, we'll turn around and go back to Nairobi."

Now, this was a pilot right out of an aerial circus. If he didn't want to fly, my reaction was that I better check my hole cards. The clock was running, the competition couldn't be far behind, and CBS had a heavy bet down on this whole road show.

At the halfway point in our flight the pilot said the weather wasn't getting any better. By now the gasoline drums were bouncing around, and none of us were feeling too frisky. I've flown to a lot of desolate places and in hairy situations, but I don't like flying in what amounts to a big egg filled with gasoline. My stomach was queasy.

I said, "Look, you're the pilot. If we have to turn back, we turn back. But it's pretty important that we go on if we can."

He said, "How important is it?"

I slapped down a thousand-dollar bill on the instrument panel. The accountants at CBS may or may not be pleased with my negotiating style, but now and then you need to make a big statement. I'm not certain how one would list this kind of bonus, but I prefer to call it incentive money. Americans believe in the incentive system.

I told the pilot, "We want to get in there badly enough that if we can land, you'll get another one just like it."

Soon we had broken through the cloud cover and saw below us the beautiful Indian Ocean. Then on the coast we saw the airport itself. Hot damn, we're here, I said to myself.

As we started a long descent to the airstrip, the pilot suddenly veered off and jerked the plane straight up and off to the right. Gasoline drums rattled around. I shouted, "What the hell is going on here?" The pilot replied with one word: "Gunfire."

And it was. Then I heard it, fairly steady firepower, too. We learned later that a small band of Pakistani troops under the U.N. flag were trying to hold the airport and were under constant harassment by one or more of the clans. At that time, they actually controlled very little of the field, and could not provide a secure landing for small aircraft.

But I give the Pakistanis credit. They were brave men, very disciplined. The gunmen they had ousted just two months ago had moved back only fifty feet or so. Half a mile away semistarving refugees subsisted on the charity of a small aid agency. They had to be wet-fed—given food already cooked—so it couldn't be looted. Relief officials were hoping the U.S. marines could quickly take control of the main road leading to the remote districts where thousands of starving people were clinging to life.

The bandits wanted to keep the airport closed—and reinforcements out—so they could run their food-extortion machine.

At that moment I was, to put it mildly, ambivalent about what to do next. The pilot was worried, quite properly, about how much fuel he had. Even if we landed safely, he had to fly out of there in bad weather. Yes, he did this for a living. He knew Mogadishu was likely to get busy, and he wanted more of our business. Still, I was worried that he might not try to put the plane down.

"You understand," he said, "that if one bullet hits this aircraft in the right place, we're a ball of flame."

Now that he put it so delicately, I shrank a bit from my gung-ho, plant-the-flag mentality. I mean, as we circled the airport, I thought about Jeannie, my children, and about the people flying with me. They had families, too. We were not there to get ourselves killed. One is acutely aware at such moments that life is not a movie.

But this was the job. We had come so far, and now we were so close. Yet what if we did get in? Would we be under fire? Could we get unloaded? Could the pilot take off again?

I was trying to make sense of this when the pilot said casually, "It seems to have settled down." This was daytime, and the shots were sporadic. The firefights might go on all night. The pilot looked around to see if there were any mortars shelling the strip, and he saw none. To my surprise he said, "We'll try it one more time."

He circled his way around, got very low, skimmed just over the beach and nearly brushed the sand dunes, and brought us in. There was no control tower, but the Pakistanis had radios and he made contact with them on his last approach. The Pakistanis asked what nationality we were. The pilot told them, and they said to come on in. There were a few scattered shots in the distance as we touched down, and light applause broke out inside the plane.

We were not surprised to see racing toward us, across the tarmac, what were known as technicals—ancient and badly battered pickup trucks, on occasion a half-wrecked Toyota. They had guns mounted behind the cab. These were lightly armored, Mad Max kind of vehicles of a very low grade. The backs of the pickups were packed with guys carrying M-16 rifles, Russian Kalashnikovs, and all kinds of small arms. Some of the gunmen wore crisscrossed bandoliers, looking like a Somali version of those old sepia photos of Pancho Villa.

So the reasonable question was what were their intentions. In previous weeks several airplanes owned by relief agencies had been stripped, their radios, seats, and tires taken—virtually anything that could be torn loose and carried off. Our pilot was armed, but he would be no match for this crowd.

The plane came to a stop, and we opened the door not knowing what to expect. It turned out that this small convoy that greeted us was a mixture. A couple of the trucks contained thugs who were looking to see what the plane had that was worth stealing. A couple had been hired by a relief agency, and Allen Pizzey had arranged with them to send in these trucks in the hope of getting us off the plane, off the tarmac, and into town.

From the plane, I had spotted a telltale grapefruit bag in one of the trucks—used for shipping CBS News film and videotape. So I figured that at least one of the vehicles was our own, or had just been stolen from us. Almost from the moment we swung open the door and started down the ladder, a relief-agency official was calling to us. "Get all your people and all your stuff off as fast as you can," he yelled. "Did you bring any gasoline?"

I said yes. Quickly, and under cover, four trucks—two of ours and two from the relief agency—formed a cordon around the plane, and we unloaded our equipment, supplies, and people. The pilot kept the plane running, got right out, and immediately went to the off wing and started pouring fuel into his tanks.

We hadn't gotten all of our supplies off the plane when one of the relief men, an Australian, gave me the signal to stop. "We can't tarry here," he said. "We have to get the hell out." The plan was to drive quickly away from the plane while the pilot took off, then fall back to the abandoned airline terminal to gather ourselves for running the gauntlet from the airport to downtown Mogadishu.

We reached the terminal, and at that point, I had a bright idea. I turned to Al Berman, senior producer of the *Evening News* and our commander in the field, and said, "You know, we've got a chance to make tonight's newscast if I can do the anchor stuff right here and we can get it on the airplane before he leaves."

So one of the technicals raced back out to the runway, and our crew asked the pilot, "Can you give us eight or ten minutes?" He said, "I can't give you a damned thing, but it will take me that long to get all the gasoline in the tanks. When I get them filled, I'm gone."

Three members of the crew were already setting up their small and

highly portable equipment. To the uninitiated, it looked like the hardware for an extraterrestrial movie. But the engineers understand every fuse and wire and knob. You give them an hour, and they literally give you the world. They send pictures up to a satellite, and another satellite back in New York or London reaches up and pulls those pictures in. I have no idea how that happens. They simply reach for the stars.

Technicals—battered old pickups with armed Somalis—were a threat to all peacekeeping forces in Somalia.

I quickly had the crew put a camera on me, and I ad-libbed an opening. We had Bob Schieffer in the studio in New York to do the newscast if everything went wrong. If we got anything on the air, it would be a miracle.

This was the opening:

This is the *CBS Evening News*. Dan Rather reporting tonight from Mogadishu, Somalia. Good evening.

This is your quintessential hellhole. There is no government, no police, only anarchy and chaos, danger and death. We are at the airport. Just arrived here a few minutes ago. There was a firefight at the end of the runway as our plane came in. Early reports: Pakistani troops engaged in a firefight with one of a kind of Mad Max vehicle with a machine gun strapped to its side that the bandits and thugs and gang leaders in this part of the world specialize in sending to test perimeter defenses. The Pakistanis' main role has been to keep this airport open and under United Nations control.

About one thousand people die every twenty-four hours here from gunfire, disease, starvation. One person will die roughly every two, two and a half minutes while this broadcast is on the air.

This is the kind of situation the Marines, followed by the U.S. Army, will be coming into.

For the official version of what President Bush is planning, we go to our Defense Department and correspondent David Martin.

It worked. In seven and a half minutes that videotape was back on the airplane and bound for Nairobi. In a Nairobi hotel we had what amounted to a miniature television-transmitting station. The staff there sent the tape off to New York, and that night's *CBS Evening News* had a broadcast anchored from Mogadishu.

Ours is a small planet, where most people measure their lives in little victories and defeats. We were in Somalia because this was an important story to tell, but our morale required a little victory, and as insiders, we cheered.

We climbed onto our trucks and began taking back roads into Mogadishu. The main street was sealed off with roadblocks. We had not gone very far when our nostrils picked up a hellish stench, and off to one side, as far as the eye could see, there were shallow graves—mostly of people who had starved, some who had been shot. The smell of human decay was worse than I thought, or remembered.

The trip was a short one. The great majority of the people we saw were women and children, living out in the open, with no water, no sewage, many of them totally naked. This was a Muslim country, and to view even a woman's bare arm or leg was once uncommon. They were skeletal, the walking dead—at least, the ones who were walking. Our cameraman, Kurt Hoeffler, videotaped it all.

I couldn't pull my eyes away from the women and children and the shallow graves. It was around two in the afternoon, and the clouds overhead indicated that we would have a sprinkle of rain later. The day was hot, humid, and rancid, and all around us was this indescribable raw sewage mixed with death.

The Somalis who had the energy looked at us as if we were the advance column of the army of deliverance. Some, we learned later, thought we were, and raised a hand or uttered a timid cheer.

We had tense moments at several roadblocks and talked and bluffed our way past them. Even as the truck was moving, the Somalis were reaching in, hands darting, trying to steal your sunglasses or whatever. If you slapped their hands away, you had to do it with a flick.

These were people with itchy fingers. Partly by keeping the truck rolling, partly with chatter, partly with threats and payoffs, our friend from the relief agency led us to where Allen Pizzey was.

Here we fell into a huge break, based mostly on the resourcefulness of Andy Clarke, a producer who had been brought in from the London bureau. Clarke was one of Pizzey's group who had flown in early and scouted the landscape. He had talked to several people, and I suppose a few dollars changed hands, which led him to a former Egyptian diplomat who owned what was left of a very small villa in Mogadishu, with a two-story stucco house and a patch of yard enclosed behind a shell-battered stucco wall. Part of the wall had been knocked down, and elsewhere there were holes the size of satellite dishes. There was a makeshift generator, a water well, and a septic tank.

But finding Mr. Egypt was a coup. He was exactly what we needed now. He was worldly, an intellectual, and not averse to making a dollar. He was curious about everything, especially television. Clarke talked him into letting us come in and set up our equipment in his yard. While the wall and gate didn't provide any real protection, it was better than leaving equipment in the open.

Mr. Egypt had a few connections with the clans and a lot of connections with the street people. If we needed dependable runners, our man could find them—none more than nine years old perhaps, but reliable. If we needed to hire guns—euphemistically called security guards—he knew where to find them. The wage scale was interesting. It went up hourly.

Mr. Egypt knew all about these things and was willing to let us take over his home—for a fee, of course. Andy set up a perimeter and an inner sanctum, where only Americans could go, to keep our equipment from getting ripped off.

When Andy asked our host if he would be willing to set up any kind of eating facility, he said yes, he could do that. He had a woman who baked bread, the highlight of each meal, and he ran a twenty-four-hour kitchen. The house had two large rooms on the first floor and two smaller rooms upstairs. We basically turned the house into a coed dormitory. Sleeping was on the floor.

Mr. Egypt moved into the maid's quarters—I don't know what happened to the maid. The key to our relationship with Mr. Egypt and his crew was what courtesies our lads could provide in return.

There was no electricity in Mogadishu, and thus no telephone service, but our people had brought along self-contained telephones. Since there was no government, and no laws, no permission was needed to set up a small dish in the backyard and attach it to one of their electronic gadgets, then search until they found a satellite. Bingo. We had mobile phones.

There were still just a dozen of us, but in two days we had created an infrastructure that functioned like a small town. As our host's curiosity about our equipment grew, I sensed a deal in the making. I understood that it had been a very long time since he had talked to his dear mother in Egypt. I made a proposal: "What if we give you the phone in our off-hours? Here's the area code for Cairo. Be my guest."

From that moment on, Mr. Egypt was bonded with CBS, which led to unexpected benefits. He had weapons of his own, which he did not advertise, to protect his home and hearth. Al Berman had served in the National Guard, and he checked out and cleaned the weapons. Then we talked about what we would do if an effort was made to storm the compound. Talking about doling out bullets can be sobering, but there is something reassuring about contingency plans, especially when you don't need them.

I was able to close the broadcast that first night—the fourth of December—with a satellite feed from our new headquarters. I described the gunfire, the stench of death that was everywhere.

Out in the Indian Ocean, several miles offshore, waited the marine amphibious vessel the U.S.S. *Juneau*. CBS had correspondent Bob Simon on board, and from the deck he reported that they could see the lights of Mogadishu. A marine commander told Simon they didn't expect any opposition when they landed, but if anyone challenged the marines, "they will be killed." The strategy was to smile and carry a big stick; to arrive on shore with such an overwhelming show of force that any potential resistance would evaporate into the desert air.

Tens of thousands of leaflets would be dropped in the next day or two, advising the Somalis that the marines were there to help, to feed, to care for the sick and starving. Success would be judged, the commander said, by shots not fired, by casualties not taken.

On Monday, December 7, I filed the following report on radio for CBS News:

"I do not intend to tell you today about millions of starving people. I do intend to tell you about *two*. West of Mogadishu there is a woman and her child. They are starving. They are waiting, bravely, staging a battle for time.

"They have heard that the Yanks are coming, coming over here. Incredible, unbelievable, but true, they are told. This mother and child hope the Americans hurry. They are Muslim. They pray to their God that the Americans come soon. Probably Wednesday. Perhaps here, they are told, where they are . . . but it may be later.

"The mother's eyes respond: Later, for *this* child, my child, later may be too late. The child is a girl . . . Harita Mohammed. One of two living children. Four of her children died in her arms—disease and lack of food. Now, this child is dying, little Harita, seven years old, weight about eighteen pounds.

"Mother and child are in a refugee camp. There is a feeding area nearby. They are too weak to get to the area and it is too dangerous for anyone to take them. The feeding area itself is cut off, isolated. Warlords and their gangsters decreed this. They kill, rob, intimidate, extort. There is no law in Mogadishu. For Harita Mohammed and her mother, no mercy.

"The message from Mogadishu is: Hurry! For Harita and her mother, it may already be too late.

"Soon, our own sons and daughters, many of America's best, will come pouring into this hellhole of a country. When someone, anyone, asks you why, tell them . . . to save the children."

THE marines landed on Wednesday, December 9, 1992, and the situation was well in hand—no resistance, so far everything going according to plan. I was broadcasting live from atop the terminal building at Mogadishu airport.

The navy SEALS (Sea, Air, and Land Service) had swept ashore first, in the predawn dark, to clear the way for the marines, to make sure no mines were in the water or on the beach. And yes, the television cameras were there—sort of Hollywoodish, almost cartoonish. And if viewers at home were saying, "Well, this looks silly," in some ways they were surely correct. But the cameras were there by invitation of those behind the task force. And as inappropriate as it may seem for an assault under cover of darkness, few TV cameras can operate without lights.

I sympathized with the surprise and consternation of the SEALS. They had the look of cat burglars pinned in a searchlight. If there had been any resistance, this would have been a setting for tragedy. But the landing was well scripted and nothing tragic happened.

For the U.S. military it was a deadly serious business. No one knew how grim it might get. Hard behind the SEALS, marine reconnaissance units came ashore. They skidded onto the beach in their rubber boats, to be greeted by the Pakistani forces in the blue berets of the United Nations. Within two hours the entire marine battalion would land in the dark to secure the airfield and the port. The helicopters would flutter in at first light.

The airport was to be the linchpin of the entire operation, and the marines' first job would be to get it ready to handle a steady stream of military transports. The first landed around noon the next day, carrying the personnel and some of the equipment needed to ready the

U.S. marines land in Mogadishu's predawn darkness, only to have camera crews light their way ashore.

airport for a twenty-four-hour-a-day air-cargo operation. For now, the airport operated only in daylight and could handle only two transports at a time.

Planes alone could never bring in all the equipment that would be needed. Most of it would come on the cargo ships, waiting offshore. But the port was big enough to handle only one at a time.

On Thursday the first combat troops from the United States, the marines from Camp Pendleton, started arriving in Mogadishu and began moving into the interior. The best estimate was that another week would pass before significant quantities of food would be delivered to the starving. You tried not to think about how many more thousands would die in the meantime.

U.S. officials had stressed over and over again that Operation Restore Hope was a humanitarian mission, with the primary aim of feeding the hungry. But that is not all that it was. The first task, by necessity, had to be to establish some level of law and order in a place that would make the old Wild West look tame. Guns were simply everywhere. Merchants had their own militias. Even car-rental agencies included a gunman in the deal. This was such a way of life here that two Somalis could argue for fifteen minutes, pointing guns at each other, and not come close to pulling the trigger. Once, when a CBS cameraman was spotted taking pictures, a Somali put a gun to the back of his head. The Somali backed off when our gunman threatened to shoot first.

The technicals used by the humanitarian agencies were kept off the streets for the first forty-eight hours after the marines landed, in an effort to "prevent misunderstandings." A major problem was that the young men who rode the technicals didn't have any other way to make a living, and they needed the money to support a drug habit that left them dangerous and unpredictable. The drug they use, called khat, is chewed. It had been a part of the social fabric there for years, but the civil wars turned teenagers into chronic khat abusers. If a kid high on khat were killed by a nervous marine, there would be a distinct danger that such an incident could spark a vendetta by the young man's clan, with every foreigner considered a legitimate target.

You do not settle into a routine on such stories, in such places. You start over every day. Sometimes you follow the blood.

After the marines came ashore, I took a crew to a town even more violent than Mogadishu. It was at the southern corner of the triangle of death, where the suffering was the worst. No one had heard much about it because journalists seldom traveled there. The town was Kismayu, the second largest in Somalia. Almost no relief shipments were allowed in by the local gunmen. A UNICEF plane had been robbed at gunpoint, the pilot and crew relieved of their valuables.

Kismayu's top clan boss was Colonel Omar Gess, and word had reached us that he was annoyed because he had not been consulted about the American military intervention. He suspected that the United States, and certainly the United Nations, were plotting once again to bring Somalia under foreign rule.

"I will never accept to be colonized again," he told me on-camera. "We believe that is not the solution. We will fight anybody who wants to colonize us. We want to be independent and free."

The colonel gave us a tour of Kismayu's port, built with American aid in the 1960s. Shiploads of cigarettes, diesel fuel, and sugar managed to pass through, but no food-relief ships had docked for the last two months. The colonel said that was not his fault.

"I want to understand," I said. "You have not kept food out of this port?"

"Never," said Gess. "Never have done it."

"And you didn't loot ships in this port?"

"We never looted ships," said Gess, "and we never prohibited ships to anchor here in our port, and we don't know why it was this propaganda was made by some people."

I noticed that the colonel's motorcade featured a truck topped with a rocket launcher from an old Soviet MiG-23, a relic of Somalia's past as a pawn in the cold war.

Later he showed me some khat from Kenya, and I asked him if he chewed any. "Sometimes," he said, "when we are—when we want to work a lot of time." He added that it was not illegal, partly because nothing was illegal in a land where no laws existed.

On the second day of Operation Restore Hope, nearly a week after CBS had begun its coverage, the first shooting casualties were reported. The first blood had been shed, and a few assumptions were changing. The conventional wisdom had been that the Americans and Europeans would be welcome at first, that the trouble would start later. Later began on day two of the operation.

We were home again in January 1993, when Bill Clinton was inaugurated as President. The United States had sent 28,000 troops to the Horn of Africa, and by June, Clinton had brought home all but 4000, leaving some 1300 of these as a rapid deployment unit. The U.N. was now paying the bills, providing most of the soldiers, and shedding most of the blood.

By then the hunger among Somalis had lessened, and the U.N. estimated that hundreds of thousands of lives had been saved. But it was still a country without a government, without laws, without structure.

In October, U.S. soldiers were pinned down for nine hours, and eighteen died in an attempt to rescue a trapped Pakistani unit. It was a fraction of the number killed in Beirut or in the Persian Gulf, fewer than in the invasions of Grenada or Panama. Yet they died during what had been hailed as a humanitarian cause, and Americans were angry and bitter.

We fed the children and brought home our troops, eighteen of them in coffins. The armed clans still roam a land where anything worth stealing has to be brought in from the outside.

After not many months had passed, there were few pictures on television of people starving in Africa and few stories in the newspapers and magazines. The politicians still argued about who deserved the blame for which decision, but the rest of the country had moved on to other issues, other problems, other pictures.

OUTTAKE

THE news on August 10, 1993, was exactly the kind I hate to hear. The deaths of American soldiers on foreign soil are never easy to report, but in this case, the circumstances were especially sad.

These four young Americans—Sergeant Christopher Hilgert, Sergeant Ronald N. Richerson, Specialist Keith Pearson, and Specialist Mark Gutting—were killed by a command-detonated mine near the Mogadishu airport. "Command-detonated" means that the mine was deliberately set. Someone waited in ambush until the soldiers' vehicle passed over the prepositioned mine. Then that someone set off the mine. And the ambushers opened fire on the other vehicles in the convoy. Anyone who was in Vietnam recognizes this as a classic convoy ambush.

These were soldiers who'd been sent to help—to save children—on a humanitarian mission. Yet they had died, evidently at the hands of the neighbors of the people they'd been sent to save. It made me sick to think about it.

And the other circumstances of the mission in Somalia were by this time no more encouraging. After a bold start and the best of intentions the Somalia rescue mission had begun to seem like America's forgotten war. As Operation Restore Hope was expanded to include "nation building" and other assignments (for which I believe the military of any nation will always be unsuited), public interest seemed to decline.

Part of the lack of interest was easily understood. When I talked to Americans who weren't in the news business, they described a "blizzard" of news—it seemed as though there were too many important stories coming at them all at the same time, and often from corners of the world their geography classes had forgotten to teach. Grabbing hold of a story, digesting it, and learning more—this seemed almost impossible in the ceaseless flow of news and information.

But I believe the roots of the public's lack of awareness about the mission in Somalia lay elsewhere. We journalists were at fault. We'd come over in strength just before the marine landing and stayed in strength a few weeks. But by this time our resources had dwindled. CBS always had a camera crew in Mogadishu, but there were several nervous days when we didn't have a correspondent in Somalia. A correspondent hungry for airtime makes an effective advocate for coverage of any story, and the good ones look for ways to make each story different. Without a correspondent our ability to pitch a story in the newsroom was thus challenged. Our ability to grab the attention of the audience was even more severely challenged.

The debate was beginning to be heard that American television had "gotten us into Somalia"—a debate whose utter wrongness didn't seem to preclude its getting rewritten every couple of weeks on the op-ed pages of most newspapers in the country. They said our pictures so disturbed the American people that intervention was necessary. I pointed out that much worse pictures from Bosnia had never inspired such a strong reaction. The American people don't make the call to arms lightly; they need more than a picture to send their sons and daughters to fight and die.

I knew that the American men and women in harm's way in Somalia needed to feel that the folks back home knew and cared about what was going on—not just when things were going badly, but all the time. Otherwise, why should they be there?

So on August 10, 1993, I was honestly upset to learn of these four young Americans making the ultimate sacrifice far from home.

The death of Fred Woodruff, a U.S. intelligence operative, in the Republic of Georgia the same day only compounded my sadness. And so, with only a few minutes to airtime, I prepared a radio essay paying tribute to the five Americans who had died.

> One does not need to know the details to know this: All five of these men were Americans far from home, in lonely places, doing lonely duty, dangerous missions in dangerous places. All five were in the service of their country, in the service of their fellow Americans.
>
> This we do know: They died heroes. And attention needs to be paid.
>
> There was a time not long ago when heroes abounded in this country. Now there are few, a precious few. Why and how this came to be is an important question. But this we do know, and have been reminded in recent hours: There are, still are, Americans who believe in the fundamental American dream, in the American ideal—and are willing to fight for it, and die for it.

I wouldn't have minded a little extra time to polish my thoughts, but the radio microphone never blinks either, and the deadline was upon me. I was glad at least that I'd spoken up, recognized the service and the sacrifice these men had made.

But a short time later I had the all too rare opportunity to make my point again, once it had simmered and stewed a little. A listener in California wrote to say that while he was sorry these men had died, and was sure they were good people deserving of some kind of tribute, the word hero was so overused as to be nearly meaningless these days. These soldiers had only been doing their duty, acting on orders—nothing heroic in that, said the listener. Next time, he suggested, I ought to use another word.

I have to admit I am always pleased by this kind of letter. It indicates that the writer has really listened and thought about my reporting, and respects my intelligence enough—and knows I'll respect his or hers—to offer specific, constructive criticisms. That this criticism centered on word choice also pleased me: Eric Sevareid used to get letters from listeners praising the beauty of his writing. I'll bet not five other electronic journalists in history have gotten many letters like that; I certainly don't. But this letter, addressed to me not just as a reporter but as a writer, was as close as I'm likely to get most days.

So I wrote back:

> Dear Sir:
>
> Thank you for taking the time to share your kind words and provocative thoughts. While it's clear that some words like "hero" risk being cheapened through overuse, I cannot agree with you that the Americans I named don't fit that term.
>
> Anyone who was in Somalia before the Marines landed in December can tell you precisely what kind of heroes our service people are in the eyes of those they came to help. I walked among the refugees, many of whom were dying of hunger in their besieged campsites, and even the most jaded American would have been moved by their longing for a rescue and their absolute faith that the Americans could and would provide that rescue—if only it wasn't too late. When word spread that the Yanks were coming, hope was reborn in a country where hope had died.
>
> By every standard the five Americans I cited were heroes: "ordinary" people risking their lives, saving others, performing truly heroic actions. Each of the five (including the CIA agent in Georgia) died trying to bring peace to a needy, troubled part of the world: I call that heroism, too.
>
> Much of heroism comes from recognition of and obedience to one's duty. That these men gave their lives in the service of that duty does not deny but *confirms* their heroism.

In my radio essays I've tried to call attention to the services rendered by America's unsung heroes—soldiers, yes, but also police and firefighters, teachers, nurses, and all the people without whom suffering and misery would never end. Every now and then somebody listens, and sometimes I even get to speak my piece—*twice.*

SEVEN
Vietnam Revisited

THE memory is a kind of museum, with exhibits you can study at your leisure at any time, move on, and then come back to them. Some exhibits are refurbished regularly and always put in the best light. All my most flattering self-portraits are on permanent display. But other memories are closed off. Access denied. Special admission required.

And then you come back to the place, the person, the song or the taste or the smell that breaks open the locks, bursts open the doors, and throws you headlong into the memory.

I came back to Vietnam in March 1993 for a *CBS Reports* documentary with retired general H. Norman Schwarzkopf. Neither of us had returned to the country since before the war ended. The purpose of the documentary was to record the impressions and reactions of General Schwarzkopf, along with those of several other veterans who were also making a return trip to Vietnam. Coming to terms with the past and the present, the memories and the realities.

It was my assignment to help draw out the general. That turned out to be the easiest part of the job. The general is a big man, but he is not a stereotypical blustery warrior. He's gracious and thoughtful, with a constantly searching mind. He's had to mull over some big issues in his day, and he enjoys talking many of them out. "Stormin' Norman" isn't afraid of letting you know he's got emotions, and this wasn't going to be an easy trip for him. For me the hard part wasn't dealing with the general's memories. The hard part was discovering and dealing with so many memories of my own, seeing places where events had taken place that would haunt my dreams for twenty years.

In 1993, as our plane approaches the Saigon airport, the memories come flooding back. Ghosts walk in, including the ghosts of who and what I was, and the ghosts of illusions shattered, dreams unfulfilled.

I remember the first time I flew into Saigon, in 1964. How green the place seemed to me then! A lovely, deep emerald green.

The color would change for me during the war. In 1964, Vietnam was already a green jungle hell, a seething caldron of real mud, real blood, real death, and the screams of the wounded. It was to get worse while I was there that first time, and worse still as I returned over the years during the war.

But the first glimpse was one of lush beauty, viewed almost innocently, unaware of the horrors— and, yes, the heroism—that went on under the canopy of leaves. I was excited that first time in 1964. The green so vivid, the place so strange, the job so new.

Now, in 1993, with the war long ended, there is no excitement, not for me—and not for the general, either, I believe. I am curious, apprehensive. The museum of my memories is beginning to open up.

Once on the ground, General Schwarzkopf and I begin a tour of postwar Vietnam: Saigon, Cu Chi, Da Nang, China Beach, Tam Ky, Hue—all the places I had reported

Vietnam: Retired general H. Norman Schwarzkopf sharing memories of the Vietnam War with Dan Rather

from in the war. Everywhere we go, there are images I'd forgotten, sounds I hadn't remembered, events that had been closed off for me.

Saigon, where I covered a massive firefight in the street alongside Eric Sevareid—the great Sevareid clad only in his silk robe and bedroom slippers. (Eric has been dead not quite a year in March 1993.)

Cu Chi, where I covered a long-forgotten, bloody "battle for the treeline," with a camera mounted on the back of a jeep, and later reported one of the first stories out of Vietnam on the "tunnel war."

Da Nang, where the old marine "press camp" was headquartered in a former brothel, and where, after the "battle of the pagoda," we walked out waving a white flag and pointing at ourselves a portable battery-powered light, as if by being well lit we'd make it clear we didn't want to be shot. But we only made a better target of ourselves for the Vietcong.

China Beach, where an old woman and a child tried to blow up young marines with a booby-trapped cooking pot.

Tam Ky, where I very nearly died pinned down on my back in the muck of a rice paddy when the VC and North Vietnamese troops ambushed a detachment of marines within hours of my arrival in Vietnam.

Hue, where I spent several warm and fragrant nights in the sampan houseboats on the "Perfume River," long before the house-to-house, pagoda-to-pagoda fighting wrecked the ancient capital.

Hanoi, the unreachable during the war. I've written elsewhere about the time I spent in Laos trying to help arrange a visa to Hanoi for the late Charles Collingwood—that's when Collingwood taught me to "always wear a dark suit, white shirt, and tie when asking for something from Asian officials," to show your respect.

In our hotel in Da Nang in 1993 there is a gift shop where they sell old cigarette lighters taken off dead GIs and marines. History, mystery, anger, and paradox race through my mind as I flee the place. I can't stand it.

EVERYWHERE in Saigon there is proof that while the South lost the war, it was not conquered. Nobody calls Saigon Ho Chi Minh City. Saigon has grown by an estimated one third since the war ended. Many expensive homes have been built since I was last here, including those for rich businesspeople. Saigon today is an exotic blend of cheap modernism, entrepreneurialism, capitalism, good, evil, decadence, and traditionalism—the old, the very old.

We go back to the U.S. embassy. Memories of the desperate faces pressed against the front gate at the time of the great exodus at the end of the war. I was in the States when Saigon fell in April 1975, but I remember watching the reports, fearful I'd recognize some person I knew in the seething mob at the gate as the gate remained closed.

Now the gate is opened for us, and we go through.

Spooky, ghostly pale now. The embassy has been kept up, a little—all of the empty rooms inside, all of those offices large and small where once I interviewed American officials. The ambassadors, most memorably the elegant patrician Henry Cabot Lodge; the military attachés, the secretaries, and the CIA men. All gone now, the offices empty except for the cobwebs and the ghosts.

We go up to the roof, where the last U.S. helicopters lingered before the North Vietnamese took the city. General Schwarzkopf and I conduct one of our first interviews up on that embassy roof. The general is a patriot; I think he would prefer not to start off at the site of an American retreat. He tells me he watched the reports of the fall of Saigon, too, from his posting in Alaska. And went out and got drunk. The fall of Saigon was not an easy time for anyone who cared about South Vietnam—or the United States.

We go to President Thieu's palace. I interviewed the South Vietnamese President there during the war. Remember how he always put oil or cream on his face to soften it—how he loved the "face oil." Thieu was a very proud man and a determined fighter, which no one remembers, because he lost. You can now have your picture taken at his desk for a handful of change.

We carry loads of U.S. greenbacks. Security for it, protecting it, is a constant problem. We carry it in our shoes, strap it deep inside our thighs, tuck it in money belts, and spread it out among bags and equipment. As always when traveling in dicey places, I am carrying some gold coins. No American credit cards are allowed in Vietnam. In 1993 there are no diplomatic relations between the United States and Vietnam—not yet. So if you get into trouble, you're on your own, especially in the countryside and outlying areas.

We have also brought cigarettes. Sometimes better than gold. Marlboros in the old U.S.S.R. Kents in Romania at the height of the cold war. "555" cigarettes are the ticket in Vietnam. Why, I never know. But a few packs work wonders at roadblocks.

I GO alone to the Museum of American War Crimes. The general, of course, isn't about to go. Nobody even mentions it to him. It is a cheap, disgusting, outrageous propaganda palace. And I think it would be seen that way by most objective people.

The museum does not, by the way, give any indication of Japanese, Chinese, or French war crimes in Indochina—much less Vietnamese. About not having any mention of Vietnamese atrocities (disemboweling political and military opponents and leaving their corpses out as a warning to others), I can understand. About failing to mention the war crimes of other countries, I do not.

SOON after we arrive in Saigon, Schwarzkopf surveys the new Vietnam. "I came over here," he recalls, "for God, country, Mom, and apple pie. I came over here to fight for the liberty of a small, friendly

Captured U.S. tanks and guns are on display throughout Vietnam.
Shown here, the War Crimes Museum in Saigon.

country. The South Vietnamese airborne was a superb military organization with a lot of genuine patriots in it. So we joined them one
hundred percent. We went where they went, slept where they slept,
ate what they ate. And we wore their uniform. We really 'went native,'
if you want to call it that. For probably the first time in my entire life
I was serving where I really got no personal return whatsoever other
than the satisfaction of serving a cause. And that does something to
you." He says his first tour of duty "really was one of the happiest
periods in my entire life."

Before he had left for Vietnam, Schwarzkopf had been given a
crash course at Fort Bragg, North Carolina. He had been on the
faculty at West Point and had received a last-minute approval of his
request for combat duty.

That strikes me: He *requested* to serve in a war that would come to be
dreaded and despised by many Americans. He came determined to
do his best and proud of what he was able to do for others.

When I came to report the war, I found a lot of Americans like
Norm Schwarzkopf. And I admit to a kind of bias. The Rathers were
brought up to respect service, and service to one's country and one's
God above all. We were taught, my brother and sister and I, that there
was no higher calling than to turn your effort to the needs of the land
that made you. With most of the soldiers you met in the Vietnam War,

the commitment to service was as strongly felt, and as obvious, as the commitment young Norm Schwarzkopf felt.

Perhaps that paved the way to disappointment for many soldiers. Even for General Schwarzkopf, the war didn't continue as it began.

SAIGON is still filled with warm and fragrant nights in 1993. The rustle of bamboo. Gentle breezes come in off the Saigon River.

One evening I stand on the edge of the roof garden atop the Majestic Hotel and weep. Alone. Weep for the dead, for the names on The Wall. And for the memories.

OF ALL the memories of Vietnam, this may be the strongest, the one that stays with me the longest. The most frequent players were in my nightmares when I came home from my first year of covering the war. They came back every time I returned to report from the war zone. I have met them many times since. While walking moonlit nights in the woods along my favorite trout stream. When watching the stars at night, all big and bright, over Texas. At odd times in the quiet of my library, and amid the hustle and bustle of the newsroom. And every time I'm in Washington and even come close to The Wall.

The time was 1965, late at night. The place was a hospital ship somewhere off the South Vietnamese coast, near Qui Nhon. We were looking for a specific interview and had come to the ship seeking it. But the person we sought had already left.

I asked to be shown around, since I had never been aboard a hospital ship before. As we descended the ship's interior ladders, I had no idea of what I would find.

They led me several decks down, into a room that took up the entire deck at this level. The room was so dark—just a few subdued lights—I had to struggle to get my eyes adjusted to see.

What I saw was the recovery room for young men, brave young Americans, with fresh amputations. There were dozens of them. Heroes all. Many had multiple wounds, some multiple amputations.

Nurses moved, almost floated it seemed to me, row to row, bed to bed. The only sounds were those of water lapping at the sides of the ship—coming low, almost imperceptibly, through the steel—and the moans, groans, and quiet weeping, with the occasional crying out, a low scream of pain.

I was there, what? Maybe fifteen minutes. Standing transfixed, almost suspended in time and in space and in my own very personal state of shock, with a rush of not-to-be-held-back tears.

I recall Eric Sevareid's saying that the essence of youth is believing things last forever. Here was proof that the belief was wrong, and the beginning of the loss of the last remnants of my own youth. Never before had I experienced anything even approaching this. And never since. And I hope never ever again.

During the whole time I was there, only one word was spoken. It was spoken over and over; first you could hear it there, then over here, now back there. It was spoken in whispers by some, in moans by others, and, in a few cases, as a low shout.

The word was mother.

No one, not one of these valiant young men in their desperate hours—suffering, spared from death but perhaps not for very long, in the bowels of a dark and lonely ship—spoke any other word. None called for father, or for doctor or nurse. Only mother.

Until such a moment, we can still think of the human body as whole: the fine, graceful machine—in the image of God. We can still think of war as exciting, an adventure, a test of bravery and strength.

But at such a moment, we are stripped of such notions, and we cling to the first person we ever knew, who brought us the first love we ever knew: Mother. I thought of Jeannie, and our son, Danjack, then four years old. I thought of my own mother.

I wondered if any of the mothers of these men could have imagined such a ship—and the feats they'd have performed to keep their sons out of this place.

I could not leave the recovery room fast enough, but I have returned to the hospital ship a thousand times in my memory.

IN SAIGON I eat rice mixed with shrimp and nuc-mom sauce, the "dead fish sauce" that's a staple of Vietnamese cooking. I throw in some of my own Tabasco sauce for old times' sake.

The food tastes the way I remember it. It hasn't changed.

The general and I meet with a group of veterans who have come back to Vietnam. We shoot the discussion atop the old Rex Hotel. This is where the U.S. Military Command's daily briefings were held during the war, the infamous Five O'Clock Follies, so named by reporters because they were scheduled at 5:00 p.m. each day and degenerated into such farces: deceptive, upbeat "reports" that often, unfortunately, featured outright lying designed to mislead the American public. More often, the military was simply misleading and deluding itself. In the end, those who believed were the policymakers in Washington and those inside the military.

The White House, Defense Department, and the very top U.S. military brass have a lot to answer for about the Follies. But in wartime almost everybody has a lot to answer for about something.

The Rex Hotel looks out on the Saigon River on one side, wonderfully lighted now at night, and a choked traffic circle directly below on the other side. Cars, motor scooters, and bikes circle round and round. Nearly every scooter and bike has a young couple on it.

The rooftop of the Rex is decorated with colored lights, palm trees, caged birds. We gather around a big round table, as if we were tourists at a resort. But we aren't tourists.

At this time the Vietnamese government has decided to let small numbers of American veterans come to visit—on condition that they perform some kind of community-service work, preferably linked to the war. If the Americans blew up a building, let them come back and rebuild. That may sound manipulative. Candidly, I believe it is. But in practice it can also be a positive experience. My new friends have been working hard all day on building a health clinic.

They are a cross section—representatives of the different kinds of Americans who came to the war in Vietnam. Like most, these are good people, trying to do right, trying to understand. I haven't met any of them before tonight, but I feel I know them already.

One man had been an M-60 machine gunner, wounded at Khe Sanh on the day the siege officially ended there. His best friend was killed trying to save his life. And he spent the next thirty-four months in military hospitals in the States.

Another had served on riverboats in the Mekong Delta—for three consecutive tours of duty. Another had been a rifleman whose tour ended about six months after his second Purple Heart. Another had been a Special Forces medic. Yet another had started as a medic, was wounded, and was brought back again and again to fight with the 1st Cavalry Division, and one more time "because I'm such a good target." The last is a woman who had come to Vietnam as a Red Cross volunteer—one of a group of recreation workers nicknamed the "doughnut dollies."

They talk about the need for completion, to come full circle, to bind up wounds and finish the job. One speaks of the disparity between his memories and the present realities: "There is no war here," he says with a kind of wonderment in his voice.

I'm struck by how many of them came to care about the Vietnamese people. The Special Forces medic talks movingly about living and working among the Vietnamese, learning some of their language, and developing an abiding respect and affection for them.

There's a feeling like surprise when the Americans find that "the enemy" mourn their dead, have struggled to build families and a normal life in peacetime. One veteran has gone into the homes of some of "the enemy," been welcomed as a guest. "I think it's one of the most healing things that I've ever done," he says.

As I listen, I know that not all the Vietnamese can be good and kind. But I believe it is true that most people, in any country, even in a terrible war, want to be good, are trying to be kind. One of the veterans seems to echo some of my thoughts when he says, "I think the war just went bad. The war was bad. But the people in the country were very good."

He tells me he came back to Vietnam for the first time in 1989 because he found himself playing Russian roulette three to five nights out of the week. "Although I was going for treatment, I wasn't stopping what I was doing. I was wanting to be dead," he says. "And I thought that I needed to take a real gamble to break the habit."

That gamble, he decided, was to come back to Vietnam. And he has come again and again. This is his fifth trip since the war. He says he still feels he is missing something, speaks of searching crowds for familiar faces, although he realizes that after three decades the faces must have changed. But, he says, he is transforming his memories from a "horror show" and "getting a peace over me."

I know the horror show he's talking about. I see it myself, sometimes before I go to sleep. But I'm not here to talk about myself, and I have the feeling, more strongly now in the company of these people who have sacrificed so much for their country, that my experiences don't measure up. I am, rightly, denied entrance to Valhalla; there's no epic poetry dedicated to the war correspondent who knew when he was flying in, when he was flying home, and who never had to pull a trigger. I keep my counsel and listen to the tales of bravery and pain, of rising awareness and the certainty of triumph over sorrow, someday. These veterans are heroes still engaged in a battle longer than any they ever fought in Vietnam.

The machine gunner talks about survivor guilt—his best friend died saving his life, and within a few months, he says, more than forty other members of his company were killed. For a time he became deeply involved with the group Vietnam Veterans Against the War. But his problems grew: posttraumatic stress disorder, drinking, family problems, and still the guilt.

A friend—Nancy, the doughnut dolly who's sitting with us now—had persuaded him to write to the parents of the friend who saved his life, to make sure they knew how brave their son had been and how much gratitude he felt. Now he has become close to that family, and opening up to them has made it easier to seek counseling. He's on the mend, and a real fighter. I admire his spirit.

I also admire Nancy, who helped this man understand how important the letter to his friend's family could be. Nancy knows how important because she lost a brother in Vietnam.

She can tell me why she came to Vietnam. The reason is rage. She was angry toward the Vietnamese people—not just the government but the entire nation. I believe she blamed all of Vietnam for her brother's death. And she didn't like the anger within herself. So she came to Vietnam to heal the anger. "Vietnam is not over for me, by any means. But the anger toward the Vietnamese people is gone. They did what they had to do."

Her face is alive with emotions, many of them conflicting. It is a face I have seen many times in my reporting, the face of the survivor. I have seen her after a storm or a shooting. She is still a little stunned by what has happened, but she is blinking back the tears, summoning her strength. She is going to survive. And she's going to do better than survive—she is going to flourish, show 'em all.

"About a week ago I said I wasn't ready to give Vietnam back to the Vietnamese," she continues. "But the way I feel now, it's done with me. I don't need to come back. It's theirs. They've earned it. They can have it. I don't want it."

There are nods of assent all around the table, and General Schwarzkopf says quietly, "Vietnam's never going to be over for me, either."

We talk for a long time, remembering the dead, recalling what we have done to keep living since the war ended. We talk about guilt and pride, and most of us feel something of each for the things we did during our time here. We talk about reconciliation, and I point out that there are some who believe the past is the past, should be let go, forgotten, buried.

One of the veterans snorts. "The people that say that—number one, most of them weren't here. And number two, to hell with them. To hell with them."

There's laughter, good rich laughter that comes from down deep inside. The laughter says that the past is the foundation of the present; it can't be buried or forgotten, not reliably. It must be shored up, made sturdy, to make the present and the future more secure. These people have come back to Vietnam trying to do just that.

It's been a long journey to the roof of the Rex Hotel. A long journey, but a necessary one.

THE Mekong Delta was one of the worst of the battle areas. Mangrove swamps, triple-canopied jungle cover, beaches alongside jungle, an absolutely terrible place to fight. I don't have time to take the full Mekong River trip; I take a truncated version, alone with a guide.

Everybody who visits Vietnam now talks about their trips to Tay Ninh in the Delta. Tay Ninh was a blood-and-sweat-soaked killing ground during the war. Now its Cao Bai Temple is a major draw. There is music in the temple today, and worship services are open to the public. The temple is beautifully decorated with carvings of spiritual leaders from Buddha to Victor Hugo.

Victor Hugo? The French influence on the former French colony is still evident. And we feel that influence a little, too. The other day General Schwarzkopf quoted the musical version of Hugo's *Les Misérables*, in which the sole survivor of a rebellion wonders why he has lived when his comrades have fallen, and then sings *Don't ask me what their sacrifice was for.*

WITH the general at Cu Chi: This is difficult for me. I saw many people die here. Much of the worst of the Tet Offensive was fought here in 1968, and the infamous tunnel war, with guerrillas burrowing for miles, able to travel without being seen, to take cover and to pop up again and again to attack American troops.

The battleground has become a tourist attraction, much of it poorly staged. Some of it strikes me as downright phony, with a kind of cheap and chintzy "Disney World of the Jungle and Tunnels" quality to it, designed to emphasize how brave and brilliant the Vietcong and North Vietnamese army were, and how dumb and foolish and fooled the Americans were.

But when you see it, you don't believe it. At least I don't. They were good, but not all *that* good.

Example: As you approach the "showplace" area, there is, just off the road, "preserved" in the jungle, in full view, the almost complete remains of a "shot-down" U.S. aircraft. I can't see any evidence that the aircraft really was shot down or was shot down in this place and is the artifact it is purported to be.

And the tunnels themselves: Well, yes, there were *some* tunnels during the war. I did some reports on the tunnels. But I wonder if they were really as ingenious and widespread as the Vietnamese government now claims. The originals I saw were much smaller, tighter, and not nearly as extensive as what is now shown. The general and I are able to go down in the tunnels and explore. The general admits that during the war he was always afraid to go down in the tunnels—not because there might be Vietcong or snakes or some other danger, but because he might have gotten wedged in and then subjected to the indignity of being tugged out, Pooh Bear–style, by his men.

I believe the tunnels have been redone, reinforced, extended, to make them much more impressive. Can't prove it, but that's what I believe.

Oh, well, maybe it's natural. History is written by the victors. The British in our own Revolutionary War are still made out to be dumber and more evil than they were in fact. So the old-line, hard-line Vietnamese Communists, eager to hang on to power awhile longer, hoping to pump themselves up to look like heroes, try to make Americans look dumb and evil. Part of you wants to shrug and say so what? What difference does it make in the long run? Does it really matter? I doubt it.

But I do find it interesting that it is the Americans—not the French, not the Japanese, not the Chinese (who were much worse over a

much longer time in what they did to Vietnam), but the Americans—
who bear the brunt of all of this. This is part of what rings hollow in
all the present talk of how the current Vietnamese government really
"holds no grudge" toward Americans. The Vietnamese people are as
warm and welcoming as they can be, but the government churns out
propaganda, builds anti-American museums and tourist attractions. It
makes me skeptical, even suspicious.

COMING to Hanoi is like stepping into the past—except that I've
never been here before. The city is dominated by the old-fashioned
French colonial architecture, none of it very many stories high, and is,
as has been written, very much "a city trapped in amber," both because of the warm amber sunlight that holds the city close, up and
down the wide boulevards and among the overhanging trees, and
because here something seems to be caught motionless in the movement of history.

I come off the plane at Noi Ba Airport with the general, who is
looking grim and uncomfortable. And we are off to the capital of the
socialist republic, what was during the war the capital of the enemy.

Our ride to the city is punctuated by "soldier's rain," so called
because it is light, the kind infantrymen used to welcome because it
broke the heat while not soaking them. We are swept into the city
center on a long line of traffic. We hear the blare of horns. We dodge
pedestrians, animals, and vehicles of every description. Women in
Vietnamese straw hats carry buckets of water on poles the old-
fashioned way. Women and men carry large baskets balanced on their
heads. What most Westerners still do not grasp is how poor, how
utterly poor in material possessions, Vietnam is. The estimated annual income, on average, is about $200 per person.

Hanoi is where the government sits, but it is also where people live,
riding rickshaws and motorbikes, conducting all kinds of business
and daily affairs right on the street. They are outdoors simmering
rice, barbecuing fish and chicken. Selling gasoline from a two-liter
jug. There are outdoor barbershops: just a couple of chairs, a couple
of mirrors hung from tree limbs. Straight-razor shaves are a specialty.
I have one. Excellent. An old toothless man gives me my shave. He
does haircuts with scissors and a bowl over the head. A genuine
soup-bowl haircut. He offers to give me one. I decline respectfully.

Heavy loads are stacked sky-high on carts and bicycles. I realize this is the way much of their military supplies traveled along the Ho Chi Minh Trail during the war. All kinds of goods are being transported along the streets of Hanoi—food, machinery, snakes. The snakes are to be eaten. There's at least one place deep inside the center city where you can pick the snake you want and have it prepared to order—curbside, of course—and eat it right there. Mine tastes nothing like chicken.

I've eaten snake often, because there's a restaurant near Lake Travis, Texas, that specializes in rattlesnake steak. The place is called Hudson's on the Bend, and the chef, Jay Moore, knows a hundred ways to camouflage the taste of snake. But this snake in Hanoi does not use Jay's recipes.

I eat with my own chopsticks. I have seen that dishwashing in Saigon and elsewhere has little to do with sanitation. Filthy water in the gutter of my curbside snake restaurant is definitely not up to Mother Rather's standards. Carrying one's own chopsticks has always seemed the least one could do.

But we're not in Hanoi to sightsee. We're here to work. We look for locations.

THERE's a war museum in Hanoi, and guess which war? There are some smashed U.S. planes and helicopters, some captured tanks. The museum is, again, very heavy-handed in its propaganda. Inside the wrecked vehicles in the courtyard are stacks of GI combat jungle boots. I can see every man who ever wore them, and can't look anymore. I move away quickly.

The wreckage makes a dramatic picture, and our producer, Joel Bernstein, hopes we can shoot an interview with the general here, but I tell him it will never happen. It doesn't. The general takes one look, then gives me a look, and we leave—pronto. He is steamed. We ride around Hoan Kiem Lake. I try to talk him down, and eventually he relaxes. I understand his feelings. This really was a mistake on our part.

We stay in the Hotel Metropole, the unofficial hotel for foreigners. Run by the French, recently restored. Run like a first-class European hotel. The Vietnamese who work in the hotel have been superbly trained. Most speak both French and English. I am surprised at first to find how many Vietnamese bureaucrats speak German, but I am told that many of them were educated in East Germany.

I decide to give snake cuisine another try, and I head for the most famous snake-food restaurant in town.

This is the real thing, small, and the menu is short: snake, snake, and snake. The snake is mashed up with spices and fried. It tastes about like it sounds.

And I won't tell you about the dreams I had, despite taking double doses of Alka-Seltzer and Tums. But the whole meal, with drinks and tip included, costs five dollars. Who says you can't put a price on adventure?

Another night, dinner is in our honor, thrown at a big government place near the hotel, with the whole CBS team invited. The general understandably declines.

It is a long meal, three hours, stiff and formal. I have to carry most of the conversation. It isn't easy—there are tense moments. A ranking official, who had been junior negotiator at the Paris peace talks in the 1970s, now hopes to be the first Vietnamese representative in Washington when the trade embargo is lifted. He says, "If you think Vietnam *needs* American trade, you are badly mistaken. We can get along quite well without it."

I respond, "If you think the United States *needs* Vietnamese trade, you are also mistaken. We can get along quite well without it."

He smiles a very Vietnamese smile and repeats that he is confident America will lift the embargo—and soon. "It is simple," he says. "Americans want to make money. The urge is very strong. And so you will lift the embargo."

Translation: Americans value money over morality. I am angry. I am confident he is wrong.

In my hotel room later, I am still angry about what the Vietnamese official has said. I remember a story General Schwarzkopf told me our first day in Vietnam. In 1964, just before he shipped in, he was given a guide to Vietnam, which stressed two points: that the Vietnamese have been raised on a rice diet and therefore do not have much endurance. And, the book went on, all Vietnamese are Buddhists, and none of them drink alcohol.

The day after Schwarzkopf met his counterpart, a captain in the South Vietnamese army, he was invited into the captain's office. The captain opened his drawer and pulled out a bottle of Scotch, and they drank the whole bottle on the spot. "So much for *that* part of the little book," Schwarzkopf had said.

Shortly afterward Schwarzkopf went on his first combat operation. He was in the field, in peak condition, and carrying only a radio. With him was a Vietnamese, slight of stature, raised on a rice diet, just as the book said, and laden down with a hundred-pound pack.

"We were going down into these deep mud gullies, and then we'd have to climb out of them. There I was—panting, with my tongue hanging out. And that little Vietnamese, with that one-hundred-pound pack on his back, would walk by and wave as he scampered on ahead. So much for the endurance thing. I came back and threw that book away."

He looked across the countryside. "I decided we really didn't know much about this country, which turned out to be all too true."

I wonder if it isn't true even today—if the Vietnamese don't understand us better than we understand them.

For much of this trip Schwarzkopf's experiences and memories overlap with mine. We have spoken of friends who died, pain that was felt. There are strong similarities. But at the same time, neither of us has lost sight of the simple, drastic distinction that he was army, I was press. In the eyes of some Americans, the military's real enemy in Vietnam was the press: The press had to be deceived, deterred because the press was determined to undo the United States military operations. To make matters even worse, I was not merely press but *television* press, in what a number of people (including me) had called the television war. *Our* pictures, broadcast into America's living rooms and dining rooms, supposedly turned the tide of public opinion against the war and brought about the American loss. Most reporters have never believed this theory. We saw it as excuse-making, blame-shifting, oversimplifying of a very low order.

Now, in 1993, the general and I have been many days in Vietnam. Finally Schwarzkopf is ready to tackle the distinction between us. He begins by remembering the *first* time he returned to Vietnam during the war, and I stand back and let him run.

Rotated home after two years of duty in 1964–65, Schwarzkopf volunteered to return to combat duty in 1969. Whereas his first tour had been "one of the happiest periods [of his] entire life," the difference in military climate in 1969–70 was almost shocking.

"I'm commanding an infantry battalion, and ninety-nine percent of the people in this battalion had been drafted. They hadn't asked to go to war. They had been drafted by their country, and they had answered the call. They hadn't run away to Canada. But when they went to war, they were going to a war which they already knew was very unpopular in the eyes of the people at home.

"So right away they were being asked to go off and die in a war that was unpopular. They got over here at a time when we had started sending U.S. units home, so they were out on the battlefield and one of their principal objectives just became 'I want to stay alive until I can go home.'

"Then, amazingly, when they got back home, somehow the mood had turned, and they were being *blamed* for the war. That was wrong. These were Americans who were doing their duty. It wasn't their war. They hadn't started it. They were not the ones sustaining it. They certainly were not the ones who wanted to be here. And yet, when they got back, they were receiving the blame.

"And that, I think more than anything else, contributes to the Vietnam Veterans Syndrome. You know, we went off to do our duty to our country, and we came back home and you all somehow made us the bad guy."

When Schwarzkopf says "you all," he doesn't mean the American civilians. He means the press. He means my colleagues; he means *me.*

And there it is: the rift between us, the rift between the military and the press in Vietnam, out in the open, where we can discuss it.

He continues. "I don't think anyone can say the press lost the war. The war was lost because of a bankrupt strategy. I think that in hindsight all of us fully understand that. Many of us, at the time, blamed the press for the attitude that the American people were adopting, which caused this to become a very unpopular war and eventually caused the withdrawal. Personally, I was antipress because I felt that the reporting of my military operations was going to be slanted—not a balanced presentation.

"Was I right? In hindsight, probably not. But at the time, I felt very strongly that I could not get a fair shake. So therefore, I just avoided the press whenever possible."

He looks at me now, a hard look. I have the feeling he hasn't expressed these things very often—certainly not to a representative of the press, with his crew standing by and cameras rolling. I want to respond in the same vein.

"I can't speak for the press as a whole," I say. "But my own experience was different. In the mid-1960s I got along very well with everybody in the field. My only difficulty came with people at, or very near, the top, who time after time demonstrated that they were either dealing in sophistry or deliberately misleading the press and the American public.

"After the Tet Offensive, as public support at home withered, I'll be candid with you—as you were with me—I resented being held responsible for the war's not going well. That was our counterpart of the military saying, 'Hey, we did our job. Maybe we didn't do it perfectly, but don't blame us when things go wrong.' The press had its version of that."

Schwarzkopf nods and says, "Oh, I think so. I think we were both right and we were both wrong. It was just like anything else. In a very complicated situation like this was, nothing was all black and white. It was various shades of gray. The blame certainly cannot be placed on the press for losing the war. That's a gross oversimplification. That's a bum rap for the press to carry."

He keeps his eyes on me. In a strange way we have just declared peace, we two representatives of the military and the press, by agreeing that the war was lost neither by those in the field nor by those in the press, but by those who directed a losing strategy.

Perhaps others will not sign on to our peace. But I believe it is a just peace, and a genuine peace with honor.

ALL along the way, I have had ghosts as my companions: Eric Sevareid and Charles Collingwood, the mentors, larger than life, with a nerve and a style that made a little boy of you, filling you with wonderment and admiration and a yearning to grow up and play with the big boys.

The Vietnamese peasant woman who once aimed an ancient rifle at my heart because I'd entered her hut by accident.

The soldier from Tennessee, caught on a mine on Thanksgiving Day.

The GI who, without anyone's ordering him and while we watched dumbfounded, leaped up and single-handedly cleaned out a machine-gun nest that his whole unit had failed to finish off in half a day's fighting.

The good-hearted army nurse with a strange braided pattern tattooed on her arm. She gave me a cup of coffee and a kind word.

The tribal chief who arrived riding on a little Cambodian elephant to negotiate with an American colonel.

My wife, sweet Jeannie, raising our children and wondering what was happening to her husband among the intrigues and atrocities of a nation at war, half a world away.

The faces of Vietnamese and French and Americans, friendly and unfriendly, trusting America, trusting the press, trusting me—or not. The faces still living, but changed—and the faces long since dead. Most persistent in their haunting are the ghosts of those who died beside me.

I am not a soldier, not the marine I tried to be. A record of rheumatic fever and my own destiny saw to that. But I came to Vietnam; I saw a war. I have these memories, and these memories have become a part of me. Since the war, I don't think I've ever seen a day in my life without thinking about Vietnam. But that doesn't mean that I had managed to put the past into perspective—that I had ever managed to understand the past *as* past. Mostly, my memories were stored away, not dealt with.

But the past keeps sneaking up on you. It is always there behind you, right over your shoulder. Only by coming back to Vietnam was I able to experience the differences that change had wrought—in the country, in me, in my memory.

Many of those who went to Vietnam years ago weren't soldiers. We were reporters, nurses, doctors, businesspeople. We were, all of us, trying: trying to help, trying to see, trying to make a name, make a buck, or just get through it. But all of us had ample opportunity to be a part of a war, with the extremes of human conduct playing out all around us. Extremes of cowardice and valor, of cruelty and compassion.

It takes a long time to absorb so many extremes. Many have been able to reconcile the Vietnam of the mind with the Vietnam that is actual—some have been able to do so without returning to Vietnam, as Norm Schwarzkopf and I had to do, as the veterans we met there had to do. We needed to return to Vietnam to see that life has moved on for Vietnam and for us. We needed to smell the fish sauce in the streets and the fragrance of flowers on the water, to return to a country of death and pain and find that it's only another country.

OUTTAKE

You could be around Eric Sevareid for half a day or more, just the two of you, and he might not say anything. Oh, maybe mumble good morning or something, but other than that, nothing.

He wasn't mad or anything. That's just the way he was. Eric Sevareid, who died July 9, 1992, at seventy-nine, was eloquent on the air, but in person he was given to silence. Long silence if he was thinking, or if he just didn't believe he had anything worth saying, or if he didn't feel like talking just then.

He was out of Velva, North Dakota, by way of the University of Minnesota, Paris, and a thousand datelines long since forgotten. He had been many places, but he came home.

And he came home to Georgetown, to his own house, to die.

He knew he was dying. You could never fool Eric; he was too smart, too observant, too sensitive.

Like Ed Murrow, who hired him at CBS, Sevareid was a lifetime scholar. Murrow was the best reporter and broadcaster in the history of over-the-airwaves news. He was the classic scholar-correspondent. So was Sevareid. Eric also became a philosopher-correspondent, the only one broadcast news has produced. And he is unquestionably the best writer to come out of electronic journalism.

No one of his generation wrote more or better essays—no one, print or broadcast. Much of what he wrote about America and what it meant to be an American in the post–World War II era is as instructive today as it was the day he wrote it. Sevareid is the only broadcast journalist I know who was a correspondent in the Spanish Civil War, World War II, Korea, and Vietnam. When I visited him for the last time, he sipped tea and told how he wished he could have gone to the Persian Gulf. "Sort of," he added, "but I guess I've seen enough wars."

My mind went back to a place near Hue, early in the Vietnam

fighting. Sevareid was the first of the big-name American broadcasters to come and see for himself what we were getting ourselves into. "I don't like it," Eric told me. "I don't like it partly because I don't believe anyone has thought this damn thing through."

Sevareid always thought things through. And partly because of that, he knew about an incredible range of things: how to lead quail, how to mend a fly line, how to converse with a monarch or a showgirl, and how to stay alive in tight places.

Like Hemingway, he loved the outdoors. He went to Paris, as Hemingway did (they knew each other there). And the two wrote in similar spare, lean styles. For my money, Sevareid did it better. The man and his writings had a quiet authority and the beauty of simplicity.

He always seemed taller than he was, although he was well over six feet. He dominated rooms, seemed to dominate any landscape he occupied. He had charisma, and he was a star. But he was not so much glamorous as he was compelling.

When I saw him that last time, in his Georgetown house, with the sun shafting through the windows over a fountain-centered small back garden, he seemed at peace. He knew, in that way that Eric always knew everything, that his work was done.

When Murrow died, Sevareid wrote, as usual, the best line: "He was a shooting star; we will live in his afterglow a very long time."

Now the same might be said of Sevareid himself. But I prefer to think of him as a northern star, the Great Northern Star: constant and clear, the big, bright, quiet one.

EIGHT
A Catfish Runs Through It

WHEN I returned from Somalia, at the end of 1992, I made myself two promises. One, I would never complain again (not realistic, but we try). And two, I would get out of the office more and onto the cutting edge of the big stories.

No doubt the budget makers at CBS believe that I travel quite enough as it is. But the simple truth is that the best stories do not make office calls. You have to go get them. When I sense a big one brewing, there is inside me this feeling of the caged cat. As the years have rolled by—and many times they haven't so much rolled as bumped—that feeling has increased. I know how that must sound: "Stick a press card in my hatband and put me through to the city desk. I'm going to bust this town wide open." In truth, there is an element of that anytime you chase a story. Big stories are good theater. Time is always running out. You don't know what the ending will be.

So in the summer of 1993, I arranged to cover the economic summit in Tokyo. I told my boss, News Division president Eric Ober, that I believed I had been to every summit since they started having them. I never knew one to make real news, but this was Bill Clinton's first overseas trip—a valid reason right there. And I had another angle. I wanted to tack on a trip to China behind it. As an emerging economic superpower, China may well be the most important story of the post-communist era.

The trouble with covering an economic summit is that you have to take enough people to fill a Verdi opera. I promised to keep it lean and keep it cheap, and my bosses indulged me.

Out of the Tokyo summit came what amounted to a miniscoop, one made more interesting by events soon to unfold. We had been told before the summit that there would be no interviews until Friday, the closing day. I said, "I know, I understand, there are things the President can't talk about. But I don't want to ask him about economics. I want to ask him about the Midwest floods." Bingo. We landed an exclusive interview with President Clinton. There are few positions less attractive to a President than to be overseas when a disaster strikes at home, giving critics a chance to say he doesn't care.

The interview turned out to be no big deal, but it did bug our rivals, so we sprang for an extra ration of sake for the troops. The summit ended, and we quietly slipped off to Shanghai.

That summer of 1993 Shanghai was the most interesting city in the world, a kind of new Klondike of the Orient. It was the engine that would pull China's train. We were just getting started when I felt a big tug from another direction.

While we were in Tokyo, I had assigned my main man, Bill Madison, to monitor the storms back in the States. I knew the floods were on the borderline of being a major story. My contacts at the National Weather Service had told me that El Niño comes over the Pacific every once in a while to cause some unusual weather patterns. Now it was sort of parked over the Midwest. Bill's job was to update me hour by hour on the floods. I didn't want to be caught in China if they were building arks back in America's heartland.

Sure enough, the story broke just a few hours after we landed in Shanghai. I hated having to break away, but I told Bill to book us on the next flight out.

The trip from Shanghai to St. Louis lasted all day and night and the next morning. We flew through time zones and the international dateline and had a change of planes and a brief stop in Tokyo. I went to the gate and got instructions on how to make an international telephone call. I had to mobilize an enormous news operation to cover a big, breaking domestic story, and I had to do it on the fly.

In addition to the daily coverage, I wanted a commitment to run a major piece on *48 Hours,* our weekly documentary series. This is prime time, ferociously competitive—an hour of news competing with entertainment, and many are unwilling to tamper with its winning formula. Part of that formula is that much of the program must be planned well ahead. Now I said to Eric Ober, "Turn on a dime and we'll swarm this story. We have the team, we have the capability, and we have the story."

Ober gave *48 Hours* the green light. He wanted CBS to provide saturation coverage. Every component of the news team would make a contribution, and every program we had would make a report. Given the financial realities of the age, saturation coverage is a huge risk. But Eric realized that this was an important story, with significant impact on millions of Americans, and if anything warranted risk, it was the great flood of 1993.

I stood at the gate in Tokyo until the last second, shouting into the phone, taking orders, giving a few, trying to persuade, nudge, beg for the resources I needed to cover the floods.

There wasn't enough time to finish making arrangements, and the next chance I had to phone was from the airport in San Francisco. I remember holding a phone in each hand and Bill Madison holding a third. We were working out dozens of details, starting with hiring the best helicopter pilots available. I wanted one in St. Louis, one in Des Moines, and another anywhere along the great Mississippi. Ideally, what you look for is a retired Vietnam chopper pilot who is now flying fat cats to gambling casinos, is bored by it, and would like to relive a few of those landings in the combat zone. You pay him well and assure him he's going to have a damned good time.

On the other phone, I'm ticking off the names of the producers we want, how many cameras, and the people behind them. Our news people were already on top of the story by the time we had reached San Francisco.

There is a lot of talk in television circles about CBS not being as big as it once was. But we are still deep in experienced off-camera people: executives, news managers, producers, researchers, writers, the people with Rolodex files who know where, in St. Louis, you find a former Vietnam helicopter pilot. We had a forty-five minute layover in San Francisco, and after all the telephoning back and forth, I was thinking, Hot damn, it's going to work.

In St. Louis, a newsroom nerve center was already being set up, in the form of two connecting rooms at a Holiday Inn. From there we could assign the stories and direct the crews. Everything was coming together now. I had left China on a Sunday morning and by Monday I was ready to follow the flood.

It is critical, when you're covering something as vast as a flood, to give people an overview of the story. A hurricane is like a cobra: It strikes quickly with an awesome force and killing power. A great flood is more like a python: huge, slow, but able to wrap itself around anything in its path and squeeze the life out of it. The best way I knew to bring the viewer into the story, to recognize the vastness of the flood sweeping down the Mississippi, was from a helicopter.

Monday was a great day. We took off early, and I knew immediately that I was paired with a fabulous pilot, Gary Lusk. This is how we rigged ourselves inside the chopper: In the front there is space for two people—the pilot and our producer, Wayne Nelson, who has a great heart for a story. The producer sits next to the pilot so he can explain to him what we are trying to do. Right behind the cockpit is a compartment that seats four people. We have three—an anchor, a cameraman, and a soundman. The cameraman hunkers down in the corner farthest back, facing the cockpit, with the soundman beside him. I'm catty-corner from the camera, wearing an intrahelicopter headset. We had built in a microphone, connected directly to our videotape, as a way to override the whir of the rotor blades.

Both doors were removed from the compartment, and everyone was wearing two really strong, web safety belts. We also attached one of the cameraman's belts to the fuselage and put another around a thigh, with enough slack to allow him, if necessary, to get out the door and onto the skid of the helicopter. This would give him more range and latitude and a wider shot of the flood.

On the opposite side of the cabin, I did the same thing so I could get out on the skid. The cameraman would then be better able to frame me against the background of the shot, and have more leeway than he would have from inside the chopper.

Our opening piece was going to be what is called the establishing shot, during which I would explain to the viewer that "this is where the flooding Missouri meets the flooding Mississippi." There is an impersonality to these often distant, panoramic shots. So what you want is to take the viewer up close and personal. With no Tele-PrompTer out on the skids, my reports were ad-libbed, almost a running play-by-play. This is a sample:

> The Mississippi River is spreading like an epidemic now across Missouri, Illinois, and Iowa, with more states to be afflicted soon, and I'm still trying to grasp the dimensions. At its worst, the water stretches from one horizon to the other. The natural inclination is to marvel at the physical dimensions of this disaster. But you can't ignore the human dimensions.
>
> Over there, that's not just a house in water up to the eaves—that is somebody's home and hard work. And over there, that's not just a flooded field. It's somebody's livelihood.
>
> You know, Mark Twain used to say that the only good thing about a flood was that the streets were quiet. He said this before the development of the outboard motor. Now the streets up and down the Mississippi sound like a speedway, as neighbors zip back and forth with supplies and passengers.

On our first day of reconnaissance we rented a small boat with an outboard motor. Then we gave our viewers a tour of the flooded town of La Grange, Missouri, from water level.

The mayor, Harold Ludwig, joined us. As we passed the rooftop of one house, I remarked, "Boy, that place is really flooded out. Whose home is it?" The mayor said, "That's mine."

I asked him, with the camera running, if he would mind showing us around on the inside of the submerged house. He sort of paused and shrugged, and said, "Well, yeah, I guess we can do that." He looked at the cameraman and asked, "Can you do it? You're carrying a lot of electric equipment."

He could and we did. We climbed out of the boat and onto the roof of the house very very carefully. We eased ourselves into the water and waded on tiptoes into the house. There was just enough air to keep our noses out of the water. I could see the mayor's eyes welling up a bit as he surveyed the damage. He pointed out the living room. Then we sort of felt our way along to the next room. "This," he said, "is what's left of my kitchen."

I suddenly felt something alive brush up against my leg. I was startled, to say the least, and my first frantic thought was, I hope it's not a snake or an eel. It turned out to be a big Mississippi catfish. They are bottom feeders and, naturally, would be in the kitchen looking for food.

Mayor Ludwig had made this tour several times since the flood began, and now he was nonchalant, as if the catfish were a family pet. But you could see he was pretty torn up. It was a fine old house, a two-story Victorian in which the Ludwigs had taken great pride.

THE siege of Des Moines was under way, and so we split off part of our base camp on the outskirts of St. Louis, chartered a small plane, and took off. On July 10 the Raccoon River hit a crest of twenty-five feet. It knocked out the Des Moines waterworks and flooded most of the major downtown areas. In this day and age it is fairly unusual for a metropolitan center to be threatened. We decided to anchor *48 Hours* out of Des Moines, from the top of a van overlooking the army of people sandbagging the levee, trying to spare the rest of the inner city.

You kept coming back to the immensity of the problem—waves of water up to eight miles wide. You measure the acres of crops ruined, the billions of dollars in devastation. You watch people cry, and you weigh the tears.

Because of our mobility, we had the opportunity to see an awful lot in a short time. The Mississippi River basin, covering eight states, contains close to 15 percent of the landmass of the United States.

Eight months of rain had swelled the major rivers to record levels and brought the region to this catastrophe. People actually wondered if the floods were a sign that the world was ending.

You saw the effects on people's dreams: new cars ruined, shrubs and plants floating away. You saw farms wiped out—a family business and way of life gone forever. Often people would not have the insurance or the savings to start over.

In part, what makes these stories of natural disasters so powerful is the realization that it can happen to us—you, me. Some critics say that wrath-of-nature stories are overplayed, especially on television. But I think of the eruption of Mount St. Helens, hurricane Andrew, the San Francisco and Los Angeles earthquakes. These are stories people identify with. Can anyone not think, "There but for the grace of God . . ." These disasters truly put life in perspective: how transient and ephemeral it really is. No one gets through unscathed.

All of that was compressed and synthesized in the story of the great flood of '93. When you see all the family photographs ruined by water, an heirloom piece of furniture lost forever, or a dog you can't get out of the kennel, a horse you can't get out of the corral, a cow you can't get out of the barn, or, indeed, a person who stayed too long and got caught in the wrong place . . . you feel humbled.

Yet the setbacks, even the tragedies, are countered somewhat by heroic deeds of strangers. Firefighters, police officers, volunteers, ordinary people, entire families, hour after hour, day after day, filling sandbags and stacking them, striving to build their last lines of defense. Such sights made your heart soar, and, yes, a secret little part of you likes to think that if called upon, you could do that and you would.

This may be the lesson of the Midwest floods, that in hard and desperate times, you have to be able to depend on others, neighbors or strangers, as they did in Des Moines. The city was without running water for at least two weeks. When the waterworks plant was able to supply a limited amount of water, the residents were warned not to use it for drinking purposes for at least a month. The water was a vivid brown, like cold gravy.

One day I watched the sandbag line stretching out a quarter mile or more along the riverfront. A woman with bright red hair, green shorts, a red-striped blouse, and heavy work gloves walked past. She carried a plastic bag. She was filling it with trash.

The sandbag line was a little like an outdoor rock concert. Even though the work was tough, a great party spirit pervaded, rock music pumped out—and the crowd generated an enormous amount of trash. This woman had designated herself the cleanup crew. She'd fill a huge plastic bag with trash, then go and get another bag, fill it, and keep coming back for more, each bag bigger than she was. She did this for the whole day, long after dark, all by herself, and again the next day. Her name was Norma Buehlmann.

Finally I stopped to tell Mrs. Buehlmann I admired her dedication. She brushed aside the compliment. She was doing this, she said, even though her house hadn't been flooded. It worried her to see so many of her neighbors affected, and she wanted to help any way she could. But she didn't have time to talk; she had to get back to work.

By the end of July the flooding still had not abated. The estimate of damages had risen beyond $10 billion. And yet people who had lost most of what they had were sharing with those who had lost everything. In an era when the decline of community, of the sense of community, is so troubling, these events—floods, quakes, fires—force people to remember that we still need to be connected.

OUTTAKE

THEN: Hurricane Carla, 1961. I thought it would be worthwhile to chain myself to a tree in the middle of a hurricane. How could I report a hurricane if I'd never experienced one close up?

I tried it. It didn't work.

Now: Hurricane Emily, 1993. I am hanging my sixty-one-year-old rump halfway out of a helicopter flying over Cape Hatteras in the aftermath of Emily, a kinder, gentler hurricane to most of the world, but not in Cape Hatteras, where she left behind winds a little higher than are really optimal for helicopter flights, especially flights when you are not, as I say, entirely *inside* the helicopter, and you are no longer the twenty-nine-year-old who used to go around chaining himself to trees, and more to the point, your wife is no longer exactly enthusiastic about stunts like these and you think she's probably right. I am trying to concentrate on the story, provided I do not fall out of this helicopter as we sail over the broken matchsticks that used to be homes. And over there is a tree, uprooted and carried several yards, about the size of the tree to which I once chained myself—so securely, I thought at the time.

Then: When you are young and the hurricane is on its way, when lives are at stake, it's one thing to convince yourself to take a few risks.

Now: When you are, well, let's just say *mature,* and the hurricane has waltzed out to sea, a threat to nobody but a few seagulls, it is much more difficult to convince yourself to take risks. My father always carried a length of rope in the back seat of our car wherever he went, because you never knew when you might have to haul something or tie the radiator back on or capture Bonnie and Clyde. I used to follow his example but fell out of the habit. Now I wish I'd brought some rope on this trip. It's a long way down, and "dropping anchor" takes on new meaning at a time like this.

Then: It was as if no one had ever covered a hurricane before. My boss at KHOU in Houston suddenly got the bright idea to put the radar on television as it tracked the course of hurricane Carla—and to superimpose the radar image over a map. The viewers would be able to *see* the hurricane approach—for the first time in history.

Now: I have stopped trying to count how many hurricanes I have covered. Over two dozen, under three dozen. For hurricane Emily, I am accompanied by two other correspondents, five television producers, one radio producer, four camera operators and four sound operators, one news writer, plus unnumbered satellite technicians and support staff. Compared to the grand and glorious expeditions of yesterday, this is a bare-bones crew. We have not brought along makeup artists or senior management, both deemed essential as recently as ten years ago.

Then: There are things in the air—charged particles, velocity, fear—that drive a young man. My adrenaline would pump; my heart would thrill. The winds rose and buffeted me, and the sea splashed higher. This was dangerous; this was exciting.

Now: There is salt in the air, and my glasses are getting a thick coating every few minutes. I am wondering where I can find a little shelter to change into my contact lenses.

Then: I came to the attention of the network and was described as "Dan Rather, up to his ass in water moccasins" by Walter Cronkite, who did much of his growing up in Texas and knows his water moccasins. Hurricane reporting can be a genuine public service: You warn people to get out of the way and tell them when it's safe to go home. There aren't many stories that are of more direct importance to people's lives. But, I thought at the time, it can also be good for your career.

Now: In a speech to college students in Chicago, I say, "Be sure to tell your parents: Dan Rather did not advise you to chain yourself to a tree in the middle of a hurricane just to advance your career."

NINE
The Weapon in the Box

I HAVE been described in print as someone with a "never-ending, consuming passion for news." That description is dead solid perfect.

In many ways my career at CBS has been a puzzlement. I was tagged as too intense to be an anchorman, too inclined to get into a confrontation over the odd event, too bull-headed. Yet more than a dozen years have passed since I succeeded Walter Cronkite, and to the surprise of many, myself included, I am still here. I am among the lucky few who get to make a living acting out their childhood dream. I make no apology for how corny that may sound. Anchoring the news is a peculiar world of makeup and hair and the right necktie. You are under a huge magnifying glass, aware at all times that if the sun catches that glass at the wrong angle, it can burn you to a crisp in a nanosecond.

But over the years I have been storing up a few observations and concerns about the business of news. So when I was asked to speak to the Radio and Television News Directors Association and, in particular, to honor the memory of Ed Murrow, who had begun the traditions left in my custody, I accepted.

I looked out across my audience, the men and women who directed the news at stations throughout America, meeting now, in late September of 1993, in Miami. To this group, decades earlier, Murrow had given the best-known speech he ever made, the greatest ever by any broadcaster.

As part of my appearance, I had been asked to introduce a video-tape tribute to Murrow. "Almost sixty years after he started—almost thirty years after his death—he is still the best, in broadcasting or print," I said. "He reported, he led, he made the best broadcasts of his time. They include the *This Is London* broadcasts during the Battle of Britain, the radio reports from the death camp at Buchenwald, and the television programs on Joseph McCarthy and on the *Harvest of Shame*.

"Edward R. Murrow was not only the patron and founding saint of electronic news and the best-ever practitioner of it. He also set standards for excellence and courage that remain the standards the world over. Murrow was, in short, a hero.

"Murrow made his memorable speech to the news directors in Chicago, October 15, 1958. In it, he criticized what commercial television was becoming, and challenged himself, his colleagues—and all of us—to do better. Ed Murrow said of television: 'This instrument can teach, it can illuminate; yes, and it can even inspire. But it can do so only to the extent that humans are determined to use it to those ends. Otherwise, it is merely wires and lights in a box. There is a great and perhaps decisive battle to be fought against ignorance, intolerance and indifference. This weapon of television could be useful.' "

With those words, the camera flashed upon the screen both a biography and a fond remembrance of Murrow. As I watched, I was thinking about Murrow's speech. It was risky, and he knew it; a bold shot, and he knew it. That was part of the Morrow style. And I went on to share those thoughts with the professional descendants of the people Murrow had addressed thirty-five years earlier.

"[Murrow] began [his 1958] speech with the modest speculation that, 'This just might do nobody any good.' I don't think Ed Murrow believed that. It was a call to arms—the most quoted line is the one about 'wires and lights in a box,' but the more important line is 'This weapon of television.' Ed Murrow had seen all kinds of battles, and if *he* lifted *his* voice in a battle cry, surely some of his own colleagues would hear him and heed him.

"I wasn't in Chicago that night. I was in Houston, serving my apprenticeship in news, a beginner in radio and television. I hadn't met Murrow yet. I could only read about his speech in the newspapers, but I absorbed every word. In my own little Texas bayou and pine tree world of journalism dreams, Murrow became protean, titanic, huge. There were other great ones: William L. Shirer, Eric Sevareid, Charles Collingwood, and Douglas Edwards; and later Walter Cronkite—men of courage and skill and great intelligence. But Murrow was *their* leader.

"As he had been for many others, Murrow had been my hero when I was just a boy. Across the radio, across the Atlantic, and across half the United States, his voice came, the deep rumble and the dramatic pause just when he said, 'THIS . . . is London.' I never got that voice out of my head. It was like a piece of music that has never stopped playing for me. Murrow told me tales of bravery in time of war, tales more thrilling than *Captain Midnight* or *Jack Armstrong* because these were *true*.

"He talked about the bravery of soldiers and citizens. He never made a big fuss about his own bravery. But even as a little boy, I knew it took bravery just to stand on that rooftop, with the bombs raining down thunder and lightning all around him . . . or to go up in that plane—*D-for-Dog*—with the ack-ack and the Messerschmitts all about. And I never forgot that Murrow did all this because he wanted me and my family, and all of us back home in America, to know . . . the truth. For *that*, for our knowledge of the truth, he risked his life.

"In my mind, then and now, neither Achilles nor King Arthur, not Pecos Bill or Davy Crockett, surpassed a hero like that.

"The Murrow I met years later—person-to-person, if you will—was everything I wanted that hero to be. He was a quiet man: tall, strong, steady-eyed, not afraid of silence. What separated Ed Murrow from the rest of the pack was courage.

"Ed Murrow had courage. He had the physical courage to face the Blitzkrieg in London. He had the professional courage to tell the truth about McCarthyism. And he had the courage to stand before the Radio and Television News Directors Association, and to say some things those good people didn't want to hear, but needed to hear.

"In our comfort and complacency, in our (dare we say it?) cowardice, we, none of us, want to hear the battle cry. Murrow had the courage to sound it anyway. Thirty-five years later, however uncomfortable, it's worth pausing to ask—how goes the battle?

"How goes the battle for quality, for truth and justice, for programs worthy of the best within ourselves and the audience? How goes the battle against 'ignorance, intolerance and indifference'? The battle not to be merely 'wires and lights in a box,' the battle to make television not just entertaining but also, at least some little slice of time, useful for higher, better things? How goes the battle?

"The answer, we know, is 'Not very well.' In too many important ways, we have allowed this great instrument, this resource, this weapon for good, to be squandered and cheapened. About this, the best among us hang their heads in embarrassment, even shame. For too long we have answered to the worst, not to the best, within ourselves and within our audience. We are less because of this. Our audience is less, and so is our country.

"Ed Murrow had faith in our country's decision to emphasize, from the beginning, commercial broadcasting. He recognized commercial broadcasting's potential, and its superiority over other possibilities. But even as he believed in the freedom of commercial radio and television, Ed Murrow feared the rise of a cult that worshiped at the shrine of the implacable idol, Ratings. He feared that the drive to sell, sell, sell—and nothing but sell—was overwhelming the potential for good, the potential for service.

"He decried the hours of prime time as being full of 'decadence, escapism and insulation from the realities of the world in which we live.' As you let that sink in, let's remember that he was talking about programs like *I Love Lucy* and *The Honeymooners*. These are the programs that had Ed Murrow worried.

"In 1958, Murrow was worried because he saw a trend setting in: avoiding the unpleasant or controversial or challenging. Shortening newscasts and jamming them with ever-increasing numbers of commercials. Throwing out background, context, and analysis, and relying just on headlines. Going for entertainment values over the values of good journalism, all in the belief that the public wouldn't accept anything other than the safe, the serene, and the self-evident.

"Murrow knew that belief was wrong. He had seen how honest, mature, and responsible American listeners and viewers could be when programming itself was honest, mature, and responsible. Reducing the amount of real-world reality on television, Murrow argued, was unconscionable.

"But Murrow did not just offer criticism. He also offered solutions.

Importantly, Murrow proposed that news divisions and departments not be held to the same standards of ratings and profits as entertainment and sports. Private profit from television is fine, but there *should* be a responsibility to news and public service that goes with it; this was the core of Murrow's case.

"In the end, Murrow could not bring himself to believe that the battle about which he spoke so eloquently could be won. He left electronic journalism believing that electronic news in America was doomed to be forever overwhelmed by commercialism and entertainment values. About that, I hope, I believe, Murrow was wrong. The battle is dark and odds-against. But it is not irreversible—not yet. To prevent it from being so requires courage.

"A few, just a few, good men and women with courage—the courage to practice the idealism that attracted most of us to the craft in the first place—can make a decisive difference. We can be those men and women. If the people in this room tonight simply agreed, starting tomorrow, to turn it around—we would turn it around.

"Tomorrow is a new day. We toil and are proud to be in this craft because of the way Edward R. Murrow brought it into being. We can be worthy of him—we can share his courage—or we can continue to work in complacency and fear.

"Cassius was right: *Men at some time are masters of their fates:/ The fault, dear Brutus, is not in our stars,/ But in ourselves . . .*"

THE initial reaction was stunned silence. Then the audience clapped dutifully for about thirty seconds—and then, as Bill Madison remembers it, they rose all at once, as if they all understood at the same time, and *whoosh,* they were on their feet.

This is a flattering recollection that I can't actually verify: I was already halfway out the door. But they brought me back into the ballroom to see a genuine standing ovation, a warm and supporting gesture from the men and women I'm proud to call colleagues.

Unfortunately, a very few in management below the top privately chose to hear the criticism as a personal attack. Some others chose simply to hear the criticism and ignore the plea for improvement. Some of them treated it simply as "Dan in one of his moods." A couple suggested that they'd have felt better if they'd seen a text of the speech before it was delivered.

It's true I'd held the speech close to my vest all the way. As I came into the ballroom, only I knew exactly what I was going to say. But this wasn't just the worry that word would leak out. The truth is that the words I wanted to speak were so personal, so very much from and of my heart and my experience, that I didn't want to share them until I was ready.

I haven't worked in journalism for more than forty-five years without caring how the work is done. My work is important to me, and the work that's done by others around me is important to me. Not only because I'm a professional but because I'm an American.

I've been to countries where the people don't have a free press, where reporters with strict professional standards are thrown in jail or killed. Those Americans who believe the American "Media" is biased would do well to sample the newspapers, radio, and television of other countries where the "news" is prescreened, preapproved, predigested, a simplified view of limited scope, only that part of the truth that somebody else wants you to know.

Through the years Edward R. Murrow and other dedicated, responsible American journalists have believed that the American people were mature enough and wise enough to handle the truth. That belief is one I fervently share. It got me into journalism, it's kept me in journalism, and it'll keep me here as long as I have my health and a story to report.

OUTTAKE

THE weekend before Valentine's Day, 1994, your reporter went to a wedding. My young friend Suzanne Meirowitz, now a producer of the *CBS Evening News,* found the man of her dreams, Bob Nederlander, and had a storybook wedding. Suzanne couldn't have looked prettier, Bob couldn't have looked prouder, and together—surrounded by loving family and friends—they were as happy as any couple I've ever seen. Outside, there was cold and snow, one of the worst snowstorms of the impossibly snowy winter, but inside was a scene as warm and romantic as you could hope for.

I wish I could tell Suzanne it will always be so—and at every wedding, don't you always think, Maybe, maybe *this* time for *these* lovers it *will* always be so—maybe the joys of this moment can translate to a lifetime of love and happiness right out of the storybooks.

But the storybooks almost always stop just before the wedding. You never find out how Snow White handled a career and raising kids. Snow White would've become Queen, you know—she *would* have had a career. But you never find out how she faced down the killer flu that swept through her whole family when she'd got a big report due at the office the next day. You never find out how Snow White and Prince Charming settled disagreements or what happened on days when Prince Charming . . . *wasn't.*

That weekend, at Bob and Suzanne's wedding, the rabbi said a lot of good things: about patience, about sticking out the tough times, just the way we'd stuck out the snow. And you remember that there's togetherness, knowing that I'd never have been able to stick out the tough times if Jean hadn't been right there, patiently sticking them out beside me.

But there's also *dancing*—and for my newlywed friends on that Valentine's Day, that would have been my best gift. I'd tell my friends to take a minute to dance together whenever you can. At the wedding I took a spin around the floor with my own dancing partner for most of four decades. And in my eyes Jean wore glass slippers and a golden gown—a storybook bride all over again.

Real life is hard on storybook love. But sometimes the dreams really do come true.

JOSEPH E. PERSICO

NUREMBERG

INFAMY ON TRIAL

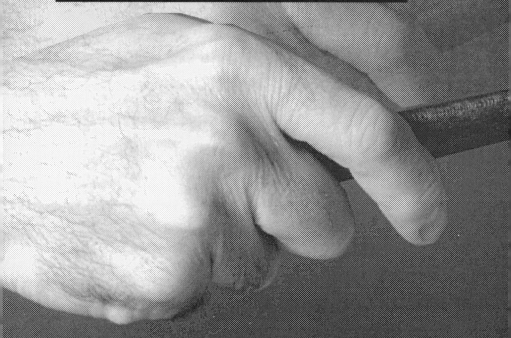

. . . A small door opened in the rear of the dock, and the rumble of conversation halted. Out stepped Göring, Ribbentrop, and Hess. They blinked under the bright lights and made their way uncertainly toward the dock. Behind them, against the wall, stood six American sentries, arms folded behind their backs.

As the rest of the defendants filed in, [journalist] Janet Flanner started taking notes: "You look at Nuremberg, and you are looking at the result of the war. You look at the men in the dock, and you are seeing the cause."

—*Nuremberg*

CHAPTER I
PRELUDE TO JUDGMENT
1

Nuremberg, October 15, 1946. Willi Krug cocked an eye at the battered alarm clock he kept within arm's reach on the floor. Five thirty—still dark out, with only the pewter light of the moon angling down from the barred window and spilling through the open doorway of his cell. The rare sound of a truck revving and pulling out of the prison yard had awakened him. Earlier his sleep had been broken by the noise of hammers banging and the muffled shouts of GIs.

Willi swung his legs off the cot and started pulling on his clothes—cast-off U.S. Army fatigues dyed black for prison staffers like himself. He left his cell and paused on the catwalk. An uneasiness swept over him. The hammering in the night, the sound of the departing vehicle—this could be the day. Ever since the sentences had been handed down two weeks before, on October 1, the unknown had hung over the prison like a cloud.

He began making his way down a stairwell strung with chicken wire to prevent suicide leaps. He had made this dawn descent every day for nearly fourteen months, ever since the defendants had been sent here for trial. It was an odd existence that Krug led—confined to prison yet not a prisoner, something more than a trusty, but still less than the well-fed American jailers for whom he worked.

In the last days of the war he had been a corporal attached to a field kitchen in the German Twelfth Army, which had been deployed to halt the Russian advance on Berlin. Willi's concern had not been whether they could stop the Red Army. That hope was forlorn. His

aim had been to keep himself out of Russian hands. He had eventually succeeded, along with hundreds of thousands of his comrades,
thanks to a man now caged in this prison, Grand Admiral Karl Dönitz.
Dönitz had succeeded Adolf Hitler at the end and, with all lost,
had determined to drag out the surrender negotiations the few precious days that allowed Germans like Willi to flee west and entrust
their fate to the expectedly more tender mercies of American and
British captors.

After his surrender to the American Ninth Army, Willi managed to
have himself selected to serve as a trusty at an improvised prison in
Bad Mondorf, Luxembourg. There he was astonished to find himself
among German leaders whom he would have once considered as
remote as the stars. When over a dozen of them were shipped to
Nuremberg to be tried as war criminals, Willi was given a choice: He
could be released and go home, or else work for the Americans in
Nuremberg. For Willi Krug home was the bombed-out shell of an
apartment building in Schweinfurt—rubble that had entombed his
wife and child. He gratefully seized the offer of a roof over his head
and regular meals.

On the main floor of the cellblock he looked out on a familiar
scene. On either side of the corridor stood the GI guards, one to a
cell, condemned to stare at their charges through a square porthole
in the door. Usually the guards greeted him with "Hey, Willi, *wie
geht's,* you old kraut" and other fractured German gibes as he passed
by. His arrival was the signal for the guards to turn off the spotlights
that they directed through the portholes onto the sleeping prisoners'
faces. But this morning's air of anxiety had tempered even these
brash young Americans, and they let him pass with bare nods.

He headed for the basement to fill the tin washbasins that he
brought to each cell every morning. En route, he passed cell 5 and
glanced in. He briefly caught sight of the Reichsmarschall's square
face, defiant chin, long, sharp nose, and thin lips. Hermann Göring
lay there, hands resting outside the blankets, regulation style, so the
guard could see them. Willi hurried by. He was required only to
dispense cold water for washing up. But when he had time, he liked
to heat the water for the Reichsmarschall, particularly this morning,
when he wondered if he might ever perform this small kindness
again.

HERMANN GÖRING HAD NOT BEEN asleep when Willi Krug passed by. He had slept fitfully that night. The Amytal and Seconal pills that Dr. Pfluecker always gave him had failed. He too felt the foreboding, and with far more reason than Krug had. The guard snapped off the hated light, and Göring allowed his eyes to open. His exposed hands were cold. He felt scant desire to rouse himself and closed his eyes again.

He might well have been recalling the other war, the war of his early manhood. One memory always stood out as crisply as the sun on that July morning in 1918. Three months before, their squadron commander, the legendary Baron Manfred von Richthofen—creator of the Flying Circus, single-handed destroyer of eighty enemy planes—had himself been shot down and killed over France. Göring, with twenty-one kills to his credit, fully expected to be the Red Baron's successor. Instead, the squadron went to a by-the-book flying bureaucrat, Wilhelm Reinhardt. Göring, impatient and impetuous, had been judged lacking in the steadiness required of a commanding officer.

That July morning he and Reinhardt had been sent to Adlershof field to meet Anthony Fokker, the builder of German warplanes. Göring spotted an awkward-looking biplane in a corner of the airfield. What was that? he asked Fokker. Just an experimental craft, Fokker said. He wanted to fly it, Göring announced. After a quick explanation of the controls, he found himself bumping along a grassy runway and nursing the aircraft aloft. He beat up the field, flying at times almost at zero altitude. He looped and spun and yawed and, finally, after a breathtaking pass down the runway on canted wings, brought her in and jumped out of the cockpit before an astonished crowd.

Reinhardt's pride demanded that he too take up the plane. He was, after all, commander of Richthofen's Flying Circus. The spectators watched Reinhardt streak toward the sun. And then it happened: A resounding crack, and the left wing simply drifted away from the fuselage. That was how Hermann Göring, at the age of twenty-five, became commander of the Flying Circus.

A polite tapping on the cell door broke Göring's reverie, and he sat up with a start. Framed in the porthole was the sad, smiling face of Willi Krug, announcing that he had brought the Reichsmarschall his water. Göring reluctantly threw off the covers and took the washbasin. He set it on the table, bent over, and splashed the water over his face. It was, he noted, agreeably warm.

2

Washington, April 1945. The train of events that put Hermann Göring into a Nuremberg jail cell had been set in motion a year and a half before by a phone call from the White House to the Supreme Court. Samuel Rosenman, speechwriter and confidant of President Franklin D. Roosevelt, was calling Associate Justice Robert H. Jackson. Rosenman asked if he might stop by Jackson's chambers. The call came barely two weeks after America had been staggered by the sudden death of FDR, whose successor was an as yet unknown quantity, Harry S. Truman.

On his arrival Rosenman gave Jackson's secretary, Elsie Douglas, a courtly nod and smile. Mrs. Douglas was an attractive blond widow of early middle age, who combined a good nature with brisk efficiency. She ushered Rosenman into a wood-paneled chamber.

Jackson rose and greeted his visitor warmly. The two men embraced almost as members of a family still feeling a grievous loss. Jackson motioned his guest to a leather armchair and asked his secretary to bring in coffee and to hold all calls.

They talked for a time about the death of the president. Then Rosenman came to the point. He had been in England with Prime Minister Winston Churchill, he said, just three days before FDR died, to discuss what was to be done with the Nazi leaders when the war in Europe ended, as it soon must. Rosenman's eyes crinkled as he repeated a story that Churchill had told him. In his last meeting with Stalin, Churchill had remarked that whenever they captured one of the Nazi bigwigs, he ought to be summarily shot. With that, Stalin announced sanctimoniously, "In the Soviet Union, we never execute anyone without a trial." Churchill responded, "Of course, of course. We should give them a trial first." Rosenman and Jackson roared with laughter: The Soviet butcher insisting on due process, while a champion of Western civilization called for drumhead justice.

Rosenman was not sure what the president had really wanted— when he said "president," he still meant Roosevelt. At times, Rosenman recalled, FDR had also leaned toward shooting the Nazi leaders out of hand. But in February at Yalta, FDR, Churchill, and Stalin had all gone on record as favoring the law. There would be war-crimes trials soon, Rosenman announced, and Truman wanted Jackson to prosecute for the United States. Rosenman explained that Truman had not forgotten Jackson's earlier reputation as a formidable prosecutor.

Jackson was an old Washington hand, and he accepted that whenever a president did something, there was a good reason and then there was the real reason. Was one of his Supreme Court rivals trying to get him off the bench? Would this assignment mean leaving the Court? he asked. Of course not, Rosenman replied. Jackson wanted the weekend to think the matter over. Fair enough, Rosenman answered, and rose to take his leave.

THE man Truman wanted to prosecute war criminals was unique in the history of the twentieth-century Supreme Court: Robert Jackson did not possess a law degree. He had been born fifty-three years before on a farm in rural Pennsylvania. His father, William, was a self-taught, self-made entrepreneur, who always had his hand in something—a sawmill, a hotel, a stable of harness-racing horses. Jackson's mother, Angelina Houghwout, was descended from an old Dutch family that had been in America since 1660. When young Bob was five, the Jacksons moved to the Jamestown area of western New York State, and there he was raised in a world long since vanished, reading the Bible, singing hymns, and learning his letters from *McGuffey's Readers.*

Young Bob spent a year at Albany Law School on money borrowed from an uncle, and received a certificate of completion but not a degree. Thereafter he settled in Jamestown, population 31,000, and over the next twenty years became a success in his small corner of the world, representing banks, railroads, and industry. But a populist streak in him also propelled Jackson to defend, without a fee, a poor black accused of stabbing a white farmer to death; his client went free. By 1932 Bob Jackson was prosperous, a pillar of Jamestown society, married to his law school sweetheart, Irene Gerhardt, and the doting father of a son, William Eldred, and a daughter, Mary Margaret.

In a single evening fate conspired to remake his life. Jackson had gone to a Jamestown Democratic fund-raising dinner. In that spring of 1932 the burning issue for Democrats was the massive corruption in the administration of New York City's bon vivant mayor, Jimmy

Walker. To Jackson's dismay not a single speaker made any reference to the Walker scandals. When it was his turn, Jackson said that this omission was a disgrace. "It comes perilously close to putting the state Democratic party in Walker's back pocket," he warned.

Months later New York's governor, Franklin Roosevelt, was elected president and Bob Jackson was invited to Washington by Henry Morgenthau, Roosevelt's treasury secretary. Jackson's Jamestown speech had taken courage, and that's what the president was looking for.

Thus it was that Bob Jackson entered the New Deal. He started in the White House, drafting tax legislation, and soon was receiving appreciative "Dear Bob" notes from an admiring FDR. His rise was swift. Roosevelt named him head of the antitrust division in the Department of Justice, then solicitor general, in which capacity he argued the government's cases before the Supreme Court. Then, at age forty-seven, Bob Jackson became U.S. attorney general.

In 1941, when the Supreme Court's chief justice, Charles Evans Hughes, resigned, Jackson was a candidate to become his successor. Roosevelt was pressured instead to name a sitting associate justice, Harlan F. Stone, as chief justice. But the country lawyer from Jamestown was named associate justice when Stone moved up to the top spot.

ON SUNDAY afternoon, three days after Rosenman's proposal, Jackson sat alone in the study at Hickory Hill, his rambling home in the Virginia hunt country. He recalled the attempt to punish war criminals after World War I—a fiasco. The victorious Allies had drawn up a list of over 4900 potential defendants and quickly trimmed it to 901 names. Of these, twelve men were ordered to trial by a German court in Leipzig in 1922. Three of the twelve simply failed to appear. Charges were dropped against three more. The remaining six got off with laughably light sentences.

Now President Truman was asking Jackson to become part of an effort to try again, this time through an international tribunal. There were no precedents, no existing body of law, not even a court. The risks to Jackson's career were high, the rewards uncertain. The course of prudence was to turn Truman down. Yet the truth was that Jackson had become bored on the Supreme Court. The titanic legal battles of the '30s over Roosevelt's New Deal legislation were over. The main arena now was abroad, in a world turned upside down by war. Jackson picked up the phone and dialed his son, Bill, a recent graduate of Harvard Law School and now a navy ensign assigned to a Washington desk job. He told Bill he was inclined to take Truman's offer, and as his first staff appointment, he wanted to hire Ensign Jackson. "Not bad for your first case," the father added. Bill hesitated briefly. It meant leaving his recent bride for an uncertain period, since the trial would be held in Europe, and wives, his father made clear, were not coming. Jackson went on, "You'll be defending me on this one long after I'm gone. That's one reason I want you there. Anyway," he added, "I expect we'll be home before Christmas."

ON MAY 2, 1945, Robert Jackson was named the American war-crimes prosecutor. By then his greatest prey had escaped him: On April 30, in a bunker twenty feet below the Berlin sewer system, Adolf Hitler took his own life. That left Reichsmarschall Hermann Göring as the top-ranking Nazi. Göring, creator of the Gestapo and the first concentration camp, had last seen Hitler in the bunker at a maudlin birthday party held for the Führer ten days before his suicide. At that point the Russians were one mile away, yet Hitler refused to leave the doomed capital. Göring felt no such compulsion and explained to Hitler that he had to head south to organize the defense of what was left of Germany. Hitler gave Göring a cool handshake and a look that suggested he smelled treachery and cowardice.

Göring flew from Berlin to Berchtesgaden, and there made a fateful decision. Hitler, by remaining in Berlin, would soon be dead or captured. Göring retrieved from his safe his copy of the Führer decree dated June 29, 1941. Its meaning was unmistakable: In the event of Hitler's death or incapacity Göring was to become leader of the Reich. He fired off a telegram to the bunker saying that unless he heard otherwise, he was taking over the nation's leadership. It was a rash gamble, and Göring lost. An enraged Hitler read the message as absolute proof of treachery. Göring's keenest enemy, Martin Bormann, secretary to the Führer, seized the moment and issued orders to the political police in Berchtesgaden to have Göring shot. Upon discovering the execution order, Göring did what Willi Krug and hordes of other ordinary Germans were doing in those waning hours of the war—he headed for the American lines.

JUSTICE JACKSON EAGERLY READ the document before him—only six pages, plus a cover memo—bound in a blue folder with TOP SECRET stamped across it. A week had passed since his appointment as American prosecutor, and he had begun with virtually nothing. Yet here, condensed in a few pages entitled "Trial of European War Criminals," he detected a brilliant start. He flipped back to the cover memo to note again the author's name: Colonel Murray Bernays, Special Projects Branch, Department of War.

MURRAY Bernays, a handsome, impressive-looking man with cavernous eyes, had been living with the issue for the previous nine months. In 1944 President Roosevelt had handed the War Department responsibility for figuring out how to bring war criminals to justice. Secretary of War Henry Stimson directed Assistant Secretary of War John McCloy to come up with a plan. But the war was still far from won, and more urgent problems occupied McCloy's thoughts. The order was bumped down to lower levels, until it finally landed in a three-man catchall unit called the Special Projects Branch, headed by Colonel Murray Bernays.

Bernays' life had been a model immigrant success story. His Lithuanian Jewish parents had brought him to America in 1900, when he was six years old. A brilliant student, he graduated from Columbia Law School and was eventually associated with a prestigious New York law firm. He had married Hertha Bernays, a niece of Sigmund Freud's, and found it advantageous to take her name. He had left a prosperous practice to join the army.

On September 15, 1944, just a week after Bernays received the war-crimes assignment, he slumped back in his chair in his office in the War Department, the job done. He had expected the task of inventing legal machinery for bringing mass murderers and aggressors to justice to be monumental. Two traps especially had to be avoided: He did not want an approach that bogged down in an attempt to deal individually with thousands of SS flunkies who had beaten a prisoner to death or loaded the gas chambers, nor did he want legal machinery that would allow the top leaders to escape simply because there was no blood directly on their hands.

The idea, beautiful in its simplicity, had struck him like a burst of light. The Nazi regime was a criminal conspiracy. The whole Nazi movement had been a deliberate effort to arm for war, seize the lands of other nations, steal their wealth, enslave and exploit their populations, and exterminate the Jews of Europe. If the whole movement was a criminal conspiracy, then those who created it were, ipso facto, criminals. This part of Bernays' net caught the ringleaders, the masterminds. His second inspiration had been to declare Nazi organizations criminal as well. They included the party, the SS, the Gestapo. This would catch the lower-level war criminals. If you could prove that the SS was a criminal organization, then you need only demonstrate that a man belonged to the SS and hand down appropriate punishment.

To this Bernays brew Secretary Stimson added the idea that the waging of aggressive war was a crime itself, an idea suggested by his trusted friend and former law partner William C. Chanler. Germany was a signatory of the 1928 Kellogg-Briand Pact for the renunciation of war as an instrument of national policy. Germany, by breaking the treaty, was not waging legitimate war when invading its neighbors; it was committing murder, assault, and destruction of property.

President Roosevelt liked Bernays' thesis: Nazism as a criminal conspiracy. He also liked Chanler's contribution: aggression as a crime. He wanted the combined plan circulated to a few key administration officials for their reaction.

HERBERT Wechsler frowned at the folder, stamped TOP SECRET, resting on his desk in the Justice Department. Wechsler's boss, Attorney General Francis Biddle, had passed it along to the subordinate whose judgment he trusted most. Before the war Wechsler had been a distinguished legal scholar at the same Columbia Law School that had produced Murray Bernays, and he found Bernays' scholarship slapdash and superficial. What was this conspiracy nonsense? Any international court was obviously going to have to include the major Allies: America, Britain, Russia, and France. Yes, Anglo-Saxon law recognized criminal conspiracy, but the concept did not even exist in the courts of France, Germany, or the Soviet Union.

And defining acts as criminal after they had been committed? That was ex post facto law, bastard law. And declaring that whole organizations were criminal? Some had members numbering in the millions. This meat-axe approach was fraught with potential for injustices, and Wechsler intended to tell the attorney general so.

At this point neither Wechsler nor Biddle knew that they were fated to play roles at the trial or that the flaws Wechsler believed he detected in Bernays' grand design would haunt them to the end.

Bob Jackson still found the Bernays plan inspired. He invited Bernays to his Supreme Court chambers in order to meet him. After they concluded their talk and Bernays departed, Jackson dictated into his diary, as was his habit, the high points of the day. The final entry was that he intended to hire Murray Bernays as his executive officer.

3

ON THE other side of the world another lawyer, Hans Frank, contemplated the irony of his existence. When Frank was a young man, his single driving obsession had been to make himself a respected figure in his profession. Instead, at age forty-five, he was sitting in a prison cell, running his thumb along the edge of a gardener's knife and hoping it was sharp enough to slit his wrist.

His body ached. Before dumping him here in the Miesbach jail in Bavaria, American GIs had formed a double line seventy feet long and forced Frank to run the gauntlet under a hail of kicks and punches. His tormentors were combat veterans of the Seventh Army's 36th Regiment, who days before had passed through the concentration camp at Dachau. Hans Frank, they had learned, was the Jew Butcher of Cracow, a man said to be engaged in work similar to what they had just witnessed.

Lilli Gau, it seemed to Frank, had been the motive force behind the decisions that had led him to this fate. She was the beautiful daughter of a rich Munich industrialist, the girl Frank had loved from boyhood. Frank's roots were not remotely similar to hers. His mother came of peasant stock, and his father was a lawyer of suspect ethics.

Hans had just taken his law degree at the University of Munich and had joined his father's practice. Forever seared into his memory was the day when the police came and arrested Frank senior for embezzlement. Even before the scandal, the Gau family had disapproved of the shady lawyer's son. Now the thought of their daughter's marrying the son of a jailbird horrified them. A marriage was quickly arranged between Lilli and a suitable magnate. Hans rebounded into a marriage with Brigitte Herbst, the daughter of a factory worker.

After his marriage Frank vowed he would expunge the stain of his father's disgrace. He would achieve recognition and respectability as a professor of law. In the meantime, with one child and another on the way, Frank had to earn a living. In October 1927 he read a classified ad in the Nazi Party organ, the *Völkischer Beobachter.* A dozen storm troopers had broken into a Berlin restaurant where a party of Jews was having dinner. They proceeded to tear the place apart. The police were called and the storm troopers arrested. The *Völkischer Beobachter* was looking for a lawyer to defend these "poor party members without means." Strapped though he was financially, Frank made a rash gamble. He wrote to the paper saying that he would take the case without a fee. He then traveled to Berlin and got the rowdies off with a light sentence.

After the trial he stopped by the Nazi Party office, where Adolf Hitler himself appeared to meet this youthful prodigy of the law. "You must come and work for the party," he told Frank. "But," Frank demurred, "I'm planning an academic career." Hitler waved aside the objection. By the age of twenty-eight Frank was the Nazis' chief counsel. His party work won headlines, and soon other clients flocked to his Munich office.

In 1930, at age thirty, Hans Frank was elected to the Reichstag. The Nazis came to power in 1933, and he continued to prosper. By 1939 he was Germany's minister of justice, the highest-ranking jurist in the land. He often wondered what Lilli Gau would think of him now.

When the war broke out, Frank joined his Bavarian regiment as a lieutenant. Within weeks after Poland's defeat, he was summoned to Hitler's private railway car in Silesia to discuss an assignment more suitable to his talents. After the meeting Frank raced back home and burst into his wife's dressing room. "Brigitte," he exclaimed, "you are going to be the queen of Poland!" As Frank explained, a huge chunk of western Poland had been absorbed into the Third Reich. The Soviet Union had taken a slice of eastern Poland. What remained in the middle, some forty percent of the original country, was to be ruled by Frank as governor-general, although he would have to share some of his authority with Reichsführer Heinrich Himmler, head of the SS, which ran the concentration camps that would keep the Poles in line. Where would they live? Brigitte wanted to know. In Cracow, he told her, in a palace.

At his first sight of Wawel Castle, the ancient seat of Polish kings, Frank behaved like a child given a huge toy. Resplendent in a personally designed uniform with flaring breeches and black boots, he bounded up the steps to the main entrance, trailed by adjutants. He entered the throne room, its walls cloaked with medieval tapestries. Here, he decided, he would hold official receptions. Nearby he found a slightly smaller room, its twenty-foot walls sheathed in tooled red leather. This would be his private office.

Frank knew Himmler's priority well and was eager to please. Thus his first official act as governor-general was to order all Polish Jews to report to German labor offices for assignment. But Nazi Jewish policy was ticklish for Frank. An intelligent, cultivated man, he did not believe the Nazi Party's crude anti-Semitic claptrap. More troublesome, Frank had a dark secret: Though he had been raised as a Catholic, he was part Jewish. Frank overcompensated with zeal. On his first anniversary at Wawel Castle, he invited his staff to the throne room for a celebration. There he took the center of the floor and reviewed the year's progress, achieved in great part, he said, because so many "lice and Jews had been eliminated." As he spoke, a young bespectacled officer scribbled furiously—Frank had ordered that everything he said in public or in his office was to be recorded in a diary for posterity. They had met their quota, Frank boasted, by deporting 1.3 million Poles for forced labor in Germany. And "at the current level of permitted rations, some 1.2 million Jews could be expected to die of hunger." That was not enough, he went on. "We must obliterate the Jews. Somehow or other we will achieve their extermination."

CRACOW was to have been their Camelot, and in the beginning Brigitte Frank reveled in the glittering social life her husband inaugurated, with its stream of Nazi luminaries to whom she played hostess. She relished her trips to the city's Jewish section and up to the Warsaw Ghetto. She loved the hand-sewn camisoles the Jews made, the furs, gold, and carpets that, in their desperation, they would sell for practically nothing. Frau Frank was greedy but not insensitive. The reports sent back to Germany about the improved lot of the Poles under her husband's leadership were contradicted in the wizened face of every child she saw and by the Jewish corpses littering the ghetto streets. The undisguised hatred that greeted her every appearance in Poland began to depress her. And so she retreated to her country home in Schliersee in Bavaria and had the Polish loot shipped to her.

Hans Frank became lonely, and by late 1941, despite the surface glitter of his life, he was close to a nervous breakdown. On Himmler's most recent visit the Reichsführer had confronted Frank with proof of massive corruption in his administration. Himmler told Frank he was willing to drop the investigation on one condition: Frank was to turn over all police functions in Poland to the SS. Frank knew that this meant unfettered exploitation of the Poles and accelerated extermination of the Jews. He wrote a letter to the chief of the Wehrmacht, Field Marshal Wilhelm Keitel, asking to be returned to military duty. Keitel, known as the Führer's lackey, immediately showed the letter to Hitler, who read it and said, "Out of the question." Frank thereafter accepted Himmler's conditions. The flow of Jews to the concentration camps quickened.

Then, when all seemed hollowest, a letter arrived. The familiar handwriting jolted him. It was from Lilli Gau, whom he had not seen in twenty years. It began "My Dearest Hans," and in it she appealed to him for help. Her son had been killed on the Russian front, and she begged him to find out the details. Frank immediately set his staff to work on the case. Then he flew to Germany and personally delivered his finding to Lilli at her home in Bavaria. The electricity between them still crackled, and he found her husband surprisingly tolerant. Lilli took an apartment in Munich for their love nest, and Frank flew from Cracow almost every month to be with her.

He felt as if he had been reborn. In Poland he may have signed a pact with the devil to keep Himmler at bay, but in Germany he could again be the man he had started out to be—a champion of the law.

In June 1942 he made a speech to the Academy of German Law, the likes of which had not been heard since Hitler had taken power. Germany, Frank said, must return to the rule of law. No civilized nation could permit the arbitrary arrests, the imprisonment without due process, carried out by the Gestapo and the SS. He made three similar speeches, one at his alma mater—the University of Munich— to the wild cheering of the law students.

Frank was summoned before the Führer, expecting the worst. Hitler told him that he could excuse an occasional lapse of judgment. In the future, however, Frank was to confine his speeches to Poland and to the party line. Frank returned to Poland and dutifully delivered up the conscript workers to the labor czar, Fritz Sauckel, and the Jews to Himmler. Most of the latter, he knew, were sent to a camp some thirty miles from Cracow called Auschwitz.

In early 1945, as the Red Army thrust deep into Poland, Frank fled Cracow and returned to his home in Schliersee. He took with him, among other art treasures, Leonardo da Vinci's masterpiece *Lady with an Ermine*, stolen from a Polish museum. He also brought along his diary, totaling 11,367 pages. When the Americans found him in May, he put up no resistance, since he was convinced he had a strong hand to play. First he led Seventh Army officers to a cellar and told them he was turning over twenty-two priceless works of art, including the Leonardo, works he said he had been protecting from the Russian barbarians. He also gave the Americans his diary. It was all there—the words that would save him, his improvement of the lives of the Poles, his fights with Himmler, his brave law speeches in Germany. Certainly, the Americans would see through the pro forma anti-Semitic rabble-rousing. It was simply the lip service any Nazi official was expected to spout in order to keep his job.

Instead of receiving gratitude from the Americans, Frank was beaten, spat upon, and thrown into the back of a truck for the trip to the Miesbach prison. In the truck he took out an army knife and slashed at his throat. An alert GI pried the knife from his hand. The cut was superficial. A military doctor bandaged his neck, and the trip continued.

Now he sat in the Miesbach prison—a pasty man with thick lips, thinning dark hair, and dark-rimmed sad eyes—the gardening knife clutched in his right hand. As he drew it across his left wrist, a GI burst into the cell and flung him to the ground, thwarting his second suicide attempt. Hans Frank had been saved for eventual transport to Nuremberg, where he would face trial for war crimes.

ROBERT Jackson's resources were undeniably thin: a six-page master plan, a secretary, his son and a friend as aides, and a potential executive officer in Murray Bernays. Bernays impressed him, but Jackson was disappointed by the rest of the War Department. The department staff had collected only sketchy data on scattered atrocities, hardly the quality of evidence to form a successful prosecution.

And then Senator Alben Barkley, who had returned from a trip to a recently liberated concentration camp, tipped him off to where the gold lay. The key was a proud man, a power in his own right, and wooing him could be tricky. Jackson was prepared to chance it. He told Elsie Douglas to ring up the Office of Strategic Services and arrange a lunch date for him with General "Wild Bill" Donovan.

Until now Jackson had known little of Donovan or of his creation, the hush-hush OSS. The pudgy, modest-looking general had been the most decorated American officer to come out of World War I. He had gotten rich between the wars in a gilt-edged New York law practice. In this war he had built the OSS from nothing into America's first intelligence service.

The OSS, Donovan explained at their meeting, had field operations throughout Europe. His people had been tracking potential war criminals since 1942 and had accumulated substantial dossiers. Furthermore, he had every imaginable specialist within his ranks: scientists, linguists, and, best of all, some of America's brightest young lawyers.

As Donovan talked, Jackson considered a bold gamble. Wild Bill not only had an organization in place, but knew how to open doors throughout Washington and the military. Jackson took the plunge. Would Donovan possibly consider becoming his lead prosecutor? The general said, "I'll think about it."

THE war in Europe had ended in the ancient cathedral city of Reims, France, in a sterile red brick school building. On May 6, 1945, General Eisenhower gazed out a second-floor window as a U.S. Army command car pulled up bearing an eagerly awaited party.

General Alfred Jodl, small, trim, erect, stepped from the car. He was escorted into a room, where he sat down with Eisenhower's deputies, since the supreme commander had refused to negotiate with a Nazi general. Jodl's instructions from Grand Admiral Karl Dönitz were to stall as long as possible before surrendering. Every hour gained would mean more German units could escape the clutches of the Russians and surrender instead to the British and Americans.

As Jodl dragged his feet through the deliberations, Eisenhower lost all patience. He directed his aides to inform Jodl that if Jodl didn't sign the instrument of surrender, the Western front would be sealed. Fleeing Germans would then march into gunfire instead of POW cages. The game was over. At 2:38 a.m., May 7, Jodl affixed his signature to the terms of surrender, to take effect in forty-eight hours. Six years of war in Europe were about to end.

Afterward Jodl returned to Flensburg, Germany, where Grand Admiral Dönitz was headquartered. There he learned that the stalling strategies had allowed over 900,000 German soldiers originally facing the Russians to reach the American and British lines.

Dönitz had set up his government in Flensburg, near the Danish border, just days after succeeding Adolf Hitler as führer. He had placed a bust of Hitler on his dresser in the captain's stateroom of the Hamburg-American line's steamship *Patria*, where he had established his living quarters. A slight, gray man, he might well have passed for a small-town pharmacist. This unprepossessing figure had, however, been the terror of the Atlantic. Karl Dönitz had invented the "wolf pack" submarine strategy, which had sunk 2472 Allied ships. Hitler had called him the Rommel of the Seas and eventually gave Dönitz command of the German navy. Why Hitler had chosen him, a simple sailor, to succeed as führer mystified Dönitz. He had been an outsider, hardly one of the old party fighters. He had accepted the appointment with the same spirit that had governed his entire naval career: obeying an order was an officer's highest duty.

On May 23, 1945, British tanks rolled into the Flensburg town square. A British officer arrived at Dönitz's office and asked the admiral to gather his ministers in the lounge of the *Patria*. On their arrival General Eisenhower's personal representative, Lowell W. Rooks, announced, "Gentlemen, I am empowered by the supreme allied commander to inform you that the Flensburg government is dissolved. You have one half hour to pack one bag before you are taken to places of detention." Rooks then drew a list from his pocket and read off the names of the men who would be taken to Bad Mondorf as defendants in future war-crimes trials.

When his name was called, Dönitz summoned the discipline of a lifetime to mask his shock and outrage. He caught sight of an equally stunned Jodl as the general's name was called. Also swept up as war-crimes suspects were Field Marshal Wilhelm Keitel, chief of staff of the armed forces; Alfred Rosenberg, the philosopher of Nazism; and Hitler's armaments chief, Albert Speer.

THE June sun was blazing at Washington's National Airport, and the air shimmered off the tarmac, enveloping the silvery hull of an Army Air Forces C-54C transport fitted out for VIP service. Robert Jackson motioned to Elsie Douglas to mount the portable stairs to the plane. As she started up, he gave her hand a squeeze, knowing that she was uneasy. It was her first flight. The rest of the party—seventeen lawyers, secretaries, and assorted staff—fell in behind Jackson for the trip to London.

Inside the plane, Jackson signaled for U.S. Army colonel Robert Storey to sit next to him. Storey, a Texas lawyer before the war, was a mild-mannered, balding man in his fifties, who had, in the final months of the war, carried out an OSS mission with the Red Army. As the Soviets advanced into Germany, he had witnessed war-crimes trials communist style. Jackson valued this experience, and he liked Storey. Thus he had enlisted the man for his staff.

As the plane became airborne, Jackson began questioning Storey about his Soviet adventure. The Russians, Storey explained, would put the accused on the witness stand, convict him by confession, and execute him, usually before the sun went down. Often the condemned were not war criminals at all, but simply opponents of communism. Jackson should know, he warned, that the Russians understood only one language: power.

The trial of war criminals, Jackson was convinced, must not be seen as an exercise in vengeance. It must signal not simply the triumph of superior might but the triumph of superior morality. Jackson was in a position to fashion a future in which aggressive warfare would no longer be accepted as the extreme edge of political activity, but would be dealt with as a crime. If he succeeded, that could be the greatest leap forward in the history of civilization.

On arriving in London, the Jackson party checked into Claridge's hotel. To one who had never witnessed war, the bomb damage in London was sobering. This brave city, pockmarked and bleeding, with thousands of innocent dead, confirmed Jackson's sense of mission. War-crimes trials were a splendid idea, he thought.

ROBERT JACKSON AND BRITAIN'S attorney general, Sir David Maxwell-Fyfe, chatted as they entered Church House, which the British government had provided for the Allied war-crimes negotiations. Maxwell-Fyfe was a dark-skinned man in his mid-forties, thickset and heavily jowled. "Swarthy and ugly," was how he described himself, "and my waistline has launched a career of its own."

The delegations from the Big Four powers—Great Britain, France, the Soviet Union, and the United States—seated themselves at a table in the conference room. The others seemed to expect Jackson to take the place at the head of the table. The Americans had pressed hardest for trying war criminals; they held most of the defendants in custody. Jackson presented the agenda. What the delegates faced was the legal equivalent of drafting the Ten Commandments, he began. Every nation had its criminal statutes. But for the world at large, none existed. They had to invent a court and give it authority. They had to agree on procedures. They had to write a statute that would describe the crimes the defendants had perpetrated and the penalties for conviction.

Jackson looked around, judging the colleagues from whom he would have to extract a consensus: the Britishers—probably reasonable; the French—inscrutable; the Russians—likely obstructive. General Donovan had provided a profile of the principal Russian negotiator, Major General of Jurisprudence Ion Timofeevich Nikitchenko. Nikitchenko, fifty years old, had gone to work in a Donbass coal mine at age thirteen. He escaped during the communist revolution by becoming a Red Army soldier. Afterward he took a law degree at Moscow University and rose to his present position. Jackson knew the facts, but could read nothing in that broad Slavic face with its steel-gray, unblinking eyes.

FOR ten days the delegates wrangled. Jackson was looking forward to escaping, at least temporarily, to check out possible trial sites on the Continent. This evening he was stretched out in his suspenders and stocking feet in his sitting room in Claridge's, dictating to Elsie Douglas. He wanted to get down on paper where the negotiations stood before he left London.

Their greatest problem, he said, was to overcome criticism that they were creating ex post facto law. Obviously, the Nazis had committed naked aggression and unspeakable acts. But what *laws* had they broken? What statute could a prosecutor cite? Yes, Germany had signed the Kellogg-Briand Pact, outlawing war. Germany had signed peace pacts with Poland and the Soviet Union. Germany had also signed the Treaty of Versailles, as well as the Hague Convention of 1907 and the Geneva Conventions of 1929. Jackson read off Germany's violations of these solemn agreements. If no punishment followed violation, what was the point of august figures gathering in world capitals and signing all these treaties? Jackson warmed to his argument. "Let's not be derailed by legal hair-splitters. Aren't murder, torture, and enslavement crimes recognized by all civilized people? What we propose is to punish acts which have been regarded as criminal since the time of Cain and have been so written in every civilized code."

To THE Continental Europeans it seemed that the Anglo-Saxons were trying to ram an alien court system down their throats. General Nikitchenko listened as Jackson and Maxwell-Fyfe explained adversarial law, with its opposing attorneys, direct examination, and cross-examination before a judge who acted as umpire. That was not how it was done in his country, he said. The French agreed. Their judges did not demean themselves by prying battling lawyers apart like a referee at a prizefight. Judges took all available evidence, sifted it, weighed it, and arrived at their decisions. Lawyers were merely to help the accused prepare a defense. They had little role in the court itself, Nikitchenko concluded in a lecturing tone. And this matter of pleading guilty or not guilty: Were they really going to allow a man like Ernst Kaltenbrunner, responsible for the Gestapo and for concentration camps, to stand up in a court of law and declare himself not guilty?

When at last they adjourned, Maxwell-Fyfe invited Jackson to his club. They might as well accept it, Sir David said over lunch; they were going to wind up with a hybrid. At least they had agreed on the number of judges: four principals—one representing each country—and four alternates. Multiple judges provided the Continental touch. Sir David regarded it as a major victory that they had finally been able to persuade the Russians and the French to accept the adversarial system of opposing lawyers. They had also agreed on three of four votes to convict, causing Nikitchenko, who had fought for easy convictions, to howl. And they had a name for the court: the International Military Tribunal (IMT).

Jackson asked what he thought they should do when the accused raised the defense that they were simply carrying out superior orders. That, Sir David said, could not be permitted; the whole prosecution case would collapse. The Germans under Hitler had operated under the concept of *Führerprinzip:* What the leader ordered, his subordinates carried out. If they allowed the defense of "superior orders," they would be able to convict only Adolf Hitler, and he was dead.

Jackson remained uneasy. In the final months of the Italian campaign an American GI had gunned down defenseless German prisoners and escaped punishment through a "superior orders" defense. Sir David countered with the statement printed in the paybook of every German soldier: He was not required to obey an illegal order. If that was true for a corporal in the Wehrmacht, why would it not apply to those immediately under Hitler?

What would surely give them the devil of a time, Maxwell-Fyfe went on, was *tu quoque*—the "so did you" defense. If the crimes they were defining applied only to the Germans, how would they escape history's verdict that the trial was not justice, but merely victor's vengeance? Atrocities had been committed on all sides.

Tu quoque, Jackson said, had to be another unacceptable defense. It implied that because some murderers went free, then all murderers must go free. The Nazi murders had been committed on an unimaginable scale. How could the world simply walk away from the deaths of six million to ten million people? But how did Jackson suggest they get around *tu quoque?* They would simply state that *tu quoque* was inadmissible, Jackson suggested. Sir David looked at his guest with renewed respect. He had not anticipated Yankee pragmatism.

ERNST Kaltenbrunner had been chief of the Reich Central Security Office (RSHA), the component of the SS that controlled the Gestapo, the criminal police, and the SD, or security service. He was what people expected in a Nazi. He was six feet six. His neck rose directly from his shoulders to his head without tapering. Huge hands dangled at his sides. His horseface was seamed by a thin, cruel mouth and a scar that cut a purple swath across his left cheek.

At the war's end Kaltenbrunner had been hiding in a chalet in the Austrian Alps, where a patrol from the U.S. Third Army stumbled upon him. The lumbering giant, just another kraut officer to General

Patton's GIs, surrendered meekly. Twelve days after his capture Frau Rosel Plutz heard on the radio that the Americans had arrested a high-ranking SS officer. To ingratiate herself with the victors, she immediately went to the American military government office at Nordhausen. She had been a typist, Frau Plutz said, at a concentration camp called Dora-Gestapo. One of her duties had been to type death sentences. The signature that appeared on all of them—that of Ernst Kaltenbrunner. Soon afterward he was bundled into an army truck and taken to Bad Mondorf.

4

NOT until early July did Jackson manage to disentangle himself from the London negotiations long enough to look for a trial site. He traveled in a Dakota transport plane with his son, Bill, and Wild Bill Donovan. By July 7 they had checked out Wiesbaden, Frankfurt, and Munich, where they met with Ike's deputy, General Lucius Clay. He had a better alternative, Clay said as they reboarded the Dakota.

Jackson dozed off briefly, only to be wakened by Clay, pointing earthward. That was it, the general said. Jackson gazed out the starboard window. He had seen the bomb damage in London, the ruins of Frankfurt and Munich. But nothing had prepared him for the urban corpse below. Where were they? he asked. Where Jackson would likely find his courthouse, Clay said. That was Nuremberg.

Until the war Nuremberg had preserved its medieval aspect. Tourists loved scaling its eleventh-century watchtowers and walking along the banks of the gently winding Pegnitz River. Some might have found the gingerbread charm of the city cloying, but most delighted in Nuremberg's houses, with their high-pitched, red-tiled roofs and carved dormers, and gables crowned with painted wooden statuettes.

Nuremberg had given Germany its first railroad line and the world its first pocket watch and clarinet. It was a toy-making center famed for exquisite miniatures—perfect replicas of trains and tiny cannons that actually fired. Nuremberg had also given Germany her greatest artist, Albrecht Dürer. Emperor Charles IV had christened Nuremberg his *Schatzkästlein*—the treasure chest of his kingdom.

It was in Nuremberg that the Nazis had found their spiritual home.

By 1933 the annual Nuremberg rallies had become the chief celebration of Nazi life—weeklong extravaganzas choreographed by Hitler's brilliant young architect, Albert Speer. The night sky lit up like a giant bonfire as party faithfuls from every corner of the Reich bore their torches through the ancient streets. Their destination was Zeppelin Field on the edge of town, a massive stadium that held a quarter of a million people arrayed in ranks of hypnotizing precision, shouting themselves into an orgiastic frenzy at the words of Adolf Hitler.

This was also the city where the Nuremberg Laws had been proclaimed—statutes that deprived German Jews of their rights, their property, and eventually their status as human beings. From the time the RAF had first struck in October 1943 until the war's final raid, Nuremberg was bombed eleven times, its marshaling yards, locomotive shops, and tank factory destroyed. In the final siege American infantry divisions pounded the city with an artillery barrage, followed by five days of house-to-house fighting.

After the surrender an American military government team surveyed Nuremberg and declared it ninety-one percent destroyed. Of 130,000 original dwellings, only 17,000 had survived intact. Nuremberg was a city without electricity, public water, public transportation, telephone, mail, or telegraph service. Yet there survived on its western edge a huge, frowning structure, the Justizgebaude—the Palace of Justice—the courthouse of the government of Bavaria.

THE Jackson party landed at an airfield outside Nuremberg designated by the military as Y28. A motorcade of staff cars and jeeps snaked out to the runway to meet them. The ride into town proved a grim confirmation of what Jackson had glimpsed from the air. Shabbily dressed people, heads bent, faces vacant, wound their way through trenches of rubble. The few standing walls along the route were plastered with signs warning GIs against fraternizing with German nationals.

The motorcade slowed and turned into a gateway in a wrought-iron fence. Jackson stared up at a three-story stone building capped by a steeply pitched roof. Most of the windows were blasted out. The yard was littered with spent cartridge cases, and the façade of the courthouse was pitted with bullet holes. A U.S. Army colonel approached and introduced himself as their escort. He informed the party that

Nuremberg at the time of the trial. Having sustained eleven Allied bombing raids before the end of the war, it was a city reduced almost to rubble.

the Palace of Justice had taken five hits, with one bomb plunging from the roof to the basement.

Inside, they found the walls blackened by fire and the floors wet from burst water mains. The colonel led them up a stairwell to the third floor, to room 600, the main courtroom. Over the entry was a sculptured tablet representing the Ten Commandments.

As they entered, a group of GIs came to desultory attention. A keg of beer sat on what had been the judge's bench. Behind the bench a sign proclaiming TEXAS BAR was flanked by several pinups. Only the ornate chandeliers and a huge baroque clock reminded the visitors of the Texas Bar's previous incarnation as a courtroom.

Back outside, the colonel led the party across a driveway to a twenty-foot brick wall. Behind that wall, he explained, were four wings of cellblocks fanning out from a center core, with enough cells to accommodate 1200 prisoners. The prison was currently full of ordinary criminal defendants. One wing, however, could quickly be cleared for war criminals. The best hotel in Nuremberg, the Grand, was also standing miraculously intact. In this virtually dead city, General Clay pointed out, were a courthouse, a jail, and a first-class hotel. That, Jackson observed, was precision bombing.

As the motorcade began its crawl back through the defiles of destruction, Jackson wondered how they could ever hope to operate amid this chaos. Clay said he would make a start. He could have General Patton move in 15,000 German POWs in the next forty-eight hours to clear the streets.

EARLIER Jackson had worried about a dearth of evidence. Now, thanks to Wild Bill Donovan's OSS, a river of documents was pouring in. In June, Jackson had named Colonel Robert Storey as chief of a new documents division, set up in Paris while the trial site was being decided.

In mid-July, Storey received an urgent phone call from an OSS ensign named English. The naval officer had been sent to scour Eastern Europe for documents. He was calling, he said, because a German nobleman, Baron Kurt von Behr, chief aide to Nazi Party philosopher Alfred Rosenberg, had revealed the hiding place of forty-seven crates of Rosenberg's files. They were in a cellar below the baron's sixteenth-century castle. This extraordinary find was followed by a tip from a German archivist that led to the Harz Mountains and 485 tons of diplomatic papers. And in a salt mine in Obersalzburg, GIs discovered the Luftwaffe's records, along with art that Hermann Göring had looted from all over Europe.

Late in July another bombshell burst. The keystone of the Bernays thesis was that the Third Reich had carried out a deliberate conspiracy to commit aggression. But how to prove it? Storey explained to Jackson, who was back in London again, that one of his researchers had found the notes of a General Friedrich Hossbach, Hitler's adjutant, recording a meeting at the Reich Chancellery in Berlin on November 5, 1937. The meeting involved Hitler, Göring, Foreign Minister Konstantin von Neurath, Grand Admiral Erich Raeder, and a handful of other top leaders. According to Hossbach's notes, Hitler told his subordinates that he was about to reveal "my last will and testament." Germany's 85 million people, he said, represented Europe's purest racial entity. The country's present boundaries were inadequate to serve this population, a condition that "justified the demand for more living space." In short, since her neighbors were unlikely to give up their soil to Germany, the country was left with no recourse but acquisition by aggression. There it was, from the Führer's lips.

All this material gave Jackson an idea. The Allies could convict the Nazis simply by introducing German documents in evidence. Witnesses would be far less convincing than anything the Nazis themselves admitted in writing.

His greatest enemy throughout the war, Albert Speer explained to a Frankfurt symposium on "The Organization of German War Production," had been bureaucratic inertia and stupidity. The American and British officers nodded knowingly as the former armaments minister of the Third Reich continued. A forty-year-old architect, Speer was a legend to insiders on both sides of the war, the wunderkind who had increased German production of weapons sevenfold in only three years. He had reached his peak output just ten months before the war ended, despite crippling shortages and incessant bombing. The Allies wanted to know how he had done it.

Though Speer had been arrested along with the rest of the Dönitz government, he sensed early on that he held a special interest for the Allies. He was aware that Wernher von Braun and other German rocket scientists were saving their skins through knowledge they possessed and the West wanted. Maybe his freedom too could be bought by what he held in his head.

Along with intellectual brilliance and limitless energy, Albert Speer possessed charm. People were drawn to this handsome, cultivated man. Adolf Hitler had liked him; the Twentieth of July plotters, who tried to kill Hitler, had wanted Speer in their government. Now the Allies seemed to be succumbing to this combination of usefulness and attractiveness, and Speer had been transferred to a comfortable incarceration near Versailles. From Versailles he had been sent to Frankfurt to lecture to his former enemies.

The session ended on a note that left his listeners stunned. Nazi Germany, Speer claimed, had been only a year or two away from producing an atomic bomb. The delay, he added with disarming contrition, served Germany right, since Germany had driven out so many of her most brilliant scientists, particularly Jewish physicists. When his talk ended, the audience gave Speer a standing ovation.

Outside the meeting room, a British lieutenant was waiting. Speer was to report to the commandant's office before returning to house custody. He felt no alarm. They were probably going to ask him to repeat his lecture somewhere else, maybe in England or even America. On his arrival at the office, the commandant informed him that he was under arrest as a major war criminal.

LESS than three weeks had passed since Jackson's visit to Nuremberg. The challenge now was to persuade the other countries' delegations to accept the city. Jackson returned there on July 21, this time with Sir David Maxwell-Fyfe, French representative Robert Falco, Wild Bill Donovan, Bill Jackson, Elsie Douglas, and Murray Bernays. Nikitchenko, under orders from Moscow, had refused to come. The Soviets were holding out for Berlin, in their zone of occupation.

Bernays was pleased at being included. Jackson was a magnet for ambitious people, and the whole operation was getting crowded at the top. Still, it was Bernays' concept that guided them all. There had to be a place for him.

Jackson was relieved to have Maxwell-Fyfe along. He had recently come close to losing his strongest ally. In July, Sir David's Conservative Party had lost power in the first British general election since the war. Churchill was out, and Maxwell-Fyfe was no longer attorney general. His Labour Party successor, Sir Hartley Shawcross, had been named Britain's chief war-crimes prosecutor. But Shawcross was more interested in the anticipated social revolution at home and had asked Maxwell-Fyfe to stay on as Britain's de facto chief prosecutor.

Nuremberg looked as stricken as before, though General Clay had made good on his offer to clear the streets of rubble. Donovan's OSS had come up with Captain John Vonetes to scout for housing and dining facilities in the battered city. A fast-talking Cornell graduate, Vonetes was that breed of soldier who could turn up Scotch for the party, nylons for the ladies, gasoline for the junket. Just don't ask too many questions. At Jackson's request Vonetes arranged a luncheon at the scarred but still elegant Grand Hotel. The British and French, who had not dined so well in years, were suitably impressed. Vonetes had also located nearly one hundred relatively undamaged homes for the trial staff. For Jackson he had found a castle—the manorial seat of the Faber-Castell family, Europe's pencil magnates. Jackson took a quick tour through its rococo interior, replete with cherubs clutching pencils, and bathrooms with tubs, as Jackson put it, "not quite big enough for swimming pools." The press would be all over him for living in such splendor, he concluded. They ought to use the castle to billet reporters. "They're the only ones who can live here without being ridiculed, because they control the laughs," he said.

The British and French delegates agreed that the trial of the Nazi war criminals should be held in Nuremberg. It had a courthouse, housing, a prison. As for the Russians and Berlin, they were out of luck: Jackson had a 3–1 vote.

On August 8 the Allied representatives were ready to sign an agreement to try war criminals in an international court. The document, nine pages long, was called the Charter of the International Military Tribunal. The IMT Charter defined four crimes: conspiracy to carry out aggressive war; the actual launching of aggression; killing, destroying, and plundering during a war not justified by "military necessity"; and "crimes against humanity," including atrocities against civilians, most flagrantly, the attempt to exterminate the Jews. Murray Bernays took the document back to his office and read it with pride. The heart of it was Article 6, expressing his idea that Nazism constituted a criminal conspiracy.

By the time the Allies signed the charter, they had finally agreed on who was to be tried. They had come up with a list of twenty-three major war criminals. Hermann Göring topped it, followed by Hitler's foreign minister, Joachim von Ribbentrop, who had managed to escape the Allied dragnet until June 13, when the son of a business partner turned him in. The last führer, Admiral Dönitz, also made the final list, along with General Jodl, signer of Germany's surrender. Others included Rosenberg, Speer, Kaltenbrunner, and Hans Frank.

The Americans held most of these men, but the Russians insisted on producing their own defendants. Two men in Soviet hands— Grand Admiral Erich Raeder and Hans Fritzsche—were thus added. Raeder had been Dönitz's predecessor as head of the German navy. Fritzsche had been a third-string operative in Josef Goebbels' propaganda apparatus. They were the best the Russians could produce.

The day after the agreement was signed, Murray Bernays was walking down the hall to his office, when he met Colonel Storey and several other recent Jackson appointees. They moved by him with barely a nod. Increasingly, Bernays was being brushed aside. He went to Jackson's office and asked if he might be relieved of his duties and return home to the States.

Bernays had become a pain to the Jackson staff. They were compromisers, adroit legal politicians. He was seen by them as a zealot who resisted any changes in his original idea, who reveled in legal combat. Jackson agreed instantly.

That night Bernays wrote to his wife, "I'm not to blame if these glory thieves made away with my property. They're practical men. I'm only a dreamer." He settled his affairs and was soon on his way.

5

THE only instruction First Lieutenant Robert G. Denson had been given on Sunday, August 12, 1945, was to fly his C-47, *Jinx*, to an airstrip near Bad Mondorf to take on "classified cargo." Denson jumped from the hatch to the ground just as several ambulances emerged from a side road. The first one pulled up, and an army colonel leaped out. Something in the officer's appearance brought Denson to immediate attention. The colonel wore a green, brilliantly shellacked helmet and rows of ribbons and kept a riding crop tucked under his arm. His round face possessed a severity heightened by steel-rimmed glasses and a thin mouth under a pencil-thin mustache. He asked if Denson was prepared to load. By now the drivers had begun opening the rear doors of the ambulances.

Denson looked on in puzzlement as several middle-aged, unshaven, haggard-looking men in disparate dress emerged and shuffled listlessly toward his plane. Only one had any bounce in his step. The stout, smiling figure gestured toward *Jinx* and said in heavily accented English, "Good machine." Denson's eyes popped. He recognized Hermann Göring. His classified cargo obviously comprised the Nazi war criminals he had been reading about.

The officer who had addressed Denson was Colonel Burton C. Andrus, recently commandant of the Bad Mondorf prison. Just before the IMT Charter was signed, Andrus had received secret orders to bring the leading Nazis from Bad Mondorf to Nuremberg and to assume command of the prison there. Now Andrus surveyed his charges, sitting on the pulldown seats that lined the fuselage. He studied the broad back of Hermann Göring, standing in the rear of the plane using the portable urinal. As Göring came back, he peered out a window. "Well, my friends, take a good look at the Rhine," he said. "It's probably the last time we'll ever see it." The others laughed weakly at the Reichsmarschall's joke. Sitting down, Göring caught the eye of Colonel Andrus, and mutual contempt flared between them.

The antipathy had begun the moment Göring arrived at Bad Mondorf. Andrus had stared at the puffed, sweating, smiling face of his prisoner in near disbelief. Göring, at 264 pounds packed over a five-foot six-inch frame, came accompanied by a valet and sixteen pieces of matching luggage. The luggage contained, along with a trove of jewelry, over 20,000 paracodeine pills, of which Göring took 20 a day, an addiction resulting from a prescription for an excrutiating toothache suffered in 1937.

Andrus put Göring on a diet and gradually withdrew the paracodeine. By the time they left Bad Mondorf, the Reichsmarschall was sixty-five pounds thinner and drug free. As Göring regained his health, his restored wit and intelligence made him a formidable adversary. During an early strip inspection at Bad Mondorf, he had deliberately left a cyanide capsule in his clothes to be found and to distract the Americans from other capsules he had secreted elsewhere. Next to Göring on the plane sat General Jodl, and next to Jodl, Field Marshal Wilhelm Keitel, Hitler's chief of staff for the armed forces. Opposite them sat the former foreign minister, Joachim von Ribbentrop. In the forward part of the plane a small humpty-dumpty figure leaned out and gave Andrus a hopeful smile. Weeks before, Walther Funk, former president of the Reichsbank, had come to Andrus, eyes brimming with tears. There was something he had to get off his chest, he told the colonel. Jews had been murdered for their gold teeth. The gold, Funk confessed, had been deposited in his Reichsbank.

Next to Funk sat Arthur Seyss-Inquart, Reich commissioner for conquered Holland. When Seyss-Inquart first took up his duties in 1940, Holland had 140,000 Jews. By the end of the war 8000 remained. Among the dead was a girl three months short of her sixteenth birthday, Anne Frank, who died at the Bergen-Belsen concentration camp.

The presence aboard the plane of the old man with the imperious manner puzzled Andrus. Hjalmar Horace Greeley Schacht had been reared in America by German immigrant parents. The family eventually returned to Germany, where the brilliant Schacht became president of the Reichsbank. He was Funk's predecessor. Schacht had been found by the Americans in Dachau, where he had been sent for his alleged role in the Twentieth of July plot to assassinate Hitler. Why was he being flown to Nuremberg to face trial as a war criminal?

One German aboard the plane enjoyed Colonel Andrus' total confidence. Dr. Ludwig Pfluecker, who had initially been brought to Bad Mondorf because he spoke English, was in his seventies, a neurologist drafted into the German army medical service. Pfluecker had agreed to come to Nuremberg under the same conditions as Willi Krug and the other POW prison workers. He was to live in the prison and be available twenty-four hours a day. It was a way, for the time being, to survive. Pfluecker's presence comforted Andrus, since, above all, the colonel had one objective: to keep these men healthy and alive until judgment day.

CAPTAIN Daniel Kiley had one thing in common with his new boss, Robert Jackson: Neither man held a degree in the profession he practiced. Kiley had studied architecture at Harvard just long enough to know that he needed no formal education to pursue his visions. What he did best was devise the optimal use of space. This was what he had been doing in Washington as the thirty-year-old head of his own firm, developing wartime housing. Later he was recruited into Bill Donovan's OSS and became chief of the Presentations Branch, which, among other tasks, built mock-ups of clandestine targets.

Kiley's appearance belied his character. He was delicate, almost elfin-looking, and weighed no more than 130 pounds. The slight frame, however, pulsated with energy and contained a will of steel. "I never take no for an answer," he liked to say. Now his assignment was to restore the Palace of Justice for the war-crimes trials.

When Kiley arrived in the courtyard of the Palace of Justice, a broad-chested army colonel eyed him uncertainly, as though this were not the man he had expected. The colonel introduced himself as John F. Corley, commander of the 1st Division's battalion of engineers, and added that whatever Kiley wanted, he would get. Kiley nodded curtly and headed wordlessly to the courthouse.

After two hours of scouring the building, Kiley and Corley reemerged into the courtyard. Kiley turned to the colonel. He wanted carpenters, plasterers, electricians, plumbers, recruited locally or flown in if necessary. They would need 250 German POWs as laborers. They were going to double the size of the courtroom, vertically and horizontally. He wanted the rear wall taken out and the attic cut into for a visitors' gallery. He wanted office space for 600 personnel. And they would need cabinetmakers to build office furniture.

Colonel Corley scribbled on a notepad. They would also need glass, tiles, brick, and plywood, Kiley went on. Corley interrupted to ask where in this ravaged city they would find these materials. There were factories around Nuremberg, Kiley said. Just put them back into operation. He turned and headed for a waiting car.

THEY looked so forlorn, these onetime Goliaths of the Reich, Hans Frank thought. Here was Field Marshal Keitel, once the very model of a Prussian Junker officer, the discolorations visible where the insignia had been ripped off his uniform, still clicking his heels every time Göring passed by. And Wilhelm Frick, a lawyer like himself, drafter of the Nuremberg Laws, wearing an incongruous plaid sports jacket. Most pathetic were head of the Nazi labor unions Robert Ley and

Above, Colonel Burton Andrus, prison
commandant, in the walkway that joined
the prison to the Palace of Justice.

Right, the Palace of Justice, with the four prison
buildings behind it. The defendants occupied the
right-hand wing. To the right of that wing is the
gym, where the executions would be carried out.

Left, cellblock C,
where the defendants
were held. To prevent
suicides, guards were
posted around the
clock at each cell and
chicken wire enclosed
the upper tiers so that
no prisoner could leap
to the stone floor
below.

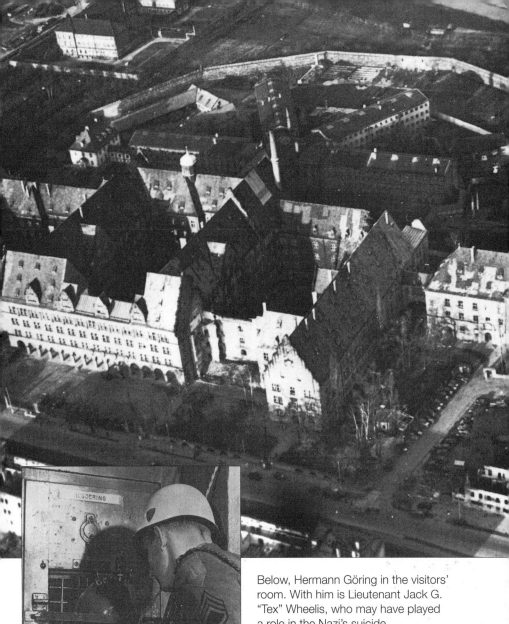

Below, Hermann Göring in the visitors' room. With him is Lieutenant Jack G. "Tex" Wheelis, who may have played a role in the Nazi's suicide.

Above, Hermann Göring's cell. A spotlight positioned at the porthole of each cell door was trained on the prisoner during the night, while he slept.

publisher Julius Streicher, who had arrived at Nuremberg with only the clothes on their backs. The U.S. Army had issued them dyed black fatigues, class X, which meant "unfit for further use." Their belts, suspenders, and shoelaces had been taken away. On August 12 they had been marched into C wing, one of four cellblocks that radiated from a central core in the prison, behind the courthouse. Cells lined both sides of the wing and ran up three tiers.

Of all the prisoners, it was Streicher whom Hans Frank loathed most. A short, bald, powerfully built man of sixty, Streicher was founder and editor of *Der Stürmer*, the anti-Semitic newspaper that read on a comic-book level. Frank would not have been caught dead reading Streicher's rag.

A German-speaking U.S. sergeant called off their names and assigned each prisoner a cell. Frank entered number 14. Immediately to the right, Frank spotted a toilet in an alcove, with no door, no toilet seat. An iron cot with a filthy mattress occupied the left wall. Opposite it, on the other side of the cell, was a table, and at the back a small barred window exposed a patch of gray sky.

Frank was startled by the slamming of an iron bolt. He walked to the door and looked out of a square porthole. A pair of GI eyes stared back. This was not going to be Wawel Castle.

COLONEL Andrus heard a tapping on his office door. His visitor was Major Douglas Kelley, an army psychiatrist. The army had recognized that sound minds had to be produced before the IMT, along with sound bodies, and so Kelley had been assigned to the prison. Headshrinkers, as the colonel called them, were an alien species to this career soldier. He had been relieved, however, to find Dr. Kelley a genial, witty man and not some brooding behavioral mystic.

Kelley asked for a few minutes of the colonel's time. Once they had the prisoners settled in, Kelley said, they should set up a small library for them. It was the kind of request that rankled Andrus, and he reminded Kelley of his principal mission—to keep Andrus advised of suicidal tendencies among his charges. That was precisely the problem, Kelley explained. They had to keep the prisoners' minds occupied. Andrus relented: "All right, I don't want them to go stir-crazy. A guy could go nuts in a little cell with what some of those boys have on their minds."

CORPORAL EMILIO DIPALMA, A combat veteran of the 1st Division, lacked enough discharge points to be shipped home. He had been assigned to report to the 6850th Internal Security Detachment (ISD), the military force that operated the Nuremberg prison. On a late August afternoon DiPalma found himself standing with a dozen other soldiers in the exercise yard between C wing and a building the GIs used as a gym. A sergeant's bellow brought them to attention. A party of officers emerged from cellblock C. In the lead strode a colonel, his uniform pressed to razor-edged sharpness, a riding crop tucked under his arm.

Colonel Andrus ordered the men at ease. They were, as of now, he informed them, part of the ISD, and it was going to be a proud unit, charged with a historic task: guarding the worst criminals mankind had ever known. The first thing that they, as "sentinels," had to understand was that these men were prisoners of war. Their rank did not matter. When a sentinel entered a cell, the prisoners were to stand.

The colonel's continual reference to them as sentinels, not guards, made DiPalma uneasy. The word had an unwelcome spit-and-polish ring to it. Sentinels, Andrus went on, would pull twenty-four hours on and twenty-four hours off. When they were on duty, they would spend two hours on the cellblock and four hours off. Each guard was responsible for four cells. No more than thirty seconds were ever to elapse before a sentinel peered through the porthole directly into the cells to observe his four prisoners. A sentinel's chief responsibility was to keep these men alive. At no time were the prisoners to be allowed to talk to one another or to the sentinels. Nor were the sentinels to talk to one another.

The rest of Andrus' talk was a drone of daily routines. Breakfast at 7:00 a.m. Afterward defendants mop and clean their cells. Lunch at 12:00, supper at 6:00. Cold showers once a week. Library privileges in the afternoon. Lights out at 9:00 p.m., at which time prisoners were to turn in their glasses, pens, and watches—anything that could cut or stab. Cells were to be inspected whenever prisoners were out of them, including a good look inside the toilet bowl. "Failure to obey will be considered a court-martial offense."

The voice became almost paternal. "Just about all of you men have seen combat," the colonel said. "You've seen the bodies of your buddies on the roadsides, the cemeteries where your friends will never earn enough points to get home. These prisoners are the men who put them there. Your job is to see that they survive long enough to be brought to justice. That is all."

ON SEPTEMBER 5, 1945, Jackson was back in Washington to consult with the president. Jackson was impressed by Harry Truman. Not that the man possessed a shred of the grandeur of his predecessor—quite the contrary. It was the quiet confidence with which this common man filled the shoes of a giant that won Jackson's admiration.

Truman needed to appoint a judge and an alternate to the Nuremberg court. What did Jackson think of Francis Biddle, the recently dismissed attorney general, as principal judge? Jackson was caught off guard. Biddle had served only briefly on the federal bench and, in Jackson's estimation, did not qualify for the IMT. Instead of responding to Truman's suggestion, Jackson raised a couple of names, including that of John J. Parker, a distinguished judge on the Fourth Circuit Court of Appeals. Parker had missed getting on the Supreme Court in 1930 by a heartbreaking single Senate vote. Truman said that he would happily name Parker, but as the alternate.

The next day Jackson got a call from Francis Biddle, who asked if he could come out to Hickory Hill. The Jacksons and the Biddles were part of a tight Washington social set and were often in each other's homes. Still, Jackson did not want Biddle at Nuremberg and thought that his lukewarm reaction had dissuaded the president from naming him.

Not so. The man who came to Hickory Hill was a lean, tanned Philadelphia aristocrat, aloof in appearance but unaccustomedly humble this day. Biddle said he thought they ought to have a chat in light of their probable close professional relationship in the future. He had been killing time since being dropped as attorney general, and Truman's offer had arrived like a life ring thrown to a drowning man.

The way Truman had fired him had been clumsy and painful, Biddle went on. Of course, he had worked against Truman's nomination for vice president in 1944, and he supposed that was why Truman resented him. But to fire him by a phone call from a White House staffer? That was poor form. That was not how these things were done.

Jackson listened to the story. It included just the sort of Main Line condescension that would have made Truman dislike Biddle. But now Jackson understood why Biddle had been given the Nuremberg judgeship: It was Truman's bad conscience.

Since Biddle was going to take the job, Jackson said he hoped that Biddle would fly to Germany as soon as possible. Organizing a four-power bench from scratch was going to take time. Biddle said he understood, and as soon as he could put together some sort of staff, he would make arrangements to get to Germany quickly.

MAJOR Kelley persuaded Colonel Andrus that the prisoners needed exercise. On the first day in the exercise yard, Göring disregarded the colonel's no-talking rule and delivered a pep talk to his fellow inmates. They were in prison, he said, for one reason only: They had lost the war. But someday a grateful nation would honor them with marble sarcophagi. "Shut up and spread out!" a guard barked.

The military men walked in single file—Dönitz, Keitel, and Jodl—purposeful and silent. In another corner the untouchables milled uncertainly: Streicher, founder of the Jew-baiting *Der Stürmer*, running in place, working up a sweat that glistened on his bald, neckless head; the towering Kaltenbrunner, chief of Reich Central Security, lurching from group to group; runty Fritz Sauckel, labor "plenipotentiary" of the Reich, the man who had herded millions of workers from their homelands and delivered them to the Nazi war machine. The loner by choice was Hjalmar Schacht, the banker whose haughty air made clear that he had no business among such people.

"Time's up!" a sergeant shouted, and the ragtag collection formed into a single line to return to the cellblock.

THE first thing Robert Jackson observed on his return to Nuremberg was that the nonfraternization rule was being torn to shreds. On the way in from the airfield, his party—young Bill, Elsie Douglas, and housing officer John Vonetes—was driven along a street that had become a flesh market, with knots of GIs and German women engaged in intimate negotiations. The party was heading for the suburbs, and Vonetes had commandeered for Jackson a sixteen-cylinder Mercedes-Benz touring car that had formerly belonged to Joachim von Ribbentrop. He would keep this car for ceremonial occasions, Jackson said, but for everyday use he wanted something less ostentatious.

They entered Dambach, a village on the western edge of Nuremberg. The huge car slid to a stop before a buff-colored stucco home at 33 Lindenstrasse. The door was opened by a stout woman, who introduced herself in English as Mrs. Hassel. "I am your housekeeper," she said. Her attitude was servile, except when she addressed the rest of the staff, which included a maid, a cook, a waiter, and three gardeners.

Vonetes conducted Jackson's party to the bedrooms on the second floor. In the master bath Jackson noted the shower, sitz bath, tub, and bidet, which, he observed, would allow him to bathe standing, sitting, lying, or squatting, according to his mood. What did Jackson think of his billet? Vonetes asked. The house, Jackson said, combined all that was god-awful in Teutonic taste, but it would do fine.

JOHN Harlan Amen, head of Jackson's interrogation division, had brought a formidable reputation to Nuremberg. As Brooklyn district attorney, he had successfully prosecuted the notorious Louis "Lepke" Buchalter of Murder Incorporated, the outfit that killed for a fee. But his specialty had been nailing crooked politicians. Amen was hard-driving, hard-living, hard-drinking, and a womanizer, with a penchant for the dramatic. He was also engaged in a rivalry with the more placid Bob Storey, head of the documents division, for Jackson's favor.

Amen rushed to Jackson's unfinished offices with a letter he was sure Jackson would want to see immediately. The handwriting was cramped, the English stilted, yet Jackson found the message electrifying. Joachim von Ribbentrop had written that he was ready to take responsibility for the actions of the leaders jailed with him. If Ribbentrop was ready to take responsibility for the crimes of the regime, then they would be acknowledged, per se, as crimes, and the prosecution was halfway home. But Ribbentrop had set a condition. He would take responsibility, he wrote, only if the Allies dropped the trial. They would cross that bridge when they came to it, Jackson told Amen. In the meantime he intended to interrogate this prisoner himself.

As they threaded their way through scaffolding and carpenter's horses on the way to the interrogation room, Amen briefed Jackson. Ever since his arrest Ribbentrop had been acting bizarrely, writing to Winston Churchill, offering to go to England to explain why war between the British and German peoples had been a tragic error. He babbled incessantly about the titled Britons he expected to call in as witnesses in his defense, including King George VI and Lady Astor. In

Amen's opinion Ribbentrop's mental stability was questionable. Jackson stopped before room 55 and braced himself for his first face-to-face encounter with a Nazi.

Ribbentrop jumped to his feet as Jackson entered. The former foreign minister wore a shapeless gray suit and a frayed shirt with no tie. The two Americans sat down behind the interrogators' table, facing Ribbentrop, and Jackson posed his first question.

JACKSON's annoyance was visible, his face flushed and his voice harsh. Specifically, what was Ribbentrop taking responsibility for? Jackson asked. Ribbentrop continued to emit a verbal fog, as he had done for the past fifteen minutes. "Let's try again," Jackson said. "Do you take responsibility for the war of aggression?" Of course not, an injured Ribbentrop answered. What about the violation of treaties? Ribbentrop's answer was unintelligible. "Do you at least take responsibility for the foreign policy of the Third Reich?" Jackson asked. Again Ribbentrop demurred, saying that he did not know the Führer's foreign policy. Jackson rolled his eyes in disbelief.

Striding angrily toward his office, Jackson told Amen this was the last time he expected to set foot in the interrogation room. The waste of time with Ribbentrop had convinced him that the documentary route was the best way to convict these people. Jackson's words troubled Amen. He had hoped this firsthand experience would hook Jackson on the importance of calling witnesses. Instead, documents, the domain of Amen's archrival Robert Storey, were winning the day.

THE corporal responsible for the last four cells on the second tier of cellblock C on Friday morning, October 5, was leaning sleepily against the stairwell when Willi Krug appeared at 6:30 a.m. with his washbasins. Willi smiled and nodded as he passed by. Seconds later he let out a cry. The startled soldier came running.

Colonel Andrus was shaving when he received the call from the duty officer. Within twenty minutes he was entering cell 110. Andrus studied the bloated, purple face of Dr. Leonardo Conti, chief of health in Himmler's SS. Conti was known as the "mercy killing doctor," specializing in quick, painless injections that eliminated inmates of asylums, jails, and homes for the aged. He was not a major defendant, but was being held for later trial. Conti had fashioned a noose from a towel, tied one end to a bar in his window, and jumped off his chair. Burton Andrus had lost his first prisoner.

The plan agreed upon at headquarters command was that Conti would be taken to the base hospital, where he would be pronounced dead of unknown causes *after* his arrival. A report of the actual manner of his death, classified top secret, was spirited back to Third Army headquarters in Heidelberg.

6

IN 1940 RUDOLF Hess had been deputy führer, the third-ranking Nazi in Germany. That August he had been visited by his old professor from the University of Munich, Dr. Karl Haushofer. The professor taught geopolitics and believed that the Anglo-Saxons and Germans, possessing superior blood, were destined to rule the world. He was the seminal influence on young Rudolf's thinking.

He was unhappy, the professor told Hess, that Germany was at war with England. When Germany went to war against Russia in the east, as she inevitably must, she would face a geopolitical disaster. England would bring in the might of the United States from the west, and Germany would be crushed between two jaws. Somehow Germany had to make peace with the British, and Haushofer had an idea. His son, Albrecht, was a friend of the duke of Hamilton's, and the duke was in contact with Churchill and King George. Haushofer proposed that his son write to the duke through a woman he knew in neutral Portugal, and suggest that Albrecht and Hamilton get together in Lisbon. Hess thought the idea was splendid.

The letter was sent on September 23, 1940, but it was intercepted by British censors. Such correspondence to an English nobleman, now on active duty with the RAF, aroused the suspicions of British intelligence. Hamilton was closely questioned about the letter and his relationship with Albrecht Haushofer.

As weeks went by with no response, an obsession began to take root in the mind of Rudolf Hess. Flying was Hess's passion. Secretly he persuaded Willy Messerschmitt, the aeronautical engineer, to let him fly his company's still secret ME-110 fighter plane. Over a cup of coffee one morning, Hess bet the engineer that he could not add two more fuel tanks to the plane without losing maneuverability. Messerschmitt took up the challenge. An ME-110 was refitted, and Hess was ready to attempt what he called his "one great deed."

On April 27, 1941, Hitler announced to his inner circle his intention to invade the Soviet Union in eight weeks. Here was the professor's nightmare come true. On May 10, a quiet Saturday afternoon, Hess drove out to the company's Augsburg field, wearing a Luftwaffe uniform. He dared not confide his intention to anyone except his aide, Karlheinz Pintsch, and Professor Haushofer. Yet Hess was sure Hitler would approve of his mission.

Hess had the mechanics at the Messerschmitt works roll out the ME-110. He handed Pintsch a letter to deliver personally to the Führer. In it he described his intention to seek out an Anglo-German peace. Hess added that if his enterprise failed, "it will always be possible for you to deny all responsibility. Simply say that I was out of my mind." By 5:45 p.m. he was airborne, with 900 miles of night flying ahead of him. His destination was Dungavel Hill, thirty miles south of Glasgow, ancestral seat of the duke of Hamilton.

Five hours later he approached his objective. Hess doubted that he could land the plane without being shot out of the sky first. And so, from an altitude of 20,000 feet, he made his first parachute jump. David McLean, a Scottish plowman, discovered Hess in a field of barley. As the Scot approached, Hess smiled and announced in English, "I have an important message for the duke of Hamilton."

AFTER reading Hess's letter, a stunned Hitler was uncertain how to handle the affair. Yes, peace with England. But the number three Nazi dropping unannounced into the enemy camp? No one was going to take this lunatic seriously. Hitler issued a statement on May 12 that read, "Party member Rudolf Hess has set out on an unauthorized flight from Augsburg and has not yet returned. A letter he left behind unfortunately shows traces of a mental disorder, and it is feared that he was a victim of hallucinations."

Thus far, though, Hess's wild gamble appeared to be succeeding. The morning after the flight, he actually had a conversation with the duke of Hamilton. He was subsequently interrogated by British officials of escalating rank, up to Home Secretary Lord Simon. And then his fortunes began to decline. His proposal that Germany would leave the British Empire unmolested in exchange for German domination of Europe struck the British as laughable. Churchill ordered him treated like any other high-ranking POW. For the next four and a half years Hess occupied a succession of British jails and military hospitals, a figure judged somewhere between eccentric and mad.

Yet on October 9, 1945, Rudolf Hess was flown to Nuremberg to stand trial as a major war criminal. True, he had been a high-ranking member of the Nazi Party. Hess's real crime, however, had been to antagonize the Soviet Union. Through its spy in Britain, Kim Philby, the Soviet secret police had quickly learned the details of Hess's mission. When six weeks later Germany invaded the Soviet Union, the Russians had no doubts: Hess was clearly Hitler's agent in a scheme to get England out of the conflict so that the Germans could fight the Russians in a one-front war. Thus when the Allies began negotiating the list of major war criminals, the Russians insisted they wanted Hess.

Since learning that he would be tried, Hess had had plenty of time to rehearse the stance he would assume. In England, after accepting the failure of his mission, he had decided that he had to protect the Führer. If Adolf Hitler had said that Rudolf Hess was crazy, then Hess would make the lie credible. Furthermore, he had to behave in a way that would reveal no Reich state secrets useful to the enemy. His best strategy, he had reasoned, was to claim amnesia. The pose had served him well in England. How could the Allies try, much less convict, a man in Nuremberg who did not remember anything?

ROBERT Jackson and General Donovan dined in early October at the Grand Hotel, where the OSS chief had taken a room. He was furious, Jackson told Donovan. First he had urged Francis Biddle to come to Europe as soon as possible. Instead, Biddle had chosen to take his sweet time, coming over on the liner *Queen Elizabeth*. Now it looked as if Biddle had maneuvered himself to become president of the court. That, Donovan said, would never do. The Americans already dominated the show. They had to give the court a more international flavor. Biddle had to be derailed, the two men agreed.

THE converted Lancaster bomber could scarcely have carried two less similar passengers than the judge the British government had selected for the war-crimes trial and his alternate. The alternate, Sir

Norman Birkett, was far from happy. Before his elevation to the bench Birkett had been the most famous trial lawyer in England. When Wallis Simpson wanted to divorce her husband so that she could marry King Edward VIII, she went to Birkett. At six feet three inches tall, with undisciplined red hair, hatchet features, and misaligned teeth, he looked as if the various parts of his anatomy had been assembled from different persons. The ungainliest of men, he also possessed a lively wit and effervescent charm.

Initially, the lord chancellor of England had asked Birkett to be Britain's principal judge at Nuremberg. Three days later the lord chancellor called with distressing news: The Foreign Office insisted on a lord justice for the post. Would Birkett be willing to take the alternate position? Birkett was trapped. To say no would appear unpatriotic. He accepted, but wrote in his diary that night, "I cannot record the secret anguish this has been to me . . . to become an alternate because of the snobbishness of the Foreign Office."

The twitchy energy of Norman Birkett was nowhere present in the man who had supplanted him. Sir Geoffrey Lawrence was sitting across the aisle of the Lancaster, placidly leafing through the cattle breeders' quarterly. An unruffled calm emanated from this rotund, glowingly bald, Pickwickian figure. With his wing collar and black suit, Sir Geoffrey might have stepped from another age. He was currently lord justice of appeals, a position he held almost as a hereditary right.

THE judges from the four nations met for the first time on October 13 in Berlin, as a sop to the Russians. As soon as they could pick a chief justice, however, they would be on their way to Nuremberg. To Francis Biddle, his expected election as president of the IMT fed a hungry ego. He had been fired as attorney general. He was nearing sixty. Nuremberg was likely his last chance. If he presided over this trial, his name would surely achieve a certain immortality. Besides, the Biddles were blue bloods through and through and not accustomed to being passed over.

The four-power Allied Control Council, which ran occupied Germany, threw a cocktail party for the judges and alternates in Berlin. Robert Jackson flew up from Nuremberg, but not for the sociability. Midway into the party, he took Francis Biddle to a quiet corner.

Jackson said he understood that the British were prepared to support Biddle as president of the court. That would not do; the Americans were too dominant. The French role in the war had been too minor to merit the presidency, and the Soviets' right to judge aggressors was already shaky. What Biddle must do, Jackson continued, was to persuade the French to throw their support to a Briton. Biddle's disappointment was deep, but he accepted Jackson's logic. The next day Sir Geoffrey Lawrence was elected president of the IMT.

JOHN Harlan Amen did not know what to make of the new prisoner. Rudolf Hess, sitting opposite Amen in the interrogation room, certainly looked like a mental case. The protruding brow and sunken eyes gave his gaze a disturbing intensity. Amen had seized the opportunity to interrogate Hess the moment the prison psychiatrist, Major Kelley, had told him that Hess was claiming amnesia. Amen had stared down hundreds of lying, forgetful, crooked local officials in his racket-busting days. "When did you get the idea of losing your memory?" the American asked in his best break-the-witness style.

"You imagine I think it would be a good idea to lose my memory to deceive you," Hess answered.

"If you didn't remember your crimes, that would make it tougher for us, wouldn't it?" Amen said. "You say you can't remember your wife's name, yet the British told us you wrote to her all the time."

"Ah yes, I received letters from her, so I copied the name from the envelope. In my trial, I will be fighting for my skin," Hess added, "and the only weapons I will have are my brain and my memory. Do you think I would deliberately give them away?"

The man had the cunning of a trapped rat, Amen concluded. Still, he planned a surprise for this afternoon, and it ought to prove whether or not Hess was faking.

HESS was marched back into the interrogation room after lunch to face his mentor, Dr. Karl Haushofer, and Hermann Göring. Göring beamed as though he had found a long-lost brother. "Rudolf, you know me," Göring said, springing forward to take his hand. Hess's eyes were unfathomable. "Who are you?" he said dully. "But," Göring said, "we were together for years! I was supreme commander of the Luftwaffe. You flew to England in one of my planes. Don't you remember?" "No," Hess answered. "I have lost my memory."

Amen motioned to Dr. Haushofer. The old man looked at Hess with tears in his eyes. He had news of Hess's family, he said. "I have seen your wife and your little boy. He is seven now, you know." Hess muttered only, "I don't remember." "The little boy is now a big boy," Haushofer went on, "a wonderful little man." Hess shook his head. He did not remember anything.

As the session ended, Göring rose and grumbled, "He's crazy."

UNTIL now their status had been ambiguous. Technically, they were prisoners of war. For the military men this made sense. But for Funk, a banker? Or Franz von Papen, briefly Germany's chancellor? Julius Streicher, a publisher of anti-Semitic trash? On October 19, 1945, their status would become all too clear.

The instrument of change was Major Airey Neave, a twenty-nine-year-old Englishman with a boyish countenance. Colleagues described him as looking twenty and acting forty. Neave was also a British legend. He had been captured in France in 1940, escaped, was recaptured and thereafter subjected to the mercies of the Gestapo. Later Neave had led the most spectacular break of the war, out of the supposedly escapeproof Colditz Castle, from which he made his way back to England in 1942.

Neave was by profession a lawyer and had been picked by the president of the court, Sir Geoffrey Lawrence, to assist the bench. He had barely settled into the Grand Hotel, when he received a message to report to the American judge, Francis Biddle, in the dining room. He found Biddle lunching with the American alternate, John Parker, who greeted Neave in a warm North Carolina accent. Biddle's tone was brusque, his manner patrician. "Major Neave, is it? You look remarkably young." Biddle informed Neave that the following day he was to deliver the indictments to the prisoners and help them find lawyers.

On the morning of October 19 a party consisting of Neave, Colonel Andrus, Dr. Kelley, an interpreter, and two GIs loaded down with bulky copies of the indictments entered the cellblock. Andrus wanted Kelley along to note whether delivery of the charges seemed to affect any of the prisoners emotionally. The door of the cellblock clanged shut behind them, and Neave felt a shiver of memory. He had prepared a little speech: "I am Major Neave, the officer appointed by the International Military Tribunal to serve upon you a copy of the indictment in which you are named as defendant. I am also here to advise you as to your rights to counsel." They stopped before the first cell, and Neave braced himself to meet Hermann Göring.

The public image of jolly Hermann, the fat favorite of the German masses, had led Neave to expect an evil buffoon, a malignant clown. Instead, he found a man with quick, ferretlike eyes and a body still too heavy for his short frame. As Göring began to scan the indictment, Neave explained his right to have a lawyer. "I have nothing to do with lawyers," Göring said. He had lived as a law unto himself for years. "You find one for me," he instructed Neave. As they were about to leave, Dr. Kelley suggested that Göring might want to write on the indictment his reaction to it. He handed Göring a pen. Göring wrote in quick, bold strokes, "The victor will always be the judge and the vanquished the accused."

The party moved on to the next cell. Rudolf Hess jerked himself to attention like a robot. Neave was astonished at the gauntness of the man. He handed Hess the indictment. Hess tossed it on the table. His eyes rolled. He began to groan, and fell to the bed, clutching his stomach. "Cramps," Andrus said wearily. "That's the latest." After making his set speech, Neave started to leave. Kelley handed Hess a pen and asked him to write something on the indictment. "I can't remember," Hess wrote in a surprisingly neat hand.

They continued down the corridor to the cell of Wilhelm Frick, drafter of the Nuremberg Laws. "The most colorless man in the place," Kelley observed. Then to Julius Streicher, who met them with hands poised arrogantly on his hips. Streicher looked at Neave's list of possible lawyers and said, "Jews, these are all Jew names, and I know the judges are Jews too."

Neave braced himself before the next cell. The brutal figure of Ernst Kaltenbrunner loomed in the doorway. What impulses drove men like him, the executive-suite officials of the factories of extermination? Neave wondered. He left Kaltenbrunner's cell in disgust. The giant had flopped onto his cot, sobbing, "I want my family!"

Dumpy Walther Funk also cried on reading the indictment. "Be a man, Funk," Andrus said. The Hitler Youth leader, Baldur von Schirach, suggested to Neave the sort of man that molests little boys. Ribbentrop's untidy cell actually stank. After hearing Neave out, the onetime foreign minister handed him a scribbled list of British aristocrats. "They can give evidence of my desire for peace," he said. Robert Ley, head of the Nazi labor unions, screeched, "Why don't you just line us up against a wall and shoot us?"

Neave found it taxing to be civil to Seyss-Inquart. The Britisher had spent the final months of the war in Holland on the banks of the river Waal. Every night Dutch resistance fighters had crossed the river bearing tales of mass death by starvation and of atrocities in the part of Holland still under Seyss-Inquart's control.

The military men—Dönitz, Keitel, and Jodl—behaved stoically. Admiral Dönitz said that he wanted a certain German naval lawyer, Otto Kranzbuehler, to defend him. Neave noticed that Field Marshal Keitel wore carpet slippers. He remembered standing barefoot for hours on a cold stone floor in the Gestapo prison in Plotsk, after his recapture, until his feet went numb. Neave had responded to the soldier's duty to try to escape. A fellow officer like Keitel must have understood that duty. Yet this man had signed orders that sent brave British POWs to their deaths for doing exactly what Neave had done. Keitel had issued orders that meant death to thousands of Russian POWs as well, and mass shootings of innocent civilians as hostages.

The next cell meant another emotional jolt for Neave. He had been imprisoned in Nazi jails in Poland, where Hans Frank had ruled. Frank began speaking breathlessly: "It's as though I am two people, the Frank you see here and Frank the Nazi leader. I wonder how that other Frank could do those things." Andrus told Frank to save his soul baring for Dr. Kelley and to listen to Major Neave.

The prison had turned a monochrome gray with the failing of the afternoon light. Neave felt drained. There remained one more cell to visit: the one housing Albert Speer. Speer, who had only recently arrived in Nuremberg, had been distressed to discover Fritz Sauckel in a nearby cell. Sauckel, the conscript labor czar, represented Speer's greatest danger. Which of them would be found most responsible for what the Allies were calling the slave labor program—Sauckel, who had recruited the workers, or Speer, who had used them?

Speer was cool, dignified, and spoke fluent English. He knew that the first move of his survival strategy must strike just the right note— that of accepting manly responsibility and expressing genuine contrition. "This trial is necessary," he said. "There is a common responsibility for such crimes, even in an authoritarian state." Dr. Kelley asked politely if Speer would mind writing that sentiment on his indictment.

They were no longer a disparate collection of captives. They were now criminal defendants whose trial was scheduled to begin November 20, Neave informed them. They would still be interrogated, but were no longer required to respond. What surprised him was how eager most of them were to keep talking.

AFTER delivery of the indictments Major Kelley went directly from cellblock C to his office, down the hall from Colonel Andrus. He felt frustrated as prison psychiatrist by his inability to speak German. But waiting in his office was a solution to that problem. The man rose gravely and introduced himself as Captain Gustav Gilbert.

Gustav Mahler Gilbert spoke fluent German, learned from his Austrian immigrant parents. Though a psychologist, Dr. Gilbert had spent part of the war interrogating POWs. When he learned that an interpreter with a background in psychology was needed at Nuremberg, he seized the chance for a transfer. Interpreting meant an underuse of his talents. Still, Nuremberg offered access, as he was later to write, "to history's most perfectly controlled experiment in social pathology." What made civilized human beings join the Nazi movement and do what they did? Here he might find the answers.

7

KEITEL and Jodl had worked together for so long that they were closely attuned to each other's moods. As they walked the exercise yard one morning, Jodl detected a heaviness in the field marshal's step. Keitel had been interrogated the day before, and Jodl asked in a whisper what he had been questioned about. "The Commando Order," Keitel said out of the side of his mouth. Jodl nodded. That was bad.

When Amen had grilled him about the Commando Order, Keitel thought the colonel would understand an officer's duty to obey orders. Amen's response had stunned him. Under the IMT Charter obedience to orders was not an acceptable defense. How, Keitel wondered, could he ever make these people understand the force of Adolf Hitler's will? That August morning in 1942 was typical. They were in the Wolf's Lair, the Führer's headquarters in an East Prussian pine forest. On the agenda was a recent Canadian commando raid on the Nazi-occupied French coast at Dieppe. Hitler, in a rage, fumed that these commandos were not soldiers. They were thugs. They had bound German prisoners with a noose tied around the neck and the other end tied in back to their legs, so that with every movement they strangled themselves. They had violated the Hague Convention.

A month after Dieppe twelve British commandos were captured in Norway on a mission to blow up a power station. Henceforth, Hitler announced, all commandos were to be shot, even if they were in uniform and surrendered willingly. Hitler directed Keitel and Jodl to get the word out to the armed forces in a formal order. Both understood the rashness of this act, but they had also witnessed the futility of resisting Hitler. Other officers had been sacked for opposing the Führer. The Commando Order was issued, over Keitel's signature, on October 18, 1942.

This order had not been the first corruption of Keitel's soldierly ethic. Earlier, in October 1941, soon after the invasion of Russia, Hitler told the senior staff that Russian guerrilla operations had to be stopped. Fifty to one, one hundred to one—that was a proper price for every German soldier the guerrillas killed. Furthermore, political commissars assigned to Russian units were to be liquidated upon capture. Keitel was to issue orders to that effect.

Keitel had gone to his quarters and drafted the Reprisal Order and Commissar Order. One month later, 2300 Russian civilians were executed in retribution for ten German soldiers killed and twenty-six wounded in a guerrilla attack. The original orders, with Keitel's signature, were now in the Palace of Justice documents room.

Keitel on occasion had tried to stand up to Hitler. After issuing the infamous execution orders, he offered his resignation, and when that failed, he considered suicide. But he always came back, held in thrall by Hitler's hypnotic powers.

Keitel had also paid a crushing personal price to this regime. His youngest son had been killed in action, another was missing, and the third was held prisoner, all on the Russian front. Yet his doglike devotion to Hitler never really flagged. Keitel had been in the room on the twentieth of July when the plotters' bomb miraculously failed to kill Hitler. It was Keitel who carried him from the shattered building, crying, "My Führer, my Führer. Thank God you're alive."

Major Kelley took Captain Gilbert on his first round of cell visits. As they entered cell 5, Hermann Göring, speaking serviceable English, asked, "Do you know what you have if you have one German? You have a fine man. If you have two Germans, you have a bund. Three Germans? You have a war!" Göring slapped his thigh and roared with laughter. Kelley mentioned that they had seen Hess earlier. "Ah, Hess." Göring shook his head. "When the Führer announced that he would be next in line after me, I was furious. I told Hitler, how could he give that nincompoop such a position? The Führer said, 'Hermann, be sensible. When you become führer, *poof!* You throw Hess out and name your own successor.' The Führer had a genius for handling men, you know." Kelley asked what Göring thought about Hitler's committing suicide. Was that not the act of a coward? Not at all, Göring responded. It was unthinkable to imagine the head of the German state sitting in a cell like this awaiting trial as a war criminal.

Gilbert hazarded a question. What about his own death? Was he concerned? "What is there to be afraid of?" Göring said grimly. "I have given orders to hundreds of thousands of men to go into battle knowing full well many would not come back. Why should I, their leader, cringe when called on to face the enemy?" He gave out a joyless laugh. "I know that I'm going to hang. But fifty years from now they will erect statues of me all over Germany. Big statues in the parks." He paused and then started laughing again. "One Englishman? You have an idiot. Two, a club. Three, an empire!"

Over dinner that night, Kelley asked Gilbert if he knew what psychological treasure was at their fingertips. Of course, Gilbert answered. He himself had been thinking of a study of the Nazis based on visits to their cells. Kelley noted that they had the raw material for a major book, a collaborative effort. He wanted Gilbert to start taking notes after the cell visits. Gilbert did not mention that he had already recorded every word of Göring's that he could remember.

General Donovan had been in the Far East for weeks, out of touch with Nuremberg. Jackson was alarmed by the way Donovan had moved in since his return. It was not a raw power grab; rather, it was the magnetic loyalty the man generated. The OSS veterans still seemed to think that his wishes amounted to orders.

Later in October, Jackson called a meeting of the top prosecution

staff. Donovan immediately suggested the priority order of business—
to choose the first witness and who would examine him. That suggestion, Jackson said, started on precisely the wrong foot, and he described the advantages of the documents approach.

Donovan shook his head. He had been talking to reporters, he said,
and documents struck them as deadly dull. If the people in this room
wanted the world to listen, they had better put some flesh-and-blood
witnesses on the stand. Jackson was not eager to have his authority
challenged in a staff fracas. He brought the meeting to an early close.
On the way out, he suggested that Donovan come to his place for
dinner that night. He had an excellent cook.

The dinner went well as long as they stuck to small talk. Donovan
ate with zest, particularly Frau Hassel's *Apfelstrudel*. Afterward they
retired to the music room, where Donovan pressed his case. Jackson
was unpersuaded. Documents, unlike witnesses, did not have faulty
memories or commit perjury, he said. Of course they would call a few
witnesses. But by relying essentially on documents, they could convict
these people with their own words. Donovan abruptly announced
that it was time for him to leave.

Jackson watched Donovan's car pull away, knowing he had probably
alienated the general. Still, he was certain he was on the right track.
Besides, it had been a long time since he had examined a witness in
court, and the documentary approach seemed far less daunting.

HERB Wechsler, the Columbia Law School professor who was Judge
Biddle's chief assistant, sat poring over an appeal. General Jodl was
demanding documents relating to Allied war crimes. The request was
just what Wechsler had feared from the first moment he had read
Murray Bernays' plan. Jodl was saying, If we committed war crimes, so
did you. If we are being tried for them, why aren't you? Emotionally,
Wechsler wanted to see these people punished. But as a legal scholar,
he found the law sacred and immutable. In a world of pure justice
Jodl had a point. Yet the charter drafters had already decided that *tu
quoque* would not be accepted as a defense.

Wechsler was wrestling with this issue when he got a phone call
from Biddle. Luise Jodl, the general's wife, had just turned up at the
Palace of Justice. Would Herb please see what it was all about?

The cool detachment Wechsler felt when faced with a legal riddle deserted him at the prospect of confronting the wife of an accused Nazi. He entered a small office to find a GI guard and a woman wearing a mannish overcoat. She was not stylish or beautiful, but her unaffected dignity struck him. She rose and introduced herself in fluent English. He guessed her to be in her mid-thirties, a good twenty years Jodl's junior. Married for only a year and a half, Luise Jodl had previously worked as a secretary in the German High Command (Oberkommando der Wehrmacht, or OKW) and had been a friend of Jodl's first wife, Anneliese. She had nursed Anneliese through a terminal illness, until the woman's death in the spring of 1944.

She had walked, Frau Jodl told Wechsler with a self-conscious glance at her battered shoes, virtually all the way from Berchtesgaden to be near her husband. She had found a room in a half-destroyed house and was sharing it with the wife of Field Marshal Keitel. She had come here to do everything in her power to save her husband. She wanted Wechsler to tell her what that might be.

Wechsler, noting her command of English, told her that an English-speaking secretary would be a tremendous advantage to her husband's lawyer. Did Jodl have a lawyer yet? Professor Franz Exner of the University of Munich was an old friend of the Jodl family, she said. Could Mr. Wechsler engage him for her husband? Wechsler said he would ask Major Airey Neave, who was busy locating lawyers for other defendants, to try to track down Exner. And he would try to arrange a job for Frau Jodl with her husband's lawyer. She thanked him, and they parted with a handshake.

Back in his office, Wechsler wondered why he had been so sympathetic, until he reflected on Jodl's plight. He knew the charges the man faced, particularly his role in transforming Hitler's manias into military orders. He also knew that he would have to recommend to Biddle that Jodl's request for documents on Allied war crimes be denied because of the IMT's position on *tu quoque*. No, he was not doing too much for an admirable woman whose husband, he suspected, would end up on the gallows anyway.

HANS Frank told Dr. Kelley and the new man, Dr. Gilbert, that he believed he was undergoing a moral regeneration. "I tell you," he said, "the scornful laughter of God is more terrible than any vengeance of man. Here we are, the would-be rulers of Germany, waiting

to be tried as common criminals. Is that not proof of God's amusement with men who lust for power?"

On October 20 Frank made up his mind. He begged the guard to
summon Father Sixtus O'Connor. Before the war the Catholic priest
from Oxford, New York, had been an outstanding student at the
University of Munich. He was currently serving his smallest congrega-
tion ever—the six defendants who had been born Catholic.

Days afterward, with Frank kneeling on the stone floor of his cell
and with Willi Krug holding a tin washbasin of holy water, Father
O'Connor rebaptized Hans Frank.

On October 23 Gilbert and Kelley visited the cell of Robert Ley, the
puffy, red-faced, alcoholic former chief of the German Labor Front.
He appeared to live in a permanent state of distress. This afternoon
they found Ley unusually agitated. Flinging his indictment to the
floor, he cried, "Am I supposed to defend myself against crimes
which I knew nothing about?" He plastered himself against the cell
wall and spread his arms out. "Stand us against a wall and shoot us,"
he said. "But why should I be brought before a Tribunal like a c—,
c—" "A criminal?" Gilbert offered. "Yes," Ley said, dropping his
arms. "I can't even say the word."

Afterward Gilbert went to the prison office to record the conversation. He always provided a copy of his notes to Kelley, who assured
him that this material was pure gold for their book.

On the evening of October 25 Second Lieutenant Paul Graven,
twenty-one years old, had taken over as duty officer on cellblock C. He
had gone to the prison office and barely ten minutes later the corporal of the guard burst in on him. The lieutenant had better take a look
at Robert Ley. Graven hurried to cell 9 and peeped through the porthole. The toilet was in a tiny alcove to the right, and only Ley's feet
were visible. Graven called to him, but there was no answer. He flung
open the bolt of the door and went in. Ley was seated on the toilet,
bent forward, his face swollen and blue-black, his eyes bulging. Around
his neck he had looped a strip of towel and tied it to a water pipe
against the wall. Ley had stuffed a rag into his mouth to stifle any cry
and had apparently leaned forward until he choked to death. Burton
Andrus had lost his second prisoner, this time a major defendant.

The Leonardo Conti suicide had been successfully hushed up, but Ley's death would be impossible to keep from others in the cellblock. The next day Andrus ordered his deputy, Major Fred Teich, to assemble the prisoners in the corridor. The colonel said to them, "When unpleasant news needs to be published, as in this case, I myself will do it. Ley has killed himself. He gained time to do this by giving the appearance of making a call of nature."

When Andrus sent the prisoners back to their cells, he directed his staff to meet with him immediately in his office. Security was obviously not tight enough, he began. From now on instead of one guard for four cells, they would post one on each cell. Two hours on, four hours off. And never during those two hours was the guard to take his eyes off the prisoner.

Gustav Gilbert found the letter painful to write. He had not seen his wife, Matilda, since the fall of 1943. He had a fifteen-month-old son, Robert, whom he had never seen. He now had enough discharge points to go home, but instead, he was staying on in Nuremberg. The idea of a book on the psychopathology of the Nazis had proved irresistible. How could he turn his back on this chance? He hoped Mattie would understand. He went to mail the letter and returned to his office, where he learned that the colonel was looking for him.

Colonel Andrus greeted Gilbert with forced bonhomie and asked the captain to have a seat. He appreciated, he said, that Gilbert was doing fine interpreting. But that was only half the job. What he also needed was "an observer," Andrus said. He wanted Gilbert to hang around with the prisoners in the exercise yard, win their confidence, become a friend. Pick up whatever they said. And if it proved interesting, report back to the prison commandant immediately.

Andrus wanted him to be a spy, Gilbert realized. At one time he might have found the idea repugnant. Now, instead, his mind was racing. Of course he would be happy to report on the defendants in the prison, he said. But imagine what they could learn, once the trial began, if Gilbert could also have access to the courtroom. Andrus liked the idea and said that he would try to obtain permission from Sir Geoffrey Lawrence, the chief justice and president of the court.

One more point, Gilbert said. Would not all this have a better chance of succeeding if instead of being simply an interpreter, he could be designated as prison psychologist? Gilbert's request was all right with him, Andrus replied, if it was okay with Major Kelley.

When the day's work was done, Gilbert suggested that he and Kelley have a drink at the Grand. It was not the kind of invitation the taciturn Gilbert ever extended, and Kelley was delighted to accept. At the hotel bar, Gilbert described his conversation with the colonel. Kelley did not instantly embrace the idea of the new title and of Gilbert alone getting access to the courtroom. But if they were going to do a book, Gilbert's observation of the defendants' behavior in court would obviously be valuable. Of course Gilbert could consider himself the prison psychologist, Kelley said.

THE trial was only two weeks off, and the world press began descending on Nuremberg. CBS's Howard K. Smith arrived in late October. Despite a boyish demeanor, he was already an old European hand. He had been reporting from Berlin when America entered the war, and had managed to get out of Germany one hour before the border was sealed. After the war he had succeeded the legendary Edward R. Murrow as the network's European chief.

Smith arrived at a press camp unlike any he had ever known. The U.S. Army had taken Robert Jackson's offhand remark literally. It had turned the castle of the Faber-Castell family into a press billet. Smith gazed at what was a heavy-handed version of a fairy-tale castle—gray, massive, with stout round towers and turrets.

The GI house manager led him upstairs, where the pleasant prospect of palatial living collapsed. Correspondents were jammed twenty to a room and sleeping on army cots. The bathrooms were ornate, but there were only four of them to serve what would eventually swell to over 300 correspondents. Smith stretched out on an unoccupied cot.

ONE of the defendants was not on cellblock C. Though indicted, he was still living at home—an old man suffering from hardening of the arteries, incipient senility, partial paralysis, incontinence, and impaired speech. His name was Gustav Krupp, of the arms dynasty. German industrialists, Robert Jackson knew, had connived in bringing Hitler to power because they knew he would break the communists. Without the businessmen's complicity, there could have been no Third Reich. But the problem with having Krupp personify the guilt of his class was his physical incapacity, already verified by a team of doctors. Jackson was undaunted. Gustav Krupp had a son, Alfried, who throughout the war had served as president of the Krupp works. Jackson had petitioned the court to indict Alfried if it could not try his father. On November 14 the issue brought the court into its first formal sitting in Nuremberg. The Krupp family lawyer argued the injustice of indicting a man because his father could not stand trial, while Jackson argued that the German industrial class bore criminal guilt for the war and must be tried.

After the hearing the members retired to what had been designated as the Judges' Room, to debate their decision. Sir Norman Birkett shuddered in disbelief. Jackson's argument, he said, was abhorrent. "This is not a football match. You don't simply field a reserve because one of the other players is sick." Jackson's petition was denied.

"PLUS vite! Plus vite!" Colonel Dostert shouted. Faster! Faster! Leon Dostert, former head of the French department at Georgetown University, had recently been an interpreter for General Eisenhower. He was also a champion of the still unproven IBM simultaneous-interpreting system, and he had set up a mock courtroom in the attic of the Palace of Justice, with one person playing the prosecutor, another the defendant, another a judge. Dostert was testing an applicant for the job of interpreter to see if she could keep up with the testimony of a "witness." Speed was the acid test. An interpreter could not delay more than eight seconds before starting to translate. Otherwise too many words backed up. One of Dostert's assistants had developed a practical test, asking candidates to reel off in two languages the names of ten trees, ten birds, ten medical terms, ten farm implements. They were looking for breadth of experience as much as language mastery and were always surprised by the number of city people who could not name ten farm implements in any language.

Dostert had decided that the best work was done when the interpreter listened in his or her native tongue and translated into the second language. The interpreter first had to understand perfectly what was being said and then could usually find suitable words in the second language to express the thought.

Dostert had dispatched his deputy, Alfred Steer, a gifted linguist, to scour Europe for the talent they needed. Steer raided the League of

Nations in Geneva. But he found that many interpreters there were accustomed to translating from written documents and unable to adapt to the pressure of interpreting on the spot. Steer had better luck at the Paris international telephone exchange. The operators were used to everyday foreign conversation under time pressure. In the end, whatever the candidate's background, only one prospect in twenty had the mental agility to listen and talk at the same time.

With the latest candidate dismissed, Dostert went searching for the architect Dan Kiley, restorer of the Palace of Justice. Robert Jackson was hounding him. Everything depended on having the interpreting system in place on opening day, November 20. Dostert found Captain Kiley downstairs in the courtroom supervising the installation of the witness-box. Had the IBM equipment arrived yet? he asked frantically. Kiley answered with an unflustered no.

FIVE days before the trial was to begin, a C-47 carrying a team of IBM engineers and a cargo of six crates landed at the Y28 airfield. The simultaneous-interpreting equipment, including 550 headsets for court officials and visitors, had gone wildly astray, some of it ending up in Peru. When the gear finally arrived, Colonel Dostert badgered Dan Kiley to get it installed. Kiley was already juggling a dozen crises. Most recently, a section of the courtroom floor had fallen through to the basement. The architect was getting by on four hours' sleep a night, usually on his office couch. Kiley assured Dostert that his interpreting system would be in place on opening day.

8

COULDN'T that woman leave anything alone! Robert Jackson bellowed. He was in the glass-enclosed conservatory upstairs at the house on Lindenstrasse. Elsie Douglas came running in and gasped when she saw the mess. The chief prosecutor had organized in piles the documents he was drawing from for his opening speech. Their busybody housekeeper, Frau Hassel, Jackson said, had insisted on opening the windows to air out the room. A storm had come up, and now all his carefully ordered papers were in disarray. Mrs. Douglas was already on her hands and knees reassembling the scattered sheets. Jackson slumped into a chair and watched her deftly retrieve order from chaos.

"Melancholy grandeur," Jackson said. That was the tone he wanted in the opener. He considered this speech, he said, the most important act of his life. He wanted it to proclaim to the world "the why of Nuremberg." They retreated to his study. He took an armchair, while Elsie sat at a desk with her steno pad. "Germany became one vast torture chamber," he began. "The cries of its victims were heard round the world." She was always surprised at how his words took on a finished quality as soon as he started to dictate.

"CHAPLAIN," Colonel Andrus said, eyeing his latest staff arrival, "just remember, you are here to fulfill the requirements of the Geneva Convention. You are to provide spiritual counseling. You are not here to convert anybody." The man standing before Andrus, Major Henry F. Gerecke, was a portly fifty-four-year-old Lutheran army chaplain from St. Louis. Raised on a farm in a German-speaking family in Missouri, Gerecke spoke an unsophisticated version of the language. He had joined the army at an age when most men were content to stay home. Two of his sons had been badly wounded fighting against the men he was about to meet in the cellblock.

The Protestant prisoners found the new chaplain, with his modest demeanor and everyman looks, the kind of simple clergyman that the Nazi regime would have crushed. Field Marshal Keitel, however, immediately took to him. Keitel had a sense that Gerecke, unlike his captors, did not despise him.

After the cell visits Andrus introduced Gerecke to Father Sixtus O'Connor. O'Connor took Gerecke's hand. "At least we Catholics are only responsible for six of these sinners," he said with a grin. "Your side has fifteen chalked up against you." Gerecke laughed. He suspected that he and the priest were going to get along.

GUSTAV Gilbert was recording the answers of the defendants to an IQ test he and Kelley had scheduled—a German version of the Wechsler-Bellevue Adult Intelligence Test. With the trial only days off they knew that any distraction would help reduce the prisoners' anxiety. And the test results would make a fascinating contribution to their book.

Göring attacked the test like a brash, bright schoolboy. On the memory portion, repeating increasing strings of numbers, he could remember up to eight numbers forward and six backward. "Come on, Doctor," he begged, "give me one more chance." He had already done the best of all, Gilbert told him. Sixty-nine-year-old Hjalmar Schacht, ordinarily so arrogant, confessed to Gilbert that he was weak on simple arithmetic. The genius who financed the remilitarization of Germany? Gilbert asked. Schacht answered, "Any financial wizard who is good at arithmetic is most likely a swindler."

On a scale in which 100 indicated average intelligence and 120 to 140 was to be expected of university graduates, Streicher scored the lowest, 106. The highest raw score, 141, was achieved by quiet, scholarly Arthur Seyss-Inquart, the Reich commissioner of the Netherlands. But with an adjustment for age Schacht came out on top, with 143. Gilbert was surprised that the extraordinarily able Albert Speer scored only a modest 128. The test, Gilbert knew, was a limited tool. Hans Frank, at 130, scored considerably lower than the third-ranking Göring, at 138. Still, Gilbert had dealt with both men, and Frank was clearly Göring's superior in his grasp of philosophical abstractions, social issues, and aesthetic nuance.

NUREMBERG had become an emotional life raft for General Donovan. True, Donovan had returned from a stay in the Far East to find most positions of power at the trials already staked out. And after the uncomfortable dinner at Jackson's home, he was well aware that his honeymoon with the chief prosecutor was over. Still, he was grateful to have a place to land. Harry Truman viewed a postwar OSS as an incipient American Gestapo and had virtually killed off the intelligence agency that was Donovan's reason for being. The general's restless energies now sought a new outlet at the Palace of Justice, where he roved the halls making small talk with secretaries. Then his break came—a letter from Hjalmar Schacht. The wily Schacht buttered up Donovan, calling him "an officer of high standing," then asked if Donovan would be interested in looking at "a brief summary of the underlying reasons and conditions of the dreadful Nazi regime." Donovan, a seasoned courtroom lawyer, could smell a defendant ready to turn state's evidence a mile away. If he could get Schacht to testify against the others, that would be a major breakthrough.

When Göring learned that Donovan appeared open to offers, he

NUREMBERG: INFAMY ON TRIAL

too seized the opportunity. He sent word that he was willing to testify against Ribbentrop, Kaltenbrunner, Schacht, Speer, and Streicher, all of whom had crossed him at some time over the years. Göring's price was that he be given an honorable death before a firing squad instead of a shameful death at the end of a rope. Donovan could envision the spectacle: the Nazi leaders consuming one another before the world. He began interrogating Schacht and Göring personally.

Jackson got wind of what was happening when John Harlan Amen came complaining about Donovan's horning in on his territory. Was he or was he not the head of the interrogations operation? Amen wanted to know. Jackson faced a painful dilemma. He knew all too well his debt to Donovan. Yet he resented the interference and disapproved of the direction in which Donovan wanted to take the trial. Jackson sent Colonel Storey to find out what role precisely Donovan had in mind for himself. Donovan was insulted, especially since Jackson had used Storey, an OSS veteran, to run this errand.

Jackson thereafter invited Donovan to his office. It was still "Bob" and "Bill," but the tension in the room was palpable. Jackson raised the issue of Donovan's contacts with Schacht and Göring. "I don't want any deals," Jackson said. A prosecutor might plea-bargain and turn one accomplice against another to crack an ordinary criminal case. But such courtroom shenanigans had no place in an international tribunal involving profound moral issues.

Get up in that courtroom and tell the Germans that their leaders are guilty because we say so, and they won't believe it, Donovan countered. But put the most popular man in the Third Reich on the stand and get a public confession from him, and that will convince everybody. "Bill, you may be right," Jackson said. "But it so happens that I have the responsibility. And I'm going to try this case by indisputable documentary proof."

The next day Donovan received a note from Jackson saying that he saw no further use for him in any position of prominence in the trial, "because of our different viewpoints." Wild Bill had been fired. He did not go quietly. He called on Francis Biddle and told him that the trial would be flat as Kansas with all that paper evidence, that Jackson was a poor manager, and that the prosecution office was a shambles. Nor was he talking behind Jackson's back, he made clear; he had said the same things in a letter to Jackson.

THE MONTH BEFORE, THE RUSSIANS had made a social splash with an October Revolution party. Now Andrei Vyshinsky, the Soviet deputy foreign minister, had arrived for the trial's opening, and it was Jackson's turn to repay the Russians' hospitality, at the Grand Hotel. Vyshinsky had a fearsome reputation as the chief prosecutor in the Soviet show trials of the '30s. Jackson found him a fascinating contradiction—one minute denouncing the West with standard communist clichés, and the next, an exuberant, witty companion. When Jackson extended his invitation to the Russian, he thought it prudent to mention that the IMT justices would also be present and that Vyshinsky should say nothing bearing on the trial.

Between dessert and coffee Jackson rose and made a gracious toast to the guest of honor. Then Vyshinsky rose, vodka glass in hand. Standing off to his right was a shy-looking young man named Oleg Troyanovsky. Son of the first Soviet ambassador to the United States and a graduate of Dartmouth College, Troyanovsky had been dispatched to Nuremberg as an interpreter for the bench.

Vyshinsky emptied his glass and said, "Vodka is the enemy of man, and therefore it must be consumed!" The guests cheered and followed his example. He then raised a refilled glass and said, "Here's to the conviction of all the men who will go on trial next Tuesday." Oleg Troyanovsky looked uncomfortable but rendered the words into English. Vyshinsky spoke again. "May their paths lead directly from the courthouse to the grave," Troyanovsky translated, and a few nervous titters were heard. Justice Parker whispered loudly to Colonel Storey, "I will not drink a toast to the conviction of any man, regardless of his guilt, before I hear the evidence."

Riding back to Lindenstrasse, Robert Jackson slumped in the back seat of his car, deep in thought. After the fiasco at the Grand, he was trying to fathom the behavior of Vyshinsky and, indeed, of most of the Soviets—by turns bombastic, self-conscious, boorish, charming. All that boozing—what was it about? Some Americans thought it was a trick to loosen their tongues for the benefit of Soviet intelligence. Jackson thought not. The Russians, with their revolution, had been left with a proletarian leadership. The heavy drinking was designed to lower the socializing to a level where they were comfortable. Their conduct led Jackson to one inescapable conclusion: The Russians suffered a national inferiority complex.

THE DAY BEFORE THE TRIAL WAS TO open, the Palace of Justice was a hive of crises. Dan Kiley was supervising the last-minute laying of the courtroom carpet. He left the installation crew long enough to check out the pressroom installed on the floor below. There William L. Shirer, who with Howard K. Smith was reporting for CBS, sat at a typewriter pounding out a story. Germany had been Shirer's beat throughout much of the rise of Nazism, and in returning for its burial, he felt a satisfying symmetry. He was now reporting his impressions after touring the city. "Nuremberg is gone," he wrote, "a vast heap of rubble beyond description and beyond hope of rebuilding." He had hitched a ride out to Zeppelin Field and stood before the grandstand, where he had heard Hitler speak in 1937. He remembered the throngs of Germans shouting themselves hoarse as Hitler proclaimed, "The German form of life is definitely determined for the next thousand years."

As Shirer wrapped up his story, he turned to a German journalist working next to him and asked how much interest his people had in the trial. "Oh, they think it's all propaganda," the German replied.

COLONEL Y. V. Pokrovsky, the Soviet deputy prosecutor, came into Jackson's office with the usual shield of belligerence carried by Soviet bearers of bad tidings. The trial would have to be postponed, Pokrovsky announced. General Roman Rudenko, the Soviet chief prosecutor, was in Berlin and ill. He had come down with malaria. Jackson experienced simultaneous incredulity and rage. This trial was not going to be derailed at the eleventh hour, he said. To start without the general, Pokrovsky warned, would be viewed by the Soviet Union as an affront. With that, he withdrew.

General Nikitchenko delivered a similar message to his fellow justices. Jackson got word to come to a meeting in the Judges' Room that afternoon to resolve the crisis. In the meantime he instructed Elsie Douglas to call the army medical office and find out what the likelihood was of anyone coming down with malaria in Berlin.

Jackson's press-relations man, Gordon Dean, soon learned of the latest Russian monkey wrench. He explained to Jackson that he was supposed to brief the press within minutes on trial arrangements. Should he cancel? Jackson told him that everything was to proceed as though the trial would start on time.

JACKSON ARRIVED AT THE JUDGES' Room, where he met Sir Hartley Shaw-cross, just arrived from England. Though Shawcross intended to al-low Maxwell-Fyfe to conduct day-to-day prosecution business, he had, as England's chief prosecutor, decided to handle the opening. Also present was General Rudenko's deputy, Colonel Pokrovsky. Jackson, still baffled by the Russians' behavior, informed the justices that he had it on good medical authority that contracting malaria in Berlin was near impossible and that he wanted the trial to proceed. They need do nothing that involved the Russian prosecution, Jackson noted, until Rudenko arrived. In the meantime could not Pokrovsky stand in for Rudenko?

Shawcross, perfectly groomed, was handsome as a matinee idol. He rose. If a delay was what the Russians wanted, he observed languidly, perhaps the court should grant it. Jackson looked dismayed. But, Shawcross added, the Russians must take full responsibility before the world for delaying the trial of Nazi war criminals.

Just before this meeting, Pokrovsky said, he had received good news. Because of recent medical advances, General Rudenko was making a remarkable recovery. He could be in Nuremberg in days. Pokrovsky sat down, wearing a sickly smile. The trial would com-mence on schedule the following morning.

CHAPTER II
THE PROSECUTION CASE
1

THE defendants were awakened on November 20, as on every other day, by the crashing of washbasins and raucous GI repartee during the changing of the guard. By 9:00 a.m. they were milling about the corridor, some in their prison-made suits, the military men in uni-forms with insignia stripped away. Göring wore one of three dove-gray Luftwaffe uniforms he had brought to Nuremberg.

Colonel Andrus arrived, and the duty officer brought the prisoners to attention. There were only twenty men instead of the expected twenty-one. Kaltenbrunner had been taken ill. "Hitch 'em up," the colonel ordered. The escorts handcuffed the prisoners. The party marched out of the cellblock and entered a covered wooden walkway connecting the cellblock to the courthouse. As the last man filed out, Andrus shouted to the remaining guards, "Search the cells."

The defendants waited by an elevator in the courthouse basement. The guards were to take off the cuffs, Andrus ordered, and bring the prisoners up three at a time.

BUSES, jeeps, and command cars jammed the courthouse yard. The honor guards of four nations stood at attention as Sir Geoffrey Lawrence's black limousine arrived. The chief justice of the Nuremberg trials stepped out wearing a long blue broadcloth coat, a bowler, and a prim smile for the photographers. His short, rotund figure disappeared into the throng.

POWs were still sweeping up sawdust as the correspondents from twenty-three nations filed into the press gallery. Among them were Janet Flanner and Rebecca West, covering for *The New Yorker;* the novelist John Dos Passos for *Life* magazine; Marguerite Higgins for the New York *Herald Tribune;* and Smith and Shirer for CBS.

The courtroom had achieved the "melancholy grandeur" that Jackson sought. Heavy sage-green drapes, dark paneling, and thick carpeting contributed to the solemn aura. The muted effect was broken only by the harsh fluorescent lighting and a few touches of color provided by the flags of the four nations behind the bench.

A small door opened in the rear of the dock, and the rumble of conversation halted. Out stepped Göring, Ribbentrop, and Hess. They blinked under the bright lights and made their way uncertainly toward the dock. Behind them, against the wall, stood six American sentries, arms folded behind their backs.

As the rest of the defendants filed in, Janet Flanner started taking notes: "You look at Nuremberg, and you are looking at the result of the war. You look at the men in the dock, and you are seeing the cause." The voice of the marshal interrupted. "Atten-shun! All rise. The tribunal will now enter!" The British and American justices, wearing black robes, came through a small door. The two French justices—Henri Donnedieu de Vabres and his alternate, Robert Falco—wore robes adorned with white bibs, ruffles at the wrist, and a touch of ermine. The Russians—General Nikitchenko and his alternate, Lieutenant Colonel Alexander F. Volchkov—were resplendent in chocolate uniforms with green trim and gold shoulder boards.

At 10:00 a.m. sharp, chief justice Sir Geoffrey Lawrence rapped his gavel, a handsome piece of oak that Francis Biddle had brought, thinking he would preside over the court. "This trial, which is now to begin," Sir Geoffrey began in a precise, metallic voice, "is unique in the annals of jurisprudence." The first order of business, he announced, would be the reading of the indictment.

The catalogue of Nazi duplicity and barbarism, recited by the prosecutors of each nation, occupied the entire morning. Simultaneous translations were provided through earphones for all the participants and for the press. A young French lawyer, just months out of a concentration camp, began his turn tremulously: " 'Out of a convoy of 230 Frenchwomen deported from Compiègne to Auschwitz in January 1943, 180 were worked to death within four months,' " he recited. " 'Over 780 French priests were executed at Mauthausen. . . .' " Keitel bowed his head. Ribbentrop dabbed at a sweating brow. Funk sobbed softly. Göring sat with a bored expression, occasionally writing on a piece of paper. He was keeping track of the number of times his name was mentioned in the indictment.

After two and a half hours Sir Geoffrey Lawrence adjourned the court for lunch. Colonel Andrus realized that he had made no plans for the defendants' meal. He hastily summoned his aides and ordered that the prisoners be fed in the courtroom. For the next hour they enjoyed a treasured taste of freedom, chatting freely among themselves for the first time since their captivity.

The afternoon session continued with the reading of the indictment. The room became hot and airless. Robert Jackson, itching to get back to editing his address, which he would deliver the next day, headed for the exit.

After the court adjourned for the day, Ray D'Addario, an army photographer, brought his camera down to the courtroom floor to take shots of the now empty chamber. As he focused on the bench, another army photographer appeared in his viewfinder. The GI was stealing Sir Geoffrey's oak gavel. "Are you crazy?" D'Addario shouted. "Put that thing back." "Like hell," the man responded, shoving the gavel into his pocket. "This is history!"

Right, members of the International Military Tribunal included (left to right) Ion Timofeevich Nikitchenko, Sir Geoffrey Lawrence, Alexander Volchkov, General William L. Mitchell (court administrative officer), Francis Biddle, and Sir Norman Birkett.

Left, Rudolf Hess, third-ranking Nazi, who claimed to have lost his memory of the war years, then gained it back suddenly during the trial. Behind him is Gustav Gilbert, the prison psychologist.

Right, the courtroom. Seated in the foreground are the prosecutors. At the far left is the prisoners' dock, with tables for the defense attorneys in front of it. At the far right is the bench and at the center rear the witness stand. Against the back wall, in the left corner, are the interpreters' booths.

Above, Robert H. Jackson (foreground), the chief prosecutor at Nuremberg and a U.S. Supreme Court justice. Behind him is the colorful British prosecutor Sir David Maxwell-Fyfe.

Right, British major Airey Neave, chosen to assist the Nuremberg justices, was known for leading the most spectacular escape of the war, from supposedly escapeproof Colditz Castle.

The next morning Elsie Douglas tucked a snowy handkerchief into Robert Jackson's breast pocket and stepped back to examine her handiwork. Bob certainly looked splendid.

The touring car waited in front of the house. Waxed to a fine sheen, it had been brought out for the occasion. The driver opened the back door for Jackson, Mrs. Douglas, and young Bill. As the car began rolling, Mrs. Douglas handed Jackson a freshly typed copy of his speech with the latest corrections. To the first page she had clipped a slip of paper on which she had written in red ink, "Slowly!"

The reading of the indictment ended by midmorning. Sir Geoffrey Lawrence announced that the defendants were now to enter their pleas, and called first upon Hermann Göring. Göring made his way to the center of the dock and began to read a typed statement. He was cut off by a sharp rapping. In the absence of a gavel Sir Geoffrey was tapping a pencil on the bench, the sound resonating through a microphone. "I have already explained," he remarked tartly, "the defendants are not to make a speech." Göring angrily snapped, "I declare myself, in the sense of the indictment, not guilty." The other defendants, in various forms, made the same plea: *"Nicht schuldig."*

All eyes turned to a distinguished figure in a morning coat and striped trousers making his way to the prosecutor's stand. Robert Jackson gazed around the room with imperturbable calm and set his text on the lectern. "May it please your honors, the privilege of opening the first trial in history for crimes against the peace of the world imposes a grave responsibility," he began. "The wrongs which we seek to condemn and punish have been so calculated, so malignant, and so devastating that civilization cannot tolerate their being ignored, because it cannot survive their being repeated."

He wanted the legitimacy of the court recognized. "Either the victors must judge the vanquished, or we must leave the defeated to judge themselves," he said. "After the first world war, we saw the futility of the latter course." He signaled the prosecution's strategy. "We will not ask you to convict these men on the testimony of their foes," he said. "There is no count in the indictment that cannot be proved by books and records." The accused, he noted with a brief smile, "shared the Teutonic passion for thoroughness in putting things on paper."

After Jackson had spoken for two hours, Sir Geoffrey Lawrence declared a recess for lunch. Colonel Andrus had arranged a dining room for the defendants in the attic of the courthouse. Göring dominated the room, rather like a coach bucking up a losing team at halftime. The defendants bolted their lunch and crowded at the attic windows. They had seen virtually nothing but prison walls for too long. Today they could look beyond the shambles of Nuremberg and see the Pegnitz River leave the city behind and wind through forests and fields toward the mountains. Their eyes drank in the view.

BACK in the courtroom, Jackson took a document from Elsie Douglas' outstretched hand. He wanted to read to the court, he said, a few excerpts from the diary of the defendant Hans Frank: " 'The Jews must be eliminated. Whenever we catch one, it is his end.' " Jackson turned a page, and the rustle could be heard in the silent room. " 'Of course I cannot eliminate all the Jews in one year's time.' " Frank's head lowered as his words from Wawel Castle echoed in the mouth of an American prosecutor.

Mrs. Douglas next handed Jackson a large leather-bound book. He was quoting from the report of the German general Jürgen Stroop entitled "The Destruction of the Warsaw Ghetto," Jackson explained. He read of German troops turning flamethrowers on apartment buildings and of Jews jumping to their deaths from smoking upper stories. He paused. "These are things which have turned the stomach of the world." The defendants—all but Hess—listened through their earphones in rapt attention, eyes open wide.

Jackson turned to the bench. "And let me make clear that while the law is first applied against German aggressors, the law includes, and if it is to serve a useful purpose, it must condemn, aggression by any other nation, including those which sit here now in judgment." Jackson picked up his text and returned to his seat.

THE defendants filed out the door and into the elevator. The force of Jackson's words was not wholly responsible for their subdued state. Frank's lawyer, Alfred Seidl, had just passed a note to his client, which Frank shared with the others. Just four days before, a British court had sentenced eleven concentration camp officials to death. If minor Nazis fared thus, what must be their own fate?

JACKSON WAS MOBBED. HOWARD K. Smith told him that he had never understood until now what had been the fate of his disappearing Jewish friends. Shirer said Jackson's words had sent shivers down his spine. Possibly the most erudite man on Jackson's staff, Colonel Telford Taylor concluded that Jackson's opener marked the pinnacle of legal writing thus far in the century. The next day the word from Charlie Horsky, Jackson's special assistant in Washington, was music to the prosecutor's ear. The speech had made the front pages of *The New York Times* and the Washington *Post*—in long stories that quoted generously from Jackson's text.

Shortly afterward Sir Hartley Shawcross, Great Britain's chief prosecutor, delivered an opening address that nearly equaled Jackson's in eloquence. Shawcross read from an eyewitness report on the fate of the Jews in the Ukrainian town of Dubno: " 'The people put down their clothes in fixed places, sorted according to shoes, outer clothing, and underwear. They stood around in family groups, kissed each other and said farewells. They went down into the pit, lined themselves up against the previous victims and were shot.' " As Shawcross spoke, Fritzsche, the radio propagandist, buried his face in his hands.

General Rudenko arrived in time to deliver the opening argument for the Soviet Union. The Russians had counted the pages in Jackson's speech and made Rudenko's speech one page longer. The moment Rudenko took the prosecutor's stand, Göring and Hess tore off their earphones, as if members of one gang had suddenly found a member of a rival gang daring to accuse them.

2

ROSE Korb, Colonel Andrus' new secretary, loved her job. Just turned twenty-three, out of Hammond, Indiana, she suddenly had a ringside seat at history. She found Andrus, by turns, stern or fatherly, but thoughtful on the whole, and she liked him. Another advantage of her job was that she was the first to meet the new men assigned to the 6850th Internal Security Detachment and could report on them to her roommates in the apartment building known as Girls' Town. She particularly liked Jack G. Wheelis, a strapping and ruggedly handsome second lieutenant who had joined the ISD two months before. Wheelis had told Rose, with a drawl and a grin, to call him Tex. Colonel Andrus had plans for Wheelis. A brawny Texan with a commanding presence, he certainly looked like a leader. Andrus was going to appoint him assistant operations officer.

THE sphinxlike Jodl was the least popular prisoner. Keitel was the neatest. Hess and Ribbentrop ran neck and neck for sloppiest. One of the most popular was Speer. But it was Göring who was fast becoming the guards' favorite. He would ask them where they came from and whether their rations were adequate, as though he could do something about it. Privately, the young Americans' lack of decorum disgusted him, as when they addressed him bluntly as Göring. Still, it served his purposes to win them over. This day, November 27, Göring was expecting to meet his lawyer, Dr. Otto Stahmer, in preparation for the next session of the court. He heard one of the guards shout, "Bring Fatso to the visitors' room."

The room was split down the middle by a mesh screen, with chairs along either side. Sliding plastic slots allowed defendants and lawyers to pass documents back and forth through the screen after a guard examined them. Tex Wheelis was on duty this morning, and Göring went after him like a politician after a voter. So the lieutenant was from Texas? Good hunting there, he had heard. Did the lieutenant like to hunt? It was the Reichsmarschall's passion. There was wonderful shooting around his estate at Carinhall. Too bad he could not show the lieutenant around it.

Stahmer arrived—a large man in his seventies. He let the guard frisk him, then took his place opposite Göring. Göring told Stahmer in German that he believed Wheelis was a friend.

WHEN the defendants filed through the door into the dock at five minutes before 10:00 a.m. on November 29, Göring took his seat and looked up to meet the gaze of a short, thickset man with close-cropped gray hair. *"Guten Morgen, Herr Reichsmarschall,"* the man said in perfect German. Göring looked at him blankly and asked, "Do I know you?" Of course, the man explained; he had worked for Göring at the Prussian Ministry of the Interior years before. His name, he said, was Robert Kempner. In 1933 he had been general counsel to the Prussian police, and Göring, as minister of the interior, had fired

him. Why? Göring asked warily. Because, Kempner said, he had successfully prosecuted storm troopers before the Nazis took over. He
had also urged dissolution of the Nazi Party and the arrest of Adolf
Hitler for treason. And, Kempner added, he probably had been fired
because he was part Jewish. Göring glared belligerently. Kempner
moved down the dock and stopped again.

"Guten Morgen, Herr Doktor Frick," Kempner said. The usually phleg-
matic Wilhelm Frick looked up, startled. He remembered Kempner
all too well. Frick, after succeeding Göring as minister of the interior,
had deprived Kempner of his German citizenship and had him
thrown into a concentration camp. Kempner had fled Germany long
ago and was now an American citizen attached to Jackson's staff. He
was in charge of the Defense Rebuttal Section, charged with anticipat-
ing the arguments of these men in the dock and preparing counter-
evidence to crush them. Kempner resumed his seat at the prosecutors' table and sat back to enjoy the morning's proceedings.

THE trial had been getting bogged down. As a legal strategy, Jackson's documentary approach was unassailable. As drama, it had become stultifying. Colonel Storey had his assistant prosecutors introducing documents wholesale, often without having them read in
court. As a result, press play of the trial was dwindling. But during the
recess the spectators saw a new face approach the prosecutor's stand.
Navy commander James Donovan was about to provide Jackson's answer to the complaint that his paperwork prosecution was too dry.
"May it please the tribunal," Donovan began, "I refer to document
2430 PS, a motion picture entitled 'Nazi Concentration Camps,' which
the United States now offers into evidence. It was compiled from
motion pictures taken by Allied military photographers as the armies
in the West liberated areas in which these camps were located."

The courtroom went dark and a projector began whirring, delivering images to a screen on the wall behind the witness stand. Later
generations might become hardened by repeated exposure to these
sights, but scenes of bulldozers shoving corpses into mass graves were
being seen for the first time by this audience. Jack Taylor, an American navy lieutenant captured on an OSS mission behind the lines,
appeared in the film and described the Mauthausen extermination
camp. Prisoners were compelled to carry huge stones out of a quarry

on their backs until they died of exhaustion, he said. Occasionally, guards amused themselves by dropping a prisoner back to the bottom of the quarry. This was called parachuting. Quiet weeping sounded in the courtroom. A woman fainted and had to be carried out.

Film taken by the Germans themselves was shown next. One reel had been shot at a camp near Leipzig. Some 200 prisoners were shown being herded into a barn. SS men then doused the building with gasoline and set it afire. The few prisoners who escaped were mowed down by machine guns. Captain Gilbert jotted down the defendants' reactions: Keitel wipes brow, takes off headphones; Frank trying to stifle tears; Speer swallows hard; Dönitz bows head; Göring leans on elbows, yawns.

The films went on for over two hours, a phantasmagoria of broken, charred bodies, ribs protruding, legs like sticks, eyes gaping. When it was over, silence hung like a pall over the room. Sir Geoffrey Lawrence rose and left almost at a run, without adjourning the court.

ON THEIR return to the prison, Göring could always tell by the rearrangement of his few personal articles that his cell had been searched during his absence. He feared most that the Americans might also have gone through his luggage, stowed in the prison baggage room, two doors down from him. Two cyanide capsules were concealed there—one in a jar of face cream, another in his ultimate hiding place. He could only hope that they were still there. In order to go to the baggage room himself, he would have to be accompanied by a guard, and he did not want to draw attention to his cache.

GILBERT and Kelley waited until after supper before going to the cells to get the defendants' reactions to the films. Hans Fritzsche sat, head hung low, on the edge of his cot. For years his voice over the radio had stirred Germans to a hatred of the Jews. "No power on heaven or earth will erase this shame from my country," he said quietly. Wilhelm Frick, who had drafted the Nuremberg Laws, said he didn't understand how such things could have happened.

General Alfred Jodl refused to talk to his visitors. But before lights out, he wrote a note for Dr. Exner, his lawyer, to pass to his wife, Luise. "These facts are the most fearful heritage which the National Socialist regime has left the German people," he told her. He assured

Luise that he knew nothing of such matters. He would, he said, "not have tolerated it for a single day."

While Kelley and Gilbert visited the cells, Robert Jackson was at home preparing a surprise.

On November 30 Hermann Göring's face displayed mingled shock and contempt as General Erwin Lahousen marched to the witness stand. Field Marshal Keitel's face expressed terror. A tall, gaunt, palely poetic man, Lahousen, in better times, had been an intelligence officer attached to the German High Command.

Documents had already been introduced that established Germany's aggressive intentions against Poland. Lahousen's appearance, Jackson believed, could lend a human dimension to the charge. Jackson had assigned the old gangbuster, John Harlan Amen, the direct examination of Lahousen. Lahousen testified that in mid-August 1939 he received an odd order from his superior—the chief of Abwehr intelligence, Admiral Wilhelm Canaris—to provide Polish uniforms, weapons, and false papers for a secret operation planned by Heinrich Himmler. The order smelled fishy to Lahousen. He nevertheless complied.

As soon as he heard reports that Polish troops had attacked a German radio installation at Gleiwitz, Lahousen became suspicious. The next day Canaris revealed to him the full story. An SS team had forced concentration camp prisoners to don Polish uniforms, then shot the men in front of the radio station, making it appear that Poles had attacked it. Hitler had his provocation for invading Poland.

Amen introduced the transcript of a meeting between Keitel and Canaris. The document made it clear that the Gleiwitz scheme had originated with the SS. But it was Keitel who had approved the army's participation and who had ordered Canaris to come up with the uniforms for the synthetic attack that launched World War II.

Lahousen continued on the stand, implicating Göring, Keitel, and Jodl in the destruction of Warsaw, the drafting of the Reprisal Order, and the extermination of the Polish intelligentsia, nobility, and clergy. Cross-examination of him by the defense attorneys revealed their clumsiness with the unfamiliar technique. They merely elicited further testimony so damaging that they stopped questioning the general.

When Lahousen had finished, Sir Geoffrey Lawrence declared a recess. The court was to be cleared of all visitors, he announced. A delicate issue was about to be decided in closed session: the competency of Rudolf Hess to stand trial. His behavior raised reasonable doubt—eating while lying on the floor, goose-stepping in the exercise yard, and reading novels in court. Three weeks before, at the court's request, Hess had undergone examination by a ten-man panel of psychiatrists from America, Great Britain, and the Soviet Union. The panel concluded that Hess's amnesia would "interfere with his ability to conduct his defense and to understand the details of the past." The final decision, however, rested with the justices.

During the recess before the hearing, Captain Gilbert approached Hess in the dock. Gilbert was convinced of the authenticity of the man's amnesia but thought he ought to warn him of the likely consequences. If the justices found Hess incompetent to stand trial, he wouldn't be coming to court anymore, Gilbert advised, and he would soon be separated from the other defendants.

Hess looked stunned. In the few minutes before the court would resume, he had to make a decision. He had already spent four and a half years in an alien, unsympathetic land. For the past two months, however confined, he had lived again among his compatriots, speaking his native tongue. Even coming into court daily represented more sociability than he had known in all those years.

The marshal shouted, "Attention." The justices returned, and Sir Geoffrey Lawrence declared the court back in session. He gestured toward Hess's lawyer, Gunther von Rohrscheidt. Rohrscheidt began to explain why his client should not stand trial, quoting extensively from the psychiatric panel's report. As the lawyer spoke, Hess scribbled a note and signaled to a guard to take it to Rohrscheidt. The lawyer glanced at it but kept on talking. Hess began gesturing wildly for Rohrscheidt to stop. Chief justice Lawrence, unable to ignore the defendant's behavior, asked Rohrscheidt if Herr Hess might speak for himself. Hess rose, and a microphone was brought to him. His manner was calm, the voice steady. "Mr. President," he said to Lawrence, "henceforth, my memory will again respond to the outside world. The reasons for simulating loss of memory were of a tactical nature. My capacity to follow the trial, to defend myself, is not affected." A stunned Lawrence quickly adjourned the court.

As REPORTERS RUSHED TO FILE THE news, Douglas Kelley and Gustav Gilbert hurried to Hess's cell. They had believed in the man's mental impairment. Their professional reputations were on the line. They found Hess smiling calmly, the mad stare absent from his eyes. He spoke easily, answering in detail their questions about his youth, his conversations with Hitler, his flight to Scotland.

The two men left, subdued. Kelley ventured that Hess's amnesia was still real. It was this sudden cure that was the hoax. He was aware of cases, he said, where amnesia patients, in order to preserve their ego, claimed that they had only pretended loss of memory.

The Saturday morning after Hess's turnabout, the justices announced their decision on his competence. Hess would stand trial.

In November, Ernst Kaltenbrunner had suffered a mild stroke and had been taken to the hospital. Sufficiently recovered now, he had been returned to his cell the previous weekened. On Monday, December 10, he made his first appearance in the dock.

Kaltenbrunner had come into prominence in 1942, when Czech agents tossed a bomb into the Mercedes sports car of Reinhard Heydrich, head of the RSHA, the Nazi police apparatus. Himmler picked Kaltenbrunner, then a relatively unknown SS leader, to succeed Heydrich. Kaltenbrunner had substantial shoes to fill. Heydrich had masterminded the phony Polish attack on the Gleiwitz radio station for Himmler. Heydrich had been in charge of the Einsatzgruppen—the extermination squads that followed the German armies into Poland and Russia. Heydrich had drafted the protocol for the "Final Solution of the Jewish problem."

Kaltenbrunner may have lacked Heydrich's icy finesse. He may often have been drunk. But he went at his duties—chief of the Gestapo, the concentration camps, the SD (an intelligence agency)—with crude energy. Even the inevitability of defeat had not tempered his zeal. As the Allied armies plunged into Germany, he had sent out an order to the concentration camps: "The liberation of prisoners or Jews by the enemy must be avoided. They must not fall into their hands alive." Just eleven days before the war ended, he informed Franz Ziereis, the Mauthausen commandant, that his quota was still 1000 Jews to be killed daily. When time ran out, he ordered Ziereis to herd all remaining prisoners into a tunnel, seal off the entrance, and suffocate them. Even Ziereis blanched at this last order and did not comply. When the desperation of his plight had pierced even Kaltenbrunner's alcoholic fog, he played his last card: He ordered the surrender of Mauthausen and its survivors to General Patton. It was this final order that he was counting on to save him.

KALTENBRUNNER'S appearance that afternoon triggered a three-alarm press alert and a correspondents' stampede for the courtroom. The photographers were particularly pleased—Kaltenbrunner was a Nazi out of central casting. He lumbered into the dock with a lopsided smile on his long horseface. He put a hand out to General Jodl, who refused to take it. He greeted Hans Frank, but Frank turned away. He took his place next to Keitel, who suddenly felt a need to talk to Ribbentrop. Kaltenbrunner spied his lawyer, Kurt Kauffmann, a fellow Nazi. He rose, leaned over the rail of the dock, and put out his hand. Kauffmann clasped his hands behind his back and gave Kaltenbrunner a brief nod.

Chief Justice Lawrence called the court to order. The first business this afternoon was to hear the plea of Ernst Kaltenbrunner, he announced. Kaltenbrunner rose, looking like a helpless giant. Throughout his captivity he had taken the position that he was only nominally responsible for the Gestapo and the concentration camps. His superior, the late Reichsführer Himmler, had his own people who actually ran those operations. Kaltenbrunner merely sat on top of them in an organization chart. His true role, he intended to convince the court, had been to run the SD. In a voice totally at odds with his brutal appearance—a voice smooth, cultivated, and reasonable—he said, "I am not guilty."

David Low, an artist for *The New York Times*, took out his sketch pad and began to limn a brute. He sketched in Kaltenbrunner's long purple "dueling scar." Like so much about the man, the scar was a fraud. It had been earned not in a test of manliness, but against a windshield in an auto accident after a drunken spree.

THE bulletin boards around the courthouse were avidly read. To visitors they were like a playbill, announcing what dramas would be performed next and who would enact the featured roles. The December 11 posting indicated that the case against slave labor was scheduled next. The prosecuting attorney was Thomas Dodd, a former FBI man who stirred mixed feelings at Nuremberg. Socially, Dodd was a boon companion, a raconteur, enlivening an evening with well-told stories. To his more erudite colleagues he was a lightweight who used their work to prop up his own thin legal scholarship. All were eager to observe his first performance in the arena.

As he moved to the prosecutor's stand, Dodd cut an impressive figure, with steel-gray hair, a classic profile. The most uneasy men in the dock this day were Albert Speer and Fritz Sauckel. Their respective guilt for the death and suffering inflicted by the slave labor program had become a topic of hot debate in evening bull sessions at the Grand Hotel. Dodd's performance could resolve the debate.

Fritz Sauckel sat in the dock in a state of emotional befuddlement. He was the least imposing figure among the defendants—a little man with a shining dome, sad brown eyes, and a silly mustache patterned after the Führer's. He was as puzzled to find himself on trial as he had been to discover that Germany had lost the war. What pained Sauckel most was that no one at Nuremberg seemed to understand his logic. How could he be guilty of crimes against working people when he himself had sprung from the working class?

He was fifty-one years old, the son of a mailman and a seamstress. Raised in a strict religious home, he had gone to sea as a boy of fifteen and sat out World War I in a French prison after his merchant ship was captured. When he came home in 1919, Germany was convulsed by Communists and right-wingers battling for the souls of unemployed workers like Fritz Sauckel. "I could not be a Communist," he told his Nuremberg interrogators, "because Marxism states that religion is the opiate of the masses, that private property is theft." On the other hand, he could not join the conservative political movements, "because they ignored people of my station." Then he had heard Adolf Hitler speak. "I had found a man who could create a union of all German people whatever their level, whatever their calling." He joined the party and became an energetic, if unimaginative, recruiter. By 1927 he was gauleiter—district party chief—of Thuringia. He had risen not by flair or connections, but by tireless, plodding effort. He remained a gauleiter until a fateful day in 1942. Sitting with Sauckel in the dock, four places to his left, was the man responsible for what happened that day.

Left, Albert Speer, Hitler's youthful architect, who became armaments minister and dramatically increased Germany's arms production using conscript labor.

Above, Nazi roundup of Jews from the Warsaw Ghetto. Part of the trial's photographic record.

Right, Fritz Sauckel, conscript labor czar, who "recruited" millions of foreign workers and delivered them from their homelands to the Nazi war machine.

In 1942 Albert Speer had just been appointed armaments minister. A principal task he faced was to move labor where it was most needed. But the gauleiters refused to give up workers from their regional fiefdoms to send to other districts. Speer persuaded Hitler that the regime needed a labor czar, someone who could break the grip of the gauleiters, preferably someone from their own ranks whom they would heed.

In March 1942 Fritz Sauckel found himself with Speer and Hitler in the Reich Chancellery in Berlin. "This has been a brutal winter," Hitler said, pacing. "We've suffered a heavy drain on our vehicles, trains, fuel. We've taken heavy manpower losses. We can only keep pace if every German enters either the military or the armaments industries." He looked directly at Sauckel. "This is a gigantic job. And you, Sauckel, are going to perform it." He was to be, Hitler said, plenipotentiary-general for the allocation of labor. He would have unconditional authority to issue orders to commissioners of occupied lands, to heads of civil agencies, even to generals and admirals, direct- ing them to round up the labor needed. The job could not be done with German manpower alone. Sauckel was to raise 1.6 million for- eign workers in the next three months, Hitler ordered. Sauckel shifted uneasily. Did not conscription of foreigners violate interna- tional law? he asked. That was not Sauckel's concern, Hitler replied.

Tom Dodd was proving a dramatic courtroom performer. With well-controlled emotion he read into the record document 294 PS, which described how a Sauckel manpower directive was carried out in the Soviet Union. The author of this report was Sauckel's fellow defendant Alfred Rosenberg. "You cannot imagine the bestiality," Rosenberg had written Sauckel. "The order came to supply twenty- five workers, but no one reported. Then the German militia came and began to set fire to the houses of those who had fled. People who hurried to the scene were forbidden to extinguish the flames. In- stead, they were beaten and arrested. The militia went through the adjoining villages and seized laborers. Among them are lame, blind, and aged people. We are now catching humans like dog catchers used to catch dogs."

As Dodd went on, Sauckel waited to hear Speer's role in all this. The way the system had worked, manufacturers would inform Speer of their labor needs. Speer would aggregate such requests from all industries and direct Sauckel to come up with the required number of workers. Sauckel merely saw himself as Speer's procurer.

Speer was forever demanding more and more workers. Sauckel suspected that he was hoarding labor far beyond his needs, while the army desperately sought more men. At one point Sauckel added up all of Speer's pending demands, and they totaled more workers than the entire German economy required.

A despondent Sauckel listened to Dodd pour on the incriminating evidence and wondered why nothing was said of his efforts to have foreign workers treated decently. In one directive to recruiters, he had written, "Underfed slaves, diseased, resentful, despairing and filled with hate, will never yield that maximum of output which they can achieve under decent conditions." Sauckel waved to attract the attention of his counsel, Robert Servatius. Servatius must make clear that he, Sauckel, had not been responsible for working conditions. That was Speer's bailiwick.

The Führer had given Sauckel an impossible job, and only one defendant in the dock knew how hard he had tried to get out of it. During the war Admiral Dönitz had been astonished by a radio message from a U-boat skipper reporting a stowaway: Fritz Sauckel. Sauckel begged to be allowed to stay aboard, but Dönitz had ordered the sub to bring Sauckel back.

Sauckel traced his final fall from grace to August 4, 1944. With the Allies securely entrenched in France, with the Red Army closing in from the east, Hitler had decided that a plenipotentiary for total war was required to maximize manpower. He called a meeting of Speer, Sauckel, Keitel, and the propaganda minister, Josef Goebbels. Goebbels immediately began attacking Sauckel. Sauckel had allowed millions of Germans to stay in soft civil service jobs. He had failed to mobilize Germany's women. Why, Goebbels said in disbelief, 500,000 females were still working as charwomen! He said he would be happy to take on the additional burden of plenipotentiary for total war. Hitler nodded and quickly added that this was a splendid idea. Goebbels was going to be in charge of the total war effort, Hitler announced, and Sauckel had better do as he was told. After that day Sauckel had toiled as hard as ever, but he had been invited to no more high-level meetings. He never saw Hitler again.

THE PLACE TO ESCAPE WHEN THE day's work was done was to the Marble Room in the Grand Hotel, where the food was good, the drinks large, and both were subsidized by Uncle Sam. Five dollars easily financed an evening of dining and drinking, and the waiter would be happy with a two-cigarette tip. Major Airey Neave, who in the end had found counsel for all the defendants, threaded his way through the jeeps and command cars that clogged the hotel's entrance as the sounds of orchestra music filtered out into the street. Herr Meyer, the manager, always smiling, greeted him, and Neave entered the Marble Room.

Zarah Leander was singing *"Der Wind hat mir ein Lied erzählt."* Leander had been a singer and film star of some prominence. Now her voice had a mechanical quality, like a piano roll played too often. Her gown, once fashionable, was now frayed and faded. Years before, even months earlier, she would have been singing the same refrain for storm troopers and party stalwarts.

Neave made his way around the dancers to a table, where he joined British friends. Under the festive disorder the Marble Room had a traceable structure. American men dominated the room, usually sitting together, though they might have with them as many British women as American. The American women were easy to spot. They were smartly dressed, spared the six years of clothes rationing that European women had undergone. At one American table Tom Dodd, fresh from his presentation of the slave labor case, held court in an ebullient mood.

Neave was struck by the contrast between the horror revealed in the courtroom during the day and the determined merriment of the Marble Room at night. He sat down, and his companions asked what Neave thought of Dodd's performance. Whatever their respective guilt, Neave observed, the contest between Sauckel and Speer was going to be influenced by social class. Look at the men on the bench. Then look at Speer and Sauckel. Whom would they invite to their club? A companion disagreed. The Speer-Sauckel case would revolve around another question: Who had been the motive force in the slave labor operation—Sauckel the slave trader or Speer the slave driver? If it had been the latter, then it seemed hard to believe that Speer could suffer a lesser fate than Sauckel. Neave hoped the bench could be that objective.

3

DURING the glory days Heinrich Hoffmann had often stayed at the Grand Hotel with Adolf Hitler. Now Hoffmann occupied a cell in the Nuremberg prison. As Hitler's personal photographer, he had been shrewd enough on his arrest to bring with him a cache of photos. Since he was the only one who knew what they portrayed, he managed to have himself made a trusty and was given the job of indexing the pictures. Hoffmann had a son-in-law in the dock: Baldur von Schirach, the Hitler Youth leader. This relationship, however, did not prevent Hoffmann from happily gathering photographic evidence against Schirach or his former colleagues.

Hoffmann was supervised by Richard Heller, a thirty-year-old navy lieutenant and lawyer who spoke a smattering of German. The first time Heller saw Hoffmann, the old man was lost in an oversized set of army fatigues. Yet a twinkle shone in his eye as he introduced himself with a flourish as "Professor Hoffmann, doctor of fine arts."

Hoffmann constantly badgered Heller, saying that there was no reason to keep him locked up. He knew where tons of photographs were hidden, and he could be far handier to the prosecution if he were free. Heller persuaded his superiors to allow him to take Hoffmann on a photographic hunting expedition.

No sooner had they set out for Munich than Hoffmann piqued Heller's curiosity by mentioning that it was he who had introduced Eva Braun to Hitler. He had been running a photography shop in Munich at the time, he said, and felt uneasy about Hitler's interest in young girls, particularly in Hoffmann's seventeen-year-old daughter, Henriette. Hoffmann deliberately steered the Führer to another seventeen-year-old—his shop assistant Eva Braun. What the "professor" didn't say was that much of his business had been in pornographic pictures. His models had been girls who worked in second-rate bars, including Braun, who had become both his assistant and his mistress. He had happily handed Eva over to the Führer.

When Hoffmann and Heller arrived in Munich, the German indeed unearthed a photographic lode. Afterward they went to Dachau, then continued on to Berchtesgaden. By the time the trip ended, they had found enough photos to fill two army trucks. On their return to Nuremberg, Heller concluded that there was no further need to cage Hoffmann and arranged lodgings for him.

ON DECEMBER 13 Tom Dodd again demonstrated his talent for the dramatic. The evidence that he planned to introduce was concealed by white sheets on the prosecutors' table. The first exhibit, he explained, was the result of an order that had gone out in 1939 from Standartenführer Karl Koch, commandant of the Buchenwald concentration camp. Koch had ordered all tattooed prisoners to report to the dispensary. Those with the most interesting and artistic tattoos were put to death by lethal injection. Dodd whisked the sheet from U.S.A. exhibit 253. The exposed, pale, leathery objects with the designs of ships and hearts still visible, Dodd said, were human skin. The Buchenwald commandant's wife, Ilse Koch, now confined here in the Nuremberg jail, liked to have the tattooed flesh tanned and fashioned into household objects, like lampshades.

U.S.A. exhibit 254, Dodd continued, originated with the punishment the Nazis reserved for Poles who had sexual relations with German women. Those caught were hanged, Dodd said, pulling away the sheet from the next exhibit. From a distance it was not easy to identify the fist-size nut-brown object. It was, Dodd explained, the shrunken head of an executed Pole, used as a paperweight by Koch. As Dodd took his seat, the stillness in the courtroom was interrupted only by nervous coughing.

The defense spokesman, looking shaken, put off cross-examination until the next day. In the morning Kaltenbrunner's counsel, the tall, combative ex-Nazi Karl Kauffmann, argued that in a Continental court the prosecutor is expected to produce evidence both favorable and unfavorable to the accused. Yet on the matter of Standartenführer Koch the prosecution conveniently omitted one salient fact: The Buchenwald commandant had been condemned to death by an SS court.

Subsequently, the prosecution demonstrated that Koch had indeed been convicted by an SS court, but not for torturing, mutilating, and murdering inmates of Buchenwald. Those acts were not crimes in the SS canon. Koch had been condemned for embezzlement of SS funds and for killing a fellow Nazi in an argument.

During the lunch break Gustav Gilbert circulated among the defendants while they ate. Ribbentrop, sitting next to Frank, asked if Hitler might have known of the terrible deeds revealed in court. "It would not have been possible otherwise," Frank answered. "They were done at his orders." Göring leaned back from a neighboring table and gave Frank a murderous look. But Frank went on. "Hitler got us into this," he said, and added that the Führer had then abandoned them through suicide. Gilbert observed Göring's mounting anger. Too often the defendants were guarded when talking in the Reichsmarschall's presence. Frank had broken ranks.

Göring rose and took Gilbert aside. "I don't want to exaggerate my love for the Führer," he said quietly. "You know how he treated me at the end. But I think in the last year or so he just, well, he left things up to Himmler." Heinrich Himmler was indeed the most chilling figure in the Hitler entourage—a remote, self-contained enigma who had accumulated terrifying power. The death camps, the Gestapo, the Einsatzgruppen—all the components of terror had been in his grip. Now he was conveniently dead, having taken a cyanide capsule after his capture, making the perfect scapegoat.

Baldur von Schirach, leader of the Hitler Youth and gauleiter of Vienna, also spoke to the psychologist. "After today it's all over," he said in flawless English. "I wouldn't blame the court if they just chop off all our heads, even if a couple of us are innocent. What are a few more among the millions already murdered?" Gilbert wondered if Schirach too might be ready to stand up to Göring.

THE morning of December 20 was bitter cold. Secretaries and prosecutors, translators and journalists, their breath visible in the air, filed into the courthouse. The more compassionate among them wondered how the Nurembergers were getting by in the coldest European winter in living memory.

Two days before, the prosecution had begun the most novel part of the original Bernays plan—the attempt to prove that Nazi organizations were criminal. There were seven: the Nazi Party leadership, the Reich cabinet, the SS, the Gestapo, the SD, the SA (the storm troopers, or Brownshirts), and the High Command. The Americans alone held some 200,000 potential war criminals, and individual trials of so many were impractical. Thus Jackson had seized on the concept of group guilt.

The Allied Control Council had issued Edict 10, making clear that any member of an organization found to be criminal would be subject to penalties ranging up to death. Four and a half million Germans had belonged to the SA alone. Potentially, half the families in Germany had members who would be touched by Edict 10. Letters poured into the Palace of Justice from POWs, wives, mothers, and children. The message was virtually unchanging: Franz or Dieter or Klaus was not a criminal but merely a guard or a clerk or a cook, doing his duty.

The organization case had an unexpected effect. Robert Kempner, head of the Defense Rebuttal Section, had surveyed Germans of all classes and found near unanimity: They wanted the defendants convicted and punished. As Kempner wrote to Jackson, "If the leaders are found guilty then the onus of guilt is removed from those who merely did their bidding."

The issue on the docket this morning was the role of the SS in conducting "medical" experiments for Göring's Luftwaffe. Pilots shot down over the North Sea had often survived the crash into the frigid waters, only to die later in lifeboats after being rescued. The problem had been brought to the attention of Dr. Sigmund Rascher, who worked out of a secret "laboratory" at Dachau.

A British prosecutor read the affidavit of a Dachau inmate, according to which Dr. Rascher ordered inmates dropped naked into freezing water. They were then plunged into hot water, warm water, or tepid water to see which method would best revive a freezing human being. The prosecutor read from Dr. Rascher's records: " 'It was evident that rapid rewarming was in all cases preferable to a slow rewarming because, after removal from the cold water, the body temperature continued to drop rapidly.' " Rascher added that most of his subjects went into convulsions and died.

The testimony ended, and chief justice Lawrence announced that court would adjourn, and resume twelve days later, on January 2, 1946, after a Christmas holiday.

ROBERT Jackson threw a Christmas party at the house on Lindenstrasse, principally for the justices, lawyers, and a few secretaries. The Russians, however, had pressed hard for an invitation for a man identified as I. V. Rasumov, chief of the Russian Translations Division.

From the instant the Soviet delegation arrived, his countrymen displayed unusual deference to Comrade Rasumov, who played the piano and told dreadful jokes.

Mrs. Douglas took over the piano and started to play "Silent Night." Glasses stopped tinkling and conversation faded as a short, blond Russian officer with a bell-like baritone began singing *"Stille Nacht, heilige Nacht . . ."* Jackson surveyed the faces of his guests. The camaraderie with the Russians pleased him. Outside this oasis of harmony, relations between East and West in Nuremberg had become increasingly chilled. The GIs posted here now were youths who had not fought against Nazism. They liked the Germans, who were tidy and hardworking, just like the folks back home. The Russians, by contrast, were incomprehensible to boys from Ohio and Tennessee.

As the last notes of "Silent Night" faded, Comrade Rasumov gave an unobtrusive hand signal, and the Russian guests left in a body. At least, Jackson thought, now they knew who ran the Soviet secret police in Nuremberg.

THE American principal justice, Francis Biddle, resented that he had not yet been able to arrange to have his wife join him. But Bob Jackson refused to buck the army's ban on spouses. Why should the brass and VIPs enjoy a privilege that occupation officials could not provide to thousands of married GIs? the army's reasoning went. Biddle was convinced, however, that personal rather than democratic impulses explained Jackson's acquiescence. Bob obviously did not want his wife there, since he had, in his secretary, all the companionship he desired. Inflaming Biddle's sense of the arbitrariness of it all was the fact that the British and French did not feel bound by U.S. Army restrictions. Chief justice Lawrence's handsome, statuesque wife sat in court every day.

COLONEL Andrus informed his staff that the defendants were to be treated no differently on Christmas Day than on any other day. There would be no special meals served. Most certainly, there was to be no exchange of gifts. However, since it might be their last Christmas, he would allow religious services. That was a damn sight more consideration than they had ever shown their victims, he noted.

On Christmas Eve, in the chapel, thirteen Protestant defendants listened to Chaplain Gerecke read the Gospel according to Saint Luke. Since his arrival the clergyman had won over his strange flock. Gerecke did not judge them; that was what they appreciated. He wanted only to reclaim their souls, an objective most of them increasingly shared. As the organist began playing *"O du Fröhliche, O du Heilige,"* they joined Gerecke in subdued voices, except for Göring, who belted out the song.

Before Major Kelley slipped away for the Christmas break, he and Gus Gilbert talked about their book. They were onto something big, Kelley said. They were going to produce a magnum opus. Sometimes, though, the arrangement seemed a bit lopsided to Gilbert. He was monitoring the defendants in the dock and making the most of the cell visits. Kelley received a copy of every note Gilbert took. Yet it was Kelley who was going away for the holidays, while Gilbert continued to work.

Field Marshal Keitel was on Gilbert's Christmas Day rounds. The psychologist had learned from prosecutor Tom Dodd that a remorseful Keitel had recently considered pleading guilty, but Göring had bullied him out of it. The old soldier, Gilbert thought, might need some spine stiffening.

Keitel stood at rigid attention. "I thank you from the bottom of my heart for this Christmas visit," he said. "You are the only one I can really talk to." The conversation drifted to Hitler's wrongheadedness in attacking the Soviet Union in 1941. He himself had been convinced that the invasion was a blunder, Keitel said. Had he made this opinion known to Hitler? Gilbert asked. Keitel was silent.

What interested Gilbert most was how a member of a caste steeped in a code of honor could have drafted instruments like the Commando and Reprisal orders. Cruelest of all was *Nacht und Nebel*—the "Night and Fog" decree—intended to terrorize resistance movements. Suspects were arrested in the middle of the night, secretly shot, and never heard of again. As Hitler put it, "They disappeared into the night and fog." Keitel had issued the *Nacht und Nebel* order.

"I am dying of shame," Keitel told Gilbert. "I only wish I had spent more time in the field. I spent too much time in Hitler's company. Please let me talk to you once in a while, as long as I am not yet a sentenced criminal," Keitel pleaded as Gilbert rose to leave. Snapping to attention once more, the old soldier wished Gilbert a happy

Christmas. In a sense Gilbert pitied Keitel. He had behaved criminally, thinking he was behaving correctly. Now, with that illusion stripped away, he stood naked before his sins.

Not so with the next soldier on Gilbert's visiting list. Gilbert agreed with Kelley that General Jodl was their most impenetrable case. The general was sitting erect at his desk, his face pinched, his cold blue eyes peering at nothing. He stood and clicked his heels. Gilbert was reminded again of what a small man Jodl was physically.

Gilbert asked how men of honor could have signed such brutal orders? Jodl answered that the prosecution's naïveté surprised him. When a directive to the armed forces began "The Führer has ordered," it meant that the command had been given orally by Hitler and that he and Keitel had merely committed it to paper, not invented it. "And if we had disobeyed, we should have been arrested, and rightly so," Jodl observed. "A soldier's obligation is to obey orders. That's the code I've lived by all my life."

Gilbert asked about what went on in the death camps. He had no idea about ninety percent of it, Jodl said. "It's impossible for me to understand what kind of beasts could have been in charge of the camps and actually have done those things."

Gilbert got up to leave. "Germans, obeying orders, no doubt."

THE why still gnawed at Gus Gilbert after every cell visit. They were not dealing with the denizens of some savage society. Hans Frank could spout yards of Schiller's poetry. Speer could move comfortably at any social level. Seyss-Inquart was a man of powerful intellect. Frick was trained in the law. It would be hard to pick out most of these men as war criminals from a gathering of Rotarians. If he and Kelley could not explain their behavior, then all they could present in their book would be the riddle but not the key.

Gilbert had learned that thirty-nine SS men were being held in the former concentration camp at Dachau awaiting execution after having been convicted by an American military court. The Nazi defendants at Nuremberg were the leaders, able to distance themselves from the actual crimes committed. None of them had shoved anyone into a gas chamber, shot a prisoner in the neck, or injected a human guinea pig with a lethal drug. The men at Dachau, by contrast, were the journeymen of the death trade, one of them having killed 20,000 himself. By studying them firsthand, Gilbert thought he might better understand the murderous impulses of Nazism. And so he arranged to spend part of the Christmas break at Dachau.

On his arrival Gilbert found a sanitized charnel house. He interviewed and administered intelligence tests to twenty of the condemned men. Their IQs, he found, averaged 107, in the "dull normal" range. Many, he learned, had been unemployed before Hitler became chancellor. After they had experienced powerlessness, the opportunity to dominate others had enormous appeal to them. What dismayed Gilbert most was their self-pity. They had simply carried out their assignments as ordered, and Himmler, escaping via suicide, had left them holding the bag.

Two days later Gilbert boarded a train back to Nuremberg. He believed that he now understood at least one piece of the puzzle. Every one of the condemned men at Dachau had confirmed it. Germany was a society where people did what they were told. You obeyed your parents, your teachers, your clergymen, your employer, your superior officer, your government officials. To produce a Dachau, an Auschwitz, a Buchenwald required not a few sadists, but hundreds, even thousands of unquestioning, obedient people.

One of the condemned SS men had complained, "We didn't dare oppose the orders of the Führer or Himmler." The excuses of the workaday killers and of the men on cellblock C were identical.

ONE morning after Christmas, Albert Speer lay on his cot staring at cracked walls covered with flowing figures and animals he had sketched with a piece of soft coal given him by a guard. He rose, went to the square porthole, and asked the guard to inform the colonel's office that he would like to meet with Dr. Hans Flächsner, his defense counsel. Speer treated everyone with courtesy. It worked. None of the guards called Speer by derisive nicknames. He was always "Mr. Speer" or "Herr Speer."

The Speers had been a leading family in Mannheim. Albert's father and grandfather had been architects. Born in 1905, Speer grew up in a fourteen-room apartment, attended by butlers, maids, and a chauffeur in purple livery. When he was thirteen, a fortune-teller at a fair predicted that he would win fame and retire early. He had never been entirely able to drive the seer's prediction from his mind.

One day in 1931, while Speer was teaching architecture at the Institute of Technology in Berlin, his students urged him to come to a lecture. They proceeded to a shabby room over a workingmen's beer hall. Speer expected a roughneck demagogue. Instead, he found himself entranced by Adolf Hitler. The next day he joined the Nazi Party.

Through party connections he won a commission to design a Nazi district headquarters. Hitler, by now chancellor, found the work impressive. He chose Speer to stage the Nuremberg rally of 1933. Speer was next asked to build the Reich Chancellery and Hitler's private residence in Berlin. He became Hitler's personal architect, closeted alone for hours with the most powerful man in Europe. He sat next to Hitler at the theater and dined with him in the best restaurants— heady stuff for a man just twenty-eight.

Speer occasionally glimpsed the dark side of his new master, but he was, by his own admission, "intoxicated by the desire to wield pure power, to order people to do this or that, to spend billions." Hitler made it all possible. In 1942 he appointed Speer minister of armaments and chief of construction, in control of 2.6 million workers. As Speer later absorbed the naval production program, he directed 3.2 million workers. By the time he wrested aircraft production from Göring and became minister of the economy, 12 million Germans and foreigners worked under Speer. By age thirty-eight he had fulfilled half of the fortune-teller's prophecy.

To run a country's arsenal was, by itself, no war crime. But Speer might have to explain actions less easily defended. In December 1943 he had visited a plant carved out of the Harz Mountains, the manufacturing site of Germany's secret rocket weapon, the V-2. The dank limestone caverns held over 50,000 slave laborers. Once these workers entered the caves, they remained for three months, working seventy-two hours a week, fed a daily diet of 1100 calories. Sanitation facilities and housing barely existed. Because of the dampness and air pressure, the workers' muscle and bone tissue deteriorated quickly. Some spaces were so low that the men worked stooped over, until they could no longer stand up straight. Deaths in the plant averaged 180 a day.

Speer also visited the Mauthausen extermination camp, where prisoners hauled stones up out of the quarry until they dropped dead of exhaustion. He had explained to his American interrogators that he had gone there to inspect a site for a new railhead and had seen only a small part of the camp. He had witnessed no atrocities.

Hardest to explain away, he knew, would be his relationship with Heinrich Himmler. As procurement of workers became more difficult, Speer had gone to Himmler, who controlled hundreds of thousands of people in the concentration camps, and asked him for 400,000 workers from Auschwitz. Speer could hardly disclaim knowledge of the nature of the camp. Earlier a friend, Karl Hanke, the gauleiter of Lower Silesia, had warned him. He had seen death in battle, Hanke said, but never had he witnessed anything to compare with Auschwitz. Speer should never accept an invitation to go there. Speer had not pressed for details.

His captivity had given Speer abundant time to examine how a man of his cultivation had slipped into this moral ditch. His conscience, he concluded, had been elbowed aside in the desperate arms race he was running against the Allies. His fixation on production blurred all human feeling. He was, he admitted to himself, fonder of machines than of people.

Defending his behavior as munitions chief was near impossible. His salvation, he was convinced, lay in his actions during the last months of the war. Toward the end Hitler had issued an order that everything in the path of the Allied armies be destroyed—every factory, bridge, power plant, road, and mine. "If the war is lost," Hitler told Speer, "the people are lost too. It is not necessary to worry about the fundamentals that the people will need for a primitive future existence. Those who survive the war will, in any event, be only the inferior. The best have fallen." In his scorched-earth order, Hitler had finally and fully revealed his maniacal nature to Speer.

The war was indeed lost, and Speer's practical mind was already on postwar Germany. The country's industrial base must not be destroyed. On his own authority Speer ordered high explosives, intended for blowing up iron and coal mines, to be hidden. He had pistols issued to factory workers to defend their plants. He ordered the armed forces not to destroy rail lines and bridges. In the meantime he begged Hitler to rescind this policy of national suicide. By late March, 1945, he had made some headway: He persuaded Hitler that only military considerations should determine which facilities would be blown up. On April 10 Speer wrote a speech revealing the hard truth to the German people. The war was lost. No fresh armies, no miracle weapons were going to save them. They were to destroy nothing vital to rebuilding the nation. He was waiting only for the right moment, he told himself, to deliver the address over the radio.

Still, for all his disillusionment, Speer had felt an overpowering urge to see the Führer one last time. He flew into besieged Berlin, landing near the Brandenburg Gate. He made it to the Führerbunker as Russian shells were slamming into the Reich Chancellery, which he had built. Hitler kept him waiting until 3:00 a.m. and then displayed no interest in anything Speer said. The visit ended with Hitler examining Speer with cold, protuberant eyes, then extending a limp hand. He expressed no gratitude for what Speer had done for Germany, no good wishes for his family. All that he said in a barely audible voice was, "So you're leaving. Good. *Auf Wiedersehen.*"

To the very end Speer had been unable to turn his back on Hitler. And he had never found the right moment to deliver his brave the-war-is-lost speech to the German people.

AT 3:00 P.M. the escort guard took Speer to the visitors' room, where Flächsner was waiting behind the wire mesh. Speer spoke quietly, guiding his lawyer through his defense strategy—how, for example, they should play the mistreatment of conscript workers and the visit to the death camp. Understatement and contrition were to be the watchwords. He had one strong, persuasive case that Flächsner must hammer at: Here was a man who had stood up to Hitler and his diabolic orders. The judges must see him as a man who had risked his life to salvage his nation's future. And he had an even more compelling story to tell. Speer's voice dropped to a whisper. Did Flächsner know that Speer had once tried to assassinate Hitler?

TO THE men on cellblock C, New Year's Day was indistinguishable from all others. Joachim von Ribbentrop, thin, haggard, was rummaging through the documents that littered his cell, desperate to find something proving the secret protocols he had engineered with Stalin. The pact with the Soviet Union had marked the acme of his career. It was one of the rare times that he had been able to sell Hitler on a foreign policy. In March 1939 the idea had struck Ribbentrop that the Nazis and the Communists might find common ground. Less than five months later the pact that jolted the world was signed. Germany and the Soviet Union agreed on the spheres where each would dominate, and Stalin, in effect, gave Hitler the green light for the invasion of Poland.

How close Ribbentrop had come to missing his eminent role in the Third Reich. At age seventeen he had immigrated to Canada in pursuit of a girl and to seek his fortune. He had lost the girl but had fallen in love with the country, staying on, holding several jobs along the way—bank clerk in Montreal, newspaper reporter in New York.

But in 1914, when the war broke out, the pull of the fatherland proved too strong. Ribbentrop returned to Germany and to war. He won a commission and afterward courted Anneliese Henkell, daughter of a champagne magnate. He went to work as a salesman for his in-laws and benefitted from his one genuine talent—a knack for languages. When he was thirty-two, he had himself adopted by an aunt whose husband had been knighted. Thus plain old Joachim Ribbentrop became Joachim von Ribbentrop.

He had not entered Hitler's orbit until 1932. In a dazzling display of name-dropping, he persuaded Hitler that he knew all the best people in Europe. When Göring learned that Hitler intended to appoint this "champagne salesman" to a high diplomatic post, he urged Hitler to make it Rome. Any Nazi could get by in that sister Fascist state. Instead, Hitler sent Ribbentrop to the Court of Saint James's. At dinner parties Ribbentrop launched into monologues, aping Hitler's words and mannerisms but lacking the magnetism. Soon the word was out that the German ambassador to Great Britain was a boor and a bore, and was welcomed in one corner of English society only—among the Nazi sympathizers, anti-Semites, and the peace-at-any-price set.

Down the corridor from Ribbentrop at Nuremberg was the man who had inadvertently helped elevate him to foreign minister in 1938. Konstantin von Neurath at the time held the post himself. Horrified at Hitler's intention to make war, he said so, and thereafter Hitler wanted someone more pliant in the Foreign Office. Joachim von Ribbentrop fit perfectly. Ribbentrop substituted energy and ambition for competence and intelligence. His single original triumph had indeed been the Soviet-German pact, and now he was desperate to produce a copy of its secret clauses so that he could demonstrate the duplicity of the Russians and their unfitness to judge him as a war criminal.

He was seeing his lawyer, Dr. Fritz Sauter, today, and he hoped Sauter had found a copy. Sauter was a famous advocate in Germany, and Walther Funk and Baldur von Schirach had also hired him. Sauter possessed an ego to match Ribbentrop's. During the visit he treated Ribbentrop with professional coolness, informing his client that he had not been able to unearth the secret passages of the German-Soviet nonaggression pact.

When Ribbentrop returned to his cell, he demanded to see the duty officer. He wanted Fritz Sauter fired as his defense counsel. The man had failed to wish him a happy New Year.

4

At 10:00 a.m. on January 2, chief justice Sir Geoffrey Lawrence reconvened the International Military Tribunal. His pink, cherubic countenance glowed after a vacation spent at his beloved Hill Farm in Wiltshire. Back in November the man had been judged a mediocrity. Now his simplicity was seen as the attribute of an uncluttered mind, a secure ego, and a strong, if understated, will. His evenhanded treatment of prosecution and defense alike had begun to persuade the defendants that this courtroom, room 600, might be a genuine arena for truth seeking and not necessarily the anteroom to the gallows.

Colonel Storey continued the case against the criminal organizations, presenting evidence against the Gestapo and making a botch of it. His idea of prosecuting was to introduce documents as though the sheer weight of the paper would tip the scales. When he became lost in this swamp of his own making, he might read the same document twice or prove the same point with five different documents. The chief justice, his patience wearing thin, strove to keep Storey on track.

To the court's relief a fresh face took the prosecutor's stand after lunch. Lieutenant Whitney Harris was a thirty-three-year-old lawyer whose film-star handsomeness belied a serious character. He had won this courtroom appearance for his work on the Ernst Kaltenbrunner case. As the day drew to a close, Harris was describing "the ninth crime for which Kaltenbrunner is responsible": the mass liquidation of prisoners at Dachau and other camps only days before they would have been liberated by the Allies.

The following morning John Harlan Amen replaced Harris at the prosecutor's stand for the direct examination of the next witness—SS General Otto Ohlendorf, a ranking member of the SD, which carried out intelligence, covert operations, and liquidations. Ohlendorf was in this courtroom only because of Harris' initiative. Harris had initially interrogated him in order to obtain evidence against Kaltenbrunner. One answer had piqued his curiosity: Ohlendorf had said that in 1941 he had headed Einsatzgruppe D in the East. Knowing the murderous reputation of the Einsatzgruppen, Harris had fired a question from out of the blue: "How many people did you kill?" The answer staggered him.

As they talked, Harris concluded that this man should not merely be providing background for the Kaltenbrunner case; he belonged in court testifying against him. When Colonel Amen saw a copy of Harris' interrogation, he claimed Ohlendorf for his own.

The witness now walked to the stand, wearing an unpressed gray suit. Amen's opening questions were calculatedly dull—queries about Kaltenbrunner's place in the RSHA organization chart. Then abruptly Amen asked how many people Einsatzgruppe D had killed. "In the year between June 1941 and June 1942 the Einsatz troops reported ninety thousand people liquidated," Ohlendorf answered. Did that include men, women, and children? Amen wanted to know. Yes, Ohlendorf replied. Amen next asked if mass shooting was the only method of execution. No, it was not. Ohlendorf explained that Reichsführer Himmler had noted that shooting women and children placed a terrible strain on the Einsatz personnel, especially family men. Therefore, beginning in 1942, women and children were gassed instead, in closed vans. Walther Funk closed his eyes as Ohlendorf began explaining how the dead victims' gold and jewelry were shipped off to the Reich Ministry of Finance.

During the defense attorneys' turn to cross-examine, British prosecutor Sir David Maxwell-Fyfe listened attentively. He was famous for his own traplike questioning. Kaltenbrunner's lawyer, Kurt Kauffmann, kept hammering at Ohlendorf, trying to get him to admit that Kaltenbrunner had no authority to issue orders to concentration camps. Didn't such orders go directly from Himmler to the head of the Gestapo, Heinrich Müller? Ohlendorf replied that Kaltenbrunner fit directly into the chain of command. As Müller's superior, he could relay orders from Himmler or initiate his own. Kauffmann, Sir David knew, had committed a classic cross-examination blunder: He had asked a question to which he did not know the answer.

The next defense examiner was Egon Kuboschok, substituting this day for Speer's attorney, Dr. Flächsner. Did Ohlendorf know, Kuboschok asked, that Albert Speer had taken actions to sabotage Hitler's scorched-earth orders? Ohlendorf answered that he did. Did Ohlendorf know that the Twentieth of July plotters had wanted Speer in their government? Yes, he did, Ohlendorf admitted. Finally, Kuboschok asked if the witness knew that Speer had planned an attempt on Hitler's life toward the end of the war. Excited whispers swept the courtroom. Göring turned and glared at Speer. No, Ohlendorf said skeptically, he had never heard of such a plan.

Albert Speer listened, satisfied. Kuboschok had been less skillful than his own lawyer would have been. Still, the seeds of his defense strategy had been planted.

Chief justice Lawrence called a brief adjournment. Instantly Göring was clambering over the chairs, thrusting his face next to Speer's. How dare he break up their united front against the prosecution? Göring shouted. What united front? Speer answered, turning away as the guards pulled Göring back to his seat.

FRANCIS Biddle had seen a name crop up from time to time and had written in the margin of the document he now held, "Who is he?" The name was Adolf Eichmann. This afternoon Biddle's curiosity was satisfied. An American prosecutor, Smith Brookhart, had begun questioning the next witness, an SS colleague of Otto Ohlendorf's named Dieter Wisliceny. Brookhart elicited from Wisliceny that in August 1942, he had gone to see Adolf Eichmann, head of the RSHA section dealing with Jewish matters. Wisliceny told Eichmann that he was being pressured by Slovakian officials to find out what had happened to 17,000 of their Jews deported to Poland. Eichmann finally admitted that the Jews were dead. How could that be? Wisliceny wanted to know. Extermination of the Jews was official policy, passed down from the Führer to Himmler to the RSHA, Eichmann explained. A disbelieving Wisliceny asked to see the order. Eichmann then took a document from his safe and showed it to him. This, Wisliceny said, was the first time he had heard of the Final Solution.

Brookhart shifted the questioning to Kaltenbrunner. Kaltenbrunner had not been RSHA chief when the Final Solution began, he noted. But, he asked Wisliceny, after Kaltenbrunner took over, was there any change in the extermination policy? "There was no diminution or change of any kind," the witness answered. Did Kaltenbrunner know personally his subordinate who directed the Final Solution? There was no doubt of it, Wisliceny said. Kaltenbrunner and Eichmann were fellow townsmen from Austria. Late in the afternoon Brookhart posed his last question: "Did Eichmann say anything as to the number of Jews that had been killed?"

"He said he would leap laughing into the grave," Wisliceny answered, "because the feeling that he had five million people on his conscience would be for him a source of extraordinary satisfaction."

REPORTERS checking the bulletin board on Friday, January 4, found the prosecution taking on the German High Command. Of all the organizations indicted, conviction of this group seemed the most difficult. Names like the Gestapo and the SS were synonymous with fear and horror. But the High Command? These were generals, admirals—the men who direct wars that politicians begin, in Germany, as in any nation. The prosecution had to prove not only that these professionals waged war but that they had played a hand in starting it and then fought it criminally. The prosecutor of the High Command was to be Colonel Telford Taylor of the United States.

From the moment Taylor approached the stand, his performance attracted attention. He was an arresting presence—slim, wavy-haired, handsome, with the air of a poet in uniform. His powers of reason held the court spellbound as he traced the corruption and transformation of an honorable officer corps into an unsoldierly, dishonorable tool of Hitler's. Taylor had set himself a minimum objective. It might be impossible to prove the entire High Command guilty, but he was determined to convince the tribunal that individual German generals could be war criminals.

On Monday, January 7, Colonel Taylor asked the court's permission to read a document into the record. As he did so, Otto Nelte, Keitel's lawyer, threw a quick glance at his client. The old soldier sat expressionless, like someone standing on a track who did not hear the train coming. " 'General Anton Dostler, on or about 24 March 1944, in the vicinity of La Spezia, Italy,' " Taylor read, " 'did order to be shot summarily, a group of United States Army personnel.' " ﹀

A fifteen-man team had slipped ashore behind the lines in northern Italy to blow up a railroad tunnel. The men were in uniform on a legitimate military mission when they were captured. On Dostler's orders they had been shot without a trial. Dostler had defended his action by saying that he was carrying out the Commando Order, signed by Field Marshal Keitel. Dostler, Taylor pointed out, had been tried by a military court in Italy and executed the month before.

Taylor went to the prosecution table and picked up another document. Keitel and his ilk, Taylor continued, would have the court believe that failure to carry out the Führer's wishes was not an option: They must shoot or be shot, as it were. That was untrue. The paybook of every German soldier made clear that to carry out, knowingly, an illegal order was a crime. Perhaps the bravest German soldier of all, Field Marshal Erwin Rommel, on receiving the Commando Order, had simply burned it.

As SOON as the court adjourned that afternoon, Captain Gilbert sped from the dock to the court reporters' room. He was looking for a statement against the High Command made that day by a witness named Erich von dem Bach-Zelewski, a general in the Waffen SS. The reporter who had taken the testimony flipped through his notes, then typed out the passage Gilbert wanted: "I am of the opinion when, for years and for decades, the doctrine is practiced that the Slavic race is an inferior race, and the Jews are not even human, then such an explosion was inevitable." The "explosion" that Bach-Zelewski had referred to was his role in putting down guerrilla resistance in Russia. The defense on cross-examination tried to have Bach-Zelewski establish that only outfits like his own SS—not soldiers in the regular army—had slaughtered people en masse. But the witness had spread guilt over the whole German war machine.

When Gilbert had heard Bach-Zelewski say that the Jew was not even considered human, something clicked into place. The search for the why of ingeniously organized, routinely administered mass murder consumed Gilbert. His visit to Dachau had furnished one

NUREMBERG: INFAMY ON TRIAL

piece of the puzzle: a culture that fostered unthinking obedience. Bach-Zelewski's statement provided a second piece. Ordinary Germans would not kill innocent human beings. But what if they had been bombarded for years with propaganda that the Slav or the Jew was not a true human, but a corruption of the race, responsible for Germany's woes? What if this attitude was the official government position? What if the very laws of the land denied to Jews the rights available to the lowliest German? Then a personality conditioned to unquestioning obedience, told to rid society of such pestilential vermin, could find the rationale to do it. These two factors explained much of the why, Gilbert concluded. Still, there had to be more.

THE prosecution's case against the organizations had ended. Their defense would take place later. Next on the court's schedule was the prosecution of individual defendants. On January 8, documents incriminating the first batch—Göring, Hess, Ribbentrop, and Keitel— fell like a blizzard. The prosecutors went after the defendants one by one, like ducks in a shooting gallery. January 9 was Alfred Rosenberg's turn. The philosopher of anti-Semitism and author of a book on the blood superiority of the German race was on trial for his roles as minister for the Occupied Eastern Territories and chief of the art-looting operation. Then on January 10 came Hans Frank. The arguments against him, taken from his own diaries, struck like hammer blows. He took such a pounding that Captain Gilbert, standing to the left of the dock, could virtually see the man buckle.

INTEREST in the trial was waning, and Howard K. Smith had a fresh idea for a broadcast. Back home, women had filled countless jobs as the men had gone off to war—the Rosie the Riveter phenomenon. Here at Nuremberg, Smith had observed that easily half of the 600 American staff members were women, employed not only as secretaries but as researchers, interpreters, and translators. Two lawyers on the American prosecution staff were women. In his report Smith told America about WAC major Catherine Falvey, who was going home to run for the Massachusetts state legislature. He described Harriet Zetterberg, a brilliant thirty-year-old law review graduate of the University of Wisconsin, known for preparing masterly briefs. What passed unnoticed, except perhaps by Zetterberg, was that she did not appear before the court. That role was reserved for the men on the staff. She was married to another prosecution lawyer, Daniel Margolies; because of the ban on spouses, the couple posed as unmarried and "living in sin" in a room at the Grand Hotel.

Zetterberg and Margolies had spent the Christmas break tracking down a physician, Dr. Franz Blaha, in Czechoslovakia. On Friday, January 11, the doctor testified.

Early in the war, Blaha had been arrested by the Nazis and committed to Dachau, where, as a physician, he was ordered to perform autopsies. What struck Margolies and Zetterberg, as the doctor took the stand, was the innate dignity of the man. Blaha was asked if he had ever seen any of the defendants at Dachau. The question was critical. Most of them had denied any knowledge of concentration camp operations. Blaha pointed and intoned the names "Rosenberg, Frick, Funk, Sauckel."

On January 12 the prison had taken on its Saturday afternoon aura, with the drama of the courtroom temporarily suspended and life reduced to the limits of a concrete cube. In his cell Speer eagerly awaited Dr. Gilbert's visit. He was determined to break Göring's hold over his fellow defendants, particularly after the way Göring had attacked him in court. Speer understood clearly what the prosecutors and the bench hoped for from the defendants—not Göring's bid for unified defiance, but individual confession and remorse. Speer was trying to bring the more pliable defendants along with him onto that course. He had high hopes for the youth leader, Baldur von Schirach. Earlier Frank too had seemed to be safely in the penitents' corner. But after the prosecution mauled him, Frank began wondering aloud whether he should make his last stand with Göring rather than with people who despised him. Speer marveled at Göring's capacity to intimidate without possessing a shred of real power. That was what he wanted to talk about to Gilbert.

Kaltenbrunner might also be enlisted as a penitent, Speer believed. And Speer would much rather have him as an ally than as an adversary. Only Kaltenbrunner knew what had really happened to Speer in the days after the Twentieth of July plot. After the plot had failed, Kaltenbrunner came to see him. In a safe at Bendlerstrasse, the High Command headquarters, Kaltenbrunner said, his people had found

Above, Jewish children held for medical experiments
at Auschwitz. Part of the trial's photographic record.

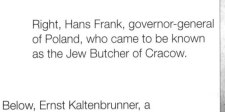

Right, Hans Frank, governor-general of Poland, who came to be known as the Jew Butcher of Cracow.

Below, Ernst Kaltenbrunner, a lumbering giant with a scarred faced, whose responsibilities included the Gestapo and the death camps.

Below, two inmates at the crematorium in the Mauthausen extermination camp.

a description of the government the plotters had intended to install. He took out an organization chart and handed it to Speer. In a box labeled ARMAMENTS Speer's name appeared in neatly printed letters. Speer quickly pointed out a penciled notation alongside the box that read "If possible." The plotters might have wanted him, but he had wanted no part of them, he said. With that, Kaltenbrunner gave him an enigmatic smile and left.

The next day Speer summoned his senior staff to a "loyalty meeting." In past speeches he had shunned party bombast. This day he praised Hitler's leadership to the skies and expressed his undying faith in the "Führer's greatness." He expected the same loyalty to Germany's leader, he said, from anyone who worked for him.

Hitler, of course, knew what Kaltenbrunner knew. That Speer's life was spared could only be explained by the rarest of Hitler's emotions: He felt genuine affection for Albert Speer. Would the giant who had whimpered for his family keep quiet about Speer's eager display of loyalty after the plot? Speer could only hope so.

On Gilbert's arrival Speer greeted him warmly in fluent, though accented, English. A rapport had grown between the two men. "You know," Speer said, "it is not a good idea to let the defendants eat together. That is how Göring keeps whipping them into line."

After Gilbert left the cellblock, he pondered Speer's point and decided to suggest a new arrangement to Colonel Andrus.

CAPTAIN Drexel Sprecher was thirty-one, a tall, broad-shouldered, open-faced American whose boundless energy fueled a life of hard work and hard play. Sprecher had been deeply disappointed when Robert Ley's suicide cheated him of his first major prosecution. Thereafter he had been assigned Hans Fritzsche, the propagandist, and now Baldur von Schirach. Schirach, as the former leader of the Hitler Youth, hoped to pass himself off as little more than the German equivalent of the national director of the Boy Scouts. Sprecher was developing a far darker record.

The accused Nazi war criminal was, in fact, three-quarters American. Schirach's grandfather had immigrated to America, served as a major in the Union army, lost a leg at Bull Run, and was an honorary pallbearer at the funeral of Abraham Lincoln. The grandfather married an American heiress and then returned to Germany. Schirach's

father had also married an American woman, who traced her fore-
bears to a signer of the Declaration of Independence. Now members
of the DAR were writing to the courts, pleading for clemency for
Baldur von Schirach.

Schirach's father had been director of the National Theater in
Weimar, and young Baldur grew up in a world of poetry, theater, and
music. The economic disaster that followed World War I, however,
cost the senior Schirach his job. As the family's fortunes plunged,
Baldur began reading such anti-Semitic tracts as Henry Ford's *The
International Jew*, and by age eighteen he had become that rarity—a
cultured storm trooper.

In 1933 Hitler had named Schirach, then twenty-six years old,
leader of German youth. From this post he wove a net that snared
nearly every German boy and girl. At age ten boys were inducted into
the Jungvolk and the girls into the Jungmädel. By age fourteen the
boys became full-blown Hitler Jugend and the girls entered the Bund
Deutscher Mädel. At eighteen the boys became party members. By
1939 Schirach's fiefdom numbered 9 million young people, presum-
ably pursuing health, beauty, and culture.

Sprecher recognized that heading a movement of robust, march-
ing, singing boys and girls could hardly be viewed as a war crime; he
hoped to convict Schirach on the basis of the ultimate purpose of all
his efforts. Schirach was charged with conspiracy to commit aggression, and the very songs the Hitler Youth sang on Alpine hikes rang
with aggressive intent:

> *If all the world lies in ruins,*
> *What the devil do we care?*
> *We will still go on marching,*
> *For today Germany belongs to us,*
> *And tomorrow the world.*

Sprecher's strategy was to add the evidence proving conspiracy to
a still blacker count against Schirach: count four—crimes against
humanity. In 1940 Hitler had made Schirach gauleiter of Vienna. For
the youth leader this was at last a grown-up's job, and with enviable
perquisites, including a magnificent villa with seventeen servants.
Soon after, Schirach informed Hitler that there were 60,000 Jews in
Vienna unfit for work. At the same time, the city faced an acute

housing shortage. Hitler ordered that Schirach deport his Jews to the government-general of Poland. Schirach later boasted, "I see this as an act contributing to European culture." Schirach's cultural contribution resulted in the death of these tens of thousands of Jews in Auschwitz. That was the case Sprecher hoped to make—that Schirach had helped shape a generation of Germans to carry out barbarities, with himself as a model.

THE first time Otto Kranzbuehler had shown up at the courthouse gate, the guards had been alarmed—Admiral Dönitz's lawyer was wearing the full naval uniform of the defeated enemy. The dashing thirty-nine-year-old Kranzbuehler was a *Flottenrichter*, a fleet judge, in the German navy. Major Neave had located him in the legal office of a German minesweeping unit that the British allowed to function to clear ports on the North and Baltic seas. At Nuremberg, Kranzbuehler insisted on his right to wear the uniform, since it was the Allies who had kept him on active duty. He hoped to register the point that most Germans had simply fought for their country; this was the role in which he intended to cast his client, Dönitz, when the case against him began.

The hallways of the courthouse were virtually deserted this Sunday afternoon as Kranzbuehler made his way to the visitors' room to discuss last-minute strategies with the admiral. Dönitz was already waiting. He was not an easy client; the moment the man opened his thin lips, any suggestion of the kindly grandfather vanished. His voice had the whine of a dentist's drill. He retained the habit of command, unbroken by his months of confinement.

Kranzbuehler had gone to the documents room days before to obtain copies of the evidence the prosecution expected to introduce. Now he went over the documents with the admiral. The Laconia Order would be the most troublesome, he said. The order, issued by Dönitz after one of his subs sank the British transport *Laconia* in 1942, forbade German naval vessels to pick up survivors, even to help them into lifeboats or give them food and water.

The only reason he had issued the order, Dönitz told Kranzbuehler, was that American aircraft had attacked his submarines while the crews were trying to rescue the *Laconia*'s survivors. He knew for a fact that the American navy operated essentially under the same conditions as the Laconia Order. Yes, Kranzbuehler said, but the admiral had to understand that, fair or not, this court would not entertain a defense of *tu quoque*. The prosecution could also be expected to introduce evidence that Dönitz had been a staunch supporter of Hitler and Nazism. The day after the Twentieth of July attempt on Hitler's life, Dönitz had gone on the radio. "An insane clique of generals," he had said, "instigated this cowardly attempt at murder." That was not the speech he was concerned about, Dönitz said. Did the Americans have the address he had made on the struggle against Jewry? In it he had said, "I would rather eat dirt than have my grandson grow up in the Jewish spirit and faith." Fifty-two copies of the speech had been run off. Fifty-one had been destroyed. Did the prosecution have the last copy? Dönitz asked. Kranzbuehler said that he did not know.

THE British had felt all along that the Americans were hogging the stage. They particularly believed that the German navy was their game. They, after all, had fought the real fight against the Kriegsmarine. Thus, on Monday, January 14, barrister-at-law H. J. Phillimore opened the case against Grand Admiral Karl Dönitz. Dönitz was charged with complicity in waging aggressive warfare and with crimes committed during the war. As Phillimore introduced the issue of the Laconia Order, Major Airey Neave listened with bitter memories. A friend of his, with wife and baby, had drowned when the ship went down. The prosecutor next moved to Dönitz's role in passing along Keitel's Commando Order to the German navy. As a result, captured British commandos had been shot without trial.

So far the evidence against the admiral had dealt only with military actions. The next phase of the prosecution moved Dönitz into a less savory realm. He had stoutly maintained that he knew nothing of the horrors of the concentration camps. The prosecutor introduced documents proving that Dönitz had personally requested 12,000 camp inmates to work in navy shipyards.

On cross-examination Kranzbuehler countered the charges as skillfully as the evidence permitted. Still, when the day was over, Kranzbuehler was mortified by the revelations of room 600. He had been a career legal officer in the navy since 1934. Had he known nothing of what had gone on? In that case, he must be an idiot. Had he been part of it? In that case, he must be a criminal. Had he known yet done nothing? In that case, he must be a coward. The choices—idiot, criminal, or coward—all left Kranzbuehler depressed.

FEW could miss the symmetry. On January 16 Robert Kempner opened the prosecution case against Wilhelm Frick, the man who had turned Hitlerian grudges into German law. Frick, the most colorless of the defendants, had headed the Ministry of the Interior and had drafted the laws that drove Kempner from Germany.

As early as 1924, Frick had introduced two then shocking bills in the Reichstag: one barring Jews from holding public office and another forbidding mixed marriages with Jews. He was merely trying to correct an imbalance, he had argued. The Jew was too powerful. By 1933, with Hitler in power, Frick signed the Enabling Law, giving Hitler the right to promulgate any measure without the Reichstag's approval. Frick further signed a decree that established that the Nazi Party controlled the German government and not the other way around. Hitler's authority was now total, and Frick had given the patina of legality to despotism.

Kempner began reciting the decrees ratified at the 1935 Congress of the Nazi Party in Nuremberg. Jews were deprived of their citizenship. They were denied employment, first in journalism, then in medicine, dentistry, and law. They were forbidden to own property. In 1943 Frick signed a decree placing the Jews completely outside the law. You could do what you wanted to a Jew without fear of punishment. This codified persecution became known collectively as the Nuremberg Laws. When the first laws were promulgated, there had been 10,000 Jews in Nuremberg. At the end of the war there were ten.

CAPTAIN Gilbert had considered escaping for the weekend. The psychologist was emotionally burned out after months of standing in court all day and making nightly and weekend cell visits. He was worried, however, about the stability of Hess and Ribbentrop. Weekend or not, he decided, he would have to see them.

For a time after his electric November 30 announcement that his memory had returned, Hess had stopped reading novels in the courtroom; his performance on the number-memory test had improved. But now he was reading in court again.

This day Gilbert again administered the number-recall test. Hess slipped from a recall the previous time of eight digits forward and seven backward to five forward and four backward today. He had difficulty remembering witnesses who had testified just days before. Gilbert left the cell and proceeded to the prison office to write his assessment. "The current apathy and memory failure," Gilbert wrote, were "part of a reaction to the final smashing of the ideology which had supported his ego and now faces him with an intolerable choice between accepting a share of the guilt of Nazism or rejecting his Führer. He'll probably end up by rejecting reality again."

Shortly after Gilbert left, Hess received another visitor—the court's liaison man, British major Airey Neave. Neave arrived in the midst of a minor tumult. Hess had just flung his mess kit, full of food, at a junior officer who dared peer into his cell. Why, Hess asked Neave, had he been left without a lawyer for a week? The major explained, as he had several times already, that Hess's counsel, Gunther von Rohrscheidt, had slipped on the ice and broken his leg. As soon as Neave was gone, Hess demanded a pencil and paper from his guard. He was going to write a letter to the members of the court, he said. He had no faith in Rohrscheidt. He wanted him dismissed.

All correspondence from the defendants to the court had to pass through Colonel Andrus' hands. The colonel had just read Gilbert's latest evaluation of Hess as "passive suggestible . . . a gullible simpleton." He was eager to read what this "passive suggestible" personality had written to the IMT. "I draw the attention of the court," Hess's letter read, "to the fact that I have now been a whole week without a defending counsel, while I have not been permitted the right to which the statute entitles me of pleading my own case. In consequence, I was prevented from questioning even a single witness during this period." It hardly seemed the letter of a "gullible simpleton," Andrus thought. He forwarded it to Sir Geoffrey Lawrence.

ON SUNDAY, January 27, the day after the Hess visit, Gilbert went to see his other problem patient, Joachim von Ribbentrop. Sauckel and Kaltenbrunner collected stamps. Keitel played solitaire. Göring slept. Ribbentrop fidgeted. Gilbert found the man a whirlwind of unfocused energy—pacing his cell, scribbling furiously on a sheet of paper, wadding it up and flinging it to the floor. He was driving his counsel mad. They would adopt a line of defense, and the next day Ribbentrop would deny that he had agreed to it. Ribbentrop would demand a certain witness and then reject that person. In Gilbert's view the erratic behavior reflected a collapsed ego, one that had had the supporting timbers yanked away.

Gilbert tried to associate this Ribbentrop with the man described by one of his former subordinates: "He would require his entire staff to line up at an airport and wait for five or six hours, even in the rain, until his plane arrived. He would appear and greet us with a frozen smile, raise his hand in the Heil Hitler salute, and be driven off. He was extremely theatrical. He treated us like dogs."

THE trial had not been under way for more than an hour on Monday, January 28, when Sir Geoffrey Lawrence appeared to be on the verge of sleep. Charles Dubost, the French deputy prosecutor, was droning away as he called on a listless parade of witnesses. During the war Dubost had been a judge by day and a Resistance leader by night, adept at blowing up trains and bridges. Now the man had about him a weariness reflected throughout much of the French delegation. The principal justice, Henri Donnedieu de Vabres, looked magnificent, with his medieval dress, long gray hair, and drooping mustache, but never said anything, never asked a question. Airey Neave, who admired the French, thought perhaps their mood reflected the exhausted state of their country. The French staff had not been paid for almost three months.

Suddenly the torpor in the room lifted. Something about the woman in the tailored dark blue suit approaching the stand commanded attention. Marie Claude Vaillant-Couturier, age thirty-three, stood erect, exuding dignity. Dubost began drawing out her story. When France fell, Vaillant-Couturier had been an antifascist journalist. In 1942 she was arrested, interrogated, and ordered to sign a false confession. "I refused to sign it," she told the court. "The German officer threatened me. I told him I was not afraid of being shot. He told me, 'We have means at our disposal far worse than being shot.' " Soon afterward she found herself packed on a train with 230 other Frenchwomen, en route to Auschwitz.

Vaillant-Couturier was assigned to a sewing block at the camp. "We lived right where the trains stopped," she said. "Consequently, we saw the unsealing of the cars and the soldiers letting men, women, and children out. We saw old couples forced to part from each other, mothers forced to abandon their young children. All these people were unaware of the fate awaiting them. Those selected for the gas chamber were escorted immediately to a red brick building."

As Dubost urged her gently on, the woman's head bowed. Her voice became barely audible. "One night, we were awakened by horrible cries," she said. "The next day we learned that the Nazis had run out of gas and the children had been hurled into the furnaces alive." Dubost asked her how many of the 230 Frenchwomen in her train survived Auschwitz. Forty-nine, she answered.

After she was dismissed, the woman walked past the dock and stopped within feet of Hermann Göring. As she wrote later, "I looked at each of them in turn. They looked like ordinary people, with a normal human side, which somehow didn't surprise me. At Auschwitz, one of the SS used to bring sugar to a five-year-old gypsy boy after he gassed the boy's mother and sister."

The next morning the witness was François Boix, a tall, lean, intense man. Boix had survived the Mauthausen concentration camp because he was a professional photographer. His appearance promised no letup in the grim chronicle of camp life.

Charles Dubost asked if while at Mauthausen, Boix had ever seen any of the defendants. "Speer," the witness replied. During the interrogation phase Speer had admitted to being at Mauthausen but only on the periphery, to consider construction of a railhead. Dubost asked Boix when he had seen the munitions chief. In 1943 Boix answered. "I did not see him myself, but the head of the identification department took a roll of film with his Leica, which I developed. I recognized Speer and some SS leaders." Some of the pictures, Boix said, had been taken at the Mauthausen quarry. "There are even pictures which show him congratulating Franz Ziereis, the commandant of Mauthausen, with a handshake," Boix added.

Documents were introduced to establish that Speer had worked with Himmler to obtain camp inmates for arms production. Minutes from a Central Planning Board meeting recorded Speer's words: "There is nothing to be said against the SS putting known slackers into concentration camps. There is no alternative."

As the court adjourned, Speer recognized that the day had been a disaster. He had been placed squarely at Mauthausen and in association with the commandant, Ziereis, a sadist known to take pleasure in carrying out executions personally. To be linked as well to Himmler was to be stained ineradicably. For the first time Albert Speer felt brushed by the wing tip of the angel of death.

5

MAJOR Kelley abruptly announced that he was going home on points. On learning of his impending departure, Gilbert cornered the major and expressed his own surprise. Kelley explained that he was going home to pursue a new interest; he was going to write a book on racial prejudice. But what about their project? a stunned Gilbert asked. Kelley put an arm around Gilbert's shoulder. "Look, Gus," he said, "there's been a big fall-off in the public's interest in this trial." Gilbert asked Kelley where he could reach him after his discharge. He did not know, Kelley said, but he would be in touch.

After Major Kelley left, Gilbert discovered that he had taken all the handwritten originals of the autobiographies they had asked the defendants to write. He had also taken a copy of all of Gilbert's notes on his cell visits. What Gilbert did not yet know was that Kelley had already approached an American publisher about a book of his own on the twenty-one men in the cells at Nuremberg.

ON FEBRUARY 6 the prosecution opened the case of the stolen art treasures. The plunder of France had begun on June 21, 1940, when Göring had accompanied Hitler to the forest of Compiègne. Here the Germans savored the sweet revenge of having the French surrender in the very railway car where the Germans had been forced to capitulate in 1918. Afterward Göring slipped away to the Jeu de Paume in the Louvre Museum in Paris, where he covetously eyed the works of Rubens, Fragonard, and Velázquez. The Reichsmarschall and Hitler, both considering themselves connoisseurs, came up with a scheme whereby Germany would become the "protector" of Europe's art treasures. The key was Alfred Rosenberg, a pompous man who had peddled philosophical rubbish about the blood superiority of the German race. Rosenberg was party chief for ideological training and education, and three months after the conquest of France, Hitler gave Rosenberg the right to confiscate art anywhere in occupied Europe.

The philosopher created Einsatzstab Rosenberg to carry out his new art-looting mission. His operatives followed simple procedures. If a desired painting, sculpture, or carving belonged to foreign Aryans, the owners were compelled to sell it. If it belonged to Jews, it was merely taken. The latter task was facilitated by the fact that thousands of French Jews had fled or been driven from their homes. Rosenberg's proudest report to the Führer described 69,619 Jewish apartments in Paris emptied of their contents, filling 29,984 freight cars with art and fine furniture.

The prosecution possessed a document written by a Dr. Hermann Bunjes revealing how Göring had benefitted from Einsatzstab Rosenberg. Dr. Bunjes, an art historian, had been engaged as Göring's personal agent in France. Seven months after the fall of Paris, Göring ordered Bunjes to meet him on his arrival at the Jeu de Paume. As Göring went through, he would tap his baton on the works to be sent to Germany. An uncomfortable Bunjes pointed out that Rosenberg's activities contravened the Hague Convention. Göring blew up, his voice echoing throughout the museum: "My orders are final! These art objects at the Jeu de Paume are to be taken to Germany immediately. Those for me are to be loaded into two railroad cars and attached to my private train."

Göring had always contended that he was merely holding the works of art until a gallery could be erected for the German people, that he meant to pay for everything. But, as he once put it, "My collector's passion got the better of me."

ON MONDAY morning, February 11, a Soviet prosecutor, General N. D. Zorya, was attempting to establish that Germany's invasion of the Soviet Union represented criminal aggression. The Russians had suffered far more at the hands of the Nazis than any other people. Their military and civilian dead totaled over 20 million. Zorya read into the record an affidavit taken in Moscow from German field marshal Friedrich Paulus, who had surrendered at Stalingrad. In the statement Paulus swore that he had had personal knowledge of Germany's aggressive intent.

The very mention of Paulus stirred bitter memories for the Germans. Jodl, Speer, Dönitz, even Göring—any of the shrewder minds in the dock—had recognized that after the defeat at Stalingrad in 1943, the war could not be won. The Germans had suffered horrific losses. The people were told that Field Marshal Paulus had fallen in battle with his troops. Actually, Paulus had gone over to the Russians, and he subsequently broadcast speeches urging German soldiers to give up the hopeless struggle. His name became synonymous with treachery. But from Paulus' standpoint he was no traitor. His Sixth Army had been surrounded. Hitler promised that Göring's Luftwaffe would come to Paulus' relief, but the planes never came. Still, Hitler had ordered the field marshal to fight on to the last man. In Paulus' judgment Hitler had condemned 300,000 Germans to starvation, sickness, freezing cold, and, ultimately, death or Russian captivity. He could find no reason to remain loyal to such a leader.

Otto Stahmer, Göring's lawyer, objected. The affidavit was merely a piece of paper coerced from a traitor general. It proved nothing. If Paulus was such an important witness, let the prosecution produce him so that the defense could cross-examine him.

The Soviet chief prosecutor, Roman Rudenko, rose, a barely concealed smile on his face. He would indeed like to call Field Marshal Paulus as a witness, Rudenko told the court. In fact, he could produce him that afternoon. Chief Justice Lawrence asked if he was hearing correctly. The Soviet prosecutor replied that Paulus had been secretly flown to Nuremberg and was now waiting in Rudenko's quarters.

As SIR Geoffrey Lawrence called the court to order, a white-helmeted guard opened the door and a lone figure appeared—lean, dignified, wearing a dark blue suit that could not conceal the bearing of a soldier. The defendants' attention was riveted.

Roman Rudenko conducted the questioning. He first established that a Russo-German nonaggression pact had been in force between August 1939 and June 1941. What, he asked, had General Paulus been doing during that period? In September 1940, Paulus explained, he had been named a deputy chief of the general staff. He had been assigned to develop an operation ultimately known as Barbarossa, a surprise attack on the Soviet Union. "Who of these defendants," Rudenko asked, "was an active participant in initiating the war of aggression against the Soviet Union?" Paulus surveyed the dock. "As I observed them," he said, "they were the chief of the OKW, Keitel, the chief of operations, Jodl, and Göring, as commander in chief of the air force."

As chief justice Lawrence declared a recess, a ruckus broke out in the dock. Göring was shouting to Stahmer, "Ask that dirty pig if he knows he's a traitor." At the other end of the dock Fritzsche was telling Schacht, "You see, that's the tragedy of the German people, right there. Poor Paulus was caught between the devil and his duty. If a man like that could betray his country, there must have been something wrong with the country."

It was February 13, Jackson's birthday, and Mrs. Douglas had planned a little surprise party, with the justices and senior staff stopping by as soon as court adjourned. First she wanted Ray D'Addario, the signal corps photographer, to take Jackson's picture. He was just about to shoot, when Mrs. Douglas started combing Jackson's hair. The photographer clicked off several frames.

Among the staff the closeness of Jackson and his secretary was well known. To him Elsie was professionally indispensable and his trusted confidante. And she was sensitive to appearances. D'Addario received a call from Mrs. Douglas after the party. Any photographs of her combing Jackson's hair were to be destroyed, she instructed, including the negatives.

The case announced on the bulletin board for February 14 made everyone uncomfortable but the Russians. They had insisted on charging the Germans with the Katyn massacre—the murder of thousands of Polish POWs in a forest near Smolensk in Russia. The Americans and British had hoped against hope that the Soviet Union would drop the charge. The Western lawyers had strong evidence suggesting that the Russians, not the Nazis, had murdered the Poles. The Soviets appeared to be seizing a chance to palm off on the Nazis a war crime of their own.

On Saturday, February 16, Captain Gilbert was told to report to Colonel Andrus as soon as court adjourned. On his arrival Andrus handed him a new regulation, growing out of Göring's disruptive behavior, particularly during the Paulus testimony. He already knew what Gilbert was going to say, Andrus observed—this new rule would have a bad psychological effect on the defendants' morale. But Sir Geoffrey Lawrence was on his back—Göring was a threat to the dignity of the proceedings. Gilbert finished reading the document, hardpressed to conceal his delight. This was essentially the isolation plan that Speer had suggested and that Gilbert had recommended to the colonel weeks before. Gilbert returned to his office to begin an agreeable task—reducing the influence of the inmate Hermann Göring.

The defendants were taken to the prison basement for their weekly shower and strip search. In the meantime their cells were searched and sprayed for vermin. Gilbert decided to break the news on their return to the cellblock. He had the duty officer line them up in the corridor. The privilege of speaking to one another had been abused, he explained, particularly in recent courtroom outbursts. Gilbert knew that the closest they came to normal socializing was in the lunchroom in the courthouse attic, time that they treasured. In the future, however, they would have lunch there in six separated dining spaces. To what he called the "youth lunchroom," Gilbert assigned Speer, Fritzsche, Schirach, and Funk. His strategy was to have Speer and Fritzsche wean the other two from Göring's influence. Next he set up an "elders' lunchroom," to include Dönitz, Neurath, Schacht, and the aristocratic Franz von Papen, who had briefly been chancellor of Germany. The dynamic here was to have the others work on Admiral Dönitz's loyalty to Hitler. To the next room he assigned Frank, Seyss-Inquart, Keitel, and Sauckel. His hope was that Frank might crack the loyalty of his companions. Raeder, Streicher, Hess, and Ribbentrop were to dine together. Streicher's odious presence, Gilbert believed, would neutralize the other three. Jodl, Frick, Kaltenbrunner, and Rosenberg were put together because their lack of affinity might defuse any mischief. Hermann Göring was to dine alone. Göring cursed at the news, but virtually all the rest were pleased. Gilbert had not realized how much they all feared Göring.

ROMAN Rudenko was no fool, and when the Soviet prosecutor seemed to be one, it was usually because of actions—such as the raising of the Katyn issue—forced on him by Moscow. It pained Rudenko to realize that his people, who had suffered so incomparably at the hands of the Nazis, had failed thus far to win commensurate sympathy among the other Allies.

On Monday afternoon, February 18, Rudenko launched his effort to make known the truth of the Soviet ordeal. The opening salvo was to be a film entitled *Documentary Evidence of the German Fascist Invaders.* An early scene showed a city square filled with bodies stacked as evenly as Christmas trees. A close-up revealed bloody bandages on dead Soviet soldiers. The narrator read the words of a German commander from a captured document: " 'I once again inform you that hereafter each officer has the right to shoot prisoners of war.' " The scene lent meaning to a cold statistic: of 5.7 million Soviet POWs taken by the Germans, 3.7 million died in captivity.

Long shots of acres of bodies were interspersed with close-ups of weeping mothers gently patting the faces of their dead children. Captured German films showed naked women herded into a ditch and shot by German guards, who then smiled for the camera.

The justices had heard testimony on Auschwitz; now they saw film. Thousands of neatly sorted pairs of shoes, hundreds of battered suitcases with names stenciled on the sides, mounds of human hair silently passed across the screen. The American alternate justice, John Parker, who believed the Russian claims of atrocities to be exaggerated, asked to be excused. He was not feeling well.

Rudenko spent the next five days producing eyewitnesses and survivors. One man described the fate of the people of the village of Kholmetz. A German army officer had ordered the villagers to dig up mines in a road with farm tools. All were killed. Another Soviet prosecutor presented evidence entitled "Crimes Against Culture and Scientific Treasures." At Yasnaya Polyana, the estate of Leo Tolstoy, a German officer used the author's books as firewood. When told there was plenty of wood around, he replied that he preferred the light of Russian literature. The home of Tchaikovsky was used by the Germans as a motorcycle garage and heated by burning the composer's manuscripts. Using the Germans' own reports, the Russians proved that these were not isolated incidents, but the product of a deliberate policy to obliterate Russian culture.

The testimony, after six straight days, became repetitious. Still, a change had come over the court, as though the justices recognized that something more than law was at work here. The Russians needed this outpouring as a catharsis, the opportunity to say at last to the world, This was our sorrow.

For the Americans, with their nation spared, the reasons for Soviet bitterness and truculence became more understandable. This was the equivalent of an enemy invader's embarking on a deliberate campaign to destroy every trace of American culture between New York City and Chicago, and using the Lincoln Memorial as a latrine.

ON ENTERING the courthouse on March 6, the *Pravda* correspondent Boris Polevoi ran into young Oleg Troyanovsky, the interpreter. An alarmed Troyanovsky was carrying an armful of newspapers. "Look at this," he said, holding up an English paper headlined SIR WINSTON CALLS FOR UNITED FRONT AGAINST SOVIET UNION. The former British prime minister had made a speech the day before at a small college in Fulton, Missouri, claiming, "From Stettin in the Baltic to Trieste on the Adriatic, an iron curtain has descended across the continent." Churchill had pronounced the death of the wartime alliance and was calling for Western resistance to communist expansion.

That day, with the completion of the Soviet presentation, the prosecution rested its case. While the moment should have sounded a chord of doom for the defendants, it was, by a quirk of fate, ending on a note of hope. True, the Allied prosecutors had achieved what they had set out to do. The four counts in the indictment had been proved indisputably and repeatedly, mostly through documentary evidence that the Germans had generated themselves. Yet an undercurrent of excitement coursed through the dock as the defense counsels held up their newspapers so that their clients could read the headlines.

At the morning recess it was as if a dam had broken. The defense lawyers rushed to their clients, and a cheerful babble ensued. Göring virtually did a jig in the dock. "Mark my word," he said. "They'll be fighting among themselves before sentences can be pronounced on us." The washed-out, wrung-out Ribbentrop suddenly displayed his old hauteur. "I always expected it," he said. "Churchill is no fool. He knows we Germans are closer to him than the Reds." Hess dropped his catatonic stare and leaned over to Göring. "You will yet be the Führer of Germany," he predicted.

In cellblock C, Dr. Pfluecker made a happy observation on his final rounds. That night there were fewer requests for sleeping pills.

CHAPTER III
THE DEFENSE
1

THE defense was due to begin its case on March 8. The back of winter had been broken. The days were turning warmer, and weeds had begun to sprout in the ruins of the city. On the evening of March 7 several defense attorneys gathered at a tavern near the courthouse to drink beer and discuss the opening of their case the next day. The Anglo-Saxon forms of law still fit them like a poorly tailored suit. Even the point of the trial puzzled them. Was it an honest effort to elicit guilt or innocence? Or was it a victor's spectacle? Admittedly, the fairness of the IMT's chief justice, Sir Geoffrey Lawrence, was beyond question. The German attorneys were given access to the same documents as their opponents. They were allowed virtually unlimited time to confer with their clients. They were well paid—by the Allies. But why? Why would victors go through this protracted and costly exercise? It fit nothing in the Germans' experience.

THE visitors' gallery was filled to overflowing. Göring, dark star of Nazism, was expected to take the stand as the first defense witness. Instead, the first person Otto Stahmer called was Luftwaffe general Karl B. Bodenschatz, an old flying pal from Göring's Richthofen squadron and, later, the Reichsmarschall's liaison to Hitler. Bodenschatz's testimony was intended to establish that after 1943, Göring had stood discredited before Hitler and no longer exercised any significant power. Field Marshal Erhard Milch, the former plane production chief, came next. Other witnesses followed. It was not until the afternoon of Wednesday, March 13, that Göring would take the stand.

Dr. Pfluecker came to see Göring the night before. He found his patient agitated, sitting at his table, a dog-eared sheet of paper in his hand. Hans Fritzsche, as a professional broadcaster, had analyzed the failings of previous German witnesses and had written out his "Suggestions for Speakers." The Germans were often mistranslated, Fritzsche noted, because they used long sentences with the verb at the end and because they spoke too fast. They should speak slowly, use short sentences, and move the subject and verb as close together as possible. Göring was now memorizing Fritzsche's advice.

He greeted his visitor gratefully. Dr. Pfluecker's attentions always buoyed him. He asked if he might have a stronger sedative that night. He doubted that he would sleep a wink. Pfluecker reminded him of the difference between natural sleep and drugged sleep. He must be alert the next day. Göring settled for his regular pill.

At 2:30 P.M. Stahmer rose from the defense-counsel table and called his witness. Göring moved with a determined stride toward the witness-box, clutching a thick purple folder. His dove-gray uniform was freshly pressed but hung poorly—he had lost seventy-six pounds in captivity. His face was flushed as chief justice Lawrence asked, "Will you repeat this oath after me: I swear to God almighty and omniscient that I will speak the pure truth and will withhold or add nothing." Göring raised his right hand, trembling visibly, and repeated the oath in a quavering voice.

Did Göring believe that the Nazi Party had come to power legally? Stahmer asked. Göring proceeded to give a well-organized history of the rise of Nazism, barely glancing at his notes. "Once we came to power," he said, "we were determined to hold on to it under all circumstances. We did not want to leave this any longer to chance, to elections and parliamentary majorities." The words were ice water flung in the face of the court. No apology, no evasion, no softening marked his recital. Once in the saddle, he explained, the party had intended to eliminate the Reichstag, to end individual rights.

Stahmer cued Göring to explain where the idea had come from to combine the ceremonial head of state and the head of government in one person, Adolf Hitler. That was simple, Göring explained. They had taken their example from the dual roles of the president of the United States. Concentration camps? Stahmer asked. Göring described in detail why and how he had started them. How could the party rule until it had established order and how could it maintain order with its deadly enemies, particularly the Communists, running free? "It was a question of removing danger," Göring said. "Only one course was available, protective custody." He spoke for over two hours, moving from stage fright to confidence to obvious relish in his own performance.

JANET Flanner left the courthouse stunned. She sat in the press bus, digesting the meaning of Göring's debut. On arriving at her quarters, she began her column for *The New Yorker*. She had witnessed, she wrote, "one of the best brains of the period of history when good brains are rare." Göring, however, she concluded, was "a brain without a conscience."

GUSTAV Gilbert accompanied the defendants back to the cellblock. The guards had to restrain the others from gripping Göring's hand and treating him like an athlete who had just saved the game. Dönitz turned to Speer. "You could see, even the judges were impressed," he said. Speer had to agree. Gilbert later stopped by Göring's cell. The man was sitting on his bed, his supper untouched. He could not eat a thing, he told Gilbert. He was too excited.

GÖRING was back on the witness stand at ten the next morning. The Nazi regime, he said, was being vilified for imposing rigid obedience on its followers. In the prosecution's argument this pyramid of unthinking submission from the top downward ended in places like Auschwitz and Mauthausen. But the *Führerprinzip*—the leadership principle—was merely sound management, Göring asserted. "Authority from above downward and responsibility from the bottom upward." Was this concept adopted only by power-crazed Nazis? Göring asked. "I should like to mention some parallels," he said. "The *Führerprinzip* is the same principle on which the Catholic church and the government of the USSR are both based."

Göring waited until the third and final day of his direct examination to rebut the prosecution's charges against the Luftwaffe. The world had been horrified at the German bombing of Rotterdam *after* the Netherlands had surrendered. It was true, Göring said, he had sent a squadron to bomb Rotterdam. But when the Germans learned that surrender negotiations were under way, they fired red flares into the sky to ward off their bombers. The first group did not understand the signal and, unfortunately, struck the target. The two groups behind did understand and turned back. Rotterdam had not been an atrocity, Göring argued. It had been a tragic error.

Göring next dealt head-on with the issue of how he had acquired his art treasures. "I decided that after the war, or at some appropriate time, I would found an art gallery, either through purchase, or gifts, or through inheritance, and present this art to the German people." For the first time since he had taken the stand, the snickering from the audience was audible.

It was late afternoon, Friday, March 15. In the final question, Stahmer asked if Germany had behaved any differently from her Allies in observing the rules of civilized conflict. Instruments like the Geneva and Hague conventions, Göring said, had been overrun by modern warfare. "At this point, I should like to say the very words which one of our greatest, most important opponents, the British prime minister Winston Churchill, used: 'In the struggle for life and death, there is, in the end, no legality.' " Göring had the words wrong, but the sentiment was uncomfortably close. Sir Geoffrey Lawrence adjourned the court. Hermann Göring had spoken, virtually without interruption and largely without notes, for over two and a half days. His cross-examination would begin after the weekend.

Sɪʀ Norman Birkett, Britain's alternate justice, had written to a colleague back home, "The first really great dramatic moment of this trial will come when Göring is cross-examined by the American prosecutor, Jackson. It will be a duel to the death between the representative of all that is worthwhile in civilization and the last important surviving protagonist of all that was evil. In a sense, the result of the trial depends on that duel."

On Monday the courtroom was packed as it had not been since opening day. Most of the morning was consumed by the defense counsels, who were finishing up Göring's direct examination, asking questions of him designed to absolve their clients. Göring readily obliged, manfully assuming responsibility for virtually everything. Not until 12:10 p.m. did Sir Geoffrey Lawrence ask, "Do the chief prosecutors wish to cross-examine?"

Jackson moved to the prosecutor's stand with confident pugnacity. He studied Göring on the witness stand. Göring stared back like an air ace gauging the enemy before a dogfight. "You are perhaps aware that you are the only living man who can expound to us the true purposes of the Nazi Party and the inner workings of its leadership," Jackson said. Maxwell-Fyfe, the British prosecutor and a legendary cross-examiner, heard the bland query with surprise. It was not how he would have begun—but Jackson, no doubt, had a hidden strategy.

"I am perfectly aware of that," Göring answered. Jackson asked Göring if it was not true that people were thrown into concentration camps without recourse to the courts. Göring began a lengthy answer, but Jackson interrupted, trying to limit him to yes or no. Göring shot back that he needed to explain. Jackson shut him off. He started asking Göring another question, when he saw Biddle whisper to Lawrence. Sir Geoffrey nodded, then stopped Jackson in mid-query. "Mr. Jackson, the tribunal thinks the witness ought to be allowed to make what explanation he thinks right in answer to this question." Jackson flushed angrily. The ruling was contrary to cross-examination custom, and he was convinced that Biddle was pulling Lawrence's strings. The prosecutor impatiently tapped his pen on the stand as Göring was allowed virtually to lecture the court at will.

Jackson next asked, "Now, was the leadership principle supported and adopted by you in Germany because you believed that no people are capable of self-government, or that you believed that some may be, but not the German people: or for that matter whether some of us are capable of using our own system but it should not be used in Germany?" Not only Göring but the justices looked baffled. He did not understand the question, the witness said, but he would attempt to answer it anyway. Maxwell-Fyfe could still discern no overarching strategy in Jackson's approach.

Göring appeared to be enjoying himself, like a prizefighter who has yet to feel his opponent's glove. He was also shrewdly exploiting an advantage. Between Jackson's long-winded questions and the translations, Göring had ample time to frame his answers, especially since he understood the questions in English before they were translated. Jackson was deprived of the cross-examiner's classic tactic: He could not crowd the witness with quick, hard, successive questions.

As the court adjourned for lunch, a journalist in the press gallery gestured toward Jackson and whispered, "Saved by the bell." Jackson's deputy prosecutors, who had come to watch their champion, filed out of the courtroom eyeing one another uneasily.

Throughout the afternoon Göring continued to respond adroitly, displaying a phenomenal memory and, thanks to the court's indulgence, having all the time in the world to exercise it. Justice Birkett feared the great duel was being lost. At the end of the day Maxwell-Fyfe came over to Jackson, his hand outstretched, and said, "Well done." It was a courteous gesture. What Maxwell-Fyfe could not say was that Jackson, after four years on the Supreme Court and years spent amid the legal bureaucracy of the Justice Department, had been too long out of the gladiatorial arena. The cross-examiner in him was rusty.

THE duel resumed the next day. At one point Jackson quoted from a document designed to show that Göring had violated the Treaty of Versailles by planning "the liberation of the Rhineland." Göring possessed a copy of the same report. He pointed out that Jackson had mistranslated it. The document dealt not with the Rhineland, but with the Rhine River. And it spoke not of "liberation," but of "clearing" the river of impediments to navigation in case of mobilization. Göring, it turned out, was right.

Still, were these actions not intended as part of a secret plan to rearm the Rhineland? Jackson asked. Göring snapped back, "I do not think I can recall reading beforehand the publication of the mobilization preparations of the United States." Jackson looked to the bench. "I respectfully submit to the tribunal that this witness is not being responsive in his examination!" Sir Geoffrey Lawrence looked to Biddle, then upheld the decision to let the witness have his say. Jackson appeared on the verge of apoplexy. Biddle whispered to Lawrence that this was probably a good time to adjourn for the day.

JACKSON saw no point in delaying further. The source of his torment had to be confronted. He did not bother to return to his office, but went straight to Biddle's chambers. There he found both Biddle and Parker. Biddle greeted him calmly and offered a seat. He preferred to stand, Jackson said. He could come to no other conclusion, he began, than that Biddle was deliberately trying to thwart him. He had not left the U. S. Supreme Court to come here and be sabotaged by his own countrymen. "I'd better resign and go home," Jackson announced. No, Biddle said. He and Parker both had enormous admiration for the job Bob Jackson was doing. The decisions on Göring were not personal. They were designed only to give the man no alibis when the trial ended. And that goal would best serve them all—the justices and the prosecution. Jackson left, hardly mollified.

That night, writing to his wife, Katherine, Biddle held nothing back. "Jackson's cross-examination, on the whole, has been futile," he wrote. "Göring listens to every question, takes his time, answers well. Bob doesn't listen to the answers, depends on his notes, always a sign of weakness." And Biddle could not suppress his delight in his own role. To the world Sir Geoffrey Lawrence might seem the master of the courtroom. But, Biddle wrote, "I do really run this show and have won on every point."

THE next day Jackson resumed his questioning. At one point he took a sheaf of documents in hand, decrees, he said, signed by Göring. Had he not issued a decree that a Jew could sell a business only with government permission? Göring said yes. Did Göring sign a decree that Jews might not own retail businesses, sell handicrafts, or form co-ops? Again Göring agreed. Jackson kept up the steady drumfire. Did Göring order Jews to surrender all their jewelry and gold to the government? Sequester Jewish property in Poland? Bar Jews from compensation for damage caused by German forces? At long last, Birkett thought, Jackson sounded like a cross-examiner.

Göring put one hand over the other to stop the trembling. Was it not true, Jackson pressed on, that on July 31, 1941, Göring signed the decree directing Reinhard Heydrich, head of the RSHA at the time, to plan a solution to the Jewish question? Göring protested that the document had been incorrectly translated. The word *Endlösung,* he said, had been rendered as "final solution" when it should have been "complete solution." He thereby robbed the document of the incriminating semantic power that "final solution" had acquired. Actually, the phrase had been accurately translated in the first place.

The prosecutor moved the questioning to *Kristallnacht*—November 9, 1938—when storm troopers and Nazi hooligans looted and destroyed 815 Jewish shops and 76 synagogues and arrested 20,000 Jews. Jackson read into the record the grim inventory of destruction from a report submitted to Göring the day after the rampage. Next Jackson nailed Göring with proof of his art looting and his role in the wholesale pillaging of resources from the Soviet Union. He finally had Göring reeling. A drumfire of hard, specific charges revealed the defendant as a coarse, venal, anti-Semitic co-architect of the worst evils of Nazism.

And then Jackson let him get away. He accused Göring's Luftwaffe of destroying the house of the American ambassador during the bombing of Warsaw. The charge stood so dwarflike next to the horrors of mass murder and slave labor that it appeared as if Jackson were, willy-nilly, reading a list of pro forma questions prepared by some junior aide. To prove the bombing charge, Jackson introduced alleged Luftwaffe aerial photographs. Göring was allowed to examine them. He turned them over. The backs of the photographs were blank: no date, no place, no identification, no authentication—unacceptable evidence in virtually any court of law.

FRANCIS Biddle wrote his wife that Jackson looked "beaten, full of a sense of failure. I have repeatedly asked Bob to the house, but he never comes and I am afraid we are no longer friends." He believed Jackson's grievance stemmed from their reversed roles. Now it was Jackson the courtroom supplicant and Biddle judging on high from the bench.

Whatever the ultimate verdict in room 600, the verdict at the Grand was clear: Göring had proved a brilliant villain and Jackson a flawed hero.

THE next prosecutor to cross-examine Göring would be Sir David Maxwell-Fyfe. On the eve of his court appearance Sir David stayed up into the early morning hours preparing himself, determined to break through Göring's armor plating of ego and brains. The elements of cross-examination were as natural to Maxwell-Fyfe as breathing, beginning with rule one: Ask only questions to which the answer is known. The objective was not to elicit information, but to get incriminating facts into the record. Rule two: Abandon a losing line of questioning. Rule three: Ignore the clever asides, the sallies and impertinences. Hang on to the essentials like a bulldog with its teeth buried in the enemy's throat. Jackson had depended on moral outrage. Sir David intended to outplay his opponents.

He would lead off with an issue that the men on the bench could

Left, Grand Admiral Karl Dönitz, chief of the German navy and the man Hitler chose as his successor.

Above, General Alfred Jodl, operations chief of the German armed forces, whom the Russians insisted upon including among the major war criminals.

Below, Field Marshal Wilhelm Keitel, chief of staff of the German armed forces, who was derided by the Nazis as Hitler's lackey.

Above, Hermann Göring, the Nazi second only to Hitler, in the dock.

feel and grasp. He was convinced that he had found his opening in the Sagan affair, in the fate of the RAF fliers who had escaped from Stalag Luft III. For the British principal justice and his alternate these were not anonymous corpses bulldozed into a ditch—they were sons, classmates, brothers.

The Sagan affair had begun on March 14, 1944, when seventy-six RAF POWs managed to burrow their way out of Stalag Luft III, at Sagan in Silesia. Hitler, at his Berchtesgaden retreat, became furious on getting the news. The escape was the third from Sagan in two weeks, he yelled at Keitel. "Dozens of officers have escaped," he went on. "In view of six million foreigners who are prisoners and working in Germany, these officers are leaders who could organize an uprising." On their recapture, Hitler ordered, the escapees were to be turned over to Himmler's secret police for "special treatment."

Twenty of them had been retaken within two hours and returned to Sagan before Hitler's tirade. Three were never accounted for, and three eventually made it to Sweden. The remaining fifty were caught in various parts of Germany, loaded aboard trucks, and told that they were being returned to Sagan. They were let out at remote places to urinate, at which time Gestapo agents shot them. Their bodies were cremated, their ashes displayed at Sagan as an example to others.

Maxwell-Fyfe took the prosecutor's stand late on the afternoon of March 20. He resumed the next morning. Sagan had been a crime known to Göring's chief subordinates, Sir David noted. "I am suggesting to you that it is absolutely impossible that in these circumstances you knew nothing about it."

"Field Marshal Milch was here as a witness," Göring answered, "and, regrettably, was not asked about these points."

Maxwell-Fyfe's memory was as good as Göring's. "Oh, yes he was," the prosecutor shot back. "Milch took the same line as you, that he knew nothing about it. Both you and Milch are now trying to shift the responsibility onto the shoulders of your junior officers." The attack on his honor jarred Göring. "That is untrue," he shouted. "You did nothing to prevent these men from being shot," Sir David snapped back. "You cooperated in this foul series of murders."

Maxwell-Fyfe was crowding Göring, barely waiting for the answers to be translated before firing off the next question. Göring's sneers and brittle asides were nowhere evident. Beads of sweat glistened on his brow. "I did not hear about this incident until after it occurred," he insisted. In fact, he had been on leave at the time of the Sagan escape. The prey had been led to the pit. Sir David tumbled him into it. True, the Reichsmarschall had been on leave until March 29, 1944, he said, reading from Göring's personnel files. But the executions of the Sagan fifty had gone on until April 13.

Chief justice Lawrence adjourned for lunch. During the break Airey Neave, twice escaped from German prison camps himself, approached Maxwell-Fyfe, smiling broadly. "You've got him," Neave said. "I know how that must feel to you," Sir David answered.

That afternoon Göring returned to the witness stand. "Let me remind you of the affidavit of Hoettl of the RSHA," Maxwell-Fyfe began. (Wilhelm Hoettl was an assistant of Adolf Eichmann's.) "He says that approximately four million Jews have been killed in the concentration camps, while an additional two million met death in other ways. Are you telling this tribunal that a minister with your power in the Reich could remain ignorant that this was going on?"

"These things were kept secret from me," Göring said. The victim again stood on the edge of the pit. Sir David began quoting from a report made to Göring in 1942: " 'There are only a few Jews left alive. Tens of thousands have been disposed of.' " Göring insisted that he had only known of "a policy of emigration, not liquidation of the Jews." The answer rang so hollow that the old cross-examiner knew this was the moment to stop. He resumed his seat. The Russian prosecutor Rudenko took over, and the Frenchman Auguste Champetier de Ribes completed Göring's cross-examination the following day.

That Friday evening, as Captain Gilbert made his rounds, he found Göring in an edgy state. "I didn't cut a very pretty figure, did I?" he said. Gilbert was quick to agree. "Don't forget," Göring continued, puffing on his pipe, "I had the best legal brains of America, England, France, and Russia against me. And there I was, all alone. I bet even the prosecutors think I did well." The odd mixture of anxiety and egotism intrigued Gilbert. Which, in the days to come, he wondered, would take the upper hand in the soul of Hermann Göring?

RUDOLF Hess's defense was scheduled to follow Göring's. The prosecutors were making bets as to whether this erratic figure would take the stand himself. It had been only four months since Hess had told the court that he had faked amnesia for tactical purposes. Captain Gilbert believed Hess's memory was genuinely faltering again.

Gilbert visited Hess on Sunday, March 23, the day before his defense was set to begin. The deep-set eyes seemed to rove unanchored beneath the massive black brows. But Gilbert was familiar enough with the man's history to know that this rattling husk had once been a serious figure.

Rudolf Hess had not lived in Germany until he was fourteen. His father had been a successful export-import merchant living in Egypt, where Rudolf was born. During World War I, Hess served in the infantry and then as a pilot. He first heard Hitler speak in the back room of a tiny tavern in Munich, and he decided to enroll as the sixteenth member of the Nazi Party on July 1, 1920.

When Hitler's 1923 putsch failed to bring down the Bavarian government, Hess happily followed his Führer into prison, where he fed Hitler ideas, one of which was Lebensraum—living space—later used to justify Germany's attempts to absorb its neighbors. On his release from prison Hess became Hitler's secretary. When the Nazis came to power, he was named deputy führer and Reichsminister without portfolio. No domestic public law, decree, or rule could be issued without first passing through Hess's hands.

As he rose in power, Hess could finally indulge the peculiar drives that pulsed beneath his conventional exterior. He took up vegetarianism and nature cures. He irritated Hitler by bringing his own health foods to dinner meetings. In the mid-'30s Hess invited the Führer to his new home in Isartal, a fashionable Munich suburb. Party legend had it that this visit cost Hess the position of successor to Hitler. The Führer was said to have found Hess's home in such unremitting bad taste that he decided no such person could ever lead Germany. That was when Hitler turned to Göring as his successor.

Now, as Hess sat in his cell, Gilbert asked him if he had made a decision about testifying in his own defense. No, he said, he would not testify. He did not want to be embarrassed by his bad memory. And he did not want to be questioned by people he disliked.

HESS had acquired a new lawyer—Alfred Seidl, an ex-Nazi and an ex–army officer. Seidl was relieved by his client's decision not to testify. But what was Seidl to do this Monday morning to defend Hess? A diversionary feint was the best strategy, he concluded. He came into the court with three copies of a "document book," which proved to be a pasteup of newspaper articles criticizing the Treaty of Versailles. Seidl and the prosecution argued as to the admissibility of this material, until Sir Geoffrey Lawrence could stand it no longer. However unjust the defense might find the treaty, Lawrence said, was Seidl saying that it justified the war the Nazis started and the horrors that followed?

Seidl next sought to introduce the recently unearthed secret protocol from the German-Soviet nonaggression pact, under which the two countries divided up Poland and allowed the Russians to seize the Baltics. His intent was to demonstrate the unfitness of the Soviets to sit in judgment on Rudolf Hess or any German. Seidl eventually managed to get the protocol introduced, where it lay inert, neither supported nor rebutted. With this limp performance Hess's defense ended.

Since Hess had not taken the stand, he could not be cross-examined. The shrewder lawyers recognized his nonappearance as a remarkable instance of being crazy like a fox. The eccentric in a rumpled tweed suit may have sat out the war, but he had been a charter Nazi, the planter of the aggressive seed of Lebensraum. His silence, however, spared him the cross-examination that Göring had gone through on the Jewish question and other damning matters.

Captain Gilbert had been uneasy ever since Major Kelley had departed, leaving no address. But in mid-March he received a letter from him. The trial was evidently going to drag on much longer than expected, Kelley wrote. Consequently, he might go ahead with a Nuremberg book of his own—in addition, of course, to their joint project, in which his interest had revived. By the way, would Gus please forward to him transcripts of the trial as it progressed? Gilbert experienced the sinking sensation of a man whose partner was going in to collect the reward while he was still out chasing the desperadoes.

Gilbert told Kelley that he, too, might write a book of his own. And he was sorry, but the administration had clamped down on trial transcripts. He was allowed only one copy and, consequently, would not be able to oblige Kelley. He closed saying that he was delighted to know that Doug was still at work on their material.

Lately, Gilbert thought increasingly of going home, but he could not leave Nuremberg, not yet. As he put it bluntly in a letter to Kelley, "I want to see them hang." In the meantime he was going off to meet Göring's wife. No one Kelley could talk to in the United States could match that kind of raw material.

EMMY Sonnemann Göring, a bosomy, warmhearted, generous woman, was the Reichsmarschall's second wife, an actress whom Göring married in 1935. By that time he had become the second-ranking figure in the state after Hitler. He lived like an Aryan pasha, with a palatial estate northeast of Berlin built with government funds. He called it Carinhall, after his first wife.

Emmy had numerous Jewish friends in the theater, and as the anti-Semitic decrees of the '30s began to wreck their lives, she asked her husband to intervene. Her special pleading put Göring on the spot with his regime. Still, he helped occasionally, enriching himself along the way by taking a bribe to get a Jew out of a concentration camp or secure a passport. He did perform one act of common decency: He arranged for two Jewish sisters to get out of Germany with their money. The sisters had tenderly cared for young Göring after he had been badly wounded during the failed 1923 putsch. If not for them, he would have bled to death.

After the war Emmy Göring was briefly arrested. Upon her release she, Göring's little daughter Edda, and a niece went to live in a shack in Sackdilling Forest near Neuhaus. It was here that Gus Gilbert traveled to see her.

He arrived on Saturday, March 23, armed with cigarettes for the mother and candy for the child. As Edda happily scampered off with her candy, Emmy said, referring to Hitler, "Can you imagine that madman ordering that child shot?" It was the opening Gilbert had wanted. What he hoped to have by the time he left were weapons to break through Göring's emotional defenses and get him to acknowledge guilt and renounce Hitler. Emmy spoke bitterly of the days after Göring left the Führerbunker in Berlin, how he and his family were to be executed because Hermann had been "disloyal." Göring had gone wild with rage, she said, cursing Hitler so savagely that she feared their guards would shoot him on the spot.

It amazed him, Gilbert said, in view of the fact that the whole world now knew Hitler was a monster, that her husband persisted in remaining loyal to his memory. "The only reason I can imagine," Gilbert offered, "is that he does it to spite a foreign court trying to judge him." One had to understand Hermann's sense of honor, Emmy said. Today Germany was full of hypocrites saying they had never supported Hitler. "And Hermann wants to show that he, at least, is not backtracking like a coward," she said. But wasn't her husband putting himself in a terrible light by this blind loyalty? She took out a handkerchief and wiped her eyes. "That is the one thing on which we cannot agree. Loyalty to a man who would murder my child?"

ON HIS return to Nuremberg on Sunday night, Gilbert went directly to Göring's cell, bearing a letter from Emmy. He mentioned his recent visit. Emmy was distressed, he said, by Göring's stubborn fealty to a man "who ordered you arrested and shot at the end, and little Edda too." Göring shrugged. He did not believe Hitler had ever ordered him shot. "That was the work of that dirty swine Bormann," he said. Gilbert pressed on. His wife was desperate to see him, if only for a few minutes. She wanted to talk him out of his misguided notion of loyalty. "My wife can influence me in lots of things," he said, "but as far as my basic code? Nothing can sway me." These matters were in the realm of men, he declared. "It's not a woman's affair."

GILBERT's visit had unsettled Göring. The psychologist's words had forced him to consider the posture he had taken. But the alternative to defiance was the belly-crawling contrition of a Speer or a Frank, and that was not for Hermann Göring. He was fidgeting on the edge of his cot, glaring angrily at the ever present face in the square porthole. Colonel Andrus had recently added a new security measure—all chairs were taken from the cells during the night. PFC Vincent Traina was leaning on the little shelf that hung outward from the port. Göring came up to the door and ordered, "Get me my chair!" The guard, jolted from his reveries, rapped Göring's hand with a blackjack and told him to sit down. Göring began cursing and shrieking, "I have rights!" The guard flung the door open, went in, and again ordered Göring to sit. Göring continued a torrent of abuse. Traina beat him on his shoulder and then on his upraised hands with the blackjack. Fritzsche, from the opposite side of the corridor, shouted for help. The duty officer came running. The fracas was duly reported to Colonel Andrus. His sentinel, Andrus ruled after an investigation, had "acted quite properly."

Riling his keepers was not a policy Hermann Göring could afford. He needed not antagonists, but friends, like Tex Wheelis. He had already given Wheelis a handsome watch. Within the next few days he managed to have a gold cigarette case extracted from his luggage in the baggage room, and he gave it to the lieutenant.

2

JOACHIM von Ribbentrop, once foreign minister of the Third Reich, was scheduled to begin his defense on Tuesday, March 26. The week before, Ribbentrop's new lawyer, Martin Horn, had cornered Captain Gilbert during a midmorning recess. He asked Gilbert if he had noticed anything strange lately in his client. The doctor no doubt knew, Horn said, that Ribbentrop had sent a letter to the tribunal offering to have himself tortured to death in expiation for Nazi atrocities. Yes, Gilbert said, he did know. Clearly, Horn went on, the man was suffering a nervous breakdown. Gilbert smelled an insanity plea and excused himself.

Horn found Ribbentrop as exasperating as had his predecessor, Fritz Sauter. The defendant's attention could not be focused long enough to proceed from A to B, before he was shooting off to Z. Ribbentrop paced constantly in his cell, rifling through papers for the one document that would save him and that he could never find. Horn had tested the insanity ploy because his client seemed to him a plausible candidate.

The evening before Ribbentrop was to begin his defense, he was led to the visitors' room for a final conference with Horn. As they faced each other through the chicken wire, Horn passed a single sheet of paper through the slot to his client. Earlier Ribbentrop had written a note to Göring asking that he testify in his behalf. Göring had attended Hitler's key foreign policy sessions and could attest that the foreign minister had always tried for peaceful diplomatic solutions, Ribbentrop believed. He snatched at the letter. Göring had drawn a line through Ribbentrop's request and had written at the bottom, "I am only aware that Ribbentrop advised in favor of war."

DREXEL SPRECHER WAS MAKING HIS own last-minute preparations to rebut the Ribbentrop defense and discussing strategy with John Harlan Amen over dinner at the Grand. Sprecher had initially assumed that he would be helping Jackson cross-examine Ribbentrop. But when he went to talk to the chief prosecutor, he found Jackson miserable with a head cold, impatient, and irritable. Colonel Amen would be handling the cross-examination, Jackson informed Sprecher. Sprecher started to express his disappointment, when Jackson cut him off. That was all there was to it, he said. Sprecher wondered why Jackson was leaving the ring. Had the Göring experience shaken him that badly?

FOR his first witness Martin Horn called Baron Gustav Steengracht von Moyland. The baron had run the Foreign Office while Ribbentrop was running after Hitler. In the witness-box he performed a useful, if humiliating, function for his old chief. Ribbentrop had repeatedly told him, the witness testified, that Hitler needed no foreign minister. He, Ribbentrop, was merely the Führer's traveling secretary.

Fräulein Margarete Blank, Ribbentrop's personal secretary, was next. Horn asked what her boss's attitude was toward Adolf Hitler. "Herr von Ribbentrop always showed the greatest admiration and veneration for the Führer," she said. "In carrying out the role set him by the Führer, Herr von Ribbentrop showed utter disregard for his own interests." The prosecutors could barely contain their laughter. No one asked to cross-examine Fräulein Blank. What she had said could scarcely be improved upon.

On April 1 Ribbentrop took the stand. After direct examination by Horn, John Harlan Amen went after the witness with his customary ankle-biting ferocity. But it was Sir David Maxwell-Fyfe whom the audience had crowded the visitors' gallery to watch. Ribbentrop, during direct examination, had protested his innocence of Hitler's aggressive intentions. He had in his hand, Sir David said, a document dated March 15, 1939, surrendering the remaining part of Czechoslovakia to Germany. "Will you agree that the document was obtained from Czechoslovakia's president by the most intolerable threats of aggression?" the prosecutor asked. "No," Ribbentrop answered. But what further pressure could you put on the head of a country, Sir David asked, than to threaten that you would march in, and also bomb Prague? "War, for instance," Ribbentrop answered primly. "War!" Sir David said in disbelief. "What is that *but* war?" Hjalmar Schacht, former head of the Reichsbank, leaned over to Gilbert, standing near the dock. "Ribbentrop should be hanged for stupidity," he whispered.

The next day, Ribbentrop faced the French and Russian cross-examiners. During Rudenko's turn the Russian asked Ribbentrop, "Do you consider the seizure of Czechoslovakia an act of aggression?" "No," Ribbentrop answered. "Poland?" "No." "Denmark?" "No." "Norway?" "No." "Greece?" "No." "The Soviet Union?" "No." Ribbentrop was dismissed and returned to the dock. "You were not even interesting," Göring muttered.

IF COLONEL Andrus had a model prisoner, it was Field Marshal Keitel, the man who never complained. This stoicism, however, won Keitel little credit among his countrymen. Göring described him as "a sergeant's mind in a field marshal's body." To Keitel life seemed an unbroken chain of misery: his youngest daughter dead of tuberculosis in 1940, one son killed and two more missing in Russia, his home destroyed in an air raid, his wife surviving on the charity of friends. In the end, the man for whom all the sacrifices had been made repaid him with scorn. Hitler had written in his final testament that Keitel and the High Command were responsible for Germany's defeat.

Early in the trial his lawyer, Otto Nelte, had tried to convince Keitel to confess. Even if they found him guilty, a soul-baring admission could mitigate his sentence. Keitel had agreed to consider the idea, but first he needed to consult with Göring, which he did in the exercise yard. Out of the question, Göring had told him. They had to present a united front. After a sleepless night Keitel had told Nelte no. Even in Nuremberg he still obeyed orders.

Admittedly, Keitel cut an imposing figure as he walked, shoulders squared, to the witness-box to begin his defense on April 3. His outward bearing, however, seemed merely to mock the craven man within. Sir David Maxwell-Fyfe waited his turn to cross-examine Keitel, like a lion resting between feedings.

Otto Nelte rose from the defense table. His intention was to follow the Göring example—to ask his client questions eliciting full, self-serving answers. Who had been responsible for the sins laid at the feet of the German armed forces? Nelte asked. Keitel paused, then spoke firmly: "As a German officer, I consider it my duty to answer for all I have done. The men in the front lines cannot be charged with guilt while the highest leaders reject responsibility. That is wrong and unworthy." The defendants in the dock sat up. The justices leaned forward. This was a Keitel none of them had expected to hear.

Nelte pointed out that Keitel's name appeared on the most odious orders. "What," the lawyer asked, "can you say in your defense?" "I bear the responsibility for whatever resulted from those orders," Keitel said. Nelte raised the issue of Keitel's role in passing along Hitler's order to execute the escaped Sagan RAF fliers. He had initially tried to avoid reporting the escape to Hitler, Keitel said, but Himmler had already informed him. Keitel thereafter argued against having the escapees shot, which merely made him the target of Hitler's wrath. He did at least talk Hitler out of shooting the men who had already been returned to Stalag Luft III, he explained. But in the end, he admitted, he had caved in to Hitler's demand for death.

KEITEL's defense now entered the fourth day, and Roman Rudenko led off the cross-examination. To him Keitel's sudden nobility was poor recompense for the suffering the man's orders had inflicted on the Soviet people. He read from document R-98—the Reprisal Order, issued by Keitel, under which fifty Soviet hostages had been shot for every German soldier killed by partisans. Rudenko asked if Keitel considered this a proper order. Sweat beaded Keitel's brow. He had originally called for shooting five to ten hostages, he explained, but Hitler had upped the figure to fifty. Rudenko read from the same document: " 'The troops are, therefore, authorized and ordered to take any measures without restriction, even against women and children.' " Did not "any measures" include murder? "Yes," Keitel admitted, barely audible, "but not of women and children."

Now it was Maxwell-Fyfe's turn to cross-examine. He questioned Keitel about Robert Paul Evans, a British seaman, age twenty, who had ridden a torpedo into a Norwegian fjord in an attempt to destroy the German battleship *Tirpitz*. What in the name of all military tradition had that boy done wrong? Maxwell-Fyfe asked. Was this not a remarkable act of courage? "There is nothing wrong," Keitel agreed. "I recognize that it is right, a perfectly permissible attack." All the same,

Robert Paul Evans on his capture had been shot under Keitel's Commando Order. "What I want to understand is this," Sir David went on. "How did you tolerate all these young men being murdered?" He had explained, if not justified, his failure to resist Hitler in previous testimony, Keitel said. But much of what he had gone along with was "against the inner voice of my conscience."

Sir David seized on the phrase. "Can you tell the tribunal the three worst things you had to do which were against the inner voice of your conscience?" It was a wild stab, the kind of self-incriminating question that a defendant usually dodges. Keitel, instead, spoke calmly, looking straight ahead, as though examining his face in an unseen mirror. First, he said, were "the orders given for the conduct of the war in the East, which were contrary to the accepted usages of warfare." He cleared his throat. "The question of the fifty RAF fliers. And, worst of all, the *Nacht und Nebel* decree. I personally thought that to deport individuals secretly was much crueler than a death sentence." Maxwell-Fyfe had no further questions. Keitel's expression suggested a man from whom a heavy burden had finally been lifted.

3

AFTER the prosecution had rested its case, a mass exodus of staff had taken place. Telford Taylor had gone to Washington in mid-February, acting virtually as a recruiting sergeant. Jackson formally appointed Taylor, a man of acknowledged brilliance, to succeed him as chief counsel for the subsequent trials of hundreds of concentration camp operators, Nazi "scientists," and assorted butchers, and Taylor was promoted to general. But he had little luck signing up lawyers. It was now peacetime. The men had come home and were not eager to leave again. Taylor informed Jackson of the one recruitment incentive that would work—he could persuade lawyers to sign on if they could bring their families.

That spring the army at long last lifted the ban on spouses. Francis Biddle immediately sent for his wife, Katherine, who arrived in April with Elzie Wechsler, wife of Biddle's chief aide, Herb Wechsler. Biddle left the quarters he had shared with justice Parker and took one of the handsomest houses still standing—the Villa Conradti.

To OBSERVERS ERNST KALTENBRUNNER was the most detestable of the defendants. Alone among them, he had set his hands directly on the levers of extermination. Adolf Eichmann, now understood to be the engineer of extermination and who had managed to slip through the Allied dragnet, was a Kaltenbrunner subordinate and friend. As chief of the RSHA—the Reich Central Security Office—serving directly under Himmler, Kaltenbrunner had been responsible for the SD and the Gestapo, which had dispatched people to the camps. His defense began on April 11.

Kaltenbrunner's lawyer, Kurt Kauffmann, spare, tall, had the hot eye of the fanatic. As soon as his client was sworn in, he plunged ahead. "You are aware that you are under extremely serious charges," he said. "The prosecution connects your name with the Gestapo terror and the atrocities of the concentration camps. I now ask you, do you assume responsibility for the counts as charged?"

The lawyers at the prosecution table looked on with admiration. Few of the Germans seemed to have grasped the dynamics of the Anglo-Saxon adversarial system, the duel of wits between lawyers. But Kauffmann appeared to have absorbed a defense fundamental: Get the worst out under direct examination. Steal the cross-examiner's thunder. Kaltenbrunner answered that, technically, he accepted responsibility for actions carried out in his domain. "I know the hatred of the world is directed against me," he went on, now that Himmler, Gestapo chief Heinrich Müller, and Oswald Pohl, who ran the concentration camps, were all dead. But his liability was solely technical. These men had been the actual evildoers. Kauffmann asked about his client's signature on thousands of orders sending people to the camps and to their death. "Not once in my whole life did I ever see or sign a single protective custody order," Kaltenbrunner answered. The signatures were facsimiles or had been typewritten.

"You will admit this statement of yours is not very credible," Kauffmann observed, and he read from a document indicating that Kaltenbrunner had ordered the execution of a team of OSS agents captured in uniform behind the lines. He asked his client to explain. "Out of the question," Kaltenbrunner answered. Such behavior would have been "a crime against the laws of warfare." Kauffmann referred to earlier testimony by a camp guard that Kaltenbrunner watched while the gas chamber was demonstrated on Mauthausen inmates. "I never saw a gas chamber," Kaltenbrunner answered. "I did not know they existed at Mauthausen." Under Kauffmann's relentless pounding Kaltenbrunner began shrieking his answers.

Maxwell-Fyfe and the other prosecutors recognized that they had overestimated their man. It was not that Kauffmann had picked up the subtleties of the adversarial system. He had learned only the prosecutorial side of it. Sir David himself could not have done a better job of incriminating Ernst Kaltenbrunner.

Lieutenant Commander Whitney Harris, the young American prosecutor who had helped build the case against Kaltenbrunner, could scarcely believe his good fortune. The British, he learned, had Rudolf Franz Ferdinand Hoess in custody. Harris arranged to have Hoess transferred to Nuremberg, where Harris interrogated him for three days. What Hoess revealed was staggering even by Nuremberg standards. But what to do with the information? Harris wondered. The prosecution's case had already ended. Then, incredibly, Kaltenbrunner applied to have Hoess appear as a witness in his defense. Why he had done so was a mystery, unless he hoped to diminish his own guilt by comparison with someone whose deeds were even blacker: Rudolf Hoess had been the commandant of Auschwitz.

In the end, Whitney Harris was deprived of the full reward of his enterprise. If there was any cross-examining of Hoess to be done, a senior prosecutor, John Harlan Amen, would do it. Meanwhile, Harris watched from the sidelines as Kurt Kauffmann, Kaltenbrunner's lawyer, invited Hoess to tell his story.

In the summer of 1941, Hoess began, he was commandant at Auschwitz, a new concentration camp built on farmland in Poland. He was enlarging the camp to accommodate 100,000 prisoners, whom he expected to employ in agriculture. Instead, he explained, "I had to go to Himmler in Berlin where he imparted to me the following: 'The Führer has ordered the Final Solution of the Jewish question. We, the SS, have to execute it.' " Hoess still did not fully understand what he was supposed to do. Shortly afterward Adolf Eichmann came and explained Hoess's new duties in greater detail. He would get a better idea, Eichmann told him, by visiting a camp at Treblinka, near Warsaw.

In the course of Hoess's recital only one point was of any possible value to the defendant. Kurt Kauffmann elicited that while Hoess was commandant of Auschwitz, Ernst Kaltenbrunner had never visited the camp. For the prosecution this admission was a cheap price to pay for the right to cross-examine Hoess.

Hoess looked bored as John Harlan Amen read from the affidavit Whitney Harris had taken from Hoess describing his visit to Treblinka. In it Hoess explained that he had been unimpressed by the Treblinka operation. It had taken the commandant there six months to eliminate 80,000 Jews using monoxide gas. Hoess had a better idea. One of his Auschwitz guards had accidentally taken a whiff of Zyklon B, a chemical disinfectant used in the camp laundry. The man had passed out instantly. Hoess and his staff tested the Zyklon B on Soviet prisoners of war locked in a room, and it worked. The substance was dropped from a hole in the ceiling, and within three to fifteen minutes the victims were dead.

Hoess built gas chambers to accommodate 2000 inmates at a time, compared to Treblinka's 200. He had two large crematoria built, with four double ovens heated by coke. With these facilities "it was possible to get rid of ten thousand people in twenty-four hours," Hoess affirmed. In all, Hoess disposed of some 2.5 million people during his tenure at Auschwitz. But he made clear that he had not tolerated gratuitous cruelty. His men were there to exterminate people, not to torment them.

AT THE end of the day Captain Gilbert went to Hoess's cell. The man's face retained the same expression of ennui that the courtroom spectators had seen. "I suppose you want to know if my thoughts and habits are normal," Hoess said. "What do you think?" Gilbert asked. "I am entirely normal," Hoess answered. "Even while doing this extermination work, I led a perfectly normal family life." Hoess did admit to one peculiarity: "I always felt happiest alone. I never had a friend." He had enjoyed most the period after the war, when he was a fugitive hiding on a farm, with horses as his sole companions.

Gilbert asked Hoess whether the Jews he had murdered had deserved their fate. He had never in his life heard anything else, Hoess explained. His whole education had taught him that the Jew was Germany's enemy. Anyway, it did not matter. He was an SS man. "We were all so trained to obey orders without thinking that the thought of disobeying never occurred to anybody. I never gave much thought to whether it was wrong. It just seemed a necessity."

For Gilbert it had all fallen into place at last. The puzzle of why was complete. Talking to the condemned SS prisoners at Dachau, he had concluded that institutionalized slaughter demanded a culture that placed obedience above thinking. In the testimony of Bach-Zelewski earlier, another piece of the puzzle had slipped into place: You can do it when you are persuaded that you are killing not people, but pernicious, subhuman creatures. The final piece had been provided by Hoess, the man who "never had a friend," who preferred the company of horses to that of people. Gilbert began writing: Rudolf Hoess was "outwardly normal, but lacked something essential to normality, the quality of empathy, the capacity to feel with our fellow man." Hoess had described the millions at Auschwitz not as people, but as "shadows passing before me." Combine unthinking obedience, racism, and a disconnection from the kinship of mankind, and you could produce an Auschwitz commandant.

His arrival at a solution that satisfied the mind served only to depress Gilbert's spirits. Every society had its authority-driven personalities. Bigots existed all over. And schizoids, dead to normal feeling, walked the streets everywhere. The distinction in Nazi Germany had been that these people had not functioned on the margins of society. They had run it.

HANS Frank's defense represented something of a personal investment to Captain Gilbert. What he hoped for on the stand was admission of wrong, remorse, repentance. To Frank's credit he had been virtually the first to stand up to Göring's bullying. His reborn Catholicism, with its promises of an afterlife, seemed to have given him reason to die, if not to live. But the man was subject to manic swings. After a recess in the Hoess testimony, Gilbert had overheard Frank tell Rosenberg, "They are trying to pin the murder of two thousand Jews a day in Auschwitz on Kaltenbrunner. How about the eighty thousand deaths from the atomic bombing of Japan? Is that justice?" Frank's spine, Gilbert feared, was malleable.

Frank was sworn in on the morning of April 18. His lawyer, Alfred Seidl, small, fussy, unimpressive, had been dubbed Mickey Mouse by Göring. "Did you," Seidl asked, "ever participate in the annihilation of the Jews?" In truth, Frank could evade. He had run no death camps, and he had hated Himmler. "I say yes," Frank responded, his voice tremulous. "And the reason I say yes is because, having lived through the five months of this trial, my conscience does not allow me to throw the responsibility solely on minor people. I myself never installed an extermination camp for Jews . . . but we fought against Jewry for years; and we indulged in the most horrible utterances. My own diary bears witness against me." He paused, then spoke with quiet force. "A thousand years will pass and still Germany's guilt will not have been erased."

Gus Gilbert heard the answer with something that fleetingly approached admiration.

THE court went into Easter recess on April 19 and was to resume on April 23. On April 22 Harlan Stone, the chief justice of the United States Supreme Court, collapsed while reading a dissenting opinion and died. Jackson's friends were instantly on the transatlantic telephone with one message: If he wanted to succeed Stone as chief justice, he must come home at once. Robert Jackson was a romantic with a realistic streak. He wanted the chief-justiceship desperately. But how could he walk out on the unfinished business in Nuremberg to lobby for a job in Washington? It was unseemly. He could only stay in Nuremberg and hope for Harry Truman's nod.

The trial resumed. Among the defendants in the dock, Wilhelm Frick, onetime minister of the interior, had only one distinguishing feature: the incongruous checkered sports jacket he wore. The man was capable only of parroting stale Nazi dogma; thus his lawyer, Otto Pannenbecker, had no intention of putting him on the stand. On April 24 Hans Gisevius was called instead. Since he had worked for Frick, he might at least be able to establish that the man had exercised no real power. But under cross-examination Gisevius had happily admitted that Hermann Göring had ordered a subordinate to murder Gregor Strasser, a rival to Hitler in the Nazi Party; that Kaltenbrunner was more dangerous as chief of the RSHA than the dread Reinhard Heydrich; and that Field Marshal Keitel had been kept fully informed of the emergence of death factories in the East. Of the man he had supposedly come to defend, Gisevius said that the Twentieth of July plotters, had they succeeded, would certainly have had Frick on the list of Nazis to dispose of. By the end of the testimony Göring was on his feet, cursing the stupidity of Pannenbecker for calling Gisevius as a defense witness.

HERB Wechsler, Jim Rowe, Adrian Fisher, and Bob Stewart acted as law clerks to the court, helping the justices determine, for each defendant, which charges had been proved and which disproved. With the prosecution and the defense of a half-dozen defendants completed, this staff began preparing draft verdicts. The premier question, because it dealt with the most monstrous crime, was to determine who bore responsibility for the Final Solution. In the carloads of documents the one piece of paper that forever eluded the prosecution was a direct written order from Hitler setting the machinery in motion.

ON APRIL 26 Julius Streicher—a man who washed his face in the toilet bowl, who talked dirty to children, who was even reviled by his fellow defendants—was put on the stand. The British cross-examiner, Mervyn Griffith-Jones, tore Streicher's defense apart with a rapier tongue. At one point he noted that Streicher, in *Der Stürmer,* had referred to the Jews as "a nation of bloodsuckers and extortionists," and asked, "Do you think that's preaching race hatred?" "No," Streicher answered. "It is just a statement of fact."

"IF WE can't convict Hjalmar Schacht, we can't convict anybody on the industrial side," Robert Jackson told Telford Taylor. Taylor listened in dismay. What was so crucial about the industrialist case? Taylor wondered. The industrialists, Jackson believed, had conspired to put Hitler into power. They had conspired to rearm Germany, and for what purpose but to wage aggressive war? Punishment of the industrialists was key if the conspiracy strategy was to hang together.

Taylor was convinced that the conspiracy theory was obsolete, but he knew there was little he could do to dissuade Jackson. Determined to claim Schacht's scalp, Jackson had decided to go into the pit again for the cross-examination. He had chosen, Taylor believed, an elusive target.

In all these months in court, Hjalmar Schacht, his steel-gray hair parted in the middle, his neck corded, had assumed a pose that suggested he was trying to avoid being contaminated by his colleagues in the dock. Back in the fall he had told an interrogator, Lieutenant Nicholas Doman, "Young man, do you know why I am here? I am here because Justice Jackson wants an innocent man who can be acquitted to prove this is a fair trial." On April 30 Schacht sat in the witness-box, not as one facing his accusers, but as one eager to share his brilliant insights with lesser mortals.

It cannot have harmed Schacht that of all the defendants, he was the only one to testify in English. He had been born Horace Greeley Hjalmar Schacht, named after the crusading American journalist. His father had lived in America for several years before resettling in Germany. Hjalmar Schacht was considered the financial wizard responsible for bringing Germany's catastrophic inflation under control in the '20s. On coming to power, Hitler had shrewdly named him president of the Reichsbank and, later, minister of the economy. Now sixty-nine, he was, according to the IQ test, the most intelligent man on trial.

During cross-examination Jackson intended to destroy Schacht's denials that he helped plan and carry out aggressive warfare. The prosecution had a 1934 decree signed by Hitler and naming Schacht secret plenipotentiary-general for the war economy. Jackson also had proof that Schacht's schemes had indeed financed Germany's rearmament, that he had made speeches praising Hitler, that he had called people who patronized Jewish shops "traitors," and that he had contributed money to the Nazi Party.

The Nazis, however, had inadvertently provided Schacht with a powerful defense. Although not part of the Twentieth of July plot against Hitler, he had been arrested after the attempt and had ended up at Dachau. Trying to convict of war crimes a man who had spent ten months in a concentration camp tested Jackson's prosecutorial gifts to the utmost.

WINTER had suited the trial. The leaden skies, gray rubble, and wan faces in the dock blended in melancholy harmony. Now spring had come. The windows of the courtroom were thrown open, and the stagnant air gave way to the fragrance of hawthorn.

Tom Dodd was again the toast of the Grand Hotel. On Friday, May 3, he had shattered the defense of Walther Funk. Round, soft, weeping, dark-jowled Funk might have seemed an unworthy adversary, a preposterous war criminal. His weak bladder had gotten him out of the German army during World War I. At Nuremberg he often had to be led from the courtroom to the men's room. This unlikely figure, however, had become minister of the economy, succeeding the old wizard Schacht. Funk was, in fact, bright and capable. But he had been known best in party circles as a bon vivant who savored good Scotch, risqué stories, and all-night revelry. Though he was married and liked to play the lecher, Funk had discreetly chosen his own sex for his most intimate companionship.

The worst thing he had done was to draft a law in the '30s barring Jews from operating retail businesses, a blow that had doomed tens of thousands to poverty or flight. What hovered over Funk at Nuremberg, however, was something more tangibly horrifying. After the conquest of Frankfurt a U.S. Army film unit had made a motion picture of unusual deposits in the vaults of the Reichsbank—heaps of gold eyeglass frames, gold rings, gold watches, and gold teeth. The prosecution had shown the film in court.

On the witness stand Funk had denied any knowledge of these deposits. In cross-examining him, Dodd read from an affidavit given by Emil Puhl, Funk's assistant at the Reichsbank, claiming that Funk had accepted valuables collected by the SS in the East. Funk insisted that Puhl's affidavit was a lie. Why did they not produce the man himself? Funk protested. Puhl would clear his old chief. "Many people deposited valuables, although the bank was not required to look into them," Funk said petulantly. "Nobody," Dodd observed, "ever deposited his gold teeth in a bank."

Emil Puhl did, in fact, testify later. Funk did know about the SS deposits of valuables, Puhl told the court, and they were, he said, *Schweinerei*—they smelled bad from the start.

On May 8 Grand Admiral Karl Dönitz was sworn in. His lawyer, Otto Kranzbuehler, was a familiar figure around the courthouse, as the only German permitted to wear his full uniform. As a career naval officer, he looked upon the Dönitz case as a defense not simply of the admiral but of the German navy. To Kranzbuehler the most dangerous piece of paper in the prosecution's hands was the Laconia Order, which his client had issued to the submarine fleet on September 17, 1942. The order—not to rescue survivors of sunken ships—was a seemingly heartless directive. The facts, however, were that the *Laconia*, a well-armed British merchantman, had been sunk by submarine *U-156* in the South Atlantic, and the U-boat captain, finding the sea full of survivors, wired Dönitz for instructions. Dönitz dispatched two more submarines to aid in the rescue operation. The three subs took survivors aboard until they were full, and towed the rest in lifeboats toward land. During this rescue operation an American Liberator bomber arrived on the scene and began attacking the *U-156*, which was flying a large Red Cross flag. The submarine took a hit amidships. Enraged by what he regarded as Dönitz's misguided compassion, Hitler demanded that the safety of the U-boats take priority over all else. Thus it was that Dönitz had issued the aid-no-survivors order.

Otto Kranzbuehler had read the *tu quoque* prohibition of the IMT Charter. It said, in effect, that even though the Allies might have committed wrongs, this did not excuse the Germans. There had to be a way around this provision. Five weeks before, he had petitioned the court to allow him to seek an affidavit from Admiral Chester Nimitz, commander of the U.S. Pacific Fleet. "I in no way wish to prove that the American admiralty in its U-boat warfare against Japan broke international law," Kranzbuehler argued. "On the contrary, I am of the opinion that it acted strictly in accordance with international law." He was not saying that we Germans did wrong, but so did you; rather, he was saying, you did right, and so did we.

The British, French, and Russian justices had been ready to reject these legal acrobatics, but Francis Biddle was intrigued by Kranzbuehler's ingenuity. He used his accustomed influence over Lawrence to win approval for the petition. Nevertheless, weeks had passed and still no affidavit from Nimitz had arrived.

During these weeks Kranzbuehler had not been idle. Sixty-seven German U-boat captains were still imprisoned in England. All sixty-seven had signed a statement averring that Admiral Dönitz had never ordered his crews to kill survivors; they had been directed not to rescue them. Kranzbuehler had managed to have the statement accepted into evidence.

On Thursday, May 9, with still no word from Nimitz, the cross-examination began. Maxwell-Fyfe read from Dönitz's speeches, exposing him as a rabid anti-Semite. He proved that Dönitz was well aware of the existence of concentration camps. Had he not requested

12,000 inmates to work in his shipyards? And Dönitz was the man Hitler had found most worthy to succeed him.

The day after Dönitz's defense ended, Admiral Nimitz had gone to his office at the Navy Department in Washington. Commander Joseph Broderick of the judge advocate general's office read from a list of questions provided by Kranzbuehler. Did U.S. submarines in the Pacific attack merchantmen without warning? Yes, Nimitz said without hesitation, except for hospital ships. Under whose authority? By order of the highest naval authority, the chief of naval operations, dated December 7, 1941, Nimitz responded. Did American submarines rescue survivors? U.S. submarines did not rescue survivors, Nimitz said, if such action would place the submarine at risk. The deposition was soon on its way to Kranzbuehler, who introduced it into evidence.

REPORTERS had observed the odd relationship for months: two former commanders of the German navy sitting side by side, day after day, barely exchanging a glance. Seventy-year-old Grand Admiral Erich Raeder had been indicted, along with the propagandist Hans Fritzsche, at the insistence of the Russians because they too wanted to produce war criminals, and these were the best they could unearth. Thereafter prosecution researchers had to scramble to find evidence to match the charges. The case finally prepared alleged that Raeder had violated the Treaty of Versailles by building up the German navy; that he had been present at the Hossbach Conference, where Hitler laid out his aggressive intentions; and that he had been party to the plan to invade Norway. The most curious document in the prosecution's possession was the Moscow Statement, which surfaced on May 20, when Soviet deputy prosecutor Colonel Y. V. Pokrovsky introduced it during cross-examination. Raeder had made it while in Russian captivity, and Göring, Dönitz, and Keitel did not fare well in it. But Raeder was unconcerned by the bridges he had burned in court. When the day ended, he told Gilbert, "Naturally, I will be hanged or shot. I have no desire to serve a prison sentence at my age."

CAPTAIN Gilbert was apprehensive as Baldur von Schirach—at thirty-nine, the youngest major war criminal—took the stand on May 23. If Gilbert had made one strategic contribution to this trial, he believed it had been to split up the defendants and to isolate Göring so that the others would be free of his intimidation. Yet Gilbert knew that Schirach was capable of extraordinary self-delusion. Schirach had once explained to the cell guard Emilio DiPalma, "You see, our Hitler Youth was the same as your Boy Scouts." To which DiPalma, a combat veteran, replied, "I never saw a Boy Scout take apart an automatic rifle and reassemble it in one minute flat."

Schirach's counsel began by deliberately raising his client's worst offenses. He drew an admission that Schirach knew about the mass exterminations in the East. He asked Schirach to comment on the testimony of Rudolf Hoess. Those millions of murders were not committed by Hoess, Schirach said in a firm voice. "Hoess was only the executioner. The murder was ordered by Adolf Hitler." The defendants looked toward the witness-box as if controlled by a single string. "It was my guilt, which I will have to carry before God and the German nation, that I educated the youth of our people for a man who committed murders a millionfold." Baldur von Schirach had displayed a spine that few had believed he possessed.

Back in the cellblock, Gilbert sought out Albert Speer's reaction. Speer said he was delighted to see Göring's united front collapsing, as first Keitel, then Frank, and now Schirach accepted personal guilt and condemned the regime. Of more immediate concern to Speer, however, was the testimony of the next defendant, Fritz Sauckel.

RОВЕРТ Servatius hurried through the Palace of Justice to the visitors' room, where he was to have a last-minute meeting with his client. The fifty-two-year-old defense lawyer had won a reputation in court for being logical and reasonable. He sat down on the other side of the mesh screen and went directly to the point. He was going to throw the toughest possible questions at Sauckel concerning the forced labor program. Better he should do it than the prosecution. Did Sauckel understand? Sauckel nodded eagerly. And do not babble, Servatius warned. Speak slowly. Use short sentences. Give the interpreters a chance to keep pace.

On Tuesday, May 28, when Sauckel entered the witness-box, Servatius began quoting Sauckel's words at a meeting of the Central Planning Board. Sauckel had boasted that when necessary, his agents resorted to shanghaiing foreign workers. Explain this statement, Servatius said. Sauckel looked stunned, as though a parent had delivered an unexpected slap. His speech revealed a provincial, uneducated German, and he was pausing at every word.

As the day wore on, Servatius made some headway, getting evidence into the record that his client had issued directives calling for the decent treatment of workers and that Sauckel himself controlled no troops, but depended on others to carry out his roundups.

The subject foremost on everyone's mind was broached the next day. "What was the relationship of your office to Speer's?" Servatius asked. At last Sauckel spoke clearly and directly: "My office had to meet the demands made by Speer."

A worse moment for Speer occurred when Servatius called as a witness Max Timm, a Sauckel deputy. The lawyer asked the witness, "Could Speer give orders to Sauckel?" Timm gave a rambling answer. Servatius pressed harder. "Could Albert Speer give orders and instructions and did he give them?" "Yes," Timm answered.

FEW noticed the flowers on the witness-box the morning of June 3 until General Alfred Jodl took the stand. Underneath the small vase of pink and white phlox a note in a familiar hand read, "Calm, oh so calm, my dear. Do not lose your temper." Jodl smiled at his wife, Luise, in the visitors' gallery, then resumed his customary mask. As secretary to her husband's lawyer, Franz Exner, Frau Jodl was occasionally able to get into court to see Alfred.

In the beginning Alfred Jodl had not appeared on all the Allied war-criminal lists. But the Russians had wanted him indicted, for he had transmitted to German armies in Russia Hitler's orders for virtually unrestricted barbarism. The Americans had eventually settled on him to round out the list of defendants in keeping with Jackson's philosophy of collective guilt. Thus Göring represented the Nazi leadership and the Luftwaffe, Schacht the industrialists, Keitel the general staff, Dönitz the navy, Kaltenbrunner the SS, and Jodl the army.

On the stand Jodl's defense was that he had tempered Hitler's worst impulses. It was true. Unlike Keitel, who would be nodding before he knew what the Führer was saying, Jodl did speak out. He protested to Hitler when some eighty American POWs were murdered by SS troops in Belgium during the Battle of the Bulge. Jodl was the model officer, unafraid to undergo fire whether in the face of the enemy or a megalomaniac leader. But, as prosecutor Geoffrey Dorling Roberts was bent on proving, Jodl also displayed the other face of the German militarist—indiscriminate obedience to an order.

If Maxwell-Fyfe was the scourge of the defendants, his countryman "Khaki" Roberts was close behind. Roberts was a huge man, swathed in yards of double-breasted serge. He had a large mustache and large square teeth, which he flashed at his prey in smiles of exuberant contempt. Wasn't Jodl's claim that he opposed brutal orders hypocritical? Roberts asked. He turned to a document signed by Jodl ordering troops in the East to punish guerrilla actions "by such terror as to eradicate every inclination to resist." Barely pausing for Jodl's answer, Roberts attacked again. Were those not Jodl's words, uttered just before the blitz? "Terror attacks against English centers of population will paralyze the will of the people to resist." And after the plot against Hitler, didn't Jodl make a speech to staff officers in which he said, "The twentieth of July was the blackest day that Germany has yet seen and will remain so for all time"? "Why," Roberts asked, "was it such a black day for Germany when someone tried to assassinate a man who you now admit was a murderer?" Before Jodl could complete his response, Roberts shouted, "Do you still say that you are an honorable soldier, a truthful man?" Without waiting for a reply, Roberts turned and walked back to the prosecutors' table.

On June 6 President Truman named Fred Vinson, his treasury secretary, as chief justice of the Supreme Court. Robert Jackson took it without complaint, yet some of his associates thought they saw deep disappointment in the man for having been passed over.

On June 10 a limping Arthur Seyss-Inquart, crippled in a long-ago mountaineering accident, approached the stand. As his testimony unfolded, the contradictions amazed the court—the mild manner, the terrible deeds, the quiet speech, the horrific record. The subjects raised by his counsel on direct examination merely positioned the witness in the gunsights for his cross-examiner. Seyss-Inquart emerged as a man who had brutalized his fiefdom of occupied Holland. Under what Seyss-Inquart regarded as his firm but humane rule, 41,000 Dutch had been shot as hostages, 50,000 died of starvation, and fifty-six percent of Dutch Jews perished.

Seyss-Inquart had neither lied nor pleaded in his testimony, but had assumed a fatalist's resignation. When he rode down the courtroom elevator that day with Hanz Fritzsche, he observed that it did not matter how he behaved: "Whatever I say, my rope is being woven from Dutch hemp."

FRANZ von Papen began his defense on June 14. However, Albert Speer, Göring's chief rival for the soul of the defendants, would take the stand within a week, and suspense was beginning to mount.

The man presented an anomaly—an indicted war criminal who could easily have walked straight from the dock to dinner with the justices. Speer tested the court's powers of objectivity. Could they discern the fine fault line of guilt between this brilliant, attractive figure and the lumpen Fritz Sauckel? Or, as one reporter put it, when babies born to women on forced labor transports had been thrown from the train, who was most responsible—Sauckel, who had conscripted the women, or Speer, who had demanded them as workers?

On June 20, the eve of his defense, Speer again reviewed his assets. What hard truths had he told Hitler when others pretended the war could still be won? What action had he taken when Hitler ordered Germany destroyed in a pointless Armageddon? What heroic solution had he plotted while others trembled in the Führer's presence? He and his lawyer, Hans Flächsner, had gone through it all, rehearsing the questions that would elicit the most beneficial answers.

Speer had instructed Flächsner to get the Sauckel business out of the way quickly. Thus early in the direct examination Flächsner asked Speer if he disapproved of Sauckel's recruitment of labor. On the contrary, Speer answered, "I was grateful for every worker he provided me with." Flächsner noted that Sauckel had claimed he worked for Speer. Would the witness please comment? It was the question at the heart of the matter. Speer hesitated, then plunged in. "Of course, I expected Sauckel to meet the demands of war production," he said. But he did not control Sauckel, as proved by the fact that he did not get all the workers he requested.

Sauckel tried to signal his lawyer, Robert Servatius. Sauckel had told his interrogators months before that Speer had actually stockpiled workers, hoarding more than he could possibly use.

Speer had saved the afternoon for his masterstroke. Since he had held a "technical" ministry, Flächsner asked, "Do you wish to limit your responsibility to your sphere of work?" "No," Speer answered. "This war has brought an inconceivable catastrophe. I, as an important member of the leadership of the Reich, share in the total responsibility." The statement—so at odds with the self-pitying moral blindness of a Ribbentrop, a Kaltenbrunner, a Sauckel—pleased the court.

Speer went on. By March 1945, "Hitler intended, deliberately, to destroy the means of life for his own people if the war were lost." Though Hitler was ordering German industry razed, Speer explained, he had made the perilous decision to thwart him and to preserve a base on which a defeated people could rebuild their country. He made sure that the court understood the high price of such defiance. Hitler had had eight officers shot for failing to blow up the bridge over the Rhine at Remagen, Speer pointed out. Other defendants had condemned Hitler—Frank with strident emotionalism, Schirach with abject apology—but Speer did so with manly composure.

Earlier in the trial, Speer's lawyer had briefly mentioned his scheme to assassinate Hitler. Speer said that he now wanted to discuss that issue, not to cast himself in a heroic light, but only to show how thoroughly he had become convinced of Adolf Hitler's insane destructiveness. Speer explained that he knew of a hidden air-intake shaft in the Reich Chancellery garden that ventilated the Führerbunker below. In February 1945 he asked the head of his munitions department, Dieter Stahl, to procure a poison gas, which he intended to drop into the ventilating system. When Speer revisited the site in March, he found a twelve-foot chimney protecting the ventilator. From that point on, he banished all further thoughts of killing Hitler.

For his closing Speer took the rhetorical high ground: "The sacrifices made on both sides after January 1945 were senseless. The dead of this period will be the accusers of the man responsible for the continuation of that struggle." That man was Adolf Hitler.

Captain Gilbert had been much moved by Albert Speer's contrition. He stopped by the man's cell that night and found him deathly pale, stretched out on his cot, holding his stomach. He was exhausted, Speer explained, and suffering painful cramps. "That was quite a strain," he said, "but I'm glad I got it out of my system. I spoke the truth and that's all there was to it."

ON FRIDAY AFTERNOON, JUNE 21, the courtroom filled as spectators gathered to watch Robert Jackson cross-examine Speer. "Will you tell me," Jackson asked Speer, "whether you were a member of the SS?" "No," Speer answered, "I was not." Jackson went on, "You filled out an application at one time, or one was filled out for you and you never went through with it, I believe. . . ." Jackson trailed off, to the surprise of the prosecutors. They had indisputable proof that Speer had been a member of the SS. Jackson, however, did not press the matter.

He asked Speer about German production of poison gas. Yes, Speer explained, three factories had been working on a gas of extraordinary lethality, but when he had learned Hitler might actually use it, Speer claimed, he ordered production stopped.

"Is it not a fact," Jackson asked, "that in the circle around Hitler there was almost no one who would stand up and tell him that the war was lost, except yourself?" Jaws dropped among the British prosecutors. "That is correct to a certain extent," Speer answered modestly.

The questioning turned to Speer's final visit to Hitler. That fact, Speer knew, was a weak patch in the fabric of his defense. He had said earlier that he had planned to assassinate Hitler. Yet afterward he had taken enormous risks to fly into doomed Berlin to see the Führer. Why? Jackson asked. "I felt," said Speer, "that it was my duty not to run away like a coward, but to stand up to him again."

That was a new twist. Speer's visit had but one purpose: to bid a final farewell to his leader. But Jackson accepted the reply and went on to another area. "This policy of driving Germany to destruction after the war was lost had come to weigh on you to such a point that you were a party to several plots, were you not?" Speer had been a party to no plots, but saw no reason to disagree. Jackson reached his final question: "You as a member of the government acknowledge a responsibility for its large policies but not for the details of their execution. Is that a fair statement of your position?" "Yes, indeed," Speer answered. He could not have phrased it more profitably himself. Speer's defense ended following cross-examination by a Russian deputy prosecutor. As he left the stand, his stomach pains ended as well.

AIREY Neave left the courtroom much dismayed. He had expected the Sauckel-Speer controversy to turn on social class—the mailed fist for one defendant and the velvet glove for the other. But Speer had performed brilliantly, and the admirable side of his character appeared to have touched Jackson. The American prosecutor had made no attempt to question him about his awareness of the extermination of the Jews or about his presence at the Mauthausen concentration camp. Speer had been allowed to talk of the production miracles he had performed, testimony that cried out for cross-examination on the role slave labor played in these feats. He had not been asked.

By the end of June the Nuremberg story had slipped to the back pages of the newspapers. The names of the only two defendants left to testify—Konstantin von Neurath and Hans Fritzsche—struck no fearsome images. Neurath, at seventy-three the oldest defendant, was exhibiting incipient senility. He had been Ribbentrop's predecessor as foreign minister and, like Papen and Schacht, had lent a patina of respectability to the Hitler regime.

In 1939 Hitler named Neurath protector of Bohemia and Moravia in Czechoslovakia, nominally above the SS and Gestapo. But these organizations carried out their grim work ignoring him. A handful of reporters in the press gallery suffered hours of Neurath's rambling rationalizations, and then his defense ended.

Hans Fritzsche was the second defendant provided by the Russians. He had headed the radio division in the Nazi Propaganda Ministry. Drexel Sprecher had applied his notable energy over several months trying to prove that Fritzsche used his broadcasts "to advocate, encourage, and incite" war crimes, particularly offenses against the Jews. But in a confidential memorandum Sprecher admitted that the evidence was "utterly inadequate."

On the 166th day of the trial, Fritzsche left the stand. The last man in the dock had completed his defense.

4

As he headed for the Judges' Room this July morning, Robert Jackson felt better than he had in months. The next time he spoke in the courtroom, it would be in the realm where he was master— delivering the American prosecution's closing speech. Now, however, he had to resolve a debate over the time to be allotted to the defense

attorneys for summations. He was painfully familiar with the stupefy-
ing lengths to which they could go, and the Germans were asking for
unlimited time. Jackson had polled his fellow prosecutors, and they
agreed that three days was ample time for the defense to sum up. He
was bringing this recommendation to the justices this morning.

Francis Biddle was coolly aloof, Sir Geoffrey Lawrence seemed impatient, and the French justices' expressions revealed nothing. Only
the two Russians were openly sympathetic to Jackson. Finally Sir
Geoffrey ruled. He had given the defendants no reason to attack the
fairness of this trial thus far. He was not about to give them that
opportunity now by gagging them. Biddle nodded. Otto Stahmer, Sir
Geoffrey said, as spokesman for the defense, had asked for one day
per defendant. If that meant summations lasting three weeks, so be it.

On July 4, when the defense summations began, Jackson's worst
fears were confirmed. A few glassy-eyed reporters studied the floor
and ceiling as Otto Stahmer explained why Hermann Göring was
innocent. "When by the advent of the Renaissance and the Reforma-
tion," Stahmer droned on, "the spiritual basis of the medieval order
was broken . . ." Jackson could take no more and left. Stahmer was
beginning his client's defense in the sixteenth century.

THE posters had long since become faded and tattered—some
200,000 of them, bearing the photograph of Martin Bormann, plastered on walls, trees, telephone poles, and boxcars all over Germany.
Bormann was a wanted man. As the Führer's secretary, he had exercised only borrowed power, but he had wielded it with ingenious
malice. He had been particularly energetic in transmitting orders to
shoot captured Allied fliers. His proximity to Hitler and his rabid
hatred of Jews and Slavs meant that he had full knowledge of the
regime's foulest crimes. The problem with the Bormann case was that
the man had disappeared in the last days of the war. The prosecution,
nevertheless, wanted Bormann indicted, and the court had agreed.
On July 6 the defense summations were interrupted so that the court
could try Bormann *in absentia*.

TWO voluble men sat drinking in the Marble Room of the Grand.
Lieutenant Tex Wheelis was telling Captain John Vonetes, the American housing officer, how well he got along with the defendants.

Göring was a friend of his, Wheelis claimed. The Reichsmarschall had given him gifts, like this watch with his facsimile signature, he noted, flashing it before Vonetes. There was only one thing wrong with prison duty in Nuremberg, Wheelis confided. "It's the guy I have to work for." Vonetes knew Colonel Andrus, but made no comment.

IN THE waning days of July, Robert Jackson stayed home and worked on his closing speech. In the rough draft he hit Göring on virtually every page. He denounced the industrialists, thus paving the way for Telford Taylor's prosecutions of them after his own departure. Above all, he wanted the speech to proclaim to the world that the Nazi conspiracy to conquer, exploit, and exterminate had been proved.

These passages formed the muscle and sinew of his text. But he enjoyed just as well playing with language, testing aloud in his rich baritone the lyrics of condemnation: "Ribbentrop, that salesman of deception"; "Rosenberg, Nazism's intellectual high priest"; "Kaltenbrunner, the grand inquisitor"; "Funk, banker of gold teeth, the most ghoulish collateral in history." He asked Elsie Douglas to find a volume of Shakespeare. He wanted the famous lines between Gloucester and Lady Anne from *Richard III* for his peroration.

The defense summations ground on for a full three weeks. The last one was delivered by Alfred Seidl for Rudolf Hess on July 25. Next the prosecution would have its final word.

ON THE morning of July 26 the defendants left their cells to hear the prosecution's summation. Robert Jackson was to speak first. Sir Hartley Shawcross, supplanting Maxwell-Fyfe on this key occasion, would succeed Jackson, followed by Auguste Champetier de Ribes for France and, finally, Roman Rudenko for the Soviet Union. The visitors' gallery and the press area were once again thronged.

The ex post facto issue had to be dealt with early, Jackson began, not necessarily to persuade the court, but to satisfy world opinion. Naturally, the defendants' "dislike for the law which condemns them is not original," he noted. " 'No thief e'er felt the halter draw with good opinion of the law.' " He had staked his prosecution on the conspiracy theory, and he pronounced it proved beyond a doubt in the words of the conspirators themselves.

He pointed to Schacht, sitting in his customary pose, legs crossed, arms folded, head turned away. "Twenty days after the seizure of power, Schacht was host to Hitler, Göring, and some twenty leading industrialists," Jackson noted. He described the financier as "a Brahmin among the untouchables. Schacht always fought for his position in a regime he now affects to despise."

Only Göring came in for more killing fire. The Reichsmarschall stopped counting after Jackson's references to him surpassed forty. Jackson indicted the other defendants in turn: "the zealot Hess," "Keitel, the willing tool," and "Dönitz, the legatee of defeat."

Albert Speer listened with a surface calm. Suddenly Jackson was quoting him. As Speer himself had said on the stand, Jackson noted, "the sacrifices made on both sides after January 1945 were without sense." And Speer had made clear that the monster responsible for these squandered lives was Adolf Hitler. Yes, Jackson had used Speer's words, but not against him. Was it possible to dream of acquittal?

Elsie Douglas had located the passage from Shakespeare and listened intently as Jackson approached his peroration. "These defendants now ask the tribunal to say that they are not guilty of planning, executing, or conspiring to commit this long list of crimes and wrongs," he began. "They stand before the record of this trial as blood-stained Gloucester stood by the body of his slain king. He begged of the widow: 'Say I slew them not.' And the queen replied, 'Then say they are not slain. But dead they are.' If you were to say of these men that they are not guilty, it would be as true to say that there has been no war, there are no slain, there has been no crime."

The hush in the courtroom was complete. Airey Neave and justice Birkett exchanged nods. Jackson might have his superiors in the thrust and parry of the game. But in finding the words that captured the majesty of justice, they had just witnessed the master.

IN THE afternoon session chief justice Lawrence called on the patrician Labourite Sir Hartley Shawcross. In a summation approaching Jackson's in eloquence, Sir Hartley called not simply for the defendants' conviction but for the death of them all. The French and Russian prosecutors also closed by demanding capital punishment.

Only the defense of the seven indicted Nazi organizations and brief final statements by the defendants remained. The interrogations unit, its work done, had been disbanded. Robert Jackson felt sufficiently comfortable to turn the direction of the prosecution temporarily over to Tom Dodd while he went home. Jackson had left his seat on the U.S. Supreme Court in May 1945 to become chief counsel for the prosecution of Axis war criminals. Now it was time to remind the Court that he was still a member.

For two months the Nuremberg justices' aides had been evaluating the evidence and preparing preliminary verdicts. Sir Norman Birkett, the great pen on the bench, had completed an early draft of the final judgment. The justices had met to review his effort while the last defendant, Hans Fritzsche, was still on the stand. They had immediately grasped a nettle in the case: the conspiracy theory. The prosecution was relying on documentary evidence to prove that several of the defendants conspired to launch an aggressive war. The French justice Donnedieu de Vabres, who never asked a question in court and rarely uttered a word in their private sessions, spoke out. A conspiracy, he said, connotes participation among more or less equal parties. The defendants would be the first to laugh at the notion of Streicher, Funk, Frick, and Sauckel as Hitler's conspiratorial peers. It was ridiculous, the Frenchman said. Judge these men by what they have done, he cautioned, not by what they allegedly planned to do. Drop the conspiracy charge.

Birkett paced agitatedly. He too had disliked the conspiracy charge, he said, but as the trial unfolded, he had come to see Jackson's larger objective. If individuals were convicted only for individual acts, the trial would never rise above the level of an ordinary criminal prosecution. What they wanted to present to the world was the condemnation of a regime deliberately embarked on war. To drop conspiracy was to lose the trial's moral grandeur.

What Göring and Company Talk About in Their Cells, the headline promised in the August 25 London *Sunday Express*. hitler's stomach cause of all the trouble; when ribbentrop wanted a medal; why hitler delayed marriage, the subheads read. The *Express*'s source was Dr. Douglas Kelley, described as "Chief Psychiatrist at the Nuremberg Trials." The article quoted Göring, Hess, and Ribbentrop, divulging heretofore unrevealed secrets from inside the prison.

Colonel Andrus tossed the clipping at Gustav Gilbert and asked what he knew about it. Gilbert answered that he knew nothing about the origins of the Kelley story. Did Gilbert know that his psychiatrist friend was on the lecture circuit back in the States, criticizing the trial? The colonel said he intended to investigate this business and he expected Gilbert's cooperation.

To Gilbert even more alarming news had come earlier. Since Kelley appeared to have struck off on his own, Gilbert had started to shape his cell-visit notes into his own book, entitled *Nuremberg Diary*. He had engaged a literary agent, who had negotiated a contract with the publisher Farrar, Straus. The agent had recently cabled Gilbert to tell him that Kelley was negotiating with Simon and Schuster. It had become a race, with Kelley holding the better post position: He had completed whatever research he intended to use, while Gilbert was still making cell visits over 3500 miles away. The best card that Gilbert held was a half-finished manuscript. He gave it to a friend returning to the States and asked him to take it to his agent.

ON AUGUST 31 the defendants made their final statements. They did so in the order in which they had been indicted, and Göring moved to the middle of the dock first. Why was he in the dock being treated as a common criminal? Göring began. Let his judges have no illusions. "Since the three greatest powers on earth, together with other nations, fought against us, we finally were conquered by tremendous enemy superiority." Justice had nothing to do with this trial.

Hess was next. He asked if he might remain seated "because of the state of my health." He spoke in a reedy voice of his days in England: "The people around me during my imprisonment acted toward me in a way which led me to conclude that these people somehow were acting in an abnormal state of mind. . . . Some of the new ones who came to me in place of those who had been changed had strange eyes. They were glassy like eyes in a dream." The justices exchanged uneasy glances. Göring jammed Hess with his elbow and told him to stop. "Shut up," Hess shot back. "It was my pleasure that many years of my life were spent in working under the greatest son which my people produced in its thousand-year history," Hess concluded, folding his arms, chin uplifted.

Major Airey Neave had measured these men since the day he had delivered their indictments. Some had grown. Some had not. Ribbentrop was among the latter. What Germany had attempted, Ribbentrop said, was what Britain had done in sweeping a fifth of the globe under her wing of empire, what America had done in occupying the New World, what Russia had done in spreading her dominion from Europe to Asia. He finished with a trace of the old hauteur.

Keitel was one who had grown, Neave believed. His tragedy, Keitel told the court, was "that the best I had to give as a soldier, obedience and loyalty, was exploited for purposes which could not be recognized at the time . . . and that I did not see that there is a limit set even for a soldier's performance of his duty. That is my fate."

Frank had moved the court earlier with his fervent indictment of Nazism. Today he began, "On this witness stand, I said that a thousand years would not suffice to erase the guilt brought upon our people because of Hitler's conduct of this war." That guilt, he continued, "has already been completely wiped out." It was canceled by the mass crimes "which have been and still are being committed against Germans by Russians, Poles, and Czechs." Frank had recanted. At the last minute a man who might have helped Germany shed the destructive myths of its past had instead chosen to poison the future.

Walther Funk wept and passed himself off as little more than a bank teller. Sauckel described having spent Christmas with the conscript workers he was accused of exploiting. Jodl justified German reprisals against "partisans who used every means which they considered expedient." Seyss-Inquart inventoried the health, insurance, and infant-welfare programs he had introduced into Holland.

Speer's steady, confident voice compelled silence in the courtroom. What would be Hitler's place in history? he asked. "After this trial the German people will condemn him as the originator of their misery and despise him." How could so advanced, so cultured, so sophisticated a nation as Germany have fallen under Hitler's demonic sway? The explanation was modern communications, Speer explained—the radio, the telephone, the teleprinter. No longer did a leader have to delegate authority afar to subordinates exercising independent judgment. Given modern communications, a Hitler could rule directly and personally through puppets.

"This war has ended on the note of radio-controlled rockets, aircraft approaching the speed of sound, atom bombs and the horrible prospect of chemical warfare," Speer went on. "In five to ten years, this kind of warfare will offer the possibility of firing rockets from continent to continent with uncanny precision. Through the smashing of the atom, it will be possible to destroy a million people in New York City in a matter of seconds. A new large-scale war will end with the destruction of human culture and civilization. That is why this trial must contribute to the prevention of such wars in the future. May God protect Germany and the culture of the West."

In the hush that followed, Neave sensed that the spectators had listened to Speer not as a man pleading for his life, but as one who had something valuable to tell them, someone with a vision born of redemption. In truth, Neave noted, Speer had said not a word about himself or his guilt.

Han Fritzsche made his statement, and Sir Geoffrey Lawrence adjourned the court. The last of ninety-four witnesses had been heard, the last of over 4000 documents entered into evidence. The next time the defendants filed into room 600, it would be to learn their fates.

CHAPTER IV

JUDGMENT DAY

1

ON MONDAY, September 2, the justices met to begin final debate on the verdicts. Legal adviser Jim Rowe briefed them on security measures. The phones would be disconnected while they deliberated. Any wastepaper, unwanted notes, or unused copies of documents were to be placed in special bags to be burned. To protect the justices, bulletproof cars were being arranged. Sir Geoffrey Lawrence reminded his colleagues of their ultimate responsibility and read aloud from Article 27 of the IMT Charter: "to impose upon a defendant, on conviction, death or such other punishment as shall be determined to be just."

Justice John Parker raised the question of the alternates' role in determining the verdicts. Sir Geoffrey had already consulted with the other principal justices and decided that on test votes all eight men— principals and alternates—would vote. On final votes only the four principals would take part. Nikitchenko again proposed that two out of four votes be sufficient to convict. He was overruled. Three of four votes would be required for a finding of guilty.

Henri Donnedieu de Vabres asked that if the judgment was death, might they not consider the firing squad for the military defendants? Nikitchenko objected. The bullet was the fate of honorable adversaries, not of butchers. For once, the Russian prevailed. Death sentences, the court decided, must be carried out by hanging. With the last of the ground rules set, they began to vote on the verdicts.

DURING the deliberations the halls of the Palace of Justice rang with an incongruous sound—the peal of children's laughter. Colonel Andrus had decided it was safe to allow family visits for the defendants. The justices agreed and asked the army to provide travel permits, transportation, and meals in a special canteen in the courthouse.

Emma Schwabenland, an American civilian employee who managed the visitors' center, moved briskly, matching defendants with wives and children. She admired the colonel for allowing the visits but was disappointed that he had insisted on keeping up the mesh screen. He had been adamant: no touching, no kissing, no hand-holding— that was how weapons and the means of suicide were delivered.

The little girl with the thin legs and her father's broad face stood on a chair reciting poems and singing songs her mother had taught her for the occasion. Nearly a year and a half had passed since Hermann Göring had seen his wife and his daughter, Edda. Emmy, so vivacious in the past, looked as faded as the old print dress she wore. Her eyes darted nervously at the guards, while little Edda burbled. "Daddy," she asked, "when you come home, will you wear all your medals in the bathtub like everybody says you do? I want to see them all covered with soapsuds."

Hans Frank awaited his family with a divided heart. Brigitte had written to him of their hand-to-mouth existence, of their children begging on the streets. When she told them that they would be able to visit their father, the eldest girl, Siegried, responded, "Oh, they haven't shot him yet?" Frank's wife, his onetime queen of Poland, was now thin, hard-faced, and shabby.

Hjalmar Schacht sat as he did in the dock—erect, aloof, but with the satisfied smile of an old man who knows he has surprised his audience. His wife, an art expert thirty years his junior, was undeniably striking. Smiling at him were his two scrubbed, blond daughters, four and five years old.

Rosenberg's wife spoke to him, while his daughter waited in the hallway. Chaplain Henry Gerecke tried to talk to her there. The girl was thirteen and precociously pretty. Would she like to pray with him? Gerecke asked. "Don't give me that prayer crap," the girl answered. A startled Gerecke asked if there was anything else he might do for her. "Yes," she said. "How about a cigarette?"

Back in the cellblock, the unvisited defendants waited. The Russians claimed they had been unable to find Frau Raeder, who lived in the Soviet zone of Berlin. Hess refused to see visitors. "I do not wish my family to see me in this state of indignity," he had told Andrus. Keitel said he had disgraced himself and could not face his wife.

TEX Wheelis leaned into the porthole, chatting with Hermann Göring while the cell guard stood aside. Göring congratulated Wheelis on his promotion to first lieutenant. Göring had two large suitcases, a small valise, and a hatbox in the baggage room. As the duty officer this day, Wheelis had the key. From this luggage Göring's third gift to Wheelis had been retrieved—a pair of fine gray gloves.

THE justices voted on the last verdicts on Thursday, September 26. On Friday four officers checked into the Grand Hotel: Brigadier General Roy V. Rickard, U.S. Army; Brigadier Edmund Paton Walsh of Great Britain; Major General Georgi Malkov of the Soviet Union; and Brigadier General Pierre Morel of France. They formed the Quadripartite Commission for the Detention of War Criminals. They had come to Nuremberg to plan and supervise executions.

ROBERT Jackson returned to Nuremberg on September 18 and stepped into a backlog of administrative headaches. Reporters complained that only a pool would be allowed to cover executions. The recently arrived Quadripartite Commission wanted seats on the courtroom floor when the verdicts were delivered. That struck Jackson as having the hangman sit in court holding a noose. The commission would occupy the gallery with the other visitors, he decided.

Sir Geoffrey Lawrence reviewed the special precautions Colonel Andrus was taking for judgment day. On the day the verdicts were to be handed down, Andrus would have a doctor in the basement, in addition to two guards who would be standing by in the elevator with a stretcher and a straitjacket in case any defendant went berserk. After the men returned to the cellblock, he intended to implement new cell assignments: third tier, term sentences; second tier, life sentences; first tier, death sentences.

MONDAY, September 30, broke sunny and clear. The bulletproof cars arrived at the courthouse, sirens wailing, led by jeeps spiked with machine guns. The eight justices exited between protective files of armed infantry; 1000 troops circled the building, and sharpshooters stood silhouetted on surrounding rooftops.

In the Judges' Room, the two Frenchmen donned their gowns and placed ruffled jabots around their necks. Nikitchenko's and Volchkov's chocolate-brown uniforms displayed razor-edge creases. Biddle had abandoned natty waistcoats and bow ties in favor of a dark gray suit and robe. His mood was somber. Lawrence appeared relaxed, his voice cool as he went over their final instructions. He would lead off, reading the passages of the judgment describing Nazism's rise to power. Donnedieu de Vabres and his alternate, Robert Falco, would trace Germany's aggressions country by country. Biddle would handle the conspiracy charge, and Parker would recite the most horrifying passages of the judgment—the crimes against humanity. The Soviets would deliver the judgment on slave labor and Nazi organizations. Lawrence picked up a thick black notebook. The others fell in behind him as he headed for the small door that opened onto the bench in room 600.

THE visitors shifted restlessly as the justices droned on, in effect recapping the history of an age. Not until 4:00 p.m. did Lieutenant Colonel Volchkov announce the verdicts on the organizations: the Nazi Party leadership, "criminal"; the SS, "criminal"; the Gestapo and the SD, "criminal." That league of Brownshirt bullies, the SA, was acquitted for having lost significance after the '30s, as was the Reich cabinet. The High Command was not judged criminal, since so few officers were involved that individual trials were preferable.

The court's guilty verdicts meant that anyone who was a member of the convicted organizations after 1939 was automatically a war criminal. Biddle, however, had successfully lobbied for exemptions for anyone drafted into membership or who had no knowledge of the organization's criminal purposes. No member of a convicted organization was punished solely on the strength of the tribunal's verdicts. To critics the organization cases had largely been a pointless exercise.

THE verdicts would be delivered first, chief justice Sir Geoffrey Lawrence announced the next morning, followed by sentencing. The twenty-one men in the dock were to remain seated while they heard the judgments on the four counts applicable to them: conspiracy to commit aggression, the commission of aggression, crimes in the conduct of warfare, and crimes against humanity.

" 'The defendant, Hermann Göring, was the moving force for aggressive war, second only to Adolf Hitler,' " Sir Geoffrey began. Göring created the Gestapo and concentration camps, before releasing them to Himmler. He signed the harshest anti-Semitic decrees. " 'He directed Himmler and Heydrich to "bring about a complete solution of the Jewish question." ' " And, Sir Geoffrey added, he was a thief.

Göring, his uniform immaculate, ground a fist into his jowl as Sir Geoffrey continued: There was nothing to be said in mitigation. The tribunal found Göring guilty on all four counts.

Rudolf Hess refused to put on his earphones and rocked back and forth as his verdict was read. It was true, the chief justice said, that this man acted abnormally and suffered from lapses of memory. " 'But there is nothing to show that he is incapable of defending himself.' " Hess had not participated in the physical abominations of the Reich. He had, however, been part of the original Nazi collusion, and he had signed decrees dismembering Czechoslovakia and Poland. Hess was guilty on counts one and two: conspiracy to commit, and the commission of, aggression.

In the press gallery *Newsweek*'s correspondent, James P. O'Donnell, jotted down impressions of the next defendant: "Ribbentrop in worst shape of any man on dock . . . looks as if noose already around neck . . . sweating." The tribunal found the former foreign minister guilty on all four counts.

Field Marshal Keitel sat up like a cadet as his name was called. " 'Superior orders, even to a soldier, cannot be considered in mitiga-

tion where crimes so shocking and extensive have been committed,' " the chief justice read. " 'Guilty on all four counts.' "

Kaltenbrunner wore his customary hangman's scowl. Witnesses
had placed him at Mauthausen, the chief justice read, and " 'testified
that he had seen prisoners killed by the various methods of execution, hanging, shooting, gassing.' " Guilty on counts three and four.

Nikitchenko read the judgment on Rosenberg: " '21,903 art objects seized in the West,' " " 'stripping Eastern Territories of raw
materials,' " " 'cleansing the occupied territories of Jews.' " Guilty
on all four counts.

The verdict for Hans Frank, read by justice Biddle, began well
enough. " 'Most of the criminal program charged against Frank was
put into effect through the police. It may also be true that some of the
criminal policies did not originate with Frank.' " But, Biddle continued, as governor-general of occupied Poland, the defendant had
cooperated in every brutal policy. When he took over, there were 2.5
million Polish Jews. When he left, there were 100,000. Guilty on
counts three and four.

The torpid Frick, onetime minister of the interior, was found guilty
of three of four counts.

Streicher nibbled on K rations as Sir Geoffrey Lawrence resumed
reading the judgment. " 'Streicher's incitement to murder and extermination,' " he said, " 'clearly constitutes persecution on political
and racial grounds and constitutes a crime against humanity.' "
Guilty on count four.

Walther Funk sank almost below the dock as Nikitchenko revived
images of steel boxes full of gold teeth in the Reichsbank vaults. Then
he read, " 'Funk was never a dominant figure in the various programs
in which he participated.' " The justice's words hinted at mitigation
of sentence, but in the end, Funk was found guilty on three counts.

Robert Jackson believed the next defendant was the linchpin required to hold the conspiracy case together. He had told his staff he
regarded Hjalmar Schacht as the most contemptible individual on
trial. "Schacht had freedom of choice. He could have gone with or
against the Nazis. He did more to bring them to power than any other
single individual." Jackson was not alone in this sentiment. William L.
Shirer, in the press gallery for CBS, was convinced that the regime
could not have risen without Schacht's misapplied genius.

Francis Biddle read the verdict. Hjalmar Schacht was acquitted on all counts. Jackson might well believe that it was Biddle out to thwart him again. In fact, Schacht had escaped through a 2–2 voting deadlock. Biddle had voted with Nikitchenko for conviction.

The courtroom was abuzz at an acquittal. After ten guilty verdicts in a row, it had begun to seem that the trial was indeed an elaborate exercise in vengeance. Schacht had cockily predicted his exoneration. He accepted it now without a trace of emotion.

Admiral Dönitz's prospects also looked brighter as Donnedieu de Vabres began, " 'The tribunal is not prepared to hold Dönitz guilty for his conduct of submarine warfare against armed British merchantmen. Nor was he guilty of ordering the killing of survivors.' " Dönitz, however, had set up zones in which his U-boats could sink anything in sight, a clear violation of the Treaty of London on naval warfare. He had also passed along the Commando Order and sought to use concentration camp labor in shipbuilding. He was guilty of counts two and three—commission of aggression and military atrocities. His predecessor as chief of the navy, Grand Admiral Raeder, was judged guilty of counts one, two, and three.

Just days before, Biddle had received a letter from Baldur von Schirach's wife, Henriette. "Our children love America," she had written in English. "It is their grandparents' country. They have a merry imagination of the ice cream and Walt Disney movies. Do I have to tell my children that this America let your father die the most disgraceful death a man can find?" Biddle, reading the verdict, could well ask how many children among the 60,000 Jews that Schirach had shipped to the East had dreamed of ice cream and Walt Disney movies. The court found him guilty on count four—crimes against humanity.

" 'Sauckel argues that he is not responsible for the excesses in the administration of the slave labor program,' " Biddle read. " 'He testifies that insofar as he had any authority, he was constantly urging humane treatment. There is no doubt, however,' " the justice went on, " 'that Sauckel had overall responsibility for the slave labor program, which he had carried out under terrible conditions of cruelty and suffering.' " Guilty on counts three and four.

Jodl sat in defiant dignity as Donnedieu de Vabres recounted his guilt in drafting plans for aggressive warfare and in passing along the Commando and Commissar orders. " 'He cannot now shield himself behind the myth of soldierly obedience at all costs,' " the justice concluded. Jodl was guilty on all four counts.

Suave Konstantin von Neurath, Ribbentrop's predecessor as foreign minister, had helped bring the Nazis to power and had signed death orders put before him by the SS in Czechoslovakia. Guilty on all four counts. Seyss-Inquart, Reich commissioner of the Netherlands, who sent 65,000 Dutch Jews to die, guilty on three of four counts.

Robert Jackson watched Speer, usually so cool, looking tortured, his face a mass of blotches. If he could acquit one defendant, Jackson had concluded, it would be this man. " 'Speer's activities do not amount to . . . preparing wars of aggression,' " Biddle declared. Not guilty of counts one and two. As for atrocities against soldiers and civilians—counts three and four— " 'Speer knew when he made demands on Sauckel that they would be supplied by foreign laborers serving under compulsion. He used concentration camp labor in the industries under his control.' "

To Airey Neave it seemed that the court had found Speer's guilt equal to Sauckel's, until the justice read, " 'Speer himself had no direct administrative responsibility for the program. He was not directly concerned with the cruelty in the administration of the slave labor program. He carried out his opposition to Hitler's scorched-earth program at considerable personal risk.' " Speer was declared guilty on counts three and four. The chief burden for enslaving millions had, however, been placed on Fritz Sauckel. If any sentences less than death were to be handed down, Speer had reason to hope.

Two more acquittals followed. Franz von Papen was found innocent, and Hans Fritzsche, third-rung radio propagandist, was also acquitted. Martin Bormann was convicted *in absentia*. Sir Geoffrey adjourned the court at 1:45 p.m. They would reconvene for sentencing after lunch.

At 2:50 P.M. the justices' door opened, and Sir Geoffrey Lawrence emerged. At his nod the others took their seats. Simultaneously, Hermann Göring, flanked by two white-helmeted guards, entered from the door behind the dock. He looked deathly pale. Sir Geoffrey began to read: " 'Defendant Hermann Göring, on the counts of the indictment on which you have been convicted, the International Military Tribunal sentences you to death by hanging.' " Göring, expressionless, turned on his heel and disappeared through the door.

Rudolf Hess swayed aimlessly, his eyes fixed on the ceiling, again refusing to put on earphones. " 'The tribunal sentences you to imprisonment for life,' " Sir Geoffrey Lawrence announced.

When chief justice Lawrence sentenced Joachim von Ribbentrop to hang, the man slumped, as if taking a body blow. Wilhelm Keitel heard his death sentence and nodded curtly—a subordinate who has just received an order.

"Tod durch den Strang"—death by the rope—Kaltenbrunner heard through his earphones. The same fate befell Alfred Rosenberg.

Hans Frank heard his death sentence and held out his hands in wordless supplication. Wilhelm Frick heard the same sentence with impassivity. Julius Streicher virtually trotted forward, spread his legs wide, and stuck out his chin. *"Tod durch den Strang,"* came over the interpreters' circuit.

Walther Funk and Admiral Raeder received life sentences, Baldur von Schirach twenty years, and Admiral Dönitz ten years. Fritz Sauckel bore an expression of a terrified animal after hearing his sentence: death. General Jodl heard his death penalty, tore off the earphones, and stalked out. Von Neurath received fifteen years; Arthur Seyss-Inquart, death.

Speer emerged through the door. On seeing him, Francis Biddle felt his gloom lift. The vote for Speer's death had been deadlocked at 2–2, with Biddle and Nikitchenko in favor. That night Biddle had not been able to sleep. The case continued to trouble him. Speer, Biddle had finally concluded, was impressionable, idealistic, and prone to hero worship. The next morning he changed his vote. " 'The tribunal sentences you,' " Sir Geoffrey Lawrence announced, " 'to twenty years' imprisonment.' "

Speer felt as if he had been snatched from the edge of an abyss. But as the cold handcuffs encased his wrists and he was marched back to the cellblock, his mood began to shift. Yes, truth and contrition had succeeded in defeating the hangman. But twenty years? He would be an old man before he was free. Lies, smoke screens, and dissembling might have worked better after all.

In the courtroom the missing Martin Bormann was sentenced to death *in absentia*. After 315 days the work of the tribunal was complete. The war-crimes trial had ended.

2

UNCERTAINTY compounded the anxiety of the condemned eleven. The Allied Control Council, which governed Germany, had ruled that the executions were to be carried out fifteen days after sentencing. But did the ACC mean exactly fifteen days later or at some point after fifteen days had elapsed? The defense lawyers were unable to tell their clients exactly when they could expect to die.

As soon as she learned her husband's fate, Luise Jodl sent a telegram to Winston Churchill:

> YOU HAVE ALWAYS BEEN PROUD OF BEING A SOLDIER. YOU WERE THE MAST, WHEN, IN DEADLY PERIL, ENGLAND KEPT THE FLAG FLYING. MAY I, AS THE DAUGHTER OF A BRITISH-BORN MOTHER, APPEAL TO YOU AS A SOLDIER, TO GIVE YOUR VOICE OF SUPPORT FOR THE LIFE OF MY HUSBAND, COLONEL GENERAL JODL, WHO, LIKE YOURSELF, DID NOTHING BUT FIGHT FOR HIS COUNTRY TO THE LAST.

She dispatched similar pleas to General Eisenhower and Field Marshal Montgomery.

A UNITED Press reporter tracked down General Eisenhower at a castle in Ayrshire, Scotland. On the whole he was pleased with the verdicts, Ike said, although "I was a little astonished that they found it so easy to convict military men."

"If the war had gone the other way, General," the reporter asked, "do you think they would have hanged you?"

"Such thoughts you have, young man," Ike answered.

THE corridors of the Palace of Justice were eerily silent. The staff had fled as from a sinking ship. By noon of the day after the verdicts, the British delegation, luggage in hand, had assembled at the Y28 airfield for the flight back to England. Sir Geoffrey Lawrence deflected reporters' questions about the verdicts and shifted the conversation to his pleasure at returning to Hill Farm in Wiltshire.

As for Robert Jackson, by the time his plane reached the mid-Atlantic, he was experiencing profound contentment. He looked around at those who had helped him survive the ordeal—Bill, Elsie Douglas, his colleagues—and assessed the past year. Whatever the failures, the aggravations and defeats, the balance was clear. He had been told that his opening speech would live in the annals of court-room eloquence, and he tended to believe it. As he later wrote to assistant prosecutor Whitney Harris, "The hard months at Nuremberg were well spent in the most important, enduring work of my life."

The French and the Russians soon left too. Nikitchenko and Rudenko had earned the respect, even the affection of their Western colleagues. The Russians' departure, however, had an eye-for-an-eye quality—avenging the Germans' conduct in the Soviet Union. When the U.S. Army went to reclaim the houses where the Soviets had lived, they found them stripped of everything movable—furniture, light fixtures, bathtubs and toilet bowls, and every spoon, dish, cup, and saucer. It was all loaded aboard trucks, headed for the Soviet zone.

ON OCTOBER 1 Lieutenant Tex Wheelis was appointed property officer in charge of the defendants' baggage room. Four days later Hermann Göring requested a meeting with his defense counsel, Otto Stahmer. Göring brought a blue briefcase with him into the visitors' room. It was a gift for his lawyer, he told the guard. The guard immediately summoned Major Teich, Colonel Andrus' deputy, who examined the briefcase, found it empty, and allowed Stahmer to keep it. Teich, however, did not remember anyone's obtaining the re-quired written permission for Göring to enter the baggage room to get Stahmer's gift. Someone else must have retrieved it for him.

Soon afterward Stahmer got word to Emmy Göring that he had been able to arrange one last visit with Hermann. She was logged into the visitors' room at 2:45 p.m. Göring's first questions were about Edda. Did she know of the sentence? Did she understand what it meant? Yes, Emmy answered, Edda knew that her father was going to die. There was something worse than dying, Göring told her. It was the form of death these foreigners had imposed on him. Of one thing she could be sure, Göring said. "They will not hang me."

GUSTAV Gilbert wanted out. After the sentencing on October 1, he had waited in cellblock C to get the condemned men's reactions. It was the logical end of his work, the circle completed. After that he could not get home soon enough. He submitted a request to Colonel Andrus to go home.

The heaviest emotional burden the defendants now bore was not knowing when they would die. Sixteen of them had appealed to the Allied Control Council—their last hope for clemency. The IMT Charter granted the ACC power to reduce, even to commute, sentences. On October 9 the ACC met in closed session for three and a half hours. They made their decisions, but chose not to inform the prisoners immediately.

THE Quadripartite Commission, in charge of planning the executions, questioned Colonel Andrus about his arrangements for a hangman. He explained that Master Sergeant John C. Woods was coming down from Landsberg. A thoroughgoing professional, Woods had "dropped" 347 men in a fifteen-year army career, most recently the Dachau SS murderers.

The colonel obtained fresh briefings on the prisoners' mental health from Lieutenant Colonel William Dunn, recently assigned as prison psychiatrist, and on their physical condition from Dr. Pfluecker and an army physician, First Lieutenant Charles J. Roska. Several of the condemned men, they reported, were taking cold morning showers, and most were joining in the exercise period— except for Göring, who never left his cell.

HANS Frank remained Father Sixtus O'Connor's prize convert. Frank might have partially reneged on his renunciation of the Nazi regime, but he had held faithful to his return to the church. His present circumstances were such a mockery of the prestige he had sought all his life that he had no quarrel with his death sentence. An end to thinking and feeling was, he told the priest, a gift.

KEITEL pleaded with Dr. Pfluecker to use his influence to stop the mournful music. Every night the organist played "*Schlafe, mein Kindchen, schlaf ein*"—"Sleep My Little One, Sleep." The song reminded Keitel of his lost sons, dead or missing in the invasion of the Soviet Union, which their father had helped launch.

Pfluecker promised that he would speak to Colonel Andrus about the organist. Alone in his cell, Keitel understood fully, at last, the old proverb "Hell is truth seen too late." He had served evil with the same soldierly devotion with which he would have served good. His crime was that he had made no distinction.

COLONEL Andrus delivered the news to the prisoners after church services on Sunday, October 13: The ACC had rejected all appeals for clemency. The day before, he had checked the latest psychiatric reports on his wards. Lieutenant Colonel Dunn had warned of potential difficulty with Sauckel and Ribbentrop; he described the latter as "a house that was not built of very good material originally and was now in the process of disintegration." As for Göring, Dunn reported, "He will seize any opportunity to go out fighting."

Alfred Jodl, on the other hand, received word of the ACC decision with customary stoicism. He knew of Luise's efforts—another dream to be dashed. Winston Churchill had replied that he had passed her communication to Clement Attlee, the new prime minister. Montgomery had reacted similarly. Her telegram to Eisenhower had been returned with a note: "Addressee has left town. No forwarding address."

ON SUNDAY evening Gilbert made a last visit to the prison, asking the condemned men how they felt about the denial of their appeals. Sauckel displayed the most palpable fear of dying. He had always done what he was told, to the best of his ability, he said to the psychologist. How could he now be a condemned criminal? Yet as Gilbert discussed the collapse of Sauckel's appeal, a ray of reality appeared to penetrate that modest intelligence. "We have an old saying, Doctor," Sauckel said. " 'The dogs will always catch the slowest one.' "

Göring lay on his cot, apathetic yet curiously alert about certain matters. He questioned Gilbert closely on one point: Was there absolutely no possibility that he would be allowed to face a firing squad? None, Gilbert answered. It was just as well, Göring said. He had heard the Americans were poor shots.

His rounds completed, Gustav Gilbert left cellblock C for the last time.

ON MONDAY, October 14, the cellblock bustled with the customary morning routine for all but Göring, who lingered in the corridor, talking to Tex Wheelis, while the other prisoners mopped their cells.

The guards liked having Lieutenant Wheelis on duty. His supervision was marked by an amiable laxity. Göring next spoke intently to Dr. Pfluecker, until the guards locked him up again.

In his cell Göring could slip his hand into the cavity where the flush pipe entered his toilet bowl. There he would find the cold, hard, reassuring tip of the cartridge. Inside was a glass vial of cyanide. How the cartridge had traveled from the baggage room to its present hiding place was known only to him. It was probably Tex Wheelis who was an unwitting accomplice, retrieving from that room the gifts Göring had given to him and to Stahmer.

MONDAY afternoon Colonel Andrus found Master Sergeant John C. Woods, the Third Army executioner, waiting in his office. The potbellied, ruby-faced sergeant commanded a certain awe wherever he served. Woods said that he had been told he would do the job early on Wednesday, the sixteenth. True, Andrus said. The Quadripartite Commission was meeting at this moment to determine the exact hour and the disposition of bodies and personal effects.

Andrus reminded Woods that secrecy was vital. They did not want to trigger any fuss by the Germans—demonstrations, escape attempts, or uprisings. Woods explained that he had managed to get his team and equipment into town unobserved, traveling by back roads during the night, avoiding the reporters who had virtually staked out the city. His crew was now waiting at the Nuremberg military district headquarters.

Andrus handed Woods a list of the heights and weights of the eleven condemned men. A basketball game would be under way tonight in the makeshift gym next to the exercise yard, Andrus said. That was the best time to slip into the yard. The noise of the game would help cover Woods' arrival.

WILLI Krug, on the third tier, was awakened after midnight by hammering and the sound of voices but soon fell back asleep. Dr. Pfluecker heard the noise too, as did Albert Speer, whose speculations sent a chill down his spine.

WHILE his men assembled the equipment in the gym, Woods ran his hands over the ropes, flexing them until he was satisfied that he had achieved the right elasticity. He should have tested them with weights first, but could find none in the prison. He began weaving the nooses. By the time he finished, the hammering was stilled.

In the middle of the gym stood three gallows, painted black, eight feet high, each approached by thirteen wooden steps. Woods mounted the first gallows and shifted his weight, testing its stability. A metal hook hung from the crossbar. Woods attached a noose to the hook. A lever jutted from the floor. Woods yanked it. The trapdoor opened with a metallic screech. He gave the lever a drop of oil. He repeated the ritual at each of the scaffolds.

One more task remained. His men strung a black curtain at one end of the gym and, behind it, placed coffins and stretchers. By then dawn was washing away the night. They piled into their vehicles and drove out of the prison yard.

3

THE day began like any other in the fixed round of their lives. Willi Krug collected the washbasins; the prisoners cleaned their cells and breakfasted on oatmeal and coffee. For all the surface calm, they kept asking Krug, Was this the day?

The POW barber came to Hermann Göring's cell first, as usual. The escort guard handed him a blade, which the barber inserted into Göring's razor. The escort and the cell guard chatted about baseball. As the barber was leaving, Göring asked him, Could this be the day?

Ribbentrop complained of insomnia to the army physician, First Lieutenant Roska. Roska said that Dr. Pfluecker would bring the usual sedatives that evening. The former foreign minister read to him a letter he had just written to his wife: "Millions have fallen. The Reich is destroyed and our people lie prostrate. Is it not right that I too should fall? I am perfectly composed and will hold my head high, whatever happens. I will see you in another world." Roska was impressed that this "disintegrating personality" had revealed unexpected dignity.

Roska interrupted Keitel in the midst of work on his memoirs. The field marshal was downcast but told the doctor he felt fine, and went back to his writing. Tomorrow would be October 16. Five years ago, to the day, he had drafted the Reprisal Order.

Chaplain Gerecke and Father O'Connor sat in the prison office discussing the World Series game to be played that night. Gerecke was ready to put ten dollars on his hometown St. Louis Cardinals. O'Connor, ordinarily a Dodger fan, settled for the Boston Red Sox. Dr. Pfluecker listened, understanding nothing. A guard arrived and said that the colonel wanted to see them in his office.

Andrus was subdued. He had just received word from the Quadripartite Commission. The condemned men were to be awakened at 11:45 this evening. They would receive their last meal and then be taken to the gym, where the executions would begin after midnight. Could they be told now? Pfluecker asked. No, Andrus said. Until they were awakened tonight, all was to proceed normally.

THAT afternoon Father O'Connor visited Frank, Kaltenbrunner, and Seyss-Inquart to ask if they would like to make their confessions and take Communion. He read the alarm in their eyes and, to their inevitable questions, pretended that he had no information.

Dr. Pfluecker asked the corporal of the guard, Sergeant Denzil Edie, to accompany him to Göring's cell. He wanted to give Göring a light sedative, he said. Edie watched Pfluecker take Göring's pulse and give him a small white pill. Göring prodded the doctor for the latest word. The colonel's warning rang fresh in Pfluecker's ears. All he dared say was, "This night might prove to be very short." Immediately upon Pfluecker's departure, Göring seated himself at the flimsy table and began writing in a bold, vigorous hand:

> To the Allied Control Council:
> I would have had no objection to being shot. However, I will not facilitate execution of Germany's Reichsmarschall by hanging! I feel no moral obligation to submit to my enemies' punishment. For this reason, I have chosen to die like the great Hannibal.*

He signed his name with a flourish.

Hermann Göring saw himself as a man of honor. Certain people in this prison had shown him kindness at some risk to themselves, especially Wheelis and Dr. Pfluecker. He owed them something. He took

---

*Hannibal, a second-century B.C. Carthaginian general, took poison rather than surrender to the Romans.—THE EDITORS

another sheet of paper and began, "To the Commandant: I have had the poison capsule with me since the beginning of my imprisonment." He explained that he had hidden it "here in the cell so well that in spite of repeated and thorough searches, it could not be found. None of those responsible for the searches is to be blamed." The next letter was to his wife.

> My one and only sweetheart, after serious consideration and sincere prayer to the Lord, I have decided to take my own life, lest I be executed in so terrible a fashion by my enemies. My life came to an end when I bade you farewell for the last time. Ever since then, I have felt wonderfully at peace with myself and consider my death a deliverance. I take it as a sign from God that throughout all the months of my imprisonment, I was left with the means which now set me free of my temporal existence. All my thoughts are with you and Edda and my dearest ones. My last heartbeats are for our great and eternal love.

He penned a note to Chaplain Gerecke asking his forgiveness but saying, "For political reasons, I had to act this way." He placed the four letters in an envelope and put them under his blanket.

AMONG the people emerging from army staff cars in front of the courthouse was Dr. Wilhelm Hoegner, minister president of Bavaria, chosen by the Americans as a German witness for the executions. Inside the courthouse, Hoegner was directed to a room, where the witnesses were gathering. In addition to eight pool reporters and four Quadripartite Commission members, thirty others would witness the final act of the trial, including doctors, chaplains, and German civil officials, such as Hoegner. Colonel Andrus began reading seating assignments in the gym.

THE colonel had imposed a communications cutoff between the prison and the outside world. The only exception he had agreed to was one phone call to the prison office after each inning to give the score of the World Series. The game was tied, and Chaplain Gerecke, Father O'Connor, and a handful of guards impatiently awaited the next ring of the phone.

Suddenly shouts of "Corporal of the guard!" and heavy footsteps echoed down the corridor. Staff Sergeant Gregory Tymchyshyn came bursting into the prison office. "Chaplain, chaplain, there's something wrong with Göring!" he shouted. Gerecke followed the sergeant to cell 5, where Göring was lying on his back, his right hand dangling over the side of the bed, his face a sickly green. Froth bubbled in one corner of his mouth as he breathed loudly and unnaturally. Gerecke took his pulse. "Good Lord," he said, "this man is dying." Gerecke ordered a guard to fetch Dr. Pfluecker. The chaplain asked PFC Harold Johnson, the cell guard, what had happened. Johnson had seen Göring bring his arm to his face, fist clenched, as though shielding his eyes. Göring had then let his hand fall back. That was at exactly 10:44 p.m., the GI said. About three minutes later Göring had started making choking noises. That was when he had shouted for the corporal of the guard.

Dr. Pfluecker arrived as Göring exhaled for the last time. The doctor took his pulse. There was nothing to be done, he said. The army doctor, Lieutenant Roska, must be summoned. Pfluecker pulled back the blanket, revealing two envelopes resting on Göring's stomach. Captain Robert Starnes, the chief prison officer, arrived, and Pfluecker handed him the envelopes. Starnes felt something heavy in one and extracted a cartridge with a removable cap. In the other he found Göring's letters.

Dr. Roska made his way through the crowd outside Göring's cell. He was immediately struck by the odor of bitter almonds. He ran his finger around the inside of Göring's mouth and brought out tiny shards of glass. "Cyanide," Roska said.

COLONEL Andrus was giving the witnesses the order of the executions when the call came. The colonel had better get over to the cellblock right away, Captain Starnes urged. Andrus hurried to Göring's cell. He stared at the face, now a concrete gray. Andrus glanced at his watch: 11:09 p.m. He left the cell to phone the Quadripartite Commission.

The four commission members arrived within minutes and cleared the cell of all but the two doctors. Andrus asked to be excused. It was his responsibility to inform the other prisoners that their sentence was about to be carried out.

The commission members pressed the doctors for details. Cyanide acted swiftly, Roska explained. Death could occur in three to five minutes. The four men began debating their alternatives. The sensible thing, they concluded, was to appoint a board to begin an immediate investigation, and to proceed with the executions.

General Rickard came out of the cell, looking for Colonel Andrus. He saw the prisoners, each handcuffed to a guard, sitting on their cots in their cells, the doors open. A last meal of sausage, potato salad, and fruit salad rested on their laps. Few touched the food. Rickard located Andrus and told him that he needed two senior officers from the ISD to serve on an investigating board. He himself would provide the board president. One more thing—Andrus would have to tell the eight reporters in the pool what had happened.

The colonel returned to the room where he had sequestered the reporters. "Göring is dead," he began. "He committed suicide by poisoning himself." They peppered him with questions. "The Quadripartite Commission is investigating," the colonel replied. "I have no further details." They made a bolt for the door and then realized they were locked in. The executions would proceed on schedule, Andrus told them. The reporters would be taken to the gym at the appropriate time.

COLONEL Andrus walked behind Joachim von Ribbentrop the thirty-five yards from the cellblock across the exercise yard to the gym. At the entrance Andrus removed his helmet and bowed stiffly. The German, his sparse gray hair whipped by the wind, returned the bow. To Andrus' relief Ribbentrop had walked steadily, head held high, hands handcuffed behind him. The colonel remained outside the gym. He had been with these men too long to want to watch them die.

The time was 1:11 a.m. as Ribbentrop went through the door. Two of Sergeant Woods' men removed his handcuffs and retied his hands with a leather strap. Most witnesses sat at tables; a few others stood. Ribbentrop was led to the gallows on the left. Woods' plan was to use two gallows and hold the third in reserve. An American army colonel stood at the foot of the steps and asked the prisoner to state his name. Ribbentrop did so in a firm voice, then mounted the stairs. Waiting at the top were Chaplain Gerecke and a stenographer, poised to record his last utterance. Another of Woods' men bound Ribbentrop's legs at the ankles. Ribbentrop was asked if he had anything to say. "My last wish," he said, "is that Germany realize its destiny and that an understanding be reached between East and West. I wish peace to the world." Woods slipped the noose over Ribbentrop's neck and a black hood over his head. Woods stepped back and yanked the lever. The trapdoor opened with a crash, and the body disappeared.

Two minutes later Field Marshal Keitel stepped briskly up the stairs of the middle gallows, as if he were mounting a reviewing stand. As he turned around to face the witnesses, he could see the rope to his right twisting slowly. "More than two million soldiers went to their death for the fatherland before me," he said. "I now join my sons. *Deutschland über Alles!*"

After the trap was sprung on Keitel, the colonel in charge asked General Rickard if the witnesses might smoke while they waited for the doctors to pronounce the prisoners dead. Roska and a Russian physician disappeared behind the black curtain at the rear of Ribbentrop's scaffold, one carrying a flashlight, the other a stethoscope.

Fifteen minutes passed. The witnesses began to eye one another uneasily. They talked in hushed tones about the broken neck that was supposed to produce merciful, almost instant death. The doctors finally emerged. Ribbentrop was dead, Roska announced. Two GIs brought the body out on a stretcher and set it on top of a coffin behind the black curtain. The American colonel gave the signal to bring in Kaltenbrunner, who was hanged while Father O'Connor, wearing a Franciscan habit, prayed next to him.

Rosenberg died wordless. Frank faced his executioners with the beatific smile of a man happy to throw off the burden of life. Frick stumbled on the top step and had to be caught.

A commotion broke out at the entrance to the gym. Two GIs propelled a resistant Julius Streicher through the door. At the gallows he refused at first to give his name, screeching instead, "Heil Hitler!" After Streicher disappeared through the trapdoor, an eerie moan persisted. Woods descended the steps and vanished behind the curtain. Soon the moaning stopped.

Albert Speer, from his cell on the second tier, could hear the guards call out the names one by one. This time it was "Sauckel."

Standing on the gallows, eyes darting wildly, the man cried out, "I am dying an innocent man!" Jodl arrived, the collar of his tunic sticking up. He licked his lips nervously as Woods slipped the hood over his head. The last to die was Arthur Seyss-Inquart, at 2:45 a.m.

Four GIs came into the gym bearing a stretcher covered by an army blanket. They set the stretcher down between the first two gallows. The colonel asked the witnesses to come forward. As they did, he pulled off the blanket and revealed the corpse of Hermann Göring.

Lieutenant Maurice McLaughlin, the official photographer, stepped behind the curtain. No one was to doubt that these men were dead, the commission had told him. McLaughlin inserted the first flashbulb and began shooting Göring. As he worked, he noticed bloody bruises about the mouths and noses of several of the bodies.

IT WAS still dark when two army trucks pulled up alongside the gym. The eleven coffins were quickly loaded. The trucks pulled away, escorted by two unmarked cars bearing armed guards. By 7:00 a.m. the small caravan had arrived at a forbidding gray stone building in East Munich's Ostfriedhof Cemetery. The German attendants had been alerted that the bodies of several American soldiers, killed during the war, would be arriving for cremation. Each coffin bore a label. The one marked GEORGE MUNGER held the body of Hermann Göring.

When the cremations were completed, the ashes were taken to a white stucco villa in a Munich suburb. The house was now the U.S. Army's European Theater Mortuary Number One. Shortly afterward a group of army officers stood on the bank of the Contwentzbach, a stream running behind the house. They watched the mortuary staff bring down eleven aluminum cylinders. One by one the ashes were emptied into the water. The cylinders were chopped with axes and smashed flat with bootheels. The Contwentzbach carried the ashes into the Isar River, which conducted them to the Danube, which emptied them into the sea. The Quadripartite Commission had fulfilled its aim—to obliterate any corporeal trace of these men and any relic around which a shrine to Nazism might rise.

MASTER Sergeant John Woods, enjoying the glow of celebrity, held his first press conference. The coarse red face beamed. "I hanged those ten Nazis and I'm proud of it," he said. "I did a good job of it too. Everything clicked. I hanged 347 people and I never saw one go off better."

Cecil Catling, veteran crime reporter for the London *Star*, asked Woods about reports that an unconscionable amount of time had elapsed before some of the men were pronounced dead—seventeen minutes for Ribbentrop, eighteen for Jodl, a startling twenty-eight minutes for Keitel. He further had it on good authority, Catling said, that some of the men's faces were smashed. Woods looked briefly uncomfortable. Any noises heard from hanged men were reflex reactions, he said. And the blood? "Perfectly natural. That happens when the condemned man bites his tongue at the moment of the drop."

What did Catling think of Woods' performance? his colleagues asked later. Rubbish, Catling said. The men had not been dropped from a sufficient height. He had witnessed enough hangings to know that they had experienced not the instant unconsciousness of a broken neck, but death by strangulation. Catling likely had it right. The army never used Master Sergeant Woods as a hangman again.

Ten days after the executions, on October 26, the Quadripartite Commission released a terse one-page report on the suicide. The commission fully endorsed the findings of its three-man investigating board. The members accepted Göring's claim that the cyanide capsule had always been in his possession and that at various times he had secreted the capsule inside the toilet bowl, in his alimentary tract, and in the cavity of his umbilicus. The commission exonerated the cell guard and all other prison personnel of negligence.*

In Washington, Robert Jackson pondered the effect of Göring's dramatic exit on the work of the IMT. Undeniably, the suicide occupied center stage for the moment. But in time to come? The court had delivered its verdict on the accused with some dispatch—in less than a year. History would take far longer, he knew, to deliver its verdict on the IMT. The court's mission had been unprecedented—too novel, too far-reaching for contemporary judgment. Only time and its perspective could unveil the enduring meaning, if any, of those eleven months in room 600.

*The precise details of Hermann Göring's suicide can never be known. That the cyanide capsule initially entered the prison with Göring's luggage appears beyond dispute. It is not credible that he kept it in his cell throughout his captivity. The cells were searched, and fairly often, according to prison records. This author's conclusion is that Göring had conditioned a member of the prison staff, most likely Wheelis, to take items or pieces of luggage from the baggage room for him. And in the last such retrieval Göring withdrew a hidden capsule.

EPILOGUE
THE VERDICT OF TIME

TODAY, half a century later, the validity of the court is still debated. Criticisms that the IMT lacked jurisdiction, that it was imposing ex post facto law, and that it tried only the losers all contain seeds of truth. An editorial in *Fortune* magazine, written at the time, raised the point that, given the destructive power of the atomic bomb, it was futile to argue that there were "legal and proper as against illegal and improper" ways to kill hundreds of thousands of innocent people. The point is not easily gainsaid. Yet Nuremberg's defenders counter that the atomic bomb, however devastating, was used to end a war. The death factories operated by Nazi Germany exterminated people from nations already defeated. A war ending in German victory would certainly have meant not an end to mass murder, but its unfettered continuation.

The trial, in the final analysis, raises the distinction between law and justice. No saint or statesman lost his life or his freedom at Nuremberg. All the men who went to prison or mounted the gallows were willing, knowing, and energetic accomplices in a vast and malignant enterprise. They were all there for valid moral, if not technically perfect legal, reasons; but then, the murderer who gets off on a technicality has experienced law, not justice. The execution of a professional hatemonger like Julius Streicher, if legally debatable, does not begin to compare with the injustice done to a five-year-old sent to a gas chamber, an end encouraged by Streicher's race preachments. It can be argued that evil unpunished deprives us of a sense of moral symmetry in life and that to punish evil has a healthy cathartic effect, confirming our belief in the ultimate triumph of good over evil. Nuremberg may have been flawed law, but it was satisfying justice.

But did the trial have any lasting impact beyond deciding the fate of twenty-one individuals? If so, were those effects salutary? The Nuremberg legacy is mixed. The one indisputable good to come out of the trial is that it documented beyond question Nazi Germany's crimes. To those old enough to remember the first horrifying film images of piles of corpses and mass graves, it is hard to believe that this evidence of our eyes would ever be challenged. However, two generations have had time to grow up with no personal knowledge of World War II. Polls have shown that as many as twenty-two percent of all Americans doubt the Holocaust as historic fact. These people are prey to the revisionists—crackpots at best, masked racists at worst. Not a single defendant at Nuremberg ever denied that the mass killing had taken place, only that he had lacked personal knowledge and responsibility.

Another reward of Nuremberg was to destroy any Nazi dreams of martyrdom. Hermann Göring's predictions of grand statues in public squares never materialized. The Third Reich was a foul creation, and the revelations at Nuremberg made that fact palpable.

Did Nuremberg contribute to a democratic Germany? Arguably, yes, despite the disturbing emergence of neo-Nazis on the edge of German political life today. Since World War II no avowed Nazis have won significant public office in Germany. It cannot be assumed that the same flowering of democracy would have occurred had the Nazi leaders been shot out of hand and had the revelations of the trial thus never become so public.

But what of the brightest hope of the trial? Did it ever deter a single would-be aggressor? Between 1945 and 1992 the world experienced twenty-four wars between nations, costing 6,623,000 civilian and military lives. Ninety-three civil wars, wars of independence, and insurgencies have cost 15,513,000 additional lives. Until recently, no international body had been convened to try any aggressor or any perpetrator of war crimes in any of these 117 conflicts.

Then, in 1992, the ghost of Nuremberg began to stir. On October 6, the U.N. Security Council voted unanimously to establish a commission to collect evidence of war crimes in the former Yugoslavia. The annihilation by Serbia of the Muslims in Bosnia, under the chillingly familiar cry of "ethnic cleansing," outraged world opinion. On February 22, 1993, the U.N. Security Council again voted unanimously, this time to create an international war-crimes tribunal to prosecute atrocities perpetrated in the same region.

Until this moment the example of Nuremberg had remained what one philosopher called "a beautiful idea murdered by a gang of ugly facts." The recent U.N. initiatives raise cautious hopes that reports of this murder may have been exaggerated. By its very occurrence in the past, Nuremberg increases the prospects for effective war-crimes trials in our time. The world now has a legal precedent, set in the Palace of Justice half a century ago. Law that supersedes nations, and justice that penetrates frontiers, may yet be achieved. But, history teaches us, not easily.

WHAT is known of the subsequent lives of the principal figures in the trial:

BURTON C. ANDRUS: Retired from the army; became a professor at the University of Puget Sound in Tacoma, Washington; died in 1977, at age eighty-five. (In his final hours he cried out, "Göring's just committed suicide. I must inform the Council.")

FRANCIS BIDDLE: Retired; wrote his autobiography, *In Brief Authority;* died in 1968, at age eighty-two.

NORMAN BIRKETT: Entered the House of Lords in 1947; died in 1962, at age seventy-nine.

MARTIN BORMANN: Remains were tentatively identified in Berlin in 1972; declared legally dead in 1973 by a West German court.

THOMAS DODD: Served as a member of the U.S. House of Representatives, 1953–57; as a senator, 1959–71; died in 1971.

KARL DÖNITZ: Served his ten-year sentence at Spandau Prison; died in 1981, at age eighty-nine.

HANS FRITZSCHE: After his acquittal at Nuremberg, was convicted by a German court; freed in 1950; died in 1953, at age fifty-three.

WALTHER FUNK: After serving eleven years of a life sentence, released from Spandau Prison in 1957 for reasons of poor health; died two years later, at age sixty-nine.

GUSTAV GILBERT: Completed his book, *Nuremberg Diary,* which came out in 1947, shortly after Douglas Kelley's book; pursued a teaching and writing career in psychology; died in 1977, at age sixty-five.

RUDOLF HESS: Spent the rest of his life in Spandau Prison; supposedly died by his own hand in 1987, at age ninety-three.

ROBERT JACKSON: Returned to the U.S. Supreme Court; served until his death in 1954, at age sixty-two.

DOUGLAS KELLEY: Published *22 Cells at Nuremberg;* committed suicide on New Year's Day, 1957, reportedly with a cyanide capsule.

GEOFFREY LAWRENCE: Elevated to the peerage for his work at Nuremberg, becoming Baron Oaksey; died in 1971.

David Maxwell-Fyfe: Elevated to the peerage, becoming Earl Kilmuir.

Airey Neave: Became a Conservative member of Parliament; served as a key adviser to Prime Minister Margaret Thatcher; killed by an IRA car bomb in 1980.

Konstantin von Neurath: Served seven years of a fifteen-year sentence; released for reasons of poor health in 1954; died two years later, at age eighty-three.

Ion Timofeevich Nikitchenko: Nothing known beyond a Soviet report of his death several years after the trial.

Erich Raeder: Served nine years of a life sentence; released in 1955; died five years later, at age eighty-four.

Roman Rudenko: Became chief prosecutor of the Soviet Union; prosecuted the American U-2 pilot Gary Powers, shot down over the Soviet Union in 1960.

Hjalmar Schacht: After his acquittal at Nuremberg, was sentenced to eight years by a German court; was cleared on appeal in 1950; died in 1970, at age ninety-three.

Baldur von Schirach: Served his twenty-year sentence; released from Spandau Prison in 1966; died in 1974, at age sixty-seven.

Albert Speer: Served his twenty-year sentence; released from Spandau Prison in 1966; wrote two books on his life; died in 1981, at age seventy-six.

Telford Taylor: After serving as chief prosecutor at subsequent Nuremberg proceedings, returned to the United States to practice law, teach, and write; in 1992 published his account of the major Nuremberg trial.

Jack G. "Tex" Wheelis: Served with the army in Korea and later as an ROTC instructor; died of a heart attack in 1954, at age forty-one.

Lucy Grealy

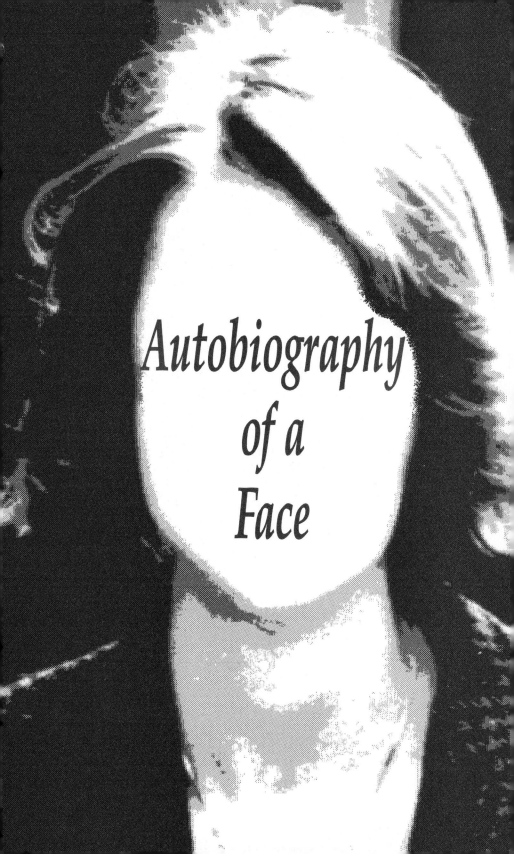

Autobiography
of a
Face

. . . "What's wrong with her face?"
The mothers bent down to
hear this question, and still bent
over, they'd look at me, their
glances refracting away as quickly
and predictably as light through
a prism. I couldn't always hear
their response, but I knew from
experience that vague pleas for
politeness would hardly satisfy
a child's curiosity.

What had happened to me was
any parent's nightmare.

—*Autobiography of a Face*

Prologue

MY FRIEND Stephen and I used to do pony parties together. The festivities took place on the well-tended lawns of the vast suburban communities that had sprung up around Diamond D Stables in the rural acres of Rockland County, New York. Mrs. Daniels, the owner of Diamond D, took advantage of the opportunity and readily dispatched a couple of ponies for birthday parties. In the early years Mrs. Daniels used to attend the parties with us, something Stephen and I dreaded. She fancied herself a sort of Mrs. Roy Rogers and dressed in embarrassing accordance: fringed shirts, oversized belt buckles, ramshackle hats. I'd stand there holding a pony, cringing inwardly with mortification, as if she were my own mother. But as we got older and Stephen got his driver's license, and as Diamond D itself slowly sank into a somewhat surreal, muddy, and orphaned state of anarchy, we worked the parties by ourselves, which I relished.

We would invariably be late for the birthday party, a result of loading the ponies at the last minute combined with our truly remarkable propensity for getting lost. I never really minded, though. I enjoyed the drive through those precisely planned streets as the summer air swirled through the cab of the pickup. When we finally found our destination, we'd clip crepe paper ribbons into the ponies' manes and tails in a rather sad attempt to imbue a festive air. The neighborhoods were varied, from close, tree-laden streets crammed with ranch-style houses to more spacious boulevards dotted with outsized Tudors. Still, all the communities seemed to share a certain carbon copy quality: House after house looked exactly like the one next to it, save for the occasional cement deer or sculpted shrub. A dog would always appear and chase the trailer for a set number of lawns—some mysterious canine demarcation of territory—before suddenly dropping away, to be replaced by another dog running and barking behind us a few lawns later.

I liked those dogs, liked their sense of purpose and enjoyment and responsibility. I especially liked being lost, tooling through strange neighborhoods with Stephen. As we drove by the houses, I gazed into the windows, imagining what the families inside were like. My ideas were loosely based on what I had learned from TV and films. I pictured a father in a reclining chair next to a lamp, its shade trimmed with small white tassels. Somewhere nearby a wife in a coordinated outfit chatted on the phone with friends while their children set the dinner table. As they ate their home-cooked food, passing assorted white serving dishes, they'd casually ask one another about the day. Perhaps someone would mention the unusual sight of a horse trailer going past the house. Certain that these families were nothing like my own, I took pride and pleasure in knowing that I had driven by their houses that day, that I had brushed against their lives, and past them, like that.

Once we reached the party, there was a great rush of excitement. The children would come running from the backyard in their silly hats; their now forgotten balloons—bobbing colorfully behind them—would fly off in search of some tree or telephone wire. The ponies, reacting to the excitement, would promptly take a crap in the driveway, to a chorus of disgusted groans.

My pleasure at the sight of the children didn't last long, however. I knew what was coming. As soon as they got over the thrill of being near the ponies, they'd notice me. Half my jaw was missing, which gave my face a strange, triangular shape, accentuated by the fact that I was unable to keep my mouth completely closed. When I first started doing pony parties, my hair was short and wispy, still growing in from chemotherapy. But as it grew, I made things worse by continuously bowing my head and hiding behind the curtain of hair, furtively peering out at the world like some nervous actor. Unlike the actor, though, I didn't secretly relish my audience, and if it had been possible, I would have stood behind that curtain forever, my head bent in an eternal act of deference. I was, however, dependent upon my audience. Their approval or disapproval defined everything for me, and I believed with every cell in my body that approval wasn't written into my particular script. I was fourteen years old.

"I *hate* this. Why am I doing this?" I'd ask myself each time. But I had no choice if I wanted to keep my job at the stable. Everyone who worked at Diamond D had to do pony parties—no exceptions. Years later a friend remarked how odd it was that an adult would even think to send a disfigured child to work at a kid's party, but at the time, it was never an issue. In fact, my physical oddness seemed somehow to fit in with the general oddness and failings of Diamond D.

The stable was a small place near the bottom of a gently sloping hill. Each spring the melting snow left behind ankle-deep mud that wouldn't dry up completely until midsummer. No one at Diamond D knew how to properly care for horses. Most of the animals were kept outside in three small, grassless corrals. The barn was on the verge of collapse, and the "staff" consisted of a bunch of junior high and high school kids willing to work in exchange for riding privileges. Mrs. Daniels bought the horses at an auction whose main customer was the meat dealer for a dog-food company; Diamond D, more often than not, was merely a way station.

The air of neglect at the stable was the result more of ignorance than of apathy. It was not as if we didn't care about the horses—we simply didn't know any better. And for most of us, especially me, Diamond D was a haven. Though I had to suffer through the pony parties, I was willing to do so to spend time alone with the horses. I thought animals were the only beings capable of understanding me.

I HAD finished chemotherapy only months before I started looking in the yellow pages for stables where I might work. Just fourteen and still unclear about the exact details of my surgery, I made my way down the listings. It was the July Fourth weekend, and Mrs. Daniels, typically overbooked, said I had called at exactly the right moment. Overjoyed, I went into the kitchen to tell my mother I had a job at a stable. She looked at me dubiously.

"Did you tell them about yourself?"

I hesitated, and lied. "Yes, of course I did."

"Are you sure they know you were sick? Will you be up for this?"

"Of *course* I am," I replied in my most petulant adolescent tone.

In actuality it hadn't even occurred to me to mention cancer, or my face, to Mrs. Daniels. I was still blissfully unaware, somehow believing that the only reason people stared at me was because my hair was still growing in. So my mother obligingly drove all sixty-odd pounds of me down to Diamond D, where my pale and misshapen face seemed to surprise all of us. They let me water a few horses, imagining I wouldn't last more than a day. I stayed for three years.

That first day, I walked a small pinto in circle after circle, practically drunk with the aroma of the horses. But with each circle, each new child lifted into the tiny saddle, I became more and more uncomfortable; and with each circuit, my head dropped just a little bit farther in shame. With time, I became adept at handling the horses and even more adept at avoiding the direct stares of the children. I knew that these children lived apart from me. Through them I learned the language of paranoia: Every whisper I heard was a comment about the way I looked, every laugh a joke at my expense.

Partly I was honing my self-consciousness into a torture device sharp and efficient enough to last me the rest of my life. Partly I was right: They *were* staring at me, laughing at me. The cruelty of children is immense, almost startling in its precision. The kids at the parties were fairly young, and surrounded by adults, they rarely made cruel remarks outright. But their open, uncensored stares were more painful than the deliberate taunts of my peers at school, where insecurities drove everything and everyone, like some looming evil presence. In those backyards, where the grass was mown so short and sharp it would have hurt to walk on it, there was only the fact of me, my face, my ugliness.

This singularity of meaning—I *was* my face, I *was* ugliness—though sometimes unbearable, also offered a possible point of escape. It became the one place to point to when asked what was wrong with my life. Everything led to it, everything receded from it—my face as personal vanishing point. The pain these children brought with their stares engulfed every other pain in my life.

The parents would trail behind the kids, iced drinks clinking, making comments about the fresh horse manure in their driveway. If Stephen and I liked their looks, we'd shovel it up; if not, we'd tell them cleanup wasn't included in the fee. Stephen came from a large, all-American family, but for me these grown-ups provided a secret fascination. The mothers had frosted lipstick and long, bright finger-nails; the fathers sported gold watches and smelled of too much aftershave.

This was the late '70s, and a number of corporate headquarters had sprung up just across the border, in New Jersey. Complete with duck ponds and fountains, these "industrial parks" looked more like fancy hotels than office buildings. The newly planted suburban lawns I found myself parading ponies on were a direct result of their proliferation.

My feelings of being an outsider were strengthened by the re-minder of what my own family didn't have: money. We should have had money. This was true in practical terms, for my father was a successful journalist, and it was also true within my family mythology, which conjured up images of fallen aristocracy. We were displaced foreigners, Europeans newly arrived in an alien landscape. If we had had the money we felt entitled to, we would never have spent it on anything as mundane as a house in Spring Valley, New York, or as silly and trivial as a pony party.

Unfortunately, the mythologically endowed money didn't material-ize. Despite my father's good job with a major television network, we were barraged by collection agencies, and our house was falling apart around us. Either unwilling or unable to spend money on plumbers and electricians and general handymen, my father kept our house barely together by a complex system of odd bits of wire, duct tape, and putty, which he applied rather haphazardly and good-naturedly on weekend afternoons. He sang when he worked. Bits of opera, slapped together jauntily with the current top-forty songs and ancient ditties from his childhood, were periodically interrupted as he patiently explained his work to the dog, who always listened attentively.

Anything my father fixed usually did not stay fixed for more than a few months. Flushing our toilets when it rained required coaxing with a Zen-like ritual of jiggles to avoid spilling the contents of the septic tank onto the basement floor. One walked by the oven door with a sense of near reverence, lest it fall open with an operatic crash.

Similarly, when dealing with my mother, one always had to act in a delicate and prescribed way, though the exact rules of protocol seemed to shift frequently. One day running out of milk was a problem easily dealt with, but on the next it was a symbol of her children's selfishness, our father's failure, and her tragic, wasted life. Lack of money, it was driven into us, was the root of all our unhappiness. So as Stephen and I drove through those "bourgeois" suburbs (my radical older brothers had taught me to identify them as such), I genuinely believed that if our family were as well off as those families, the extra carton of milk would not have been an issue.

Though our whole family shared the burden of my mother's anger, in my heart I suspected that part of it was my fault and my fault alone. Cancer is an obscenely expensive illness; I saw the bills. There was no doubt that I was personally responsible for a great deal of my family's money problem; ergo, I was responsible for my mother's unhappy life. During my parents' many fights over money I would sit in the kitchen listening, even after my brothers and sisters had fled to their bedrooms. I stayed as some kind of penance.

The parents who presided over the pony parties never fought, or at least not about anything significant—of this I felt sure. Resentment made me scorn them, their gauche houses, their spoiled children. These feelings might have been purely political, like those of my left-wing brothers (whose philosophies I understood very little of), if it hadn't been for the painfully personal detail of my face.

"What's wrong with her face?"

The mothers bent down to hear this question, and still bent over, they'd look at me, their glances refracting away as quickly and predictably as light through a prism. I couldn't always hear their response, but I knew from experience that vague pleas for politeness would hardly satisfy a child's curiosity.

After I had passed the swing sets and looped around to pick up the next child waiting for a ride near the picnic table, I'd pause confrontationally, imagining that my presence served as an uneasy reminder of what might be. What had happened to me was any parent's nightmare, and I allowed myself to believe that I was dangerous. The parents obliged me in this. They brushed past me, around me, sometimes even smiled at me. But not once in the years that I worked pony parties did anyone ask me directly what had happened.

They were uncomfortable because of my face. I ignored the deep hurt by allowing the side of me that was desperate for definition to staunchly act out, if not exactly relish, this macabre status.

Zoom lenses, fancy flash systems, perfect focus—these cameras probably were worth more than the ponies instigating the pictures. A physical sense of dread came over me as soon as I spotted the thickly padded case, heard the sound of the zipper. I'd automatically hold the pony's halter, careful to keep his head tight and high in case he suddenly decided to pull down for a bite of lawn. I'd expertly turn my own head away, pretending I was only just then aware of something more important off to the side. I'd tilt away at exactly the same angle each time, my hair falling in a perfect sheet of camouflage between me and the camera.

I stood there perfectly still, just as I had sat for countless medical photographs: full face, turn to the left, the right. I've even seen some of these medical photographs in publications. Curiously, those sterile, bright photos are easy for me to look at. For one thing, I know that only doctors look at them, and perhaps I'm even slightly proud that I'm such an interesting case, worthy of documentation.

Once, when my doctor left me waiting too long in his examining room, I leafed through my file, which I knew was off-limits. I was thrilled to find a whole section of slides housed in a clear plastic folder. Removing one, I lifted it up to the fluorescent light, stared for a moment, then carefully, calmly replaced it. It was a photograph taken of me on the operating table. Most of the skin of the right side of my face had been pulled over and back, exposing something with the color and consistency of raw steak. I wasn't particularly bothered; I've always had a fascination with gore. But I made a mental note not to look at slides from my file again, ever.

With the same numbed yet cavalier stance I waited for a father to click the shutter. At least these were photographs I'd never have to see, though I have seen one pony-party photo of me. In it I'm holding on to a small, dark bay pony. I look frail and thin and certainly peculiar, but I don't look anywhere near as repulsive as I then believed I did. There's a gaggle of children around me, waiting for their turn on the pony. My stomach was always in knots then, surrounded by so many children, but I can tell by my expression that I'm convincing myself I don't care as I point to the back of the line.

Fifteen years later, when I see that photo, I am filled with questions I rarely allow myself, such as, how do we go about turning into the people we are meant to be? What relation do the human beings in that picture have to the people they are now? How is it that all of us were caught together in that brief moment of time—me standing there pretending I wasn't hurt by a single thing in this world while they lined up for their turn on the pony, neatly, at my insistence, one in front of the other, like all the days ahead.

One

*K*ER-POW!
I was knocked into the present, the unmistakable *now*, by Joni Friedman's head as it collided with the right side of my jaw. Up until that moment, my body had been running around within the confines of a circle of fourth-grade children gathered for a game of dodgeball, but my mind had been elsewhere. For the most part I was an abysmal athlete, and I was deeply embarrassed whenever I failed to jump deftly into a whirring jump rope or, worse, when I was the weak link yet again in the school relay race. How could one doubt that the order in which one was picked for the softball team was anything but concurrent with the order in which life would be handing out favors?

Not that I considered myself a weak or easily frightened person; in more casual games I excelled, especially at wrestling (I could beat every boy but one on my street) and in taking dares (I would do just about anything, no matter how ludicrous or dangerous, though I drew the line at eating invertebrates and amphibians). I was accorded a certain amount of respect in my neighborhood because I once jumped out a second-story window. I was a tomboy par excellence.

But when games turned official under the auspices of the Fleetwood Elementary phys ed department, everything changed. The minute a whistle appeared and boundaries were called, I transformed into a spaz. It all seemed so unfair. I knew in my heart I had great potential, star potential even, but my knowing didn't translate into hitting the ball that was coming my way. I resigned myself early on, even though I knew I could outread, outspell, and out-test the strongest kid in the classroom. And when I was picked practically last for crazy kickball or crab relays, I defeatedly assumed a certain lackadaisical attitude, which partially accounts for my inattention on the day my jaw collided with Joni Friedman's head.

I do know that the ball I was going for was mine. I hadn't even bothered to call it, it was so obvious; and though it was also obvious that Joni was going to try to steal it away from me, I stood my ground. The whistle to stop playing began to blow just as the ball came toward us. I leaned forward and Joni lunged sideways, and all other thoughts were suddenly and sharply knocked out of me.

I felt the force of our collision in every one of my atoms as I sat—calm and lucid though slightly dazed—on the asphalt. Everyone was running to get on line. I assume Joni asked me how I was, but all I remember is sitting there among the blurred and running legs, rubbing the right side of my jaw, fascinated by how much pain I was in and by how strangely peaceful I felt. It wasn't the sensation of things happening in slow motion; it was as if time had mysteriously but logically shifted onto another plane. In retrospect, I think it's possible I had a concussion.

My jaw throbbed. Rubbing it with my hand seemed to have no effect: The pain was deep and untouchable. Because the pain was genuinely unanticipated, there was no residue of anxiety to alter my experience of it. Anxiety and anticipation, I was to learn, are the essential ingredients in *suffering* from pain, as opposed to feeling pain pure and simple. This alien ache was probably my first and last experience of unadulterated pain.

"Are you all right, dear?"

Interrupted in my twilight, I looked up to see Mrs. Minkin, who was on playground duty that afternoon. She fell into the category of scary adults, not someone to whom I was willing to admit distress.

"I'm fine, thank you."

And I was fine. As quickly as it had happened, the sharp ache in my jaw receded. I stood up and brushed myself off. By the time I was back in the classroom, I had forgotten the incident entirely.

I WAS reminded of it again that evening as I sat on the living-room rug earnestly trying to whip up a book report that I had been putting off for two weeks. Now, to my grave dismay, the report was due the very next day. Gradually I became aware of possible salvation: I had a toothache. This wasn't as welcome a reason for staying home from school as a cold or a fever, because it would entail a visit to the dentist. Had it been only a minor toothache, I'd probably have preferred to suffer the wrath of my teacher rather than my mother's inevitable agitation, but now that I had noticed the ache, it seemed to be worsening steadily.

The dentist and I were already well acquainted. I was cursed with terrible teeth, and Dr. Singer convinced my parents that if there was to be any chance of my adult teeth growing in normally, he must be allowed posthaste to do everything imaginable to my baby teeth. It seemed as if I went to the dentist every week for some mysterious procedure. No one likes the dentist, but what I resented most about Dr. Singer was that he made a practice of lying to me.

"Hold out your thumb, and I'll show you how I'll make your tooth go to sleep so that nothing will hurt it."

I'd hold my thumb out.

"You see, I'll put this medicine on your tooth just like I'm putting it on your thumb," he'd say as he pushed a syringe lightly into my finger, releasing a jet of clear fluid.

"It won't hurt any more than that."

Then he'd turn to his instrument tray, his back blocking my view, and switch syringes. Before I could see what flashed before me, he'd stick the needle deftly into my waiting gums. I was always surprised that a simple stream of fluid could hurt so much. Even after he had performed this dirty trick many times, I believed there must be something extraordinarily wrong with my gums.

As the evening wore on, I could no longer pretend the toothache wasn't there. Finally I went to my mother and confessed my pain. As I had expected, she was angry. Of course, she was angry at the situation, at the bother, at the possible cost, but at that age I had no way to distinguish such subtle gradations. I painfully presumed that her anger was directed at me alone.

Only when my father walked into the room and asked what was going on, did I remember my collision earlier in the day. This new information seemed to irritate my mother even more, especially when my father, characteristically trying to dissolve the tension of the situation, ventured a prognosis. "She's just got a cold in her tooth, that's all. She'll be fine in the morning."

He meant well, but his dismissal of the problem confirmed my mother's belief that she was the only one in the family who faced facts. This was true in a sense, but she never recognized that her anger scared all of us into retreat. By churning problems through her own personal mill, she kept us from ever discussing a problem outright. I was sent off to bed with two aspirins and a promise of reappraisal.

"You've got lockjaw!" my brothers pronounced happily the next morning. They were only too pleased to describe in detail how I would never open my mouth again, how everything I ate from then on would have to come through a straw.

I mumbled back to them as best I could. It was true that I had woken up with my jaw swollen and seemingly locked—it didn't hurt when I tried to open it, so much as it appeared to be stuck—but a diet of milk shakes didn't seem like such an awful fate. Primarily, however, I was excited by the idea that something really *was* wrong with me, that I hadn't been overreacting the previous night; I was authentically sick—no school definitely. I felt cheerful. My mother made an appointment for me to see the family doctor later that morning.

"Well, considering the swelling and this immobility and that she had a hard knock, I'd say it's probably fractured."

A broken jaw. This would be the first of many diagnoses and surely the one most completely off course. Dr. Cantor explained to me that if it was broken, I'd have to have it wired shut so it could heal, but first I had to go over to the hospital to have it x-rayed. I wasn't thrilled with the wired-shut part, but I was too involved with the idea of venturing off to a hospital emergency room to think much about it. My two absolute, hands-down favorite television programs were *Emergency* and *Medical Center,* and the possibility of living out one of these dramas elated me. My mother kindly indulged me as I sat on a trolley in one of the cubicles, humoring me about what an adventure it all was and how jealous my brothers would be. She told me how brave I was and how lucky we all were that this had happened to me and not Sarah, my twin sister, an avowed scaredy-cat. Sarah would have cried horrendously, but I was courageous and didn't cry and thus was good. It seemed a natural enough equation at the time.

The X rays came back. It wasn't a broken jaw, but something called a dental cyst, probably caused by the blow to my jaw forcing one of my back molars down into the gum, nicking the mandible. It was nothing serious, but they would have to operate and remove the cyst right away to avoid an infection. I went back home with my mother to collect my pajamas, and off we went to Pascack Valley Hospital, a small community hospital in the next town. Surgery was scheduled for the following day.

What I remember most from that first night in the hospital is that I didn't sleep very much. I devoted most of the time to a silly conversation about television star David Cassidy with the girl in the bed across from me. At midnight a nurse came along and taped an NPO sign to my bed: *nil per os,* nothing by mouth. I felt special, singled out, and in a condescending tone I explained to my neighbor what it meant, just as the nurse had explained it to me thirty seconds before.

EVERY hospital has its own quirky protocol. Some hospitals make you put on the surgical gown in your room; some make you wait until you reach the OR. Some anesthesia departments have rooms in which you are put to sleep; others take you right on into the operating room itself. Pascack Valley Hospital subscribed to the latter and also, bless their hearts, to the theory that it's best to knock the patient out as quickly as possible and *then* assign the IVs and other assorted needles and tubes to their final bodily destinations. Still living in the fantasy of a television show, and slightly dopey from the preop medication, I was intrigued by the sight of a real live operating room. The gleaming metal and impressive lights were exactly as I'd anticipated. My first authentic surgically masked face peered down at me.

"I'm going to put this mask over your face and give you some air to make you sleepy. It might smell a little funny."

Funny was an understatement. Through the black rubber mask came chemical fumes so alien to me that I thought I would suffocate. I struggled slightly, trying to turn my head away. Someone put a hand on my forehead, and the gesture calmed me instantly.

"Now I want you to close your eyes and breathe and relax and think about nice things. Do you have any pets?"

I began to list the names of the menagerie back home, aware that a faint buzzing was growing louder and louder. The things around me began to lose their borders. It became increasingly difficult to speak. After listing the names of two cats, I was reduced to producing only a syllable at a time with each breath.

"Close your eyes."

This was unthinkable. First, I didn't want to miss a thing, and second, what if they thought I was asleep and began cutting me open when I was merely resting my eyes? This last fear was to haunt me through subsequent operations. Even after I admitted my fear a few years later and had the whole process explained, I remained wary.

I felt nauseated. The gas was overpowering, and finally I couldn't take it any longer and rolled over to vomit. A viscous magenta liquid with swirls of green poured out, staining the white sheet. Someone put a metal basin near me. I still felt nauseated but could bring nothing else up. I lay back and closed my eyes, exhausted from the effort. A strange nurse was standing beside my bed insisting I acknowledge her visually and then, to my great annoyance, verbally. The very last thing I wanted to do was open my eyes, let alone speak to this woman, who was now asking the most ridiculous question I'd ever heard: "Lucinda, what time is it?" I wasn't used to people calling me by my full given name. With an outstretched arm she directed my gaze to a clock on the wall. This is nonsense, I thought. Couldn't she understand that sleeping was the single most desirable act in the world? She asked me again, and only to rid myself of her, I gathered my wits and told her. It was eleven ten. My first operation was over.

Six months later, sometime near Easter, I came home from school with the right side of my face swollen and hot. I'd been going to the hospital sporadically ever since the surgery to have X rays taken of my jaw. A bony knob had appeared on the tip of my jaw, just under my ear, and my mother had asked the doctor about it repeatedly.

"It's just a bony growth; it's nothing to worry about, Mrs. Grealy."

"But surely it's not normal?"

"It's nothing unusual after such surgery, Mrs. Grealy."

The doctor—who wasn't a doctor, but a specialized dentist—smiled condescendingly after each inquiry. Nothing infuriated my mother more than this condescension, which even I at nine years old recognized as endemic in the medical profession. But I was vain and proud when it came to wanting to be different from everyone else, and so far the role of patient had delivered. My teachers had given me a noticeable amount of special treatment, and I'd gained a new level of respect from my friends since going under the knife.

When my mother marched me back to Dr. Cantor's office, it was

with a sense almost of righteousness. It was obvious I had a bad infection that they could no longer ignore, and my heart thrilled when
I heard the words emergency surgery. They had to drain and clean
out the lump, which was looking angrier by the minute.

As far as I was concerned, I was still on a great adventure, the star
of my own television special. Besides, there was yet another unfinished book report looming. Something as impressive-sounding as
emergency surgery had to be worth a long extension as well as another round of presents. It seems odd to me now that a deed as
relatively easy as not crying over a needle was rewarded so lavishly,
while my herculean efforts to simply not fall apart during one of the
many family crises went completely unnoticed.

After the surgery my parents were instructed to take me to the
Strang Clinic, which translated to me as a trip to the city. I was
thrilled. I loved any chance to drive through the filthy, bewildering
streets of New York. At the Strang we met the eccentric Dr. John
Conley, a leading head and neck surgeon. After a thorough examination, he arranged to have me admitted to the children's wing of
Columbia Presbyterian Hospital, known as Babies Hospital.

WHEN a film's heroine innocently coughs, you know that two scenes
later, at most, she'll be in an oxygen tent; when a man bumps into a
woman at the train station, you know that man will become the
woman's lover and/or murderer. In everyday life, where we cough
often and are always bumping into people, our daily actions rarely
reverberate so lucidly. Once we love or hate someone, we can think
back and remember that first casual encounter. But what of all the
chance meetings that nothing ever comes of? While our bodies move
ever forward on the time line, our minds continuously trace backward, seeking shape and meaning there.

As I sat on the playground's sticky asphalt, I had experienced time
in a new way, but perhaps that memory has significance because of
the way my life has unfolded. It seems almost uncanny to me that I
didn't know. How could I not have?

It's impossible for me to revisit this twenty-year-old playground
scene and not wonder why I went right when I should have gone left
or, alternatively, not see my movements as inexorable. If the cancer
was already there, it would have been discovered eventually, though

probably too late. Or perhaps that knock set in motion a chain of physical events that created an opportunity for the cancer to grow, which it might not otherwise have found. Sometimes it is as difficult to know what the past holds as it is to know the future, and just as an answer to a riddle seems so obvious once it is revealed, it seems curious to me now that I passed through all those early moments with no idea of their weight.

Two

A T FIRST there was only the presence of the boy beneath the bed to horrify me, but before I knew it, his father was under there, and then, most shocking of all, even the doctor squatted down and tried his own ineffectual cajoling. This last bit of vaudeville was so . . . so undignified. I was mortified. The boy, a year or two younger than I, wore red pajamas with feet. Partly I felt embarrassed for the father and the doctor, but mostly I found myself deeply embarrassed for the boy. How could anyone sink so low as to hide beneath a bed? This went against every belief I held dear. One had to be good. One must never complain or struggle. One must never, under any circumstances, show fear; and above all, one must never ever cry. I was nothing if not harsh. Had I not found myself in this role of sick child, I would have made an equally good fascist or religious martyr. The subtleties of my first visit to the emergency room, where I'd been praised as good for being brave, were already arranging themselves into a personal credo. At a time when everything in my family was unpredictable and dysfunctional, with my mother recently discharged from a brief stay in a hospital herself, I had been supplied with a formula of behavior for gaining acceptance and, I believed, love. All I had to do was perform heroically, and I could personally save my entire family.

At that point heroism was still fairly easy. I'd been on ward 10 in Babies Hospital for only about an hour. Babies Hospital was nothing like the shining, clean technomiracles I was used to on television and had experienced at the newer Pascack Valley Hospital. The walls here were pale green, and the floor was dark green tiles speckled with gray, worn to an even darker shade where people had paced over the years.

All the doors were wood, and the partitions, strategically placed for viewing purposes, were made of thick sea-green glass reinforced with wire mesh. There were bars on all of the outside windows. Though the hospital was undeniably clean, a dingy air prevailed throughout. In time I came to find this dinginess comforting, more humane than the fascinating but alien landscapes of newer wards I would later visit.

I heard my name called. Again they called me Lucinda. Previously that name had belonged only to the first day of school, but now I recognized it as the property of all people in uniforms standing in the unflattering fluorescent light of hospitals. The doctor asked my parents a number of questions about my mother's pregnancy with me and about my infancy, and sometimes my mother and father had to confer with each other in order to answer. I wasn't used to seeing them pair up like this; I wasn't used to seeing them act so normal, like the parents of my friends in the neighborhood, like parents I had seen on TV. It was generally assumed that we were not a normal family, a feeling we proudly carried and tried to hide at the same time.

WE—my parents, two older brothers, older sister, twin sister, and I—had immigrated to America five years earlier, when Sarah and I were four. My father, a well-known television journalist in Ireland, had been offered a job he couldn't refuse in the States. He packed us all up and had us travel to America by ship. Unlike our earlier countrymen, who had come in steerage, we sailed on the *Queen Mary*. Surely this grand act was to be the harbinger of the riches already awaiting us. As with most of my father's gestures, that voyage was well meant, but later, when things were not going quite as well, it was referred to with scorn; and even later, after his early death, it seemed an act filled with literary bathos, and pointedly sad.

Of course, at the time it was an adventure *extraordinaire*, especially for a four-year-old gathering first memories. My brothers played Ping-Pong on a back deck and sometimes lost the ball over the side. I loved nothing better than to run and stare at its lostness in the churning water far below. The chaos held me tightly, endlessly. The most predictable memory of all, the Statue of Liberty, draws a complete blank; but I remember New York when we disembarked—rainy and filled with broken windows.

"Where are we now?" my twin sister, Sarah, and I asked our mother several days later, in our new kitchen. She stood near the sink, her hair short and ash-blond, her shirt white silk. I was convinced my mother was the most beautiful woman in the world.

"We're in Spring Valley now." She was patient with us.

"But when are we going to America?"

This struck her as funny. Her face lit up, and I knew we'd pleased her, but exactly how escaped me. Spring Valley was just a name, a place, but America—now, that was something big, a whole way of life, an idea, a piece of magic. Judging by the way everyone spoke of it all the time, I was eager to know when we were going to be there.

My older brother Sean was seventeen when we left Dublin; Nicholas a few years younger than he; and Suellen a few years younger than that. For Sarah and me Dublin was just a collection of vague shadows, but for the rest of our siblings Ireland was home. This new place to which they'd been unwillingly transported, America, could never match up. I could not even eat an American candy bar without being reminded by one of my brothers that it stood for the entire political and social inferiority of America. Television, I was told, was vastly superior back in Ireland. Their worst insult became "That's so American." If we were selfish or acted spoiled, we were "becoming American." When we used up all the hot water in the bath, that was an American thing to do. Gradually my earliest memories of Ireland transformed into pure myth. The flawless times of the family were past; I had missed them simply by being born too late. I began a lifelong affair with nostalgia, with only the vaguest notions of what I was nostalgic for.

Apart from its vulgar culture, the worst aspect of America was its politics, according to my brothers. In reaction to our conventional Republican neighborhood in a country different in almost every way from the one they knew, they became radical. Added to the list of insults along with "American" were "bourgeois" and "capitalist"; "American bourgeois capitalist" was the most searing of all. I had no idea of what these things meant, but I developed disdain for them too.

If I intuited that our family was different and in some ways superior, there were also obvious oddities about us. Schoolmates made fun of our accents. Sean had long hair and lived a hippie life, different from the lives of our neighbors' sons. My mother suffered from depression, an illness I could not understand at the time. There were always money problems, even before my father lost his job, and if nothing else, our home's drastic state of disrepair served as a reminder that there were things I had to keep from other people.

SEEING my parents act so much like, well, *parents*—other people's parents—there on Babies 10, surprised me and momentarily fooled me. They spent the entire afternoon with me, talking to doctors, talking to me and to each other. I watched the drama of the boy in the red-footed pajamas unfold as he was eventually extricated from beneath the bed, saw how his mother held him in her lap the entire time the doctor did whatever he was doing to him.

At one point I was sent down to hematology for a blood test. I also visited radiology for a chest X ray. This department was newly renovated and, unlike the rest of the hospital, was painted in bright colors. It was the only floor that actually fitted my picture of a children's hospital. Murals of cartoonish animals and clowns stared merrily at me as I walked down the halls. In the waiting room I found an absurd number of giant stuffed animals sitting dejectedly in the corners. Being all of nine years old, I disassociated myself from all this baby stuff and made a point of looking disdainful and bored. It was of paramount importance that I appear adult, strong, unafraid.

As the day wore on, I began to believe that maybe my parents really were like the other parents after all. Finally, as dinnertime approached, the intern who'd examined me earlier explained to my parents that he was going to do a bone marrow test on me. We were all standing in the hall together. I don't remember whether I was afraid of this test, but when my parents said, "Well then, we'll be off," I looked at them panic-stricken and asked, "Aren't you going to stay with me?" They looked at each other, then back at me, and said something about the traffic, and besides, I wasn't scared, was I?

I felt my face flush. Immediately I regretted all my assumptions. The embarrassment I felt then stays with me still, though, of course, it wasn't embarrassment. It was the moment when I understood unequivocally: I was in this alone.

As IT turned out, there really wasn't much to fear, at least not just then. The treatment room was small and overheated, even cozy. I lay on my stomach on the stiff, clean-smelling white sheets covering the table. The two interns who did the bone marrow test seemed bent on entertaining each other more than me, but I liked them instantly. They had a little routine down, switching into alternately squeaky and rough voices. They even thought it was funny when they pressed down on my numbed lower spine and my legs reflexively kicked the contents of a tray all over the floor. As it clattered on the green tile, I tensed, waiting for a flare of anger. Instead they laughed at themselves, made jokes silly enough that we all groaned, awarded me ludicrously high points for being such a good sport, allowed me to feel at ease, at home even.

This sense of comfort continued in the following days. There were definite problems to face here, but to me they seemed entirely manageable. My father would stop by after work to say hello when he wasn't working too late, while my mother, who hated driving into the city, came in less frequently. Some of the other parents, the ones who came in every day, felt sorry for my lack of visitors and sneaked me contraband food items. I played up to this expertly whenever I sensed a particularly orphan-sensitive audience. My mother would have been appalled if she'd known.

I felt perfectly fine. Each day one test would be scheduled, typically an intricate scan or X ray, and these were relatively painless. I made friends with the other children, quickly discovering the hierarchy on that and all other wards. The truly sick were at the top, of course, and anyone having an operation also ranked. But the real deciding factor was seniority—how long you'd been on the ward—and in this, Derek was king.

Derek was a handsome boy with a serious case of asthma. He had been in and out of the hospital many times already, and by the time I arrived, he had a week's stay under his belt. Despite his asthma, he seemed to feel fine, and the two of us together, relatively healthy and with far too much time on our hands, spelled trouble.

Afternoons were long. Sunlight pushed in past the barred windows and lay down heavily on the green floor. When the nurses shut off the bright overhead lights, you could almost hear them sigh, and this was the moment Derek and I waited for each day—nap time, when the ward was quiet and the nurses sat around their station pretending not to care what we were up to as long as we didn't make noise.

Sometimes the afternoons were planned for us. We were taken to another floor with a playroom that boasted a large, ornate dollhouse, a collector's item probably. You could only look at it from behind a glass partition. It was really a doll's mansion, with dozens of intricate rooms filled with luxuries like tapestries and fluffy feather comforters on brass beds. There were perfect little spoons and forks, and old-fashioned items like washboards and iceboxes and chamber pots. This house had absolutely nothing to do with any of our lives. Most of the children in the hospital came from the surrounding poor neighborhood, and this little house was a rarefied version of everything they would never have.

Every once in a while a movie was shown, usually just cartoons, in a lecture hall in another part of the hospital. The movie itself was generally awful, but Derek and I enjoyed making fun of it later and also guessing what was wrong with the other kids who filed in with us, pushing their IV poles, holding parts of themselves delicately. Anyone who looked truly shocking or particularly ill or sported an impressive piece of machinery was treated with respect. There was an implicit honor code: You never stared openly, you always did whatever you had to to help, you were always extraordinarily patient. Not that we weren't perfectly capable of being little brats, but in the hospital a kind of dignity reigned.

It was when nothing official was scheduled that Derek and I got up to our own tricks. At first we stayed on the ward, sneaking around in the storage room or any other place that carried a forbidden air. Gradually, we took to sneaking off the ward, where we risked getting caught by a dutiful nurse. The lobby was attractive for its gift shop. We stole get-well cards and gave them to other patients, signing them "Love and Kisses, Michael Jackson." We thought this was hysterical. A few times we ventured down near emergency. That waiting room had all the good magazines, and there we lived in eternal hope that someone covered in blood would stagger in through the door, maybe even clutching a knife sticking out of his heart. It never happened.

Though it seemed like an eternity, that hospital stay probably lasted only two weeks or so. Every day I'd have some test, and it never occurred to me to ask what was going on, what the tests were for, what the results were. At least this is how I remember it, though my mother tells it differently. In my version, when the day came, the doctors took both my parents into my room alone. They stayed in there a long time. Finally my mother emerged, explaining that I was going to have an operation on my jaw, but I could come home for the weekend first.

I remember being thrilled, as if I'd only heard the part about going home for a weekend. My mother looked at me aghast. She was acting strangely, I thought, not herself. I had to explain that it wasn't the operation I was excited about. I knew that if I went home for a weekend, I'd get special treatment, and I did. My father let me go horseback riding not once, a big treat in itself, but twice. When my sister complained about the favoritism, my father virtually snapped, an uncharacteristic response; but I was too excited by the proximity of horses, with their sweet, grimy smell, to even try to figure it out. I don't remember going to visit my school at all.

In my mother's version, when she came out of my hospital room, I jumped up, hearing only that I was going home. But after that, she says, the doctor asked to speak to me, as if I were an adult. He told me I had a malignancy. He explained they would do everything they could, that I should do my best to get well and they would help. As my mother tells it, I did go to school, where I thanked my teachers and classmates for the cards they'd sent me. I told them I had a malignancy. My mother said I seemed rather happy about it, and my teachers were shocked by my attitude. I told them all, probably with pride, that I was going to have a *big* operation now.

Some years later, I don't remember exactly how many, as my family was milling about the kitchen and I was leafing through the paper at the table, someone dated an event as something that had happened "before Lucy had cancer." Shocked, I looked up.

"I had cancer?"

"Of course you did, fool. What did you think you had?"

"I thought I had a Ewing's sarcoma."

"And what on earth do you think that is?"

My family seemed rather incredulous, but it was true. In all that time not one person ever said the word "cancer" to me, at least not in a way that registered as pertaining to me.

SUNDAY afternoons in the hospital were the stillest and longest—formless hours to be gotten through. With all the departments closed, there was none of the week's bustle. The familiar nurses were off, leaving us in the hands of aides who didn't care if we were entertained or not. There were more of the other patients' visitors to watch, obscure relatives who made the trip from out of town bearing useless flowers and ornately wrapped toys. But I grew tired of scrutinizing them, grew to recognize the swirling patterns and dynamics of every family that walked onto the ward complaining of how hard it was to park around here, how long the elevators took.

I could always count on Derek, who would appear beside me when I most needed him, decked out in his blue bathrobe with COLUMBIA PRESBYTERIAN in fading black letters across the chest. There were things about Derek I didn't understand. Though I never would have admitted it to him, I envied the fact that he lived in the city. I thought it made him exotic. Once, I awakened to find him standing over me, and two other boys peering in from the doorway. He'd kissed me. Perhaps they had wanted to watch, thinking I'd be grossed out, but my reaction obviously disappointed them. All I felt was somewhat confused as to why Derek, who looked equally confused, would want to do such a bizarre thing.

Three

N
O ONE clearly explained to me what was about to happen. Mary, the head nurse, did call me over at one point. Derek tagged along. Mary was one of my favorite nurses, always kind and always the one most likely to crack a joke as she walked into the room with that dreaded basin, the one they carried needles in. Though I didn't mind blood tests, I'd developed a fear of preop injections.

By now I'd had three operations—the latest a bone biopsy. Usually they gave two injections before taking you down to the OR, one in each thigh, and the shots hurt like bad leg cramps for several minutes. Most nurses offered the hearty and useless advice "Rub that spot hard!" or "Squeeze your toes!" But not Mary. She'd stand over you, needle poised, and announce her own joking version of comfort: "Now, this isn't going to hurt me one little bit."

I specifically asked Mary if she'd give me the injection before my fourth operation, the one that involved removing the tumor and no more than one third of the jaw. She seemed disappointed when she told me that she wouldn't be on duty for it. Late that afternoon, before she left, she called me over. "This is a big operation you'll have tomorrow. You know that, don't you?"

I'd been told it would take a whole four hours, which was certain to elevate my social status on the ward. Though I'd felt sick after my other encounters with anesthetics, I didn't comprehend what a four-hour surgery would mean. Somewhat chagrined at being spoken down to, I told her I understood everything perfectly, unaware that I hadn't a clue how sick I was or what was going to happen.

She looked me right in the eye. "Do you know you'll look different afterward?"

For Derek's sake I made a joke about bandages, about looking like the Mummy. Horror movies were a major source of entertainment for Derek and me. Between us, we'd seen every bad monster movie ever made. Mary realized she wasn't getting anywhere with me. She shifted her weight and looked down at her shoes. After a few moments of contemplation, she left.

The next afternoon, when I woke up in recovery, I couldn't quite figure out where I was or what had happened to me. My entire body ached, and when I tried to speak, nothing happened. I didn't realize I had had a tracheotomy. There was a constant loud sound of machines, and at one point I amused the nurses, who showed me how to speak by placing a finger over the hole in my throat, by asking if they could turn them off so I could get some decent sleep. My parents came in together for a minute, stood at the foot of the bed, and considered me from what seemed a long, long way away.

With no room in ICU, they decided to keep me overnight in recovery. For the first few hours I vomited up large amounts of blood I'd swallowed during the procedure. Drainage tubes drifted down onto the pillow beside me, displaying the slightly shifting red and golden fluids of my body. An IV hung over me, dripping steadily and endlessly, producing a hypnotic effect similar to that of the watery chaos I'd been drawn to off the stern of the *Queen Mary*. If I lay perfectly still, I felt no pain. I dozed and woke, dozed and woke all night, slept my half sleep with an image of myself as swaddled.

BIZARRELY, after they removed half my jaw, I limped. It was my first day up out of bed. I was back on ward 10, in my own room and with my own nurses around the clock, and I was going to traverse the entire four feet to the bathroom. This required a certain amount of preparation, of disconnecting tubes and wires.

"Why are you limping? They didn't do anything to your legs, Chicken-chops."

My mother was watching the nurse help me. I liked it when she called me Chicken-chops, the name she used with any of us when we were ill. I placed my finger over my throat.

"I don't know."

It was everything I could do just to say those three words. My non sequitur limping seemed to amuse the nurse and my mother, and eventually it amused me. None of us understood that the body is a connected thing.

FLUID was the major issue. I refused to drink enough. Or rather, that's how they perceived my inability to down more than a quarter of a glass at a time. Every swallow left me breathless; two swallows exhausted me; three and then four made me feel I should be congratulated. Instead they made an embarrassing chart and pinned it on the door, a Magic Marker record of every cubic centimeter I consumed. They thought the threats to never take out my IV would impel me, but they misjudged. I gladly would have spent the rest of my life on an IV if they would just leave me alone.

Day after day passed, and still I could barely manage a fraction of the ten glasses a day they wanted of me. Ten glasses. An unimaginable sum! How could I explain that I just wanted to lie there, becoming ever more intimate with my body?

I knew all of my body's rhythms now, all of its quirks. The smell of my wound was sweet and ever present, the skin on my elbows and heels as sore and red as holly berries. Though at first I'd dreaded the daily injections, now I welcomed the dozy contentedness they offered. I learned that all I had to do was relax, that fear was the worst part. Even the worst pains could be rendered harmless if you relaxed into them, didn't fight. I was given a full-time plug for my trachea, but I put little effort into speaking, reducing my vocabulary to only syllables at a time. I grew weaker and weaker.

They started feeding me through a gastronasal tube, which had been inserted earlier. Each mealtime a tray arrived with my name on it, a tray filled with liquefied everything, even turkey. I asked them to let me smell each container before they poured it into the tube. Aroma alone started to revive me. Finally, at about five in the morning of my tenth birthday, I tricked a nurse into giving me some orange Jell-O. It was the first thing I'd eaten in a week, and instantly I felt better.

When my whole family came to visit me for my birthday, I sat in a wheelchair and gazed at them, feeling splendid. I could tell they were shocked at the sight of me. I had been an absolutely normal nine-year-old the last time they saw me, some ten days before. My older sister spoke politely to me, as did my twin sister. They'd never been polite to me before, and I knew that a chasm had opened between us. Suddenly I understood the term "visiting." I was in one place, they were in another, and they were only pausing.

MY MOTHER was the visitor *extraordinaire*. She'd arrive each afternoon, give me whatever bit of news or information about my health she had as quickly and simply as possible, then sit down in a chair and begin knitting. She'd spend the entire visit knitting. Human presence is the important part of visiting, and she understood that. Other visitors were more awkward—friends of the family who'd stop by and stand over me for long, clumsy minutes, trying to engage me in conversation, when all I wanted was for them to sit down and not say a word.

My father was the worst visitor. He loved puns and would think of a more terrible one each day. But in the awkward silence that followed his rehearsed routine, what should he do then? Sometimes he'd put on a surgical mask and make a joke about Dr. Dad, a joke I'd seen dozens of other fathers make with their kids. Then he'd sit down and stare intently at the drip of my IV. He could sit like that for a long time. I knew how hard it was for him, and he probably knew how hard it was for me.

On certain afternoons after that first big operation, he'd come on his lunch break, though he didn't have much time to visit, with his hectic work schedule. We both knew that his visits were slow and sorrowful for both of us and that it was okay for him to come only occasionally. One day I heard his step echoing toward me down the hall. Carefully, not entirely sure what I was intending, I got into bed and closed my eyes. His loud breathing and hard-soled shoes entered the room. Silence stood over me for a minute or two. I heard hands fumble around in coat pockets, the crinkle of paper, a pen covering it with soft thips of sound. Then at once everything was leaving the room, pulling out of it and leaving behind that specific, hollow sound of emptiness. I opened my eyes and read the note I found on my night table: "Lucy, I was here but you were sound asleep. I didn't want to wake you. Love, Daddy." I felt I'd let us both off the hook, yet after that, the afternoon seemed interminable.

GRADUALLY I began to improve. I gained strength, the various tubes were removed, and walking became less of a heroic effort. I still resisted speaking, however, keeping my answers to a simple yes or no. I allowed people to believe speaking was difficult, though my mother knew better and kept at me constantly. One day Mary came in when I was alone and announced that I was much better now, that someone else needed this room and I was to be transferred to the floor above. She left as casually as she had come. A few minutes later an aide came in to help me pack. I excused myself and went into the bathroom, where I was overcome by weeping, the first tears I'd shed since I'd been in the hospital.

How could they throw me out like this? I had come to believe that the nurses liked me, that they were my special friends, yet now I was just being tossed away. Only then did I begin to realize how accustomed I'd grown to being taken care of. I hadn't even had to wash myself. And as much as I hated to concede any points to my mother, I knew I had become too passive. An ornate surge of grief came over me. Luckily, I tired easily, and the weeping could go on for only a few moments. I wiped my eyes. Ashamed of myself, I went back into the room to help the aide gather my things into a red plastic disposal bag. My mother had taken my overnight case home early on, because it took up too much room.

The new ward was laid out exactly like ward 10, but it was filled with a different kind of patient. These were teenage girls who giggled with one another and told jokes that I didn't get about the doctors, especially one Dr. Silverman, whom they all seemed to be in love with. The girls were skeletally thin; knowing nothing of anorexia, I wondered what was wrong with them.

I spent a week on the new ward, but I never committed to making friends there. Derek came up to see me once or twice, but then he too was discharged. My body started orienting itself toward home, feeling stronger and more bored every day. Though I had looked at the scar running down the side of my still swollen face, it hadn't occurred to me to scrutinize how I *looked*. I was missing a section of my jaw, but the extreme swelling, which stayed with me for two months, hid the defect. Before the operation I hadn't had a strong sense of what I looked like anyway. Proud of my tomboy heritage, I'd dogmatically scorned any attempts to look pretty or girlish. A classmate named Karen had once told me I was beautiful, and by the third grade two boys had asked me to be their girlfriend, all of which bewildered me. When Derek had delivered my first actual kiss, he had taken me completely by surprise. On the day I finally went home, I felt only proud of my new, dramatic scar and eager to show it off.

SCHOOL was already over for the year. The endlessness of summer stretched out before me, temptingly narcotic. I wasn't allowed to go swimming, because the scar on my trachea was still soft and fresh, a pink button on my throat, but I didn't really mind. I was a hero. Neighbors stopped me on the heat-rippled sidewalks to ask how I was. Evan, my closest friend from the neighborhood, and the other boys seemed suitably impressed with my hospital tales—I embellished heartily—and with my coup: I didn't have to make up the two months of schoolwork I'd missed.

One afternoon when Evan and I were playing an intricate game of jungle in his living room, his father passed through on his way to the kitchen. Pausing in the doorway, he turned and addressed me directly. I knew that his wife had died of cancer several years before, but I couldn't have imagined what went through his mind now, seeing a child with the same disease, the same prospects. He looked at me sadly for a minute before asking if I knew what chemotherapy was. I'd been told I was going to have chemo, I replied, but it had been described as simply another drug, another injection, maybe one that would make me a little flushed, no more. I'd had some unpleasant scans involving injected dyes that had transformed the world into something woozy and hot, but nothing so bad that I felt unable to face it again.

My explanation wasn't what he was expecting, but unable or unwilling to finish what he'd started, he mentioned something vague about chemical changes in my body, about how my hair might be affected. Having no idea what he was talking about and sensing something serious I'd rather not pursue, I made a joke to Evan about how my hair would turn green, my eyes purple. This was the second time an adult had tried to approach me directly about my situation, and it was the second time I had refused to tackle it.

DEATH became part of my vocabulary when I was six. The family's pet gerbil had died, and with my sister Suellen, who was twelve at the time, I was disposing of the body behind the house. The gerbil lay on top of a brown paper bag from the A&P, soon to be his final shroud. When I touched him, I couldn't believe how hard, how cold he was. Susie picked him up by his tail, and the sunlight suddenly illuminated the dullness of his still open eyes. A strange idea entered my head, an idea so preposterous it couldn't be true. How could it be? Surely, Susie would laugh at me for even suggesting it, but I felt I had to make sure anyway, for my own peace of mind.

I paused for a moment, considering how best to phrase it. I went for the negative approach.

"People don't die, do they?"

She looked at me with the surprise I'd hoped for, the faintly amused look that told me my fear was unfounded, but her response became proof positive that one should never ask a twelve-year-old sister anything. With glee in her voice she commenced to describe in great detail how you went into the cold dark ground, how the skin fell off your bones, how your eyes fell out. In a truly inspired touch, she began singing: *"The worms crawl in, the worms crawl out,/ In your stomach and out your mouth."*

I don't blame her. I was an easy mark, and had I been in her position, I'd have done the same thing. For a twelve-year-old with a younger sister, cruelty is de rigueur.

As we stood there, Susie had no idea what she had just implanted in the deepest part of me. No one had any idea, not my parents or teachers or friends, because there was no way I could discuss it. At night I dreamed of being carted off and left alone in a dark, cold room filled with bones, bones that would wake up once I was in there and dance around me. There was a small dark hole in the steps in front of our house that led nowhere in particular, but in my new dreams it became the gateway to a world that terrified me, a world where people had no heads, or if they did, they were filled with worms and beetles. This was what awaited me; there was no way I was going to escape death, and as the days passed, I became more and more frantic.

Why had we been born if this was the terrible end we had to look forward to? My six-year-old self was privately obsessed with my terrors and questions, when salvation appeared in the most surprising place—the television show *Laugh-In*. A repeating skit, mixed in with sexual and political innuendos that were over my head, showed a ragged, exhausted man climbing to the top of a large mountain. At the peak sat a man with a long gray beard. The climber would ask the guru, "Oh, master, what is the meaning of life?" Of course, the answer was always a silly one, usually resulting in the climber's falling off the mountain. Then I saw a National Geographic program that located this mountain, with its guru, in an actual place called Tibet. Immediately I went to my father. He was in the living room reading, sitting on the red couch that was so accustomed to his body that it obligingly hollowed to hold him more comfortably. After his death I used to curl up into this space and lie there with the cats, the warmth of his physical dent as reassuring as some ghostly hand in my hair.

"Daddy, how much would a plane ticket to Tibet cost?" I asked, offering no explanation for my question.

He scrunched up his forehead to let me know he was thinking. Looking down at his palm, he pretended to do calculations, muttering to himself. After a minute of this, he turned and looked at me as he would an adult. "One million dollars," he announced as seriously as I had asked him. I thanked him. For a six-year-old, one million dollars was about as unintelligible as one hundred, but I decided to start saving. I understood it might take some time, possibly years.

Gradually my obsession with death was replaced with new, daily discoveries about what it meant to be alive. But for a long time I put myself to sleep at night by imagining the mountain, the long, arduous climb. I counted off each step the way other people counted sheep, and each night that I made it to the top, I'd ask my question, yearning to hear the answer. Truth was something that existed; it was just that it lived far away.

I had long since forgotten the trauma of the gerbil when I became ill, and the idea that death had anything to do with me directly didn't even enter my mind. It wasn't so much avoidance as the simple belief that nothing bad would ever, could ever happen to me. Sometimes I wonder if it wasn't this disbelief that kept me alive. Despite my knowing that people died, it never occurred to me that I might personally be implicated.

Later, as a teenager, I worked in a library, and one day as I was reshelving books in the medical section, a book on pediatric oncology caught my eye. Pulling the heavy thing out, I laid it on the table and looked up my cancer, Ewing's sarcoma. I read a brief description of the various manifestations of it, followed by a table of mortality rates. A reasonable chance of survival was given at five percent.

Five percent. I felt obliged to say something, but no one was around, and I didn't know what to say anyway. Placing my hand on my neck, feeling the pulse there, I stood for some minutes on the verge of moving or speaking or sitting or *something*. Then the impulse passed. Finally someone walked into the room, breaking the silence with the squeak of winter boots, and I reached for another book to shelve.

Four

FOR two years I drove with my mother into New York City five days a week, every week, for radiation treatments, plus—on most Fridays, with periodic "vacations"—chemotherapy as well. Then for another half year we went in once a week to finish out the chemotherapy. My mother worked mornings in a local nursing home and would come to pick me up at our house at midday. We got into the car in our suburb, drove for just under an hour through the relative countryside of the Palisades Parkway, propelled ourselves across the Hudson via the George Washington Bridge, and found ourselves deposited smack in the middle of city streets.

During the drive my mother and I were usually engulfed by our own private inner travels, the radio's sound filling the front seat like an anesthetic. Once we went through the customary parking ordeal, we walked the few blocks to the hospital in silence. This was the routine we fell into, and it seemed natural to both of us.

The radiotherapy department existed deep in the guts of the hospital in a specially built section with cement walls many feet thick. Chris, my radiotherapist, explained that careful regulations made the walls so thick. She placed her hand on the otherwise innocuous pale yellow plaster and told me in reverent tones about the care one had to take around radiation. She wore a thick green smock made of lead. She let me hold it once, and it seemed to weigh as much as I did.

Radiation treatment itself was a breeze, about as complicated as an X ray. I'd get up on the table, and Chris would don her lead smock and turn out the lights. Bulbs inside the clunky machine hanging from tracks on the ceiling would shine down on my face, to be aligned with the Magic Marker X's drawn on my neck and face. "Hold your breath!" The command would come from somewhere in the corner, and I'd inhale as deeply as I could, almost always thinking about a movie I'd seen, a maritime disaster in which the hero had to swim a long distance underwater in order to save everyone else. I'd held my breath along with him, wondering if I too had it in me to save the others. Believing that one should be prepared for any emergency, I went about trying to improve my breath-holding capacity, and lying there on the gurney in radiotherapy seemed as good a place as any to practice for a disaster at sea. As the machines over my head clicked and whirred softly, my body swelled with air, trembling almost imperceptibly with the desire to let it all fall away from me. Just when I was about to abandon all hope and let the salty water fill my lungs, Chris's voice would sound from the dark corner.

"Breathe!" The overhead lights would come on, Chris would appear and help me off the table, and it was all over until the next day.

If it was Monday, Tuesday, Wednesday, or Thursday, that was the whole procedure. I'd find my mother in the waiting room, and we'd head home, hoping to avoid rush-hour traffic. Friday was different. Every Friday, usually around three o'clock, was my appointment with Dr. Woolf at the chemotherapy clinic.

Despite Evan's father's early warning attempts, I went in to my first appointment with Dr. Woolf completely unprepared. The only thing that really worried me about chemo was the prospect of weekly injections, because that's all I thought it would be—an injection. If I had been blind to warnings about chemo, once I entered the clinic, I got my first intimations of what was about to happen.

In sharp contrast to the new radiotherapy department, the chemotherapy clinic was old-looking, drab. The waiting area was on one side of a much used hall, a main thoroughfare for the hospital. It was completely open, like a lounge. The couches and chairs were covered in dark green vinyl; the floor was black tile with white traces that were almost worn out of existence. My mother wasn't allowed to smoke, which drove her insane, especially since week after week for two and a half years we had to wait at least two hours past the scheduled time before my name was called.

The other people in the waiting room fascinated me. We all looked exhausted, though relative health seemed to vary widely. Some looked bloated and sluggish, others were thin as rakes, and almost everyone was in some stage of losing or growing in hair. Hats, scarves, and wigs covered the naked scalps. On that first visit I felt apart from the rest of them, felt a million miles away.

When we were finally in Dr. Woolf's office—my mother ready to scream from the long wait—we encountered his telephone, apparently a permanent appendage. He could carry on conversations with my mother, me, his nurse, his secretary down the hall, and someone on the phone simultaneously; he had it down to an art. My mother thought him incredibly rude, and she was right. Dr. Woolf's manner was gruff and unempathetic. The first time he examined me, I could only flinch at his roughness as his large fingers pressed hard into my abdomen, pried open my still stiff mouth. His appearance didn't help. Tall, large-featured, and balding, he had a big white spot on his forehead, which caught the light in a sinister way. He scared me.

His office was as drab as the waiting room but was saved by a large, multipaned window that looked out onto a well-tended courtyard with banks of blue flowers and ivy-clenched trees. I spent a lot of time looking out that window. I spent a lot of time forcing myself to look out that window, because even on that first visit I knew that this room was no place for me. I wanted nothing to do with the treatment table, which was too tall for me to get onto by myself, or the two 60-cc syringes waiting patiently in their sterile packets.

This first examination was more thorough than the ones I would later receive. I was asked to strip down to my underwear, which I did, feeling humiliated and exposed. While the doctor talked to the nurse, my mother, and the person on the phone tucked beneath his chin, he prodded me with his hands, hit me just slightly too hard with his reflex hammer, and spoke far too loudly. He got out a tourniquet and wound it tightly around my arm, pinching the skin, just like a kid on the playground giving an Indian burn; and despite every ounce of strength I could muster, I began to cry. Not loudly, not even particularly heartily, just a few simple tears, which were as accurate and prophetic as any I'd ever shed.

The butterfly needle, named for the winglike holds that fanned out from its short, delicate, bodylike cylinder, slipped into my arm, a slender pinch I barely felt. Because it was inserted into the crook of my arm, I had to sit with my arm rigidly straight. I began to grow warm. For a split second, a split of a split second, the sensation was almost pleasurable. But immediately it was too much. I felt the lining of my stomach arc out and pull spastically back into itself, like some colorful sea anemone that had been disturbed.

It was an anatomy lesson. I had never known it was possible to feel your organs the way you feel your tongue in your mouth. My stomach outlined itself for me; my intestines, my liver, parts of me I didn't know the names of began heating up, trembling, creating friction and space by rubbing against the viscera, the muscles of my stomach, my back, my lungs. I wanted to collapse, to fall back onto the table or, better yet, go headfirst down onto the cold floor, but I couldn't. The injection had only begun; this syringe was still half full, and there was a second one to go. My head began to hurt. I squinted around the office, not the least bit surprised to see a yellow-green aura surrounding everyone and everything.

My body, wanting to turn itself inside out, made wave after wave of attempts to rid itself of this noxious poison. I shook with heaves so strong they felt more like convulsions. Someone lifted a metal basin to my face, and I quickly deposited into it everything my digestive system owned, and when that wasn't enough, I came up with the digestive juices themselves. My stomach now was empty, but the spasms still came, my stomach pressing inward, squeezing ever harder.

Gradually the waves of vomiting subsided, leaving behind an unacted-upon nausea that seemed to involve not just my stomach but all of me, even my feet, my scalp. Someone helped me put my clothes back on; I don't remember the walk back to the car.

The sky was so blue it was almost transparent, and it moved seamlessly outside the window as I lay in the back seat. The trip home was straightforward: from the bridge onto the parkway, then off the parkway, down a few streets, and up the driveway. From this unfamiliar vantage point, without the normal visual landmarks, I stared at the sky and attempted to guess where we were. Over the years I perfected the mental drive, could do it even when I was half asleep, even when the rhythm was interrupted by a sudden need to vomit into the kitchen mixing bowl my mother placed on the floor of the car.

That first time I arrived home, I remember feeling not quite so bad. I'd begun to feel less nauseated, or at least better able to control it. My father suggested I eat something, some ice cream perhaps. My head swimming, I sat at the kitchen table and ate several spoonfuls, my parents looking at me expectantly.

"It wasn't so bad, was it now, Lucinda Mag?" my father asked.

I shook my head no, purposefully bringing another spoonful up to my mouth. My stomach rebelled. I stood quickly and made my way over to the sink, where I threw up. For some reason I started to cry. My mother put her hand on my head and tried to soothe me, and when I was done, she began to explain that there was no need to cry, that everything would be all right, that I mustn't cry.

How could she know I would take her so seriously? She went on to explain how disappointed she was that I'd cried even before Dr. Woolf had put the needle into me, that crying was only because of fear, that I shouldn't be afraid—it would be all right. It was one thing to cry afterward, because she knew that it hurt, but why did I cry beforehand? Hadn't I always been so brave before?

I looked out the kitchen window over the sink. Immediately outside, the overgrown, sloppy fir trees prevented any clear view of the front lawn or street. Sometimes the briefest moments demand that we live the rest of our lives in reference to them. What did my mother mean? Part of me knew then, and still knows, that she was afraid for me. If somehow she could convince me not to be afraid, we could rally around the truism she had grown up with: There was nothing to fear but fear itself. My mother didn't know how to conquer what I was afraid of, nor could she even begin to tell me how to do it for myself. Instead, out of her own fear, she offered her own philosophy, which meant in this instance that I should conquer the fear by not crying. It was a single brief sentence, a fleeting thought she probably did not mean and doesn't even remember saying, but I, who would have done anything to find a way out of this pain, would never forget it. As I made my way downstairs to my room, I resolved to never cry again.

I kept my bedroom dark and watched the light from my television change color on the wall beside me. Every hour or so I felt a great urge to lean over and retch into the mixing bowl on the floor. I drank water constantly so as to have something to throw up. As soon as the vomiting was over, I'd feel whole continents better, and the intense nausea that had been unendurable only moments before was suddenly bearable. I'd lie back on the pillow, feeling both energized and exhausted. Gradually over the next hour the feeling of unbearableness would return—subtly, insidiously—until I again had to lift myself up and hang over the side of the bed. This went on all night.

The second day was better. The cycle between bouts of nausea would gradually extend, so that I was throwing up only every four hours, every six hours, only three times during the night. The third day was the breaking point. I could actually eat something innocuous, like tapioca. Sometime during the late afternoon, relief would come. A flicker at first, only a moment, but for that brief moment I understood I was going to get better, that this was going to end. I sat up in bed, felt the strength of my body support me. Another moment would go by, and I'd feel ill again; but an hour, maybe two hours later, the feeling would return, stay for just a few breaths longer before abandoning me. So it would go on through the evening. When I woke up on the fourth day, I felt a little weak but glorious and high—that sanguine, comfortable feeling one gets after performing some great physical feat. I had swum the Channel. I had climbed Mount Eiger.

I sat up, listening for the sounds of my mother's footsteps, the clicking of the dogs' nails on the tiled floor. A tree obscured my window, shattering the light into patches on the dirty glass. I didn't understand how I could have overlooked the sheer joy of these things for so long, how the intricate message of their simplicity had escaped me until just this moment. This weightless nowness, this ecstasy could sometimes last me all day, at least until that afternoon, when it was time to go back to the hospital for the radiation treatment, which, as I've said, didn't seem so bad—not really, anyway.

The fifth day was Tuesday, my favorite day of all. All but completely recovered, with everyone else away at school or at work, I was free to wander about the still house, form intimate relationships with the cats and dogs, who regarded me nonjudgmentally as I tracked their movements over the living-room floor, sleepily following the inexorable arc of the sun. Tuesday, still far away from Friday, was futureless, thought-less, anxiety free.

The house empty was a different place from the house occupied. With so many brothers and sisters, I'd never had many opportunities for privacy. I liked to go into my mother's closet for the sheer pleasure of smelling her, at the same time knowing how annoyed she'd be. I became a snoop, going through everyone's drawers, looking for clues to how other people lived their lives. I'd lie on my sister's bed, look out her window, and think, So this is what she sees when she wakes up. What was it like to be somebody else? I went into my father's bed-room, dark and cluttered, and saw all the bits of paper, the stray ties, as marks of how little he was touched by his personal surroundings. In my brother's room I found magazines with pictures of naked women, fascinating to me for reasons I couldn't determine. His room seemed the most alien of all. Even when I lay down on his bed and saw what he saw, I knew I wasn't even close.

The long, elliptical mornings of invading other people's privacy seemed endless, but eventually I'd hear the car drive up to the house and know it was time to leave for the city. Except for Fridays, I looked forward to the drive. I pretended I was riding alongside the road with great, graceful swiftness on a large, black, gleaming horse, its sensu-ous mane tangling in my face, the rhythm of its hooves a hypnotic lecture on how to arrive someplace entirely different.

Inexorably, Friday, or D-day, as we began calling it, would ap-proach. I'd wake up early, as always, but I did not want to get out of bed, even to go lie on the floor with my best friends, the dogs, who, I imagined, understood my suffering and whose wet tongues licking my face weren't random or casual, but full of sympathy.

The second week of chemo was worse, in that I knew what to expect. This presented a curious reversal of fear for me, because with other types of pain, the fear of not knowing usually brought more suffering than the thing itself. This was different. This was dread.

We went through the whole routine again—the endless waiting, Dr. Woolf's eternal phone call, his strong hands on my body. I tried not to look at the syringes beside me, but when I looked out the window, Dr. Woolf passed in front of my line of vision, casually hold-ing a syringe in the air. When I looked down at the floor, I somehow chanced to look at the exact spot where Dr. Woolf sent a brief spurt of fluid out of the syringe to clear the needle of air. I took it as a sign to cry, which I did, ashamed of myself, unable to meet my mother's eyes as she began telling me not to, to hold it back.

The tourniquet went on, and it began all over again, just like the week before, except that this time when I got home, I went straight to bed. I didn't even try to eat anything as grotesque as ice cream. I felt that my mother was disappointed with me. I hadn't gone straight to bed last time. Why was I doing it this time? She came to my room and sat on the edge of my bed. She looked tired but beautiful, always beautiful to me: her makeup exact and perfect, the redness of her lips, the faint hue of her powder, the musky smell of her perfume.

"You can't let this get you down, you know. I know it's hard, but don't give in to it. You were not so bad last time. Make sure that what you're feeling isn't just in your head."

She sat there a moment longer, staring at me sadly, before asking if there was anything else. When I said no, she stood up and left me alone with the television. My father had rigged up a buzzer to the kitchen, which I could press if I needed anything.

My father also bought me toys, not because he believed for a second that they would sufficiently compensate me, but because it was as close a gesture as he could manage. He didn't really have the stomach for the treatments, and only on the rare days when my mother was ill or busy would he take me in for chemotherapy. His rhythm was entirely different from my mother's. We arrived late, so there was not as much waiting time. Once my name was called, he'd accompany me into the office and exchange greetings with Dr. Woolf, but as soon as I was asked to take off my clothes, he'd turn to me and say, "Right then, I'll go get the car." Perhaps in part he was embarrassed to see his daughter half naked, but I knew he did not want to see me suffer.

He'd jangle the keys at me, just as he did with the dogs, whose excitement at that familiar sound approached heart attacks. He'd smile and announce, "I'll be right back," adding, "This way you won't have to walk so far when it's over. I'll double-park and come get you."

I watched his back as he left, and felt relief, because his embarrassment and awkwardness caused me as much pain as they did him. There was no blame in those moments, no regrets, no accusations, not even despair. Those things came later, when I learned to scrutinize and judge the past. As an adult, I wonder how he could have left me alone in there; but as a child, I knew the answer to this clearly and knew that as soon as he was out of the room, I was, if nothing else, free to respond as *I* chose. And as Dr. Woolf turned to me with his tourniquet, I turned to him with my unfettered grief.

It was harder to maintain a sense of transcendence during the appointments with my mother. She stayed in the room and, despite my repeated failures, insisted that I not cry. But one summer day—it must have been summer, because we were all hot and red-faced—I remember my mother bending beside me. The needle was in my arm, and I was feeling the first hot flushes in my stomach. "Don't cry," she was whispering to me, as if it were a secret we were sharing. Dr. Woolf's voice was resonating over our heads, talking to neither one of us. Perhaps it was something in her voice that day, maybe it was the way everything shone and vibrated with the heat, but for the first time in a long time I lifted my eyes from the still empty basin and looked at her. Her own eyes were filling with water, tears that would never fall, but hovered there, only inches from my own.

Suddenly my perception of the world shifted. I wasn't the only person in the world who suffered. My mother, to my profound discovery, was suffering not just because of me but also for me.

Moments never repeat themselves exactly. Simply because I understood something important and graceful there on the examination table didn't mean that only seconds later I wasn't back in another moment in which I hated myself for crying, for not being strong enough. The comfort I'd gained from understanding my mother's pain was both fleeting and insidious. When the next injection came, the next bout of crying, and I *wasn't* able to not suffer, I felt I had only myself to blame, that I had failed in some unknowable, spiritual way. In my mind, I didn't have what it took. I didn't deserve to be comforted.

Five

NEXT to the garage there was a small island of grass between the sea of driveway asphalt and the front walk of cement. Smack in the middle, a fir tree splayed its boughs just high enough off the ground for me to sit in the shade beneath them, the earth dark and sweet smelling. To the south I was able to survey what amounted to my version of a grassy plain; to the north a jungle of thick moss grew up around a gutter drainpipe. This was my kingdom. Plastic animals bought at the local drugstore inhabited it, and together we lived our urgent lives.

The lion, my favorite, had muscles permanently rippled into his hard plastic body. He lived in the cave I built for him out of stones, not far from the gutter drainpipe. Every morning I took him out of the fresh grass bed I'd made the previous night, and together we surveyed the island, checking on the other animals safely tucked into their own domiciles. The aardvark was stashed beneath the tree, the ibex and giraffe were installed on the border of the grassy plain, the zebra roamed between the jungle and the plain, and the snake I relegated to the rocks near the tip of the island. The animals never came inside the house, never left the island, which to me was the most authentic aspect of their lives.

My mother insisted that I wasn't taking very good care of them when I complained that one of the dogs had chewed on my giraffe or zebra during the night. How could I explain why it was crucial for me, safe in my bed at night, to think of them out there, living their continuous lives regardless of my presence. I especially loved the nights when the weather became wild, imagining my animals braving the elements, the wind howling and rain beating down. Every morning I had the distinct sense that I was simply opening the door on an ongoing world, constant and sure, even if I was stuck inside, too sick to get out of bed.

When I wasn't on my island, I was riding for the pony express—though sometimes I was a Martian sent to this planet on a surveillance mission. As an alien, I could transform myself anywhere, anytime. Sometimes I would take on human form and walk among a race that mistook me for one of their own. Sitting in the car or a waiting room, I'd examine everything around me carefully. What exactly was this peculiar ritual of the tollbooth? What was the significance of the different types of footwear? The whole trick was to forget myself.

The only time I was ever completely myself was on Fridays. There was no way to escape the pain. Yet with each successive visit to Dr. Woolf's examining room, my feelings of shame and guilt for failing not to suffer became more unbearable. The physical pain seemed almost easy in comparison. Was this how my body dealt with the onslaught, veering the focus away from itself, insisting that its burden be lessened by having my mind take on more than its fair share? Whatever the process was, it worked—worked in the sense that I became adept at handling my pain.

Afterward I'd lie in bed and concentrate on letting the tremors run their course, until they'd gradually leave me, exhausted but still alive. Some pain, like the pain of a needle or the site of an operation, is specific: It announces itself in no uncertain terms. Often I tried to balance the pain out with the rest of my body, a sort of negotiation in which I'd isolate one section. I'd lie there and list to myself the parts that didn't hurt, trying to feel them, aware that normally I'd have no reason to "feel" my body or know it so intimately.

At times I was desperate and could find no solace anywhere. Nothing seemed to work, and the weight of being trapped in my own body made it difficult to lift even a hand off the sheets. Pain centered in my head was the most difficult to deal with. It's one thing to ignore your arm or your stomach, but ignoring your head isn't quite so simple. The radiation treatment was beginning to take its toll, and open sores began appearing all over the insides of my cheeks. The first time I felt them was while eating a bowl of tomato soup. Each mouthful stung, and since no one had told me that radiation burns were a common side effect, I suspected the soup of being no good. When I thought no one was looking, I carried my bowl from the living room, where I was eating in front of the television, into the bathroom, where I overturned it into the toilet, flushing it away. I didn't want to say anything to my mother, because I was afraid she'd see this as yet another of my ploys to not eat. I was losing weight rapidly, and everyone seemed to be shoving food in my face, food I had little interest in. Eating had become a monumental effort. Simply finishing one boiled egg was tantamount to an act of heroism.

Now there was a new item on the already long list of why it was hard to eat: Not only did I have trouble chewing and swallowing, not only was my stomach in turmoil half the time, but now it actually hurt to put food into my mouth. As the radiation treatment went on, I could eat only the blandest of foods. Fruit was out of the question; drinking orange juice felt as if I were rinsing my mouth out with battery acid. I lived almost exclusively on oatmeal, disgusting protein drinks that practically had to be forced down my throat, and endless dozens of junk-food chocolate-cream rolls, my mother's welcome bribe for the protein drinks. I loved eating entire boxes of these disgustingly sweet things slowly and with embellished delight in front of Susie and Sarah, who were eternally on some new diet.

AFTER every six weeks, I was admitted to the hospital, to my beloved Babies 10, for a five-day course of intensive chemotherapy. I actually looked forward to these times in the hospital. The doctors set up the IV and administered the yellow fluid slowly and continuously, which didn't make me feel as intensely ill as the weekly injections of a concentrated dose. And if I did feel ill, I simply threw up in my basin and lay back in my white bed, secure in knowing that no one cared too much if I threw up or not, cried or not. I felt free and sovereign. As a "regular customer," I knew the nurses, the routines, and the jargon, and often found myself explaining things to the rookie doctors who rotated on and off the ward. With no school responsibilities to speak of, no family tensions to deal with, I considered going into the hospital something just short of a vacation.

At home it was different. Those long quiet mornings in the house still gave me pleasure, but as soon as any family members entered the front door, tension and shame accompanied them. Unable to locate my unhappiness within the difficult and complex relationships we shared, I thought that it all originated with me, that I was somehow at fault. If I couldn't overcome my growing depression, I deserved it, and how unfair of me to inflict it upon everyone else, upon my mother especially.

I was willing to try anything to get out of the weekly chemo shots. The only way to do this was to be too sick to withstand them. Holding a thermometer up to a light bulb, and other elementary school tricks, were ancient history. I had to be *really* sick, had to have a measurable increase in my white blood cell count, indicating an infection.

My first experiment in making myself ill came about innocently. It was a Thursday in early winter, and everyone was asleep except my father, who was working late again. Icy rain was falling all over the state. News reports warned people not to drive if they could avoid it. The temperature was hovering at just thirty-two degrees.

I lay in bed thinking about my island, and suddenly I was overcome with a desire to go outside and see how my animals were faring in the storm. I got out of bed and pulled down my long flannel nightgown, which had bunched up around my waist. Without bothering to put on shoes, I walked toward the garage door and let myself out as quietly as possible, trying not to waken the dogs. I felt the chill run up my legs.

My animals were fine—just where I'd left them. Standing there, only a few feet from the door, I began to shiver. That's when it hit me that if I stayed outside, I was going to catch cold. I was going to get sick, perhaps even sick enough to raise my white blood cell count. It seemed like the perfect plan. Walking into the dark backyard, I found a spot where I knew that no one inside the house would be able to see me, and lay down on the cold wet grass. I tried looking up at the black, chalky sky, but the rain kept splashing into my eyes, forcing me to close them. How long would I have to stay out here? What would I do with the evidence of my wet nightgown? The cold began to get painful, and my teeth chattered.

My nightgown soaked through, making it almost transparent. I lay there until I couldn't stand it anymore, until my fingers were stiff and red and starting to swell. Once inside again, I pulled off my nightgown and hung it over a chair. If my mother found it, I would tell her I'd thrown up on it and washed it myself in the sink. It was sensuous and delicious to be back in my warm bed, the sheets absorbing the water from my naked skin. I fell asleep almost instantly, a rarity for me.

The next morning I woke up and saw the wrinkled nightgown still on the chair and remembered what had happened. Sitting up, I tried to gauge how I felt. Did I have a fever? Was my throat sore? No. I felt perfectly fine. In fact, I felt better than I had all week, which seemed like the cruelest joke, seeing that it was Friday and in only twelve hours I would be right back in this same bed, throwing up.

I sought out different ways of getting sick. I experimented with drinking dishwashing liquid, but all that did was make me *feel* ill without actually *being* ill. My pet project was inhaling water. Once, while nauseated, I'd inhaled some of my own vomit, and my lungs had reacted instantly with a case of pneumonia. If I could somehow get a small amount of fluid into my lungs, I figured I'd be set. I filled the bathtub and on the count of three submerged my head. Breathe, I'd tell myself, *breathe*. I saw it as a battle of my own will. I saw it as a test of forcing myself. I'd lie there until I ran out of breath, reemerge for air, then sink back under again, firmly telling myself that this time I was going to do it. When I finally found it in myself to open my mouth underwater, my body would automatically heave itself up, sputtering water. The violent coughing I couldn't suppress prevented the water from reaching my lungs. The water in the bathtub sloshed around me and splashed over the sides, and the white towels, soaked from mopping up the floor, hung like flags of surrender over the tub.

Most drastically, I experimented with scratching my arms with rusty nails I found lying on the street. A case of tetanus—the lockjaw everyone thought I'd had in the beginning—still seemed preferable to chemo. I remember sitting on the stone steps in our backyard one afternoon, the summer sun glaring down. I was listening to the screams of the neighborhood children I hardly ever played with anymore and trying to scratch myself with the top of a dirty tin can. While I could raise a good welt, I never scratched forcefully enough to break the skin or draw blood. Something always held me back, and for the longest time I thought it was cowardice.

LETTERS from strangers all across the country started arriving in the mail. Somehow my name had found its way onto a Catholic prayer list. The letters—on colored stationery bordered with flowers, cats, intricate motifs—were usually short, written in rounded hands. All of them assured me that Jesus loved me, and if I loved him, he would take on his share of the burden. Letter after letter advised me to think happy things: think of kittens, of foods I like to eat. My family got a kick out of reading these letters. With our bitter, cynical air we mocked them, laughing at their naïveté. Every letter promised a prayer said in my name.

I laughed along with my brothers and sisters, but part of me longed for the world of those letters, just as I longed for the world I watched on television, on *Father Knows Best* and *The Brady Bunch*. I fantasized about these shows, imagining what would happen if one of their children got sick. Everything would be talked about, everything dealt with. No one would ever lose his temper. No one would go unnoticed.

Along with the letters came pamphlets: Christian publications mostly geared toward children. They told stories of a mysterious stranger who appeared on the doorsteps of troubled families, a stranger with a special shine to him, a kind look, and a light in his eyes. A quality of calmness and fairness infused the difficult tasks the stranger performed, whether mediating an argument between parents or helping an invalid. He glowed with love and peace and understanding. After a few days he would leave the family, having impressed upon them how they too could be happy if they let God into their lives.

In the privacy of my room, I decided I wanted this light, this peace, this glow. But the scenarios always ended the same way, with the stranger leaving and the troubled family left alone to ponder and resolve to change. I always wanted to turn the page, to know what the troubled family could actually *do* in order to believe. After all, I was sold. I wanted to have Jesus help me out and make me good and strong and pure—all of the things I was sure I wasn't. But exactly how was I supposed to do this?

Sooner or later we're all driven to this point. In secrecy, away from my family and our shared scorn over the letters and their simplistic sentiments, I sat down in my bedroom on the blue carpet and asked, "God, if You exist, prove it to me."

What was I expecting? A voice, a verbal affirmation? A physical one? A sudden light maybe? I looked up into the air above my head for it. I knew I only half expected an answer. Was my partial belief preventing God from speaking to me? Didn't I have to fully believe? Or did all this simply mean that there *was* no answer? I hugged my knees close to my chest and rocked back and forth. I couldn't bear to think that everything I was going through didn't actually have meaning.

I resolved to believe, even in the face of this lack of response. Was it possible to prove my worthiness by repeatedly asking the question, even in the brunt of this painful silence? In the same way that I was sure I could prove my love, and lovability, to my mother by showing her I could "take it," I considered the idea that what God wanted was for me to keep trying and trying, no matter how difficult it was. My goal, and my intended reward, was to understand.

LIFE became more complicated at home when my father lost his job in the news department at ABC. The loss of his job meant the loss of his medical coverage. Luckily, my mother's job was able to take up part of my coverage, but we were still in a bind. Family life became more tense. Days were filled with phone calls and letters and endless forms. Nights were filled with even more arguments about money.

For some inexplicable reason the new coverage, so inadequate in so many ways, paid for an ambulance to transport me to the hospital each day. The notion thrilled me. But the day the ambulance actually pulled up in front of our house, I felt self-conscious as I walked down the lawn. Some neighbors had come out to see what was happening and stood there watching. "I'm not really that sick," I wanted to tell them. "This is just a big joke." Though I knew I'd lost weight and was a bit pale, I never considered myself all that sick. It didn't occur to me until then that people might actually pity me. The idea appalled me.

Horrified as I was that people might feel sorry for me, I also knew that I possessed a certain power. After all, people noticed me. Wherever I went, even just to the store with my mother, I could count on some sort of attention, and I discovered that people were embarrassed when I caught them looking at me. I stared right back at these strangers with my big blue eyes, which appeared even bigger now that I'd lost weight and now that, without bone to shape it, the right side of my face was starting to sink in. They always looked away quickly, trying to pretend they hadn't been staring.

If this type of attention wasn't always comfortable for me, it nonetheless further defined me. Most people struggle all their lives to avoid fading unnoticed into the crowd, but this was never my concern. I was special. Being different was my cross to bear, but being aware of it was my compensation.

In a few weeks my father got a new job, at CBS, and I was again covered by his medical insurance, meaning no ambulance. I was relieved. My mother and I once more took up our daily drives to the hospital. The whole way there, I stared out the window and, as before, imagined myself on a horse, galloping along the strip of grass beside the road, jumping the irrigation ditches and road signs.

Six

EARLY on in the treatment my hair began to fall out. Although I had been warned, I was taken by surprise the first day I reached up to sweep my hair back and found my hand full of long blond hair. I guess I'd never believed this really would happen. I was sitting in the car with my mother, and I started to cry. At a loss to say anything that would truly comfort me or stop my hair from falling out, she re-minded me that I had known this would happen, that I shouldn't get so upset—as if foreknowledge of an event could somehow buffer you from its reverberations. Feeling, again, that I had failed simply by being upset made me cry harder.

I'd never thought much about my hair. I had been complimented on it, but such remarks had never particularly interested me. More often than not, my hair seemed like a bother to me, something that got in the way when I wrestled or climbed trees. But now? When I undressed at night, I heard the static of my sweater as I pulled it over my head, then saw the long strands on the collar waving in the breeze of the electricity. I'd sit up in bed in the morning and look down at the tangles of hair on my pillow. Once an aggressive, careless brusher, I now patted at my head with a comb very carefully and very gently.

Involved as I was with the process of losing my hair, I somehow ignored the change in my appearance. I knew I was going bald; I knew I was pale and painfully thin; I knew I had a big scar on my face. In short, I was different-looking, and I knew my face had an effect on other people. But I was still keeping myself ignorant of the details of my appearance. I must have known intuitively it was better this way.

I spent a very long time not acknowledging that I was going bald, even as I swept my own hair off the dog's black coat after a particularly vigorous hug. I was young—only ten, almost eleven. Sex appeal be-longed to toothpaste commercials, while sex itself was still a mysteri-ous thing, clues to which could be found in the pages of my brother's magazines. I looked at myself in the mirror with a preoccupied pre-adolescent view, which is to say that I looked at myself but didn't judge myself. When the first taunts were thrown at me, usually by some strange kids in the supermarket parking lot, more often than not I was able to come back with an insult far more sarcastic and biting than their own rather unimaginative "Baldy" or "Dog Girl." I under-stood that their comments were meant to impress one another more than to harm me. I possessed a strong sense of myself—and I lived vividly in my world of hospitals and animals and fantasy. I had no sense of myself in relation to the "normal" people I walked by every day. I was naturally adept at protecting myself from the hurt of their insults, and I felt a vague superiority to them—for the moment, anyway.

Sometimes when I was in the hospital, days or even a week would pass before I was well enough to get up and wash my hair. I hated the way it got oily and tangled from lying on it so long. That first morning when I could get up and wash it was always a great relief. But finally one morning when I asked my mother to help me wash it, she looked at me sorrowfully and suggested in a kind voice, "Maybe it's time to cut it." And that's what we did. She borrowed a pair of scissors from the nurse's desk, and while I sat in a chair, she snipped off what remained of my hair.

The next morning my mother came in with a hat, a small white sailor's hat, which I put on and almost never took off for the next two and a half years. Sometimes my hair grew several inches and was perfectly presentable, but I knew it was only going to fall out again, and I refused to be seen in public without my hat. My hat. It became part of me, an inseparable element of who I thought I was.

My hat was my barrier between me—and what I was vaguely becoming aware of as ugly about me—and the world. It hid me, hid my secret, though badly; and when people made fun of me or stared at me, I assumed it was only because they could guess what was beneath my hat. It didn't occur to me that the whole picture, even with the hat, was ugly; as long as I had it on, I felt safe.

As the teasing continued, both from strangers and from the very boys whom I'd once regarded as friends, I began to suspect that something was wrong. I identified the problem as my baldness, an outside force beyond my control. I assumed that once the problem was solved, once my hair grew back in, I would be complete again, whole, and all of this would be over, like a bad dream. I still saw everything as fixable.

DURING this time my mother was working in a Hasidic nursing home, and most of her co-workers were Hasidim. Hasidic custom dictates that once a woman is married, she must cover her hair. This used to be done with kerchiefs, but now most of the women wore wigs. I imagine they grew tired of their wigs the same way other women grow tired of their clothes, because there seemed to be a surplus of discarded wigs in the community. As my mother's friends became aware of my predicament, they generously began to donate these hand-me-down hairpieces. The first time my mother came home with a wig, we all had a good time playing with it, trying it on ourselves first and then on the cats. When I put it on, I looked as ridiculous as my brothers and sisters, not to mention the cats, so it was all a big joke.

But more wigs kept coming home with my mother. Sometimes it seemed she had a new one every day, and each was more atrocious than the last. When her friends asked how the wigs had worked out, my mother politely but truthfully told them that none of them fitted me properly. One of my mother's closest co-workers offered the services of her wigmaker, who would measure my head and make one "just the way I wanted it." Not wanting to appear ungrateful, I, coached by my mother, thanked this woman and agreed to go for a fitting, with the unspoken understanding between my mother and me that I did not really want a wig.

We drove to New City, a nearby town with a large Jewish population, and found the store in a small cluster of shops. I'd never been to a "parlor" before, and I'd envisioned a fancy salon filled with glamorous women. But the room was harshly lit with long overhead fluorescent bulbs, and instead of Warren Beatty, whom I'd seen in *Shampoo,* we were greeted by a small old man who was bald himself. He affectionately beckoned me to sit in a chair facing a mirror framed with carved pink-and-gold flowers.

"So, the little girl wants a wig, eh?"

He smiled at me in the mirror. I shriveled inside, mortified beyond any realm I'd previously thought possible. He turned to my mother, and they began speaking. I kept watching him in the mirror, not because I was fascinated by him, but because I didn't want to look at myself. I knew the moment was coming when he'd ask me to take off my hat. I knew there was nothing I could do about it except pretend I didn't care; and when he turned back to me and the moment finally came, I took off the hat as nonchalantly as possible and placed it in my lap. I kept my gaze directed at him in the mirror while he took out a measuring tape and ran lines over the various angles of my head.

After the measuring, he went to the back room to get samples. Knowing I'd had long blond hair, he brought back wigs of varying lengths and shades of blond. He placed each one in turn on my head and discussed with my mother which types were closest to my "natural" state.

Now it was unavoidable; I had to look at myself in the mirror. As each wig was put on and adjusted, both the man and my mother would ask me what I thought. All I could manage was a sullen nod or shake of the head. Looking at myself in these wigs horrified me.

How long was this going to go on? How many wigs were there in the world, anyway? Though inside I was growing more and more petulant, I made halfhearted efforts to look happy; and when the last wig was finally tried on, I actually smiled when the old man asked how I liked it. I hated it. At last the issue of cost came up, which in my mind signaled the end of this charade. I knew my mother would never want to pay for something as ludicrous as a wig, and besides, hadn't we more or less agreed we weren't really going to get one? The man quoted an astounding sum. I sat in the chair, my feet swinging, ready to leave, and watched my mother and this man talking. To my great amazement I saw a look on my mother's face that seemed to say she was actually considering ordering one of these overpriced, custom-made patches of hair. When we finally left the store, it was with a promise that she would think it over and call him tomorrow.

Once we were in the car, I thought she would look at me and we'd both laugh, but instead she turned and addressed me seriously. "Well, do you want one? It's a lot of money, but if you want one, I'll buy it for you."

What had happened? I thought we'd only gone to be polite to her friend. I didn't know how to reply. Back at home, she called her friend to tell her what had happened, and I heard her say, "It was the first time in a long time I've seen her smile. She hasn't smiled in so long."

So that was it. Normally, I was intuitive and could guess what was going on behind people's words and actions, but if my own mother could be so wrong about me, how could I know I wasn't mistaken in my own interpretations?

To keep the situation from getting too far out of hand, I went to my mother and told her outright that I didn't want a wig, that I thought they were ugly. She looked relieved because of the expense, but as she looked at me and smiled, I thought again of what she'd said on the phone. I smiled at her, sick in my heart at this newly discovered chasm opening up between me and the rest of the world. But I insisted I was okay, happy even, that the wig was a big joke. She smiled back at me even more broadly, relieved to see my old self, and for that moment I was happy, content that I could at least give her that.

I kept on wearing my hat. But I couldn't shake the image of my face staring back at me with that grotesque halo of a wig. Had they meant it when they'd said, "Now, doesn't that look nice?" Or were they lying to me? Perhaps they hadn't wanted to hurt my feelings. It was dawning on me that I might look much worse than I had supposed.

One morning I went into the bathroom and shut the door, though I was alone in the house. I turned on the lights and very carefully, very seriously, assessed my face in the mirror. I was bald, but I knew that already. I also knew I had buckteeth, something I hadn't given too much thought to until this moment. My teeth were ugly. And, I noticed, they were made worse by the fact that my chin seemed so small. How had it gotten that way? I rooted around in the cabinets and came up with a hand mirror and, with a bit of angling, looked for the first time at my right profile. I knew to expect a scar, but how had my face sunk in like that? Was it possible I'd looked this way for a while and was only just noticing it? More than the ugliness I felt, I was suddenly appalled at the notion that I'd been walking around unaware of something that was apparent to everyone else. A profound sense of shame consumed me.

I put the mirror away, shut off the lights, went back into the living room, and lay in the sunlight with the cats. They didn't care how I looked. I made a silent vow to love them valiantly, truly, with an intensity that would prove I was capable of, worthy of . . . I wasn't sure what, but something wonderful, something noble, something spectacular. I repeated the same vow to the dogs.

I WAS still experimenting, unsuccessfully, with making myself ill. Pneumonia remained my pet plan, though I was unable to inhale the water. The one time I actually got out of having chemotherapy, I wasn't even feeling particularly sick. But the blood test showed a high white blood cell count, and I was overjoyed when the doctor decided I should be put into isolation for a bit. A porter came down to the clinic to collect me in a wheelchair. I loved riding in wheelchairs, and I waved gaily to Dr. Woolf as I was chauffeured past him.

"Better not look too happy," my mother advised me. Immediately I went into my waif mode, a style I'd been perfecting for some time. Since becoming aware of my odd appearance, I'd decided to use it for all it was worth to have an effect on people.

Isolation wasn't such a thrill after all. Because my admission was unexpected, I hadn't come prepared with books or toys, and, horror of horrors, the room had no television. I kept opening the door to stick my head out, but someone always yelled at me to shut it and get back into bed. I felt perfectly fit. How could I really be ill? Lying face-down on my bed, I felt my hipbones jut down into the overstarched sheets. Sleep was a long way off. I saved myself only by pretending I was a prisoner put in the hole, which I'd read about in a book.

That week was the exception, though. Most weeks Friday was still D-day. The chemotherapy became my entire life for two and a half years. To fill the time as I waited to see Dr. Woolf, I'd go to the public bathroom down the hall. It was an old bathroom with only two stalls. Each stall door was wooden and closed on the inside with a silvery metal latch. There was no graffiti anywhere in the bathroom except on these latches. Someone had scratched onto each rectangular piece of metal a message. Sitting on the toilet in the first stall, you could read "God Is Near," and in the second, "Be Here Now." I sensed that it had been done a long time ago.

Since I still spent my private moments trying to engage God in conversation, alternately attempting to barter Him into answering my questions and silently trying to listen to the answer, these communications seemed important to me.

Each Friday I'd plod down to this bathroom, killing time before the inevitable, and I'd pause for a moment before the two doors, trying to decide which message I wanted to read. "God Is Near." Well, okay, how near? Did this mean He was near in the way someone is near when they're coming toward you—not yet here but expected sooner or later? Or did it mean He was near but not showing his face, present but unseeable? "Be Here Now." I didn't want to be here now. My wanting was inconsequential. I *was* here now, whether I liked it or not. But something about this saying attracted me, either despite or because of its seeming simplicity, and two out of three times I went for door number two.

Some weeks I stared at it dumbly, thinking only of the impending injection. Some weeks I continued with my fantasy life: The pony express rider seeks relief in the town's saloon. The alien ponders the wonders of waste disposal. Some weeks, especially when it was hot, I thought of nothing as I leaned forward, pressing the coolness of the inscribed metal against my forehead, and wept.

Seven

HAVING missed most of fourth grade and all but a week or so of fifth grade, I finally started to reappear at school sometime in sixth grade during my periodic "vacations" from chemotherapy. I'd mysteriously show up for a week or two weeks or sometimes even three or four, then disappear again for a couple of months.

Most of the sixth-grade class consisted of children I'd grown up with. They were, for the most part, genuinely curious about what had happened to me. They treated me respectfully, though there was a clique of boys who always called me names. "Hey, girl, take off that monster mask. Oops, she's not wearing a mask!" This was the height of hilarity in sixth grade, and the boys, for they were always and only boys, practically fell to the ground, besotted with their own wit.

The school year progressed slowly. I felt as if I had been in the sixth grade for years, yet it was only October. Halloween was approaching. Coming from Ireland, we had never thought of it as a big holiday, though Sarah and I usually went out trick-or-treating. For the last couple of years I had been too sick, but this year Halloween fell on a day when I felt quite fine. My mother came up with the Eskimo idea. I put on a parka, made a fish out of paper, which I hung on the end of a stick, and wrapped my face up in a scarf. My hair was growing in, and I loved the way the hood rubbed against it.

We walked around the neighborhood with our pillowcase sacks, running into other groups of kids and comparing notes: The house three doors down gave whole candy bars, while the house next to that gave only cheap mints. I felt wonderful. It was only as the night wore on and the moon came out, and the older kids, the big kids, went on their rounds, that I began to realize why I felt so good. No one could see me clearly. No one could see my face.

For the end of October it was a very warm night, and I was sweating in my parka, but I didn't care. I felt such freedom. I waltzed up to people effortlessly and boldly; I asked questions and made comments the rest of my troupe were afraid to make. I didn't understand their fear. I hadn't realized just how meek I'd become, how self-conscious I was about my face until now, when it was obscured. My sister and her friends never had to worry about their appearance—or so it seemed to me—so why didn't they always feel as happy as I felt that night?

Our sacks filled up, and eventually it was time to go home. We gleefully poured out our candy on the floor and traded off. Because chewing had become difficult, I gave Sarah everything that was too hard for me, while she unselfishly gave me everything soft. I took off my Eskimo parka and went to my room without my hat. Normally I didn't feel that I had to wear my hat around my family, and I never wore it when I was alone in my room. Yet once I was alone with all my candy, I felt compelled to put my hat back on. I didn't know what was wrong. I ate until I was ready to burst, trying hard to ignore everything except what was directly in front of me: the chocolate melting beneath my fingernails, the candy so sweet it made my throat hurt.

THE following spring, on one of the first warm days, I was playing with an old friend, Teresa, in her neat and ordered backyard when she asked, completely out of the blue, if I was dying. "The other kids say that you're slowly dying, that you're wasting away." I looked at her in shock. Dying? Why on earth would anyone think I was dying? "No," I replied in the tone of voice I'd have used if she'd asked me whether I was the pope, "I'm not dying."

When I got home, I planned to ask my mother why Teresa would say such a thing. But just as I was coming through the front door, she was entering from the garage, her arms laden with shopping bags. She took a bright red shirt out of a bag and held it up against my chest.

"Turtlenecks are hard to find in short sleeves, so I bought several."

I was still a tomboy at heart and cared little about what I wore, so long as it wasn't a dress. But turtlenecks—why on earth would I want to wear turtlenecks in the spring? I didn't ask out loud, but my mother must have known what I was thinking. She looked me straight in the eye. "If you wear something that comes up around your neck, it makes the scar less visible."

Genuinely bewildered, I took the bright-colored pile of shirts down to my room. Wouldn't I look even more stupid wearing turtlenecks in the summer? Would they really hide my scar? I hadn't taken a good, long, objective look at myself since the wig fitting. I remembered feeling upset by it, but I conveniently didn't remember what I'd seen in that mirror, and I hadn't allowed myself a close scrutiny since.

I DONNED MY SHORT-SLEEVED turtlenecks and finished out the few months of elementary school. I played with my friend Jan at her wonderful home with its several acres of meadow and, most magnificent of all, a small lake. There was a rowboat we weren't allowed to take out by ourselves, but we did anyway. Rowing it to the far shore, a mere eighth of a mile away, we'd "land" and pretend we'd just discovered a new country. With notebooks in hand, we would log our discoveries, overturning stones and giving false Latin names to the newts and various pieces of slime we found under them.

Jan had as complex a relationship to her stuffed and plastic animals as I had to mine, and when I slept over, we'd compare our intricate worlds. Sometimes, though, Jan wanted to talk about boys, and I'd sit on my sleeping bag with my knees tucked up under my nightgown, listening patiently. I never had much to offer, though I had just developed my very first crush. It was on Omar Sharif.

Late one night I'd stayed up and watched Dr. Zhivago on television with my father. Curled up beside him with my head on his stomach, I watched the images of a remote world, a world as beautiful as it was deadly and cold. For weeks I pictured the ruined estate where Zhivago wrote his sonnets, aware that the true splendor of the house was inextricably bound to the fact that it was ruined. I didn't understand why this should be so, nor why reimagining this scene gave me such a deep sense of fulfillment mingled with such a sad sense of longing.

Elementary school graduation day approached. I remembered being in second grade and looking out on a group of sixth graders preparing for graduation. It had seemed like an unimaginable length of time before I'd get there. But now I was out there mingling in the courtyard. So much had happened in four years. I felt so old, and I felt proud of being so old. During the ceremony I was shocked when the vice principal started speaking about me, about how I should receive special attention for my "bravery." As he spoke, I could feel my face turning red. Here I was, the center of attention, receiving the praise I'd been fantasizing about for years, and all I could feel was intense, searing embarrassment. I was called up onto the platform; everyone was applauding. In a daze I accepted the gift Mr. Schultz was presenting me with, a copy of The Prophet. I could barely thank him.

Later, alone in my room, I opened the book at random. The verse I read was about love, about how to accept the love of another with dignity. I shut the book after only a page. I wanted nothing to do with the world of love; I thought wanting love was a weakness to be overcome. And besides, the world of love wanted nothing to do with me.

THE summer passed, and junior high school loomed. Jan, Teresa, and Sarah were all very excited at the prospect of being "grown-ups," of attending different classes, of having their own locker. Their excitement was contagious, and the night before the first day of school I proudly marked my assorted notebooks for my different subjects and secretly scuffed my new shoes to make them look old.

Everyone must have been nervous, but I was sure I was the only one who felt true apprehension. I found myself sidling through the halls, trying to pretend that I didn't notice the other kids—almost all of them strangers from adjoining towns—staring at me. Having seen plenty of teen movies with their promise of intrigue and drama, I had been looking forward to going to the lunchroom. As it happened, I sat down next to a table full of boys.

They pointed openly and laughed, calling out loudly enough for me to hear, "What on earth is *that?*" "That is the ugliest girl I have ever seen." I knew in my heart their comments had nothing to do with me; it was all about their appearing tough and cool to their friends. But these boys were older than the ones in grade school, and for the very first time I realized they were passing judgment on my suitability, or lack of it, as a girlfriend.

My initial tactic was to pretend I didn't hear them, but this only seemed to spur them on. In the hallways, where I suffered similar attacks of teasing, I simply looked down and walked more quickly, but in the lunchroom I was a sitting duck. The same group took to sitting near me day after day, even when I tried to camouflage myself by sitting in the middle of a group. They grew bolder, and I could hear them plotting to send someone to sit across the table from me. I'd look up from my food and there would be a boy slouching awkwardly in a red plastic chair, innocently asking me my name. Then he'd ask me how I got to be so ugly. At this the group would burst into laughter, and my inquisitor would saunter back, victorious.

After two weeks I broke down and went to my guidance counselor to complain. I thought he would offer to reprimand them, but instead he asked if I'd like to come and eat in his office. Surprised, I said yes, and that's what I did. I felt safe eating in that office, but I also felt lonely, and for the very first time I definitively identified the source of my unhappiness as being ugly. A few weeks later I left school to reenter chemotherapy, and I was almost glad to go back to it.

My INNER life became ever more macabre. Vietnam was still within recent memory, and pictures of the horrors of Cambodia loomed on every TV screen and in every newspaper. I told myself again and again how good I had it in comparison, what a wonder it was to have food and clothes and a home and no one torturing me. I bombed and starved and persecuted my own suffering right out of existence.

I had the capacity of imagination to momentarily escape my own pain, and I had the elegance of imagination to teach myself something true regarding the world around me; but I didn't yet have the clarity of imagination to grant myself the right to suffer. If there was a more important pain in the world, it meant my own was negated. I thought I simply had to accept the fact that I was ugly, and that to feel despair about it was wrong.

Halloween came around again, and even though I was feeling a bit woozy from an injection a few days before, I put on a plastic witch mask and went out with Teresa. I walked down the streets, suddenly bold and free: No one could see my face. I peered through the eye slits and did not see one person staring at me, ready to make fun of my face. I breathed in the condensing, plastic-tainted air behind the mask and thought that I was breathing in normalcy, that this freedom and ease were what other people felt all the time. Assuming this was so, I again named my own face as the thing that kept me apart, as the tangible element of what was wrong with my life and with me.

At home, when I took the mask off, I felt both sad and relieved. Sad because I had felt like a pauper walking for a few brief hours in the clothes of a prince and because I had liked it so much. Relieved because I felt no connection with that kind of happiness. I didn't deserve it and thus I shouldn't want it. It was easier to slip back into my depression and blame my face for everything.

HANNAH was a cleaning woman in Dr. Woolf's office. Her domain, when she wasn't polishing the floors or disinfecting the metal furniture, was an oblong room just a few doors down from Dr. Woolf's.

During the last year of chemotherapy I'd grown considerably weaker, and sometimes walking the few blocks to the car after the injection seemed an insurmountable task. On bad days my mother would leave me in Hannah's care while she went to fetch the car. Hannah would sit me down in a chair next to a small table with a kettle and some cups on it, kneel in front of me, and ask, "How do you feel?" Looking her straight in the eye, I'd confidentially report, "My nose hurts."

I later learned that the chemo affected my sinuses, but as far as I could tell, Hannah was the only one who believed this comic complaint. She'd nod sympathetically and offer me a cup of tea, and I would politely refuse. Beyond a cup of tea, there was nothing she could offer me. But her gaze soothed me. With Hannah I felt a vague sense of camaraderie, imagining that both our little lives were made miserable by these unknowing, cloddish doctors. As ill as I felt, I always liked sitting there with her, imagining our parallel lives clicking quietly along like two trains beside each other, with similar routes but different destinations.

When I played with Jan or Teresa—my friends from that time now indelibly labeled "before"—they treated me the same way they always had, though perhaps with an air of delicacy that seemed unnatural for all of us. They asked me questions about the physical effects of my treatment: how much it hurt, why I was so skinny, when my hair would grow back. I loved to answer with vigor and embellishment. A third of my answers were shaped by the braggart's love of a good tale, another third by my instinctive knowledge that they'd never understand what it was really like, and a third by my own unawareness of what it was like a great deal of the time.

I realized how different these conversations were from the ones with my friends on ward 10, my friends from "after." People who weren't ill or involved in the daily flow of hospital life had their own ideas of what it was like to be ill. It seemed impossible to tell them how it really was, and I didn't particularly want to do so. I was confident that as soon as I was back on ward 10, my friends and I would redefine for each other what it was like to be sick.

I felt as if my illness were a blanket the world had thrown over me; all that could be seen from the outside was an indistinguishable lump. And somehow I transformed that blanket into a tent, beneath which I almost happily set up camp. Not that this meant I was actually happy—not in any normal definition of the word. "For God's sake, stop looking so morbid all the time" became a familiar phrase in my house. Whenever anyone else was present, I felt incapable of being anything other than a depressed lump. It was only when I was alone that my ability to relish life surfaced.

Each week, with the first glimmer of returning strength after the days of vomiting, I discovered that, for me, joy could be measured in negative terms: of what I *didn't* have, which was pain and weakness. My greatest happiness wasn't acquired through effort, but was something I already had, deep and sonorous, inside of me. I also saw that most people, never having experienced intense physical discomfort on a regular basis, didn't—couldn't—know this.

I viewed other people both critically and sympathetically. Why couldn't they just stop complaining so much, just let go and see how good they actually had it? Everybody—from my mother to the characters I read about in books (who were as actual and important as real people to me)—was always looking at someone else's life and envying it. I wanted them to stop, to see how much they had already, how they had their health and their strength. I imagined how my life would be if I had half their fortune. Then I would catch myself, guilty of exactly the thing I was accusing others of.

ONCE, during a week of intensive chemotherapy toward the end of the two and a half years, I was sent to another ward, as 10 was already full when I checked in. It was late at night, always a bad time in the hospital, but especially on this ward, which was notoriously understaffed. Often there was only one nurse and a handful of aides to take care of everyone. This was particularly bad news if you had an IV. They were still using butterfly needles inserted into the back of your hand and taped down to the skin. The chances of the needle's puncturing the vein were high, and I'd learned to keep that hand absolutely still, even in my sleep. Worse, however, the limited staff often neglected to refill the IV bottles regularly, and they would dry up in the night, causing the needle to clot with blood. Many nights I had to be woken three or four times in order to be restuck with a new butterfly. I learned not only to sleep without moving, for fear of hitting the needle out of place, but also to sleep in two-hour shifts so that I could wake up and check the bottle's fluid level myself.

This particular night I woke up on that strange ward and looked at the IV bottle in the light coming in through the city window. To my relief, it was still half full. I had to go to the bathroom. I tried to assess if I could walk the few feet unaided and decided I couldn't. Pressing the call button for a nurse, I sighed, realizing it wasn't a buzzer system, as they had on other floors, but simply a bulb that would light up over my door in the hallway. Chances were good that no one would see it for some time. I waited. I waited and waited and even tried calling out, but my voice couldn't carry that far. My roommate slept soundly, still heavily sedated from her operation that morning.

How much time passed I don't know, but I had to make a decision: Get up and walk, or pee in the bed, as I'd done once before in a similar situation. I wasn't going to go through that embarrassment again. All I had to do was be strong, I told myself, and I could make it to the bathroom. Sitting up and slipping down to the floor was fine as long as I did it slowly. Grabbing my IV pole, I began the seven or eight feet to the bathroom. My IV clinked against the metal pole as I pushed it along, and as I neared the foot of my roommate's bed, I understood I would never make it. Tiredness so overwhelmed me that I even forgot I had to go to the bathroom. Could I make it back to my bed? It was too far. Suddenly afraid I was going to faint, I crouched down to the floor. I'm okay, I told myself. I'm okay.

I thought that if I could just rest like that for long enough, I'd regain the strength to make it back to bed. The five feet might as well have been five miles. My knees began to ache, and afraid that I might fall even from this crouch position, I gingerly lay down on the floor. My hipbones and elbows hurt against the hard floor. If I lay here long enough, would someone come by and see me? Maybe that someone would sweep me up in his arms, place me back in bed, put a comforting hand across my forehead, and whisper something sweet and consoling in my ear.

Until that moment I had believed in the dramatic possibilities my tragedy called up. But now the floor was cold. The floor was just so cold. I didn't want to lie there anymore; and even though it would take a herculean effort to ease myself up, I didn't want to wait for someone to come rescue me. I suddenly had a glimmer of what the person had meant when he scratched that message into the bathroom door: "Be Here Now." I felt a bottomless sense of peace, of stillness. I decided it was simply a matter of will, that if I really concentrated, I could make it back. And I did. It took a long time, and I don't remember anything once I was back in bed. I must have fallen asleep immediately, only to be woken a little while later by an aide answering my call light at last.

"Do YOU realize this is the last six weeks?" my mother asked late one Thursday afternoon while preparing dinner.

"What?"

"The last set of shots. Only six more, and then all this will be over. What a relief. You must be overjoyed."

I was shocked. Over? It was almost over? "Thank God for that," I said, using a phrase she employed all the time.

I went down to my room and lay on my bed, utterly confused. Why wasn't I overjoyed? I was almost thirteen years old. I'd been doing this since I was ten; I barely remembered what life had been like before. No more shots; no more Dr. Woolf; no more throwing up. Why wasn't I happy? I didn't want it to continue, did I? No, I knew I didn't, but life after chemo seemed unimaginable. As hard as it was to admit this to myself, I was afraid of its ending, of everything changing. I wouldn't be special anymore; no one would love me. Without the arena of chemotherapy in which to prove myself, how would anyone know I was worthy of love? I lay there turning these things over and over in my mind, more perplexed than I'd ever been in my life.

Counting off the days became an obsession. Thirty-eight more days until the last shot. Thirty-two more days. Fifteen more days. Three days and eighteen hours. Forty-eight hours and nineteen minutes. Three hours. Sixteen minutes. Now. I walked into Dr. Woolf's office, and it didn't seem in any way special or different. Dr. Woolf was all business as usual—on the phone, talking in five directions at once. For only the second time, I looked at the syringes in the basin. One was filled with a red solution the color of Kool-Aid. I watched him attach the needles, watched him walk carelessly around the room with them, still on the phone. Then he put the phone down and put the tourniquet on and rubbed my arm with a cotton ball, the smell of rubbing alcohol filling the air. As usual, it took a few stabs to find a vein.

The hot flashes came, followed by the familiar nausea, and I painfully retched up the single Thorazine pill I'd been given an hour before. It was meant to help the vomiting. Slowly I realized that I wasn't crying. Not crying had become the goal of my visits to the chemotherapy clinic. But now I felt absolutely nothing. My mother was praising me for being so good. I looked at her and at the beautiful window behind her. Robotically I looked back to my arm, to Dr. Woolf's huge hands changing syringes. Nothing. I felt only a void.

Then it was over. My mother and Dr. Woolf were talking. I couldn't hear them, though they were right next to me. I was looking at the ceiling. It was peeling, and there was a water stain just off to the right. Funny, I thought. All that time looking around and never noticing the ceiling. Had I never looked at it, or had I looked at it dozens of times, only now really *seeing* it? My mother finished speaking with Dr. Woolf and turned toward me; then she too, before helping me off the table, wordlessly looked up for a moment, following my gaze.

She went off to get the car, and I was ushered into Hannah's room. "How do you feel?" she asked. I began to cry. Just a little bit at first, but soon I was sobbing. I tried to stop, but it was out of control, and I gave myself over to it. Hannah bent over and put an arm on my shoulder for a second. Then, without asking, she busied herself making me the cup of tea she'd been offering me for years. Though I didn't think it was possible, I cried even harder.

A few minutes later Hannah handed me the tea in a mug with a picture of the Statue of Liberty on it. Slowly the crying began to stop. I felt so tired all of a sudden, but quietly tired, in a restful way, not the usual exhaustion. By the time my mother returned, I had stopped, not because of any effort on my part, but because the crying had run its course. We said good-bye to Hannah and walked out. Among the people on the streets, bending their heads down into the cold wind, no one seemed to notice or care that this day was different from others.

Eight

ONE day, when I had a full three or four inches of hair, I was leaving the house with Susie. At the last minute I turned and ran back up the stairs, calling out, "Just a minute while I get my hat."

"You don't need it anymore, Lucy. Your hair is fine," she called back, frustrated that we were going to be late.

I stopped in the middle of the stairs, genuinely surprised. Running my fingers through my hair, I had to admit she was more or less right. It wasn't nearly as long as it used to be, but I wasn't bald. I went out with her into the world, bareheaded for the first time in years. A warm breeze parted my hair and stroked it like a caress. We went to the store, and people gave me second looks, as they always did, but not one person called me Baldy.

The next day I went to school bareheaded, and no one mentioned it. Had I been wrong in thinking that I needed to hide behind my hat? Had it all been a mistake on my part? Except, people still looked at me. Though I had given up eating in the lunchroom, there were relentless daily attacks of teasing in the hallways. Girls never teased me, but out of the corner of my eye I could see them staring. Groups of boys were what I most feared, and I gladly ducked into an empty doorway if I saw a group coming my way that looked like trouble.

MY RELIEF—tinged with regret—at leaving the familiar world of the hospital didn't last long. The radiation had been very hard on my teeth, and saving them would require a lot of specialized work. Only a few months after I naïvely thought I'd said good-bye to Columbia Presbyterian Hospital forever, we had to again start driving in once or twice a week for what turned out to be two years of dental work.

There was, however, the benefit of getting out of school. By now I hated school with a vengeance and continually told lies about my health in order to stay away. Anything, just not to have to face those boys each day.

The various procedures, including at least a dozen root canals, kept me in pain most of the time. Codeine was prescribed. We kept the prescription bottle in a kitchen cabinet, and within a short while, I was taking pills almost constantly. I looked forward to the pleasant, sleepy feeling they offered. Aware that I was taking more than I should, I would alternately ask my mother and then my father to refill the prescription in order to keep my high consumption less conspicuous. All of this came to an abrupt end one day when my mother caught me shaking out no less than six times the prescribed number of pills into my palm. From then on I had to make do with aspirin.

My inability to open my mouth wide caused problems whenever anyone wanted to work on my back teeth, and it was decided that I should be admitted to the hospital and have a whole slew of work done all at once under general anesthesia. This idea was fine by me.

This was my fifth operation, a number that seemed high at the time. On the morning of the operation, the nurses came with the preop injection needles. This was the worst part of all. Yet it gave me pleasure to think that the boys who teased me openly at school and the adults who stared at me covertly elsewhere would never be able to stand this pain. My whole body was tense and my stomach upside down, but I was convinced that because I did not admit these things, it meant I had a chance at *really* being brave, not just pretending.

After the operation I remember throwing up and feeling terribly weak, though joyously relieved it was all over. In post-op the specially trained nurses checked on me every ten minutes. I was too groggy to sense what was going on, but I relished the aura of attention, the cool hands on my warm arms, the I-won't-let-anything-bad-happen-to-you voices, the notion that I was somehow special. Afterward, back in my room, I dozed and woke for hours, each time more panicked than before at being all alone. I'd make up some excuse to ring for a nurse, just to have someone enter the room. I began to wish that the operation weren't over, that I was still asleep on the stretcher with a crowd of people hovering near me.

Later, as I underwent more and more operations, even when I was home in my own bed, upset about how much I hated my face, I could put myself to sleep by imagining myself lying on a stretcher. I could almost hear the movements of strangers in comfortingly familiar uniforms all around me, the distant beeps that were really heartbeats.

At school the taunts were becoming only harder to take. Somehow I had reasoned that if a bad thing happened often enough, it would get easier. It worked with pain, so why wasn't it working with teasing? Every time I was teased, which usually happened several times a day, it seemed incrementally more painful. I was good at pretending I hadn't heard, but I could sense myself changing, becoming more fearful. Before, I'd been an outgoing person, but now meeting new people was laced with dread. Except for the one time I went to my guidance counselor to complain, I discussed this with no one. Besides, I reasoned, what could I do about it? I was ugly, so people were going to make fun of me. I'd just better get used to it. But I couldn't. No matter how much I braced myself, the words stung every time.

One afternoon I went to the hospital for some outpatient surgery. A tooth in the back of my mouth had to be pulled, and I was knocked out for about ten minutes. Afterward I waited in recovery for my mother to take me home. When she came in, she pulled the blood-soaked gauze out of my mouth and gasped. In the course of the surgery two of my lower front teeth had been partially knocked out, leaving two very ugly stumps. Apparently no one had been planning to tell us about this complication, and it was only by chance that my mother discovered it while we were still there. Justifiably, she exploded in anger. The surgeon's response was predictably patronizing, and a full-fledged battle ensued as I sat there feeling a bit woozy.

Once home, my mother, still fuming, turned to me and said, "You don't have to go to school tomorrow if you don't want. I understand that you might not feel very good about the way your teeth look." We looked straight at each other. Something had just happened, but I wasn't sure what. All I'd ever wanted was to be left alone and allowed to stay at home. I had spent a great deal of energy trying to convince her that I had to stay at home because of some counterfeit physical ailment, and suddenly it wasn't what I wanted at all.

She stood over me in the living room, the cats howling for their dinner because we'd returned home so late, and offered me— What? Compassion? As I think of it now, I'm certain her offer to let me stay home was an attempt to understand what she must have known instinctively. But it was too late. I'd already given up that fight. I understood my mother's offer only as barbed verification of what I believed to be the indisputable truth: I was too ugly to go to school. I pretty much stopped going to the seventh grade, and though my grades were mediocre, I was moved along to the eighth.

I RELISHED that summer as no other. My friend Jan and I took our infatuation with horses to ridiculous proportions. We spent all of our playtime pretending we were horses, galloping around her yard, jumping over whatever obstacle we could set up. Whoever got around better was given a homemade blue ribbon, and afterward we would kneel on her lawn and dare each other to graze.

Jan's parents were paying for her to take riding lessons, and I was filled with envy. We couldn't afford them. Sometimes she'd invite me to go with her, and I would, though I hated the superior tone she took with me then. I went because the very presence of horses over-whelmed me, filled my whole body with a sensation so physical and complete that I'd be transported during those hours. Jan started boasting that her parents were going to buy her a horse and that maybe, just maybe, she'd let me help her take care of it.

Jan never got her horse, but that summer, shortly after my four-teenth birthday, I got my job as stable hand at Diamond D. It was the perfect environment for me. Most of the other hands were girls who were a couple of years older than I was, and there were two boys, Sean and Stephen. The girls were nice enough to me and eventually be-came my friends, though I never felt completely at ease with them. They were raucous and wild, and I loved them for this. Epithets the likes of which I'd never heard even from my own wild brothers flew from everyone's lips. There was a glorious delight in getting as muddy and dirty as possible and in the tired ache from trying to hoist bales of hay, however ineffectually. As the summer wore on, I got tanned and gained weight and grew physically stronger every day.

I loved how basic the needs of the animals were, how they had to be fed and watered even if you were tired or hot or late. There was a primacy to it, a simplicity I recognized from coping with pain, a meaning that did not extend beyond the confines of one's body.

I kept my new world, with its physical pleasures and new social experiences, hidden from my family, who did not seem particularly interested anyway, though they were glad I'd found something "healthy" to do with my time. School was coming around again, and I actually looked forward to returning. Horse fever is common among junior high school girls, and I thought my new job at the stable might improve my status. Everyone at the barn was preparing to return to school, including Jeanne, who was boy crazy and had a crush on Sean.

The day before school began, some six of us girls were sitting on top of the hay pile. Jeanne stood on top, pointing to each person and asking, "If Sean asked you out, would you go with him?" The girls were mixed in age and in physical development, Jeanne being the oldest, at sixteen. Alison and I, at fourteen, were the youngest. Alison looked fourteen, but I, my body still reeling from the effects of che-motherapy, looked about ten. Puberty was still a year away. Jeanne seemed to be asking everyone systematically, but she wasn't actually thinking of asking me, was she? Sean would never ask me out.

Finally, Jeanne turned to me and, only because she didn't know how to politely leave me out, asked the question. I hesitated, not sure how to respond, but then Chris—another of the girls—came to my aid and answered for me. "Why would Sean want to go out with her?"

"Well, I'm just asking," Jeanne replied. I shifted uncomfortably on the hay, glad Chris had spoken for me. This was the moment when I knew definitively that I would never have a boyfriend, that no one would ever be interested in me in that way. I suppose I had learned this already from the boys at school, but never had I actually expressed it in real terms to myself.

Because I was never going to have love (this realization, too painful to linger over, I embraced swiftly and finally), I cast myself in the role of Hero of Love. Instead of proving my worth on the chemotherapy table, I would become a hero through my understanding of the real beauty that existed in the world. My face may have closed the door on love and beauty in their fleeting states, but didn't my face also open me up to perceptions I might otherwise be blind to?

Beauty had nothing to do with the ephemeral world of boys—of this I felt sure. This was driven home to me when junior high school started again and I watched my twin sister and her friends begin their puberty. They put on blue eye shadow, blow-dried their hair, and spent interminable hours at the local mall. My own notions of what made a woman beautiful were more classically oriented: If I could look like anyone in the world, it would be either Marlene Dietrich or Botticelli's Venus. I definitely did *not* aspire to look like Farrah Fawcett.

At school the old gang of boys appeared to have dispersed, and I was free to eat in the lunchroom again. But a new group had formed, and they tracked me down every day between fourth and fifth periods as I went from gym to English class, which were at opposite ends of the school. Their teasing was the most hurtful of all because it wasn't even directed at me but at a boy named Jerry.

"Hey, look, it's Jerry's girlfriend. Hey, Jerry, go on, ask your girlfriend out." I heard Jerry meekly protest. I knew that calling me his girlfriend was just about the most malicious insult the other boys could level at him. What morons, I thought. What misguided morons. Martin Luther King, Jr., one of my heroes, had said, "I will not allow my oppressors to dictate to me the means of my resistance." That seemed like a far truer thing, a far deeper thing. I wanted to hate those boys, but I tried to forgive them. I thought that if I could do this, the pain they caused would be extinguished. I was shooting for nothing less than sainthood; often, after my daily meeting with them, I only ended up hating myself instead.

The horses remained my one real source of relief. When I was in their presence, nothing else mattered. Horses neither disapproved nor approved of what I looked like. All that counted was how I treated them, how my actions weighted themselves in the world.

IN THE middle of the school year, several months before my fifteenth birthday, I went to see Dr. Conley, the surgeon who had removed my jaw, to discuss plans for reconstructing it. I had known all along that something was going to be done to "fix" my face, but up until this point I don't think I had really believed it.

Without the threat of chemo or dental work, being in a doctor's office seemed so simple and easy. As Dr. Conley examined me, he held my head in his hands, touching my face as no else had in years. It was the closest I ever got to experiencing trust.

After the examination he sat down and explained to me that the biggest obstacle to reconstruction would come from all the radiation treatments I'd undergone. Irradiated tissue tends not to take grafts too well and presents a higher rate of reabsorption; even if the graft wasn't actually rejected, it might simply be "taken back" by my body and shrink down to nothing.

He proposed a technique that involved the use of "pedestals," which would require several operations. In the first operation two parallel incisions would be made in my stomach. The strip of skin between these incisions would be lifted up and rolled into a sort of tube with both ends still attached to my stomach, resembling a kind of handle. This was the pedestal. The two incisions would be sewn together, like a seam. Six weeks later one end of the handle would be cut from my stomach and attached to my wrist, so that my hand would be sewn to my stomach for six weeks. Then the end of the tube that was still attached to my stomach would be severed and sewn to my face, so that now my hand would be attached to my face. Six weeks after that, my hand would be cut loose and the pedestal, or flap, as they called it, would be nestled completely into the gap created by my missing jaw. This would be only the first pedestal. The whole process would take several, plus additional operations to carve everything into a recognizable shape, over a period of about ten years altogether. Ten years! I was horrified. I would be twenty-five years old in ten years—ancient. Any hope I'd allowed myself died right then.

My despair worsened a few days later when I went to the library with my father. While he picked among the fiction, I went to the nonfiction department and secretly looked up books on plastic surgery. I found photographs of the pedestal procedure. The people in the photographs looked like freaks. Worst of all, the final outcome made them look exactly like what they were: people with alien bits of flesh sewn to them. I was so frightened I could not get my breath. Was this what my life was going to be? I felt utterly without hope, completely alone and without any chance of ever being loved. Feeling as if I had uncovered some horrible secret, I went to meet my father. As we drove home together, he asked me what was wrong, but I couldn't tell him. At home I went to my room, where I wanted desperately to cry, but even the tears were numbed back. I lay frozen on my bed until my mother called me for dinner. For the first time, I wished I were dead.

RELIEF came in two unexpected ways. The first occurred some months later, toward the end of eighth grade, when Kelly, a girl I had met at the stable, had to move to another state. Unable to take her horse, an ex-racehorse named Sure Swinger, she arranged with my parents to give him to me. I'd never understood just how quickly, how splendidly and suddenly, reality could change.

The second form of comfort came in the person of Dr. Daniel Baker, a younger associate of Dr. Conley's. He and some other doctors were working on a new reconstruction technique: microsurgery to graft vascularized free flaps. This state-of-the-art surgery involved taking a large chunk of soft tissue, probably from my groin, and sewing the whole thing, veins and all, onto the jaw area. This not only dispensed with the multistage pedestal procedure but it also offered a greater chance that the graft would survive, because the new tissue would have its own blood supply. Dr. Baker explained that it would be best to wait another year or so, perhaps until I was sixteen, so that I could grow some more first. I would have to have a major operation followed by lesser ones to shape the graft, but Dr. Baker seemed to think there was a good chance of achieving "a near normal jawline."

I can still see my father's reaction as he stood in Dr. Baker's office beaming. I had never mentioned my fears concerning my face to my father, and in my solipsism I had never thought that he might share my unhappiness. The halo of joy that surrounded him now was a revelation to me, and his joy made me feel better.

Maybe life was going to be all right after all. Maybe this wasn't my actual face at all but the face of some interloper, some ugly intruder, and my "real" face, the one I was meant to have all along, was within reach. I began to imagine my "original" face, the one free from all deviation, all error. I believed that if none of this had happened to me, I would have been beautiful. I looked into the mirror closely and imagined the lower half of my face filled out, normal. Reaching my hand up, I covered my chin and jaw, and yes, even I could see that the rest of my face really was beautiful. As soon as I took my hand away, the ugliness of the lower half canceled out the beauty of the upper half, but now this didn't matter so much: It was all going to be "fixed."

What would it be like to walk down the street and be able to trust that no one would say anything nasty to me? My only clues were from Halloween and from winter, when I could wrap the lower half of my face in a scarf and talk to people who had no idea that my beauty was a lie. To feel that confidence without the threat of exposure—how could I possibly want anything more? If they thought I was beautiful, they might even love me. *Me* as an individual, as a person.

I'd rationalized my own desires for so long that I was genuinely perplexed as to whether this sudden and glorious sense of relief at the prospect of having my face fixed was valid. Was the love that I'd guarded against for so long going to be the reward for my suffering? I had put a great deal of effort into accepting that my life would be without love and beauty, in order to be comforted by Love and Beauty. I did not trust the idea that happiness could be an option.

For a few months I settled into a routine of living what felt like two separate lives. Days were filled with school, where I tried to be as fiercely intelligent as I could. My armor would be my academic prowess. The second life took place after school and all day during the summer, when I went to my horse, Swinger, with whom I was conducting nothing less than a romantic relationship.

We went on long rides through the woods, and I would tell him everything I knew and then explain why I loved him so much, why he was special, different from other horses, how I would take care of him. After the ride I would take him to graze in an empty field. I would lie down on his broad bare back and think I was the luckiest girl alive. Best of all was when I happened to find him lying down in his stall. Carefully, so as not to spook him, I'd creep in and lie down on top of his giant body, his great animal heat and breath rising up to swallow my own smaller heat and less substantial air.

WHEN school started again, my ninth-grade English class began reading poetry. Our first assignment was Theodore Roethke's "My Papa's Waltz." I read it dutifully the night before class and recognized in the image of the father's hand and the boy's bewilderment something beautiful and important, something that vaguely had to do with my own family. And as I recognized myself, I also realized the precision of language. The poem's power over me came from the author's unassailable ability to say what felt so right and true. I tried to say this in class the next day, but my teacher wanted us to talk about whether or not the boy in the poem loved his father. As we spent the forty minutes debating along those lines, what I knew about my love for my own father seemed to grow only more distant.

Earlier in my childhood, when my father came home late at night, he would shout greetings to everybody as he came through the door, and Sarah and the dogs and I would go running to greet him. But eventually only the dogs would get up to greet him, while Sarah and I tossed off distracted greetings from our seats in front of the television set. One evening I had a terrible premonition of the time, after Sarah and I had grown up and moved out and the dogs were long dead, when he would come home and there would be only his own voice echoing emptily up the stairs. I felt a strange chill, almost as if I had seen a ghost. From that day on, I made a point of greeting him at the top of the stairs. I saw this in terms of my future absence from his life; it never occurred to me that he would ever be absent from mine.

Just seven or eight months after that premonition, I had an experience of death. Only four months after I received him, Swinger developed an infection in his hoof. I watched carefully as Gene, one of the adult employees of the stable, gave Swinger the prescribed penicillin injection in his neck. Then I went down to the tack room to put something away. When I returned to the ring where Gene was leading Swinger, I realized something was terribly wrong. Swinger was falling down and trying to get back up, only to fall down again. Finally he could not get back up at all.

A crowd had gathered, and everyone was shouting and trying to rouse him; but his legs were sticking almost straight out and trembling, and his eyes were rolling into the back of his head. Gene shouted at me to run and get a blanket from the barn. I tore away to get the blanket off its rack. With it in hand I ran back to the ring, but as I got closer, I saw that everyone was just standing there, not shouting anymore. Gene reached the gate before me and held it shut and wouldn't let me in. I looked at him and burst into tears. I allowed Gene to hold me as I sobbed. I smelled the sweat on his clothes and looked toward Swinger and knew that he had died.

Someone called my mother. When she came to pick me up, for some reason I was frightened by the prospect of her reaction: Would she be mad? Naturally, she was very sympathetic, but I couldn't shake the feeling of shame. When we got home, I went wordlessly down to my room and watched television in a stupor of grief. My mourning was so untouchable that I had no clue as to what to do with it. Perhaps Swinger had died because I loved him too much. Why else would God allow the being I loved more than myself to die like that?

I WAS stricken over Swinger's death for several months, but time eventually did perform its healing task, and gradually I became excited at the prospect of getting another horse, promised by my parents. I knew that money was still an issue and that this new horse might not materialize straightaway, but I knew they would not go back on their word. Then sometime after Christmas my mother received a phone call from my dad's boss, explaining that he had gone to the hospital because of stomach pains. My first reaction was that this would put a wrench in my new-horse plans. My mother was certain it was nothing at all, maybe just his ulcer acting up again. But he was still in the hospital the next day—they were keeping him for tests—and he was there the day after that and the next day too. My mother started visiting him every day, yet the rest of us stayed behind, assuming he would be out the very next day.

The weeks turned into months. He had pancreatitis: No one would say if he would get better or not. One day toward the end of March my mother came home and told us they'd put my father on oxygen. Inwardly I shuddered. Everything I knew about hospitals told me that this was a bad thing. My father was going to die, and as bad as this knowledge was, it was made worse by my notion that I was the only one who understood it. My family was not the sort to openly discuss things. Though we all must have been hurting, we did not speak of my father except with a forced optimism.

My father's bedroom was a disaster area, filled with stray papers and dirty socks and odd cups and occasional forks. I went in and surveyed it all—just as I'd done when I was younger and he was away at work— but now I was looking for something else. Now I was looking for something that would explain my father's life to me. I couldn't find it.

The whole time he was in the hospital I went to visit my father only once. Even after all these years, I don't understand why we stayed away. Were we so adrift in our own sea of grief that we were able to convince ourselves that it was better this way? He grew more and more disoriented. My mother reported that he had become paranoid, talking about Germans and the dogs the Germans had set on him when he was a prisoner during World War II. He'd been a pilot in the RAF, and we had a dashing, fuzzy photo of him in his flak suit, smiling. It pained me to think that now, near the end of his life, he was reliving this nightmare, as alone as he had been the first time. We spent the next couple of weeks waiting. Every time the phone rang, the whole house went silent.

I was dreading the inevitable phone call; I knew that Sarah would break down and cry, but I didn't know what everyone else would do. I wanted my father to die and for there to be no fuss, no outbreaks, no displays. I was terrified.

When the call did come at last, some six weeks before my sixteenth birthday, my mother answered the phone at the far end of the kitchen. My brother Nicholas was sitting at one end of the table, Sarah was sitting at the other end, and I was standing in the doorway. Susie was away at college, and my brother Sean was living in California. Sarah, Nicholas, and I remained motionless as we listened to my mother speak, thanking the doctor for all he had done, and when she got off, she told us matter-of-factly and very sadly what we already knew. To my surprise it wasn't Sarah who cried but Nicholas. He put his head down on the table and wept, and all I could think of was that I didn't expect this, just as I didn't expect Sarah to sit there so calmly.

I turned my head and looked at the painting on the wall next to me. It was a head of Christ painted by Sean, one I'd passed several thousand times, yet I felt I was seeing it for the first time. I'd never noticed how much brown he'd used in the thorns, how much gold for the skin. It all seemed so very odd. Did grief heighten vision, or was it only an illusion, a way to distance myself from what was happening?

Along with sadness a sense of relief followed my father's death. At least we weren't waiting anymore. I was sitting in the kitchen a couple of days after my dad's funeral. Perhaps we were still in shock, but Sarah and I were laughing hysterically over a new joke we'd heard, and just as we were in the thick of it, the phone rang. It was my surgeon, Dr. Baker. I was shocked to hear his voice, for he was nothing less than a monumental figure in my life; but when he offered his condolences, all I could do was jauntily reply, as if he'd just apologized for stepping on my shoe, "Oh, that's all right. It doesn't matter." As soon as I hung up the phone, I realized what I'd done. But as I told Sarah about the call, the two of us burst into laughter again.

THAT June, a few weeks after my sixteenth birthday, I went into New York University Medical Center for my first reconstructive operation, my first microvascularized free flap. I liked this hospital: It was newer and better staffed than Columbia Presbyterian, and I was no longer relegated to the children's ward. My ward was devoted to plastic surgery, and I was shocked to see how many people were having their noses done, their faces lifted.

The woman in the bed next to me was having her breast reconstructed after a mastectomy, and she insisted on telling me all about her scars and her feelings of ugliness. I had no patience with her lament. Her face was beautiful, and she had a husband who brought her a dozen red roses. It was true she was missing a breast, but I didn't see how that mattered as long as she had these other things. I realized she was genuinely suffering, but she was mistaken, I thought. Her problems lay in her perception. Talking with her only strengthened my conviction of the importance in this world of having a beautiful face. Still, I liked her, and I liked being treated as an adult by another adult. We ordered out for Chinese food, for what I kept calling my last meal. "No, no, don't say that," she said, trying to reassure me. I just couldn't get her to see that I was joking; I could tell she was new at this hospital stuff.

The anesthetist came to see me that night and decided that it might be hard to intubate me—insert a breathing tube into my windpipe—so he would do it while I was awake. It didn't sound like a big deal, and I didn't think twice about it.

The next morning, however, as I lay dazed on the stretcher, they tried passing a tube up one nostril. It didn't hurt, but when it reached the back of my throat, I gagged. They pulled it out and tried the other nostril. By now I was upset, but I lay as still as I could. That nostril didn't work either, so they decided to go straight through my mouth. This required prying my mouth open and keeping it open, which hurt like hell, but worse was that at each attempt to pass the tube, my airway was temporarily blocked and I couldn't breathe, which put me into a panic. The preop medications were slowing my reactions, but I instinctively started to struggle. When two nurses came and held me down, I started to cry and struggle even more. They must have sedated me further, because my reactions grew more sluggish.

Suddenly everyone seemed to disappear, and I was left in peace—floating but still crying hard. I looked up, and there was Dr. Baker looking down at me. He reached out his hand and placed it on my forehead, replicating the gesture I'd received during my very first operation. I was calmed instantly, as if all my sorrows existed within that one single point on my forehead. And then I was asleep.

WHEN I awoke, I was in a lot of pain, but the pain was in my hip, where the graft came from. I reached up to touch my face. I felt a large, warm, very soft mass where there used to be an indent, and a complicated trail of stitches. When my mother came to visit, she asked how I felt, and I responded with a question.

"What does it look like?"

"Well, dear, it's a bit hard to tell. It's very swollen."

"But do you think it will be all right?"

"Well, he's definitely filled it out. But it's so swollen now, you have to wait and see."

I didn't want to wait. After she had gone, I asked a nurse for a mirror. Sitting up was too painful, so I lay there and held the mirror above me, staring up at an image I only vaguely recognized. "Swollen" was an understatement. This new thing on my face was huge. What repulsed me most was a large strip of foreign skin, much paler than my facial skin, running along the lower half of my new jawline. Surrounded by dozens of minute stitches, it looked just like what it was—a patch. I handed the mirror back to the nurse, thanked her, and went back to sleep.

When I woke up again, I tried to remind myself that it had been only a few hours since the surgery and that I couldn't judge the end result by what I had seen in the mirror. There would be more operations to revise the graft. I knew better than to expect perfection; yet I had not anticipated how *foreign* it would look. I shut down, tried not to think about my face. When I did think about it, I projected my thinking forward to the next operation, the one that would fix this one.

After the first few hours I was taken out of intensive care and sent to special care, which was one rung lower on the attention scale. There were three other beds. The one directly across from me was empty. In the one next to that, kitty-corner from my bed, was a girl who, I found out from eavesdropping, was dying from a brain tumor. Relatives came and gave her presents, which she opened with a blank, unknowing face. When she spoke, her words were unintelligible. In the bed next to mine a teenage boy named Michael was recovering.

Michael's first comment to me was about my stuffed kangaroo, which my mother had bought for me and which all the nurses commented on. He said dryly that my kangaroo had usurped his monkey as the cutest toy on the ward. His monkey hung from a bar at arm's length above his bed. He was only a year older than I was, but he seemed to have lived a whole life already.

Michael would reach up to the bar hanging over his bed and use his arms to hoist himself up. He didn't wear a pajama top, so when his back was momentarily off the bed, I could see his muscles flex. He told me he had dived off the top of a two-story building into a pool and had hurt his back.

"Why'd you do that?"

"I don't know," he answered, looking up at the ceiling. "It was a friend's pool," he said after a moment, as if that should somehow clarify the situation.

Whenever he spoke, he sounded slightly bored, slightly distant. But he talked with me quite a bit over the next couple of days, and I always felt privileged that he was speaking to me at all. If he were at school, would he be one of the boys who made fun of me? I stole sideways glances at him—his long wavy hair, the stubble on his chin and upper lip—and thought that probably, yes, he would be.

One night Michael refused to take a particular pill, and the doctor came to argue with him about it. Michael fought with the doctors all the time, always questioning them and refusing to do things he didn't want to do; he was my complete opposite. It was the middle of the night, and the main overhead lights were off. His curtain was drawn, and I saw Michael's and the doctor's shadows thrown against the yellow curtain. The pill Michael was refusing to take was something he needed for his stomach. His voice was rising in protest, and then, inexplicably, he started crying and screamed at the doctor to leave. As the doctor left, I lay there, wondering if I should say something.

A few minutes later a nurse came to empty his urine catheter bag. I knew he had one—I had one too—but I'd never thought about how it might work with a man. The nurse didn't close the curtain properly, and when I looked over, I saw for the first time an adult male's penis. It was only then that I acknowledged that Michael, at the age of seventeen, was permanently paralyzed, all because of a stupid trick.

I couldn't help but compare his situation to my own. Michael had lost something he was never going to get back; my face had only changed into the next shape it was meant to have. I could not dare to think I might actually want or like that shape, but I had a sudden realization that to have it at all meant something.

Two days later I was transferred to a regular ward. I promised Michael I would come visit him, but I never did. As soon as I was back on the ward filled with nose jobs and jowl tucks, I grew fearful of my distorted face again and put Michael and his predicament out of my mind. I was walking to the bathroom by myself now, and each time I opened the door, I saw my own face reflected back at me. Was that really me? I considered the whole operation a failure, and when the doctors came around and told me how well it was healing, how good it looked, my heart sank. We were speaking two different languages; if this looked good, then what I thought would look good must be an impossible dream. I felt stupid for having had any expectations or hopes at all.

Nine

IT WAS only when I got home from the hospital that I permitted myself to look more closely at my new face. It was still extremely swollen (it would be for months), and a long, thin scar ran the length of it. In the middle of the scar was the island of pale skin from my hip. Placing my hand over the swollen and discolored parts, I tried to imagine how my face might look once it was "better." If I positioned the angle of my face and the angle of my hand and the angle of the mirror all just right, it looked okay.

Actually, in my mind my face looked even better than okay; it looked beautiful. But it was a beauty that existed in a possible future. This strange fantasy of beauty became something very private, a wish I would have been ashamed to let anyone in on. Primarily it was a fantasy of relief. When I tried to imagine being beautiful, I could only imagine living without the perpetual fear of being alone, without the great burden of isolation, which is what feeling ugly felt like.

The beginning of high school was a couple of months away. Each day I checked my face in private. I expected to have a second, revising operation before school started, but as it turned out, I would have to wait at least another three months. What was the point if I still had to walk into a new school on the first day looking like this?

There was only one solution, and that was to stop caring. I became pretentious. I picked out thick books by Russian authors and carted them around with me. Sometimes I even read them. *Anna Karenina. The Brothers Karamazov.* I read *Jude the Obscure* simply because I liked the title—and anything else that sounded difficult and deep.

On the first day of school I rode the bus, entered my strange homeroom, and went through my day of classes as invisibly as possible. By now my hair was long, and I walked around with my head bent, my dark blond hair covering half my face. Having decided against seeking anything as inconsequential as social status, I spent the days observing my peers with a perfectly calibrated air of disinterest. I remained the outsider, like so many of the characters I had read about, and in this role I found great comfort.

For the most part I was left alone. People were more mature, and it was rare that anyone openly made fun of me. One day when I went to my English class, I found lying on my chair a copy of Hermann Hesse's *Siddhartha*, his version of the story of the Buddha. My notions of Buddhism were sketchy, but the opening pages immediately reminded me of the messages of grace, dignity, and light that I'd encountered long ago in Christian publications. I'd almost forgotten about my quest for enlightenment, my imagined momentous meeting on a mountaintop with the great guru. Now I took it as a sign that someone had left this book on my chair. Desire, with all its painful complications, I decided, was something I should and would be free of.

Two months after school started, the long-awaited revision operation was scheduled. I started focusing on the date, believing that my life would finally get started once I had the face I was "supposed" to have. Logically, I knew that this was only one of many operations, but surely it would offer a hint of how it was all going to turn out.

When I woke after the operation, I reached up and felt the suture line. A few hours later, recovered enough to walk unaided to the bathroom, I geared myself up to look in the mirror. Apart from looking as if I'd just gotten over a bad case of flu, I looked just the same. The patch of paler skin was gone, but the overall appearance of my face was no different from before.

I blamed myself for the despair I felt creeping in; again it was a result of having expectations. I must guard against having any more. So what if my face was ugly. So what if other people judged me for this. That was their problem, not mine. This line of reasoning offered less consolation than it had in the past, but it distanced me from what was hurting most, and I took this as a sign that I was getting better at detaching myself from my desires.

When I returned to school, I had resolved that my face was actually an asset. It was true I hated it and saw it as the cause of my isolation, but I interpreted it as some kind of lesson. What was there to learn from a face as ugly as mine? At the age of sixteen I decided it was all about desire and love.

Over the years my perspective on what it was all about has shifted, but the most important point then was that there *was* a reason for this happening to me. I no longer felt that I was being punished, as I had during the chemo. Perhaps my face was a gift to be used toward understanding and enlightenment. This was all noble enough, and I tried my best, but for the most part I was as abysmal at seeking enlightenment as I had once been at playing dodgeball. And as much as I wanted to love everybody in school and to waft esoterically into the ether when someone called me ugly, I was plagued with petty desires and secret, evil hates.

I hated Danny in my orchestra class because I had a crush on him and knew that he would never have a crush on me. I not only harbored hatred for Danny, I also hated Katherine, the girl in orchestra *he* had a crush on. Trying to repress that feeling, I found myself hating Katherine's cello, of all things, which she played exquisitely well. The cycle eventually ended with me: I hated myself for having even entertained the absurd notion that someone like Danny could like me.

WHEN my father's insurance money came, and before we learned of our tax debt, my mother generously kept her promise and bought me another horse. I called her Mare. I kept her at Snowcap, a better-kept stable than Diamond D. There I seriously undertook learning to ride. I fell in love with Mare just as I had with Swinger, and again I had bad luck. Not long after I got her, she broke her leg while turned out in a field. As she limped pathetically onto a trailer, I knew she would have to be put down. Again my heart was broken, but this time I saw it in much more self-pitying terms. I told myself that anything I loved was doomed, and even as I was aware of my own overblown melodrama, I took a strange comfort in this romantic, tragic role.

Luckily, the owners of Snowcap permitted me to continue on at the barn as their exercise rider. This was ideal. Not only did I get to ride horses for free, but it also gave my life a center. I withstood school all day, knowing I would go straight to the barn afterward. I relished the physicality of riding, performing acts I was good at, feeling a sense of accomplishment. I spent as little time at home as possible.

During tenth grade I had one more operation to work on shaping the free flap, and the results seemed as ineffectual to me as the last time. The following summer I spent every day with the horses. One day, when it was too hot to get much accomplished, I went along for the ride on an errand with some people from the stable. We got caught in traffic on the main road, and as we crept along at a snail's pace, a bakery storefront caught my attention. It reminded me of something I couldn't quite put my finger on. Then I remembered that I had been to this town years earlier with my father. He loved to go out for a drive on a Sunday and explore the area, and Sarah and I loved to accompany him. We'd sing songs with him, songs from his own distant childhood, and we could both hear a strange, sad love in his voice as he sang. Unexpectedly, and consciously for the first time since his death, I missed my father.

The one time I had visited him in the hospital, I had had to wait in the hallway briefly. The smells and sounds were so familiar—the sweet disinfectant, the aroma of overcooked food, the metallic clinks of IV poles. Yet I was only visiting, passing through, not sure how to act. Now, more than a year after his death, I again didn't know how to act. I didn't want to ignore the grief or even get over it, because that would mean I hadn't loved my father. When my horses died, I had cried almost continuously for days. The loss was pure and uncomplicated. Loving my father had been a different matter. I finally and suddenly found myself consumed with a longing for his presence.

I started imagining my father visiting me in the hospital. With all my might I strained to hear his footsteps approaching, the rustle of his clothes as he stood near me, his cough to see if I was awake. I'd imagine opening my eyes very slowly, very carefully, and try to see him. All I could conjure was the vaguest of outlines.

SPENDING as much time as I did looking in the mirror, I thought I knew what I looked like. So it came as a shock when I went shopping with my mother one afternoon toward the end of that summer and saw my face in the harsh fluorescent light of the fitting room. Pulling on a new shirt, I caught a glimpse of my reflection in a mirror that was itself being reflected in a mirror opposite, reversing my face as I usually saw it. I stood there motionless and realized how asymmetrical my face was. How had that happened? Reaching up to touch the right side, where the graft had been put in only a year before, I saw clearly that most of it had disappeared. I felt distraught at the sight and even more distraught that it had taken so long for me to notice.

I felt like such a fool. I'd been walking around with a secret notion of promised beauty, and here was the reality. When I saw Dr. Baker a few weeks later, I wanted desperately to ask him what had gone wrong, but I found myself speechless. Besides, I knew that the graft had been reabsorbed by my body—the doctor had warned me it might happen. Dr. Baker spoke of waiting a few years before trying any more big operations, of letting me grow some more. We spoke about a series of minor operations that would make readjustments to what was already there, but there was only vague talk of any new grafts, of putting more soft tissue or bone in place. Sitting in his expensively decorated office, I felt utterly powerless. Realizing I was going to have to change my ideals and expectations was one thing, but knowing what to replace them with was another.

That summer I started riding horses for my boss, Hans, in local schooling shows. In practices I always wore a helmet with my hair hanging loose beneath it, but etiquette required that during shows my hair be tucked up beneath the helmet, out of sight. I put this off until the last minute. The simple act of lifting my hair and exposing my face was among the hardest things I ever had to do—as hard as facing Dr. Woolf, harder than facing operations. Certainly no one at the show grounds was going to make fun of me, but I was beyond that point. By then I was perfectly capable of doing it all to myself.

The habits of self-consciousness, of always looking down and hiding my face behind my hair or my hand, were so automatic by now that I was blind to them. When my mother pointed out these habits to me in the hope of making me stop, telling me they directed even more attention to my face, she might as well have been telling me to change the color of my eyes.

I fantasized about breakthroughs in reconstructive surgery, about winning the lottery and buying my own private island. And there were still acts of heroism waiting to be thrust upon me, whole busloads of babies to be saved. Then a wise older man—there had to be at least one out there—would read about my heroism in the papers, fall in love with my inner beauty, and whisk me away from the annoyance of existence as defined by Spring Valley High School.

During the eleventh and twelfth grades I had several small operations. Each time I was wheeled down to the surgical wing, high on the drugs, I'd think, Now, now I can start my life—just as soon as I wake up from this operation. And no matter how disappointed I felt when I woke up and looked in the mirror, I'd simply postpone happiness until the next operation. I knew there would always be another operation, another chance for my life to finally begin.

In the wake of my recurring disappointment I'd often chide myself for thinking I'd ever be beautiful enough, good enough, or worthy enough for someone else's love, let alone my own. Who cared if I loved my own face if no one else was going to? What was beauty for, after all, if not to attract the attention of men, of lovers? When I walked down a street or hallway, sometimes men would whistle at me from a distance, call me "Baby," yell out and ask me my name. I had a good figure, and my long blond hair was pretty. I would walk as fast as possible, my head bent down, but sometimes they'd catch up with me or I'd be forced to pass them. Their comments would stop instantly when they saw my face, their sudden silence potent and damning.

Life in general was cruel. The only way to tolerate it, to have any hope of escaping it, I reasoned, was to know my own strength, to defy life by surviving it. I had already read a great deal about the Holocaust, but now we were reading first-person accounts by Elie Wiesel and Primo Levi in social studies. I was transported by their work, and the more I absorbed of their message, the more my everyday life took on a surreal quality. Now everything, *everything*, seemed important: the tastes of salt and peanut butter and tomatoes, the smell of car fumes, the small ridge of snow on the inside sill of a barely open window. I thought that the way to live in the present moment, to resee the world, was to continuously imagine a far worse reality. At these moments the life I was leading seemed unimportant, uncomplicated. Sometimes I could truly find refuge in the world of my private senses.

After the section on the Holocaust my class moved on to art history. One day I walked into class late and found the lights off. My teacher was just about to show slides. Giacometti's sculptures flashed on the wall, their elongated arms simultaneously pointing toward and away from the world, while their long legs held them tall and gracefully but tenuously. Matisse's paintings seemed to be about how simple it was to see the world in a beautiful way. Picasso's were about how complex, how difficult, beauty was.

The poems we read in English class had similar effects on me. My taste was not always sophisticated, but I did read poetry by Keats, Emily Dickinson, and Wallace Stevens, which moved me in ways I couldn't understand. I would read Keats's "Ode to a Nightingale" and feel that something important was being said, but the moment I tried to examine the words, dissect the sentences, the meaning receded.

Senior year I applied to and was accepted at Sarah Lawrence College with a generous scholarship. Not sure what to do with my life, I decided to work toward medical school. The day senior-class yearbook photos were taken, I purposefully cut school, and I threw away all the subsequent notices warning that unless I attended the makeup shoot, my photo would not appear in the yearbook.

Ten

CERTAIN people go through radical outward changes their freshman year of college. This is especially true at Sarah Lawrence, with its enrollment of only eight hundred and a program decidedly focused on liberal arts. The college is only an hour from Spring Valley, so my mother drove me there. She helped me carry boxes up to my dorm room, said good-bye, and drove away. From across the parking lot outside my window I could hear a Herman's Hermits song blaring out, *"Something tells me I'm into something good."* I took it as an omen. For days beforehand I'd been a nervous wreck, but suddenly I felt I belonged. It was an unusual, curious feeling.

Sarah Lawrence is something of a satellite of New York City's Lower East Side. Some students dressed entirely in black or sported bizarre haircuts, while others wore, with enviable grace and style, exotic, ruined clothes that looked as if they'd washed up onshore after the *Titanic*'s New Year's Eve party. Everyone cultivated an air of being an outsider, beyond it all, utterly cool. I fell for these appearances instantly. Rather than snubbing me, everyone was extraordinarily nice and even interested in me. I was amazed to observe myself so at ease, ready and able to make contact with people. Within hours I was having intense discussions about life, art—all the topics I'd been craving for so long.

Yet for all the deep conversations, one's looks still were of paramount importance. Only the aesthetic had changed. In many ways the fashion of cool was every bit as rigorous and unforgiving as the fashion of fitting in had been in high school, only here the rigor depended upon a higher degree of individuality. With amazing predictability the freshman class went through its first-semester transformations. I was no exception.

Some of us, after Thanksgiving break, left our embarrassing old chinos and Docksides at home, and arrived back on campus completely vamped out in retro punk: dyed magenta hair and green fingernails and long black skirts. Others went for oversized dresses from their grandmother's closets, strange little hats with feathers, pearl necklaces that hung to their navels. I went with the I-don't-care, I'm-an-artist look, which required that everything I wore come from the Bargain Box, the local thrift store, and cost no more than a dollar fifty. Extra points went to anything I found lying on the street.

At the heart of this antifashion statement was poetry. Still set on medical school, I had signed up for the required science courses, but I had to fill out my schedule with something in the humanities. My mother urged me to take one of the writing workshops the school is well known for, and deciding that fiction would be too much work, I chose a poetry course. In the first semester I was hooked.

Reading and writing poetry brought together everything that had ever been important to me. I could still dwell in the realm of the senses, but now I had a discipline, a form for them. Rather than a way to create my own private life and shun the world, the ability to perceive was now a way to enter the world. Language itself, words and images, could be wrought and shaped into vessels for the truth and beauty I had so long hungered for. Poetry became a religion for me.

By the end of my freshman year I'd gained a reputation as one of the better poets on campus, which aided the development of my artistic persona. How trivial to actually think about one's appearance. The attire of my fellow scruffy artists told the world to recognize them as geniuses too preoccupied to care about anything as mundane as clothes. But for me, dressing as if I didn't care was an attempt to show the world I wasn't concerned with what it thought of my face. In my carefully orchestrated shabbiness, I was hoping to beat the world to the finish line by showing that I already knew I was ugly. Still, all the while, I was secretly hoping some potential lover might notice I was wearing my private but beautiful heart on my stained and fraying sleeve.

IN TRUTH there was little danger of meeting someone who might actually desire me, and not just because of my looks. The female-to-male ratio at school was three to one, and much of the male population was, for varying reasons, unavailable.

That summer I was looking forward to a second free-flap operation, but it wasn't to be. My mother had to leave her job at the nursing home, which meant I no longer had medical insurance. And to ease her financial burden, she had decided to sell the house, which required a great many repairs and a general sorting out. After weeks of filling out forms and spending hours on the telephone on hold, I eventually received Medicaid. I went to see Dr. Baker, and together we decided to postpone surgery until the following summer.

The house was sold early in the fall of my sophomore year. For years our poor old dilapidated house had been nothing but an embarrassment, and I'd underestimated its value to me as a reliable source of comfort, as a place I could always go. Now, to my surprise, I missed it. I experienced a strange kind of orphanhood that worked its way into my writing. The word "home" kept cropping up in my poems. When school vacations came around, I'd often spend them as the guest of friends instead of at my mother's new, smaller apartment.

In sharp contrast to high school, I now possessed a large number of decidedly wonderful friends. Through them I discovered what it was to love people. There was an art to it, I found. It required the effort of always seeing them for themselves and not as I wished them to be. I was on equally good terms with politically radical and openly hedonistic people, friends who were concerned deeply with the spiritual and those who could not care less about it. Generally, they didn't mix with one another, though most shared the quality of being on the fringe. To be on the fringe at a school as fringy as Sarah Lawrence was itself an accomplishment, but it was this very quality that I loved most about my friends. They wore their mantles as outsiders with pride, and their self-definition was the thing that put me at ease with them. I didn't feel judged. I felt acceptance I had never experienced before and was able to genuinely open myself to the love they offered.

As SOPHOMORE year drew to a close, I went to see Dr. Baker about setting up the next operation. I was full of hope, but as it turned out, Dr. Baker had far too much work right then to do the operation himself. He was handing me over to a team of two surgeons at St. Vincent's Hospital, down in Greenwich Village. They were very capable, he assured me. I wanted to know if this change had anything to do with my being on Medicaid now, but I felt too abashed to ask.

Things went badly right from the start. I went into St. Vincent's during a heat wave, and the air-conditioning in my room was broken. I woke up after the operation in a sweat. Still delirious and in intense pain, I pulled off the sheets to see that rather than the normal line of stitches along my hip, where they'd taken the graft, there was a long row of thirty or forty large metal staples. It looked as if someone had sawed my leg off and then put it back on with an office stapler. That sight upset me, but when I tried to speak, I found they'd given me a tracheotomy—another surprise.

Coming out of eight hours of anesthesia takes a long, unpleasant time. I kept surfacing into consciousness, taking note of one detail, such as the staples, then sinking back down again. I couldn't understand why I had staples in my leg, and I was never conscious long enough to learn that it was simply an experiment in wound closure. I kept hallucinating gruesome scenes in which nurses were attacking me with pliers. My whole body kept shaking, and I could not stop crying. I felt like a small child. I didn't feel safe.

At some point in the night I found it difficult to breathe. I wrote out a note to the nurse, who said she would tell the doctor. An hour later it was worse; I wrote another note, and finally a doctor arrived to draw an arterial blood sample to check my oxygen level. A long time went by. I was frightened. When the doctor returned and started taking another blood sample, I was only dimly aware of him. His voice sounded muffled as he said hello to another doctor, who walked in and asked, "Didn't you just do a blood gas a little while ago?" I could hear them talking as if through water. "Yeah," he replied congenially, "but I didn't believe anyone's oxygen level could be that low." However unable I was to communicate with the outside world, this comment jolted my inside voice awake. Oh, my God, I thought, brain damage—I'm going to have brain damage.

Several people were having a conversation about what to do with me, but I couldn't concentrate on it. Then someone leaned down to tell me they were going to take me to intensive care, that I was going to be put on a respirator. Now this, I thought, sounds like an excellent idea.

After I was finally put on the respirator, it was discovered that I had pneumonia. I spent a hellish week in intensive care, where the lights were on twenty-four hours a day, the air-conditioning was still broken, and every once in a while the alarm on my heart monitor would go off for no apparent reason. It always jolted me right off the sheets. I had to wait for someone to come give it a whack before it would stop.

WHILE in the hospital, I had been so ill that I hadn't put much effort into thinking about my appearance. My mother had been given the use of an apartment on the Upper East Side for the summer, and afterward I went to stay with her. One whole living-room wall was covered with mirrors. I walked into the apartment and almost fainted at the sight of me. The graft had been applied not just to one side of my face but from one ear to the other, and was swollen to the size of a football. The visage I saw staring back at me was undeniably repulsive. The feeling was confirmed for me whenever I went out on the street. People would stop in their tracks and stare at me. One afternoon a beggar ran up behind me, demanding money. I stopped and turned around to look at him. He stopped in midsentence, looked at me for a second longer, then politely apologized and handed me a dollar bill before turning away, muttering to himself. My self-esteem reached the bottom of the deepest, darkest pit.

I was promised a revision operation before going back to school, and I placed all my hope on that. I spent a lot of time sitting alone in the kitchen giving myself pep talks—diatribes on the meaning of life.

One afternoon the phone rang. It was Steven, one of my friends from college. When he asked how I was, I tried to answer, but all that came out was choking tears. "Hang on," he said, "I'm coming to get you." An hour later the bell rang. When I opened the door, I expected to have to go into a long explanation about why I looked the way I did, but before I could start, Steven announced we were going dancing that night. Dancing? Was he serious? He was. He had just come out as a homosexual, and he told me I was the only one he trusted enough to accompany him to the gay clubs. It was important, he said. He was counting on me to support him.

My own sexuality completely on hold, I found myself in a world composed of sex. I felt both safe and amazed by my sudden proximity to dozens of half-naked men on the dance floor. The club was called The Monster, and the sex here had nothing to do with me. No one took any notice of me—I was without value in this world. I put all my energy into learning to dance. My teachers were some of the great anonymous masters of the mid-'80s dance-club scene. I spent my first few visits watching before finally getting up enough nerve to go out on the floor myself. Never in a million years would I have been able to do this in a heterosexual club, but here, what the hell? I learned the balance between letting loose and keeping control, allowing my body to react impulsively to the beat and directing that impulse into movement. It was all about rhythm, about finding the place where the music's rhythm met my own. Every once in a while I would think fleetingly that this must be what it was like to act sexually in the world.

THE summer following my sophomore year came to an end, the grotesque swelling came down, and I had a revision operation. Though I didn't feel particularly good about my image, I didn't feel bad about it either. This was a momentous step forward, and I decided to push myself one step further. I cut my hair. I knew it was the only way I would ever stop hiding behind it. Starting off with a long bob, I worked in small stages, every few weeks making it shorter and shorter. By the end of my junior year it was only a few inches long. I'd been trying for an androgynous effect, and with my slight figure shrouded in baggy clothes, I was often mistaken for a boy. During that year the free flap was slowly reabsorbed, as the last one had been. Once again, I had nothing to show for the operation but the scarred donor site. Finally, the summer before my final year at college, I was scheduled for a bone graft.

The graft would be nonvascularized, meaning a lump of bone would be taken from my hip, ground up, and then, like clay, fashioned into the rough shape of a jaw. The effects of this operation were immediately apparent and remarkable, because bone doesn't swell. I remember limping out of bed to the bathroom and not believing my own eyes. Could that really be me? For weeks afterward I kept putting my hand up and checking to make sure it was still there—an actual jaw. For the first time in memory, I actually looked forward to seeing myself in the mirror, seeing a face I liked.

What puzzled me was that I still didn't feel attractive, despite what all my friends were telling me. Wasn't my fear just supposed to fall away? Wasn't someone supposed to fall in love with me? Wasn't life supposed to *work* now? Where was all that relief and freedom that I thought came with beauty?

Eleven

THE general plot of life is sometimes shaped by the different ways genuine intelligence combines with equally genuine ignorance. I put all my effort into looking at the world as openly, unbiasedly, and honestly as possible, but I could not recognize my own self as a part of this world. Personally, I felt meaningless, or, more precisely, I felt I meant nothing to anyone.

Even though I now possessed many rich friendships—had people who valued me—not having a lover meant I was ultimately unlovable. Rather than finding affirmation in knowing my friends loved me, I turned it against myself: If so many people thought I was such a lovable person, the fact that I still wasn't able to get a lover proved I was too ugly. Whatever sense of inner worth I developed was eroded by the knowledge that I could only compensate for, but never overcome, the obstacle of my face. At times I was so lonely I was amazed I didn't just expire right there on the spot.

Not surprisingly, I saw sex as my salvation. If only I could get someone to have sex with me, it would mean that I was attractive, that someone could love me. I never doubted my own ability to love, only that the love would ever be returned. The major reason I was still a virgin when I graduated from college was obviously the lack of genuine opportunities combined with my crippling lack of self-esteem, but I persisted in seeing it as proof that I had lost out on the world of love only because of my looks.

ALL of this would change when I went to graduate school. Having long given up on the idea of going to medical school, I applied to master of fine arts programs in poetry. If sex wasn't going to be my salvation, writing and poetry would be. But within two days of arriving at the University of Iowa, I met the man who would become my first lover. There was no doubt I was an easy mark. On the surface Jude was everything I imagined I wanted: an older, handsome writer who drove an antique sports car and had a quirky personality. On the whole he was, as he loved to hear me describe him, terribly dashing.

The relationship was a disaster. I never for a moment thought I was in love with Jude or that he was in love with me, but it was a highly charged sexual relationship. At his prompting, I began dressing more like "a woman," although I still could not bring myself to use the first-person pronoun and the word woman in the same sentence. At first I felt like an impostor, but as time wore on, even I had to admit I had a sexy body. I went from looking like a boy to wearing miniskirts, garter belts, and high heels. It was just as much a costume as dressing androgynously had been, and even though these new dresses hid none of my curves, they hid my fear of being ugly. I thought I could use my body to distract people from my face. It made me feel worthy. I even got dressed up to go to the supermarket.

All of my parading around couldn't hide the fact that the bone graft was slowly going the way of the other grafts. I didn't really notice it until the day after Jude broke up with me. Looking in the mirror, I saw the telltale signs and felt a huge dread come over me. This is when I began dressing in earnest slinkiness. I began spending two hours a day at the gym, imposing a killer regime on myself. My body was one thing I had control over. If I had put a tenth of the energy I spent obsessing over my face and my body into my work, I could have written *War and Peace* ten times over.

Bent on proving I was desirable, I started collecting lovers, having a series of short-term relationships that always ended, I was certain, because I wasn't beautiful enough. I became convinced that anyone who wanted to have a real relationship with me was automatically someone I didn't want. It was the classic Groucho Marx paradox: I didn't want to belong to any club that would have me as a member.

Dr. Baker and I decided to try another soft-tissue free flap. So much of the original irradiated tissue had been replaced with nonirradiated tissue that he felt there was a good chance this graft would stick. But a few months before the operation, I discovered that Medicaid would not pay my hospital bills. The accumulated reasons ranged from my not living in the state where the operation was to be performed to my being a full-time student with a teaching fellowship.

Dr. Baker suggested I go to the University of Iowa hospital for a consultation with the head of plastic surgery, who was an old friend of his. Perhaps there was a way for him to do the operation.

The surgeon was from the old school. Of course my free flaps had shrunk, he told me; they always did. He suggested sticking with the pedestal method that Dr. Conley had outlined for me so many years before. He was very enthusiastic, explaining about all the different incisions he'd make and how I could stay in the hospital for the six weeks when my hand was sewn to my stomach and then to my face. I felt totally repulsed, and ashamed of my repulsion.

Not wanting to be rude, I told the surgeon that I probably couldn't go through with the operations because of the money involved. "Oh, don't let that worry you. You wait right here." He disappeared for a long fifteen minutes, returning with a hospital financial officer, who outlined a payment plan for the three major operations and the minor follow-up, as well as the extended inpatient stays. When he had finished, he assured me that with payments of only a hundred dollars a month I could pay off the original bill and all the accumulated interest by the time I was forty-two. He was very affable, and I shook his hand, telling him I'd think about it.

I stayed calm until I reached the street, when I broke into a run and didn't stop until I got home, four miles away. Then I started to hyperventilate. There was no way I was going to put myself through those operations, let alone have the pleasure of paying them off just when I should rightfully be starting my midlife crisis, like everybody else.

There I was with my short skirts and sharp mind and list of lovers, trying so hard to convince myself that maybe all I really needed to do was learn how to treat myself better. Forget all that now, though, because here was the ugly truth. I felt I had been shown a mirror of what my life really was, what I really was, and I did not want to look. I was someone whom doctors talked to about sewing her hand to her face. I was trying to believe there really wasn't all that much wrong with me, but here were my worst suspicions, confirmed.

Lying in my usual abject heap on the living-room carpet, a pose I adopted in dire times, I mouthed the words "I'm tired. I don't want to do this anymore." For once, I didn't adopt either a noble or a catastrophic interpretation of events. It was reality, after all. I did have cancer once; I did have a disfigured face now. There was no denying these things. I felt pulled in two different directions. I had tasted what it was like to feel loved, to feel whole, and I had liked that taste. But fear kept insisting that I needed someone else's longing to believe in that love. No matter how philosophical my ideals, I boiled every equation down to these simple terms: Was I lovable or was I ugly?

I KNEW THAT ONE WAY OR ANOTHER I would have an operation. After a great deal of finagling, I managed to find funding for the next free flap from a charity, through the New York University Center for Reconstructive Surgery. Dr. Baker did the operation that summer, and it was the usual story of hope and disappointment. I looked horrendous for a few months, then I looked better, and just as I was getting used to the new face, the graft started disappearing. I thought about trying another bone graft, but when I discovered that there was a limit to the number of times I could apply for funds, I decided to give it up. This was me, this was my face—like it or lump it.

I opted for a geographic cure, deciding to go live in Europe once school was finished. I took on extra jobs, worked around the clock, and in a few months saved two thousand dollars and bought a ticket to Berlin. An old college friend was living there, which seemed as good a reason as any to pick that destination.

WEST Berlin, the Wall still intact at the time, fueled every romantic notion I had about living the bohemian life. I lived in a flat heated by giant prewar porcelain stoves, with no proper bathroom. I applied for jobs teaching English at various schools and went to Kreuzberg—a poor, run-down area near the Wall—for very cheap German lessons, which I took along with a roomful of Turkish immigrants. While waiting to hear about jobs, I spent my days sitting in cafés, trying to write the ultimate poem about beauty and truth.

Living in a country where I didn't speak the language suited me just fine. Everything was an adventure, including buying milk at the corner store. I maintained a romantic picture of myself as an expatriate artist until all my job possibilities fell through. Running low on funds, I decided to go to London and live with my sister Susie. I figured I'd find work more readily in a country where I spoke the language.

Usually cities offered me the refuge of anonymity, but everything felt different in London. Though I'd toned down my fashion sense quite a bit since Iowa, I still enjoyed wearing clothes that showed off my figure. Groups of men, mostly young and drunk, would spot me from a distance and follow me, catcalling. It was like junior high school all over again. As soon as they got near enough to see my face clearly, they'd start teasing me, calling me ugly, thinking it hysterically funny to challenge one another to ask me out on a date. I always stayed calm and kept right on walking, but it was exhausting. One evening, after I'd come home visibly upset from some teasing, my sister mentioned a surgeon named Oliver Fenton. While I was in Iowa, just after my last failed free flap, she'd read about a new method for plastic surgery he was working on, known as a tissue expander. She had written to him and asked whether this new procedure might be of any benefit to me. He called her back himself and told her he thought it might work. Then she had called me from London, but I was very doubtful, and I soon forgot all about him. Now she mentioned him again—how nice he'd sounded on the phone, how it couldn't hurt to at least go see him. He lived in Aberdeen, Scotland, seven hours by train from London. In all likelihood I would have skipped it if Susie hadn't generously offered to buy the ticket as a present.

FENTON explained the whole procedure to me. First he would insert a tissue expander, to be followed by a vascularized bone graft. Because the bone graft would have its own blood supply, the chances of its being reabsorbed were minimal. The procedure would take at least six months to finish; I knew enough about plastic surgery by then to know this probably meant a year. Telling him I'd think about it, I boarded the train back to London. In the dining car I encountered yet another pack of drunken men willing to judge my looks for me.

I was frightened at the idea that none of Fenton's proposed operations would work. But—again but—how could I pass up the possibility that they might work, that at last I might finally fix my face, my life, my soul? And thanks to my Irish passport and socialized medicine, the operations would be free. Remembering the cruel comments of those men on the train, I called up the doctor and told him yes.

AN EMPTY balloon was inserted under the skin on the right side of my face and then slowly blown up by daily injections of a few milliliters of saline solution into a special port beside my ear. The objective was to slowly stretch out the skin so that there would be enough of my own skin to pull down and cover the bone graft. The whole process took about three months, and I spent the entire time in the hospital.

The others on the ward took it upon themselves to teach me about Scotland. The dialect was almost impenetrable at first, but I wasn't half bad at understanding it by the time I left. Certain patients became my good friends, and after they were released, they took me for day trips to the beautiful countryside surrounding Aberdeen.

I was happy to be in the hospital, relieved not to have to go out into the world looking this way. My face transformed on a daily basis into something rather monstrous. I knew my appearance was strange, but there were other people on the ward with tissue expanders, and I never felt the need to explain or feel ashamed of my appearance.

The big day finally came, and, in what turned out to be an almost thirteen-hour operation due to some unforeseen difficulties, the tissue expander was removed and a graft from my hip put in. I was severely disoriented when I woke up, a feeling exacerbated by the morphine they were giving me. I was overtaken by a brutal paranoia, convinced that because I had chosen to do this to myself, I deserved everything I got. Such long operations are rare, and I don't think the staff was aware of this side effect. I was a complete wreck, and no one knew how to reassure me. It wasn't until Susie came up from London a couple of days later to visit me that the paranoia began to wear off.

Because of the bone taken from my hip, I was very lame for a long time. I tried not to think about the results of the surgery. There were more revision operations to come. After a few of them my face was beginning to look acceptable to me; the new graft was solid and didn't seem to be in jeopardy. But then something unexpected happened: The original bone on the left side of my jaw, which had also been heavily irradiated, was starting to shrink, probably spurred by the stress of such a large operation. The doctor proposed putting a tissue expander in on the left side, followed by yet another free flap.

I could not imagine going through it *again*, and just as I'd done all my life, I searched for a way to make it okay, make it bearable—for a way to *do* it. I lay awake all night on the train back to London. I realized then that I had no obligation to improve my situation, that I didn't have to explain or understand my life, that I could simply let it happen. By the time the train pulled into King's Cross Station, I felt able to bear it yet again, not entirely sure what other choice I had.

I moved to Scotland, partly to be near the hospital and partly because I wanted more independence. Eligible for social security benefits, I was able to get my own, albeit very cold, flat. When I arrived at the hospital to set up a date to have the tissue expander inserted, I was informed that I would spend only three or four days there after the initial procedure. Almost in a whisper I asked if I would be staying in the hospital for the three months of expansion time. No—I was to come in every day to the outpatient ward. Horrified by this prospect, I left there speechless. I would have to live and move about in the outside world for three months with a giant balloon stuck in my face.

I went into the hospital, had the operation, and went home at the end of the week. The only things that gave me any comfort during the months I lived with my face gradually ballooning out were my writing and my reading. I wrote for hours each day and lost myself reading everything from Kafka to Jackie Collins. Luckily, it was cold, so when I walked to the hospital, I could wrap my whole head in a scarf. As the tissue expander grew and grew, this became harder to do. I stopped going out except to the hospital and to the little store around the corner to buy food. I knew the people who worked there, and I kept wondering when they were going to ask what was wrong. I assumed they thought I had some massive tumor and were afraid to ask.

Finally I couldn't stand the polite silence any longer. I blurted out my whole life story to the man behind the counter. I was holding a bottle of milk, letting the whole saga stream out of me, when the bells tied to the door jangled. The man who walked in was completely covered with tattoos. I stopped in midsentence and stared at him. He stopped in mid-stride and stared at me. There were lush jungle scenes all over his face, neck, and hands. I don't know why, but I felt immensely sorry for him. We finally broke our mutual stares. I paid for my milk, he bought a pack of cigarettes, and we walked out together, turning different ways at the corner. After that, I walked the streets of my dark little Scottish city by the sea and knew without doubt that I was living in a story Kafka would have been proud to write.

THE one good thing about a tissue expander is that you look so bad with it in, that no matter what you look like when it's finally removed, it has to be better. I had the graft and some revision operations, and by that summer even I had to admit I looked better. But I didn't look like me. Something was wrong. Was *this* the face I had waited for through eighteen years and almost thirty operations? I couldn't make what I saw in the mirror correspond to the person I thought I was. It wasn't only that I continued to feel ugly; I simply could not conceive of the image as belonging to me. I'd been through twelve operations in the three years I'd been living in Scotland. Fenton was running out of things to do to me. Was this it? Even as people confirmed that this was now my face, even as people congratulated me, I felt that the person in the mirror was an impostor. Why couldn't anyone else see this?

The only solution I could think of was to stop looking. It wasn't easy. I'd never suspected just how omnipresent our own images are. I became an expert on the reflected image—how it can spring up at you at any moment from a glass tabletop, a well-polished door handle, a darkened window, a pair of sunglasses. I perfected the technique of brushing my teeth without a mirror; grew my hair in such a way that it would require only a quick, simple brushing; and wore clothes that were easily put on, with no complex layers or lines that might require even a minor visual adjustment. I did this for almost a year.

THE journey back to my face was a long one. Between operations, thanks to some unexpected money inherited from my grandmother, I traveled around Europe. I kept writing. I returned to Berlin and sat in the same cafés as before, but now without my image, without the framework of "when my face gets fixed, then I'll start living." I felt there was something empty about me. I didn't tell anyone—not my sister, not my closest friends—that I had stopped looking in mirrors. I found that I could stare straight through a mirror, allowing none of the reflection to get back to me.

Unlike some stroke victims who are physically unable to name the person in the mirror as themselves, my trick of the eye was the result of my lifelong refusal to learn *how* to name the person in the mirror. My face had been changing for so long that I had never had time to become acquainted with it, to develop more than an ephemeral relationship with it. It was easier to think that I was still not beautiful enough or lovable enough than to admit that perhaps these qualities did not belong to this thing I thought was called beauty after all.

Without another operation to hang all my hopes on, I was completely on my own. And now something inside me started to miss me. A part of me, one that had always been there, organically knew that I was whole. It was as if this part had known it was necessary to wait so long—to wait until the impatient din around it had quieted down, until the other internal voices had grown exhausted and hoarse—before it could begin to speak, before I would begin to listen.

ONE EVENING NEAR THE END OF MY long separation from the mirror, I was sitting in a café talking to a man I found quite attractive when I suddenly wondered what I looked like to him. What was he actually seeing in me? I asked myself this old question, and startlingly, for the first time in my life, I had no ready answer. I had not looked in a mirror for so long that I had no idea what I objectively looked like. I studied the man as he spoke; as reluctant as I was to admit it, the only indication in my companion's behavior was positive.

And then I experienced a moment of the freedom I'd been practicing for behind my Halloween mask all those years ago. As a child, I had expected my liberation to come from getting a new face to put on, but now I saw it came from shedding something, shedding my image.

I used to think truth was eternal, that once I *knew*, once I *saw*, it would be with me forever, a constant by which everything else could be measured. I know now that this isn't so, that most truths are inherently unretainable, that we have to work hard all our lives to remember the most basic things. Society is no help. It tells us that we can be most ourselves by acting and looking like someone else, only to leave our original faces behind to turn into ghosts that will inevitably resent and haunt us. As I sat there in the café, it suddenly occurred to me that it is no mistake when sometimes in films and literature the dead know they are dead only after being offered that most irrefutable proof: They can no longer see themselves in the mirror.

Feeling the warmth of the cup against my palm, I felt this small observation as a great revelation. I wanted to tell the man I was with about it, but he was involved in his own thoughts and I did not want to interrupt him, so instead I looked with curiosity at the window behind him, its night-silvered glass reflecting the entire café, to see if I could, now, recognize myself.

About the Authors

JOYCE EGGINTON, daughter of a London newspaper executive, pursued her own career in journalism, first as a writer in Britain, then as the New York correspondent for the London *Observer.* She has since become known for her in-depth investigations of contemporary American tragedies, including *From Cradle to Grave,* the story of an upstate New York woman whose nine children all died under suspicious circumstances. *Circle of Fire* is Egginton's fourth book published in the United States.

Born and raised in rural Texas, **DAN RATHER** had his first brush with journalism as a newsboy, hawking papers on a street corner. He eventually earned a degree in journalism and by 1962 joined the staff of CBS News, where his ability to sniff out a story became legendary. **MICKEY HERSKOWITZ,** a Texas-based writer, has co-authored autobiographies with baseball great Mickey Mantle, sportscaster Howard Cosell, and others. He also worked with Dan Rather on his earlier best seller, *The Camera Never Blinks.*

JOSEPH E. PERSICO was a teenager in upstate New York during the Nuremberg war-crimes trial. He was intrigued by the event as it unfolded and has been fascinated by it ever since. To research his book, the author drew upon previously unpublished documents and interviewed people who had never before talked about their roles at Nuremberg. Even the accounts of his subjects' thoughts and feelings are drawn directly from their own writings and oral  histories. The author of several critically acclaimed biographies, Persico is currently working with General Colin Powell on his autobiography.

 **LUCY GREALY** had her last reconstructive surgery when she was twenty-eight. She then became a Bunting Fellow in poetry at Radcliffe College. Today she teaches writing at Sarah Lawrence College and lives in the SoHo district of New York City. Her poems and essays have appeared in numerous publications. *Autobiography of a Face* is based upon an article she wrote for *Harper's* that won a coveted National Magazine Award. In addition to writing, her life is filled with travel, friends—and, yes, dates.

CREDITS